PUBLICATIONS OF THE

FOUNDATION FOR FINNISH ASSYRIOLOGICAL RESEARCH

NO. 30

STATE ARCHIVES OF ASSYRIA

VOLUME XXIII

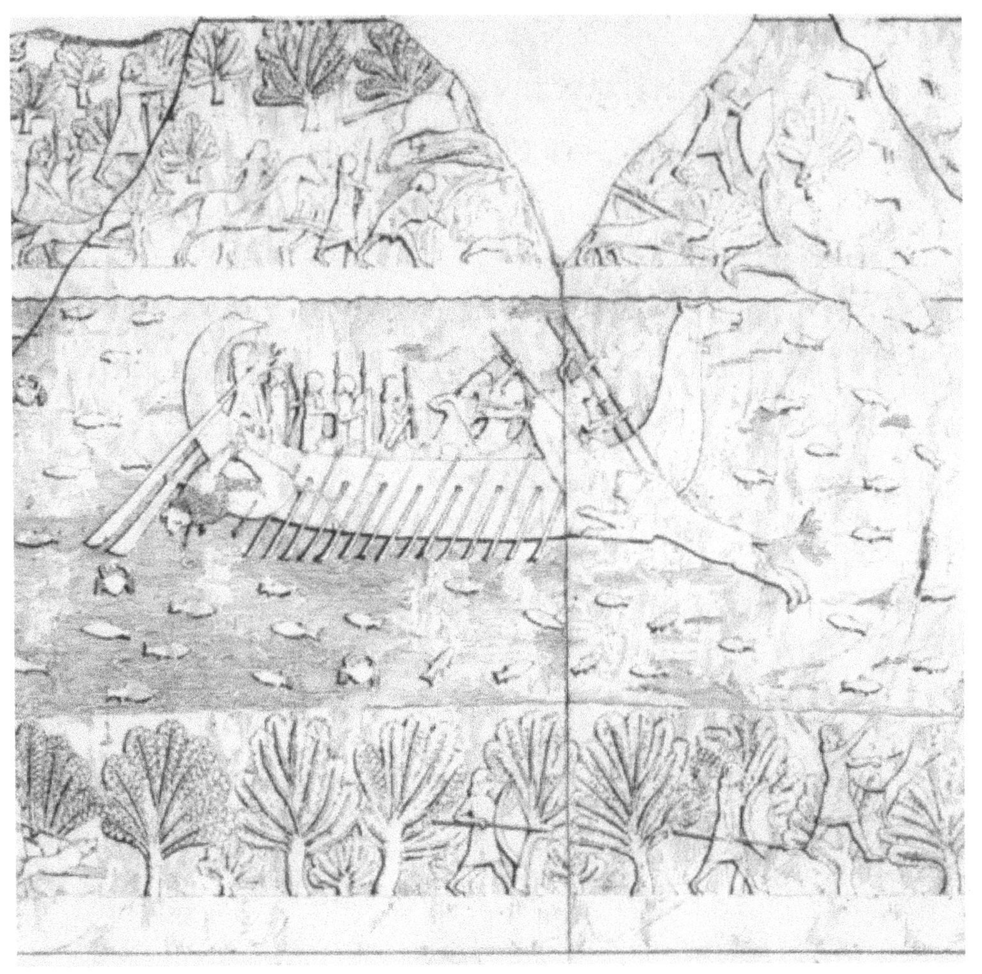

FRONTISPIECE. *Lion hunt from a galley.* Or. Dr. V, 22.

STATE ARCHIVES OF ASSYRIA

Published by the Neo-Assyrian Text Corpus Project, Helsinki

in association with the

Foundation for Finnish Assyriological Research

VOLUME XXIII

Mikko Luukko and Greta Van Buylaere

SUPPLEMENT TO SAA I-XXII

Letters, treaties, literary texts, legal and administrative documents, astronomical reports, oracle queries, and rituals

THE NEO-ASSYRIAN TEXT CORPUS PROJECT

Published with the support of the
Foundation for Finnish Assyriological Research

and the Assyrian American Association of San Jose, CA

Set in Times
The Assyrian Royal Seal emblem drawn by Dominique Collon from original
Seventh Century B.C. impressions (BM 84672 and 84677) in the British Museum
Typesetting by Greta Van Buylaere
Indices by Simo Parpola
Cover design and typography by Mikko Heikkinen

Printed in the USA
Distributed by Eisenbrauns,
an imprint of Penn State University Press

ISBN 951-570-001-9 (Whole Series, Paperback)
ISBN 951-570-002-7 (Whole Series, Hardbound)
ISBN 978-951-51-8583-9 (Volume 23, Paperback)
ISBN 978-951-51-8584-6 (Volume 23, Hardbound)
ISSN 1798-7431 (PFFAR)

SUPPLEMENT TO SAA I-XXII

LETTERS, TREATIES, LITERARY TEXTS, LEGAL AND ADMINISTRATIVE DOCUMENTS, ASTRONOMICAL REPORTS, ORACLE QUERIES, AND RITUALS

Edited by

MIKKO LUUKKO

and

GRETA VAN BUYLAERE

Illustrations

edited by

JULIAN READE

THE NEO-ASSYRIAN TEXT CORPUS PROJECT

2024

In memory of
Frederick Mario Fales
23.5.1946 – 15.4.2024

FOREWORD

The State Archives of Assyria Project was initiated in 1986 to make the incompletely and inadeqately published royal archives of the Neo-Assyrian Empire finally available to specialists and the general public in readable and reliable editions. The publication plan, adopted already years before the official launching of the project, involved identifying, transliterating, copying and digitising all unpublished Neo-Assyrian archival texts in the collections of various museums; converting them, along with the published material, into a searchable database; creating software for manipulating the data and automating the publication process; and dividing the texts into chronologically and topically coherent groups to be converted into individual volumes in international collaboration.

By 2003, eighteen volumes of the SAA series had been published, but for various reasons it took 20 more years to publish the remaining four volumes. Meanwhile, new texts had been discovered in archaeological excavations, numerous joins had been made to the published tablets, many inadvertent omissions from published volumes had become apparent, and scores of small fragments of little value remained unpublished, necessitating the publication of the present supplementary volume.

We are grateful to both authors for undertaking to edit this volume, which largely consists of fragments but also contains many important and fascinating texts. The make-up and history of the volume are explained in more detail in the preface and the introduction.

The State Archives of Assyria Project expresses its thanks to the Trustees of the British Museum, the Oriental Institute of the University of Chicago, and the département des Antiquités orientales of the Musée du Louvre for permission to publish cuneiform tablets and illustrative materials in their custody, and to the staff of the Near East Department of the British Museum for their wholehearted and enthusiastic cooperation. We also thank the University of Helsinki for supporting the Project in various ways since its inception.

Helsinki, January 2024 Simo Parpola

PREFACE

The State Archives of Assyria (SAA) series presents modern text editions of over 5,000 Assyrian and Babylonian archival texts written on cuneiform tablets. These editions, including transliterations and English translations, were compiled by Professor Simo Parpola and his team. The tablets were primarily excavated at Nineveh (Kuyunjik), but also at Nimrud (Kalhu) and Assur, the capitals of the Neo-Assyrian Empire. In 1987, Parpola published the first volume of SAA entitled *The Correspondence of Sargon II, Part I. Letters from Assyria and the West.* Now, more than thirty-five years after this landmark publication, followed by twenty-one more volumes, the SAA series is coming to an end.

Over the years the need for an SAA supplement has become apparent for several reasons, the most important being the new joins (and a few old joins), some new finds, previously overlooked tablets, and – for the sake of completeness – the importance of publishing some of the more fragmentary material from Nineveh. This supplement has therefore been produced out of necessity.

The preparation of an SAA volume is a collaborative effort. Parpola outlined the procedure for the preparation of an SAA volume before the publication of the first SAA volume as follows: "Once enough texts to make up a volume have been entered, printouts and indices are run and sent to the respective editor, who provides collations and other corrections, translations and an introduction."[1]

Apart from the partly different collection process of the texts for this publication, the aforementioned procedure was also followed in this final volume. The Project's database, which contains transliterations of the majority of the texts published in this volume, was created by Professor Simo Parpola and his assistants, and later augmented with transliterations of all Neo-Babylonian letters published in CT 54, which Professor Manfried Dietrich generously made available to the SAA project in digital form.

With Simo Parpola's help, I have collected the material for this book over an extended period, using the database of the Neo-Assyrian Text Corpus Project, and recent publications of colleagues for those texts that are being republished between the covers of this book. Additionally, more texts were transliterated by me, and many transliterations were updated to reflect the latest joins.

At a later stage, I carefully checked all the transliterations of the texts to be incorporated, including those in the Project's database and other sources. Subsequently, I prepared English translations of the texts and the standard critical footnotes for the publication. Lastly, I wrote this concise introduction. As the texts in this book cover a more mixed group thematically than any of the previous volumes, only a brief overview of the published texts is provided in the introduction. Under the subheading *Texts Included and Excluded*, I explain the reasons for publishing or not publishing the texts. For the preparation of this book, Greta Van Buylaere and I were able to collate many tablets kept in the British Museum in 2023, for which we are very grateful, but we have not seen any originals from sites other than Nineveh.[2] However, any shortcomings are probably my own.

As stated above, the database is the cornerstone of this volume. Although I took the primary responsibility for its preparation, its completion would not have been possible without the contributions of Simo and Greta. In addition to his role as director of the Neo-Assyrian Text Corpus Project and his meticulous work in transliterating many texts for the Project's database, Simo was also indispensable in resolving many difficult passages in the volume. I cannot thank him enough for his encouragement and positive attitude during the project. Greta had previously edited several texts in this volume, namely nos. 10, 12, and 18, and we had published nos. 275-277 together. Therefore, it seemed natural to collaborate on this book, for which she has also translated many other texts. Greta will provide a more detailed discussion of no. 21 elsewhere. Her insightful comments on the preliminary proofs of the texts, the critical apparatus and the introduction were greatly appreciated and have been incorporated into the manuscript. In addition, Greta completed the collations and drew the copies published in this volume. This included some of the more challenging passages, which led to fruitful discussions between us. Greta's crucial role extended to handling most of the technical matters, especially text formatting, masterfully reproducing the complex layout of SAA in Word.

For their help in making this final volume a reality, I am pleased to thank Dr. Julian Reade, who, as always, from the beginning to the end of the series, has done a great job in selecting the illustrations for this SAA volume; Professor emeritus Grant Frame (UPenn, Philadelphia), who ceded to SAA 23 a group of texts originally allocated to SAA 22[3]; in a few instances I have profited from the editions of eBL, directed by Professor Enrique Jiménez (LMU Munich), for which I am grateful. I am indebted to Professor Jacob Lauinger (Johns Hopkins) for making photographs of Tell Tayinat version of Esarhaddon's Succession Treaty available to me; Dr. Jeanette Fincke for making many joins on Babylonian tablets that form an integral part of this volume; Professor Daniel Schwemer (JMU Würzburg) for answering some of my questions and for allowing me to do part of the research for this volume in Würzburg; Dr. Bastian Still for telling me about BM 29391 a long time ago at UCL; the staff of the Department of the Middle East of the British Museum and Dr. Jon Taylor in particular for accommodating Greta and me to collate many of the tablets in the BM published in this volume; Dr. John MacGinnis for first-hand information on the new Marduk Ordeal fragment from Nineveh; Dr. Mary Frazer for allowing me to see the manuscript of her book on Akkadian royal letters in advance of its publication; Dr. Jamie Novotny (LMU Munich) for his help in adapting the volume to the *Open Richly Annotated Cuneiform Corpus* (Oracc) and Professor Steve Tinney (UPenn) for hosting all the texts published in the *State Archives of Assyria* series online at Oracc. There are certainly others to whom we also owe a debt of gratitude, and we apologise to those we may have forgotten on this occasion.

The world has undergone significant changes since the 1980s, when preparations for SAA commenced. Technology has come a long way since the days before the World Wide Web. Nowadays, almost everything in Assyriology is digitised, and the offprints of articles have all but disappeared, replaced by pdf files. Today, even traditional print books are being "threatened" by e-books and audio books, and artificial intelligence, or programmes supported by it, are set to have a profound impact on our field. In any case, the main question in all of this may be one of distribution; thanks to the WWW we have never seen more efficient and widespread distribution, and we no longer need mass-produced physical objects for our message to reach all corners of the known world, but essentially in the spirit of spreading the word and getting our message heard we continue along the same path that was paved, for example, by Esarhaddon's Succession Treaty and many stelae of the Assyrian Empire.

Given the vicissitudes of funding, it was perhaps fortunate that in the 1980s no one knew how long it would take to prepare the *State Archives of Assyria* series.[4] Since the Neo-Assyrian Text Corpus Project has not received proper funding since 2001, this volume has been prepared on a tight budget. I am grateful to the Foundation for Finnish Assyriological Research and Rochelle Yousefian of the Assyrian American Association of San Jose for their support of this endeavour.

Espoo, November 2023 Mikko Luukko

CONTENTS

INTRODUCTION

This supplement to SAA I-XXII completes the publication of the *State Archives of Assyria* (SAA) series. It offers a wealth of published and unpublished archival texts and, with the additions to SAA 3, a group of texts that can be characterised as more literary in nature. The main purpose of this introduction is to provide a brief overview of the contents of the volume.

A Glance Backwards

In the 1850s, the discovery of thousands of clay tablets from Nineveh (Kuyunjik), the capital of the Assyrian Empire, was one of the most astonishing discoveries of the ancient world. Later, archaeological fieldwork at Assur in the early twentieth century and at Kalhu/Nimrud (for the purposes of SAA, especially the 1952 season) proved that the success recorded in Nineveh was not sporadic, but that the intellectual legacy of the ancient Assyrian Empire can be found in many sites. As a result, many fascinating archival texts excavated outside Nineveh deserve to be published or republished in SAA.

The systematic publication programme for the textual remains of the Assyrian Empire began at the latest in the late 1980s with the critical editions of the State Archives of Assyria (SAA) and Royal Inscriptions of Mesopotamia, Assyrian Periods (RIMA 1-3, 1987-1996). This was followed by Studien zu den Assur-Texten (StAT, since 1999), Keilschrifttexte aus Assur literarischen Inhalts (KAL, since 2007) and Royal Inscriptions of the Neo-Assyrian Period (RINAP, 2011-2023).[5] However, as precursors to these publication series, the Cuneiform Texts from Nimrud (CTN, since 1972) and the seminal monographs by Nicholas Postgate, Neo-Assyrian Royal Grants and Decrees (1969) and Taxation and Conscription in the Assyrian Empire (1974), and Simo Parpola, Neo-Assyrian Toponyms (1970) and Letters from Assyrian Scholars to the Kings Esarhaddon and Assurbanipal I (1970) and II (1983), set the standards and paved the way for all subsequent publications.

Although there is still some work on the textual cuneiform material found in the earlier excavations,[6] the publication series have thoroughly revolutionized the field and made the Neo-Assyrian period the largest and most popular period within Assyriology. All of these works have contributed enormously to our understanding of the Assyrian Empire.

However, not all the unearthed archival texts of the so-called Assurbanipal's library or libraries are yet edited and fully available to the specialists and the wider public. This volume attempts to enhance the state of the Neo-Assyrian and Neo-Babylonian archival texts by publishing the remaining previously unpublished fragments from Nineveh. In addition, as with many other SAA volumes, it adds to the picture by updating some scattered archival texts from other Assyrian sites. Essentially, the update also includes the (re)publication of various archival texts from Nineveh for which scholars have been able to rejoin additional pieces after their first State Archives of Assyria publication, thus providing more information.

Letters and Other Archival Texts – A Succinct Overview of the Contents

Neo-Assyrian and Neo-Babylonian letters or their fragments make up the bulk of the texts. However, some years ago it became apparent that it was necessary to include all the surviving archival texts of the various sub-genres, as well as the updates and improvements made to the texts after their corresponding publication in the SAA volumes.[7] As a result, in addition to letters, the book includes treaties, literary texts, queries to the sun god, astrological reports, legal transactions and administrative texts, as well as grants and decrees. The purpose of this volume is to offer some well-preserved tablets to counterbalance the badly broken material, so that a more balanced and fruitful presentation of the material could be achieved.

The Neo-Assyrian and Neo-Babylonian texts published in this volume are for the most part numerically small fragments that contribute to the completion of the preserved archival texts from the so-called 'Assurbanipal's' royal library or libraries.[8] However, the volume also contains intact or almost intact tablets. The texts are arranged in chapters according to their genre, with chronology as another important factor, and where possible, as before, personal dossiers or a thematic grouping also play a role, but since there are no extensive dossiers in this volume, this principle has more to do with the order in which the texts are presented.

Many of the fragments included in this volume were originally published in cuneiform hand copies in two important books:

• Dietrich, M., Cuneiform Texts from Babylonian Tablets in the British Museum, Part 54: *Neo-Babylonian Letters from the Kuyunjik Collection* (London 1979), and

• Parpola, S., Cuneiform Texts from Babylonian Tablets in the British Museum, Part 53: *Neo-Assyrian Letters from the Kuyunjik Collection* (London 1979).

Most of the fragments in the two volumes edited here have not been translated elsewhere, except for those treated by Harper in his out-of-date ABL. In addition to CT 53, CT 54 and the ABL fragments, this volume also offers a group of high K(uyunjik) numbers and additional pieces from other Kuyunjik collections.

Apart from the two very specific corpora of SAA 9 (Prophecies) and SAA 19 (Nimrud Letters), this volume adds texts to almost all previous SAA volumes, but it is not the first or only volume to do so. In fact, SAA 14 462-479 were additions to SAA 6;[9] SAA 15 274-287 were additions to SAA 1 and SAA 5; SAA 16 157-176 were additions to SAA 10 and SAA 13; SAA 18 124-142 were additions to SAA 10 and SAA 13. On the other hand, SAA 19 contained cross-references to letters previously published in SAA 1, SAA 5, and SAA 15, which belong to the corpus of SAA 19.[10]

This volume (re)publishes several joins, including previously unpublished pieces. Since the archaeological discovery of the Nineveh tablets, scholars have been able to make hundreds and thousands of joins. Traditionally, various means have been used to join fragments, including the study of visual similarities between pieces, their shared geographical, prosopographical and topical or thematic parallels.[11] Unsurprisingly, most joins were made between the pieces belonging to the same Kuyunjik sub-collection. However, recently it has become more difficult to make joins in the corpus of archival texts. Indeed, many of the fragments in this book are by their very nature very generic and no longer offer easy cases for combination with other pieces. Certainly, more joins will be made between the remaining fragments, and this process will benefit from artificial intelligence or other machine-reading innovations or automated functions that are being developed.[12] It should be noted that, whenever possible, we have retained the earlier SAA titles of the texts for which further pieces were joined after their first SAA publication.

In NA, thanks to the extensive Sargon correspondence, there are more 8th-century letters excavated at Nineveh and Nimrud than 7th-century letters, but in NB, interestingly,[13] the reverse is true, with the surviving letters to Esarhaddon and Assurbanipal outnumbering those to Sargon (and Tiglath-pileser III).[14] In many cases, however, when we are dealing with small fragments it is often methodologically tenuous to distinguish between 8th and 7th century letters. Apart from this volume, SAA 3, 10, 13 and 21 also offer a mixture of NA and NB texts, mainly letters.

The additional letters to the ten previously published volumes of letters are divided into two main groups (Chapters 1 and 3), to which are added two further chapters with extensive unattributed NA and NB sections (Chapters 2 and 4). The main criterion is chronological, and the two groups are those of Sargon II (Chapter 1) and, with due reservation, of his son Sennacherib, and those of their successors (Chapter 3), i.e., Esarhaddon, Assurbanipal and, at least in theory, the later kings. It should be stressed, however, that in many cases there is currently no methodologically sound way for distinguishing between the two groups (there is likely to be a high margin of error in Chapters 2 and 4).[15]

Several letters speak directly of warfare and violence (nos. 49, 72, 74, 75[16], 78, 80, 122, 195, 204, etc.), but mostly the events they refer to cannot be pinpointed. Of these, no. 72 is an extremely interesting, but badly damaged letter, which tells us of the measure taken by the unknown sender to adopt the son and daughter of a deportee after a battle or skirmish. Otherwise, for example, few letters concentrate on images or statues (nos. 14 and 77). The recurring problem with small fragments is the contextual uncertainty of who is doing what, where and why. But even in their present state they give us snippets of information and an idea of what was going on in Assyria.

Ch. 1: The Correspondence of Sargon II: Additions to SAA I, V, XV and XVII

In this chapter, the division into the previous volumes is roughly: nos. 1-8 (SAA 1), nos. 9-16 (SAA 5), nos. 17-28 (SAA 15) and nos. 29-41 (SAA 17). The chapter begins with fragmentary royal letters and includes, for example, a letter from the chief victualler (no. 8, previously only edited in German). The chapter offers eight previously edited SAA letters with additional joins (nos. 1, 6, 10, 21,

29, 31-33), of which a letter (no. 21) describing Merodach-baladan's plot with Marduk-šarrani is perhaps the most tantalising, and the many joins for no. 33 have transformed the text, which still contains several gaps.

Ch. 2: Fragments of Unknown Authorship and Broken Letter Openings and Endings

Unfortunately, this volume is characterised by a large number of fragments and few complete texts. This chapter is obviously related to Chapter 1, but also to Chapters 3 and 4. Nos. 42-67, 94-95, 97-112 contain unattributed NA and nos. 68-93, 96 corresponding NB letters. Thus, the total of 112 texts in the first two chapters is divided into 72 NA and 40 NB letters.[17] The chapter concludes with fragmentary letter beginnings and endings, of which only no. 96 can be attributed to a sender, Ahu-iqiša, about whom nothing certain can be said.

Ch. 3: The Correspondence of Esarhaddon, Assurbanipal and Later Kings Additions to SAA X, XIII, XVI, XVIII, XXI and XXII

The division into the previous volumes is roughly as follows: nos. 113-118 (SAA 10; nos. 115 and 118 are NB), no. 119 (SAA 13), nos. 120-124 (SAA 16),[18] nos. 125-134, 139 (SAA 18 and SAA 21, all NB), 135-138 (SAA 22). The chapter provides four previously edited SAA letters with newer pieces (nos. 113, 127-129), including a new edition of the letter relating to the successful conspiracy to kill Sennacherib. Perhaps the most interesting addition to the scholarly letters of SAA 10 is the one describing a ritual that may relate to a death in a temple (no. 115). The only addition to SAA 13 is a fragmentary letter on teams (of horses) by Nabû-šumu-iddina (no. 119), whose numerous reports on horses are published in this volume. Certainly the highlights of this chapter are the "Sasî letter" (no. 120) and an anonymous conspiracy letter in NB (no. 126), already published by Weidner in 1954; two remarkable letters, previously available only in German translation. These two letters, together with no. 123, are the clearest denunciations in the volume. No. 140 is not, strictly speaking, an addition to any previous volume, for it is a dramatic post-Assurbanipal letter in NA about the death throes of Assyria.

Ch. 4: Fragments of Unknown Authorship

This chapter is closely related to Chapter 3, but possibly also to Chapters 1 and 2. Nos. 141-162, 225 are unattributed NA and nos. 163-224 are corresponding NB letter fragments. This gives a total of 34 NA and 79 NB letters for Chapters 3 and 4. No. 154 is an exceptional tablet, previously only edited in Italian, with two private letters on one tablet, and the only complete tablet with the names of the sender and recipients preserved in this chapter of unattributed fragments.

Apart from the letters of the king(s) of Assyria (tentatively nos. 1-5, 7, 125, perhaps also nos. 134 and 144), most of the other letters published in the first four chapters of the volume were sent to the kings of Assyria.[19] Only nos. 39, 70, 83, 123, 12é7, 130-131, 134, 140-141, 154-155, 157, 163-164, 199, 225 are letters that were clearly not addressed to the king, or very unlikely to have been: many of them use "you" forms and the sender addresses "my lord" rather than "the king, my lord". One letter addressed to the palace scribe (no. 157) and another in which he is mentioned (no. 176) are not surprising, as they are consistent with his responsibility for the state archives of Assyria.[20]

Ch. 5: Neo-Assyrian Treaties and Loyalty Oaths: Additions to SAA II

There are only four texts in this chapter, but the last one is the most remarkable for its sheer size, duplicating the longest text in the entire SAA series.[21] The first one, no. 226 is Assurnasirpal II's fragmentary treaty that has been recently published by Stefan Jakob as KAL 9 68. Its curse section may have served as a model for Esarhaddon's Succession Treaty. The two treaty fragments of Sennacherib, nos. 227-228, first published by Eckart Frahm in his KAL 3, are likewise very welcome additions to the slowly but surely growing number of Neo-Assyrian treaties or their fragments. These early seventh-century treaty fragments are of great interest because they show that their standardised wording served as a model for later treaties,[22] such as Esarhaddon's Succession Treaty. All in all, the comparison between the different exemplars, even when they are just small fragments, seems to be fruitful and attests to a strict continuity within this genre. Further, a captivating detail in a treaty imposed by Sennacherib is that Esarhaddon, whose name is broken away, though readily to be restored, is not defined in the same way as Assurbanipal later as the "great crown prince designate" (*mār šarri rabiu ša bēt-rēdûte*), but "only" as the "crown prince designate" (*mār šarri ša bēt-rēdûte*). Neither Esarhaddon nor Assurbanipal was the eldest of his brothers.

The Tell Tayinat version of Esarhaddon's Succession Treaty (no. 229) was discovered in 2009 and promptly published by Jacob Lauinger.[23] The importance of this new large four-column tablet cannot be overstated, as it has stimulated research into the Neo-Assyrian treaties and opened up new avenues of investigation.[24]

Ch. 6: Court Poetry and Literary Miscellanea: Additions to SAA III

In addition to royal ideology, the Assyrian language/dialect was an important criterion for the inclusion of a literary text in SAA 3. However, this was not used as an exclusive, rigorous method, as texts associated with certain Assyrian kings but written in SB/NB were also included in SAA 3.[25] Nevertheless, the additions in this chapter may appear somewhat more haphazard and arbitrary than in other chapters. However, this chapter does provide some of the highlights of the volume, such as a literary letter praising Assurbanipal's exploits in Elam (no. 235) and an earlier composition telling us of the victories of Assurnasirpal II in the west (no. 233) and the exploits of Shalmaneser III (no. 234). Other texts in this chapter also relate to the Elamite campaigns of Assurbanipal (no. 237,[26] possibly also no. 236). Other relevant texts can be described as god-list-like texts (no. 230) or prayers to the specific gods (nos. 231 and 232). In this chapter, texts from Assur play an important role together with those from Nineveh, e.g., the recent discovery of a Marduk Ordeal fragment from the Maški Gate in Nineveh (no. 240) illuminates few details of this fascinating text. The fragmentary but interesting no. 241 seems to refer to the early relations between the Assyrians and the Arameans.

Ch. 7: Queries to the Sungod: Additions to SAA IV

Especially thanks to the many joins by Jeanette Fincke, this chapter now edits or re-edits fourteen queries to the sun god (nos. 245-258). The improvements are mainly in the details, but they are important. One fragment (no. 245) concerns Ursâ of Urartu, about whom only two queries were previously known (SAA 4 18-19). Nos. 258 (Mullissu) and 260 ((liver) omens) add new details to this sub-corpus. The last two texts in the chapter deal with extispicy omens and are not standard queries, although they are closely related.

Ch. 8: Astrological Reports to Assyrian Kings: Additions to SAA VIII

The chapter edits and re-edits (thanks to three joins by Jeanette Fincke) altogether six astrological reports sent to the kings Esarhaddon and Assurbanipal (nos. 263-266, 268-269), and a hemerology (no. 262), the first edition of which, as SAA 8 38, left much room for improvement. Chronologically, no. 267, a fragmentary tablet from the reign of Adad-nerari III, does not belong to SAA 8 or to this chapter, but thematically this curiosity, which reports on a lunar eclipse, is an interesting addition. Moreover, this chapter also includes a fragment of rather uncertain character referring to a stylus and written objects (no. 270) and four texts that are rituals or likely related to them (nos. 271-274). Three of them were already drawn by Dietrich for CT 54.

Ch. 9: Legal Transactions of the Royal Court of Nineveh: Additions to SAA VI and XIV

Most legal documents and contracts are, of course, ideally published as fully as possible in the archives. Here the additions to SAA 6 and 14 provide some unusual documents, especially those of nos. 279-281. No. 279 is a unique text that is difficult to classify. It tells us of crimes committed in Nuhub, possibly near Assur, but it is uncertain what, apart from its geographical location, links all its details. No. 280 is a tablet from Borsippa in which Assurbanipal clarifies the status of Nabû-le'i. In terms of officials and their professions, this document provides one of the most impressive lists of witnesses from the Neo-Assyrian period. No. 281 is a court record or a statement for the court that specifies crimes against an anonymous person.

Unlike in SAA 6 and SAA 14, this chapter also includes five documents in NB: three slave-sale documents drafted in Nineveh belong to Ubaru's dossier, the already mentioned Assurbanipal's decision concerning Nabû-le'i's status in Borsippa and a further fragment of what may be an Assyrian-influenced legal contract (nos. 275-277, 280, 283). These documents are important witnesses of

Assyrian and Babylonian interaction, i.e., how flexibly conventions could be borrowed between the two dialects or languages.

Ch 10: Imperial Administrative Records: Additions to SAA VII and XI

This chapter presents three texts previously published in SAA 7 and 11 with new joins (nos. 286-287 and 290). Because of its special nature and general interest, a funerary text of an Assyrian king of uncertain identity (no. 288), recently edited by Theodore Kwasman, has also been included in this volume. Of course, it could have been presented as an addition to the literary texts of SAA 3, but most of the partially preserved text reads like an inventory list. Indeed, this chapter contains various lists, whether of persons, professions, women, chariot troops, sheep, towns and villages, or messengers. The nature of the last two very fragmentary texts of the chapter is open to interpretation (perhaps fragments of a letter and a legal document).

Ch. 11: Grants, Decrees and Gifts of the Neo-Assyrian Period: Additions to SAA XII

The penultimate chapter of the volume offers two short fragments from Assur that have been previously published in German by Eckart Frahm in his KAL 3. No. 297 provides a partial duplicate of Sennacherib's votive donation (SAA 12 86) that dedicates personnel to the Akitu Temple he had built outside Assur. The fragment comes from almost the beginning of the tablet and may have been a draft or a sketch giving a more succinct description of the deed. No. 298 is an even smaller NA piece of a decree of an unknown king (perhaps Adad-nerari III) on offerings and preserves part of the curse section and refers to the regular offerings of the Aššur temple at Assur.

Ch. 12: Assyrian Royal Rituals and Cultic Texts: Additions to SAA XX

The final chapter closes with two fragmentary royal rituals. The first is a Middle Assyrian fragment which may relate to the "Royal Coronation Ritual" (SAA 20 7 = KAR 135+), but opinions of its status vary.[27] This piece preserves the remnants of two columns describing the king's pious acts towards his gods in the Aššur Temple of Assur by providing them animal sacrifices and precious gifts (especially stones). The second, very badly broken fragment seems to be part of another royal ritual because it mentions a day date, someone or something entering the king's presence, Šeru'a-eṭerat (Esarhaddon's daughter and Assurbanipal's sister), Kandalanu (king of Babylonia), as well as king of Elam and tables that were most likely meant for offerings or a royal banquet.

All texts published here are also available online at the State Archives of Assyria Online (SAAo) under the Open Richly Annotated Cuneiform Corpus (Oracc) website.[28]

On the Present Edition

Texts Included and Excluded

As far as the texts published in this volume are concerned, we could not entirely avoid certain arbitrariness in their selection. The texts included and excluded from SAA 21 and SAA 22 also determined the content of this volume.[29]

a) New joins to previously published SAA texts:

Since the State Archives of Assyria editions of several texts, more joins relevant to SAA have been made. The many joins made by Jeanette Fincke, to whom we owe our gratitude, are especially worth singling out here.[30] In fact, most of the tablets that have been joined after their first SAA publication are worth republishing in their more complete form. However, some recent joins also add too little information that their republication is not necessary in print form, but it is enough to update these online (http://oracc.museum.upenn. edu/saao/corpus). In theory, all such joins combining two previous SAA numbers together were considered for republication in this volume, but in practice this did not seem essential. The list below records the new (or old) archival joins included and excluded in this volume.[31]

b) Inclusions (see also the list of joins at the end of the book):

• No. 1 = SAA 1 10 (K 622 + K 1981 = ABL 306 + CT 53 221) + K 16512 (CT 53 784; join by A. Livingstone, 16/10/1989); the small joined piece affects r.5-9

• No. 6 = SAA 1 70 (K 4304 = ABL 107) + SAA 5 282 (K 7517 = CT 53 387; join by S. Parpola, later physically confirmed by G. Van Buylaere, --/3/2009)

• No. 10 = SAA 5 55 (Sm 807 = ABL 741) + SAA 5 61 (K 5609 = CT 53 296; join by G. Van Buylaere 15/11/2007)

• No. 21 = SAA 15 189 (K 5333B = ABL 1024) + SAA 15 208 (K 9813 = CT 53 408; join by G. Van Buylaere 17/11/2008)

• No. 29 = SAA 17 16 (K 12954 = ABL 838) + K 13130 (CT 54 251; join by J. Fincke, 11/9/2003); K 13130 affects lines 1-10 and improves many readings in these lines

• No. 31 = SAA 17 165 (K 1942 = CT 54 41) + SAA 17 166 (K 13025 + K 16584 = CT 54 238; join by J. Fincke, 16/12/2005)

• No. 32 = SAA 17 169 (Sm 1915 = ABL 1067) + K 13853 (CT 54 261; join by J. Fincke, 6/8/2003); the small fragment slightly improves lines 1′-8′ of the obverse

• No. 33 = SAA 17 180 (K 7527 = CT 54 203) + K 5510 (CT 54 124) + K 7519 (CT 54 202) + Sm 1793 (CT 54 422) + Bu 91-5-9,30 (CT 54 558; joins by J. Fincke, 6/8 and 8/8/2003 and 30/11/2005); thanks to Fincke's joins the tablet has now 21 + 17 partially preserved lines

• No. 113 = Part of SAA 10 223 (Sm 1761 = part of CT 53 130) + SAA 16 167 (Sm 1851 = CT 53 855; join by G. Van Buylaere 26/11/2010)

• No. 127 = SAA 18 51 (K 1969 = CT 54 46) + K 16935 (join by J. Fincke, 12/12/2005); lines 2-e.8 were fragmentary before K 16935, which now helps to reveal an interesting blessing

• No. 128 = SAA 18 100 (1880-7-19, 28) + K 21923 (join by J. Fincke, 13/12/2003); K 21923 improves many of the readings on the left-hand side of the tablet, both obverse and reverse

• No. 129 = SAA 18 182 (Bu 91-5-9-,072 = ABL 717) + Bu 91-5-9,023 (CT 54 556) + Bu 91-5-9,238 (the latest piece, SAA 18 182, was joined to others by J. Fincke 14/8/2003); the tablet is still partially fragmentary, but it now counts forty lines, covering its full height on both sides, instead of eighteen lines as before

• No. 239 = SAA 3 25 (K 4449 = AfO 18 382) + K 10319 (CT 54 219; join by J. Fincke, 29.11.2005); the rejoined piece adds eight more lines to the end of column II and seven more lines to the beginning of column Rev. I

• No. 246 = SAA 4 36 (83-1-18,539 = AGS 10) + SAA 4 123 (Sm 1880 = PRT 79; join by J. Fincke, 8/9/2003)

• No. 247 = SAA 4 108 (K 11492 = AGS 50 + Sm 412 = PRT 26) + Sm 684 (CT 54 404; join by W. von Soden, 6/4/1979); small Sm 684 adds signs to obverse, lines 16, 18-19, and to reverse 1-3, challenging some older restorations

• No. 248 = SAA 4 131 (K 11464 = AGS 134) + SAA 4 181 (82-5-22,487 = AGS 128; join by G. B. Lanfranchi, 27/7/1982; cf. AfO 31, 333)[32]

• No. 249 = SAA 4 297 (K 12213) + K 4720 (join by J. Fincke, 18/11/2005); K 4720 adds four lines to both the obverse and reverse of the tablet, and a lower edge of two lines in between

• No. 250 = SAA 4 299 (K 8880) + SAA 4 331 (K 1423; join by J. Fincke, 18/11/2005)

• No. 252 = SAA 4 316 (K 4728 = PRT 103) + SAA 4 340 (K 8909; join by J. Fincke, 18/11/2005)

• No. 253 = SAA 4 324 (K 396 = PRT 110) + K 21929 (82-3-23; join by J. Fincke, 18/11/2005); small K 21929 affects lines 9-13 of the obverse

• No. 254 = SAA 4 327 (K 3791 = PRT 108) + K 16276 (join by J. Fincke, 18/11/2005); K 16276 adds eight-line beginnings to the obverse and clarifies that the end of the reverse was uninscribed

• No. 255 = SAA 4 341 (K 4766 = CT 54 69) + 82-5-22,70 + K 14308; the latest join (R. Borger 19/7/1990) adds legible signs to r.1-4, and the number of lines on the reverse is now plus 1. The lines of the new piece that relate to the obverse of the tablet (lines 8ff) are destroyed

• No. 264 = SAA 8 280 (K 1309 = RMA 181A) + SAA 8 286 (83-1-18,301; join by J. Fincke, 22/11/2005)

• No. 265 = SAA 8 283 (K 4708 + 10298) + K 5712 (join by J. Fincke, 22/11/2005); the latest piece concerns lines 7-8, r.1-3

• No. 266 = SAA 8 475 (K 13012) + SAA 8 510 (K 5723; join by J. Fincke, 21/11/2005)

• No. 286 = SAA 7 24 (K 1473 [ADD 827] + K 10447 [ADD 914]) + K 1944a [ADD 1135]) + K 15604 (CT 53 674). The latest join, K 15604, binds the other pieces together, including K 1944a, clarifies the number of lines of the tablet and improves the readings of lines 5-12

• No. 287 = SAA 7 150 (K 7702 + 13029 + 13198 + 13752) + SAA 7 179 (K 18554; bottom right corner of the multi-column tablet; latest piece was joined by T. Kwasman, 4/6/1993)

• No. 290 = SAA 11 123 (K 1995 = ADD 852) + K 19290

c) Exclusions: the following joins are not worth republishing in this volume because the improvements in them are minimal and only affect a small number of lines; they can be consulted in their updated form at Oracc (http://oracc.museum.upenn.edu/saao/corpus):

• SAA 4 119 (K 11523 = AGS 27) + SAA 4 256 (K 11529 = AGS 165) (join by J. Fincke, 3/9/2003); the join concerns r.1′-5′ and confirms the previously restored readings

• SAA 8 400 (Ki 1904-10-9,262 = BM 99230) + Ki 1904-10-9,321 (BM 99289; join by J. Fincke 22/11/2005); the join concerns lines 3-7 and confirms the previously restored readings

• SAA 8 410 (K 973) + K 15005 (join by J. Fincke 15/11/2005); a small flake slightly improves r.5-7

• SAA 10 161 (K 5463 = ABL 928) + K 22015 (join by J. Fincke 13/8/2003); a small flake slightly improves lines 9-12

• SAA 10 244 (Ki 1904-10-9,48 = BM 99019 = ABL 1388) + Ki 1904-10-9,341 (BM 99309; CT 53 979): join by Th. Kwasman in 1983; the join confirms the previous restorations in r.1-4

• SAA 14 131 (Rm 53 = ADD 338) + K 20536 (join by Th. Kwasman 19/4/1982); the join affects lines 2′-7′ but it does not really improve the readings

• SAA 17 14 (K 7526 = ABL 837) + K 19980 (join by J. Fincke, 19/8/2003); the small new piece confirms the previous restorations

• SAA 17 141 (K 5474 = ABL 748) (+) SAA 17 142 (Sm 501 = ABL 1052; join by S. Parpola, 17/7/2002); this is a perplexing and disputed case; see C.B.F. Walker in the critical apparatus to SAA 17 141, p. 121. In addition to Walker's observations, the joined tablet is very high, and the dimensions seem not balanced but disproportionate.

There are also later copies of royal letters from Nineveh which are not included here because their originals were not Neo-Assyrian but concerned the Assyro-Babylonian relations of the preceding period; these include ABL 924+, ABL 1282, ABL 1283, recently edited by Mary Frazer in her Akkadian Royal Letters in Later Mesopotamian Tradition (Leiden - Boston 2024).[33] Nor is it necessary here to publish other comparable historical letters such as CT 54 432 (Sm 2116) + 1912-05-13,2,[34] BM 45642 (81-7-6, 35)[35] and BM 28825 (98-11-12, 1).[36] Similarly, a later, well-known letter from Sîn-šarru-iškun to Nabopolassar, first edited by Lambert, is now re-edited by Frazer and not published here.[37]

Two small treaty fragments VAT 12374 and VAT 9424 from Assur, published by Frahm in KAL 3 as nos. 70 and 71, duplicate SAA 2 6, lines 54-62 and 509-516 respectively. However, unlike the large Tell Tayinat tablet, these small fragments do not offer anything new to Esarhaddon's Succession Treaty and are not worth publishing anew here.

The following archival fragments – most of them letter fragments – from Nineveh were examined and considered for inclusion in this volume, but in their present state they are too broken and insignificant for publication. We have therefore discarded them. However, if in the future they are joined with other pieces, they may be worth publishing elsewhere:

ABL 1254 (Bu 89-4-26,100); ABL 1271 (Sm 584).

CT 53 243 (K 5390), 256 (K 5491), 273 (K 5534), 279 (K 5546), 302 (K 5833), 361 (K 7456), 373 (K 7486), 379 (K 7412), 383 (K 7503), 433 (K 12016), 493 (K 13141), 514 (K 14243), 523 (K 14579), 545 (K 14610), 547 (K 14615), 555 (K 14632), 587 (K 14688), 594 (K 14968), 595 (K 14978), 597 (K 14983), 600 (K 14996), 609 (K 15019), 613 (K 15066), 645 (K 15335), 648 (K 15370), 663 (K 15402), 680 (K 15611), 682 (K 15613), 687 (K 15619), 692 (K 15634), 694 (K 15637), 699 (K 15641), 701 (K 15664), 703 (K 15648), 709 (K 15666), 723 (K 16043), 728 (K 16049), 732 (K 16057), 736 (K 16063), 742 (K 16079), 746 (K 16087), 750 (K 16103), 753 (K 16097), 762 (K 16472), 771 (K 16484), 773 (K 16487), 783 (K 16511), 788 (K 16518), 791 (K 16526), 796 (K 15636), 800 (K 16552), 801 (K 16554), 804 (K 16569), 819 (Sm 572), 820 (Sm 636), 828 (Sm 861), 831 (Sm 1173), 838 (Sm 1574), 843 (Sm 1633), 849 (Sm 1741), 853 (Sm 1833), 854 (Sm 1844), 913 (Sm 1855), 971 (Ki 1902-5-10,034).

CT 54 44 (K 1958), 72 (K 5060b), 94 (K 5409b), 115 (K 5451b)[38], 134 (K 5548), 146 (K 5596), 153 (K 5615), 158 (K 5632), 159 (K 5633), 166 (K 5646), 197 (K 7461), 200 (K 7504)[39], 213 (K 8745), 228 (K 11790), 281 (K 14969), 283 (K 15024), 291 (K 15070), 311 (K 15392), 327 (K 15697), 329 (K 15700), 332 (K 15703), 336 (K 15707), 339 (K 15710), 343 (K 15715), 344 (K 15716), 346 (K 16086), 352 (K 16114), 353 (K 16117), 354 (K 16118), 355+ (K 16121 + K 8632)[40], 362 (K 16131), 365 (K 16134), 368 (K 16137), 370 (K 16140), 372 (K 16142), 374 (K 16580), 381 (K 16597), 382 (K 16598), 383 (K 16599), 384 (K 16600), 385 (K 16601), 389 (K 16606), 392 (K 16612), 394 (K 16614), 399 (Sm 452), 400 (Sm 481), 403 (Sm 632), 408 (Sm 1174), 411 (Sm 1254), 413 (Sm 1381), 416 (Sm 1615), 417 (Sm 1626), 418 (Sm 1631), 421 (Sm 1735), 426 (Sm 1836), 427 (Sm 1843), 444 (Rm 2,489), 458 (80-7-19,336), 471 (81-2-4,382 + K 4247 + K 8492 + K 13760 + K 15375)[41], 480 (81-2-4,498), 488 (81-7-27,255), 491 (82-3-23,046), 525 (83-1-18,505), 531 (83-1-18,709); 537 (83-1-18,736), 546 (83-1-18,826), 550 (83-1-18,868), 552 (83-1-18,882), 563 (Bu 91-5-9,070), 568 (Bu 91-5-9,124), 572 (Bu 91-5-9,226), 573 (Bu 91-5-9,227); 576 (Bu 91-5-9,237), 577 (Bu 91-5-9,239), 578 (Th 1905-4-9,071 = BM 98565), 585 (Ki 1904-10-9,284 = BM 99252).

K 1967, K 5391, K 5513, K 5532, K 7132[42], K 7293, K 10919, K 14800[43], K 15097, K 15346, K 15426, K 15600, K 15620, K 15624, K 15627, K 15630 + K 16544,[44] K 15631, K 15647, K 15651, K 15652, K 15653, K 15656, K 15657, K 15658, K 15663, K 15667, K 15669, K 15671, K 15672, K 15673, K 15674, K 15676, K 15677, K 15680, K 15684, K 15694, K 16041, K 16052, K 16054, K 16061, K 16065, K 16067, K 16101, K 16102[45], K 16486, K 16488, K 16493, K 16494, K 16495, K 16497, K 16502, K 16505, K 16508, K 16513, K 16519, K 16520, K 16524, K 16525, K 16528, K 16530, K 16533, K 16535, K 16537, K 16538, K 16540, K 16541, K 16542, K 16543, K 16546, K 16547, K 16548, K 16549, K 16557, K 16558, K 16559, K 16560, K 16561, K 16563, K 16564, K 16566, K 16567, K 16570, K 16573, K 16574, K 16575, K 16577, K 17527, K 17622, K 18007, K 18843, K 19353, K 19501, K 19630, K 19965, K 19973, K 19975, K 19978, K 19983, K 19990, K 19992, K 20220, K 20556, K 20559, K 20567, K 20568, K 20905, K 20913, K 21950 (82-3-23), K 21951; 79-7-8,268; Ki 1904-10-9,287 (BM 99255).

Sm 618, Sm 839, Sm 1142, Sm 1619, Sm 1625, Sm 1714.

The Order of Texts in This Volume

The order in which the texts are presented follows as closely as possible the practice of previously published SAA volumes, to which they are complementary. As the letters in the first four chapters and other texts are additions to previous volumes, the book does not offer complete individual dossiers. In fact, only a small proportion of the letters are from identified senders, which has resulted in extensive unattributed sections. However, the sorting criteria are the same as before and relate mainly to prosopography (starting with the royal letters), geography, themes in the texts, and chronology (e.g., the important but sometimes rough division of the letters into Chapters 1-2 and Chapters 3-4). Another important criterion is numerical, since the two chapters of the letters follow the previous order of publication (Ch. 1 = SAA 1, 5, 15, 17; Ch. 3 = SAA 10, 13, 16, 18, 21, 22) and the internal numerical order of each of these volumes, in which the additional texts to these volumes now appear. There is no serious attempt to organise unattributed letters, but they often follow their respective CT 53, CT 54 and/or ABL numbers. Small letter fragments with introductory formulae or closings are part of Ch 2 without any particular sorting.

The numerical order of the other chapters is also largely based on their original order of publication, but the additions to the volumes which form a natural unit in terms of their genre (SAA 6 and 14 as well as SAA 7 and 11) belong together. There is a slight deviation in the arrangement of chapters, where the additions to SAA 4 (queries to the sun god) come before those of SAA 8 (astrological reports). However, in contrast to other chapters, they both offer reports that rely on the disciplined interpretation of signs and omens. In all these non-letter chapters, the numerical principle is also applied in relation to the previous order (for other prevailing criteria, see the original volumes).

Transliterations and Translations

The primary purpose of the transliterations and translations is to establish a reliable standard text. Despite the difficult funding situation, many texts from Nineveh have been collated specifically for this volume, some of them several times. In addition, we have used photographs provided by The Ashurbanipal Library Project, available on the websites of the British Museum (https://www.britishmuseum.org/collection) and the Cuneiform Digital Library Initiative (https://cdli.mpiwg-berlin.mpg.de/), together with previous publications, to make the editions as decent as possible. It should be stressed, however, that texts from sites other than Nineveh have not been collated.[46]

The transliterations, addressed to the specialist, render the text of the originals in Roman characters according to standard Assyriological conventions in the customary SAA style. Results of collation are indicated with exclamation or question marks. Single exclamation marks imply correction of incorrect readings found in earlier editions and/or copies. Definite scribal errors corrected in the transliteration are indicated with double exclamation marks, while question marks indicate uncertain or questionable readings.

Restorations and emendations have generally been made sparingly, but in a few cases we have taken the liberty of suggesting more thorough restorations for the understanding of a text. Broken portions of the text and all restorations are enclosed within square brackets both in the transliteration and translation. Parentheses enclose items omitted by ancient scribes. Uncertain or conjectural translations are indicated by italics. Scribal omissions and interpretative additions to the translation are enclosed within parentheses. Untranslatable passages are indicated by dots. Badly broken passages are generally only translated if the isolated words in them contain some meaningful information. The fragmentary nature of the material has resulted in an extraordinary number of texts remaining untitled.

The translations seek to render the original tenor and meaning of the letters in readable English. Personal, divine and geographical names are rendered in the conventional way if a well-established and functional English or Biblical equivalent exists (e.g., Merodach-baladan, Sargon, Nineveh); otherwise, the name is given in the transcription without length marks except for the circumflex in the final position (e.g., Nabû, Mahdê, Sasî, etc.) and in the divine name Sîn. The divine name Aššur is distinguished from the homophonous city name (Assur). Month names are rendered by their Hebrew equivalents (Nisan, Shebat, Adar), with Roman numerals indicating the place of the month within the lunar year added in parentheses. Weights and measures are whenever feasible rendered by their Biblical equivalents (mina, shekel, homer, with metric equivalents occasionally supplied within parentheses). The rendering of professions follows the Assyrian-English-Assyrian Dictionary and is a compromise between the use of accurate but impractical Assyrian terms and inaccurate but practical modern or classical equivalents.

Critical Apparatus

The primary purpose of the critical apparatus is to support the readings and translations established in the edition. It chiefly consists of references to previous editions and/or studies of the texts and collations of difficult passages. Other essential matters covered are textual parallels, scribal mistakes corrected in the transliteration, alternative readings or translations of ambiguous passages, and discussions of grammatical and lexical problems. Restorations based on easily verifiable evidence (parallels or duplicates) are basically not explained in the apparatus, conjectural restorations only if their conjectural nature is not made explicit by italics in the translation.

Collations by the editors published in copy at the end of the volume are referred to simply as "see coll.".

The critical apparatus does contain some additional information relevant to the interpretation of the texts but should not be considered a commentary and this volume is not a comprehensive study of these texts. For the convenience of the reader, references to studies of individual texts are given, but with no claim to completeness. Comments are mainly devoted to problems in the text, e.g., to the discussion of difficult passages, and the historical and technical information contained in the texts is generally kept to a minimum.

Glossary and Indices

The glossary and indices in this book have been automatically generated from the transliterated text and are for all practical purposes complete. The glossary contains all the occurrences of even the most common words arranged in alphabetic order under the relevant lemmata. The forms listed are not arranged semantically, and generally only the basic meanings of the words are given. Since the texts included in this volume are written in both Assyrian and Babylonian, the relevant forms are often to be looked up under both Assyrian and Babylonian lemmata. E.g., occurrences of the verb **wṣī* "to go out" are listed under both NA *uṣû* and NB *aṣû*, depending on the language of the text. Cross-references are provided in such cases. A complete list of logograms with their readings precedes the glossary.

The name indices are styled like the glossary. To enhance their utility, identifications are given (in parentheses) for every name whenever possible. The lemmas are given in their normalized form, which is not necessarily identical with the name form used in the translations.

NOTES

[1] Parpola, *Akkadica* 49 (1986) 22.
[2] Apart from the Nimrud tablet ND 2446, which is kept in the British Museum.
[3] See SAA 22, p. xxxi.
[4] Compare this "delay" with Parpola's optimistic view expressed in his "The Neo-Assyrian Text Corpus Project of the University of Helsinki," *Akkadica* 49 (1986) 20.
[5] Literary texts produced in the Assyrian Empire (whether authored, rewritten or simply copied by the Assyrians is not our concern here) have attracted much attention, such as those published in the Corpus of Mesopotamian Anti-witchcraft Rituals (including *Maqlû*), the *Epic of Gilgamesh*, and omens, divinatory, medical, and astrological-astronomical tablets, etc.
[6] For example, Parpola is also finishing his work on the Khorsabad (Dur-Šarruken) material together with Professors John Brinkman and Grant Frame.
[7] "All" the archival texts is a slight exaggeration, as some of them are in unpublishable condition.
[8] For example, the difference between the fragments in this volume and the mostly well-preserved tablets in SAA 22 is striking.
[9] Note also that many documents in SAA 14 (esp. nos. 174-423) are undatable.
[10] Luukko, M., "Updates to *Nimrud Letters* editions previously published in the *State Archives of Assyria* series" at https://www.ucl.ac.uk/sargon/downloads/saa19_updates.pdf exemplifies this.
[11] Probably the most informative work on the Nineveh joins and "joinology" is still Borger's Ein Brief (1991: especially pp. 46-58).
[12] Of course, this requires a large corpus. An excellent example of such a corpus and its consistent construction is eBL (https://www.ebl.lmu.de/).
[13] See, e.g., Luukko, SAAS 29 (2019) 243 and Mattila – Harjumäki, SAAB 21 (2015) 112f.
[14] Apart from this volume, eighth-century NB letters from Nineveh and Nimrud are published in SAA 17 and SAA 19 (nos. 4, 99, 117, 122, 124, 130-131, 133-150, 201-203), while seventh-century NB letters are published in SAA 10 (nos. 109-121, 154-172, 178-180, 313, 371-374), SAA 13 (nos. 4-6, 173-183, 185), SAA 18, SAA 21 (the majority, but the volume also contains about 50 NA letters) and SAA 22.
[15] For the most part our division agrees with that of Fincke's (AfO 50 [2003-2004] 147f.), but there may be some minor differences.
[16] However, the verbs for robbery and killing will have to be partially restored.
[17] Counting now tentatively no. 27 (CT 54 377) as a Neo-Assyrian letter.
[18] As a denunciation, no. 123 is thematically an addition to SAA 16, but it is also an outlier, a stray tablet of unknown provenance.
[19] There are, of course, many letters with uncertain recipients (e.g., nos. 11, 14, 21), mainly because the names have been broken away.
[20] The many tasks of the palace scribe have been discussed in Luukko, SAAB 16 (2007) 227-256. Another important palace official attested as the recipient of a letter (no. 141 = CT 53 174) in this volume is the palace supervisor (*ša-pān-ēkalli*).
[21] The first part of the text is not a duplicate to SAA 2 6.
[22] Probably drafted in 683 or 682 BCE; see Frahm, KAL 3, p. 132.
[23] J. Lauinger, JCS 64 (2012) 87-123.
[24] For example, Lauinger himself, Fales, Ponchia, Watanabe and many others have published articles inspired by this treaty text. Surely more Neo-Assyrian treaty tablets, or fragments of them, will be found in new excavations in the Near East.
[25] See Livingstone's discussion of the inclusion of a text in SAA 3, pp. xvi-xvii, xx-xxii, xxv-xxxi. Livingstone does not use the definition NB but speaks generally of "Late Babylonian". In this chapter, no. 243 may seem like an oddity. However, there is something disturbing about the somewhat clumsy and robust appearance of the fragment, and several gaps between words may suggest that it is not an ordinary letter, but perhaps something else.
[26] No. 237 (Rm 2, 455) is a letter, and formally an addition to SAA 10, but as it contains many quotations and relates to Assurbanipal's war against the Elamites, it fits in well with other such texts.
[27] See S. Panayotov, CDLN 2015:7 and the latest edition of the text by H. Schaudig in KAL 12, no.3.

[28] SAAo: http://oracc.museum.upenn.edu/saao/corpus. Oracc: http://oracc.museum.upenn. edu/.
[29] Note, however, that what is said in SAA 22, p. xxxi about the publication of ABL 1032 (K 8381) in this volume is incorrect; the letter has been published as SAA 21 144.
[30] Her work on the Babylonian tablets from Nineveh has been described in J. C. Fincke, "The Babylonian Texts of Nineveh, Report on the British Museum's Ashurbanipal Library Project," AfO 50 (2003-2004) 111-149.
[31] This volume also contains joins other than previously published SAA texts, but it is sufficient to include the former group in the "List of Joins" at the end of the volume.
[32] Further, the CDLI website, https://cdli.mpiwg-berlin.mpg.de/artifacts/240365 (accessed 29.8.2023), says "SAA 04, 246 + 263 (P240365)", but I do not know if the two small fragments really belong together. If they do, the two questions (SAA 4 263 = K 17834) come first, followed by the chain of *ezib*s (SAA 4 246 = Sm 1272).
[33] In Frazer's corpus these are referred to as A6 (ABL 924+ = K 1109 + K 3045, ms. A, but also small NB fragments forming ms. b were also found at Kuyunjik), B2 (ABL 1282 = K 2641) and C6 (ABL 1283 = K 2646). Other historical letters or their fragments that she has published with Nineveh manuscripts are A9 (K 212 + K 4448, ms. A_1; Sm 2116 + BM 104727, ms. A_2), C2 (K 8486), C4 (K 9952, ms. B), C13 (K 6411) and C14 (K 7982). Many other letter fragments in Frazer's corpus also deal with Assyro-Babylonian relations of the late second and early first millennia, with manuscripts from places other than Nineveh, and often, because of their condition, with uncertain senders and recipients.
[34] It is a Middle Babylonian literary letter, consisting of several exemplars, including two from Nineveh (Frazer's A9 just above with previous literature).
[35] A Late Babylonian copy of a letter sent from Borsippa to Assurbanipal concerning the king's request that Babylonian tablets of learning be collected and sent to him; the text is edited by Frame - George, Iraq 67 (2005) 265-270 and now also by Frazer op.cit. A11.
[36] Another Late Babylonian copy of a letter sent to or from Assurbanipal related to his request for tablets from Babylonia; see Frame - George, Iraq 67 (2005) 270-277 and Frazer op.cit. A12.
[37] W.G. Lambert, "No. 44: Letter of Sîn-šarra-iškun to Nabopolassar," in I. Spar - W.G. Lambert (eds.), *CTMMA 2: Literary and Scholastic Texts of the First Millennium B.C.* (New York 2005), 203-210, pls. 62-63 (copy by I. Spar) and Frazer op.cit. A16. See also a letter from Nabopolassar to Sîn-šarru-iškun; ibid. A17 (with previous literature).
[38] A fragment of a royal inscription; see SAA 21, p. xli.
[39] This is a fragment of an oracle query dealing with an MB *tamītu* (see eBL for details).
[40] Join by J. Fincke (6.8.2003). The NB letter now has 28 (14 + 14) partially preserved lines, but as the left part of the tablet is missing, it does not yet provide much context, mostly just single words.
[41] 81-2-4,382 (CT 54 471) is a join by Lambert in 1977 to a text he published in "The Problem of the Love Lyrics" in H. Goedicke - J. J. M. Roberts (eds.), *Unity and Diversity. Essays in the History, Literature, and Religion of the Ancient Near East* (Baltimore - London 1975) 108-115.
[42] A fragment of a hemerology.
[43] A fragment of a royal inscription; see SAA 21, p. xli.
[44] Join by Th. Kwasman (16.4.1980). This small NA fragment has only 8 partially preserved lines.
[45] Possibly a fragment of a land-grant schedule, i.e., an addition to SAA 12; see PNA 1/I 35b s.v. Adad-rēṣūwa 2.
[46] The only exception is ND 2446 (see note 2 above).

Abbreviations and Symbols

Bibliographical Abbreviations

79-7-8 etc.	tablets in the collections of the British Museum
A	tablets in the collections of Istanbul Arkeoloji Müzeleri
ABL	R.F. Harper, *Assyrian and Babylonian Letters* (London - Chicago 1892-1914)
ADD	C.H.W. Johns, *Assyrian Deeds and Documents* (Cambridge 1898-1923)
AEAD	S. Parpola - R.M. Whiting (eds.), *Assyrian-English-Assyrian Dictionary* (NATCP, Helsinki 2007)
AfO	Archiv für Orientforschung
AGS	J.A. Knudtzon, *Assyrische Gebete an den Sonnengott* (Leipzig 1893)
An	lexical series An-*Anum*
Annus Ninurta	A. Annus, *The God Ninurta in the Mythology and Royal Ideology of Ancient Mesopotamia* (SAAS 14, Helsinki 2002)
AOAT	Alter Orient und Altes Testament
ARINH	F.M. Fales (ed.), *Assyrian Royal Inscriptions: New Horizons in Literary, Ideological and Historical Analysis* (Orientis Antiqui Collectio XVIII, Rome 1981)
ASJ	Acta Sumerologica Japonica
Ass	field numbers of tablets excavated at Assur
Assur-Forschungen	*Arbeiten aus der Forschungsstelle "Edition literarischer Keilschrifttexte aus Assur" der Heidelberger Akademie der Wissenschaften* (Wiesbaden 2010)
BAM	F. Köcher, *Die babylonisch-assyrische Medizin in Texten und Untersuchungen* I-VI (Berlin 1963-1980)
Bauer Asb	Th. Bauer, *Das Inschriftenwerk Assurbanipals* (Leipzig 1933)
BM	tablets in the collections of the British Museum
Borger Ein Brief	*Sonnengott sowie Bemerkungen über „Joins" und das „Joinen"*. Nachrichten der Akademie der Wissenschaften zu Göttingen, Philologisch-Historische Klasse 1991, 2 (Göttingen 1991)
Bu	tablets in the collections of the British Museum
CAD	The Assyrian Dictionary of the Oriental Institute of the University of Chicago
Caubet Khorsabad	A. Caubet (ed.), *Khorsabad, le palais de Sargon II, roi d'Assyrie* (Paris 1995)
CDLN	Cuneiform Digital Library Notes
CRRAI	Rencontre assyriologique internationale, comptes rendus

CT	Cuneiform Texts from Babylonian Tablets in the British Museum
CTN	Cuneiform Texts from Nimrud
Dalman Aram. Wb.	G.H. Dalman, *Aramäisch-neuhebräisches Wörterbuch zu Targum, Talmud und Midrasch* (Hildesheim 1967)
Deller Zagros	K. Deller, *Ausgewählte neuassyrische Briefe betreffend Urarṭu zur Zeit Sargons II.*, in P.E. Pecorella - M. Salvini, *Tra lo Zagros e l'Urmia. Ricerche Storica ed archeologiche nell'Azerbaigian iraniano* (Rome 1984)
de Vaan Bel-ibni	J.M.C.T. de Vaan, *„Ich bin eine Schwertklinge des Königs". Die Sprache des Bēl-ibni* (AOAT 242, Kevelaer - Neukirchen-Vluyn 1995)
EA	J.A. Knudtzon, *Die El-Amarna-Tafeln* (Vorderasiatische Bibliothek 2, Leipzig 1915)
eBL	Electronic Babylonian Library
Fales and Lanfranchi Lettere	F.M. Fales - G.B. Lanfranchi, *Lettere dalla corte Assira* (Venezia 1992)
Foster Before the Muses	B.R. Foster, *Before the Muses: An Anthology of Akkadian Literature* I (3rd ed., Bethesda, MD 2005).
Frame Babylonia	G. Frame, *Babylonia 689-627 B.C. A Political History* (PIHANS 69, Leiden 1992)
Fs. Donbaz	Ş. Dönmez, (ed.), DUB.SAR É.DUB.BA.A: *Studies Presented in Honour of Veysel Donbaz / Veysel Donbaz'a Sunulan Yazilar* (Istanbul 2010)
Fs. Grayson	G. Frame (ed.), with the assistance of L. Wilding, *From the Upper Sea to the Lower Sea. Studies on the History of Assyria and Babylonia in Honour of A.K. Grayson* (Uitgaven van het Nederlands Instituut voor het Nabije Oosten te Leiden 101, Leiden 2004)
Fs. Kessler	J.M[a] Córdoba - C. del Cerro (eds.), *"Im Osten grauts, der Nebel fällt, ..." / "Amanece por Oriente, cae la niebla, ...": Karlheinz Kessler Festschrift / Homenaje* (Isimu 20-21, Madrid 2017-18)
Fs. Lambert	A.R. George - I.L. Finkel (eds.), *Wisdom, Gods and Literature: Studies in Assyriology in Honour of W.G. Lambert* (Winona Lake, IN 2000)
Fs. Lanfranchi	S. Gaspa *et al.* (eds.), *From Source to History: Studies on Ancient Near Eastern Worlds and Beyond Dedicated to Giovanni Battista Lanfranchi on the Occasion of His 65th Birthday on June 23, 2014* (AOAT 412, Münster 2014)
Fs. Parpola	M. Luukko, S. Svärd and R. Mattila (eds.), *Of God(s), Trees, Kings, and Scholars: Neo-Assyrian and Related Studies in Honour of Simo Parpola* (Studia Orientalia 106, Helsinki 2009)

Fs. Postgate	Y. Heffron, A. Stone and M. Worthington (eds.), *At the Dawn of History: Ancient Near Eastern Studies in Honour of J. N. Postgate* (Winona Lake, IN 2017)
GPA	J.N Postgate, *The Governor's Palace Archive* (CTN 2, London 1973)
Hunger Kolophone	H. Hunger, *Babylonische und assyrische Kolophone* (AOAT 2, Kevelaer - Neukirchen-Vluyn 1968)
Gr. Nr.	excavation number
IM	tablets in the collections of the Iraq Museum, Baghdad
JCS	Journal of Cuneiform Studies
K	K(onstantinopel)-Photo
	tablets in the collections of the British Museum
KAL	Keilschrifttexte aus Assur literarischen Inhalts
KAR	E. Ebeling, *Keilschrifttexte aus Assur religiösen Inhalts* I-II (Wissenschaftliche Veröffentlichungen der Deutschen Orient-Gesellschaft 28 and 34, Leipzig 1919, 1922)
Ki	tablets in the collections of the British Museum
Koch-Westenholz Liver Omens	U. Koch-Westenholz, *Babylonian Liver Omens: The Chapters* Manzāzu, Padānu *and* Pān tākalti *of the Babylonian Extispicy Series Mainly from Aššurbanipal's Library* (Carsten Niebuhr Institute Publications 25, Copenhagen 2000)
LAS	S. Parpola, *Letters from Assyrian Scholars to the Kings Esarhaddon and Assurbanipal* I, II (Alter Orient und Altes Testament 5/1-2, Neukirchen-Vluyn 1970, 1983)
Litke An-Anum	R.L. Litke, *A Reconstruction of the Assyro-Babylonian God-Lists*, AN: ^{d}A-nu-um and AN: Anu šá amēli (Texts from the Babylonian Collection 3, New Haven, CT 1998)
LKA	E. Ebeling - F. Köcher, *Literarische Keilschrifttexte aus Assur* (Berlin 1953)
LTBA	L. Matouš - W. Soden, *Die lexikalischen Tafelserien der Babylonier und Assyrer in den Berliner Museen* I-II (Berlin 1933)
Menzel Tempel	B. Menzel, *Assyrische Tempel* I-II (Studia Pohl, Series Maior 10, Rome 1981)
MG	Maški Gate (Nineveh)
MGT	Maški Gate Texts
Millard Eponyms	A. Millard, *The Eponyms of the Assyrian Empire* (SAAS 2, Helsinki 1994)
MVAeG	Mitteilungen der Vorderasiatisch-Ägyptischen Gesellschaft
NABU	Nouvelles Assyriologiques Brèves et Utilitaires
ND	field numbers of tablets excavated at Nimrud
OIP	Oriental Institute Publications
Or	Orientalia, Nova Series
PhAss	photographs taken during the German excavations in Assur

PIHANS	Publications de l'Institut Historique-Archéologique Néerlandais de Stamboul
PNA	K. Radner - H.D. Baker (eds.), *The Prosopography of the Neo-Assyrian Empire* (Helsinki 1998-)
Postgate TCAE	J.N. Postgate, *Taxation and Conscription in the Assyrian Empire.* (Studia Pohl, Series Maior 3, Rome 1974)
PRT	E. Klauber, *Politisch-religiöse Texte aus der Sargonidenzeit* (Leipzig 1913)
R	H.C. Rawlinson, *The Cuneiform Inscriptions of Western Asia* (London 1861-1884)
RA	Revue d'assyriologie
RCAE	L. Waterman, *Royal Correspondence of the Assyrian Empire* I-IV (Ann Arbor 1930-1936)
RGTC	Répertoire Géographique des Textes Cunéiformes
RIMA	Royal Inscriptions of Mesopotamia. Assyrian Periods
RINAP	Royal Inscriptions of the Neo-Assyrian Period
RlA	Reallexikon der Assyriologie
Rm	tablets in the collections of the British Museum
RMA	R.C. Thompson, *The Reports of the Magicians and Astrologers of Nineveh and Babylon* I-II (London 1900)
SAA	State Archives of Assyria
SAAB	State Archives of Assyria Bulletin
SAAS	State Archives of Assyria Studies
SAHG	A. Falkenstein - W. von Soden, *Sumerische und akkadische Hymnen und Gebete* (Zürich - Stuttgart 1953)
SANER	Studies in Ancient Near Eastern Records
Scurlock Magico-Medical Means	- J. Scurlock, *Magico-Medical Means of Treating Ghost-Induced Illness in Ancient Mesopotamia* (Ancient Magic and Divination 3, Leiden - New York 2006)
Seux Hymnes	M.-J. Seux, *Hymnes et prières aux dieux de Babylone et d'Assyrie* (Littératures anciennes du Proche-Orient 8, Paris 1976)
SKT	H. Winckler, *Sammlung von Keilschrifttexten* I-III (Leipzig 1893-95)
Sm	tablets in the collections of the British Museum
Smith	copy from the folios of Sidney Smith
StAT	Studien zu den Assur-Texten
StOr	Studia Orientalia
STT	The Sultantepe Tablets
Tallqvist Götterepitheta	K. Tallqvist, *Akkadische Götterepitheta* (StOr 7, Helsinki 1938)
Th	tablets in the collections of the British Museum
TIM	Texts in the Iraq Museum
UF	Ugarit-Forschungen
VAT	tablets in the collections of the Staatliche Museen, Berlin

Waerzeggers Ezida	C. Waerzeggers, *The Ezida Temple of Borsippa: Priesthood, Cult, Archives* (Achaemenid History 15, Leiden 2010)
WO	Die Welt des Orients
YBC	siglum of tablets in the Yale Babylonian Collection
ZA	Zeitschrift für Assyriologie
ZAR	Zeitschrift für Altorientalische und Biblische Rechtsgeschichte
ZT	siglum of tablets from Ziyaret Tepe
ZTT	S. Parpola, "Cuneiform texts from Ziyaret Tepe (Tušhan), 2002-2003," SAAB 17 (2008), 1-114

Other Abbreviations and Symbols

Asb	Assurbanipal
DN	divine name
GN	geographical name
MA	Middle Assyrian
MB	Middle Babylonian
NA	Neo-Assyrian
NB	Neo-Babylonian
NN	Uncertain personal name
OA	Old Assyrian
OB	Old Babylonian
PN	personal name
RN	royal name
SB	Standard Babylonian
coll.	collated, collation
e.	edge
mng.	meaning
ms.	manuscript
obv.	obverse
pf.	perfect
pl.	plate, plural
prs.	present
prt.	preterite
r., rev.	reverse
s.	(left) side
sg.	singular
subj.	subjunctive
unpub.	unpublished
var.	variant
!	collation
!!	emendation

?	uncertain reading
: :. ::	cuneiform division marks
*	graphic variants (see LAS I p. xx)
0	uninscribed space or nonexistent sign
x	broken or undeciphered sign
( )	supplied word or sign
(( ))	sign erroneously added by scribe
[[ ]]	erasure
[...]	minor break
[......]	major break
...	untranslatable word
......	untranslatable passage
+	joined to
(+)	indirect join
→	see also

TRANSLITERATIONS AND TRANSLATIONS

1. The Correspondence of Sargon II
Additions to SAA I, V, XV and XVII

FIG. 1. *Urartian envoys.*
BM 124802a.

1. Urarṭian Emissaries Meet Captives

K 622 + K 1981 + K 16512

1 *a-bat* LUGAL *a-na* ^{md}PA–BÀD–PAB
2 *an-nu-rig* ^{m}*man-nu–ki-i–aš-š*[*ur*]
3 LÚ*.*qur-bu-te ina* UGU LÚ*.MAH.MEŠ
4 *am-mu-ti* KUR.URI-*a-a a-sap-ra*
5 *ina pa-na-at* LÚ*.*hu-ub-te ha-an-nu-ti*
6 *ša ina pa-ni-ku-nu* NINDA.MEŠ *e-ka-lu-u-ni*
7 *a-na* URU.*ur-zu-hi-na ub-ba-la-áš-šú-nu*
8 *at-ta* UD-*mu ša e-gír-tú an-ni-tú*
9 *ta-mar-u-ni re-eš* LÚ*.*hu-ub-ti*
10 *ha-an-ni-i i-ši*! *lu et-ku*
11 *li-iz-zi-zu ina* ŠÀ UD-*me*
12 *ša* ^{m}*man-nu–ki–aš-šur* LÚ*.*qur-bu-ti*
13 *i-šap-pa-rak-kan-ni ma-a*
14 *an-nu-rig* LÚ*.MAH.MEŠ
15 *a-na* URU.*ur-zu-hi-na*
16 *iq-ṭar-bu-u-ni ma-a* LÚ*.*h*[*u-ub-tu*]
17 *nam-me-šá* LÚ*.*hu-ub-tu* ⸢*pa*⸣-[*hír*]
18 ⸢*a-na*⸣ URU.*ur-zu-(hi)-na a-*⸢*lik*⸣ [0]
e.19 [*x x x a*]-*na* LÚ*.*šá*–[UGU–URU]
20 [*ša*] ⸢URU⸣.*ur-zu-h*[*i-na*]
21 *pi-q*[*id*]
r.1 ^{m}*aš-šur*–TÉŠ–U[N.MEŠ-*ma a-sap-ra*]
2 *mu-*⸢*uk a*⸣-[*lik x x x x*]
3 *a-du pa-*⸢*ni*!⸣ [*x x x x x x x*]
4 *is-si-šú-nu* ⸢*i*⸣-[*ti-iz x x x*]
5 *ke-e-*⸢*tu*⸣ MÍ.MEŠ KU[R.*x x x x*]*x*
6 *ša* TA* LÚ*.*hu-ub-tu* [*il-li*]-*ka-ni-ni*
7 *ina* URU.*arrap-ha ina maš*!-*ka-*⸢*ni*⸣ [1-*e*]*n*! *lu kam-mu-sa*
8 TA* LÚ*.*hu-ub-*⸢*tu*! *lu*!⸣ *l*[*a*!] ⸢*il*!⸣-*la-ka*
9 *ù an-nu-rig* ⸢MÍ?.MEŠ? *ša*! *ú-ba*⸣-ʾ*u-u-ni*
10 *ú-še-ṣa-an-ni* ⸢*ina*! URU!⸣.*x*[*x u*]*b*!-*bal-u-ni*
11 TA* MÍ.MEŠ *ha-a*[*n-na*]-*ti ina* ⸢URU.*arrap*⸣-*ha*
12 *lu kam-mu-sa* NINDA.M[EŠ *l*]*e-e-*⸢*ku*!⸣-*la*!
13 A.MEŠ *li*!-*is-si-a a-d*[*i*!] ⸢É *a*⸣-[*na*]-⸢*ku*!⸣ *al-lak-an-ni*
14 GIŠ.GIGIR.MEŠ *ša* É.GAL *ša* MÍ!.M[EŠ *a*]*n*!-⸢*na*!-*ti*!⸣
15 *ub-ba-lu-ni-ni* NINDA.MEŠ *a-na* ⸢UN!⸣.[MEŠ]
16 ŠE.*ki-is-su-tú a-na* ANŠE.*ú-*⸢*rat*!⸣.MEŠ
17 *lid-di-nu*
rest (2 lines) uninscribed

ABL 306 + CT 53 221 + CT 53 784 (= SAA 1 10+)

1 The king's word to Nabû-duru-uṣur:

2 Right now I am sending the royal bodyguard Mannu-ki-Aššur to those Urarṭian emissaries: he will bring them to Urzuhina in advance of these captives who are eating bread in your charge.

8 As for you, the day you see this letter, summon these captives; they should be on the alert, standing by, and the day Mannu-ki-Aššur the bodyguard writes to you: "The emissaries have arrived in Urzuhina, set the ca[ptives] in motion," ass[emble] the captives, go to Urzuhina, and entr[ust] them [...] to the the [city-over]seer [of] Urzuh[ina].

r.1 [I am also sending] Aššur-balti-n[iše] (with the following orders): "G[o ......] in the presence [of ......] and as[sist] them!" Truly, the [*Urarṭia*]n women, who [ca]me with the captives, should stay in [on]e residence in Arrapha (and) not go with the captives!

9 But now *the women* whom he is seeking, taking out and bringing to [...], should live with these women in Arrapha, and should be given bread to eat and water to drink until I come. The palace chariots which are bringing these women are to provide the peop[le] with bread and the teams with fodder.

1 [10, r.7, 12f, 15f] See coll. [r.3, 8-10, 14] For collations, see SAA 1, p. 255a. [r.6-7] The readings are improved by a join.

FIG. 2. *Female prisoners and child.*
BM 124552.

2. Fragment Mentioning Bel-taklak

K 5630

1 [*x x x x x x x x x*]
2 [*x x x x x x x x x*]
3 *a-na* ^{m}*x*[*x x x x*]
4 ^{m}EN–*tak-lak* [*x x x x*]
5 *ṭ*[*è-mu x x x x x*]
6 7 [*x x x x x x x x*]
7 *ma-*[*a x x x x x x*]
rest broken away
Rev. blank

CT 53 300

(Beginning destroyed)

3 to [NN]
4 Bel-taklak [....]
5 *r*[*eport* ......]

(Rest destroyed or too broken for translation)

2 This fragment comes from an originally brief communication which may have been a royal order (the first line may be restored as *a-bat* LUGAL). 5 Or: "o[rder".

3. Silver Requested

K 14988

beginning broken away

1′ [*x x*] ⸢BUR? *lu* 2 *lu* 3⸣ GÚ.⸢UN⸣
2′ [*ina*] ⸢ŠU⸣ LÚ*.DUMU–*šip-ri ina* UGU-⸢*ia*⸣
3′ *še-bi-la a-n*[*a-ku* T]A* *un-na-k*[*a*]
4′ KUG.UD *x*[*x x la-din-a*]*k-ka*
5′ *a-na-ku* [*x x x x*]
6′ *ki-i* ⸢*ma*?-*a*?⸣-[*da a*]–*dan-*[*n*]*iš*
7′ *ta-ra-a-*[*man-ni-ni*?]
r.1 *a-na-*⸢*ku*⸣ GIŠ.MÁR.DA.ME
2 *ú-ṣa-ba-ka*

rest uninscribed

CT 53 598

(Beginning destroyed)

1 [...] ... send me 2 or 3 talents (of silver) [v]ia (*my*) messenger.

3 [I will give] you [...] silver [fr]om here.

5 I [...]

6 As you love [*me*] *ve*[*ry*] *much,* I will (also) increase the number of the hardwood poles for you.

4. Messengers

K 15339

beginning broken away

1′ [*x x x*] *x*[*x x x x x*]
2′ ⸢LÚ.A⸣–KIN-*i*[*a x x x x*]
3′ *i-tal-ka x*[*x x x x x*]
4′ *ina* ŠÀ URU.⸢*x*⸣[*x x x x*]
5′ ⸢LÚ.A–KIN⸣.MEŠ-*k*[*a*? *x x x x*]
6′ [*x x x*]-*ni* [*x x x x x*]

rest broken away

CT 53 646

(Beginning destroyed)

2 m[y] messenger has come [......]

4 in the town of [......]

5 *yo*[*ur*] messengers [...]

(Rest destroyed)

5. ---

Sm 417

beginning broken away

1′ *ina* U[GU *x x x x x x x*]
2′ *ina* UGU *x*[*x x x x x x x*]
3′ *a-a-ka* [*x x x x x x x*]
4′ *i-ba-áš-*[*ši x x a-ta-a*?]
5′ *la taš-pu-*[*ra x x x x x*]

6′ 1-*et a-bu-*[*tú x x x x*]
7′ *ina* UGU LÚ*.*qur-*[*bu-ti x x x*]
8′ *ha-an-nu-ti* [*x x x x x x*]

9′ *it-*[*x x x x x x x x*]

rest broken away

CT 53 816

(Beginning destroyed)

1 *Concerning* [......]

2 *Concerning* [......]

3 where [......]?

4 *there is* [... *Why*] have you not writt[en to me? ......]

6 *One wor*[*d* ...]

7 *Concerning* the body[guard ...]

8 these [......]

(Break)

3 This is a royal letter to another king, but too short for identifying the sender and recipient. r.1 GIŠ.MÁR.DA = *martû.* r.2 *ú-ṣa-ba-ka* is D prs 1st sg. of *aṣābu.*

4 2, 5 The messengers of two parties suggest a diplomatic context.

5 4-5 This may or may not be a royal letter. Thus far, the phrase *atâ lā tašpura* appears almost exclusively quoted in letters to the king. 6 One might restore, e.g., [*la tu/ú-pa-zar*?] "[(*I*) *do not conceal*] a single wor[d]".

Rev. beginning broken away
1′ *x*[*x x x x x x x x x*]
2′ *ina p*[*a-an x x x x x*]
3′ *mi-i-*[*nu x x x x x x*]
4′ *ù a*[*n-x x x x x x x*]
5′ LÚ*.*qur-bu-ti* [*x x x x x*]
6′ *ina* UGU-*hi-ia* [*x x x x x*]
7′ *a-ta-a x*[*x x x x x x*]
rest broken away

r.2 *in the pres*[*ence of* ...]
3 wh[at ......]
4 moreover [......]
5 the bodyguard [......]
6 *to* me [......]
7 why [......]
(Rest destroyed)

6. Names of the City Lords on Reliefs

K 4304 + K 7517

1 [*a-na* LUGA]L! *be-lí-ia*
2 [ARA]D-*ka* ⸢m⸣[DÙ]G!–IM–*aš-šur*
3 *lu* DI-*mu a-na* LUGAL EN-*ia*

4 *ša* LUGAL *be-lí iš-pur-an-ni ma-a*
5 MU.MEŠ *ša* LÚ*.EN–URU!.MEŠ *ša* URU.MEŠ

6 *a-ta-a la za-qu-ru* LUGAL *be-lí*
7 *ú-da hu-li-ni* [*p*]*a-ni-u*
8 *ša a-na* KUR.*man-na-*⸢*a*⸣-[*a u š*]*a*? *a-na mad-a-a*
9 ⸢*ni*⸣*-il-lik-u-ni in*[*a* É.SIG4.MEŠ?]
10 [*ša*] É.GAL *la-bir-*[*te x x x x*]
11 [*x x*] *né-e-ta-m*[*ar x x x*]
rest broken away
Rev. beginning broken away
1′ [*x x*]*x* ⸢*lu* LÚ.UŠ⸣-*x*[*x x x x*]
2′ [M]U.MEŠ LUGAL.MEŠ LÚ.E[N?–URU.MEŠ?]

3′ [*p*]*i-tu-a-te ina* I[GI *x x x x*]
4′ [M]U.MEŠ-*šú-nu g*[*a-am-m*]*u*!-⸢*ru*!⸣
5′ [*x x*]*x a-ni-*[*ni*? *x x x x-n*]*i* TA* ŠÀ
6′ [*x x x*]*x-hu*? [*x x x*]-⸢*ha*⸣ *a-na* URU.BÀD–MAN–GIN
7′ [*x x x x x*] *an-ni-tú ep-ša-at*
8′ [*x x x x x*]*x-pa-hu-ni*
9′ [*x x x x x*]*x i-ṣa-bat-su*
10′ [*x x x x x*]*x-at*

ABL 107 + CT 53 387 (= SAA 1 70 + SAA 5 282)

1 [To the kin]g, my lord: your [serv]ant [Ṭa]b-šar-Aššur. Good health to the king, my lord!

4 As to what the king, my lord, wrote to me: "Why are the names of the city lords of the cities not highlighted?"

6 The king, my lord, knows that our previous campaign which we directed to Mannea [and] Media [... *is depicted*] o[n *the walls* of] the Ol[d] Palace. We have ins[pected ......]

(Break)

r.2 [the na]mes of the kings and the [*city*] *lo*[*rds*] –

3 [di]adems in fr[ont of ...]

4 their [na]mes are c[ompl]eted.

5 [...] *w*[*e* ...] from [... *to* ...]... *and* Dur-Šarruken. This [...] has been made ......

(Rest too broken for translation)

6 For the join, see Parpola in Caubet Khorsabad p. 76, n. 115. 5 See coll. 8 Or: -⸢*ù*?⸣ *a-na mad-a-a*. r.4 For collation, see SAA 1, p. 256b (no. 70 r.1). r.5 Alternatively, the beginning may be restored as [*ú-m*]*a*?*-a ni-*[. r.6 Calah could precede Dur-Šarruken, i.e., [*a-na* URU.*kal*]-⸢*ha*⸣.

FIG. 3. *Caption inscribed on carving of Iranian city.*
Botta and Flandin, Monument de Ninive II, Pl. 145.

7. Fragment Related to the West

K 7368

beginning broken away

1′ [*x x x x x*]*x*[*x x x*]*x*[*x x*]
2′ [*x x x x x*] *iš* [*x x x*] *m*[*a-a*]
3′ [*x x x x* ^{m}]*aš-šur–ú-*⌜*ki*⌝-[*i*]*n x*[*x*
4′ [*x x x x*] ⌜*a*⌝*-ki ša i–de-en-*[*ni*$^{?}$]
5′ [*x x x x*].MEŠ *ša* KUR.*e-bir–*[ÍD]
6′ [*x x x x*]*x-ik at-ta-*[*x*]
7′ [UD-*mu ša e-gír-tú*$^{?}$ *a*]*n-ni-tú ta-ma*[*r-u-ni*]
8′ [*x x x maš*$^{?}$]*-ku ša pi-i-r*[*i*$^{?}$ *x*]
9′ [*x x x x*]*x bi is x*[*x x*]
10′ [*x x x* ^{m}*šum*]*-ma–*DINGIR LÚ*.*x*[*x x*]
11′ [*x x x x x*] *ip-qi-d*[*u-ni*]
12′ [*x x x x x x*] ⌜LÚ*⌝.*ku-*[*x x*]

CT 53 336

(Beginning destroyed)

3 [...] Aššur-ukin [...]
4 [...] as *in a laws*[*uit*]
5 [...]s of Eber-[nari]
6 [... ...]... *I have* [...].
7 [*The day*] you se[e] this [*letter*],
8 [...] *elepha*[*nt sk*]*in* [...]
9 [...] ... [...]
10 [... Šum]ma-ilu, the [...]
11 [*whom* ...] appointed
12 [...] the [...] official

7 This fragment must have come from the west, or it is a royal letter sent to the west. [6] A form of *parāku*? The pronoun *atta*, "you", cannot be excluded. [9] Possibly Š]À-*bi is-s*[*e*/*i*$^{?}$-*x*].

13′ [*x x x x x*]*-liṭ-šú-nu-u-n*[*i*]
14′ [*x x x x x* UD]U.HI.A*-šú-*[*nu*]
15′ [*x x x x x x*].MEŠ*-šú-*[*nu*]
16′ [*x x x x x x x*]*x x*[*x x*]
other side broken away

13 [... ...]... them
14 [......] the[ir she]ep
15 [......] the[ir ...]s
(Rest destroyed)

8. Chief Victualler Waters Terebinth Trees

K 4719 + K 14670
1 *a-na* LUGAL EN-[*ia*]
2 ARAD*-ka* LÚ*.GAL–*da-ni-ba*[*t*]
3 [DI]*-mu a-na* LUGAL EN*-iá*

4 [*a*]*-na* UGU (*ša*) LUGAL *be-li*
5 *ṭè-mu iš-ku-na-ni-ni*
6 *ma-a* A.MEŠ TA* IGI.2.MEŠ
7 *a-na* ŠÀ GIŠ.*gu-up-ni ša* GIŠ.*bu-ṭu-ni*
8 [*kur*]*-ru ma-a* ÍD*-šú-nu*
9 [*lu*?] *zak-ku* URU.MEŠ
10 [*it-ta*]*l-ku-ú-ni*
11 [*ina p*]*a-ni-ia i-ti-ti-su*
12 [*ma-a x r*]*u bu ṣa* [*x*] *gu*
13 [*x x x x*]*x a-ba-làh*
14 [*x x x x*]*x-ú*
15 [*x x x x x*] ÍD*-šú-nu*
16 [*x x x x x*]*x*
17 [*x x x x x-*ʾ]*a-la*
18 [*x x x x x x*]*x*
rest broken away
Rev. beginning broken away
1′ [*x x x x x x*]*x*
2′ [*x x x x l*]*u* 5
3′ [*x x* ᵐDI*-mu*]–EN–*áš-me*
4′ [*x x x x*] *ṭa-a-ba*
5′ [*a-na*] ⌜*e*⌝*-pa-še*
rest uninscribed

CT 53 230
1 To the king, [my] lord: your servant the chief victualler. [(Good) hea]lth to the king, my lord!
4 As to the order that the king, my lord, gave me: "[Le]ad water from the springs into the terebinth trees! [*May*] their canal(s) be cleared."
9 (The people of) the towns [have c]ome. They were standing [in] my presence, [saying]: "......
13 [...]... I *fear*
14 [......]
15 [...] their *canal*
(Break)

r.3 [... Šulmu]-beli-lašme
4 [...] is good [to] do.

13 E.g., *ša ú-bal*]*-liṭ-šú-nu-u-n*[*i*] or a form of *šalāṭu*.

8 Join by S. Parpola (--.6.1974). Previous edition: Menzel-Wortmann, Mesopotamia 21 (1986) 225-26. As far as we know, this is the only surviving letter by the chief victualler. 4, 11 The prepositions used are somewhat uncertain; alternatively, though less likely, [*i*]*-na* (mostly *ina* UGU) and [*a-na*] respectively. 7 The anaptyctic vowel in *bu-ṭu-ni* has many parallels in NA in similar phonological contexts. 8 Menzel-Wortmann also restores [*kur*]*-ru* and translates "... leitet auf die Stämme der Terebinthen (zur Bewässerung)!" 17 Possibly a form of *ša'ālu* "to ask". r.2 E.g., "[... o]r 5" or "[... *wor*]*k*, 5 [*servants of* Šulmu]-beli-lašme". r.3 PNA (3/II 1274) distinguishes six individuals called Šulmu-beli-lašme during the reign of Sargon II. This man is no. 5 and is described as: "Official responsible for royal fields".

COURTESY TRUSTEES OF THE BRITISH MUSEUM

FIG. 4. *Aqueduct, canal and irrigated trees.* BM 124939.

9. Urarṭian Emissaries on Their Way

K 5323 + K 14607

1 [*a-na*] LUGAL *be-lí-*[*ia*]
2 [ARAD-*k*]*a* ᵐI–DIN[GIR]
3 [*lu-u š*]*ul-mu a-na* LUGAL *b*[*e-lí-ia*]

4 [*ina* UG]U LÚ.MAH.MEŠ KUR.URI-⸢*a*⸣.[*a*]
5 [*ša* LUGAL] *be-lí iš-pur-an-*[*ni*]

6 [*x x x*] URU.*a-ú-me-ni* ⸢*x*⸣ [*x*]
7 [*x x x* T]A* URU.*lu-*⸢*ub*?⸣*-d*[*a*?]
8 [*x x*]*x-šá-ba* ÍD ⸢*x*⸣ *x*[*x x*]
9 ÍD.*di-ig-lat qa-ni* [*x x*]
10 [*ina* ŠÀ]*-bi e-tab-ru-u-*[*ni*]

11 [TA* Š]À*-bi a-na* URU.[*x x*] ⸢*x*⸣
12 [*x x*]*x-ru ša* ⸢URU⸣.[*x x x*]
13 [*it-t*]*al-ku-u-n*[*i x x x x*]
rest (about 5 lines) broken away
Rev. possibly uninscribed

CT 53 74 + CT 53 542

1 [To] the king, [my] lord: [yo]ur [servant] Na'di-il[u. Good h]ealth to the king, [my] l[ord]!

4 [As t]o the Urarṭian emissaries [about whom the king], my lord wrote to me:

6 [...] the city Aumeni ... [...]

7 [... fr]om *Lubd*[*a*]

8 [...]*šaba*, the river ... [...]

9 they have crossed the Tigris [the]re *near* [...]

11 [from th]ere to the city [...]...

12 [...]... of the city [...]

13 [they ha]ve come [...]

(Rest broken away)

9 Joined by Th. Kwasman (16.4.1980). In addition to this, the chief cupbearer Na'di-ilu (PNA 2/II 916f) sent more than ten letters to Sargon II (SAA 5 62-73 and SAA 1 98 together with Ṭab-ṣil-Ešarra, governor of Assur). [7] Although Lubda seems a surprisingly southern, though by no means impossible, location for the Urarṭian emissaries. [8] Perhaps it is another city or river mentioned at the beginning, and not, e.g., a verbal form of *ušābu*, but it is also possible to read NÍG.BA = *iqīša* as part of a name.

10. A Captured Informer

Sm 807 + K 5609

1 [*a-na* LUG]AL *be-lí-*[*ia*]
2 [ARAD-*ka*] ᵐ*aš-šur*–BÀD–IGI-*i*[*a*]
3 [*lu-u š*]*ul-mu a-na* LUGAL *be-*⸢*lí*⸣-[*ia*]

4 [LÚ.*da-a*]-⸢*a*⸣-*li-ia ša ina* ŠÀ K[UR-*i*]
5 [*šu-nu*]-*u-ni* LÚ.EME *šu-*[*ú ša*]
6 [TA* URU.*i*]*r*$^{!}$-*gi-is-ti-a-ni a-n*[*a* 0$^{?}$]
7 ⸢ᵐ⸣[*a-r*]*i-e a-na* KUR-*i i*[*l-lik-u-ni*]
8 LÚ.[*d*]*a-a-a-li-ia iṣ-ṣab-*[*tu-ni-šú*]
9 *a-sa-*[ʾ]*a-al-šú mu-ku mi-*⸢*i*⸣-[*nu*]
10 *ṭ*[*è*]-⸢*e*⸣-*mu ša* KUR.U[RI$^{!}$-*a-a*]
11 *ma-*⸢*a*⸣ [KUR].⸢*e*$^{?}$⸣-*ti-na-a-a x*[*x x x*]
12 *ma-*⸢*a*⸣ [*x i*]*l* [[*x*]] GIŠ$^{!}$ [*x x x*]
13 *ma-*⸢*a*⸣ [*x l*]*a-a ú-ṣa x*[*x x x*]
14 *it-*[*x x x x x x x x x*]
rest broken away

SAAB 16, p. 2 (ABL 741 + CT 53 296 = SAA 5 55 + SAA 5 61)

1 [To the ki]ng, [my] lord, [your servant] Aššur-dur-paniy[a. Good h]ealth to the king, [my] lord!

4 My [s]couts in the m[ountain] have captu[red] an informer [who] was g[oing from the city A]rgistiani t[o Ar]ije, over the mountain.

9 I asked him about the news of the Ur[arṭian, and he told me]: "The *E*tinean(s) [...] ......

13 [has n]ot [*yet*] come out [...]

10 Previous edition: Van Buylaere, SAAB 16 (2007) 2-3, with a new copy of the tablet.

FIG. 5. *Crossing a river.*
BM 124541.

Rev. beginning broken away
1′ [*x x x*] ⌈*x*⌉ [*x x x x x x*]
2′ ⌈*x x*⌉ *šá* [*x x x x x*]
3′ *mi-mi-n*[*i x x x x x x*]
4′ ⌈*it*⌉-*x*[*x x x x x x x x*]
5′ Í[D *x x p*]*a-an* [*x x x x*]
6′ ⌈*x*⌉-[*x x x*] *ri* ⌈*e*?⌉ [*x x x x*]
7′ *i–da-at am-m*[*u*?*-ti x x x x*]
8′ ⌈*x x*⌉ *ul* ⌈*la*⌉ *a x*[*x x x x*]
9′ ⌈*x x x x x*⌉ [*x x x x x*]
10′ *giš-ri ih-*[*x x x x x x x*]
11′ ⌈*it*⌉*-ta-lak* [*x x x x x x*]
12′ [*x*]*x ik x*[*x x x x x x x*]
rest broken away

(The reverse remains too broken for translation)

11. Ninevite Dealings

Sm 765B
beginning broken away
1′ [*x x x x x*] *a* [*x x x x x x x x x*]
2′ [*x x x x x*] MÍ [*x x x x x x x x x*]
3′ [*x x*] ⌈*ša*⌉ *x*[*x x x x x x x x x*]
4′ [*x x* ^{md}*x*]–MAN–PAB L[Ú*.*x x x x x x x*]
5′ [*x x x x*]*x-si ša* ^{m}*ba-*[*bi-i x x x x x x*]
6′ [*x x*]*-a ma-a qu-lu šar-hu ma* [*x x x x x x*]
7′ [*x x* ^{m}*ba*]*-bi-i ki-i ti-ìl-tu x*[*x x x x x x*]
8′ [*ina* URU.*n*]*i-nu-a ki-i ṣa-bit-u-ni ma-*⌈*a*⌉ [*x x x x x x*]
9′ [*x x*] *id-du-bu-ub ma-a* ^{m}*mah-*[*de-e x x x x x*]
10′ [*ma-a da*]*-a-a-la-te-šú la ši-na ši-na* [*x x x x x x*]
11′ [*x x*]*-ha ma-a ke-e-tu* URU.NINA *bi-*[*x x x x x x*]
12′ [*x ina*] UGU *pi-i ša* ^{m}*ba-bi-i is-*[*x x x x x x*]
13′ [*is-sa*]*k-nu-šú ma-a* TA* ŠÀ É.GAL *x*[*x x x x x x*]
14′ [*ma a-k*]*e-e le-pu-uš* TA* IGI [*x x x x x x*]
15′ [*x x*]*x-a ma-a a-di bé-et* [*x x x x x x x*]
16′ [*x x x x*]*-a-ni dul-*⌈*lu*⌉ [*x x x x x x x x*]

CT 53 826
(Beginning destroyed)

2 [...] *a* woman [......]
3 [......]
4 [... DN]-šarru-uṣur, the [...] official
5 [... the ...]s of Ba[bî ......]
6 [...]... says: "A fearsome silence [......]
7 [...] *when* [Ba]bî [...] a *proverb* [...]
8 when he was arrested [*in* N]ineveh [......]
9 [...] he spoke: "Mah[dê ......]
10 "They are not his [ex]cursions, they are [...]
11 [...]..., saying: "Truly Nineveh [......]
12 [... a]t Babî's behest [......]
13 [p]ut him [*in fetters*], saying: "From the palace [......]
14 ["Ho]w am I supposed to act?" *Because of* [......]
15 [...]... said: "Until [......]
16 [...] *me*, the work [......]

11 A fragment of a large letter. The amount of text missing on the right was estimated from the curvature of the tablet. [6] Cf. *rašubbu* = *šarhu* An IX 17, LTBA 2 2:170. [6, 15] These lines may mention the same person (name ending in *-a*) at the beginning. One possibility is ^{md}PA-*u/ú-a*, mentioned in a letter of Mahdê (SAA 5 74 r.5). [7] Reading *ki-i ti-an-tu* "like Tiamat/Deluge" is also possible. [8] Possibly, e.g., [*issi*(-) ...] at the end. [9] Mahdê (Ammi-hati), governor of Nineveh, eponym of the year 725. [11] Perhaps a feminine pl. stative or [URU.*kal*]*-ha* at the beginning. [16] Or, a 1st person plural stative form at the beginning.

Rev. beginning broken away
1′ [*x x* É$^{?}$].GAL *x*[*x x x x x x x x x*]
2′ [*x x x x*]*x lu ma-*⸢*a*⸣ [*x x x x x x x x*]

3′ rest uninscribed

(Break)
r.1 [... *the pa*]*lace* [......]
2 [... ...]..., saying: "[.......]"

12. Urged by the King's Sealed Order

BM 36543
1 [*a-na* LUGAL] BE-*i*[*a*]
2 [ARAD-*ka* ^{m}*pa*]*q*$^{?}$*-qa–*^{d}[UTU$^{?}$]
3 [*lu* DI-*mu a-na*] LUGAL BE-*i*[*a*]

4 [*bé-et*] *un-qi* LUGAL *né-*[*mur-u-ni*]
5 [*ina* ITI].DUL *nu-ta-mì-iš*

6 [LÚ*.*u*]*m-ma-ni ša* LUGAL *iš-pur-an-ni*
7 [*ma-a u*]*ṣ-ṣi ina pa-an* KASKAL.2-⸢*ku*⸣*-nu*

8 [*x x x* MU.]AN.NA *tak-ta-ra-ma*
9 [*x x x*]*x-tu ša* LUGAL [(*x x*)]
10 [*ma-a*$^{?}$ *r*]*a-am-mi ma-*[*a*$^{?}$]
11 [*x x x a*$^{?}$*-n*]*i-ni ša* DUM[U$^{?}$ *x x*]
12 [*x x x x*]*x-an-ni ma-*⸢*a*⸣ [*x x*]
13 [*x x x u*]*m*$^{?}$*-ma-nu-ú-ti* [*x x*]
14 [*x x x x x x* L]Ú*.*i-tu-*⸢*'a*⸣*-*[*a-a*]
15 [*x x x x x x x*] ⸢*x*⸣ [*x x x*]
rest broken away; possibly a few lines missing
Rev. as far as preserved, uninscribed

Fs. Postgate, p. 661
1 [To the king, m]y lord: [your servant *Upa*]*q-Š*[*amaš*. Good health to the] king, m[y] lord!
4 We set out [in the month] Tašritu (VII) [when] we [saw] the king's sealed order.
6 [The *sc*]*holar*(*s*) who(m) the king sent to me, [say(s): "*I*/*He*/*It* will g]o out before your *expedition*."
8 [... the y]ear *has drawn to an end*
9 [...] ... of the king [(...)]
10 [(saying): "*L*]*eave*
11 [... *w*]*e* who the *so*[*n* ...]
12 [...] *to me*, thus: [...]
13 [... *sc*]*holarship* [...]
14 [...] the Itu'e[ans]
(rest destroyed)

13. ---

K 16498
1 [*a-na* LUGAL E]N-*i*[*a*]
2 [ARAD-*ka* ^{m}*ú*]-⸢*pa*⸣*-qa–*^{d}*šá-maš*
3 [*lu* DI-*mu a*]*-na* LUGAL EN-*i*[*a*]

4 [*x x x x*]*x* ⸢DI-*mu*⸣
5 rest broken away
Rev. completely broken away

K 16498
1 [To the king], m[y lo]rd: [your servant U]paq-Šamaš. [Good health t]o the king, m[y] lord!
4 [...] *is/are well*
(Rest destroyed)

r.2 Instead of a quotation at the end of a letter, read, e.g.,]*x-lu-ma* ⸢*a*⸣-[*na*.

12 Previous edition: Van Buylaere, Fs. Postgate (2017) 659-61. The restoration of the sender's name is uncertain. If Upaq-Šamaš sent the letter, he may (or may not) be identical with the sender of SAA 5 162 and 163 and no. 13 (below).

13 Cf. SAA 5 162-163.

14. Images in Mazamua

K 15609

beginning broken away

1′ [*x*] *ṣa-la*[*m x x x x x x*]

2′ [TA*] ⸢É⸣ *ina* KUR–*za-*[*mu-a x x x x*]

3′ [*x*] *ṣa-la*[*m x x x x x x*]

4′ ⸢TA*⸣ KUR–⸢*za*⸣-[*mu-a x x x x*]

rest broken away

Rev. beginning broken away

1′ [*x x x x*] *x*[*x x x x*]

2′ [*x x*] ⸢*ša*⸣ *ina* U[RU.*x x x*]

3′ [*š*]*a* TA* ŠÀ-*bi x*[*x x x x*]

4′ [*a*]-*sa-tar re-e*[*h-ti x x*]

5′ [*la*] *šá-aṭ-ru*

rest uninscribed

CT 53 678

(Beginning destroyed)

1 [...] the *imag*[*e* of ......]

2 [from] a house in Maza[mua ...]

3 [...] the *imag*[*e* of ...]

4 from Maza[mua ...]

(Break)

r.2 [I] have inscribed those in the t[own of ... and tho]se *from* [...].

4 The re[st of the ... have not been] inscribed.

15. Fragment Mentioning Snow and Defeat

K 16066

beginning broken away

1′ [*x x x x x d*]*an* [*x x*]

2′ [*x x x x* LU]GAL *be-*⸢*lí*⸣ [0]

3′ [*ú-da ki-i*] *ku-pu-ú x*[*x x*]

4′ [*x x x x*] ⸢*x*⸣ LUGAL *be-l*[*í*]

5′ [*ina* UGU *ša*? LUG]AL *be-lí iq-*[*bu-u-ni*]

6′ [*x x x x x*] *de-ek-*[*tú*]

7′ [*x x x x x*]*x ma q*[*a-x x*]

8′ [*x x x x x*]*x-šú-nu* [*x x*]

9′ [*x x x x x* ᵐ]ᵈEN–Š[U.2-*u-a*?]

10′ [*x x x x x x*]*x-šú-nu*

rest broken away

K 16066

(Beginning destroyed)

2 [... the ki]ng, my lord, [knows that] snow [...]

4 [......] the king, m[y] lord,

5 [*Concerning what* the kin]g, my lord, sa[id]

6 [......] defe[at]

7 [......] ... [...]

8 [......] them/their

9 [......] Bel-qa[*tu'a*]

10 [......] them/their

(Rest destroyed or too broken for translation)

14 1, 3 This fragment may refer to stelae or statues. 2 "House", unless it is an abbreviated form of "temple" or "palace"?

15 3 Perhaps *q*[*ar*?*-hu*]. 4 Here the genitive ("of/to the king, m[y] lord") might work better than the nominative. 7 Perhaps, e.g., [*ina* ŠÀ-*bi-šú-nu i-du*?]-⸢*ku*?⸣, "[inflic]ted a defe[at on them]" or 2? *ma-q*[*a-rat*?] "*2 bal*[*es of straw*]". 9 The same man may or may not appear in SAA 5 196 r.3 and SAA 15 259:8′ (where the name is read differently); cf. PNA 1/II 325f. Alternatively, but less likely, it is simply a DN, "the god Bel".

16. Fragment Mentioning Si'immê

K 16080
beginning broken away
1′ [*x x x x x*] ⸢*x x x*⸣ [*x x*]
2′ [*x x x x*] *šá ga* ⸢*x*⸣ *x*[*x x*]
3′ [*x x x*] ⸢*i*⸣*-si-tú* 1 *bi-x*[*x x*]
4′ [*x x x*]*x* BÀD ⸢*x x x*⸣ [*x x*]
5′ [*x x* URU$^{?}$].*si-*⸢*im*⸣*-me-e* [*x x*]
6′ [*x x x x*]-⸢*ši*$^{?}$⸣ *e x*[*x-x x*]
7′ [*x x x x x*] ⸢*a-na* URU$^{?}$⸣.[*x x*]
rest broken away
Rev. completely broken away

K 16080
(Beginning destroyed)

3 [...] a tower, *one* ...[...]
4 [...] a wall [...]
5 [...] Si'immê [...]
(Rest too broken for translation)

17. Fragment Mentioning Merodach-baladan

Sm 589
beginning broken away
1′ [*x x x x*]*-su*
2′ [*x x x x*]-⸢*ú*⸣*-ma*
3′ [*x x x i*]*-šap-pa-ra*
4′ [*x x x x*]*-i ina* É.GAL
5′ [*x x x x*]*x* LUGAL *be-lí*
6′ [*x x x*] *ki-i ša i-qa-bu-ni*
7′ [*x x x x*] *mil-ku-ni*
rest broken away
Rev. beginning broken away
1′ [*x x* ^{md}AMA]R.UTU–A–AŠ
2′ [*x x x it*]*-tal-ka*
3′ [*x x x x*] ITI.ŠE
4′ [*x x x x*]*-lu*
5′ [*x x x x*]*x šú-ú*
6′ [*x x x nu*]*-kúr-ti*
7′ [*x x x x*]*-lak*
rest broken away

ABL 1272
(Beginning destroyed)

3 [... he will] send/write
4 [...] *in* the palace
5 [...] just as the king, my lord, orders [...]
7 [...] our advice
(Break)
r.1 [... Me]rodach-baladan
2 [... c]ame
3 [...] the month Adar (XII)
4 [......]
5 [......] he
6 [... host]ile messages
7 [...] *go(es)*
(Rest destroyed)

18. Fragment Referring to *Kibabiše* and Bit-*Zualza*

BM 30205
1 [*a-na* LU]GAL *be-lí-i*[*a*]
2 [ARAD]*-ka* ^{md}U.GUR–KAR*-i*[*r*]
3 [*lu* D]I*-mu a-na* LUGAL *be-l*[*í-ia*]
4 [*a–d*]*an-niš a-na* KUR *ša* LUGAL D[I*-mu*]
5 [ŠÀ]*-bu ša* LUGAL EN*-ia a–*[*dan-niš*]

Fs. Postgate, p. 652
1 [To the k]ing, m[y] lord: your [servant] Nergal-eṭir. [The b]est [of he]alth to the king, [my] lor[d]! The land of the king is w[ell]. The king, my lord, [can be gl]ad in[deed].

16 3 Or, e.g., *ana bi-i*[*r-ti*]. 7 Or: ⸢*a-na qur*⸣-.
18 Previous edition: Van Buylaere, Fs. Postgate (2017) 651-53. Nergal-eṭir may have been the governor of Bit-Hamban around 708 BC. He is the sender of SAA 15 65-68.

6 [*lu* DÙ]G.GA *ša ina* UGU LUGAL E[N-*ia*]
7 [*áš-pu*]*r*-⸢*an*⸣-*ni mu-uk* ^{m}*k*[*i-ba-bi-še*?]
8 [*ina* IGI LUG]AL EN-*ia il-la*-[*ka*]
9 [*la i*(*m*)-*ma-g*]*u*?-*ur la il-li*-[*ka*]
10 [*x x*] *x* [(*x*) *i*]*š*? *p*[*u*? *x x*]
rest broken away
Rev. beginning of reverse broken away
1′ [*x x x x x*] ⸢*bat*? *ta*?⸣ [*x x*]
2′ [*ša a-na*? LU]GAL EN-*ia* [*x x*]
3′ [*x x x-n*]*i šúm-ma ú*-[*x x*]
4′ [*x x x*]*x ša* É–⸢*zu*?⸣-[*al-za*]
5′ [*x x x x*] ⸢*ša*? ^{m}⸣*x*[*x x x x*]
rest (about 3 lines) broken away

6 As to what [I wro]te to the king, [my] lo[rd]: "K[*ibabiše*] will com[e into the presence of the ki]ng, my lord" — [he refu]sed to com[e].
(Break)

r.2 [... *to*/*of* the k]ing, my lord, [...] ... *if he*/*they* [...] of Bit-*Zu*[*alza*]

(rest destroyed)

19. Cultic and Economic Dealings in Der

BM 134514
1 [*a-na* LUGAL *be-lí-ia* ARAD-*ka* ^{md}UTU–EN–PAB?]
2 [*lu* DI-*mu a-na* LUGAL EN-*ia*] ^{m}⸢^{d}⸣[*x x x x*]
3 [*x x x x x x-t*]*i ša x*[*x x x x*]
4 [*x x x x x x*.M]EŠ LÚ*.⸢*qe*⸣-[*pa-a-ni*]
5 [*x x x x x x*] *kal a-na* [*x x x*]
6 [*x x x x x* T]A *mar* LUGAL [*be-lí*]
7 [*x x x x x x*]-*ni ṣib-ti š*[*a x x x*]
8 [*x x x x x x*] *ša* LÚ*.DUMU–K[Á.DINGIR.MEŠ]
9 [*x x x x x x*]-*te a-na* AN.GAL *x*[*x x*]
10 [*x x x x x x*].MEŠ *a-na* LÚ*.ŠÀ.TAM [*x*]
11 [*x x x x x x*] *ma-a* KUG.UD.MEŠ-*ni x*[*x x*]
12 [*x x x x x* LÚ*].ŠÀ.TAM *ia-a-ši iq-t*[*i-bi-a*]
13 [*ma-a x x x x*] *pa-ṭu-ru ša* UDU.HI.A
14 [*x x x x x x*]*x-ka ma-a a-na ma-da*-[*ti*]
15 [*x x x x x x*]-*bi-ma a-na gi-né-e*
16 [*x x x x x x*] KUG.UD.MEŠ *pa-ṭu-ru*
17 [*x x x x x x*]*x it-ta-an-nu-ni* : *ni*-[*x x*]
18 [*x x x x x x*]-*tú* UDU.MEŠ NITA.MEŠ *ša* [*x x*]
19 [*x x x x x x*] ⸢*a-ta*⸣-*na-áš-šu x*[*x x*]
20 [*x x x x x x x x*] ⸢*i-du*⸣-[*x x x*]
lines 21-24 obliterated
25 [*x x x x x*] ⸢*šu*⸣ *u* [*x x x x x x*]
26 [*x x x x x*]*x kam x*[*x x x x x x*]

CT 53 981
1 [To the king, my lord: your servant *Šamaš-belu-uṣur*. Good health to the king, my lord!]
2 [NN ...... the ...] *of* [......]
4 [The ...]s *and* the del[egates ......] to [...]
6 [...... Ev]er since the king, my lord,
7 [......] the tax o[f ...]
8 [......] *of* the Ba[bylonians]
9 [... ...]*s* for Ištaran
10 [... ...]s for the prelate
11 [......] "our silver *is* [...]
12 [......] the prelate tol[d] me: "The remitted [delivery] of sheep [*is*] your [......].
14 "For the tribute [......] and for the
15 regular offerings [...]
16 The [...s] have given me the remitted [payment] of silver [......]."
18 [......] *the rams of* [...]
19 [......] I have given him [...]

(Rest destroyed or too broken for translation)

19 This tantalising letter fragment clearly concerns Der (lines 9-12) and was written by the same scribe who wrote for Šamaš-belu-uṣur and Nabû-duru-uṣur (Parpola, ARINH p. 128, n. 12). The signs *iq*, LÚ*, MEŠ, *ti* and *ú* can be used as symptomatic signs for a palaeographic comparison (compare with the same in SAA 15 120 and 129). Of the two candidates, Šamaš-belu-uṣur is the more likely sender because, unlike his deputy Nabû-duru-uṣur, he corresponded regularly with the king and has other letters whose introductory formula ends with a simple greeting: *lū šulmu ana šarri bēlīya* (SAA 15 121-124, 126-127). [2] Perhaps *ma-da-t*]*i*, cf. line 14. [12] For the Babylonian rather than Assyrian spelling of *iq-t*[*i-bi-a*], for which there are parallels from Der, see Luukko, SAAS 16, p. 80. [14] The beginning may read, e.g., [(*x x*) *ina* UGU-*hi-ia it-ta*]*l-ka* [... ca]me [to me]". [18] The sequence UDU.MEŠ NITA.MEŠ is unusual.

27 [*x x x x x*]*x ú* [*x x x x x x*]
Rev. Destroyed

20. – – –

K 1381
1 ⸢*a-na*⸣ [LUGAL] BE-⸢*ia*⸣
2 ARAD-*k*[*a* ^{m}*x x x*]
3 *a-h*[*u-šú ša* ^{m}*x x x*]
4 ^{m}*a-*[*x x x x x*]
5 ^{m}[*x*]*x*[*x x x x*]
rest broken away
Rev. beginning broken away
1′ [*x x x x*] *x*[*x x*]
2′ [*x x x*] LÚ*.EN–⸢*x x*⸣
3′ [*x* MA.N]A AN.BAR *ina* ŠU.2-*šú-nu*
rest (about 3 to 4 lines) uninscribed

CT 53 176

1 To the [king], my lord: yo[ur] servant [NN], brot[her of NN].

4 N[N (...)],
5 N[N (...)]
(Break)

r.2 [...] ...; they have [*x min*]*as of iron* in their hands.

21. Marduk-šarrani Conspires with Merodach-Baladan

K 5333B + K 9813

1 [$^{m?}$*x x x x*]*x* DUMU–KÁ.DINGIR.RA.K[I]
2 [*ki-i an-ni*]-⸢*i*⸣ *iq-ṭi-bi ma-*⸢*a*⸣
3 [^{md}AMAR.UTU–DUMU.U]Š–SUM-*na iq-ṭi-bi-*[*a*]
4 [*ma-a x x x*]*-ma la-du-ak*[!]-*k*[*a*]
5 [*ma-a a-lik*[?] *mi*]-⸢*i*⸣-*nu dul-lu ša* ^{m}⸢DINGIR⸣-[*x x* (*x*)]
6 [*i-ba-šú-u-ni*[?] *is-s*]*e-e-šú e-pu-u*[*š*]
7 [*ma-a* ^{md}AMAR.UTU–LUGAL[?]-*a*]-*ni a-na* ^{md}AMAR.[UTU–A–AŠ[?]]
8 [*iq-ṭi-bi ma-a*] ⸢*a*⸣-*lik* ^{md}AMAR.UTU–M[AN–*a-ni*[?]]
9 [*x x x x*]*x-li a-na* LÚ*.E[N[?]–*x x*]
10 [*x x ma-a* ^{m}]^{d}AMAR.UTU–LUGAL-⸢*a*⸣-[*ni*]
11 [*a-na* DUMU–^{m}*ia-k*]*i-ni iq-ṭi-b*[*i*]
12 [*ma-a* ^{d}EN *u*] ⸢^{d}⸣PA *lu ú-du-*[*ú*]
13 [*šum-ma*[?] *x x*]-⸢*ú*⸣ GIŠ.GU.ZA-*ka ina qa-*[*ti-ka*[?]]
14 [*la-a*[?] *i-ka*]*r-ra-ru-u-ni ù a-*[*na*]
15 [*x x x x*]*-ub-te ša* KUR–^{d}*aš-š*[*ur*.KI]
16 [*x x x x*] *la i-haṭ-ṭa-an-*⸢*ni*⸣

ABL 1024 + CT 53 408 (= SAA 15 189 + SAA 15 208)

1 [NN], a citizen of Babylon, reported [as fol]lows:

3 "[*Merodach*-bal]adan said [to me: '...] I will not kill you! [*Go*] (and) perform [w]ith him [w]hatever work of *Il*-[... *there is*]!'

7 [*Marduk-šarra*]ni [said] to Mer[*odach-baladan*]: 'Go!' Marduk-ša[rrani ......] to the [...] official [...].

10 Marduk-šarrani (further) said [to the son of Yak]in: '[Bel and] Nabû know [*that h*]*e* shall lay your throne in [*your*] ha[nds]. Moreover, a[s to the] Assyr[ian ...] ... *does/shall (not) sin against me*.'"

20 This text may refer to the rewarding of people. [1] The spelling BE-*ia*/*iá* is rare and appears mainly in the letters of Šamaš-belu-uṣur, governor of Der (see SAA 15, nos. 115, 118, 121-122, 125-126; but see also no. 12, above), whose letters contain a greeting (see line 3), but this letter has no greeting (cf. Luukko, Iraq 74 [2012] 104, 111). [3] However, syllabic spellings of *ahu* are rare. [r.3] Reading [^{m}ARA]D–^{d}MAŠ and translating "[Urd]u-Inurta (is) in their hands" is also possible.
21 See copy p. 293. For a detailed discussion of this text, see Van Buylaere, forthcoming. [4] As copied by Parpola in CT 53 408, correcting a typographical error in SAA 15 208.

17 ⌈*ma-a a-na* DUMU⌉–^{m}*ia*-GIN *iq-ṭi-bi*
18 *ma-a* A.MEŠ *ina* URU.BÀD–LUGAL-*uk-ki la-áš*-[*šú*]
19 *ma-a a–ki-ma ta-at-tal-ka ina* UGU-*hi*
20 *ta-as-sak-na am–mar* UD-*me-ka*
e.21 *ta-ṣab-bat-su*
r.1 *ma-a* ^{md}AMAR.UTU–MAN-*a-ni a-na* ^{md}AMAR.UTU–A–AŠ
2 *iq-ṭi-bi ma-a man-nu šu-ú ša ina* KUR–*aš-šur*.KI
3 [*is-s*]*e*-⌈*ia*⌉ *i-da-ab-bu-bu-u-ni*
4 [*ma-a x*]*x-lu i-ba-áš-ši a-tu*-[x (x)]
5 [*x x x*]*x-ma ša* LÚ*.IGI *la-áš*-[*šú-ni*]
6 [*x x x x*]*x ma-a* ^{md}⌈AMAR⌉.UTU–MAN-*a-n*[*i a-na*]
7 [DUMU–^{m}*ia*]-⌈GIN *iq-ṭi-bi*⌉ *x*[*x x*]
8 [*man-nu šu-ú*$^{?}$] ⌈*ša*⌉ [*ina* KUR]–⌈*aš-šur*.KI⌉ *x*[*x x x*]
9 [*x x x x*] ⌈*x x*⌉ [*x x x x x*]
about 6 lines broken away
16 [*x x x x x x*] *me* [*x x x*]
rest uninscribed

17 He (= Marduk-šarrani) said to the son of Yakin: 'There is no water in Dur-Šarrukku. If you come and launch an attack on it, you will take it in a matter of days.'"

r.1 Marduk-šarrani said to Merodach-baladan: 'Who *speaks* [*wit*]*h* me in Assyria? I have indeed ... [...] ... [...] ... who has no witness [...]...'

6 (Erased?) Marduk-šarrani said [to the son of Ya]kin [.... *Who is*] the one who [in] Assyria [......]

(Rest destroyed or too broken for translation)

22. Fragment Mentioning Scouts and *Rab mūgi*

K 14107
beginning broken away
1′ [*x x x x m*]*a*$^{?}$*-a* ⌈LÚ.*x x*⌉
2′ [*x x x x*] *ša la* LUGAL

3′ [*x i-na*$^{?}$*-á*]*š-ši da*-⌈*ia*⌉-*li*
4′ [*x x x*]*x-ka e-tab*-[*r*]*u-ni*

5′ [*x x x* LUG]AL *be-lí* [*ú-d*]*a*
6′ [*x x bé*$^{?}$]-*et i-ra*-[*q*]*u*$^{?}$-*ni*
7′ [*x x x l*]*i-din*

8′ [*x x x*]-*ta-a* É
9′ [*x x bir*]-*te* [I]GI.2-*ia*
e.10′ [*x x x*] ⌈*a*⌉-*da-gal*
11′ [*x x x š*]*á ina* ŠÀ-*bi*

r.1 [*x x x*] ⌈*ú*⌉-*ma-a an-nu-rig*
2 [LUG]AL *be-lí*
3 [*x x x*]-⌈*a*⌉ *le-mur*
4 [(*x*) L]Ú.GAL–*mu-g*[*i*]
5 [*x x x*]*x ṭè-me*

6 [*x x x*]*x-mar*-[[*x*]]-*ri*
7 [*x x x*] DUMU-*i*[*a*] *it-tal-lak*
8 [*x x x x x*]-*ni* ⌈*x*⌉ *sa ú*
9 [*x x x x x x* LU]GAL$^{?}$
rest broken away

CT 53 512
(Beginning destroyed)
1 [... *say*]*ing*: "the ...-*official*
2 [... *is tak*]*ing* (*for himself*) [...] without (the permission) of the king.
3 Scouts [*and*] your [...] have crossed over (*the river*).
5 [... the kin]g, my lord, [kno]ws
6 [... *whe*]*re they hide*
7 [... he should] give
8 [... *w*]*hy a house*
9 [... *bet*]*ween* my [e]yes
10 [...] I *looked*
11 [...... whi]ch *there* [...]
r.1 Right now, let the [ki]ng, my lord, see *my* [...]
4 [(...)] the *rab mūg*[*i*]
5 [...] *report*
6 [......]
7 [...] m[y] son went
8 [......] ...
9 [...... *the ki*]*ng*
(Rest destroyed)

23. Fragment Mentioning Mandireans

K 15678
beginning broken away
1′ [*x x x* URU].*man-di-r*[*a-a-a x x x x*]
2′ [*x x x x*] *a-na iš*-[*x x x x*]
3′ [*x x x x*]-*ri-ip*-[*x x x x x*]
e. broken away
Rev. completely broken away

CT 53 712
(Beginning destroyed)
1 [...] the Mandire[ans ......]
(Rest destroyed)

24. Fragment Mentioning Aššur-šarru-uṣur

K 16576
beginning broken away
1′ [*x x x x*] ⸢*x x*⸣ [*x x x*]
2′ [*x x x* T]A$^{?}$ KÁ.GAL ⸢*a*⸣-[*x x*]
3′ [*x x x* ^{m}]*aš-šur*–LUGAL–PAB [*x x x*]
4′ [*x x x la*$^{?}$-*a*]*m-tu*[*h*$^{?}$ *x x x*]
5′ rest broken away
Rev. destroyed

CT 53 807
(Beginning destroyed)
2 [... *fr*]*om the gate* [...]
3 [...] Aššur-šarru-uṣur [...]
4 [... *I shall*] *pick u*[*p*...]
(Rest destroyed)

23 1 For the Mandireans on the Elamite border, cf. SAA 15 24 r.24 and 119 s.2 (Bagg RGTC 7/3/1, p. 388).
24 2 The end is probably either "t[o" or "I [...]".

FIG. 6. *Gambulean male and female prisoners.*
BM 124801c.

25. Visiting Aramean Tribes

K 1904
beginning broken away
1′ [*x x x*]–*du-ri ša x*[*x x x x*]
2′ [*x x*]*x–siq-ri a-na* LÚ*.*pu-q*[*u*]-*d*[*i*?]
3′ [LÚ*].*ru-ʾu-a-a a-na* LÚ*.*hi-in-di-*[*ru*]
4′ [L]Ú*.*gam-bu-li* *il-*[*lak*?]
5′ [*ina*?] ITI.APIN *ik-ka-aṣ-ṣ*[*ar*? *x* (*x*)]
6′ [*x x*]*x* ⸢LÚ*⸣.EN.NAM [*x x x*]
rest broken away
Rev. completely destroyed

ABL 1281
(Beginning destroyed)
1 [...]-duri who [......],
2 [...]-siqri go[es] to the Puq[u]d[u], the Ru'ua, the Hinda[ru] (and) the Gambulu.
5 [*In*] Marchesvan (VIII) it (= the troop, *kiṣru*) will *be organi*[*zed* ...]
6 [...] the governor [...]
(Rest destroyed)

26. Petition Concerning Towns and Orchards

83-1-18,782
1 *a-na* LUGAL *be-l*[*í*!*-ia*]
2 ARAD-*ka* mAD–[*x x*]
3 *lu-u* DI-*mu a-n*[*a* LUGAL EN-*ia*]
4 *ina* UGU URU.DINGIR-[*x ša* LUGAL?]
5 *ip-qid-*⸢*ú*⸣-[*ni*]
rest broken away
Rev. beginning broken away
1′ *a-x*[*x x x x x x*]
2′ *re-eh-*[*ti x x x x x*]
3′ *ú-sa-li*? ⸢*ù*?⸣ [*x x x*]
4′ URU.MEŠ *ù* GIŠ.[SAR.MEŠ *ša*?]
5′ LUGAL *be-lí-ia ú-*[*x x x*]
6e *an-nu-ra mì-*⸢*i*?⸣-[*nu x x*]
7e *ina na-gi-u ša* [*a-na* LUGAL]
8e *be-lí-ia a-hu*[*r-ú-ni*?]
s.1 [*x x x x x* LUG]AL *be-lí-i*
2 [*x x x x x x*] *ka-la-mu*

CT 53 947
1 To the king, [my] lor[d]: your servant Abi-[...]. Good health t[o the king, my lord]!
4 Concerning the town of *Ilu*-[... which *the king*] *assigned to* [me]
(Break)
r.2 I have watered the res[t of ......].
3 *Furthermore*, [...] *I* [*shall* ...] the towns and orc[hards *of*] the king, my lord.
6 Now then, *wh*[*at* ...] in the district about which I have petitioned [the king], my lord?
s.1 [....... the ki]ng, my lord
s.2 [.......] all.

25 Winckler SKT II 24 (another copy). This is either a small horizontal tablet or, if the main part preserved is the lower or upper edge, only a small part of a very large tablet. At least three of the four edges are broken off, but presumably not much is missing from the left, although more may be missing than thought, and from the right. [1] It would be tempting to restore the name of Issar-duri ([md15?]–*du-ri*), governor of Arrapha, whose letter (SAA 15 1) deals with Bel-duri (another possibility) and the Ru'uean, etc. This person, unless *dūru* is "wall", could also be the subject of the following sentence up to the end of line 4. [2] We assume a PN at the beginning ending in *siqru* (*zikru*), "utterance, command; name, fame", rather than an ethnic name. [3] The spelling LÚ.*hi-in-di-ru* also occurs twice in the royal inscriptions of Tiglath-pileser III (RINAP 1 40:5 and 47:6). [4] The spacing in this line may indicate that the right edge was not far away from the *il* sign. [5] Alternatively, perhaps "(*the ground*) will *free*[*ze* ...]/*hard*[*en* ...]", but Arahsamna seems too early for the ground to freeze in Babylonia.

26 Probably a letter by a tribal chieftain from Babylonia; this makes the language and orthography of the letter fascinating. [1] See coll. [2] E.g., Abi-[hari] (of *Gambulu*); see SAA 19 120 and 141. [4] Or: URU *an-*[*ni-e*. [5] In flawless NA, we might expect *ipqidannīni*. [r.1] *a-l*[*ik* is possible. [r.3] For *ú-sa-li*, see CAD Š/1 273 s.v. *šalû* B (*salû*), which does not record any D stem forms, but its lexical section with parallels suggests that the verb had such transitive meanings as "to water, irrigate" in the D stem. [r.4] Or [*ša*] at the end. [r.6] The spelling *an-nu-ra* is highly unusual. [s.1] *be-lí-i* is another unusual spelling, probably a mistake for *be-lí-ia*. [s.2] The letter is written in NA, but the word *kalāmu* and the sign form of *ka* are NB (also so in lines 2 and 4 when part of UGU).

27. ---

K 16588

1 [*a-na*] LUGAL *be-lí-*[*ia*]
2 [ARA]D-*ka* ^{m}AD–[*x x*]
3 [*e-piš*$^{?}$ *ṣ*]*i-bu-tú šá* [LUGAL]
4 [*lu-u* D]I-*mu a-n*[*a* LUGAL EN-*ia*]
5 [*x x*]*x* ⸢*x*⸣ [*x x x x*]
rest broken away

CT 54 377

1 [To] the king, [my] lord: your [serva]nt Abi-[..., *who fulfils* the king]'s [w]ish. [Good h]ealth t[o the king, my lord]!
(Rest destroyed)

28. ---

K 22051

1 ⸢*a-na*⸣ [LUGAL *be-lí-ia*]
2 ARAD-*ka* [^{m}*x x x x*]
3 *lu-u* D[I-*mu a-na* LUGAL EN-*ia*]

4 DI-*mu* [*a-na x x x*]
5 DI-*m*[*u a-na x x x*]
rest broken away

K 22051

1 To [the king, my lord]: your servant [NN]. Good he[alth to the king, my lord]!

4 [......] is/are well,
5 [......] is/are well
(Rest destroyed)

29. Joining the Royal Entourage

K 12954 + K 13130

1 [*ṭup*]-*pi* $^{md+}$AG–EN–MU.MEŠ ⸢*ù*⸣ ^{m}*x*[*x x x*]
2 [*a-n*]*a* LUGAL *be-lí-šú-nu lu-ú šul-mu a-na* LUGAL *be-*[*lí-ni*]

3 [M]UN *šá* AD *a-na* DUMU *la i-pu-šú* [0]
4 [L]UGAL *be-lí-a-ni i-tep-šá-an-ni a-na* É–AD-*k*[*a* 0]
5 *tu-ul-te-rib-an-na-ši ù du-un-q*[*u* 0]
6 *šá te-pu-šá-an-na-ši* KUR.KUR *gab-bi* [0]
7 *ki-i iš-mu-ú* LUGAL *be-lí-a-ni it-ta-*[*'i-du*]
8 *en-na a-du-ú* ERIM.MEŠ [0] *pah-hi-zi a*[*n-nu-ti*]
9 *šá it-ti* ^{m}*a-na*–$^{d+}$AG–⸢*tak*⸣-*lak* LUGAL [*be-lí-a-ni*]
10 *ṭè-en-šú-nu i-di* KUR [*u*]*l x* [*x x x x*]
11 *š*[*u-x*] *x*[*x*] *x*[*x x*]*x* [*x*] ⸢*a-na*⸣ *x* [*x x x x*]
12 *x*[*x x x x x x x x x x x x x*]
rest broken away
Rev. beginning broken away
1′ *ši-*[*x x x x x x x x x x x x x*]
rest broken away

ABL 838+ (= SAA 17 16+)

1 [Tab]let of Nabû-bel-šumate and [NN] to the king, their lord. Good health to the king, [our] lo[rd]!
3 [The k]ing, our lord, has done us a [fa]vour that (even) a father has not done to his son: you have introduced us into yo[ur] paternal house! And when the whole world heard the good de[ed] you had done us, they prai[sed] the king, our lord. Now then, the king, [our lord], knows the news of t[hese] insolent men who are with Ana-Nabû-taklak. The land [... n]ot [...]
(Rest destroyed)

27 1 The NA fragment no. 26 (above), with strong Babylonian influence, may be from the same sender. 3 This is an unusual phrase within an introductory formula.
28 4f *šulmu ana* ... is typical of many writers (including crown princes, governors and scholars).
29 8 Or, *pih-hi-zi*; cf. SAA 17 39:8 (see also CAD P 33a).

30. – – –

79-7-8,313

beginning broken away

1′ ⸢*x x x x*⸣ [*x x x x x x x*]
2′ *ki-i* ^{m}ZALÁG-⸢*e*$^{?}$⸣-[*a x x x x x*]
3′ *lu-ú il-x*[*x x x x x x x*]
4′ *la me-tu-ma* [*x x x x x x x*]
5′ *la*–ŠU.2 LUGAL *be-lí-*[*x x x x*]

6′ *en-na* DINGIR.MEŠ *šá* LU[GAL *x x x x*]
7′ *na-áš-par-tu šá* LUGA[L *x x x x*]
8′ *u*[*l x x*]*-li-mu-*⸢*ú*⸣ [*x x x x x*]

9′ [*x x x x x*] ⸢*x*⸣[*x x x x x*]

last line of obverse and edge broken away

r.1 [*x x x*] *be*$^{!}$*-lí*$^{!}$*-ia*$^{!}$ *nu*$^{!}$ *x*[*x x x x x x x*]
2 [*x x x*]*x šu*$^{!}$-⸢*lum*$^{!}$ *a*$^{!}$*-na*$^{!}$⸣ [*x x x x x*]
3 [*x x*]-⸢*x-a*$^{?}$⸣ *a-na* LUGAL *b*[*e-lí-i-ni x x*]

4 *na-áš-par-ta šá* LUGAL *i*[*š*$^{!}$*-pur-an-na-ši*]
5 *ki-i šá* LUGAL *ṭè*$^{!}$*-e*[*m*$^{!}$ *iš-kun-an-na-ši*$^{?}$]
6 *ni-te-pu-uš* $^{md+}$A[G–*x x x x a-na*$^{?}$]
7 URU.*pad-an it-tal-k*[*a x x x x x x*]

8 *id-da-bu-ub u*[*m-ma x x x x x x x*]
9 ⸢*x x x x x x*⸣ [*x x x x x x x x x x*]

rest broken away

CT 54 453

(Beginning destroyed)

2 when Nura[*ya* ......]
3 let ... [......]
4 are not dead [......]
5 from the hands of the king, [*my*] lord, [...]
6 Now the gods of the ki[ng ...]
7 the message *which* the king [......]
8 *no*[*t* ...]... [......]

(Break)

r.1 [...] my lord ...[......]
2 [...] health to [......]
3 [...]... to the king, [our] l[ord ...]
4 the message which the king s[ent to us], we have done just as the king ord[ered us].
6 Na[bû-...] has come [*to*] the town of Paddan(u) [......]
8 spoke, s[aying: "......]

(Rest destroyed)

31. We Have Not Sold Sinneans for Silver!

K 1942 + K 13025 + K 16584

1 ARAD-*ka* ^{m}*ul-lu-b*[*a-a-a a-na*]
2 *di-na-an* LUGAL *be-lí-*[*ia lul-lik*]
3 *um-ma-a a-na* LUGAL [*be-lí-ia-a-ma*]

4 *a-na* LUGAL *iq-ta-bu-*[*ú um-ma*]
5 LÚ.DUMU–*si-na-a-a* [*x x x x*]
6 *a-na* KUG.UD *in-na*[*m-di-nu x x*]
7 1-*me* 2-*me a-na* [*x x x x x*]
8 LUGAL ⸢*be-lí-a*⸣ [*iq-ta-bi*$^{?}$]
9 *u*[*m*$^{?}$*-ma*] *a-lik-ma* [*x x*] ⸢*x*⸣ [*x x x*]
10 [LÚ.DU]MU–*si-na-a-a a-na* KUG.[UD *x x*]
11 [*la ta-n*]*am-din at-ta ù* [*x x x*]
12 [*pu-u*]*h-hir-šú-nu-tú šá* IT[I *x x*]

CT 54 41 + CT 54 238 (= SAA 17 165 + SAA 17 166)

1 Your servant Ullub[aya: I would gladly die] for the king, [my] lord! Say to the king, [my lord]:
4 They have said to the king: "[...] Sinneans have been s[old] for silver."
7 100 or 200 for [...]
8 The king, my lord, [*said*]: "Go and [...]! [Do not s]ell the Sinneans for s[ilver]! You and [... g]ather them! Monthly [...]" —

30 2 The reading of the PN is not entirely certain, but cf. PNA 2/II 968, s.v. Nūrāia or Nūr-Aia, especially nos. 8, 10, 12, 13 (should be no. 14). 5 A form of *elû* "to go up; to slip" may be expected. 8 Perhaps a form of *šalāmu*, but another segmentation *x x*]*-li-mu* ⸢*ú*⸣-[is also possible. r. As the signs on the reverse of the tablet appear better preserved in the photograph than in the copy, it is likely that the tablet has been cleaned since Dietrich's copy. r.1–5 See coll. r.6 The PN may well be "Na[bû-šumu-lišir]"; cf. SAA 17 115 r.12f. r.7 Probably the same GN in Babylonia also appears in SAA 14 254:1′; SAA 17 115 r.12, 162 r.8′ and RIMA 3 A.0.103.2 III 21′ (Šamši-Adad V).

31 r.6 Or: "along".

13 [*x x*]*-ra šá a-na* LUGAL *iq-bu-*[*ú x x*]
14 [*x i*]*t-ta-ra-aṣ ul-t*[*u x x*]
15 [*x*]*-ka* LÚ.UNUG.[KI*-a-a x x*]
16 [*x x x*].KI *iš-hi-*[*ṭu x x*]
17 [*x x x x*].ME[Š *x x x x*]
rest broken away
Rev. beginning broken away
1′ ⸢*x x*⸣ [*x x x x x x*]
2′ *ù x*[*x x x x x x*]
3′ *il-l*[*i-ka x x x x x*]
4′ *ina pa-n*[*i x x x x x*]
5′ *it-tan-n*[*a x x x x x*]
6′ *šid-*⸢*di*?⸣ *x*[*x x x x x*]

7′ *mam-ma a-*[*na* KUG.UD]
8′ *ul n*[*i-id-din*]

13 […] what they said to the king […]
14 […] he had extended. From […]
15 N]N, the Uruk[ean …]
16 […] attac[ked …]
(Break)

r.2 and […]
3 ca[me …]
4 befo[re …]
5 sol[d …]
6 *side* […]
7 We have not s[old] any [*Sinneans*] f[or silver].

32. Seating Bel-ṣarbi

Sm 1915 + K 13853
beginning broken away
1′ [*x x*] ⸢*x*⸣ LUGAL [*x x x x*]
2′ *x*[*x x x*]*-i* URU.*te-x*[*x x x x*]
3′ *ul x*[*x x x*]*x ár-ki* [*ṭup-pi šá*]
4′ LUGAL E[N *iš-pur*]*-an-ni* ^{d}LUGAL.GIŠ!.[ÁSAL]
5′ *ki-i* KU[R!]-⸢*i*⸣ *ina áš-ri-šú* [*la-bi-ri*?]
6′ *ul-te-ši-*[*b*]*i* ^{m}ŠEŠ*–r*[*a*!*-mu*]
7′ LÚ.2*-ú šá* ⸢^{m}⸣[A]N.⸢ŠÁR!⸣–EN–[LAL*-in*]
8′ LÚ.EN.NAM *šá* U[RU.*ú*]*-pi-*⸢*i*⸣ [*x x x*]
9′ UN.MEŠ *id-duk ù* [É.MEŠ*-šú-nu*]
10′ *ih-te-pe* DINGIR *ki-i* [*x x x x*]
e.11′ *a-na* TIN.TIR.KI *it-t*[*a-x x x x*]
r.1 *a-ki* ^{m}AN.ŠÁR–EN–LAL!*-*[*in x x x*]
2 LÚ.EN.NAM *um-ma x*[*x x x x x*]
3 LUGAL *al-ka x*[*x x x x x x x*]

4 *e-re-ši* [*x x x x x x x x*]
5 *a*!!*-na* ^{d}LUGAL.[GIŠ.ÁSAL *x x x x*]
6 *in-ni-ṭ*[*ir*? *x x x x x x x x*]
7 *ù* KUR [*x x x x x x x x x*]
8 [*x*]*x x*[*x x x x x x x x x x*]
rest broken away

ABL 1067 + CT 54 261 (= SAA 17 169+)
(Beginning destroyed)
1 […] the king […]
2 […] the town *of* [……]
3 [did] not […]. After [the tablet which] the king, [my] lo[rd, sent] to me, I seated Bel-ṣ[arbi] like a moun[ta]in in his [*ancient*] place. Ahi-r[amu], the deputy of [A]ššur-belu-[taqqin], the governor of [O]pis, […] killed the people and destroyed [their houses].
10 When the god [……],
11 he we[nt] to Babylon […].
r.1 Because Aššur-belu-taqq[in …]
2 the governor said, "Go [… to] the king […]
4 ask [……]
5 for Bel-[ṣarbi …]
6 will be sav[ed …]
7 and the land […]
(Rest destroyed)

32 [2] Unless URU is a generic "town/city" here. [4, r.5] For ^{d}LUGAL.GIŠ!.[ÁSAL] = *Bēl-ṣarbi*/*ṣarbat* "Lord of the Poplar" = Nergal, a god worshipped in Bāṣu/Šapazzu, a city near Sippar, see Litke, An-Anum VI 72, and Bagg, RGTC 7/3-1, 102; cf. SAA 3 9:8, r.6. [5, r.1] See coll. [7] Or, e.g., LÚ.2*-ú šá* ⸢1⸣ [0? L]Ú?. EN.[NAM? *x x x*]?

33. Loyal Servant's Report

K 5510 + K 7519 + K 7527 + Sm 1793 + Bu 91-5-9,30

beginning broken away

1′ [LUGAL *be-l*]*i-i*[*a x x x x x x x x x*]
2′ [*al*]-⸢*ta*⸣-*si ma-a*ʾ-*d*[*a x x x x x x x*]

3′ [L]UGAL *al-ta-*⸢*nap*⸣*-pa-ra a-na i*[*a-a-ši uz-nu*]
4′ LUGAL *la* ⸢*šak*⸣*-na-an-ni a-du* [UGU *šá en-na*]
5′ LÚ.EN.NAM ⸢*i*⸣*-da-an-ni ṭè-*[*e-mi* LUGAL *be-lí*]
6′ *liš-*ʾ*a-al-šú* [^{d}]$^{+}$AG *lu-ú i-di* [*ki-i a-di*]
7′ *si-hu bar-*⸢*tu*⸣ *e-pu-šu* ⸢*ú*⸣-[*x x x x*]
8′ *ši-pir-ta-a a-na áš-ri* [*šá-nim-ma*]
9′ *tal-li-ku ú-x*[*x x x*]*x ba-šu-*[*ú x x*]
10′ *ù ga-am-m*[*a-ru*$^{?}$] ⸢*i*⸣*-ba-šu-*[*ú x x*]
11′ ⸢*ù*⸣ [L]Ú.AD.MEŠ-⸢*e-a*⸣ LÚ.ARAD.ME[Š *šá* LUGAL]
12′ *š*[*u*]*-nu ù a-*⸢*na*⸣*-ku* LÚ.ARAD ⸢*šá* LUGAL *be-lí-ia*⸣
13′ [*a-n*]*a* UGU LUGAL *be-lí-ia am-ra-ku*
14′ [^{m}]^{d}*aš-šur*–EN–⸢LAL⸣ LÚ.EN.NAM *ṭa-ab-ta-šu*
15′ ⸢*i*⸣*-ba-áš-šú i-na* ŠÀ*-bi-ia ù ki-i*
16′ [*i*]*š-pu-ra um-ma it-ti* LÚ.ERIM.MEŠ
17′ [*m*]*a-a*ʾ-⸢*du*⸣*-ú-ti* ⸢*du*⸣*-bu-ub-ma*
18′ [*t*]*a-*⸢*mí*$^{?}$⸣*-it-su-nu* ⸢*a-na*⸣ UGU LUGAL
19′ [*liš-pu*]*r-ú-ni ki-i ad-bu-bu il-te-lim*
20′ [*ina p*]*a-an* LUGAL ⸢*ki*⸣*-i id-gu-lu ṭè-e-mu*

21′ [*x x x*] *x*[*x x x x x*] *dib-bi-ni ki-i*
r.1 [*x x x x x x*] *ú-maš-ši-ru*
2 [*x x x x x x*]*-lu* LÚ.ERIM.MEŠ
3 [*x x x x x x*] *ṣu-ub-bu-tu*

4 [*x x x x x x*]*x rik-sa-ni-ma*
5 [*x x x x x x k*]*i-i ú-šal-li-mu*
6 [*x x x x x x*] LUGAL *i-te-er-bu*
7 [*x x x x x x x*] *ip-taš-hu*

8 [*x x x x x x x* LU]GAL *niš-me-e-ma*
9 [*x x x x x x a-n*]*a* LUGAL *nid-din*
10 [*x x x x x x x x x*]*-šú ù*
11 [*x x x x x x x x x*].⸢MEŠ⸣
12 [*x x x x x x x x x x x*]
13 *x*[*x x x x x x x x x x x*]
14 *ša*[*k*$^{?}$*-x x x x x x x x x x*]
15 *a-n*[*a x x x x x x x x x*]
16 *en-n*[*a x x x x x x x x x x*]
17 *šá* ^{m}[*x x x x x x x x x x*]

rest broken away

CT 54 124 + CT 54 202 + CT 54 203 (SAA 17 180) + CT 54 422 + CT 54 558

(Beginning destroyed)

1 [the king], m[y lord ......]

2 [I have r]ead man[y ......]

3 I keep writing [to the k]ing, but the king has not been paying [attention to me hither]to.

5 The governor knows me; let [the king, my lord], ask him about [my] re[port]. By Nabû [they] have made a revolt (and) rebellion, and my letter has gone to a [*hostile*] place! *There exist* [...s], and there will be *annihil*[*ation*]!

11 But (already) my ancestors were servants [of the king], and I am a servant of the king, my lord. I am devoted [t]o the king, my lord; the kindness of Aššur-belu-taqqin, the governor, resides in my heart, and when he wrote: "Speak with many men, and [let] them [sen]d their [sw]orn agreement to the king," I spoke, and it succeeded.

20 When they had become obedient [t]o the king, [......] an order

21 [......] when our words

r.1 [......] abandoned

2 [......] soldiers

3 [......] were captured

4 [......] the *agreements*

5 [...] when [...] completed

6 [......] of the king entered

7 [......] were relieved

8 May we hear [... *of* the ki]ng, so that we can give [... t]o the king.

(Rest destroyed or too broken for translation)

33 18 Although the second sign of [*t*]*a-*⸢*mí*$^{?}$⸣*-it-su-nu* would be highly unusual, so too would be reading [*t*]*a-*⸢*wi*$^{?}$⸣*-it-su-nu*.

34. Fragment Mentioning Westland, Sealand and Yakin

K 12946

beginning broken away

1′ [*x x*] ⌜*x*⌝ [*x x x x x x x*]
2′ [*x*].MEŠ *x*[*x x x x x x x x*]
3′ [*x x*]*x* KUR.MEŠ *x*[*x x x x*]
4′ [*x* KUR].MAR.TU.KI [*x x x x*]
5′ [*x x x*] 80 KUR–*tam-ti*[*m x x x x*]
6′ [*x x*].MEŠ-*ši-na* ⌜*x*⌝ *x*[*x x x*]
7′ [*x x x*]*x-ši-na iš-šá-*[*a x x x*]
8′ [*x x x*]-*šú* ^{m}*ia-ki-na x*[*x x x*]

9′ [*x x* A]D *ù* AMA *i-n*[*am*$^{?}$*-din*$^{?}$ *x x*]
10′ [*x x x*] *ù* NIN GIŠ.BA[N$^{?}$ *x x*]
11′ [*x x x x*]*x* ŠEŠ ⌜*ù*⌝ [*x x x x*]
12′ [*x x x x*] ⌜*x*⌝ [*x x x x x*]

rest broken away

CT 54 233

(Beginning destroyed)

3 [...] lands [...]
4 [...] Westland [...]
5 [...] 80 Sealand [...]
6 their [...]s [...]
7 their [... (...)]
8 *his* [...] Yakin [...]
9 [... fat]her and mother *he will g*[*ive* ...]
10 [... *brother*] and sister *a bo*[*w* ...]
11 [...] brother and [*sister* ...]

(Rest destroyed)

35. ---

K 5529

beginning broken away

1′ [*x x x x*]*x* [*x x x x x x x*]
2′ [*x x x x*] *x*[*x x x x x x x*]
3′ [*x x* LU]GAL *be-l*[*í x x x x x x*]
4′ [*x x*] *ṭè-e-*[*ma-ni*$^{?}$ *x x x x*]
5′ [*x il-ta-n*]*ap-par-ru a-n*[*a x x x*]
6′ [*x x x*]-*šú a-du-ú pa-ni* [*x x x*]
7′ [*x x x x*]-*me*-10 *ki-i* [*x x x x*]
8′ [*x x x-b*]*i i-ba-*[*áš-ši x x x*]
9′ [*x x x x*] *bi* [*x x x x x x*]

rest broken away

CT 54 130

(Beginning destroyed)

3 [... the ki]ng, [my] lord [......]
4 [...] rep[orts ...]
5 [...] they [keep s]ending. T[o ...]
6 [...] *him*. Now then [...]
7 [... x]10 *that* [...]
8 [... ther]e are [...]

(Rest destroyed or too broken for translation)

36. ---

K 5593

beginning broken away

1′ [*x x*] ⌜*x x*⌝ [*x x x*]
2′ [*i*]*t-*⌜*ta*⌝*-du-*⌜*ú*⌝ [*x x x*]
3′ *a-na* UGU URU.*x*[*x x x*]
4′ *i-qab-bu-ú u*[*m-ma x x*]
5′ *dib-bi šal-mu-t*[*u x x x*]

CT 54 144

(Beginning destroyed)

1 [...] have *pitched* (*camp*).
2 [...] are *plotting* against the town of [...]: "[...] honest words [...]

34 [6] The last visible sign may be ⌜SAG$^{?}$⌝. [6, 10] See coll.
35 [4] Or, "ne[ws]". [6] For *adû pān*(*i*), cf. SAA 17 94 r.7′ and 95 r.18.
36 [7] For *sipru*, cf. SAA 17 2:15. [10] Or, read *ù a-na-k*[*u* "And, as for me". [r.8] Unlike in Dietrich's copy, a photograph available online seems to show traces of *na*.

FIG. 7. *Assyrian army camp.*
Original Drawings VI, 16.

6′ LU[GA]L *i-di ki-*⌜*i*⌝ [*x x x x*]
7′ É *sip-ri-šú šá* [*x x x x*]
8′ *ta-at-tan-n*[*a x x x x x*]
9′ *i-na pa-an x*[*x x x x x*]
10′ *ù a-na š*[*u-x x x x x x*]
11′ ⌜*x x-ru*⌝*-nu* [*x x x x x x*]
rest broken away
Rev. beginning broken away
1′ *x*[*x x x x x x x*]
2′ *la* [*x x x x x x*]
3′ LÚ.*qur-b*[*u-tu x x x x*]
4′ *i-na bi-r*[*it x x x x x*]
5′ *ul it-*[*x x x x x x*]
6′ 1-*en* LÚ.A–KIN [*x x x x*]
7′ *la i-mah-*⌜*ha*⌝*-*[*ru x x x*]
8′ ⌜*a-na*⌝ *pa-ni-šú* ⌜*áš*?⌝*-*[*x x x*]
9′ [*x x*] *x*[*x x x x x x*]
rest broken away

6 The ki[n]g knows that […]
7 *where* his *document of* […]
8 you have given […]
9 *before* […]
10 and *to* […]
(Break)

r.3 a royal body[guard …]
4 betwe[en …]
5 not …[…]
6 one messenger […]
7 do/does not recei[ve …]
8 *to* his presence […]
(Rest destroyed)

37. Fragment Concerning Military Matters

K 15205

beginning broken away
1′ [*x x x x x x x x*]*x*[*x*]
2′ [*x x x x x x x x*] *x* [*x*]
3′ [*x x x x x x x x*]*x x*[*x*]
4′ [*x x x x x x*] ᵐDUMU–[15?]
5′ [*x x x x x x x x*]*x ni* [*x*]
6′ [*x x x x x x x* ERI]M.MEŠ [*x*]
7′ [*x x x x x x x x x x-t*]*i-šú-nu*
8′ [*x x x x x x x x*]*x-ma*
9′ [*x x x x x x x x*]*-at*
10′ [*x x x x x x x x*].MEŠ
11′ [*x x x x x x x x*]
12′ [*x x x x x x x x*]*x*
13′ [*x x x x x x x x*]*x-hu*
r.1 [*x x*] 3 LÚ.EN–KÚR
2 [*x x*] *e-mu-qí-šú*
3 [*x x-á*]*r bat-qu*
4 [*x x x*]*x* ERIM.MEŠ-*šú*
5 [*x x x*] *šá e-mu-qu*

6 [*x x ki-i*] *šá mah-ru*
7 [ᵐDUMU–15? EN].NUN *it-ti-ni*
8 [*li-iṣ-ṣu*]*r šá a-kan-na*
9 [*li-ir*]*-ku-ba ba-taq-šú-nu*
10 [*li-iṣ-bat ki*]*-i* LUGAL *be-lí-a i-qab-bu-*[*ú*]
11 [*x x a-ša*]*p-pa-rak-ku-nu-ši*
12 [*x i?-š*]*ap-pa-ra-ni*
13 [*x x x*]*-ir l*[*i*]*-še-eg-la-a*[*n-na-šú*]
14 [*x x x x x x*] *um-ma* [*x x*]
15 [*x x x x x x x*] *šá* ᵐᵈ[*x x*]
rest broken away

CT 54 300

(Beginning destroyed)

4 [......] Mar-[*Issar*]
5 [......]
6 [...... me]n
7 [......] their [...]
(Break)

r.1 [...] 3 *of* the enemy
2 [...] his forces
3 [...] *replacement*
4 [...] his men
5 [...] *who* forces
6 [... If] it is acceptable, [let *Mar-Issar* stan]d [gu]ard with us, [ri]de (horses) that are here [(and) supply] their deficit. [I]f the king, my lord, command[s, I shall s]end [...] to you.
12 [... he w]rites me
13 [...] let him deport [us]
14 [......] "[...]
15 [......] *of* [NN]
(Rest destroyed)

38. Problem with Fleeing Fugitives and Refugees

K 15342

beginning broken away
1′ [*x x*] UGU *x*[*x x x x x x x*]
2′ [*x-q*]*a* LÚ.*hal-qu* LÚ.*mu-n*[*a-ab-bi-tu*]
3′ [*x x*] ⸢*i*⸣*-hal-li-qu da-x*[*x x x x*]
4′ [*x x*] ⸢*i*⸣*-na* ŠÀ-*bi in-né-hi-i*[*s x x x x*]
5′ [*x x n*]*i-i-ri dan-nu i-na* [*x x x x*]

6′ [*x x a*]*-di* LUGAL *a-na* É–⸢DINGIR⸣.[MEŠ *x x x*]

CT 54 307

(Beginning destroyed)

2 [...] fugitive*s* (and) ref[ugee*s*]
3 [...] are fleeing ...[......]
4 [...] retreats there [...]
5 [...] a strong [y]oke in [...]
6 [... un]til the king to the temple [...]

37 r.1 The more "solemn" LÚ.EN–KÚR, rather than a simple *nakru* ((LÚ.)KÚR), also appears in SAA 17 95: from the same sender? 4 Possibly a royal bodyguard or commander of outriders in the reign of Sargon II, see PNA 2/II 738b, nos. 9, 11. r.3 A form of *kaṣāru* is possible. r.13 Note [ᵐ*ha-a-a*]*-ir* in SAA 17 95:5.

38 4 There is no N stem of *nahāsu*, thus, probably to be interpreted as *inehhis*.

7′ [*mun-dah*?]-*ṣu-ti šá* LUGAL *be*-[*lí-i-ni*? *x x*]
8′ [*x x š*]*u-ṭur-a-nim-ma šu*[*p-ra x x x x*]

9′ [^{md}*x*–D]IN-*iṭ* DUMU-*šú šá* [*x x x x*]
10′ rest broken away
Rev. completely broken away

[7] [W]rite me down [the *names of* the *fighti*]*ng* men *of* the king, [*our*] lo[rd ...] and sen[d them to me].
[9] [... DN-ub]alliṭ, son of [...]
(Rest destroyed)

39. ---

K 15698
beginning broken away
1′ [*x x* E]N-*i-ni* [*x x x x x*]
2′ [*x x*] *ù ni-ip*-[*x x x x x*]
3′ [*si*?-*i*]*t-ti ma-a*-[*x x x x x*]
4′ [*x x*]*x-na ul x*[*x x x x x*]
5′ [*x x*] *ba-ni-i* [*x x x x x*]
6′ [*x*]-*ni nit-t*[*a-din x x x x*]
7′ [*x x*] EN-*a-nu* [*x x x x x*]
8′ [LÚ.EN].NAM $^{md+}$AG–[*x x x x x*]
rest broken away

CT 54 328
(Beginning destroyed)
[1] [...] our [lo]rd [......]
[2] [...] and we [......]
[3] [*the rem*]*aining* ...[......]
[4] [...]... *not* [......]
[5] [*the nob*]*ility* [......]
[6] we gave *our* [......]
[7] [...] our lord [......]
[8] [gov]ernor (*and*) Nabû-[......]
(Rest destroyed)

40. ---

K 16110 + 82-5-22,1766
beginning broken away
1′ ⸢*a*⸣-[*n*]*a* LÚ.*x*[*x x x x x x*]
2′ LÚ.*qí-pa-a-ni* [*x x x x x*]
3′ *is-sag-gu-na* $^{m?}$*x*[*x x x x*]
4′ *a-na* LÚ.GAL!!–*ki-ṣir x*[*x x x x*]
5′ *ma-la nap-pi-š*[*u x x x x*]
6′ *it-ti-šú-nu ul* [*x x x x*]

7′ [*a-d*]*u-ú* ŠEŠ.MEŠ-*n*[*i*? *x x x*]
8′ [*x i*]*l-ta-par* LUGAL *a-n*[*a x x x x*]
9′ [*li-šá-li-k*]*a-an-na-a-šú x*[*x x x x*]
10′ [*x x x*]*x-a šá* LUGAL EN-*i-n*[*i x x x*]
11′ [*x x x*]*x ki-i it-ti* [*x x x*]
12′ [*x x x x*]*x* ⸢*x*⸣ *x*[*x x x x x x*]
rest broken away

CT 54 348
(Beginning destroyed)
[1] to the [...] official [...],
[2] the royal delegates [...]
[3] *were moving about.* [NN]
[4] to the cohort commander [...],
[5] *all* [...] *to its top* [...]
[6] [do] not [...] with them ...[...].
[7] [No]w [...] has sent *o*[*ur*] brothers [*to* ...].
[8] [*May*] the king [*let*] us [*g*]*o* t[o ...].
[10] [...]... of the king, ou[r] lord [...]
[11] [...] as with [...]
(Rest destroyed or too broken for translation)

7f Or, "who, the king [...]", e.g., "[summoned]", the imperatives are not addressed to the king, who is probably not the recipient of this letter. 8 One could restore [*ha-an-ṭiš*] "quickly" at the beginning.

39 3 Not to exclude *itti*, *ritti*, etc. Probably not *mā*, an Assyrianism. 5 Perhaps restore [DUMU.MEŠ]–*ba-ni-i*.

40 CT 54 348: Join by M. Dietrich (--.10.1965). 3 Now understood as a form of *segû*. 5 I.e., possibly *ana appīšu* > *nappīšu*. 6 *ul* is either a negation or part of a verbal form. 11 Unless "if with" or less likely here "like a sign".

41. ---

K 16126

beginning broken away

1′ [*x x x x x x*] ⸢*x*⸣ [*x x x x x x*]
2′ [*x x x*] ⸢*x x*⸣ *mu d*[*a x x x x x*]
3′ [*x x* L]UGA[L *i-dab*]*-bu-u*[*b x x x x*]
4′ [*x x x*]*x li-du-uk* [*x x x x*]
5′ [*x x x*]*x pa-šú-nu liš-kun* [*x x x x*]
6′ [*x x x*]*x mu* [*x*]*x lul-*[*x x x x*]
7′ [*x x x*] *x* [*x*] *x nam ih* [*x x x x*]
8′ [*x x x*] LÚ *x*[*x x*] *pa-ni* ⸢*x*⸣ [*x x x x*]
9′ [*x x x*]*x ba x*[*x*]*x a-na pa-*[*ni x x x*]
10′ [*x x x*]*x-ul* DINGIR SIG$_5^?$ [*x x x x*]
11′ [*x x x x x*]*x ka nu* [*x x x x*]
12′ [*x x x* LÚ.*aš-š*]*ur*.KI.ME[Š *x x x x*]
13′ [*x x x x x x*] ⸢*x*⸣ [*x x x x x x*]

rest broken away

CT 54 358

(Beginning destroyed)

3 [*is spea*]*kin*[*g about* the k]in[g ...]
4 [...] let him kill [...]
5 [...] let him *adjust* their *speech* [...]
6 [...] ... [...]
7 [...] ... [...]
8 [...] the [...] *before* [...]
9 [...] ... [...] to [...]
10 [...]... the god *is good* [...]
11 [......] ... [...]
12 [... the Assy]rians [...]

(Rest destroyed)

41 3 Alternatively, [*it-ti* L]UGA[L or [*a-na* UGU L]UGA[L. 5 Or, read *liš-kun-*[*ú* "let [them] make common cause"? 10 *ul* as a negation is possible or "a good god", which seems suspicious. Perhaps DINGIR and SIG$_5$ are the elements of a broken personal name. Or read DINGIR *u x*[*x*.

2. Fragments of Unknown Authorship

FIG. 8. *Huntsman at Dur-Šarruken (Khorsabad).*
BM 118829.

42. Mounting [...] of Gods with Sinews

K 1193
beginning broken away
1′ [*ina* UGU *x x x*]*x ša* DINGIR.MEŠ
2′ [*ša* LUGAL *be-lí iq-b*]*u-u-ni*
3′ [*qu-up-pa-ti*[?] *š*]*a gi-di*
4′ [*ina x x x x*]*x kar-ra*
5′ [LÚ.*x x x*] LUGAL *ša na-mu-du*
6′ [*ú-du-ni l*]*il-li-ka*
7′ [*gi-di* T]A ŠÀ-*bi liš-ši*

8′ [*x x*] *i-ba-áš-ši*
9′ [*ša g*]*i-di ina* UGU-*hi*
e.10′ [*la*] *kar-ru-ni*
11′ [*dul-lu*[?]] *ina pi-it-ti*
12′ [*na-m*]*ì-di-šú*
r.1 [*lil-li*]*-ka le-e-pu-šú*
2 [*gi-d*]*i ina* UGU-*hi lu-še-li*
rest uninscribed

CT 53 169
(Beginning destroyed)

1 [Concerning the ...] of the gods, [about which the king, my lord, sp]oke, [*boxes* o]f sinews are placed [in ...].

5 A [...] of the king, who [knows] the measurement, [sh]ould come (and) take [sinews fr]om there.

8 There are [...s] on which [s]inews have [not] been placed.

11 [He should co]me and do [*the work*] according to its [measu]rement, and mount [sine]ws upon it.

43. Doing the King's Work

K 1160
beginning broken away
1′ [*x x x x x x*]
2′ [*mi-n*]*u ṭè-*⸢*e*⸣*-*[*mu*]
3′ ⸢*ša*⸣ *iš-kun-ni-ni* SI[G$_5$?]
4′ ⸢*dul*⸣*-lu* LUGAL *né-pa-áš*
5′ *a-na* ⸢LUGAL⸣ EN-*ia*
e.6′ [*a*]*-s*[*ap*]*-ra*
r.1 [*mi-nu*] ⸢*ša*⸣ LUGAL *be-lí*
2 ⸢*i*⸣*-šá-pa-ra-ni*
3 *ina pi-ti le-pu-uš*
4 rest uninscribed

CT 53 167
(Beginning destroyed)

2 [Whatev]er ord[er] that was given to me – it is goo[d].

4 We are doing the king's work.

5 [I am w]r[iti]ng to the king, my lord. I shall act according to the written instructions of the king, my lord.

42 This letter fragment refers to a building or renovation context (cf. the use of sinews in SAA 19 123 and 156). [3, etc.] *gīdu* "sinew of an animal" (CAD G 66f) is a much rarer word than *šer ānu*

43 [2, r.1] Or, [*mì-n*]*u*/[*mì-nu*]. [3] *iš-kun-ni-ni* is an abbreviated form of *iškunannīni*.

44. Corvée Workers for the King

K 4301

beginning broken away

1′ [*an-nu-r*]*ig* ⸢*ú*⸣-[*ra-si x x*]

2′ [*a-n*]*a* LUGAL EN-*i*[*a a-sap-ra*]

3′ [13] *ina* IGI ^{md}PA–*x*[*x x x*]

4′ [1]1 *ina* IGI ^{m}EN–[*x x x*]

5′ 10 *ina* IGI ^{m}EN–[*x x x*]

6′ 4 *ina* UGU *is-q*[*a-ti*? *x x*]

7′ 10 *ina* KÁ–[*x x x*]

8′ 20 *ina* UGU ⸢KI⸣.[MAH? *x x x*]

9′ 4 *ina* IGI ^{m}[*x x x x x*]

10′ PAB 72 *ina* UG[U *x x x*]

11′ 8 [*ina*] IGI ^{m}SUHUŠ–[*x x x*]

12′ [*x x x*]-*ši-šú-n*[*u x x x*]

rest broken away

Rev. beginning destroyed

1′ ⸢*qa*⸣-[*x x x x x x x*]

2′ *ut-ru* [*x x x x x*]

3′ *ina* É *dul-*⸢*lu*⸣ *x*[*x x x*]

4′ [*l*]*e-pu-*[*šu*]

rest uninscribed

CT 53 227

(Beginning destroyed)

1 [I am no]w [sending x] cor[vée workers t]o the king, m[y] lord –

3 [13] are at the disposal of Nabû-[...],

4 [1]1 are at the disposal of Bel-[...],

5 10 are at the disposal of Bel-[...],

6 4 (working) on *lo*[*ts* ...],

7 10 at the gate [of ...],

8 20 (working) on the *to*[*mb* ...],

9 4 are at the disposal of [NN].

10 In all 72 (working) on [...]

11 8 are [at] the disposal of Ubru-[...],

12 [...] ... the[m]/the[ir ...]

(Break)

r.2 *extra* [......]

3 [They should] d[o] the work [...] in the *house*.

45. – – –

K 5489

beginning broken away

1′ [*x x x x x*] ⸢*x*⸣ [*x x*]

2′ [*x x x x l*]*a ú-ṣ*[*u-ni*]

3′ [*x x x x*] *la id-*[*x x*]

4′ [*mi-nu ši-ti*]-*ni a-ma*[*r*]

5′ [*a-na* LUGAL EN]-⸢*ia*⸣ [*x x x*]

rest broken away

other side destroyed

CT 53 255

(Beginning destroyed)

2 [*They refuse*] to com[e out],

3 [...] do not g[ive].

4 I will find o[ut whatever it is and *write* to the king], my [lord]

(Rest destroyed)

44 r.3 Perhaps *dul-*⸢*lu*⸣ L[UGAL.

45 2 or 3 Possibly [*la i-ma-gúr l*]*a ú-ṣ*[*u-ni*] or *la id-*[*du-nu*]; cf., e.g., SAA 5 118:9-11; SAA 19 125:17′; for the latter SAA 1 149: 8-9; SAA 16 29 r.1; SAA 19 195 s.1-2. 4 For the restoration, cf. SAA 5 19 s.1; SAA 10 101 r.8f; SAA 13 131:10f.

46. ---

K 5521

beginning broken away

1′ [*ša* MAN *be-lí*] *iš-pu*[*r-an-ni*]
2′ [*ma*]*-a pi-ti* [*x x x x x*]
3′ [*a-m*]*a-har-*[*ka x x x x*]

4′ [*šúm*?*-m*]*u* MAN *b*[*e-lí x x x*]
5′ [*x*] *iš-qa-*[*ti x x x x*]
6′ [MAN E]N*-ia* [*x x x x*]

rest broken away

Rev. beginning broken away

1′ [*x x*] *du* [*x x x x*]
2′ [*x x*] *a-du a-*[*x x x*]
3′ [*x x-b*]*i* A.ŠÀ [*x x x*]
4′ rest broken away

CT 53 267

(Beginning destroyed)

1 [As to what the king, my lord] wrot[e to me]: "[I shall re]ceive [... from you] according to [..., (and) ...]" –

4 [*If*] the king, [my] l[ord ...]

5 [...] shar[es of ... *to* the king], my [lo]rd [...]

(Break)

r.2 [...] *until I* [...]

3 [*in*] a field [...]

(Rest destroyed)

47. Details on Statues

K 5542

beginning broken away

1′ *ra-*[*x x x x x x*]
2′ É.MEŠ [*x x x x x*]
3′ *a-na* UGU [*x x x x*]
4′ *la a-ka-r*[*a-x x x*]
5′ DAGAL *ku-bur* NU.M[EŠ *x x x*]
6′ ⌜*a*⌝*-na* LUGAL *be-lí-iá* [*x x x x*]
7′ rest broken away

Rev. destroyed

CT 53 276

(Beginning destroyed)

2 houses [...]

3 *against* [...]

4 I will not pu[t ...]

5 the width and thickness of the statues [...]

6 to the king, my lord [...]

(Rest destroyed)

48. ---

K 5601

1 *a-na* LUGAL [EN*-ia*]
2 ARAD*-ka* ^{m}[*x x x x*]
3 [*l*]*u-u* DI*-mu* [*a-na* LUGAL EN*-ia*]
4 [*x*] ⌜*x nu*⌝ *x*[*x x x x*]

rest broken away

Rev. beginning broken away

1′ [*x x*]*x* ⌜*a*⌝*-na x*[*x x x x*]
2′ *il-la-k*[*a* 0?]
3′ rest uninscribed

CT 53 288

1 To the king, [my lord]: your servant [NN]. [Go]od health [to the king, my lord].

(Break)

r.1 [...] is coming to [...].

46 3 As (*ina*) *pān* is usually used as the preposition "before" in NA, we have here a present tense verbal form *a*/*i*/*ni*/*tamahhar*. 4 Or: [UD*-m*]*u* ...? 5 Or: [*x*]*-iš qa-*[*x x x x*]. r.3 I.e., perhaps restore [*ina* ŠÀ*-b*]*i*.

47 5 Surprisingly, this sequence of "width and thickness" does not appear elsewhere in SAA.

48 r.1 The most likely restoration is probably ⌜É?⌝.[GAL], "p[alace]", but L[UGAL EN*-ia*] is also possible.

49. Punishing the King's Foes

K 7323

beginning broken away

1′ [*x x x x x*]*x ši-ti*

2′ [*x x x*]*-ku*

3′ [*x x x*] *ú-ka-ṣa*

4′ [*ina* UGU *x x*].MEŠ

5′ [*ša* LUGAL *be-lí*] *iš-pur-an-ni*

6′ [*x x x x*]*-a* 1*-tú*

7′ [*x x x x*] *a-na* UGU É.SIG4

8′ [*x x x x x*]*-ba*

9′ [*x x x x*]*-*⌜*lu*⌝*-ši*

rest broken away

Rev. beginning broken away

1′ [m*x x x la pa*]*-li-hu*

2′ [*ša* LUGAL *be-lí-ia*] *a-ṣa-ba-at*

3′ [*x x x x x*] GIŠ.[ŠU?].⌜2⌝.MEŠ

rest broken away

CT 53 319

(Beginning destroyed)

1 [......] *she/it*

2 [...]...

3 [...] I will *flay*.

4 [Concerning the ...]s [about *which/whom* the king, my lord], wrote to me,

6 [...]... *one*

7 [...] *to* the wall

(Break)

r.1 I have seized [NN, who does not f]ear [the king]

3 [......] *man*[*acle*]s

(Rest destroyed)

50. – – –

K 7350

beginning broken away

1′ [*x x x x x x*]*x* ⌜*is*⌝*-si-bi*

2′ [*x x x x ip*]*-*⌜*qi*⌝*-da-ni-ni*

3′ [*x x x x*] *ú-se-rib*

4′ [*x x x x* I]TI.SIG4

5′ [*x x x x x*] *dul-lu*

6′ [*x x x x x x*].MEŠ

7′ [*x x x x x x x*]*x*

rest broken away

Rev. uninscribed

CT 53 326

(Beginning destroyed)

1 [......] he *surrounded*

2 [... ap]pointed me

3 [...] *I* made enter

4 [...] month of Sivan (III)

5 [......] the work

(Rest destroyed or too broken for translation)

51. Official Sent to Assur

K 7532

beginning broken away

1′ [*ša ina* URU].ŠÀ–⌜URU⌝

2′ [LUGAL *b*]*e-lí iš-pu-ra-šú-*⌜*ni*⌝

3′ [*x x*] m10*-i i-si-si-šú*

CT 53 385

(Beginning destroyed)

0 [NN whom the king], my [l]ord, sent [to] the Inner City.

3 [...] Addî called to him

49 [3] The fragment seems to be about corporal punishment and/or executions, an unusual topic in NA letters (but see, e.g., Radner, ZAR 21 [2015] 118-21). [6] Or, perhaps "a tower", *isītu*.

50 [3] Or: "made [me] enter".

51 [3, r.1] The two personal names are too common to be identified with any certainty.

e.4′ [*x x*]*x ú-ta-si-ku*
r.1 [*x x x*] 1 *ša* ᵐEN–IGI.LAL-*ni*
rest broken away

4 [...] they assigned
r.1 [...] one of Bel-emuranni
(Rest destroyed)

52. Transporting in Secrecy

K 10936
beginning broken away
1′ [*x x x*] ⸢*x x x x x x*⸣ [*x x*]
2′ [*x x*]*x-at nu-uk a-ta-a* [0]
3′ [*x*] ⸢*a*⸣*-na* É*-ka ta-za-bi*[*l*]
4′ [*nu*]*-uk* PAB.MEŠ*-ka e-mu-*[*ru*]
5′ *ki-i an-ni-ma* [*e-pu-šu*]
6′ [*š*]*u-u ki-i* [*an-ni-e*]
7′ [*i*]*q-ṭí-bi-a* [*ma-a x x*]
e.8′ [*x x*]*x* [*x x x x x*]
Rev. broken away

CT 53 421
(Beginning destroyed)

2 [... *it*] is [...], I said: "Why do you transpo[rt ...] to your house? Your brothers will se[e] *it* and [do] like this."

6 [H]e told me as [follows]: "[......]
(Rest destroyed)

53. Dealings with the Qedarites

K 12987
beginning broken away
1′ [*x x x x* LÚ*].GAL–KAŠ.[LUL *x x*]
2′ [*x x x x x*] *ma an* [*x x x*]
3′ [*x x x x x*] *šá hu-u*[*b-tu*?]
4′ [*x x x* ᵐ?]*ba-nu-ni* [*x x x*]
5′ [*x x*] ⸢*x*⸣ *la e-pa-š*[*u-u-ni*]
6′ [*x x*]*x* LÚ*.SAG *ša* L[UGAL 0?]
7′ [KUR.*qe-d*]*a-ra-a-a x*[*x x x*]
8′ [*x x x x x*]*x* [*x x x x*]
rest broken away

Rev. beginning broken away
1′ [*x x x x x x*] ⸢*x x x*⸣ [*x*]
2′ [*x x x x x x*] *še su* [*x*]
3′ [*x x x x x x*]*-ka-lu-*[*x*]
4′ [*x x x x x x*] *ta ra x*[*x*]
5′ [*x x x x x x*]*x* LUGAL *be-l*[*í*]
6′ [*x x x x x x*]*x* [*x*]
7′ [*x x x x* LÚ*.GAL–K]AŠ.LUL [0]
8′ rest broken away

CT 53 449
(Beginning destroyed)
1 [...] the chief cupbe[arer ...]
2 [...] ... [...]
3 [...] *who the capt*[*ives*]
4 [...] *Banuni* [...]
5 [*who*] did not d[o ...]
6 [...] a eunuch of the k[ing]
7 [*of* the Qed]arites [...]
(Break)

r.5 [......] the king, [my] lord
6 [......]
7 [... the chief cu]pbearer
(Rest destroyed)

52 ² Unless we have the end of a feminine stative form. Then the fragment could be about a woman instead of "it".

53 ⁷ Or restore [LÚ?.*qi-d*]*a-*, with the determinative LÚ as in the NB letters SAA 18 143:8, 144 r.6′, 145:7; but see also SAA 19:11 (with KUR) and SAA 4 139:12 (without determinative). This ethnic name, if correct, may suggest a 7th century context, but the chief cupbearer, on the other hand, may favor an 8th century event.

54. Fragment Mentioning the People of Dur-Šarruken

K 14582
beginning broken away
1′ [*x x x*] ⸢*li da*⸣ [*x x x x x*]
2′ [URU].BÀD–LUGAL–GIN-*a-a* [*x x*]
3′ [*x x x x x x*] *ina* ŠÀ [*x x*]
4′ [*x x x x x x x x x x*]
5′ [*x x x* LÚ].⸢A⸣–KIN [*x x x*]
6′ [*x x x x x*] *ana-k*[*u*$^{?}$ *x x*]
rest broken away

CT 53 530
(Beginning destroyed)
2 the people of Dur-Šarruken [...]
3 [......] in [...]
4 [......]
5 [... the] messenger [...]
6 [...] *I* [...]
(Rest destroyed)

55. Tablet from Babylon

K 14637
beginning broken away
e.1′ [I]M.GÍD.DA [*x x x x*]
r.1 T[A*] KÁ.DINGIR.RA.[KI *x x*]
2 [^{m}]⸢^{d}⸣30–DINGIR-*a-a* [*x x x x x*]
3 [*x-ṣ*]*u-um-ma* T[A* *x x x x*]
4 [*x x x*] ⸢*x x*⸣ [*x x x x x*]
rest broken away

CT 53 556
(Beginning destroyed)
1 a one-column tablet [...]
r.1 fr[om] Babylon [...]
2 Sîn-ila'i [......]
3 ... *fr*[*om* ...]
(Rest destroyed)

56. A Silver Dagger

K 15396
beginning broken away
1′ [*ma*]-⸢*a*⸣ *a-ta-*⸢*a*⸣ [*x x x x x*]
2′ [DUMU$^{?}$]–LUGAL *ina* ŠU.2-[*šú ṭa-ab-tu*]
3′ *e-pu-šá-an-ni* [*x x x x x*]
4′ GÍR KUG.UD *a-nu-u-tú* [*a-na ia-a-ši*]
5′ ⸢*i*⸣*-sa-ap-ar* [*x x x*]
6′ [*x*]*x* URU.*x*[*x x x x x*]
rest broken away

CT 53 660
(Beginning destroyed)
1 [sayi]ng: "Why [...] has the king's [*son*] by [his own] hand done [a favor] to me, in sending [a ...], a silver dagger and (other) goods [to me]?
6 [... ...] the town of [......]
(Rest destroyed)

55 1 Presumably this line indicates the nature of the tablet. r.3 E.g., [*mur*$^{?}$*-ṣ*]*u-um-ma* "the illness" or [*har*$^{?}$*-ṣ*]*u-um-ma* are the most the likely restorations, but is there enough space for them? Or, perhaps [*e*$^{?}$*-ṣ*]*u-um-ma*?

56 4 Interestingly, the only "silver dagger/sword/knife" in NA archival sources so far, whereas a "golden dagger/sword of gold" is a better attested ceremonial object; see, e.g., CAD P 282b and SAA 16 63:30, r.17.

57. Fragment Referring to the Deputy (Governor?)

K 16073

beginning broken away

1′ [*ma*]-*a a*-⸢*na*⸣ *x*[*x x x x x x*]
2′ [*ub*]-*bu-lu ma*-⸢*a*⸣ [*x x x x x*]
3′ [L]Ú*.2-*ú i-s*[*i-x x x x*]

4′ *ina pa-an* EN-⸢*iá*⸣ [*x x x x x*]
5′ *ur-ta-me-ú* [*x x x x x*]

6′ *ina* UGU *pi-i* ⸢É?⸣ [*x x x x*]
7′ [*š*]*a* LÚ*.2-*e* [*x x x x x*]
8′ [*x x*] ⸢*x*⸣ [*x x x x x x*]

rest broken away

CT 53 740

(Beginning destroyed)

1 [sayin]g: "[they b]ring [...] to [...].
2 "[......]
3 the deputy is wi[th ...]
4 they have released [......] in the presence of my lord [......]
6 according to the order of *pa*[*lace* ......]
7 [o]f the deputy [......]

(Rest destroyed)

58. Work for Officials

K 16473

obverse destroyed

e.1′ [*x x*]*x za-ku x*[*x x x x x*]
2′ [*ina* UG]U LÚ*.EN–*pi-qit-ta-te*
3′ [*š*]*a* LUGAL *be-lí iq-bu-u-ni*
r.1 [*e*]-*da-nu ša dul-li-šú-nu* [0]
2 [LUGAL *b*]*e-lí lu-pa*-⸢*aq*⸣-[*qid-su-nu*]
3 [*x x*]*x nu-še-ṣi* [*x x x*]
4 [*x x x x*]*x* [*x x x x x*]

rest broken away

CT 53 763

(Beginning destroyed)

1 [...] *exempt* [......]
2 [As t]o the officials about [wh]om the king, my lord, spoke, may [the king], my [lo]rd, assi[gn them a d]eadline for their work, (and) let us bring out [......]

(Rest destroyed)

59. ---

Sm 1753

beginning broken away

1′ [*x x*]*x x*[*x x x x x x*]
2′ ⸢*pa*?⸣-*ni-e q*[*ur*?-*x x x*]
3′ LÚ*.GAL–*ki-ṣir* [*x x x x*]
4′ *ša i-si-šú ú*-[*x x x x*]
5′ ^{md}PA–DIL–⸢*ba*?⸣-[*liṭ*? *x x x*]
6′ *ina* IGI ^{m}*x*[*x x x x x x x*]

rest broken away

CT 53 850

(Beginning destroyed)

1 [......] *previous* [......]
3 cohort commander [...]
4 who [...] with him,
5 Nabû-edu-*ba*[*lliṭ* ...] *in the presence of* [NN ...]

(Rest destroyed)

57 3 Or: "the deputy has [...]".
59 3 Probably a PN at the end. 5 PNA also has this hapax PN s.v. Nabû-ēdu-balliṭ. 6 See coll. (final traces not in CT 53 850).

60. Taking Care of Mares

81-2-4,455
beginning broken away
1′ ⌜*x*⌝[*x x x x x*]
2′ *la ṣab-tú* ⌜*x ni*⌝ [*x*]
3′ É *gam-mur* ⌜*x ni*⌝ [*x*]
4′ *la ṣab-tú* 4 *x*[*x x*]
5′ ⌜PAB LÚ*.*um*?-*ma*⌝-*ni* [*x*]
6′ [*x x x*]*x ša* ᵐ*x*[*x x*]
7′ [*x x x*] ⌜*x x*⌝ [*x x*]
rest broken away
Rev. beginning broken away
1′ [*x x x x*] ⌜2⌝-*me* [*x*]
2′ [*x x x*]*x ni man* [*x*]
3′ [*an*]-⌜*ni*⌝-*tú la nu-gam-m*[*a-ru-ni*]
4′ [*ma*]-⌜*a*⌝ *šúm-mu* MÍ.ANŠE.KU[R.MEŠ?]
5′ [*it-ta*]*l*?-*ka-ni is-si-*[*ni*?]
6′ [*ina* Š]À URU.MEŠ-*ni* : *ni-ha-ṣi-*[*ni*]
7′ [*x x x x*]*x* ⌜*áš*⌝ *ti sa a* [
8′ rest broken away

CT 53 898
(Beginning destroyed)

2 are not *fastened* ... [...]
3 the house is finished ... [...]
4 are not *fastened* ... [...]
5 In all, the craftsmen [...]
6 [...] *of* N[N]
(Break)

r.1 [......] 200 [...]
2 [... t]his [... *which*] we will not fini[sh]."

4 "If the mare[s have co]me, we shall take ca[re] of them with [*us* i]n the towns."
(Rest destroyed)

61. – – –

83-1-18,785
beginning broken away
1′ [*x x x x*] ⌜*x*⌝ [*x x x x x*]
2′ [*ša* LUGAL *be*]-*lí ṭè-e-*[*mu iš-ku-na-ni-ni*]
3′ [*x x x-k*]*a a-ha-ma-a-šú* [*x x x x*]
4′ [*la-a il-l*]*i-ka ana-ku x*[*x x x x*]

5′ [*x x x x*]*x* 5 6 *pa-ni-ka* [*x x x*]
6′ [*x x x*]-*hu-ra ina* GIŠ.*ṣar-*[*bi-ti x x*]
7′ [*x x x*]*x-da-ka-a ša x*[*x x x x*]
8′ [*x x x*] *su-hi-ri-ka* [*x x x x*]
9′ [*x x x t*]*a-áš-ši tu-*[*x x x*]
10′ [*x x x x*]*x ni* [*x x x x x*]
rest broken away

CT 53 948
(Beginning destroyed)
1 [As regards NN, about whom the king], my [lor]d, [gave me] ord[ers, if he com]es, I shall immobilize him. [*So far* he has not co]me. I [......]
(Remainder untranslatable)

60 r.2 Or, -*ni* MAN? r.5 Although, admittedly, *is-si-*[*ni*?] seems superfluous if correctly restored. r.7 The signs look reasonably clear, could this be a *hapax* GN: U]RU.⌜*pa*/*áš*⌝-*ti-sa*(-)*a*?
61 3 Perhaps a form of *alāku* at the beginning, e.g., [*ma-a al-k*]*a*. Note also the adverb *ahamma* "apart, separately". 8 This may be a Babylonianism against the Assyrian *sahhirīka*. Or: *suhhirī* KA. 9 Obviously two second person singular verb forms.

62. – – –

1932-12-12,597 (BM 134602)
beginning broken away
1′ *[x x-a]p-ru-u-ni ina* ŠÀ U[RU? *x x*]
2′ *[e-ru?]-bu-u-ni a-sa-par x[x x x]*
3′ *[ina* UG]U? UN.MEŠ-*šú-nu ak-t[ar?-ra]*

4′ *[x ša* LUG]AL *be-lí iš-pur-an-ni [x x x]*
5′ *[x x x]-me ša* URU.MEŠ-⸢*ni*⸣ *[x x x x]*
6′ *[x x x x] a?* ⸢*ma*⸣ *[x x x x x]*
rest broken away
Rev. completely broken away

CT 53 973
(Beginning destroyed)
1 [... have wr]itten to me (that) [... *had ent*]*ered the t*[*own of* ...]. I sent *word* and *pla*[*ced ... on the to*]*p of* their people.
4 [... as to what the ki]ng, my lord, wrote to me: "[... the ...]*s of the towns*
(Rest destroyed or too broken for translation)

63. – – –

K 18525
beginning broken away
1′ *[x]* ⸢*x*⸣ *[x x x x x x]*
2′ [U]D-27-K[ÁM *x x x x x*]
3′ *mi-i-[nu ša* LUGAL *be-lí]*
4′ *i-q[ab-bu-u-ni]*
e. uninscribed
r.1 61 *x[x x x x x x]*
2 1 *x [x x x x x x]*
3 2 *x[x x x x x x]*
rest broken away

K 18525
(Beginning destroyed)
2 (On) the 27t[h d]ay [......]
3 Wh[at is it that the king, my lord], s[ays]?

r.1 61 [......]
2 1 [......]
3 2 [......]
(Rest destroyed)

64. They Are not Speaking the Truth

K 19999
beginning broken away
1′ *i-tal-ku [x x x x*
2′ LUGAL *li-x[x x x*
3′ *ma-ta-a-[ti? x x x*
4′ ⸢*x*⸣*-l[i-x x x x*
e.5′ *ina pa-an x[x x x*
6′ DUMU ⸢*šá*⸣ *[x x x x*
7′ *pa-an [x x x x x*

r.1 9 *qa [x x x x x*
2 1 TA* ŠÀ *[x x x x x*
3 *la il-*⸢*qi*⸣ *x[x x x*

K 19999
(Beginning destroyed)
1 they went [......]
2 the king should [......]
3 land[s ......]
4 [......]
5 in the presence [......]
6 son of [......]
7 *before* [......]
r.1 9 litres [......]
2 1 from [......]
3 he has not taken [......]

62 1 Probably restore *[i-sa-a]p-ru-u-ni*. 4 The line may end in *[ma-a]*.

4 *la ke-tú pa-an* [LUGAL EN-*ia*
5 *i-da-bu-b*[*u x x x x*
6 [*x x x*]*x* [*x x x x*
rest broken away

[4] They are not speaking the truth before [the king, my lord, ...]
(Rest destroyed)

65. – – –

K 20092
beginning broken away
1′ [*x x x*]*x* [*x x x*]
2′ [*x x x*] *e* [*x x x*]
3′ [*x x x*]*x-šú-nu it-t*[*a-x*]
4′ [*x x x*]*x-du* LÚ.SAG LUGAL
5′ [*x x x*]*x e-ter-ba a-na* LUGAL? *x*[*x*]
6′ [*x x x*]-*e* GAL
7′ [*x x x*].GUR *ina* MURUB4–URU
8′ [*x x x*] ⸢*x*⸣ [*x x x x*]
rest broken away

K 20092
(Beginning destroyed)

[3] their [...] has/have [...]
[4] [...] a royal eunuch
[5] entered [...] to the *king* [...]
[6] [*of the*] *great* [...]
[7] [...] in the centre of the city
(Rest destroyed)

65 [4] Possibly a PN ending in *-du*/DU. [5] The first visible signs may be *-š*]*ú-nu*. In NA, *e-tar-ba* is expected, whereas NB would have *i-ter-ba*. Alternatively, the end could be ⸢DUMU?⸣–MAN? with some extra scratches. [7] Perhaps a PN at the beginning: "...-Ne]rgal *is* in the centre of the city".

FIG. 9. *Horses from Iran.*
Botta and Flandin, Monument de Ninive II, Pl. 135.

66. Accusations about Horses

K 5460
beginning broken away
1′ [*ina* UGU *x x x*] ⸢LÚ⸣.[*x x x x*]
2′ [*ša ina* UGU-*šú*?] LUGAL! [*be-lí*]
3′ [*ṭè-e-mu iš*]-*ku-na*-[*an-ni-ni*]
4′ [*ma-a* ^{m}*ṭu*?]-*du-te* DUMU ^{m}[*x x x*]
5′ [*x x x* ^{m}*a*]-*du-ni*-⸢*i*⸣ [*x x x*]
rest broken away
Rev. beginning broken away
1′ [*ina* UGU LÚ.3].⸢U$_5$.MEŠ⸣-*ni* [*ša a-na*]
2′ [LUGAL EN-*ia*] ⸢*a*⸣-*hu-ru*-⸢*ú*⸣-[*ni mu-uk*?]
3′ [*x x x*]-*ti ša bit-qi i*[*b-tu-qu-ni*]
4′ [*x x* LÚ].⸢3⸣.U$_5$-*ia ina* UGU-⸢*hi*⸣ [*x x*]

5′ [*x x x*]*x* ANŠE.KUR.MEŠ *ša pu-u*-[*hi*]
6′ [*ša x x-n*]*i a-di ša ma-da*-⸢*a*⸣-[*ti*]
7′ [*la a-na ta*]-*da-a-nu né-m*[*a-al x x x*]

8′ [*x x a-na*] *ši-ih-li ap-t*[*i-qid x x*]
9′ [*x x x ta*]-*hu-mu-ma la i*-[*x x x*]

10′ [*x x x x m*]*a-a la* GÍD.D[A *x x x x x*]
11′ [*x x x x x la il-l*]*i-ku* [*x x x x x*]
rest broken away

ABL 1324
(Beginning destroyed)

1 [As regards *NN*], the [..., about whom] the king, [my lord, g]ave m[e orders, saying: "...*Ṭu*]duti, son of [NN, *and* A]dunî, [...]

(Break)

r.1 [As to the '*third m*]*en*', [about whom] I approached [the king, my lord, *saying*]: "[*They are*] those who [*made*] *accusations* [...]; my 'third man' [*has been killed*] on account of it" –

5 [...] bart[er] horses, [*which are* ...], along with tribu[te] horses, [*are not* to be s]old bec[ause ...].

8 I have ass[igned ... as] a replacement, but [... the ter]ritory is not [......]

10 [... They say]: "It is not long [...]

11 [...... have not go]ne [...]

(Rest destroyed)

67. Writing Board of Aplaya

K 13188
beginning broken away
1′ [*x x x*] L[UGAL? *x x x x*]
2′ [DI-*mu*?] ⸢*a*⸣-*na* EN.NUN.[MEŠ? 0?]
3′ [*ina* U]GU GIŠ.LI.⸢U$_5$?⸣.[UM]
4′ *ša* ^{m}DUMU.UŠ-*a-a* L[Ú*?.*x x x*]
5′ *ša* LUGAL *be-lí iš*-[*pur-an-ni*]
6′ *ma-a* TA* IGI ^{m}EN–[*x x x*]
7′ A ^{m}*na-zi-ia i*-[*ṣa*?]
8′ *a-na* ^{m}EN–*ú*-⸢*x x*⸣ [*še-bi-la*?]
9′ *ma-a* GIŠ.LI.[U$_5$.UM?]
10′ [*x x x*] ⸢*x*⸣ [*x x x x*]
rest broken away

ABL 1357
(Beginning destroyed)

2 *The garrison*[*s are well*].

3 [Concer]ning the writing b[oard] of Aplaya, the [...], about which the king, my lord, wr[ote to me]: "*T*[*ake it*] from Bel-[...], son of Nazia, [*and send*] it to Bel-*u*... The writing b[oard ......]"

(Break)

66 Harper's ABL copy shows a little more than can be seen today. 2 There is a remnant of what could be interpreted as a low horizontal wedge in front of the LUGAL sign. See coll. 4 The PN is tentative. In GPA 91, there is a man called Hiniduti, and in SAA 6 37, there is a man called Ṭuduti, but both are rare names.

67 There may be three or four lines missing from the beginning of the tablet. 2 The restoration is highly conjectural, and the tablet may originate from the seventh century, when such greeting formulae were less common. 3, 9, r.3 However, the spelling GIŠ.*le*-[*'i/'u*] cannot be excluded. 4 The name Aplaya is too common to be certain who this individual was. 6, 8 It seems that there are two different individuals with Bel as the first element of the name in these lines. 7 PNA 2/II 939b, has only two attestations of the name. 8 Harper copied what can be interpreted as ^{m}EN-*ú-kaš/bi-u*, but the last two signs seem rather uncertain. Of the Bel-names in PNA, Bēl-upahhir (1/II 336b, no. 1) would be the best match contextually.

Rev. beginning broken away

1′ ^{m}E[N$^{?}$–*x x x*]*x it-t*[*al*$^{?}$*-x x*]

2′ *a-na* ⸢LUGAL⸣ EN-*ia i*[*s-sa-par*$^{?}$]

3′ *ma-a šúm-mu* GIŠ.LI.[U$_5$.UM$^{?}$]

4′ *up-ta-zi-i*[*r x x x x*]

5′ LUGAL *hi-ṭu le-mid*$^{!}$*-a*[*n*$^{!}$*-ni*]

6′ [*i–s*]*u*$^{?}$*-ri* ^{m}EN–*x*[*x x x*]

7′ [*x x x*]*x* ⸢*x x*⸣ *x*[*x x x x*]

rest broken away

r.1 B[el-...] *ca*[*me* and *w*[*rote*] to the king, my lord: "If I have concealed the writing b[oard (and) ...], may the king punish m[e]!"

6 [*Per*]*haps* Bel-[...]

(Rest destroyed)

68. – – –

K 1149

beginning broken away

1′ [*x x x x*] *li*[*d-x x x x x x*]

2′ [*x x x x*]*x x*[*x x x x x x x*]

3′ [*x x x x-t*]*i*$^{?}$ ⸢*i*⸣-[*x x x x x x*]

4′ [*x x x x*] ⸢EN⸣*-šú-nu n*[*a-x x x x x x*]

5′ [*x x x x x*]-⸢*ú*⸣ *ana* KUR.*aš*$^{?}$-[*šur*.KI *x x x x x*]

6′ [*x x x x x*]*-ú x*[*x x x x x x x*]

7′ [*x x x x* E]N$^{?}$*-šú* [*x x x x x x x*]

rest broken away

Rev. beginning broken away

1′ [*x x x x x*] LÚ.S[AG$^{?}$ *x x x x x x*]

2′ [*x x x x x*] EN*-šú-n*[*u x x x x x x*]

3′ [*x x x x* LUG]AL *iš-pu-*[*ra x x x x x*]

4′ [*x x x x a-d*]*u-ú a-n*[*a x x x x x x*]

5′ [*x x x* LUGA]L *be-lí-i*[*a x x x x x*]

6′ [*x x x x a*]*l-tap-r*[*a* (*x x x x x x*)]

rest uninscribed

CT 54 9

(Beginning destroyed)

4 [......] their lord [......]

5 [......] to *As*[*syria* ......]

(Break)

r.1 [...] the *eu*[*nuch* ......]

2 [...] their lord [......]

3 [... *of whom/which* the ki]ng, wro[te ...]

4 [... No]w [*then*] t[o ......]

5 [... *to* the kin]g, m[y] lord [...]

6 [...... I] have writt[en].

69. – – –

K 1256

two lines destroyed

3 [*x x x*]*x x*[*x x x x x*]

two lines destroyed

6 [*x x x x x x x*]*-zib*

7 [*x x x x x x*]*-bi*

8 [*x x x x x x i*]*q-bu-ú*

9 [*x x x a-na pa*]*-an* LUGAL *lul-lik*

10 [*x x x*]*x* [*x x x*]*-bi-ma*

11 [*x x x*]*x* [*x x*] *en-na a-du-ú*

12 [*x x x x*] ⸢*x x*⸣*-a šu-ú*

13 [LUGAL *be-lí-a*$^{?}$ *ṭè*]*-e-mu liš-kun-šu-ma*

14 [*x x x x-t*]*i ih-sa*

CT 54 21

(Beginning destroyed)

8 [...] spoke

9 [...] let me come [t]o the king

10 [... *spea*]*k* and

11 [......] now then, he *is* [...].... Let [*the king, my lord*], give him [or]ders *so that*

r.1, 6f Or read here 1-*en* "one" instead of ^{m}EN–. r.5 See coll. r.7 Copied by Harper as *x*]*x* ^{m}EN *x*[*x*.

15 [*x x x x x*]-*an-ni*
16 [*x x x x ú-še-t*]*i-qa-an-ni-ma*
17 [*x x x x*]-*ni ṭè-e-mu*
18 [LUGAL *liš-k*]*u*$^{?}$-*na-an-ni*
e.19 [*x x x x*] ⸢*x x*⸣ [*x x x*]
Rev. three lines destroyed
4 [*x x x x x x x-t*]*i*$^{?}$
5 [*x x x x x x x*] *ši-tu*
6 [*x x x x x x x*]-*bu*
7 [*x x x x x x x*]-*du*
8 [*x x x x x* LÚ.A$^{?}$]–KIN
9 [*x x x x x x-n*]*i*
10 [*x x x x x x x*]-*ri*
three lines destroyed
14 [*x x x x x x x*]-*mu*
15 [*x x x x x x x x*]
16 [*x x x x x x x-p*]*i*$^{?}$
two lines destroyed
19 [*x*] ⸢*x x*⸣[*x x x x x*]

[*they*] go back [*to* ...].
15 [......] me
16 [... does *not pa*]*ss* me *on* and [... *m*]*e*. [*Let the king giv*]*e* me orders [......]
(Break)

r.8 [...... *mes*]*senger*
(Rest destroyed or too broken for translation)

70. The Governor in Til-Banana

K 1910
beginning broken away
1′ [*x x x x x x*] ⸢*x*⸣
2′ [^{d}*aš-šur* ^{d}UTU $^{d+}$EN] *u* $^{d+}$A[G]
3′ [*x x x x*] *be-lí-iá*
4′ [*x x x x-d*]*u-ú*
5′ [*x x x x*] BAR *be-lí-iá*
6′ [*x x x*] *a-na* 1-*en*
7′ [*x x* L]Ú.*šak-nu*.MEŠ
8′ [*x x*]-*di su ú li* ⸢*x*⸣

9′ [*x x*]-*šú it-ti-ia*
10′ [*x*] *be-lí-ia li-il-s*[*u*]
11′ LÚ.EN.NAM *a-na*
12′ *til-li-ba-na-na*
13′ [*i*]*t-ta-lak* ⸢*ù*⸣ [0$^{?}$]
14′ *a-na ka-da-*[*am-me*$^{?}$]
Rev. completely broken away

CT 54 35
(Beginning destroyed)

2 [May Aššur, Šamaš, Bel] and Na[bû]
3 [...] my lord
4 [... ...]...
5 [...] ... my lord
6 [...] to one
7 [...] the prefects
8 [...]......
9 Let his [...] read [...] with me [to] my lord.
11 The governor went to Til-Banana and [...] to *the store*[*room*]
(Rest destroyed)

70 12 *til-li-ba-na-na* is difficult, but we are inclined to take it as a GN rather than a form of *tilpānu* "bow"; cf. a PN s.v. Bāni-Anu in PNA 1/II 265a. The GN Bananu is attested in SAA 18 68: 9 (URU.*ba-na-na*), 86 r.6 and 87: 13′ (LÚ.*ba-na-nu*) and in royal inscriptions of Assurbanipal (URU.*ba-nu-nu*).

71. I Did Not Sin

K 1912

beginning broken away

1′ [*x x-n*]*u* ⸢*x*⸣ [*x x x*]
2′ [*x x*]-*mar ina pa*-⸢*an*⸣
3′ [*x x*] *šu-ú um-ma*
4′ [*x x*] *ù* ŠEŠ–AD-*iá*
5′ [*x x*]-*ú a-na-ku ul ah-ṭi*
6′ [*x x*] *it-ti-iá ir-ta-ši*
7′ [*x i-qab*]-*ba-a um-ma* ERIM.MEŠ
8′ [*x x x*]-*ú id-di*
9′ [*x x x*] *ip-te-qid*
10′ [*x x x x*].KI-*a-a qi-bi*
11′ [*x x x x x*] *x*[*x x x x*]

rest broken away

Rev. beginning broken away

1′ [*x x x x*] ⸢*x x*⸣-[*r*]*i*
2′ [*x x x a*]-*na* LUGAL
3′ [*x x x h*]*a-an-ṭiš*
4′ [*x x x*] ⸢*x x*⸣
5′ rest broken away

CT 54 36

(Beginning destroyed)

2 […]… *before*
3 […] he is saying:
4 "[…] and my uncle
5 […], I did not sin,
6 he *had* […] with me
7 [… he sa]ys to me: "The men
8 […] he has thrown
9 […] appointed
10 […] say [to the] men of […]

(Break)

r.1 […] …
2 [… t]o the king
3 [… q]uickly

(Rest destroyed or too broken for translation)

72. Adopting a Deportee's Children

K 1983

beginning broken away

1′ [*x x x*]*x x*[*x x* (*x*)]
2′ [*x x x*] *u*$^{?}$ *i-x*-[*x x* (*x*)]
3′ [*x x x*]*x x x* (*x*) [*x* (*x*)]
4′ [*x x x a*]*k*$^{?}$-*ta-šad* ERIM.M[EŠ-*šú-nu*]
5′ [*x x x h*]*u-ub-tú ki-i*
6′ [*ah-bu-tu e*]-*gi-ra-ti*
7′ [*x x x x x*]*x-mu*
8′ [*x x x x x*]*x-ú*
9′ [*x x x x-s*]*u*$^{?}$-*ú*
10′ [*x x x x-ṣ*]*u-ú*
11′ [*x x x x x x*]*x*
e.12′ [*x x x x x*] NUMUN
13′ [*x x x*]*x* ⸢*x*⸣
14′ [*ki-i an*]-*ni-i i-ba-áš-šú-ú*
r.1 [*sa-li*]-*ma ki-i iš-kun*
2 [*aq-te-ri*]*b-šú-nu-tú ù*
3 [*šu-ú š*]*u-gu-lu-ú*
4 [1-*en*] *a*$^{!}$-*ta-lak a-na-ku*
5 [*it-ti d*]*ib-bi ṭa-bu-tu* DUMU-*šú*
6 [*a-ṣa-bat-m*]*a pi an-ni-i aq-ta-ba-áš-šú*
7 [*um-ma* DUM]U-*ú-a šú-ú um-ma*
8 [*a-na-ku*] ⸢*a*⸣-*bi-šu-ma* DUMU.MÍ-*šú*
9 [DUMU.MÍ-*ú-t*]*ú ul-ta-áš-kin-nu*

rest broken away

CT 54 49

(Beginning destroyed)

4 [*I* co]nquered [*the land*] (and) [*killed* their] soldiers. [Having taken p]risoners, [*I sent*] letters [……

(Break)

13 [*As soon as things*] were [like t]his, (and) when [pea]ce had set in, [I approach]ed them, and [there was a d]eportee –

r.4 I went, [grasped] his son [with] kind [w]ords, and said to him like this: "He is my [so]n, and [I am] his father." His daughter was established [as my daughter].

(Rest destroyed)

72 r.9 Lit., "was provided with daughtership".

73. A Border Dispute

K 5192

beginning broken away

1′ *x x x x x x x x x x x*]*x* ⸢*si*? *da*⸣ *x*[*x x x x x*
2′ *x x x x x x*]⸢*x*⸣-*ú na*-⸢*ad*⸣-*na-áš-šu*-⸢*nu*⸣ [*x x x*
3′ *x x x x x x x i*]*k*? 1.*en-šú* 2-*šú ù* 3-*šú ni*-⸢*qip*?⸣ [*x x*
4′ *x x x x x x*]⸢*x*⸣ *ul-tu* UGU-*hi as-sa-ku x*[*x x x*
5′ *x x x x x x*]-*uš ù qaq-qar-ma ul e-ri-*[*iš*
6′ *x x i*]*l-tap-ra um-ma al-la-kám-ma mi-ṣir a-ša*[*k-kan*
7′ *x x*] *mah-ru-ú šá tu-ma-aṣ-ṣi-ru-ma tas-su-q*[*u*
8′ *x x*] UGU-*hi mi-nu-ú i-na* ⸢*qa*?⸣-*bi-iš-ni* KUR *ma-ṣa-r*[*a*
e.9′ *x mi*]-*iṣ-ri-šú*-⸢*nu*⸣ *ip*-⸢*rik*⸣ *a-lak-ka šá-ni-iu-*[*u*
10′ *al-ta*]-*kan-na áš-šú mi-ni-i šá tal-la-ka a*-[*x x x x*
11′ *x x*]*x un qí-ni-ia man-nu šá il-l*[*a-ka x x x x x*
r.1 *x x*] GIŠ.HUR *i-na sa-ra-hu x*[*x x x x x x x*
2 *x x*]*x qí-it* ZI.MEŠ ⸢*x*⸣ [*x x x x x x x x x*
3 *x x x i*]*l*!-⸢*tap*⸣-*rak-k*[*a x x x x x x x x x x x*

rest broken away

CT 54 74

(Beginning destroyed)

2 [......] was given to them [...]
3 [......] once, twice and thrice *we shall trust* [...]
4 [......] therefore I am doctor [...]
5 [......] and I cannot cultiv[ate] the land [...]
6 [......] has written to me: "I will come and *demar*[*cate*] the border [...]
7 [...] the former [border] which you demarcated and chos[e ...]
8 [......] Why does the country [*not* have] a guar[d] in *qabišnu*? [...]
9 [......] he blocked their [bo]rder, *anoth*[*er*] *way* [...]
10 [...... *I have s*]*et up*, why do you come? [...]
11 [......] my *family*, whoever will co[me ...]
r.1 [......] a design *for* destruction [......]
2 [......] the end of life [......]
3 [...... s]ent to yo[u ......]

(Rest destroyed)

74. Raping and Resettling People

K 5389

beginning broken away

1′ [*x x x*] *x*[*x x x*]
2′ [*x x x*] *šá* EN LUGAL.MEŠ
3′ [*x x x*] *ma-ṭi*
4′ [*x x i-d*]*ab-bu-bu*
5′ [LÚ.GIŠ.D]A.MEŠ
6′ [UN.MEŠ KUR *in-d*]*a-zu-ma*
7′ [*ina* KUR.NIM.M]A.KI
8′ [*ul-te*]-*ši-bu*

CT 54 81

(Beginning destroyed)

2 [The *archery*] of the lord of kings is [...] defective [(and) *the enemies* are c]onspiring.

5 [The confede]rates [have r]aped [the people of the land] and [set]tled them [in Ela]m.

73 Originally a very wide tablet, according to K. Watanabe (ASJ 7 [1985] 150) a royal letter. 9 Alternatively, read *a-lak-ka šá-ni-ia-*[*nu*, "I will go, for the second time" or so. 11 But "my family" (*qinnīya*) is usually written with a geminated consonant. Perhaps from *qanû* "to acquire", although *qinītu* "acquisition" does not seem possible.

74 5 LÚ.GIŠ.DA = *a'lu* see CAD A/1 374a. 6 *in-da-zu* is pf. 3 pl. of *mazû* "to press, rape". r.2 *i-ši-ia-aṭ* (from *šâṭu*/*šiāṭu* as against Bab. *šêṭu*) is an Assyrianism. r.3 DINGIR.MEŠ, referring to Aššur as God = all the gods (= *elōhîm*), is formally plural but conjugated as singular and takes sg. object and genitive suffixes.

9′ [*x x x*].ME[Š] ⸢*x*⸣
rest broken away
Rev. beginning broken away
1′ [LÚ].⸢GIŠ.BAN.MEŠ⸣
2′ [*la i-š*]*i-ia-aṭ*
3′ [*mu-hur*]*-šú-ma* DINGIR.MEŠ *šá* LUGAL
4′ [*a-na*] UGU DUMU.MEŠ*-šú*
5′ [*ha-an-ṭiš*] *i-tar-ma* DINGIR.ME
6′ [*ši-i*]*t-tu-tu*
7′ [*it-ti-šú i-tur-r*]*u*

9 [...]s [...]
(Break)

r.1 [(The lord of kings) should not ne]glect [the ar]chery!
3 [Appeal] to Him, so the God (lit. gods) of the king will [swiftly] return [to] His children, and [the r]est of the gods [will retur]n [with Him].

75. – – –

K 5408b
beginning broken away
1′ ⸢*x x x x*⸣ [*x x x x x*]
2′ [*x*] UN.MEŠ*-šú-nu ù* [*x x x*]
3′ [*hab*$^{?}$]*-tu-ni i-ba-áš-*[*ši x x*]
4′ [*i*$^{?}$*-n*]*a* ŠÀ*-bi-šú-nu id-*[*du-ku*$^{?}$]
5′ [^{m}*x–a*]*m-ma* DUMU ^{m}*sa-*[*x x x*]
6′ [^{md}]30*–nu-ri-i* ^{m}*x*[*x x x*]
7′ [*x x*] ⸢*x x*⸣ É–DINGIR.M[EŠ *x x*]
8′ [*x x x*] ⸢*x x*⸣ [*x x x*]
rest broken away
Rev. seven totally obliterated lines

CT 54 93
(Beginning destroyed)
1 [……]
2 [x] their people and [... were rob]bed. [They] *ki*[*lled*] som[e ... fro]m their midst.
5 [...-a]mma, son of Sa[...]
6 [...] Sîn-nuri, N[N]
7 [...] ... temple [...]
(Rest destroyed)

76. – – –

K 5415b
beginning broken away
1′ [*x x x x*]*-lu* [E]RIM.MEŠ
2′ [*x x x* L]Ú.EN.NAM
3′ [*x x x x*] *um-ma a-na*
4′ [*x x x x*]*-du ul i-man-gur*
5′ [*x x x x*] *i-šem-mu*
6′ [*x x x-t*]*a* LÚ.*rak-su*
7′ [*x x x x*] *a-na*
e.8′ [*x x x iq-ta-b*]*i um-ma*
9′ [*x x x x*]*x hi-ra-a-ma*
10′ [*x x x x*] *a-na-ku*
r.1 [*x x x x*] *šu-ú*
2 [*x x x x i-d*]*i-lu*
3 [*x x x x x x*]*-qu*
4 [*x x x x x x*]*x*
5 [*x x x x x x*]
6 [*x x x x x x*]*x*
7 [*x x x x x x*]
rest broken away

CT 54 96
(Beginning destroyed)
1 […… m]en
2 [……] the governor
3 [……]: “to
4 [...] refuse to listen to [...]
6 [……] a conscript
7 [……] to
8 […… he sai]d: “Dig [...] and [...]. I

r.1 [...] he
2 […… lo]cked
(Rest destroyed)

77. Inventory of Royal Statues and Treasures

K 5416b

Obv. completely broken away

r.1 *x x x x x* URU]DU? KAB.TÚG Á *x*[*x x x*

2 *x x x*] ^{m}LÚ–ŠEŠ.GAL–GI.NA [*x x x*

3 *x x ina q*]*a-ti-šú iz-za-az-ma* [*x x x*

4 *x x ṣal*]*-ma* LUGAL ŠU.2-*šú kit-*[*pu-la x x*

5 *x x x n*]*u*?*-up-ṭir-ra* LUGA[L *x x x x*

6 *x x x ṣa*]*l-mu* LUGAL ŠU.2-*šú* [*x x x x*

7 *x x* GÚ.U]N KUG.GI GIŠ.*i*[*l-lu-ru*

8 *x x x x x x*] SAR ŠU.2 Š[U *x x x x x*]

9 *x ṣal-mu* LUGAL] ŠU.2-*šú kit-*[*pu-la x x*

10 *x x x x x x x x x* MA].NA KUG.[GI *x x x*

11 *x x x x x x x x x x*] ⸢*x*⸣ [*x x x x x x*

rest broken away

CT 54 97

(Beginning destroyed)

r.1 ......] ...... [......

2 ......] Amel-*Nergal*-kin [......

3 ...] stands [on] his [h]ands and [...

4 ... A] royal [sta]tue with fo[lded] hands [...

5 ...] A royal ... [......

6 ... A] royal [sta]tue with [...] hands [...

7 x talen]ts of gold, an *i*[*llūru*-plant ...

8 ...] ...... [...

9 ... A royal statue] with fo[lded] hands [...

10 ...... x mi]nas of go[ld ......

(Rest destroyed)

78. ---

K 5421b

beginning broken away

1′ *x x x*] ⸢*x x*⸣ [*x*]

2′ *x x x*]*x* LÚ.*e-mu-qí*

3′ *x x šu*?*-u*]*b-bi-ra*

4′ *x x x*] *ù*

5′ *x x* LÚ.*e-m*]*u-qí-šú*

6′ *x x x*] *ha-rib-ti*

7′ *x x x*]*x-šú-nu*

r.1 *x x x š*]*á-la-mu*

2 *x x x x x*]*-zib*

3 *x x* ^{m}*un*?]*-da-du*

4 *x x x*]*-ni-šú-nu*

5 *x x x*] *id-duk*

6 *x x áš-p*]*u-ram-ma*

7 *x x ina* ŠÁ] ⸢É⸣–DINGIR *a-bu-ku*

8 *x x x*]⸢*x-a-ni*⸣

rest broken away

CT 54 98

(Beginning destroyed)

2 ...] (armed) forces

3 ... *br*]*eak*!

4 ...] and

5 ...] his [fo]rces

6 ...] (lain) waste

7 ...] their [...]

r.1 ... w]ell-being

2 ...]...

3 ... *Un*]*dadu*

4 ...] their [...]*s*

5 ...] killed

6 ... whom I se]nt and brought [into] the temple

8 ...]*s*

(Rest destroyed)

77 r.5 *n*]*u*?*-up-ṭir-ra*: reading and meaning obscure. r.8 SAR may refer to an 'inscription'.

78 r.2 Probably a form of *ezēbu*.

79. Deserting from a Foreign Land

K 5629
Obv. completely broken away
Rev. beginning broken away
1′ *at-*⌈*ta-din* ^{md}⌉[*x x x x x*]
2′ *a-na da-ki-i*[*a x x x x x*]

3′ ⌈*ah*⌉*-te-liq ul-tu* KU[R *x x x x*]
4′ *ki-i an-qu-tu x*[*x x x x*]

5′ ⌈*šá*⌉ ^{d}U.GU[R] EŠ.BAR *a-ga-*⌈*a*⌉ [*x x x x*]
6′ [*x*] ^{md}30–SILIM–DÙ*-u*[*š x x x*]
7′ [*x x*]*x* ⌈*nu šá x x*⌉ [*x x x*]
rest broken away
s.1 [*x x*]*x ag mam-ma x*[*x x x x*]
2 [*x x x*]*x* ⌈*x x*⌉ [*x x x x x*]

CT 54 157
(Beginning destroyed)

r.1 I have given [...]. [NN *was plotting*] to kill m[e].
3 I fled [......]. When I deserted from the land [......]
5 that Nergal [...] this decision
6 [...] Sîn-šulmu-epuš [...]
(Break)
s.1 [...]... *some*body [...]
(Rest destroyed or too broken for translation)

80. Burying Massacred Corpses

K 7353
beginning broken away
1′ [*x x x*] ⌈*pi-šú-nu* LÚ.TIN⌉.TI[R.KI.MEŠ *ki-i*]
2′ [*iš-mu*]*-ú šu-ú e-mu-qí-š*[*ú up-tah-hi-ir*?]

3′ [*ina p*]*a-an na-de-e šá hi-r*[*a-a-ti x x x*]
4′ [*a*]*-šar šá šal-ma-a-ti šá x*[*x x x x*]
5′ [*na-d*]*u-u* 50 ANŠE.KUR.RA.M[EŠ *ina* ŠÀ-*bi*]
6′ [*iq-tib-ru*]*-šú-nu* LÚ.*bir-kab-ti šú-*[*ú x x x*]
7′ [^{m}*x x x*]*x e-mu-qu ma-la* [*ú-pah-hi-ru*]
8′ [*il-tap*]*-ram-ma* ^{m}*gal-*⌈*bu*⌉ [*x x x x x*]
9′ [*x x de*]*-e-ku* AD *šá i*[*h-li-qu x x x*]
10′ [*il-tap*]*-ra um-ma x*[*x x x x x*]

11′ [*ra-man-ga š*]*e-zib* É–AD-[*ia*? *x x x x*]
12′ [*x x x x x i*]*g-da*[*m-ru x x x x*]
13′ [*x x x x x x*] *x*[*x x x x x*]
rest broken away

CT 54 179
(Beginning destroyed)

1 [As soon as] the Babyloni[ans had hear]d their words, he [*gathered* h]is forces.
3 [Bef]ore leaving the mo[ats and ...s, the pl]ace where the corpses of [...... had been thr]own, 50 cavalryme[n *buried*] them [*there*]. A certain *aristocrat* [......].

7 [NN *dispa*]*tched* all the men that [he had assembled], and Galbu [and NN ... were ki]lled. *A father* who f[led *the massacre* wro]te to me: "[...... and s]ave [yourself]!"
11 [*My*] paternal house [......]
12 [...... c]ame to an e[nd ......]
(Rest destroyed)

80 1 Or: "(the wording of) their [tabl]et". 5 Lit. "horses". 6 LÚ.*bir-kab-ti*: hapax, perhaps a compound of *bêru* "choice, select" and *kabtu* "honoured, important". Another, probably less likely, option is "charioteer", i.e., an abbreviated compound of *bēl narkabti*.

81. Noblemen of the Enemy Country

K 13934
beginning broken away
1′ [*x x x x x*] ⌜*šá* ITI$^{?}$⌝.[*x x x x*]
2′ [*x x x x*]*x-nu šá* LÚ.U[GU–*x x*]
3′ [*x x*] ⌜*a-tam*⌝*-mar i-na* [*x x x*]
4′ [*x x* LÚ].DUMU–DÙ.MEŠ *šá* KUR *na-*[*ki-ri*]
5′ [*x x*] LÚ.SAG.MEŠ *šá* ^{md}[*x x x*]
6′ [*x x* LÚ].*sa-gan šá* LÚ.SA[G.MEŠ *x*]
7′ [*x i*$^{?}$*-n*]*a pa-ni-ia* LÚ.[*x x x*]
8′ [*x x*] ⌜*x x x*⌝ [*x x x x x x*]
rest broken away
Rev. completely broken away

CT 54 262
(Beginning destroyed)
1 [......] of the *month* [...]
2 [...]... of the *ov*[*erseer* of a ...]
3 I have seen [...]. In [...]
4 [x] noblemen of the en[emy] country [*with*] the eunuchs of [NN *and* the] *prefect* of the eunu[chs (...) *were i*]*n my presence and* the [...]
(Rest destroyed)

82. ---

K 15028
beginning broken away
1′ ⌜*x x x*⌝ [*x x x x*]⌜*x*⌝
2′ *šú-nu a-na-*⌜*ku*⌝ [*lu*]*l-lik*
3′ *man-nu šá iš-pu-ra*
r.1 [*um-ma*] LÚ.NÍGIR
2 [IGI LUGAL *ul-ta-ad-g*]*i-lu*
3 [*lu-mur x x x*] *a-ni-ni*
4 [*x x x x il-t*]*ap-ra*
5 [*x x x x x x*]*x-ka*
rest broken away

CT 54 284
(Beginning destroyed)
1 they are [......].
2 I [will] go [and find out] whoever wrote: "They [have made] the Herald [submis]sive [to the king]." We are [...].

4 [... he wr]ote
(Rest destroyed or too broken for translation)

83. ---

K 15044
beginning broken away
1′ *x x x*] *be-l*[*í-x x x x x*
2′ *x x i*]*t-ta-di x*[*x x x x*
3′ *x x*] *su-uk-ku-tú x*[*x x x x*

4′ *x a-d*]*u-ú al-ta-áp-*[*ra x x*
5′ *x x k*]*i-i a-na ṭu-*[*bi šá-kin x*
6′ *x x*] *a-na* ERIM.MEŠ *aš-š*[*ur*.KI*-a-a*

7′ *x x x i*]*h-hi-su* ŠU.2 *b*[*e-lí-x x*
8′ *x x x*]*-ma* ŠÀ*-ba-t*[*a x x x*
9′ *x x x x x*]*x-zu* UR[U *x x x*
rest broken away
Rev. completely broken away

CT 54 286
(Beginning destroyed)
1 ... *my*] lord [......
2 ... *t*]*hrew* [.....
3 ...] are silenced [......
4 Now t]hen I have writt[en ...
5 ... I]f it [seems] go[od ...
6 ...] *to* the Ass[yrian] troops
7 ... re]treated. [*My*] l[ord] will [*capture* ...] and [...] anger [...
9 ......]... the town of [......
(Rest destroyed)

81 2 E.g., *ša-muhhi-āli*, "town overseer", or *ša-muhhi-bēti*, "overseer of the household". 4 Possibly a number at the beginning. 5 One could restore *a-di* or *it-ti* at the beginning.
83 5 Or, "I]f it [is] approp[riate]"; cf. SAA 10 240 s.1 and see CAD Ṭ 117a.

84. – – –

K 15170 + K 15287

beginning broken away
1′ [*x x x x x*]*x* ⸢*ni*⸣ *x*[*x x*]*x*
2′ [*x x x x x*]*x x*[*x x x*]
3′ [*x x x x x x x x*] ⸢*x x x*⸣
4′ [*x x x x x*]-⸢*ta-ni*⸣ [*x x*]
5′ [*x x x x x*] ⸢*u* AN *x x x*⸣-*ni*
6′ [*x x x x x*]-*šú* ⸢*x x*⸣ [*x*]
7′ [*x x x x x*] ⸢É⸣.GAL *a-na* ⸢*pa-ni*⸣-*ka*
8′ [*x x x x x-s*]*a*$^{?}$-*ni um-ma*
9′ [*x x šá-ʾa-al u*]*ṣ-ṣi-iṣ*
10′ [*x x x x x x x*]*x sar šá-šú-nu*
11′ [*x x x x x x ul-t*]*e-bi-la-áš-šú-nu-tú*
r.1 [*x x x x x x x x*] *ni x*[*x x*]*x*
2 [*x x x x x in-da*]*q*$^{?}$-*tu-ni*
3 [*x x x x x x x*]-*la-áš-šú-nu-ti*
4 [*x x x x x x x*] *it-ti-šú-nu*
5 [*x x x x x x x i*]*k-lu-ú*
6 [*x x x x x x* ER]IM$^{?}$.MEŠ
7 [*x x x x x x*.ME]Š *šá* AD.MEŠ-*šú-nu*
8 [*x x x x x x*] LÚ.*qin-na-a-ti*
9 [*x x x x x iš*$^{?}$-*p*]*ur*
10 [*x x x x x x*]-*nu*
11 [*x x x x x it-t*]*i-šú-nu*
12 [*x x x x x hu-us*]-*sa-am-ma*
13 [*x x x x kit*$^{?}$-*t*]*u a-šá-ʾa-al*
14 [*x x x x x x*] *a-ga-a šu*-⸢*ú*⸣
15 [*x x x x x x*]-*nu-tim-ma*
16 [*x x x x x x*]*x ú-šeb-bi-lam*
17 possibly uninscribed

CT 54 298

(Beginning destroyed)
7 [...... of] the palace *in* your service
8 [......]: “[... *th*]*oroughly* [*investigate*]
10 [......] ... *them* [...]
11 [...... I have s]ent them [...]
r.1 [......] ... [...]
2 [...... *they fe*]*ll* to me
3 [...... *sen*]*t* them
4 [......] with them
5 [......] held
6 [...... *m*]*en*
7 [......]s whose fathers
8 [......] families
9 [...... *he sen*]*t*
10 [......]...
11 [...... wit]h them
12 [...... reme]mber and
13 [... *tru*]*ly* I shall ask
14 [...] this [...] it/he
15 [...... t]hem *and*
16 [...... s]ent to me.

85. – – –

K 15196

beginning broken away
1′ [*x x x*] *um*-[*ma x x x x x*]
2′ [*x x*]*x* É [*x x x x*]
3′ [*x* L]Ú.EN.NA[M *x x x x*]
4′ [*x x*] *ha-an-ṭiš* [*x x x x*]
5′ [*x*] *ù a-na* LUGAL [*x x x x*]
6′ [*x ṭ*]*è-e-mu-nu a-n*[*a x x x x*]
7′ [*x*] *i-na pi-ia* [*x x x x*]

CT 54 299

(Beginning destroyed)
1 [...]: “[...]
2 [...] the house [...]
3 [...] the govern[or ...]
4 [...] quickly [...]
5 [...] and to the king [...]
6 [...] our [r]eport t[o ...]
7 [...] in my mouth [...]

84 Join by M. Dietrich (--.11.1964). r.3 Possibly *ul-te-bi*]-*la-áš-šú-nu-ti*; cf. line 11′.

8′ *[aq-ta]-bi ki-i ha-[an-ṭiš x x x]*
9′ *[a-na]* LUGAL *la ta[l-li-ka x x]*
10′ *[x x]x ni x[x x x x]*
rest broken away
Rev. completely broken away

8 [I sa]id it. If you do not qu[ickly] co[me to] the king
(Rest destroyed)

86. ---

K 16130
beginning broken away
1′ *[x x]x x[x x x x x x x x]*
2′ *[x ṭ]è-em-ku-nu [x x x x x]*
3′ *[ta-ša]k-ka-na-ma a-na* LUGAL *[x x x x x]*
4′ *[x ta-š]ap-pa-ru a-na-ku al-ta[p-ra x x x x]*
5′ *[x x]x a-ga-a ul ih-haz [x x x x x]*
6′ *[x x x k]i-i e-si-ti lu-[x x x x x]*
7′ *[x x a-n]a* LUGAL *al-tap-r[a x x x x]*
8′ *[x x x]x ul ú-pa-la-[x x x x x x]*
9′ *[x x x x]x šá mah-[x x x x x x]*
10′ *[x x x x x x] x[x x x x x x x x]*
rest broken away

CT 54 361
(Beginning destroyed)

2 [You will pr]epare your (pl.) [r]eport [......] and [s]end it to the king [......].
4 I have writ[ten ...]
5 this [...] will not *take* [...]
6 [...] *let* [... l]ike a tower [...]
7 [...] I am writin[g t]o the king [...]
8 [...] will not *fright*[*en* ......]
9 [...] who/of [......]
(Rest destroyed)

87. ---

K 16593
beginning broken away
1′ *[x x x x x x]x ⸢bu x ú⸣ [x]*
2′ *[x x x x-n]id-da* GIŠ.ÙR.MEŠ [0]
3′ *[x x x x i]š-pu-ra* [0]
4′ *[x x x x]-an-ni ina ba-la-ṭ[i]*
5′ *[x x x x] ⸢x x x x⸣ [x]*
rest broken away

CT 54 379
(Beginning destroyed)

2 [...]... *log*s
3 [... he s]ent
4 [...] *me for* the life
(Rest destroyed)

88. ---

Sm 1479
beginning broken away
1′ *u a-na pa-ni-šu [x x x x x x]*
2′ *gab-bi lit-su [x x x x x x]*
3′ *ta-du-nu x[x x x x x x]*
4′ *ana* ŠÀ-*bi a-ha-me[š x x x x x x]*

CT 54 415
(Beginning destroyed)
1 and into his presence [...] all [...] his *side* [...... *that*]
3 you left to me [......]
4 to each othe[r ......]

86 2-3 The usual meaning of *ṭēmu šakānu* "to give order" is unlikely to work here. 5 Possibly "will not marry". 7 For example, a temporal adverb could be restored at the beginning. 8 I.e., perhaps *ú-pa-la-[ah/hu*.
88 3 *taddûnu* is prt. 2nd sg. subj. with assimilated ventive ending.

5′ ⸢*ù*⸣ *ra-man-gu-nu* [*x x x x x x*]
6′ [*ki*]-*i pa-na* LUGA[L *be-lí-ia*]
7′ [*mah*]-*r*[*u*] *li-p*[*u-uš*]
rest broken away

5 and yourselves [......]
6 Let the kin[g, my lord], d[o a]s [he fin]d[s] appropriate.

89. ---

Sm 1869
beginning broken away
1′ [*x x*]*x*[*x x x x*]
2′ [*x x*]*x me* [*x x x x*]
3′ [*x x x*]*x*[*x x x x x*]
rest broken away
Rev. beginning broken away
1′ [*x x*] *pa* [*x x x x*]
2′ [*x x*]*x* LÚ.GIŠ.[BAN? *x x*]
3′ [*x x x*] *a-na šul*?-*m*[*a*?-*ni x x*]
4′ [*x x* md+A]G?–BA-*šá x*[*x x x x*]
5′ [*x x x x*] AN *x*[*x x x x x*]
rest broken away

CT 54 428
(Beginning destroyed)

r.2 [...] the *arc*[*her*(*s*) ...]
3 [...] for *a pres*[*ent* ...]
4 [... *Na*]*bû*-iqiša [...]
(Rest destroyed or too broken for translation)

90. Men Revolting

Sm 1995
beginning broken away
1′ [*x x x x*] ⸢*x x*⸣ [*x x*]
2′ [*x x a*]*n*? *dah x*[*x x*]
3′ [*x x is-s*]*i-hu-ni* [*x x*]
4′ [*x x x x*]-*in*? LÚ.EN.⸢NAM⸣
5′ [*x x x x u*]*m-ma* 1.*en*
6′ [*x x x x*] *ni-iṣ-bat-ma*
7′ [*x x x x*] ⸢*x x*⸣ [*x*]
rest broken away
Rev. beginning broken away
1′ [*x x x x x*]*x*[*x x x*]
2′ [*x x x x*]*x-ku-i*[*n-ni*]
3′ [*x x x x u*]*l-tu x*[*x x*]
4′ [*x x x x*]*x man-di-t*[*i*]
5′ [*x x x iq*]-*bi um-m*[*a*]
6′ [*x x x x*] *ta-ak*-[*x*]
7′ [*x x x ki*]-*i ú-pah*-[*hi-ru*]
8′ [*x x x x*]*x nu* [*x*]
9′ [*x x x x*]*x* LÚ.ERIM.ME[Š]
rest broken away

CT 54 431
(Beginning destroyed)

3 [...*s* revo]lted against me [...]
4 [...-*ka*'']*in*, the governor [...]: "We shall seize one [...] and
(Break)

r.2 [... *they have* ...] m[e]
3 [... *f*]*rom* [...]
4 [...] *a surprise atta*[*ck*]
5 [... sa]id: "[...]
6 [...] ...[...]
7 [...] gath[ered]
8 [......]
9 [...] men
(Rest destroyed)

89 r.4 Mentioned in PNA 2/II 837a.
90 4 Possibly a PN: a governor, such as [Nabû-belu-ka'']in (of SAA 15)? r.2 Cf., e.g., *id-du-ku-in-ni* SAA 13 185:15′; *iš-ru-ku-in-ni* SAA 21 1:14; RINAP 2 41:28, 43:75; RINAP 4 48:19 (with *-ma*), but any transitive verb whose final radical is *k* could work.

91. ---

80-7-19,174

beginning broken away

1′ [*x x x x x*]⸢*x x x*⸣[*x*]
2′ [*x x a-di* UGU] *šá en-na*
3′ [*x x x x x*] KAB?-*šá bal-ṭu*
4′ [*x x x x x*]-*ru i-gu-ru*
5′ [*x x x x x*]*x* AD-*šú i-rad-di*
6′ [*x x x x x*] *ú-maš-šar-ú-ši-ma*
7′ [*x x x x x*]-*di*
8′ [*x x x ú-š*]*a*?-*an-nu-ú-ši*
9′ [*x x x x x-n*]*a um-ma*
10′ [*x x x x ul*]-*tah-li-qu*
11′ [*x x x x x-n*]*i-iá i-zi-iz*
12′ [*x x x x x-b*]*i iz-zi-iz*
13′ [*x x a-nam*?]-*dak-ka*
14′ [*x x x x i*]-*qab-ba-áš-ši*
15′ [*x x x x* ^{m}]*ta-at-tan-nu*
16′ [*x x x x x*] *mi-iṣ-ri*
17′ [*x x x x x*]*x-na-a-ma*
18′ [*x x x x x t*]*a-šak-kan-áš-šú*
19′ [*x x x x x x x x*]⸢*x x*⸣

rest broken away

Rev. beginning broken away

1′ [*x x x x x x x x*]*x*-⸢*ú*⸣
2′ [*x x x x x x x x*]*x-su*
3′ [*x x x x x x x x*]-⸢*ú*?⸣-*ma*
4′ [*x x x x x x x x*]*x* ^{d}AMAR.UTU
5′ [*x x x x x x x x*]*x* É-*šú*
6′ [*x x x x x x x ú*]-*še-ri-bu-uš*
7′ [*x x x x x x x x*]-*az-zu*
8′ [*x x x x x* LÚ.*ag*?]-*ru-ti-šú*
9′ [*x x x x x x x x*] UGU
10′ [*x x x x x x*]*x-a* IGI.DU
11′ [*x x x x x x*]-*ta-a-ši*
12′ [*x x x x x x-p*]*u-lu*
13′ [*x x x x x x*] ⸢*x dan*⸣

rest broken away

CT 54 457

(Beginning destroyed)

2 [... until] now
3 [...... *as long as*] *her* ... lives
4 [......] *hired*
5 [......] his father leads
6 [......] they will *release* her and
7 [......]
8 [... they will *ch*]*ange* her/it
9 [......]: "[...] have made [...] flee
11 [...] *be present* [*with*] my [...]
12 [...] *was present* [*ther*]*e*
13 [*I* will gi]ve you [...]
14 [... he] says to her
15 [...] Tattannu
16 [......] border
17 [... ...]...
18 [...... you] will place it/him

(Break)

r.4 [......] Marduk
5 [......] his house
6 [... ha]d him brought into [...]
7 [...... *stan*]*ding*
8 [......] his [*hi*]*red men*
9 [......] *head*
10 [......] *my* [...], leader
11 [......]... *her*
12 [... ...]...

(Rest destroyed)

91 3 Perhaps a PN, as it may be something other than "her/its *left*", which hardly makes sense here. 4 LÚ.*ag*]-*ru i-gu-ru*, "employed [a hired la]bourer" is possible; cf. r.8. 5 The subject may be defined before "his father". 9 Possibly –SUM-*n*]*a*. 11 Or: "stand [in] my [presen]ce"; cf., e.g., SAA 17 3:7. 15 Or, "you gave/have given", but Tattannu is also a common Babylonian name, though it does not occur in PNA. 18 Or: "[you] will give him [orders]". r.4 Perhaps the final element of a PN. r.7 If correct, then this form seems more Assyrian (e.g., *izzazzu*) than Babylonian (cf. SAA 15 55). r.12 Perhaps a form of *apālu*, but a noun is also possible.

92. – – –

80-7-19,341
Obv. completely broken away
Rev. beginning broken away
1′ [*x x*]*x* ⸢*x x*⸣ *x*[*x x x x x*]
2′ [*x-d*]*a šá* LUGAL *b*[*e-lí-x x x x x*]
3′ [*x* ŠÀ]-*bi* LÚ.ERIM.ME[Š *x x x x x*]
4′ [*x x*] ŠÀ-*bi-šú-nu a*-[*x x x x x*]
5′ [*x l*]*i-bu-kám-ma* [*x x x x x*]
6′ [*x-m*]*a ina* ŠÀ-*bi x*[*x x x x x*]
7′ [*x x*] *ih-li-qa x*[*x x x x x*]
8′ [*x a-n*]*a* ŠÀ-*bi* URU.*x*[*x x x x x*]
9′ [*x ki*]-*i id-du*-⸢*ú*⸣ [*x x x x x*]
10′ [*x x*]*x pal-h*[*u x x x x x*]
rest broken away

CT 54 460
(Beginning destroyed)
r.2 [...] *of/whom* the king, [*my*] l[ord ......]
3 [*fr*]*om* the men [......]
4 [*one*] *of* them [......]
5 [let] him lead [...] here *and* [......]
6 [...] *there* [......]
7 [... *who*] fled [......]
8 [... *t*]*o* the town of [......]
9 [... *havi*]*ng thrown* [......]
10 [...] *they are* afrai[d ......]
(Rest destroyed)

93. Problem with the Harvest

81-2-4,411
Obv. completely broken away
e.1′ [*x x x*] ⸢*a-na* UGU-*hi-šú šak*⸣-*n*[*u*] *x*[*x x x*]
2′ [*x x*]*x-nu ù en-na e-bu-ru ik*-[*ta-lu-ú*]
r.1 [*ki-i* Š]U.2-*su-nu ta-kaš-šá-du ina* ŠU.2-*i*-[*ka u i-na*]
2 [ŠU.2 LUGA]L *be-lí-ia i-nam-di-nu-uš ù ki-i* [*la*]
3 [*ta-k*]*aš-šá-du a-di* UGU *mi-tu-tu it*-[*tan-al-lak*]
4 [*x x*] *ù ki-i a-na ar-ra-ka*-⸢*a*⸣-[*ti x x x*]
5 [*x x i*]*l-ta-kan e-bu-ru a-ga*-⸢*a*⸣ [*x x x x*]
6 [*x x x*]*x* ⸢*x x*⸣ *x*[*x*] ⸢*x*⸣ [*x x x x x x*]
rest broken away

CT 54 473
(Beginning destroyed)
1 [...] were plac[ed] on him [...]
2 [...]... but now [*they*] have de[tained] the harvest.
r.1 [If] you catch it in their [h]ands, it will be delivered into [your] hands [and into the hands of the kin]g, my lord, but if [you don't], he will w[alk (free)] until (his) death.
4 [...] and if [it] is postponed until lat[er ...], (then) this harvest [......]
(Rest destroyed)

94. – – –

1932-12-12,617 (BM 134822)
1 [*a-na* LUGAL *be-lí-ia*]
2 ⸢ARAD⸣-*ka* ᵐ⸢ᵈ⸣[*x x x x*]
3 *lu-u šu*[*l-mu* 0]
4 *a-na* [LUGAL *be-lí-ia*]
rest broken away
Rev. beginning broken away
1′ *lu*-⸢*šá*⸣-*x*[*x x x x x*]
rest uninscribed

CT 53 982
1 [To the king, my lord]: your servant [NN]. Good he[alth] to [the king, my lord!]

(Rest destroyed or too broken for translation)

92 r.4 For example, *a*-[*na* or "I [have ...] of them" or an imperative *a*-[*mur*?.
93 2 Another *ša*]*k-nu*, "were [pla]ced", could appear at the beginning. r.4f Cf. SAA 17 152:18.

95. ---

K 22002

1 [*a-na*] LUGAL *b*[*e-lí-ia*]
2 [ARAD-*k*]*a* ^{md}P[A–*x x x*]
3 [*lu*] DI-*mu a-*[*na* LUGAL EN-*ia*]

4 [*x x*]*x ši x*[*x x x x*]
5 rest broken away

K 22002

[1] [To] the king, [my] l[ord: yo]ur [servant] Na[bû-...]. [Good] health t[o the king, my lord]!
(Rest destroyed)

96. Fragment of a Letter by Ahu-iqiša

Sm 546

1 *a-na šul-m*[*u* LUGAL ARAD-*ka*$^{?}$]
2 ^{m}ŠEŠ–BA-*š*[*a x x x x*]
3 *a-na* LUGAL [*x x x x*]
4 *a-na* ⌜*x*⌝ [*x x x x x*]
5 ⌜*x*⌝ [*x x x x x x*]
rest broken away
Rev. completely broken away

ABL 1054

[1] For the well-bei[ng *of the king*: *your servant*] Ahu-iqiš[a].
[3] [...] to the king [...]
[4] to [......]
(Rest destroyed)

97. ---

K 14633

1 *a-na* LUGAL *be-*[*lí-ia*]
2 ARAD-*ka* ^{m}*l*[*u*$^{?}$*-x x x x*]
3 ⌜*lu*⌝ *šul-*[*mu a-na* LUGAL EN-*ia*]
rest broken away

CT 53 552

[1] To the king, [my] lo[rd]: your servant [NN]. Good heal[th to the king, my lord]!
(Rest destroyed)

98. ---

K 14653

1 [*a-n*]*a* LUGAL *be-lí-ia* ARA[D-*ka* ^{m}*x x x*]
2 [*lu šu*]*l*$^{?}$*-mu a-na* LUGAL *b*[*e-lí-ia*]
3 [*x x x*]⌜*x*⌝[*x*] ⌜*e-ru*$^{?}$⌝-[*x x x x*]
rest broken away

CT 53 567

[1] [T]o the king, my lord: your serva[nt NN]. [Good he]alth to the king, [my] l[ord]!
(Rest destroyed)

95 A flake. [4] Or: IGI.

96 [1] As this is an unusual opening for a letter, the restorations are not entirely certain. [2] In this section, Ahu-iqiša is the only surviving full name of a probable sender.

98 Probably originally a wide and large tablet, since ARAD-*ka* in line 1 is typical of such letters. [3] Perhaps a form of *erābu*, "to enter", or *šēru*, "morning".

99. – – –

K 16514
1 [*a-na* LUGAL *be-lí-ia*]
2 ⸢ARAD⸣-*ka* [^{m}*x x x x*]
3 *lu-u šu*[*l-mu a-na* LUGAL EN-*ia*]
4 GIŠ.Ù[R.MEŠ *x x x x*]
5 *ina* Š[À$^{?}$ *x x x x x*]
6 UG[U$^{?}$ *x x x x x x*]
rest broken away
Rev. uninscribed

K 16514
1 [To the king, my lord]: your servant [NN]. Good he[alth to the king, my lord]!

4 Bea[ms ......]
(Rest destroyed or too broken for translation)

100. – – –

K 16503
1 *a-na* [LUGAL *be-lí-ia*]
2 ARAD-[*ka* ^{m}*x x x x*]
3 *lu* [DI-*mu a-na* LUGAL EN-*ia*]
4 *ša* L[UGAL *be-lí ina* UGU ^{m}*x x x x*]
5 ⸢LÚ*⸣.[*x x x x x x*]
rest broken away
Rev. Uninscribed

CT 53 781
1 To [the king, my lord: your] servant [NN]. Good [health to the king, my lord]!

4 (As to) what the k[ing, my lord, *wrote to me about NN*], the [...]
(Rest destroyed)

101. – – –

K 15675
1 [*a-n*]*a*$^{?}$ L[UGAL$^{?}$ EN-*ia*]
2 ARAD-*k*[*a* ^{m}*x x x x*]

3 *a-na-k*[*u*$^{?}$ *x x x x x*]
4 ⸢*i*⸣–*pa*-[*an*$^{?}$ *x x x x*]
5 ⸢*i*$^{?}$⸣-*x*[*x x x x x x x*]
rest broken away
Rev. completely broken away

K 15675
1 [*T*]*o the k*[*ing, my lord*]: yo[ur] servant [NN].
3 *I* [......]
4 *befo*[*re* ......]
(Rest destroyed)

102. – – –

K 16507
1 [*a-na* LUGAL EN-*ia*]
2 [ARAD-*ka* ^{m}*x x x x*]-⸢*a*⸣
3 [*lu* DI-*mu a-na* LUGAL EN-*i*]*a*
4 [*ina* UGU *x x x x*]-*ib-ri*
5 [*ša* LUGAL *be-lí iš-pur-a*]*n-ni*
6 [*x x x x x x*] LUGAL

K 16507
1 [To the *king*, my lord: your servant NN. Good health to the king, m]y [lord]!

4 [Concerning ...]... [about *which/whom* the king, my lord, wrote t]o me.

101 A possible opening of a letter, but the fragment is a flake.
102 4 A PN ending in *ib-ri*?

7 [*x x x x x x x*]*x*
8 [*x x x x x x x*]*x*
rest broken away
Rev. as far as preserved, uninscribed

(Rest destroyed or too broken for translation)

103. ---

K 21871
1 *a-na* LUGA[L *be-lí-ia*]
2 ARAD-*ka* [^{m}*x x x x*]
3 *lu* DI-[*mu a-na* LUGAL EN-*ia*]
rest broken away

K 21871
1 To the kin[g, my lord]: your servant [NN]. Good heal[th to the king, my lord]!
(Rest destroyed)

104. ---

Sm 959
Obv. broken away
Rev. beginning broken away
1′ *ina* ŠÀ-⌜*bi*⌝ [*x x x x*]
2′ *kam*-⌜*mu*⌝-[*su*$^{?}$ *x x x x*]

3′ *ma-a a-n*[*a*$^{?}$ *x x x x*]
4′ *ši-i* [*x x x x*]
rest uninscribed

CT 53 830
(Beginning destroyed)

r.1 [*are*] sta[ying] in [...].

2 [...] says: "She/it [...] t[o ...].

105. ---

Sm 1339
Obv. broken away
Rev. beginning broken away
1′ [*x x x x*] *ni x*[*x x x x x*]
2′ [*x x x š*]*a*$^{?}$ KUR-⌜*e*$^{?}$⌝ [*x x x*]
3′ [*x x x x*]*x* ⌜*ni*$^{?}$⌝ ŠE *i*[*na* UGU *x x x*]
4′ [*x x x*]-⌜*ú*⌝-*te ša* ⌜*a*⌝-[*na* LUGAL]
5′ [*áš-pur*]-*an-ni a-ki ša* ⌜*a*⌝-[*na-ku*]
6′ [*a-mur-ú-n*]*i* ZU-*u-ni a-sa-*[*ṭar*]
7′ [*a-na* LUGAL] ⌜*ú*⌝-*se-bi-la* [0]
rest uninscribed

CT 53 841
(Beginning destroyed)

r.2 [... *o*]*f the mountain* [...]
3 [...] ... A[s to the ... ...]s about *whom* [I wrote] t[o the king], I have wri[tten down and] sent [to the king] what I [saw] and know.

105 r.2 Alternatively, it could be a GN.

106. ---

K 7354
Obv. Destroyed
Rev. beginning broken away
1′ *x x x x*] *a* [*x x x*
2′ *x x x*]-*ú* GIŠ.SA[R *x x x*
3′ *x x x*] *ep-šá a-ni-*[*nu*? *x x*
4′ *x x-p*]*u-uš a-ta-*[*x x x x*
5′ *x ú-ma*?]-*me-ia a-a-k*[*a*? *x x*
6′ *x x x*] *be-lí liš-pur* GIŠ.S[AR? *x x*
rest uninscribed

CT 53 329
(Beginning destroyed)

r.2 […] an orcha[rd …]
3 Do […]! *W*[*e* …]
4 [… d]o. *Wh*[*y* …?]
5 […] wher[e are] my [*bea*]*sts*? […]
6 […] my lord should write, the orc[hard …

107. What NN Wrote

K 15010
Obv. entirely destroyed
Rev. beginning broken away
1′ *ša* ^{m}[*x x x x*]
2′ *iš-ṭu-*[*ru-ni*]
rest uninscribed

CT 53 605
(Beginning destroyed)

r.1 [*this is*] *what* [NN] wro[te].

108. ---

K 16098
beginning broken away
1′ [*x x x x x x x x x-n*]*i*?
2′ [*x x x x x x x x x*]-*hu*
rest broken away
Rev. beginning broken away
1′ [*x x x*] ITI.MEŠ
2′ [*i*?-*t*]*a-nu-ni-ši*
3′ [*ú-ma*]-⸢*a*⸣ *e-ṣa-na-ši*
rest uninscribed

CT 53 754
(Beginning destroyed)

r.1 [They did g]ive it [for x] months, (but) [no]w it is too little for us.

109. ---

K 16490
beginning broken away
1′ [*x x x x x*]-*ni-e x*[*x x*]
2′ [*ú-ma-a*] *an-nu-rig*
3′ [*ina pa-an*?] LUGAL EN-*iá*
e. uninscribed

CT 53 774
(Beginning destroyed)

2 Now [then *I am sending it/him/them to*] the king, my lord.

106 r.6 Not sure if "[the king] my lord".
107 r.1f The interpretation seems obvious, but interestingly no other letter ends in this way.

r.1 [*x x x x*] *ki-i ša* ⸢LUGAL⸣ *b*[*e-lí*]
2 [*i-la*]-⸢*ú*⸣-*ni le*-[*pu-šú*]
3 [*x x* LUGAL] EN [*x x x*]
rest broken away

r.1 The king, [my] l[ord], may [do] as [he dee]ms best.
3 [... the king, my] lord [...]
(Rest destroyed)

110. ---

K 16491
Obv. broken away
Rev. beginning broken away
1′ [UD-*x*]-⸢KAM⸣ T[A *x x x*]
2′ [*x x*] ⸢*ú*⸣-*qa-rab* [*x x*]
3′ [*x x li*]*b-bu* [*x x x*]
4′ [*x x x*] [*x x x*]
rest uninscribed

CT 53 775
(Beginning destroyed)

r.1 [On the x]th [day], I shall bring [...] fr[om ...].
3 [... *the king, my lord, can be* g]lad.

111. ---

Sm 121
Obv. broken away
Rev. beginning broken away
1′ [*x x*]*x x*[*x x x x x x*]
2′ [*x x*]*x a* [*x x x x x x*]
3′ [*x x*]*x* [*x x x x x x*]
4′ [*an-n*]*u-rig* [*x x x x*]
5′ [*ina*] UGU-*hi* [*x x x x*]
6′ [*x*] LUGAL EN [*x x x x*]
7′ [*x*] *be-lí* [*x x x x*]
8′ [*mi*]-*nu ša i*-[*na* UGU-*hi-ia*?]
9′ [*i-d*]*a-bu-bu* [(*x x x x x*)]
rest uninscribed

CT 53 810
(Beginning destroyed)

r.4 [N]ow [...]
5 [*Con*]*cerning* [...]
6 [...] the king, my lord [...]
7 [...] my lord [...].
8 [Wh]at is that [*they* s]peak *a*[*gainst me*]?

112. ---

K 22141
Obv. broken away
Rev. beginning broken away
1′ ⸢*x x x x*⸣ [*x x x x*
2′ LUGAL *be-lí l*[*u ú-di*?
3′ *ki-i a-n*[*a-ku x x x x*
rest uninscribed

K 22141
(Beginning destroyed)

r.2 The king, my lord, sh[ould *know* (...)] that I [......].

109 r.1 As a verb of sending or "he/they is/are coming" are the most likely options, the beginning may be restorable. r.3 This may be the last inscribed line.

110 r.3f As these are the last lines of the letter, the most common encouragement *lib-bu ša* LUGAL EN-*ia lu* DÙG(.GA) "the king, my lord, can be glad" is probably the most likely way to end the letter.

111 r.8f The interpretation is by no means certain. Or, perhaps, "[Wh]at is that [they ... *and* s]peak? [(......)]".

3. The Correspondence of Esarhaddon, Assurbanipal and Later Kings
Additions to SAA X, XIII, XVI, XVIII, XXI and XXII

FIG. 10. *Ashurbanipal with stylus instead of dagger in his belt.* BM 124876.

113. Medical Report

Sm 1761 + 1851

beginning broken away
[DI-*mu a–dan-niš*]
1′ [*a-na*] ^{md}3[0–NUNU]Z–GIN-*i*[*n*]
2′ [DI]-*mu a–dan-niš*
3′ [*a-n*]*a* ^{m}AN.ŠÁR–LUGAL–AN–KI–T[I.BI]
4′ [*ina kí*]*n-ṣi-ia ah-h*[*ur*? (*x x*)]
5′ [(*x*) *i*]*m-ma-li al-*[*x*]
6′ [(*x*)] DI-*mu a–dan-niš*
7′ [*a-n*]*a* ⸢^{md}⸣[3]0–NUNUZ–GIN-*in*
8′ [ŠÀ-*bu šá*] LUGAL EN-*iá*
9′ [*a–dan-niš*] *a–dan-niš*
10′ [*lu-u ṭa*]-⸢*a*⸣-*ba*
rest broken away
Rev. completely broken away

CT 53 130 (part of SAA 10 223) + CT 53 855 (SAA 16 167)
(Beginning destroyed)
1 Šî[n-per'']u-ukin [is *doing very very well*]. Aššur-etel-šame-erṣeti-mub[allissu] is doing very [we]ll.
4 I am sti[ll] (*praying*) [on] my [kn]ees; *I* [... *fi*]*lled with* [...].
6 [Š]în-per'u-ukin is doing very well. The king, my lord, [can be] very glad [indeed].

(Rest destroyed)

114. Another Medical Report

81-7-27,268
1 *a-na* LUGAL *be-*⸢*lí*⸣-[*ia*]
2 ARAD-*ka* ^{md}I[M–MU–PAB]
3 *lu-u* DI-*mu a-na* [LUGAL EN-*iá*]
4 ^{d}PA *u* ^{d}AMAR.UTU ⸢*a*⸣-[*na* LUGAL]
5 *be-lí-ia lik-*[*ru-bu*]
6 DI-*mu a–*[*dan-niš*]
7 *a-na* ^{m}AN.ŠÁR–[GIN–BALA.MEŠ-*a*?]
8 DI-*mu* ⸢*a*⸣–[*dan-niš*]
9 ⸢*a-na* ^{m}⸣[*x x x x x*]
rest broken away
Rev. beginning (about 7 lines) broken away
1′ *x*[*x x x x x x x x*]
2′ *x*[*x x x x x x x x*]
3′ *a-n*[*a x x x x x x*]
4′ *ša* L[UGAL *x x x x x x*]

CT 53 130 (earlier part of SAA 10 223)
1 To the king, [my] lord: your servant Ad[ad-šumu-uṣur]. Good health to [the king, my lord]! May Nabû and Marduk bl[ess the king], my lord!
6 Aššur-[*mukin-paleya*] is doing v[ery] well; [NN] is doing v[ery] well.

(Break)

r.4 of the k[ing ......]

113 Previous partial editions are SAA 10 223 and SAA 16 167. The curvature of the tablet suggests that not much is missing from its left edge. 1 The traces do not allow us to read ^{md}G[IŠ.NU$_{11}$–M]U–GIN-*i*[*n*] "[Šamaš-šu]mu-ukin" (cf. SAA 10 223:9). 2, 8-10 This line is not written as densely as other lines, and line 9 may have had more than just [*a–dan-niš*], but cf. lines 8 and 10. 4 Since this is a medical report about young royal patients, and not about the health of the sender, Adad-šumu-uṣur, an alternative such as [*ina mu*]*r-ṣi-ia*, "[*with*] my [ill]ness", seems unlikely. 5 I.e., possibly a *malû* N stem form, unless *ina malî* is "in filling (*with*)". 7 It is a little surprising that the name of the prince is repeated (also in line 1′), but this seems to be the point, an emphatic and encouraging repetition, and somehow related to what is said in lines 4′-5′. Sîn-per'u-ukin is the object-subject of at least two other medical reports in SAA 10 (199:6 [name partly restored], 222:7).

114 7 It is unlikely that the name of Assurbanipal, who appears by name only twice in SAA 10 (245:14 and 289:5), should be restored here; Aššur-mukin-paleya is a more likely candidate (see especially SAA 10 208 r.2′, 296:6, 298:6, r.3, 299:7, 300 r.5, 320:8, r.11), although his name is not written with AN.ŠÁR in SAA 10.

5′ DINGIR.ME[Š *x x x x x x*]
6′ DINGIR.ME[Š *x x x x x x*]
7′ *i-šá-*[*x x x x x x*]
8′ *šá* ^{d}A[MAR.UTU *x x x x x*]
9′ ^{d}PA *u* ^{d}[*x x x x x*]
10′ AMA–LU[GAL *x x x x x*]
11′ MÍ.^{d}[*še-ru-u-a*–KAR-*at*]
12e *ket-t*[*u x x x x x*]
13e *ù a-na* L[Ú.*x x x x*]
14e *ina* URU.*ni-*[*nu-a x x x*]

[5] The gods [......]
[6] the gods [......]
[7] ...[......]
[8] of M[arduk ......]
[9] Nabû and [......]
[10] the ki[ng's] mother [......]
[11] [Šerua-eṭerat]
[12] real[ly ......]
[13] and to [......]
[14] in Ni[neveh ......]

115. Purification of a House

K 1592 + K 20912
beginning broken away
1′ ⸢*x x x x x x x x x*⸣
2′ É *liš-bi-ṭu-ma* TÚG-*s*[*u*]
3′ *a-na* ÍD *lid-du-ú*
4′ *i-ga-ru šá it-ti-šú*
5′ *tah-ha-an-qu si-ri*
6′ *li-kun* UDU 1-*ma a-na*
7′ ÍD *lid-du-*⸢*ú*⸣ *a-na* [*x*]
e.8′ *šá* É–^{d}AMAR.UTU ⸢*x x*⸣
r.1 *u* A.MEŠ *šá* KÀŠ.⸢MEŠ?⸣ ANŠE
2 É *li-iz-ri-qu*
3 *šum-*⸢*ma*⸣ [*mi-q*]*it-ti* GAL-*tú*
4 *t*[*ak-pir-tú šá*] ⸢É⸣ *lu-še-ti-q*[*u*]
5 [LÚ.MAŠ].MAŠ ŠU.2 UGU
6 [*x x*] ⸢*x x x x*⸣
rest broken away

CT 54 27+
(Beginning destroyed)
[2] They should sweep the house and throw h[is] garment into the river.
[4] The wall, which was *squeezed* with him, should get a durable plaster, and they should throw a sheep into the river.
[7] To [the ...] of the temple of Marduk [...].
[r.1] Moreover, let them sprinkle water mixed with (*lit.*: of) donkey's urine on the house.
[3] If [the da]mage is great, they should perform the Pu[rification of the] House (ritual).
[5] [An exor]cist [should ...] hands on
(Rest destroyed)

115 Joined to K 20912 by J. Fincke (15.8.2003). This text is probably a fragment of a letter from a Babylonian exorcist, perhaps Nabû-šuma-lišir (cf. SAA 10 313), giving instructions on how to deal with an ominous death in a temple. [5] The difficult *tah-ha-an-qu* is taken as N prt. 3rd sg. f. subjunctive of *hnq* 'to strangle, constrict', Rabb. Heb. also 'to squeeze' (Dalman 1967, 154b), assuming that *igāru* is here fem. by analogy with *igartu*. [r.4] For the purification rite for a house see CAD T 85.

116. Do Not Conceal from Me What You See!

K 1161
beginning broken away
1′ [*ma-a x*] ⸢*ni ši*⸣ [*x x x*]
2′ [*ša a*]-⸢*rak*⸣ UD-*me* ⸢*ša*⸣ [0]
3′ *a-di* ⸢ŠÀ⸣ U[D].⸢*x*⸣.[KÁM *la*]
4′ *i-ba-ṭal*-⸢*ú-ni*⸣
5′ *ma-a a-t*[*a*]-⸢*a*⸣ *la-*[*a*]
6′ *i-qab-bi-iu*-⸢*ú*⸣
e.7 *ša ina* ⸢É⸣ [*x x x*]
8′ *šap-la q*[*a-ti*]
r.1 *is-si-ka ina* [UGU-*hi*]
2 *ad-bu-bu-*[*ni šu-ú*]
3 *ù ina* UGU *ša taš*-⸢*pur-an*⸣-[*ni*]
4 *ma-a ina* KASKAL–MAN [0]
5 *a-bi-ia-ad* [0]
6 LÚ.Ì.DU8 *me-me-ni*
7 [*x*] ⸢*an x*⸣ [*x*]
rest broken away
s.1 *ša ta-mar-u-ni* [TA* *pa-ni-ia*]
2 *la tu-pa-za-*[*ar* 0$^{?}$]

CT 53 168
(Beginning destroyed)

1 the [l]ong-lasting [...]...[...], which did [not] stop until the [...th] d[ay] – why don't they speak (about it)?

7 [That is about what] I secre[tly] discussed with you in the *tem*[*ple of DN*].

r.3 And concerning what you wrote to me, saying: "I will spend the night on the king's road. *Any* gatekeeper [......]

(Break)

s.1 Do not conce[al from me] what you see!

117. *Phantom of* Bel

Rm 63
beginning broken away
1′ *x*[*x x x x x x x*]
2′ ⸢*za*$^{!}$-*qi*$^{!}$-*ku*$^{!}$ $^{d!}$⸣EN$^{!}$ [*x x x*]
3′ *i-ka-ru-*[*ru*$^{?}$*-ni x x*]
4′ *a-na* LUGAL *be-*[*lí-ia*]
5′ *a-na* NUMUN-⸢*šú*$^{?}$⸣ LAL$^{!}$ *x*[*x x x*]
6′ ⸢*x*⸣ *ta*$^{!}$ *x*[*x x x*]
7′ LUGAL *be-lí a-na* [ARAD-*šú*]
8′ *iq-ṭi-bi ma-a* ⸢*at*⸣-[*t*]*a-*[*ma*]
9′ *ina pa-ni ta-az-za-az*
10′ *i-šá-daq-di-iš šá-lu-ši-ni*
11′ *ina pa-ni at-ti-ti-zi* 0$^{!}$
12′ *ú*-⸢*ma*$^{!}$⸣-*a* LUGAL *x*[*x x x*]
e.13′ ⸢*ú*$^{!}$-*da*$^{!}$⸣ *x*[*x x x*]
rest broken away
Rev. vitrified

ABL 1174
(Beginning destroyed)

2 *Phantom of* Bel [...]

3 [they] will la[y ...]

4 to the king, [my] lo[rd], to his offspring ... [...] ... [...]

7 The king, my lord, said to [his servant]: "You shall stand by (him)!"

10 Last year and the year before last I stood by (him), but now the king [...] knows [...]

(Rest destroyed)

116 This letter was probably addressed to Esarhaddon because of the relatively rare spelling of final weak verbs with the sign IA (obv. 6′ and rev. 5), which is principally attested in letters to this king, see SAA 10 23 r.12 (from Issar-šumu-ereš), 199:6′, 17′ (from Adad-šumu-uṣur), and 322 r.4 and 323:9 (from Urdu-Nanaya). The injunction "don't conceal from me what you [hear] and see" (s.1), typical of Esarhaddon, is also implicit in SAA 10 265 r.13 (from Marduk-šakin-šumi) and 286 r.8 (from Nabû-nadin-šumi). The confidential tone of the letter suggests that it was addressed to one of the king's closest advisers. The phrase *ša tašpuranni* (r.3) is also typical of letters sent by Esarhaddon (see SAA 16 2-6). [4] *i-ba-ṭal-ú-ni* is N sg. 3 subj. of *baṭālu*, with a paragogic *a* inserted after the elided *i* (**ibbaṭilūni* > **ibbaṭlūni* > *ibbaṭ*^{a}*lūni*) [7] Or: "in the pa[lace]".

117 Topically, this is an addition to SAA 10. [2, 5f, 12f] See coll. [6] Curiously, the line has been copied by Harper as if it were neatly written *iš-pur-an-ni*. [9, 11] Less likely is "You will stay in (my) entourage", since in that case *ina pa-ni-ia* would be expected, cf. SAA 10 226 r.9, 227 r.16, 228:23, etc. Note also that the writer has already "stood by" for two years.

118. Fragment Mentioning Jupiter

K 16135
beginning broken away
1′ [*x x lil-l*]*i-kám-m*[*a x x x x x*]
2′ [*x x x*]*x a-na x*[*x x x x x x*]
3′ [*x x* M]UL.SAG.ME.G[AR *x x x x x*]
4′ [*x x x*] *a-na ta-x*[*x x x x x x*]
5′ [*x x x* LU]GAL *i-t*[*a-x x x x x*]
6′ [*x x x x*] ⸢*x x*⸣ [*x x x x x x*]
7′ [*x x x x*] *it-ta-x*[*x x x x x*]
8′ [*x x x x*]*x x*[*x x x x x x*]
9′ [*x x x x x*] *x*[*x x x x x x*]

CT 54 366
(Beginning destroyed)
1 [... let him co]me an[d ......]
2 [...] to [......]
3 [...] Jupit[er ......]
4 [...] to ...[... ...]
5 [... the ki]ng has [......]
6 [......]
7 [...] ... [......]
(Rest destroyed)

119. Fragment of a Letter by Nabû-šumu-iddina

K 21982
1 [*a-na* LUGAL EN]-*ia*
2 [ARAD-*ka* ^{md}PA–MU–S]UM-*na*
3 [*lu-u* DI-*mu a-na* LUGAL] EN-*ia*
4 [*a–dan-niš a–dan*]-*niš*
5 [^{d}AG ^{d}A]MAR.UTU
6 [*a-na* LUGAL EN-*ia l*]*ik-ru-bu*
7 [*x x x x x x x*]*x-ia*
8 [*x x x x x x*]*x* LAL-*tum*
rest broken away
Rev. beginning broken away
1′ [*x x x x x x x*]*x*
2′ [*x x x x x x x*]-*ik*
rest uninscribed

K 21982
1 [To the king], my [lord: your servant Nabû-šumu-i]ddina. [The very be]st [of health to the king], my lord! [May Nabû and Marduk] bless [the king, my lord]!

7 [...] my [...]
8 [......] team (of horses)
(Rest destroyed or too broken for translation)

118 3 This fragment could also be part of an astrological report (SAA 8). 5, 7 Alternatively, these (especially line 7) could be understood as "signs/portents/omens" (*ittu*).

119 2-6 Only Nabû-šumu-iddina places the *adanniš adanniš* clause in this position (see SAA 13 78-79, 81, 83-92, 94-111, 119 and SAA 16 175) before Nabû and Marduk. 8 Cf. 5 LAL *ša sīsê* EA 9:37 and *sīsê* LAL-*at nīri* 1R 31 III 66, and see la-al LAL = *ṣimittu*, S^{a} Voc. Q 23 (CAD Ṣ 198).

120. Plotting in the Upper Echelons of Assur

YBC 11382

1 *a-na* LUGAL EN-*ia* ARAD-*ka* ^{md}PA–*ú-šal-lim*
2 *aš-šur* ^{d}UTU UD.MEŠ GÍD.DA.MEŠ *a-na* MAN EN-*ia lid-di-nu*
3 *la an-nu-u šu-u ša a-na* LUGAL EN-*ia a-qab-bu-ni*
4 *mu-uk ša la* LUGAL *i-duk-ku-ni*
5 *ina* UGU *mi-i-ni ša am-ma-ru-ni a-šá-am-mu-ni*
6 *a-na* LUGAL EN-*ia a-qa*[*b*]*-bu-ni ina* UGU-*hi šu-u*
7 UN.MEŠ *ma-a'-du-te i-zi-ir-ru-ni ina* UGU *du-a-ki-ia*
8 *i-da-bu-bu* :. *ú-ma-a ša la* LUGAL EN-*ia*
9 *iṣ-ṣab-tu-ni* 3 ITI.MEŠ *ina* É LÚ.GAR *e-ta-az-bu-ni*
10 É.GAL *gab-bu ina* UGU-*hi-ia us-sa-an-hi-ṣu*
11 *ma-a me-me-ni e-gír-tu-šú lu la i-mah-har-šú a-na* LUGAL
12 *lu la i-da-an ma-a me-me-ni di-ib-bi-šú lu la i-šam-me*

13 *ina* UGU *pi-i ša* LÚ.*šá*–UGU–URU *ša* URU.ŠÀ–URU
14 *ina* UGU *pi-i ša* ^{m}*sa-si-i an-ni-u gab-bu ep-šá-ku* LUGAL *la ú-da*
15 *ma-a ha-du-ni a-ni-nu ki-i ša* ŠÀ-*bi-ni-ni né-ep-pa-áš* [[*x*]]
16 *ma-a at-ta a-ta-a a-mì-ru šá-mi-u qa-bi-u*
17 *ú-ma-a* UD-25-KÁM *ša* ITI.GAN *ina* URU.ŠÀ–URU *az-za-az*
18 ^{m}*ab-da-a* LÚ.*šá*–UGU–URU *ir-tu-gu-man-ni*
19 *ma-a al-ka* MÁŠ.MI *ši-i la-ap-šu-rak-ka*
20 *ma-a ina* MÁŠ.MI-*ia ma-a* LÚ*.TUR *šu-u* GIŠ.*hu-ṭar-tu ina* ŠU.2-*šú*
21 TA* É–KI.MAH-*hi it-tu-ṣi-a ma-a ir-tu-gu-man-ni*
22 GIŠ.*hu-ṭar-tu an-ni-tú it-ta-an-na ma-a i-da-bu-ub*
23 *ma-a ina ṣil* GIŠ.*hu-ṭar-ti an-ni-ti ta-ka-bit ta-da-in*
24 *a-na-*⌈*ku*⌉ TA* *an-na-ka aq-*⌈*ṭi-ba-áš*⌉*-šú mu-uk ana* IGI-*ni*

Assur-Forschungen 91, 93

[1] To the king, my lord: your servant Nabû-ušallim. May Aššur (and) Šamaš give long days to the king, my lord.

[3] Isn't this so that I say to the king, my lord: "They are killing me without the king's permission." Why is it that because of what I see, hear and report to the king, my lord, many people hate me and are plotting to kill me?

[8] Now, without the king, my lord's permission, they have seized me (and) abandoned me for three months in the house of the *prefect*. They have caused the entire palace seek a quarrel against me, (saying): "Nobody should receive a letter from him (and) give it to the king. Nobody should hear his words."

[13] At the command of the city overseer of the Inner City (and) at the command of Sasî, I am *suffering* all this; (but) the king does not know it. (The city overseer and Sasî say): "(It is) our pleasure to act as we please; you, why are you one who sees, hears and reports?"

[17] Now, I was in the Inner City on the 25th of Kislimu (IX), when Abdâ, the city overseer, shouted at me, saying: "Come! Let me explain to you this dream of mine. In my dream, there was a *boy* with a *sceptre* in his hands. He came out from a mausoleum, shouted at me, gave me this *sceptre* (and) spoke: 'Under the aegis of this *sceptre*, you will become respected (and) powerful.' I said to him from here: '[Se]nd it to us, (and) I will *lay claim to* it there. He will *li*[*sten to*] your word.' [He] spoke: 'We [... the Cha]ldeans.

120 Previous edition: Frahm Assur-Forschungen, pp. 91-110 (with extensive notes). [3] We suggest taking *an-nu-u* simply as the near demonstrative (as used in r.1), "this", orthographically the most compelling choice, instead of *annu*, "approval, assent, (word of) consent". Alternatively, *an-nu-u* could be seen as a variant of *arnu*, "guilt, punishment, sin, crime". [8] Probably :. functions as a word divider here, guiding the reader. [20, 22f] *huṭāru*, *huṭārtu* "stick, staff", perhaps "sceptre", thus associated with kingship. The word is less common than *haṭṭu*, but this may be related to the frequent, ambiguous logographic writings with GIŠ.PA. [24] At the end of the line Frahm reads ^{m}*ši-ni*(?). Admittedly the problem for our interpretation is the preposition *ana*, which is otherwise always written as *a-na*, but the limited space at the end of the line may have justified a shorter variant.

e.25 [*šu*]-*pur am*-[*m*]*a*$^{?}$-*ka a-ba*$^{?}$-*gír ina pi-i-ka i-š*[*á*$^{?}$-*me*$^{?}$]
26 [*i*]-*da-bu-ub ma-*⸢*a*⸣ [LÚ$^{?}$.*ka*]*l-da-a-a ni-s*[*i*$^{?}$-*x*]
27 [*m*]*a-a* ^{m}*tukul-ti*–[^{d}MAŠ$^{?}$ TA*$^{?}$ U]GU URU.Š[À–URU]
28 [LU]GAL-*tu u* [*x x x x x*]*x-ub x*[*x x*]
r.1 *ma-a a-na an-ni-i ina bat-ti* AD *šu-u* AM[A 0$^{?}$]
2 *it-ta-an-nu-ni-šu ma-a a-na a-a-ši la id-*⸢*di-nu-ni*⸣
3 *ma-a al-ka šá-ni-tu-um-ma la-aq-ba-ka*
4 *ma-a* MUL *šu-u ina* ŠÀ AD-*šú ša* LUGAL *ka-an-ni-i*
5 *a-ta-mar ma-a ár-hiš ina* ŠÀ-*bi a-ta-mar*
6 *ma-a ú-ma-a an-nu-rig a-ta-mar-šú*
7 1-*me*-20 LÚ*.ERIM.MEŠ *na-as-qu-te* URU.ŠÀ–URU-*a-a*
8 *a-de-e is-si-šú is-sa-*⸢*ak*⸣-*nu* GUD *i-tap-šú ta-mì-tú is-sak-nu*
9 *a-na a-a-ši ma-a al-ka is-si-ni ti-ma*
10 *a-na-ku la am-ma-gúr ina* UGU-*hi šu-u* 1-*en* :. LÚ.*ag-ru*
11 LÚ.*šá*–UGU–URU *ina* UGU-*hi-ia e-ta-ga-ra* 1-*en* :.-*ma*
12 ^{m}*sa-si-i e-ta-ga-ra ma-a a-bat* MAN *ina* UGU-*hi-šú qi-bi-a*
13 *hu-us-su* DINGIR.MEŠ-*ka ú-zak-ku-ni* LUGAL *ú-da*
14 *ki-i* URU.ŠÀ–URU-*a-a gab-bu ki-i* EN–[*d*]*a-me dan-ni*
15 *i-da-ga-lu-ni-ni a-ke-e a-na-ku* KUG.UD *šul-man-nu*
16 *a-mah-har-šú-nu* TA* LÚ.*ag-ru-te an-nu-te* LUGAL *lid-bu-ub*
17 LUGAL *liš-al-šú-nu man-nu e-gu-ra-šu-nu-ni* LUGAL *li-ih-kim*
18 *šá-ni-tu a-bu-tú da-ba-a-bi i-ba-áš-ši ša a-mu-ru-ni*
19 *a-na* ^{m}LUGAL–*lu*–*dà-ri aq-ṭi-bi ma-a ina* ŠÀ *e-gír-ti*
20 *šu-ṭur bi-la ina* ⸢ŠÀ *e*⸣-*gír-ti as-sa-ṭar at-ta-na-áš-šú*
21 *šu-u it-tu-bil a-na* ^{m}*sa-si-i it-ti-din*
22 *ina* ŠÀ *an-ni-ti* LUGAL *lu e-ti-ik ki-i ina* UGU *du*$_{6}$-*li dan-ni*
23 *gab-bi-šú-nu i-da-bu-bu-ni ù* 1-*me*-20 ERIM.MEŠ *ša* ⸢*a*⸣-*na* MAN EN-*ia aq-bu-ni* LUGAL LÚ.*qur-bu-te is-si-iá*
24e [*liš-pur lu-b*]*i-la-šú-nu ina* IGI LUGAL *la-as-di-ir*
25e [*ina* ŠÀ-*bi an-n*]*i-ti* LUGAL *li-ih-kim*

Tukulti-[*Ninurta* ...]... ki]ngship and [...] [*fr*]*om* the In[ner City]. *For this*, that father (and) moth[er] have given it to him *at the vigil*; they didn't give it to me.'"

r.3 (He continued): "Come! Let me tell you another (dream). I have seen *that* star in the *well-tended* (*burial chamber of*) king's father. I saw it *briefly* there. Now I have seen it."

7 120 choice troops from the Inner City have concluded a treaty with him (Abdâ), *slaughtered* an ox (and) sworn an oath. (They said) to me: "Come, swear with us!" (but) I did not agree. Because of it, the city overseer has employed a hireling against me; also Sasî has hired one, saying: "Say the king's word against him!" Remember (though) that your gods exonerate me. The king knows that all (the people from) the Inner City regard me as a severe mortal enemy; how could I then accept a bribe of silver from them? The king should speak with these hirelings (and) ask who has hired them. May the king understand (the situation).

18 There is another matter of intrigue that I saw. I have told Šarru-lu-dari (about it). (He said): "Write it down in a letter (and) bring it to me". I have written it down in a letter (and) given it to him, (but) he brought it to Sasî (and) gave (it to him). In this matter, the king should be alert. As all of them are speaking about hard work and (because of) the 120 troops which I mentioned to the king, my lord, [may] the king [send] a bodyguard with me. [I will br]ing them (and) line (them) up before the king. May the king understand [th]is [matter].

28 *ub*, despite the *mā* of the following line, seems unlikely to be a form of *dabābu*, so the sign here may be read as *ár*. r.1 For the tentative rendering of *ina bat-ti*, cf. SAA 12 69:18, 26. Frahm reads AD-*šu u* AM[A-*šú*], although in his orthography the scribe rather systematically uses *šú* in suffixes (exceptions can be found in r.2, 17, both in verbal forms), but *šu-u* for an independent personal pronoun (lines 3, 6, 20, r.4, 10).

26e ⸢*a*⸣*-ta-a* LÚ**.da-a-a-lu ša* DUMU MÍ.*ta-ba-lit*
27e TA* ŠÀ URU.*ku-ri-gal-zi*
s.1 *ina* UGU-*hi-šú-nu il-la-ka e-gír*.MEŠ *ina* UGU-*hi-šú-nu ub-ba-la a-na* 2-*šú ku-zip-pi ša* MAN
2 ⸢*ú*⸣-[*š*]*e-ba-lu-niš-šú am-mu-rig ina* IGI LÚ.*šá*–UGU–URU *šu-u la-al-lik lu-bi-la-šú*

[26] Why does the scout of the son of the woman Tabalitu from (Dur)-Kurigalzu come to bring them letters? They are sending him two royal garments. At that time, he is in the presence of the city overseer. I will go and bring (*them*) to him.

121. Fragment of a Letter by Bel-iqiša(?)

K 15064

1 [*a-na* LUGAL] *be-lí-ia*
2 [ARAD-*ka* ^{m}EN$^{?}$–NÍ]G$^{?}$.BA
3 [*lu* DI-*mu a-na* LUG]AL *be-lí-iá*
4 [^{d}AG ^{d}AMAR.UTU *a-na*] LUGAL *be-lí-iá*
5 [*a–dan-niš a–dan-niš*] ⸢*lik*⸣*-ru-bu*
6 [*ša* LUGAL *be-lí*] *iš-pur-an-ni*
7 [*ma-a ki-ma a-n*]*a-ku a-sa*[*k*]*-nak-ku-nu*
8 [*x x x x x*] ⸢*a-ke-e* LUGAL⸣ *be-lí*
rest broken away

Rev. beginning broken away
1′ [*x x x x* LÚ**.da*$^{?}$]*-a-a-li*
2′ [*x x x x x x*] ⸢*i*⸣*–da-te*
3′ [*x x x x x x*]*-tal-ka*
4′ [*x x x x x l*]*u-u* 2 GÚ.UN 4 MA.NA
5′ [*x x x x x i*]*t-ti-di-ni*
6′e [*x x x x* LUGAL] *be-lí*
7′e [*x x x x lip*$^{?}$]*-qid šu-tú*
8′e [*x x x x x*]*-u-ni*

CT 53 612

[1] [To the king], my lord: [your servant *Bel-i*]*qiša*. [Good health to the ki]ng, my lord! May [Nabû and Marduk very greatly] bless the king, my lord.

[6] [As to what the king, my lord], wrote to me: "[After] I appointed you, [......]."

[8] How (does) the king, my lord [......]?

(Break)

r.1 [... *sc*]*outs*
2 [......] afterwards
3 [...... c]ame
4 [...... *b*]*e it* 2 talents 4 minas (*of silver*)
5 [...... h]e gave and [...].
6 [*May* the king], my lord, [*appo*]*int* [...]
7 He [......].

r.27 For the reading of (Dur)-Kurigalzu, see ibid. p. 108f.

121 1-5 The partly restored introductory formula corresponds to that of Bel-iqīša's, as in SAA 16 111, 113-114. 2 Normally *iqīša* is written as BA-*šá* in names, but see, e.g., PNA 1/II 355b s.v. Būru-iqīša. 7 The shorter variant *ana-ku* is also possible. Assuming that *a-sak-nak-ku-nu* is an unintentional metathesis for *a-sak-kan-ku-nu*. r.8 As the top and the left side of the letter may have been partially inscribed, it is not certain that this is the last line.

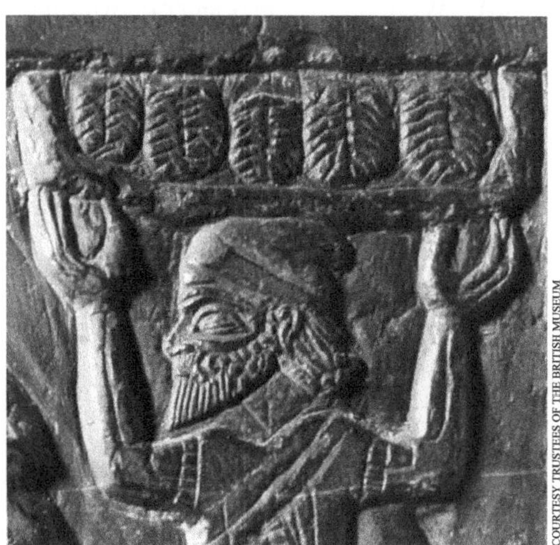

COURTESY TRUSTEES OF THE BRITISH MUSEUM

FIG. 11. *Tribute money paid as bundles of gold or silver bracelets.*
BM 118885.

122. Fragment Mentioning Umban-kidinni and Bit-Imbî

K 13122

beginning broken away

1′ [*x x x x x*] ⸢*il-lak*$^{?}$⸣

2′ [*x x x x x*]*x qi-bi*

3′ [*x x* URU.*de*]*-e-ri duk-šu*$^{?}$

4′ [*x x x* ^{m}*um-b*]*a-ki-di-ni il-la-kan-ni*

5′ [*x x x x x*]*-tu ši-i*

6′ [*x x x x x ú*]*-gam-mu-ru*

7′ [*x x x x x*]*-a il-la-ka*

8′ [*x x x x x*] ANŠE.KUR.RA.MEŠ

9′ [*x x x x x-s*]*u-te*

10′ [*x x x x x x x*]*x-a-a*

rest broken away

Rev. beginning broken away

1′ [*x x x x x x x x*].MEŠ

2′ [*x x x x x x x i*]*š*$^{?}$ LÚ*.3-*šú*.MEŠ

3′ [*x x x x*] *a x*[*x*]*x* [[]] *nu* [[]]

4′ [*x x x x*] *ina* URU.É–*im-b*[*i-i*] *šú-nu*

5′ [DUMU ^{m}*um*]-⸢*ba*$^{!}$⸣*-ki-din x*[*x x x*]*-u-ni*

6′ [*x x x x*] *ni is x*[*x x x x*]

rest broken away

ABL 1352

(Beginning destroyed)

1 *goes* [......].

2 Say [*to* ...]: Kill *him* [*in* D]er!

4 [*Before* Umb]an-kidinni comes

5 [......] it/she

6 [...... they] finish

7 [......] *is on his way*

8 [......] horses

9 [......]s

10 [...... the] *people* [of ...]

(Break)

r.1 [......]s

2 [......] the 'third men'

3 [......] ...

4 [......] *they* are in Bit-Imb[î].

5 [The son of Um]ban-kidinni [...]

(Rest destroyed)

123. Denouncing Crimes

A 3660

1 ^{m}*qa-lu-su*

2 LÚ*.SIPA–MUŠEN.MEŠ ÚŠ

3 ^{m}*ra-tu-a-a*

4 LÚ*.GAL–50

5 4 ZI.MEŠ *ina kas-pi*

6 *it-ti-din*

---

7 ^{m}*la-qe-pu*

8 LÚ*.SIPA–MUŠEN.MEŠ

9 ^{m}*ga-lul*

10 *a-na* ^{m}*ha-ga-te-te*

11 *ina* URU.*til–qa-né-e*

12 *it-ti-din*

NABU 2002/90

1 Qallussu, fowl herd, is dead. Ratuaya, the commander-of-fifty, has sold (his) 4 persons for silver.

---

7 Gallulu has *sold* La-qepu, fowl herd, to Hagatete in the town Til-qanê.

---

122 This is an addition to the dossier of Nabû-ra'im-nišešu (and Salamanu) published in SAA 16 136-145. 1 Not as well preserved as drawn in Harper's copy. 3 Perhaps restore [*ma-a ina*$^{?}$ URU.*de*]-. 4 The beginning, e.g., [*a-du* É]. For Umban-kidinni, cf. SAA 16 139:6, 140 r.7, 142:7. 7 Probably a personal name, cf. e.g., "Bur-Silâ, 'third man' of the crown prince", SAA 16 136:11. 9 E.g., *rak-s*]*u-te* "[recru]its". 10 For instance, KUR.BÀD.DINGIR.K]I$^{?}$*-a-a*, "[the] people [of Der]" or "[the Elamite](s)" are possible. r.4 Originally there may have been another sign between *-i* and *šú-*. r.5 Cf. SAA 16 138 r.8′: the tablet may be closely related to this one. Perhaps read ^{m}*um*]-⸢*ba*$^{!}$⸣*-ki-din-n*[*i*.

123 Previous edition: Donbaz, NABU 2002/90. 7-12 Like Donbaz, we take La-qepu as the object of the sentence. It seems that the sender of this brief but revealing denunciation is probably an anonymous fowl herd.

r.1 *ku-um* LÚ*.*ha-te-ni-šú*
2 LÚ*.ERIM.MEŠ *bal-ṭu*
3 *lu-bi-lu-⸢niš-šú⸣-nu*
4 LÚ*.EN.NAM *liš-al*
5 *a-ta-a* LÚ*.*par-ri*$^{!}$-⸢*ṣu*$^{!}$⸣-*te*
6 *ina kas-pi id-du-nu-na-ši*
7 EN *qa*$^{!}$-*la*
8 LÚ*.ARAD.MEŠ *ša man-ni*
9 *a-ni-nu*
(rest uninscribed)

r.1 The men are alive instead of his brother-in-law (Qallussu). Let them be brought to the governor, so he may question them. Why are the criminals selling us for silver? My lord is quiet: Whose servants are we?

124. *ilku*-Duty of the Shepherds

K 546
1 *a-na* LUGAL EN-*ia*
2 ARAD-*ka* ^{m}*ba-la-si-i*
3 *lu* DI-*mu a-na* LUGAL EN-*ia*
4 $^{d+}$EN *ù* ^{d}AG
5 *a-na* LUGAL EN-*ia lik-ru-bu*
6 *ina* UGU LÚ.IGI.UM LUGAL *be-lí*
7 *liš-pu-ra sa-ga-a-te*
8 KUŠ.*ma-za-'e il-ku*
9 [*ša*] LÚ*.SIPA.MEŠ
10 [*li*]-*ih-hur*
r.1 [*am-mar*$^{?}$] *i-ba-áš-šú-u-ni*
2 [*ina*] *kas-pi la i-da-nu-ni*
3 KUŠ.MEŠ *ša pa-ag-ri*
4 *li-hu-ru a-na iš*-QAR
5 *li-di-nu*
rest uninscribed

ABL 75

1 To the king, my lord: your servant Balasî. Good health to the king, my lord! May Bel and Nabû bless the king, my lord!

6 Let the king, my lord, write to the treasurer: [he should] receive sashes and water-skins, the *ilku*-duty [of] the shepherds. They should not sell [anything] there is. Let them receive skins from the carcases to give them as the *iškāru* dues.

r.5 Donbaz: *a-ta-a* LÚ*.ERIM$^{?}$.MUŠEN-*x-x* with note that the traces could be read as LÚ*.ERIM$^{?}$.MUŠEN-*di-te*. r.7 Donbaz reads EN *x-la*, but notes: "Perhaps can be reconstructed as EN *qa*$^{?}$-*la*. But the sign looks more like *ṣu*."

124 Previous editions: Parpola, LAS 37; Postgate TCAE, p. 248. 2 This Balasî is probably not the famous astrologer (see Parpola, LAS II, p. 43 and Postgate TCAE, p. 248). This letter is therefore an addition to SAA 16 and not to SAA 10. 7-8 Cf. Postgate TCAE, p. 68f. r.1 For this line, see Parpola, LAS II, p. 43, but the sign *i* is not broken off (ABL 75 and photo collated). Orthographically, there is hardly any difference between reading *i-ba-áš-šú-u-ni* and *i-na-áš-šú-u-ni*.

FIG. 12. *An Elamite king with bulbous royal hat.* BM 124794.

125. A Royal Order Concerning Men

Sm 545

beginning possibly broken away

1′ *a-n*[*a* ^{m}*x x x qí-bi-ma*?]

2′ *um-ma-a* [LUGAL-*ma*? 0?]

3′ ERIM.MEŠ *šá a-na* [*x x x*]

4′ *aq-bu-ú* [*x x x*]

5′ ^{m}MU–GIN DUMU [*x x x*]

6′ ^{m}BA-*šá* DUMU [*x x x*]

7′ ^{m}*ki-rib-ti* [*x x x*]

8′ [^{m}*a*?-*q*]*a*[*r*?]-*a* [*x x x x*]

rest broken away

Rev. Unintelligible

ABL 1053

1 [*Say*] t[o NN] thus says [*the king*].

3 The men whom I *ordered to* [... *are*]:

5 Šumu-ukin, son of [...],

6 Iqiša, son of [......],

7 Kiribtu [......],

8 [*Aq*]*a*[*r*]*â* [......]

(Rest destroyed)

126. Conspiracy against Esarhaddon

VAT 4923

1 *hi-ṭa-a-ti ša* $^{md+}$AG–ŠEŠ.MEŠ–SUM-*na* DUMU ^{m}*ku-up-pu-up-ti* ⸢*x*⸣

2 *a-na* AN.ŠÁR–ŠEŠ–SUM-*na* LUGAL KUR.KUR *ih-ṭu-ú* MU.NE

---

3 *ši-pir-ti šá a-na* LUGAL KUR.NIM.MA.KI *iš-pu-ru*

4 ^{m}ŠEŠ–SUM-*na* A-*šú šá* ^{md}DUMU–⸢É⸣–ŠEŠ-*ir šá-ṭir ši-pir-ti*

5 ^{m}ARAD–^{d}*su-ti-ti* GAL–É *šá* DUMU ^{m}*ku-up-pu-up-ti*

6 *um-ma* ^{d}30–ŠEŠ.MEŠ–SU-*ba ši-ma-a-ti la ta-qab-ba-a*

7 *um-ma e-mu-qu šá* ^{d}AN.ŠÁR–ŠEŠ–SUM-*na ki-i*

8 *e-mu-qu šá* ^{d}30–ŠEŠ.MEŠ–SU-*ba ma-a-da*

9 *ú-qu-šú ia-a-nu a-du-ú e-mu-qu* ⸢*a*⸣-*na*

10 *pir-ṣa-a-ti ú-ka-*⸢*lu*⸣*-ma a-šap-par-*[*á*]*š-šú*

11 *at-tu-ka* É-*šú-nu na-mu-ra-ti* [*x x*]*x*[*x*]

12 $^{d+}$AG–ŠEŠ–SUM-*na* DUMU ^{m}*ku-up-pu-up-ti* ⸢*x*⸣

13 2 [MA.NA] KUG.GI *šá* $^{md+}$EN–ŠEŠ.MEŠ–SU-*ba* LÚ.KUG.D[IM]

14 *ša* ⸢*x*⸣[*x x x x*]-⸢*ṣi*⸣ *šá* KUG.GI *šá* ^{m}NÍG.GUB

AfO 17 1ff

1 The crimes which Nabû-ahhe-iddina, son of Kuppuptu, committed against Esarhaddon, king of the lands:

---

3 The letter he sent to the king of Elam: Ahu-iddina, son of Mar-biti-naṣir, was the writer of the letter.

5 Arad-Sutiti, major-domo of the son of Kuppuptu, (says): "Sennacherib (has gone to his) fate. Don't say to me: 'The army of Esarhaddon is as large as that of Sennacherib'!

9 His army is nothing! They now have a pseudo-army. I shall send for it/him.

11 It will be yours: their house, audience gifts [...]. Nabû-ahhe-iddina, son of Kuppuptu, [...] 2 [minas] of gold *of* Bel-ahhe-eriba, the goldsm[ith] *of* [...], of gold which Kudurru,

125 As indicated in Harper's copy (also a photograph has been collated), the top of the tablet is clearly broken, but we have now tentatively interpreted line 1′ as the original line 1 (cf. SAA 17 2-3, 6; SAA 19 4, but also SAA 17 151; GPA 201 and 202). In any case, it may well be a royal letter; this interpretation is supported by line 4.

126 Previous edition: Weidner, AfO 17 (1954) 5-9; see also, e.g., Frame Babylonia 66f (discussion); date probably 680 (shortly after Sennacherib's death). [1] Cf. SAA 16 63:8-9. [2] MU.NE literally means "their names", and refers back to *hīṭāti*, beginning a list of enumerated crimes. We have therefore chosen to use the colon instead of translating it. [9] Apparently an abbreviated (*em*)*ūqušu* (cf. *emūqu* in lines 8 and 9), as in Babylonian *rab-ū/uqi* (cf. NA *rab-mūgi*), and not, e.g., a variant of *unqušu*, "his seal(ed royal order)/signet ring". [11] E.g., "receiving" or "bringing" might be expected. [11-15] Interestingly, as in no. 128, "goldsmiths" also play a role here (because of a bribe?).

15 LÚ.KUG.⸢DIM *šá x*⸣ *x*[*x x x x x x x*]
16 9 TÚG.*e-la-a-ti* 5 *ṣal-mu* LUGAL *i-na* [*x*]
17 *pa-ni* GABA-*šú-nu* KUG.GI *ši-šik-ti-šú-nu* KUG.G[I]
18 1.ŠU TÚG.IB.MEŠ *šá bi-ir-mu šá* ^{m}*bi-bé-e-a*
19 *ù* ^{m}*mar-duk* DUMU.MEŠ ^{m}*du-gul–la-ke-e*
20 *id-din-nu-ni-šú* HAR KUG.GI *šá húb-še-*⸢*e*⸣ *tam-le-e*
21 *šá* $^{md+}$EN–SUM-*na a-na* 30 MA.NA KUG.UD *id-da-áš-šú*

the goldsmith *of* [......], 9 upper garments, 5 royal images in [...], their golden pectorals, gold of their hem, 60 multicoloured garments which Bibe'a and Marduk, sons of Dugul-lakê, gave to him (and) left him a golden bracelet of Bel-iddina, inlayed with ..., for 30 minas of silver.

r.1 *an-na-a-ta na-mu-ra-ta šá a-na*
2 LUGAL KUR.NIM.MA.KI *ú-še-bi-lu*
3 *i-qab-bi um-ma* LUGAL-*ú-tu ša* AN.ŠÁR–ŠEŠ–SUM-*na*
4 *pa-ha-ta* GAL–*pi-qit-ti ú-paq-qid-ma* ⸢*li-il*⸣-*tan-ni-šú*
5 ^{m}*ah-he-e-a* A-*šú šá* ^{m}⸢DUMU.UŠ⸣-*a il-tap-ra ù*
6 *ar-ki-šú il-tap-ra an-ni-iš* ⸢*x*⸣ *i-na*
7 *mu-ṣip-e-ti š*[*u-hu*]-*ṭu a-ta-*⸢*x x x*⸣
8 *i-na la-bi-ri ki-i* ⸢*x x*⸣ [*x x x*]*x*
9 ⸢*x x x*⸣ [*x x x x x*]*x* TIN.TIR.KI
10 *ih-te-p*[*u-u x x x x*]*x e li hi*
11 KUR *la*–ŠU.2 [*x*]*x* LUGAL$^{?}$ *ul-te-lu-ú*

r.1 These are the audience gifts which he sent to the king of Elam, saying: "I will entrust the kingship of Esarhaddon to a governor and official commissioned to replace him."

5 Ahhe'a son of Aplaya wrote to me, and he wrote to me later on (as well). For this *I s*[*aw him*] s[trip]ped of garments!

8 In the old times, when [......, the ...] destroyed Babylon [and ...] ... made the land slip from the hands of the *king*.

15 A verbal form is expected at the end of the line. 20 Or: "a golden ring". r.4 Probably a D-stem form because of the plurality of the objects. r.11 Weidner's copy has a clear *ka*, not LUGAL, but we have not been able to collate the original tablet.

COURTESY IRAQ MUSEUM, BAGHDAD

FIG. 13. *Crown prince and high eunuch of Tiglath-pileser III.* Iraq Museum.

12 *en-na* 10 ERIM.MEŠ *it-ti a-ha-meš ki-i iz-zi-zu*
13 KUR *la*–ŠU.2 LUGAL *ú-še-lu-ka* ŠÀ-*bi šá* LUGAL KUR.KUR
14 *be-lí-ia*$^{!!}$ *la i-šá-hi-ṭu a-mat ma-la a-šem-mu-ú*
15 *a-na* LUGAL KUR.KUR *be-lí-iá a-*⸢*šap-pa*⸣*-ru*
16 [L]UGAL *ina* ŠU.2 ⸢*x x x x x x*⸣ [*x*]
17 *la ú-maš-šar-an-ni-ma la a-m*[*a*]*-ta*
rest blank

12 Now 10 men have been plotting together to let the land slip from the king's hands.

13 May the heart of the king of the lands, my lord, not jump! Whatever I hear, I shall send it to the king of the lands, my lord.

16 May the king not abandon men in the hands [of ......], may I not die!

127. Blessings

K 1969 + K 16935
beginning broken away
1′ ⸢$^{d+}$EN⸣ *u* ⸢$^{d+}$AG⸣ [*x x x x*]
2′ *šá a-na* UGU-*hi-šú-nu* [0]
3′ [*tu*]*k-ku-la-a-ta* [0]
4′ ⸢UD⸣.MEŠ-*ka lu-ur-ri-ku-ma*
5′ *ṭu-ub* ŠÀ-*bi ṭu-ub* UZU
6′ *ù na-mar ka-bat-ti*
7′ ⸢*a*⸣*-na* IGI SUHUŠ *tam-ti*
e.8 *liš-ru-ku-nik-ka*
r.1 ⸢*x*⸣ [*x x*]*x i-ka-at*$^{?}$-[*tam*$^{?}$]
2 [*x x x x x l*]*i* [*x x x x x*]
rest broken away
s.1 *a-x*[*x x x x x x x x x x x x x*]
2 *šá x*[*x x x x x x x x x x x x x*]

CT 54 46+ (=SAA 18 51+)

1 May Bel and Nabû [...], in whom you have [co]nfidence, lengthen your days and grant you happiness, good health, and gladness *before* the foundation of the sea.

(Rest too broken for translation)

128. Your Son Is Going to Murder You

80-7-19,28 + K 21923
beginning broken away
1′ ⸢*x*⸣ [*x x x x x x x x x x*]
2′ NUMUN$^{?}$ ⸢*x*⸣ [*x x x x x x x x*]
3′ *šá* ^{m}⸢^{d}⸣[*x x x x x x*]
4′ *šá da-*⸢*x x x x*⸣ [*x x x*]
5′ 3 ŠEŠ.MEŠ-*ni* URU.TIN.TI[R.KI.MEŠ 0$^{?}$]
6′ LÚ.KÙ.DIM.MEŠ *i-na* É [*x x x*]
7′ : *a-de-e šá si-i-hi šá x*[*x x x x*]
8′ *ki-i iš-mu-ú* 1.*en i-n*[*a* ŠÀ-*bi-šú-nu*]

ABL 1091+ (= SAA 18 100+)
(Beginning destroyed)

3 *of* [NN ...]

4 ...... [...]

5 Three Babylonian brothers, goldsmiths in the *temple* [*of* ...], when they heard about the treaty of rebellion *of* [...] one o[f them]

r.14 Text: *be-lí-šú*.

127 1 Perhaps something like "[your gods/helpers]" should be restored at the end. 3 Two signs at the end of the line under *ta* belong to the reverse and read *x*]*x-a*. 5 The trace at the end of the line may be part of the final sign of a line from the reverse of the tablet. 7 If interpreted correctly, this is an unexpected phrase. Perhaps it is related to the location of the sender (i.e., southern Babylonia?) .

128 Previous editions: Parpola, CRRAI 26 (1980) 172f and 180f; SAA 18 100; Jones, NABU 2019/53 (partial edition); Dalley and Siddall, Iraq 83 (2021) 5-7. 4 This line is difficult, but perhaps something like *šá ṭa-*ʾ*ab*$^{?}$*-ti šá x*ʾ [*x x x*], "It is good what [...]".

9′ *i-na pa-ni (ni)-ir-ti a-mat* LUGAL *i*[*q*$^{!!}$*-ta-bi*]
10′ $^{md+}$AG–MU–*iš-kun ù* ^{m}*ṣi*[*l-la-a*]
11′ *ki-i il-li-ku-nu i-šá-a-*[*lu-šú*]
12′ *um-ma a-mat* LUGAL*-ka a-na* U[GU *mi-ni-i*]
13′ *šu-ú ma-a* ⸢*a*⸣*-na* UGU ^{m}ARAD–⸢^{d}⸣[NIN.LÍL]
14′ *i-na* TÚG.KUR.RA*-šú pa-ni-šú* ⸢*i*⸣-[*ter-mu*]
r.1 *i-na pa-ni* ^{m}ARAD–^{d}NIN.[LÍL*-ma*]
2 *ul-te-zi-zi-šú um-ma a-mur x*[*x x x*]
3 *im-ma-gar ina pi-i-ka qi-*[*bi*]
4 *šu-ú iq-ta-bi um-ma* ^{m}ARAD–⸢^{d}⸣[NIN.LÍL]
5 DUMU*-ka i-dak-ka pa-ni-*[*šú*]
6 *ki-i ip-tu-ú* ^{m}ARAD–^{d}NI[N.LÍL]
7 *ki-i ú-sa-niq-šú a-na šá-*⸢*a*⸣*-*[*šú*]
8 ⸢*ù*⸣ ŠEŠ.MEŠ*-šú i-t*[*a-bak*$^{?}$]
9 *šu-*⸢*mu*$^{?}$ *šá*⸣ ERIM.MEŠ ^{m}*šar-hi-ia* $^{m⸢d+?⸣}$[*x x x x*]
10 *ù* $^{md+}$AG–ŠEŠ–APIN*-eš ki-*⸢*i*⸣ [LUGAL *x x*]
11 *la i-qi-pi* ERIM.MEŠ *šá* É ^{m}AR[AD–^{d}NIN.LÍL]
12 LUGAL ⸢*li*⸣*-šá-al-la* : *en-n*[*a a-du-ú*$^{?}$]
13 *da-ba-ba bab-ba-nu-ú šá* [*a-na* LUGAL$^{?}$]
14 *ki-i* [*i*]*m*$^{?}$*-hur-ru a-na* LU[GAL EN*-i-ni*]
15 *ki-i iš-pu-ru* LUGAL [EN*-a-ni*]
16 ⸢*x x*⸣ [*x x x*] ⸢*x x*⸣ [*x x x x*]
rest broken away

ap[*pealed*] to the king before the murder.

10 Nabû-šumu-iškun and *Ṣil*[*laya*] came and questioned [him], saying: "[What is] your appeal to the king ab[out]?" He said: "(It is) about Urdu-[Mullissu."]

14 [*They covered*] his face with his cloak and made him stand in front of Urdu-Mull[issu], saying: "Behold, [your appeal] is granted, speak with your own voice". He said: "Your son, Urdu-[Mullissu], is going to murder you".

r.5 When they uncovered his face (and) when Urdu-Mul[lissu] had interrogated him, he (Urdu-Mullissu) *l*[*ed*] him and his brothers [*away*]. The names of the men are Šarhia, [NN], and Nabû-ahu-ereš.

10 If [*the king*] does not believe [*the report*], the king should question the men of Ur[du-Mullissu's] household.

12 Now [*then*], it is excellent *news* that *he appealed* and wrote to the ki[ng, *our lord*]. The king, [*our lord, …*]
(Rest destroyed)

129. Petitioning the King Again

Bu 91-5-9,72 + Bu 91-5-9,23 + Bu 91-5-9,238

ABL 717 + CT 54 556 (= SAA 18 182+)

1 [*a-na*] ⸢LUGAL⸣ KUR.KUR *be-lí-ia*
2 [ARAD*-k*]*a* $^{md+}$AG–TIN*-su–iq-bi*
3 [AN.ŠÁR ^{d}]UTU ^{d}AMAR.UTU *u*$^{!}$ ^{d}PA EN GI.DU[B].BA
4 [*x x*]*-u*$^{!}$ *šá* LUGAL *be-lí-i*[*a*]
5 [*x x*] É.GAL*-*⸢*ka*⸣
6 [*x pa*]*-làh be-lut-ti-ka*
7 [*ù* D]I*-mu* NUMUN *šá* LUGAL *be-lí-ia*
8 [*a-na* UD.M]EŠ *da-ru-tu liq-bu-ú*

1 [To] the king of the lands, my lord: [yo]ur [servant], Nabû-balassu-iqbi. May [Aššur], Šamaš, Marduk, and Nabû, lord of the sty[l]us, ordain […] of the king, m[y] lord, […] of your palace, [fe]ar of your lordship, [and the wel]l-being of the seed of the king, my lord, [for] everlasting [day]s.

[9] Dalley and Siddall interpret this line differently: "one [*among them said*] at the first meeting: "It is a matter for the king." However, we find a sandhi spelling suggested by Parpola (1980: 177, n.16) a more likely interpretation. For comparable sandhi spellings in NA, see Luukko, SAAS 16, pp. 118-21. The problem at the end of the line is that the sign is not *iq*; see the copies in Parpola (1980) 181 and Dalley, Iraq 83 (2021) 5. Alternatively, e.g., ⸢*pi*⸣-[*i e-puš*$^{?}$/*iš-ku-nu*$^{?}$]. [11] Dalley and Siddall translate *kî illikūnu*, "When he came", but like the more common *illikūni*, the spellings of *il-li-ku-nu* refer to a plural subject (SAA 17 143:7; SAA 18 72:7′, 12′, 132 r.6; SAA 21 148 r.1; see also SAA 22 63:5′ and SAA 22 13:10′; Cole, OIP 114 18:5, 11 [both *il-lik-ú-nu*]).

129 [3, 4, 9, 11, r.14, 15] For collations, see SAA 18, p. 226a.

9 [*ul-tu*] *re*!*-eš-im-ma* ⸢UR!⸣.KU
10 [*šá* É–EN]*-šú i-ra-mu a-na-ku*
11 [*x x x*]*-tú it-ti* LÚ.SUKKAL!.⸢MEŠ⸣
12 [*x x x*] *a-de-e* ⸢LUGAL⸣ [*x x*]
13 [*x x x x*]*-ub a-mat šá x*[*x* (*x*)]
14 [*x x x x*]*-ia a-n*[*a*? (*x*)]*x*
15 [*x x x x*]*x ki-i a-ta-mar*
16 [*ù al-t*]*e*?*-mu-ú a-na* LUGAL EN*-iá*
17 [*lu-uš-pu-r*]*u*? LUGAL EN*-a*
18 [*x x x x*] *lim-hur-ú-in-ni*
19 [^{m}*x x x* DUM]U*-šú šá* $^{md+}$AG–GÁL*-ši*
20 [*x x x lil*]*-li-ku ina* ÙR*-ri-šú*
21 [*x x x l*]*i-tu-ra* ANŠE? *ù* 8 UDU.NITÁ.⸢MEŠ?⸣
e.22 [*x x*]*x x x*
r.1 [*x x x x x x x x x x x x x x x*]*-bi*
2 [*x x x x x x x x x x x x x x x*]*-x*
3 [*x x x x x x x x x x x x x x x*]*-x*
4 [*x x x x x x x x x x x x x x x*]*x-*(*x*)
5 [*x x x x x x x x x x x x x x x*]*-x-tu*
6 [*x x x x x x x x x x x x x x x*]*-nim-ma*
7 [*x x x x x x x*]*x*[(*x*)]*-ši*
8 [*x x x*]*x* ERIM.MEŠ *i-ṭib-bu-ni*
9 [*x x x*] GISKIM.MEŠ *šá lum-nu*
10 [*x x x i*]*l-li-ka-ni*
11 [*x x* HU]L?*-nu a-na* LUGAL*-*⸢*ú-tu*⸣
12 [*x x x*]*x x x x*[*x* (*x*)]
13 [*x x x*] ⸢LUGAL⸣ *be-lí-*⸢*ia x x*⸣
14 ⸢*a*⸣*-n*[*a* MU–DI]NGIR! *u mu-kin-nu-tu*
15 LUGAL ⸢EN⸣*-a*! *it-ti* ERIM.MEŠ *an-nu-tu*
16 *liš-pur-an-ni u ia-a-nu-ú*
17 LUGAL *ki-i šá i-le-'u-ú*
18 *li-pu-uš* [0]
rest (two lines) uninscribed

9 [From] the very beginning I have been a dog who loves [the house of] his [lord].
11 [...] with the viziers
12 [...] the treaty of the king [...]
13 [...] the *word of* [...]
14 [(...)] my [...] *t*[*o* ...]
15 [...] if I see [and he]ar [..., I will repor]t it to the king, my lord.
17 May the king, my lord, [*and the viziers*] receive me.
19 [May NN, so]n of Nabû-ušabši [and ...] go,
20 [*and* ...] return onto his roof.
21 *A donkey* and 8 rams
(Break)

r.8 [...] men *became* well
9 [...] signs came, indicating evil [*for* ...],
11 [... *ba*]*d* for kingship
12 [...] ... [...]
13 [... *of*] the king, my lord [...]
14 May the king, my lord, send me fo[r oa]th and testimony with these men; or may the king do as he finds best.

130. ---

K 5393
beginning broken away
1′ [*x x x x x x*] *ba x*[*x x x x x*]
2′ [*x x x x x*]*-zi* MU.AN.[N]A? [*x x x*]
3′ [*x x x x x*] *ú-šá-as-dir* [*x x x x*]
4′ [*x* ^{md}U.G]UR–ŠEŠ*-ir qaq-q*[*a-ru*? *x x*]
5′ [*x x mam-ma šá*?]*-nam-ma it-t*[*i-x x x*]
6′ [*x x x x*]*-da-ka* É*-ku-*[*nu*? *x x x*]

CT 54 82
(Beginning destroyed)
2 [......] year [...]
3 [......] *I had arranged* [...]
4 [... Ner]gal-naṣir the *lan*[*d* ...]
5 [... *someone* e]lse wit[h ... ...]
6 [...] *your* [...], *yo*[*ur* (pl.)] house [...]

17 For the spelling *lu-uš-pu-ru*, cf. SAA 17 31 r.8′. 19 Or, "[NN and so]n Nabû-ušabši". r.6 *x* KUR].NIM.MA "Elam" is a possible reading. r.9f Cf., e.g., SAA 8 502 r.15.

130 3 No *sadāru* Š in CAD S 11-17. 4, 7 No. 131 was sent by Nergal-naṣir, but there is not enough context to consider whether he is the same or a different individual as here. 5 Or, "[*no one* e]lse with [...]"; cf. SAA 13 176 r.9-10. Alternatively, restore [*mi*]*-nam-ma* "[W]hy with [......]?" 6 But if a form of *dâku*, "to kill", such as *id*]*-da-ka*, then [*mi*]*-nam-ma* is the more likely restoration in the previous line.

7′ [^{md}U.GUR–ŠE]Š-*ir a-pa-làh* UG[U *x x x*]
8′ [*šá be-lí i*]*q-bu-ú um-ma m*[*a-x x x*]

9′ [*x x x x*]*x-ir qa-ru-t*[*i x x x*]
10′ [*x x x x*].MEŠ-*e-a e-x*[*x x x x*]
11′ [*x x x x*]*x-šú be-lí iq-*[*bu-u*$^?$ *x x*]
12′ [*x x x x x*] *ina* URU.*šá-ma-*[*ú-nu x x*]
13′ rest broken away

Rev. beginning broken away
1′ [*x x x x x x x*] ⌜*x*⌝ [*x x x x*]
2′ [*x x x x x x*] NUMUN *x*[*x x x x*]
3′ [*x x x x*] ⌜*x*⌝ *lid-di-nu* [*x x x*]
4′ [*x x x x*.M]EŠ *šá be-lí-iá a-*[*x x x*]
5′ [*x x x x x*]*x-ni re-ši m*[*a*$^?$ *x x x*]
6′ [*x x x x k*]*i-i pi-i s*[*i-x x x*]
7′ [*x x x x x*]-*šú ki-i pa-n*[*i x x x*]
8′ [*x x x x x x*] É *šá da-*[*x x x*]
9′ [*x x x x x x x*] ⌜*x x*⌝ [*x x x*]
rest broken away

7 I fear [Nergal-na]ṣir. Concern[ing ... about which/whom my lord s]aid: "[...]
9 [... ...]... *invited gues*[*ts* ...]
10 my [...]s ...[...]
11 [... ...]... my lord *sa*[*id* ...]
12 [...] in Šama[*'unu* ...]
(Break)

r.2 [......] seed [...]
3 [......] let them give [...]
4 [...] *I* [... the ...]s of my lord
5 [......]... *head* [...]
6 [...... acc]ording to [...]
(Rest destroyed or too broken for translation)

131. Fragment from Nergal-naṣir to Nabû-ušallim

K 1228
1 [*ṭup-pi*] ^{md}U.GUR–ŠEŠ-*ir*
2 [*a-na* $^{md+}$A]G–*ú-šal-lim* ŠEŠ-*šú*
3 [*lu-ú* DI]-*mu a-na* ŠEŠ-*ia*

4 [*x x x x*] ⌜*x x x*⌝
5 [*x x x x*] ⌜*x x x*⌝-*ṣu*
6 [*x x x x pa*$^?$-*ši*$^?$-*r*]*a*$^?$-*at-ti*
rest broken away
Rev. as far as preserved, uninscribed

ABL 229
1 [A tablet of] Nergal-naṣir [to Na]bû-ušallim, his brother. [Good heal]th to my brother!
4 [...] ...
5 [...] ...
6 [...... *secre*]*tly*
(Rest destroyed)

132. ---

K 11687
beginning broken away
1′ [*x x x x x*] ⌜*x*⌝ *x*[*x x*]
2′ [^{m}*x*]-⌜*na-nu* ^{md}U.GUR⌝–[*x x x x x*]
3′ [*x x p*]*a-*⌜*an* ^{m}DUMU.UŠ-*a*⌝ *x*[*x x x x x*]
4′ [^{m}*šu-m*]*a-a šá* É.SAG.Í[L *x x x*]
5′ [*x*]-⌜*ri* É.MEŠ *šá* LÚ⌝.[*x*]⌜*x x*⌝[*x x*]
6′ [*x x*] *me* [*x*] ⌜*mi-ni*⌝-[*i x*]*x i-ša*[*k-kan*]

CT 54 226
(Beginning destroyed)

2 [...]nanu, Nergal-[... (...)]
3 [... *be*]*fore* Aplaya [......]
4 [Šum]aya of Esaggi[l ...]
5 [...] the houses of the [...] official
6 [... *w*]*hy does* [...] *pla*[*ce* ...]?

11 The spelling *be-lí* for *bēlā* is an Assyrianism. 12 For the proposed restoration, cf. SAA 17 152:5.
131 4 This line has more illegible traces than indicated in Harper's copy.
132 Previous edition: Vera Chamaza, AOAT 295 no. 168. Possibly a fragment from the reign of Esarhaddon. 2 Vera Chamaza interprets the first name as [Bu]nānu.

7′ [*x*]*x*[*x*] *šú* ⸢*x x*⸣ *a* [*x*] *a-na e-k*[*a-nu*]
8′ ⸢*a-na* ^{m}*si*⸣-*x*[*x x x il*]-*li-ku* [*x x*]
9′ ⸢*a-na qaq-qar*⸣ [*x x x*] *a-na a-ka*[*n-na*]
10′ ⸢*x x a*⸣ [*x x*]*x tak-la-*[*x x x*]
11′ ⸢*x x*⸣ [*x x*] *mi-nu-*[*ú x x x*]
12′ [*x x x x*]*x* ⸢*su*⸣ [*x x x x x*]
rest broken away

7 Wh[ere]to [......]?
8 [... w]ent to N[N ...].
9 [...] to the territory [of ...] *back* he[re]
10 [...] ... you *detai*[*ned* ...]
11 [...] what [...]
(Rest destroyed or too broken for translation)

133. Sheikhs Are Afraid

K 5553
beginning broken away
1′ [*x x x x x x x x x*] ⸢*x x*⸣ [*x x x x x x x x*]
2′ [*x x i-l*]*e-ʾu-ú ina* KUR ⸢LUGAL$^{!}$⸣ [*x x x x x x x*]
3′ [*x x*] ⸢*x x* LÚ⸣.ERIM.MEŠ ARAD.MEŠ-⸢*šú*⸣-*n*[*u x x x x x x*]
4′ [LUG]AL$^{?}$ LÚ.*na-si-ka-tu liš-al* [*x x x x x x*]
5′ [*i*]*t-ta-din* ⸢LÚ.*x*⸣ *ina* ŠÀ-*bi* LÚ.ERIM.M[EŠ$^{?}$ *x x x x*]
6′ ⸢*x*⸣-*i* UNUG.K[I *x x*]*x*.MEŠ *šá* 2 LÚ.*x*[*x x x x x*]
7′ *i-te-zi-*[*iz x* (*x*) *x*]*x-me-šú-nu it-t*[*a-x x x x x*]
8′ ⸢*ù* LÚ⸣.*n*[*a-si-k*]*a-ti pal-hu-ma* [*ki-i pa-an* LUGAL$^{?}$]
9′ ⸢*mah-ru* ^{m}*za*⸣-*kir* LÚ.*na-si-ku ù* LÚ.ER[IM$^{?}$.MEŠ-*šú*$^{?}$ *x x x*]
10′ [*x x*]*x* ⸢*id*⸣-*du-ú ù a-na* ŠÀ-*bi* LÚ.KÚR.M[EŠ *x x x x*]
11′ [*x x x*] ⸢*x x x*⸣ *šá qa-ra-bu a-na* LÚ.*x*[*x x x x x*]
12′ [*x x x x*]*x* ⸢*x tu*⸣ *ù i-ha-am-mu-ú x*[*x x x x x*]
13′ [*a-na e-peš q*]*a-ra-bu pa-nu-šú ki-i x*[*x x x x x*]
14′ [*x x x x x*] LÚ.KÚR GAZ *i-kaš-šad en-n*[*a x x x x x*]
15′ [*x x x x x x*]*x* ⸢MU⸣.AN.NA.ME *a-ki-*[*i x x x x x x*]
16′ [*x x x x x x x*] ⸢*x x x*⸣ [*x x x x x x x x x x*]
rest broken away

CT 54 136
(Beginning destroyed)
2 [... *as he f*]*inds best*, in the land of the king [......]
3 [...] men, the[ir] servants [......]
4 [*the ki*]*ng* should ask the sheikhs. [...]
5 [ha]s given, the ... *of* the men [*of* ...]
6 ... Uruk, [the ...]s of two [...]
7 stoo[d (and) ...] their [......]
8 *and* the s[heik]hs are afraid. [*If it is*] agreeable [*to the king*, may] the sheikh Zakir and [*his*] m[en ...]
10 [...] *threw*. *Moreover*, *among* the enemies [...]
11 [...] who [...] battle *against* [...]
12 [...] and rejoice [...]
13 "[...] is intent [on doing b]attle". If [...]
14 "[...] will kill and vanquish an enemy." No[w ...]
15 [......] years *since* [......]
(Rest destroyed)

9 Less likely "no[w]". 10 According to Vera Chamaza, "vertrauenswürdig", i.e., *tak-la* [.

133 2, 5, 6, 10 See coll. 4 Intuitively, the first sign seems quite certain, but there is no intact LUGAL sign in this letter. 6 The beginning does not look like [*p*]*i-i*. 8 If the restoration is correct, and there is enough space, one might assume that "my lord" is also included. 10 Not [*k*]*i-*⸢*i*⸣ at the beginning. 11, 13 *qarābu* in the sense of "battle, fight" is an Assyrianism. 14 LÚ.KÚR GAZ *i-kaš-šad* is a quotation from an unidentified omen text.

134. Returning People to the Sheikhs

K 1181

beginning broken away
1′ *ṭup-pi ta-mu-r[u nu-bat-ta]*
2′ *la ta-ba-a-t[a* UN.MEŠ-*ia*$^{?}$]
3′ *ina* ŠU.2 1-*en* [*i-na* ŠÀ-*bi*]
4′ LÚ.*na-si-ka-t*[*i šá*]

5′ KUR *lu-tir-am-m*[*a ka-ru-u*]
6′ *ik*$^{!}$-*ki*$^{!}$-*ia lu*[*d-di* 0]
7′ $^{md+}$AG–PAB–AŠ [*x x* (*x*)]
8′ ^{m}*na-bi-*⸢*ia*⸣ [*x x* (*x*)]
9′ ^{m}UD.NUN-*x x*[*x x* (*x*)]
10′ ^{m}*ha-bur*–[*x x x* (*x*)]

r.1 ^{m}NUMUN-*ú-tu* MIN [*x x* (*x*)]
2 ^{m}*ina–pi-i*–$^{d+}$EN MIN [*x x* (*x*)]
3 ^{m}*na-aq-*⸢*bi*⸣–^{d}[*x x* (*x*)]
4 ^{md}⸢*x*⸣–*ú-še-zi*[*b x x* (*x*)]
5 ^{m}ÉRIN.⸢TÁH$^{?}$⸣–^{d}*iš-t*[*ar*$^{?}$ *x x* (*x*)]
6 ^{md}KUR–*ra-mu šá x*[*x x* (*x*)]
rest uninscribed

CT 54 14

(Beginning destroyed)

1 (The day) you see my tablet, do not spend [a night], so I can return [*my people*] to the custody of one [of] the sheikhs [of] the land an[d] dr[op] my [sulky] mood!

7 Nabû-ahu-iddina [...],
8 Nabîya [...],
9 UD.NUN-...[...],
10 Habur-[...],
r.1 Zerutu, ditto [...],
2 Ina-pi-Bel, ditto [...],
3 Naqbi-[DN, ...],
4 DN-ušezi[b ...],
5 Nerar-Išt[ar ...],
6 Kur'e-ramu who/of [...].

135. – – –

K 15045

1 [*a-na* LUGAL KUR.KUR *be-lí-ni*]
2 [ARAD.MEŠ-*ka* LÚ.*ki-i*]*s*$^{?}$-*s*[*ik*$^{?}$-*a-a*]
3 [^{d}30 *u* ^{d}NIN.G]AL *a-na* LUGAL K[UR.KUR]
4 [*be-lí-ni*] *lik-ru-b*[*u*]
5 [UD-*mu-us-s*]*u* ^{d}30 *u* ^{d}NIN.GAL [*a-na*]
6 [TIN ZI.MEŠ] *ù a-ra-ku* UD-[*me*]
7 [*šá* LUGAL *be-lí*]-⸢*i*⸣-*ni* ⸢*nu-ṣal*⸣-*l*[*a*]
8 [*x x x x*]*x*[*x x x x x x*]
rest broken away

CT 54 287

1 [To the king of the lands, our lord: your servants, the people of *Ki*]*ss*[*ik*]. May [Sîn and Nikk]al bles[s] the king of the l[ands, our lord]. We pra[y dail]y to Sîn and Nikkal [for the good health] and long lif[e of the king], our [lord].

(Rest destroyed)

134 2 One can restore [UN.MEŠ] if one considers that the people enumerated in lines 7-r.6 are not sheikhs, but people who are to be returned to them. 5 Cf. SAA 17 152:20-21. 6 See coll. r.1f The two ditto definitions may not support the interpretation of all these people as sheikhs.

135 SAA 21 42 and possibly SAA 21 39 are letters from Assurbanipal to the people of Kissik. 1-7 For the restorations, see SAA 22, nos. 84:1-7 and 85:1-6.

136. Fragment of a Letter by Bel-ibni

K 7454

1 [*a-na* EN LUGAL.MEŠ] ⸢*be*$^{?}$-*lí*$^{?}$⸣-[*ia*]
2 [ARAD-*ka* $^{md+}$EN–*i*]*b*-⸢*ni*⸣
3 [AN.ŠÁR ^{d}UTU *u* ^{d}AMAR.UTU *a-r*]*a-ku* UD.M[EŠ$^{!}$]
4 [*ṭu-ub* ŠÀ *u ṭu-u*]*b* UZU *šá* EN [LUGAL. MEŠ$^{?}$]
5 [*liq-bu-ú a-na* UGU$^{?}$ ^{m}*i*]*n-da-bi-bi* [0]
6 [*x x x x x x*]*x a-na*$^{?}$ UGU-*hi-šú* [0]
7 [*x x x x x*]*x lul*-[*x*]*x-e-a*
8 [*x x x x x it*]-*ti-šú* ⸢*it*⸣-*ta-ši-iz-zu*
9 [*x x x x x-t*]*a*$^{?}$-*a-nu*
10 [*x x x x x x*]-*šá-a-nu*
11 [*x x x a-na* UGU$^{?}$-*h*]*i*$^{?}$-*ni*
12 [*x x x x x x*] ⸢$^{d?}$AMAR⸣.UTU
13 [*x x x x x x*]*x*
rest broken away
Rev. beginning broken away
1′ [*x x x x x x x x x x*] ⸢*x*⸣
2′ [*x x x x x x x x x x x*]*x* ⸢*ṣi*$^{?}$ MUN$^{?}$⸣
3′ [*x x x x x*] *i-ṣab-bat-ma*
4′ [*x x x x x* L]Ú$^{?}$.SANGA *šú-ú ù*
5′ [*x x x x x* 1.*e*]*n pi-i*
6′ [*x x x x x-t*]*i*$^{?}$-*šú-nu la-pa-an*
7′ [*x x x x x*]*x-qu a-na x*[*x* (*x x*)]
8′ [*x x x x x x*]*x-hi ú-kà*[*ṣ-ṣip* (*x*)]
9′ [*x x x x x na-as*$^{?}$-*p*]*an-di u*[*s*$^{?}$ *x x x*]
10′ [*x x x x x* LU]GAL *be-l*[*í* (*x x x*)]
11′ [*x x x x x x*]*x* EN.N[UN$^{?}$ (*x x*)]
12′ [*x x x x x x x*]*x* [(*x x*)]
13′ [*x x x x x x x* Í]D$^{?}$ *x*[*x* (*x*)]
14′e [*x x x x x x x*]*x šú-nu* [0]

CT 54 195

1 [To the lord of kings, my] *lord*: [your servant Bel-i]bni. [May Aššur, Šamaš and Marduk decree lo]ng life, [happiness and] physical [well-bei]ng to the lord [of kings]!
5 [*Concerning* I]ndabibi
6 [...] against him
7 [...] *my* ...
8 [...] they have stood [wi]th him
9 [...] ...
10 [...] ...
11 [... *again*]*st* us
12 [...] Marduk
(Break)

r.3 [...] he will seize and
4 [...] he is a priest and
5 [... of on]e opinion
6 [...] their [...] before
7 [...] ... to [...]
8 [...] ... he/I plan[ned (...)]
9 [... *devast*]*ation* [...]
10 [... the k]ing, [my] lord, [(...)]
11 [...] *wat*[*ch* (...)]
12 [......]
13 [......]
14 [...] are they.

137. ---

82-5-22,1772

beginning broken away
1′ [*x* (*x*) *x*] *ri* [*x x x x*]
2′ [*x* (*x*) *x*]*x da* ⸢*a*$^{?}$⸣ [*x x x x*]
3′ [*x*] *ik-lu-ú* ^{m}*x*[*x x x x x*]
4′ [*a*$^{?}$-*n*]*a* ^{m}*ma-ni-ia* LÚ.[*x x x*]
5′ [*x*]*x* KÁ *mar-rat* [*x x x x*]

CT 54 503

(Beginning destroyed)

3 [...] they held back. [PN]
4 [*t*]*o* Mania, the [...]
5 [...] mouth of the sea [...]

136 Previous edition: de Vaan Bel-ibni 337-38. Cf. Dietrich, WO 5 (1970) 182-83. [3, r.7f, 13] See coll. [4] There may not be enough space for the proposed restoration at the end. [6] Not]-*šú* as in Dietrich's copy of CT 54. [7] The sign seems certain, but the reading *lul* is uncertain. [11] Or, *i-na* UGU$^{?}$-*h*]*i*$^{?}$-*ni*. [12] Marduk can of course be part of a PN. [r.13] According to Dietrich's copy this line is already part of the upper edge.

137 Previous edition: de Vaan Bel-ibni 351-52. [4] Or, "Mania (and) the [...]".

6′ [(*x*) *i*]*l-tap-ra-ni*[*š*$^{?}$-*šú x x x*]
7′ [(*x*)] LÚ.GIŠ.B[AN$^{?}$ *x x x x*]
e.8′ [*u*]*l*$^{?}$ *i-r*[*u-ub*$^{?}$ *x x x x*]
9′ [*x x*]*x ta x*[*x x x x x*]
10′ [*x* (*x*) *x*]*x x*[*x x x x x x*]
other side destroyed

6 [h]e has sent *h*[*im* ...]
7 arc[her(s) ...]
8 *he* [*did no*]*t en*[*ter* ...]
(Rest destroyed)

138. King of Babylon, Natan and Nabû-bel-šumati

Ki 1904-10-9,298 (BM 99266)
beginning broken away
1′ [*x x x x*]-⌜*ia x*⌝ [*x x x x x x x x*]
2′ [*x* LU]GAL TIN.TIR.KI *ù* $^{m⌜d⌝}$[*x x x x x x x*]
3′ [*a-n*]*a pa-ni* ^{m}*na-tan it-ta*[*l-ku x x x x x*]
4′ [*u*]*l-tu pa-ni* ^{m}*na-tan a-n*[*a x x x x x x*]
5′ [*i*]*t-tal-ku en-na ki-i i*[*l-li-ku-ni*$^{?}$ *x x x*]
6′ [$^{md+}$A]G–EN–MU.MEŠ ⌜*di-ku*⌝ *i*[*d-de-ke*$^{?}$ *x x x x*]
7′ [*a-na* U]GU-*hi-ni* ⌜*ul i*⌝-*di* [*x x x x x x*]

CT 54 587
(Beginning destroyed)
1 [...] *my* [......]
2 [*of the ki*]*ng* of Babylon and [PN (...)]
3 we[nt] into the presence of Natan [...]
4 [f]rom the presence of Natan t[o ...]
5 [th]ey have gone. Now, when *th*[*ey came* ...]
6 [N]abû-bel-šumati *mobi*[*lized* (*his forces*) ...]
7 *he will not mo*[*ve* aga]inst us. [...]

138 Previous edition: de Vaan Bel-ibni 357-58. It is not certain whether the preserved part is the obverse or the reverse of the tablet. 2 Or: [*x* L]Ú TIN.TIR.KI.

FIG. 14. *Nubian prisoners wearing manacles.*
BM 124928.

8′ [LUGAL? TIN.T]IR.KI ⸢*il*⸣-*ta*[*p-ra x x x x x*]
9′ [*x x x x x*]*x* ⸢*x*⸣ *r*[*u x x x x x x*]
rest broken away

8 [*The king* of Babyl]on has writt[en ...]
(Rest destroyed)

139. Men Requested

83-1-18,512
beginning broken away
1′ [*x x x x*]⸢*x x*⸣ [*x x*]
2′ [*x x x x*] ^{m}*ad-ri-i*[*a*]
3′ [LÚ.EN.NAM] ERIM.MEŠ *liš-pur-na-a-*[*šú*]
4′ [*x x x*]*x*.MEŠ 10 *la e-*⸢*bir*⸣
5′ [*x x x x*] *x*.MEŠ-*ú*
6′ [*x x x x*]⸢*x*⸣ [*x x i*]*n*
rest broken away

CT 54 526
(Beginning destroyed)

2 [...] May Idriy[a, the governor], send u[s] men.
4 Some 10 [...] have not crossed (the river)
(Rest destroyed or too broken for translation)

140. All Is Lost

ZT 13284 + ZT 13285 + ZT 13286 + ZT 13287
1 [*a-na* LÚ*.IGI.DU]B E[N-*ia*]
2 [ARAD-*k*]*a* ^{m}*man-nu*–GIM– URU.ŠÀ–URU
3 [*lu*] DI-*mu a-na* ⸢EN⸣-*ia*
4 [*š*]*a* KUR.MEŠ *gab-bu* LÚ*.⸢A⸣.BA.MEŠ
5 KU[R].*aš-šur-a-a* KUR.*ár-ma-a-a*
6 LÚ*.GAL–TÚG.KA.KÉŠ.MEŠ-*ni*
7 LÚ*.EN–*pi-*⸢*qi*⸣*-ta-te* [L]Ú*.*um-ma-ni*
8 LÚ*.⸢SIMUG⸣–URUDU LÚ*.SIMUG–AN.BAR
9 *ša a-nu-tú* [G]IŠ.*til-li*.MEŠ
10 *i-kap-pa-ru-ni* LÚ*.NAGAR.MEŠ
11 LÚ*.ZADIM–BAN LÚ*.ZADIM–GAG.TI
12 LÚ*.UŠ.BAR.MEŠ LÚ*.TÚG.KA.KÉŠ.MEŠ
13 *ša bat-qu i-ka-ṣ*[*a-ru-ni*]
14 *a-na-ku a-na man-ni* [*up-ni-ia*]
15 *la-ap-ti mi-i-n*[*u la-aq-bi*]
16 *mi-i-nu lu-ra-*[*ad-di*]
17 *ki-i ša* LÚ.[IGI.DUB *iq-bu-ni*?]
18 *gab-bu ta-ri-*[*iṣ x x x*]
19 *in-nu-u* 1-*en* [*šu-ú*]
20 *a-na-ku-u ú-*[*di-ia*?]
21 *a-mu-at l*[*a-a ma-gu-ru*]
e.22 *la-a i-*⸢*šá*⸣*-*[*mu-u-ni*]

ZTT 22

1 [To the treasur]er, my lo[rd]: yo[ur servant], Mannu-ki-Libbali. [Good] health to my lord!
4 [O]f all the horses, Assyrian (and) Aramean scribes, cohort-commanders, officials, craftsmen, coppersmiths, blacksmiths, those who scour the tools (and) equipment, carpenters, bow-makers, arrow-makers, weavers, tailors (and) those who ma[ke] the repairs – to whom should I pr[ay], what [should I say], what mo[re] should I [do]?

17 Just as the [*treasurer said*], everything is *possi*[*ble* ...].
19 Our [*end* is] one.
20 (So) am I a[lone] going to die? [They pay] a[bsolutely] no he[ed to me].

9 Not ⸢EDIN?⸣.

139 2 Idriya (var. Ataraya) is known as governor of Hal[ziatbar] in the reign of Assurbanipal; cf. PNA 2/I 505b and Luukko, Fs. Postgate (2017) 328, 330.

140 Previous edition: Parpola, SAAB 17 (2008) 86-95. 17 Parpola: *ki-i ša* LÚ [*x x x x*], "Just as a man [......]", and admittedly the above restoration is conjectural.

e.23 mdPA–[GIN–PAB *ša*]
r.1 *i-si-ia* [*x x x x x x*]
2 *e-ta-rab* [*si-bar-ri x x*]
3 *šá-ki-in ina* [*x x x x x*]
4 *ina* UGU *ši-ih-*[*li x x x x*]
5 ⸢*dul-lu*⸣ [*š*]*a* GIŠ.⸢É⸣–[*x x x x*]
6 GIŠ.É–*ki-ṣir*.MEŠ [*x x x x*]
7 *ša* NÍG.ŠID.MEŠ-*ma* [*x x x x*]
8 *ša* ITI.DU6 *lu qur-*[*bu x x x*]
9 mdPA–GIN–PAB ⸢*lu*⸣ [*x x x*]
10 *ú-ma-a* 1-*en ina* ŠÀ-*bi-šú-n*[*u*]
11 *la-áš-šú a-ke-e a-qa-bi*
12 *me-me-ni ina* ŠÀ *ši-pir-ti*
13 *an-ni-ti ša áš-pur-an-ni* 1-*en*
14 *la-áš-šú* [L]Ú*.3.U5.M[EŠ]
15 *ša* IGI GIŠ.GIGIR.MEŠ *me-me-*⸢*ni*⸣
16 *la-áš-šú man-nu re-e-šu*
17 *i-na-áš-ši ina ku-me*
18 *an-*⸢*ni*⸣*-e ša si-bar-ri*
19 [*x x x*]*x šá-ki-nu-u-ni*
20 [*x x x*] *a-šá-par-u-ni*
21 [*x x x x x x x*] ⸢*x x*⸣
s.1 *ina* IGI-*ia la-áš-šú ina pi-ti mi-i-ni lu-si-pu-*[*šú-nu*]
2 *mu-a-tú ina* ŠÀ-*bi il-la-ka la-a* 1-*en* [*x x x x*]
3 [0] *ep-šá-ak*

23 Nabû-[kenu-uṣur], my associate [...] entered [......] (and) has been put [in irons] in [...].

r.4 As to [my] secon[d-best man ...] the work [o]n the [...] containers, the *bandage boxes* [......], even that of the accounts [......] of Tishri (VII) should be prese[nt ...].

9 Nabû-kenu-uṣur should be [...].

10 Now, not one of them is there. How can I command? Nobody (mentioned) in this letter that I'm sending, not one (of them) is there! There are no "third men" to supervise the chariots.

16 Who will make the muster instead of this one who is being kept in irons [...]?

20 [The *lists* that] I send [......] are not at my disposal.

s.1 According to what can they collect [them]?

2 Death will come out of it! No one [will escape]. I am done!

r.2, 18-19 One could restore AN.BAR after *si-bar-ri*. r.20 *a-šá-par-u-ni*: a 1st sg. present form (cf. SAA 5 91 r.5; SAA 19 41:6′ and 57:9) may be as likely an explanation as a preterite (Parpola, SAAB 17, p. 94).

4. Fragments of Unknown Authorship

FIG. 15. *Horses from Iran delivered as tribute.*
Botta and Flandin, Monument de Ninive II, Pl. 131.

141. Fragment of a Letter to the Palace Supervisor

K 1240
1 *a-na* LÚ*.*šá*–IGI–⌜É⌝.G[AL]
2 EN-*ia*
3 ARAD-*ka* ᵐ⌜*x-ki*?⌝-*su*
4 ⌜*lu*⌝ D[I-*mu a-na* EN-*ia*]
rest broken away
Rev. beginning broken away
1′ *be*?-*x*[*x x x*]
2′ *an-ni-te be-*⌜*lí*⌝
3′ *lu-še-bi-la*
rest (two lines) uninscribed

CT 53 174
1 To the pal[ace] supervisor, my lord: your servant NN. Good he[alth to my lord]!

(Break)

r.1 My lord should send this [...].

142. ---

K 5537
beginning broken away
1′ [*x x x*]*x* [*x x x x*]
2′ [*x x x*]-*ka a-l*[*a-x x x*]
3′ [*x x x i*]*na pur-si-t*[*e*? *x x*]
4′ [*x x* ᵐᵈP]A–*tak-lak* L[Ú*.*x x*]
5′ [*x x x-t*]*i-ši ina* UG[U *x x*]
rest broken away

CT 53 274
(Beginning destroyed)

2 *your* [...] *I* [...]
3 [... i]n a *pursītu*-jar [...]
4 [... Na]bû-taklak, the [...]
(Rest destroyed or too broken for translation)

143. Send It to the Palace!

K 7494
beginning broken away
1′ [*x x*] *at-*⌜*ti-din x x*⌝ [*x x x x x*
2′ [*ma*]-*a ina* É.GAL *še-bil še-*[*x x x x*

3′ [*ma-a*?] *ket-tu-u ši-i* TA* ⌜É?⌝.[*x x x* TA*?
4′ [É?.GA]L? *i-sa-*⌜*pa*⌝-[*ru-ni x x x x*
5′ [*x x x*] ⌜*x*⌝ [*x x x x x x x x*
rest broken away
other side destroyed

CT 53 375
(Beginning destroyed)
1 [...] I gave [......]
2 [He/they sa]id: "Send it to the palace! ...[......]
3 "It is true; [...] from the *pa*[*lace* ...
4 They (also) wro[te to me *from the palac*]e
(Rest destroyed)

141 [3] Unfortunately, the name of the sender is damaged. It is not impossible that it was Kikkisu "reed hut" (ᵐ⌜*ki*?-*ki*?⌝-*su*), but we do not know such a name; alternatively, it could be a DN-eriba name, e.g., ᵐ⌜*x x*⌝–SU.
142 [2] *-ka* may be part of a form of *alāku*. [5] Possibly *i*/*it-t*]*i-ši*, i.e., "Na]bû-taklak, the [...], took [...]".
143 [3f] Parallels for writing "from the palace" are listed in Luukko, SAAB 16 (2007) 235.

144. ---

K 10989
beginning broken away
1′ [*x x*] *ina* UG[U *x x x x*]
2′ [*a-ta*?]-*a la ta*-[*áš-pu-ra*?]
3′ [*ú-ma*]-*a an-nu-rig* [*x x*]
4′ [*ta-ka*]*l-la-šú ú*-[*x x*]
5′ [(*x*) *x-a*]*n-ni* TA* É L[Ú*.*x x*]
6′ [*x x*] *ú-še-si*-[*ib-u-ni*?]
7′ [^{m}*a-d*]*u-ni*–DINGIR LÚ*.A–[KIN?]
8′ [*x x x*] ⌈*x x x*⌉ [*x x x*]
rest broken away

CT 53 423
(Beginning destroyed)
1 […] *because of th*[*is* … Wh]y *d*[*id*] you not [*write to me*]?
3 [No]w then [… you det]ain him […],
5 […] *me*. Ever since the […] official *settl*[*ed* …],
7 [Ad]uni-il, the *mes*[*senger*]
(Rest destroyed)

145. ---

K 12979
beginning broken away
1′ [*x x x x x*]*x za* ⌈*x x x*⌉
2′ [*x x x x*]-*e ša* MAN
3′ [*x x la ú*]-*ra-ma-na-ši*
4′ [*x x x x*]*x-ri-i*
5′ [*x x x x t*]*a-ha-ru-u-ni*
6′ [*x x x x*]-*ut-ka id-da-na-ši*
7′ [*x x x x*]*x a-sa-kan*
8′ [*x x x* D]I-*mu*
9′ [*x x x x*]-*pa*
10′ [*x x x x x*]*x-tú*
rest broken away
Rev. beginning broken away
1′ [*x x x x*] ⌈*x x*⌉ [*x x*]
2′ [*ša a-na* LUG]AL EN-[*ia*]
3′ [*áš-pur-an-n*]*i nu-uk*
4′ [*x x x x*]*x-šú i-tal-ku*
5′ [*x x x i*]*m-li-ku-u-ni*
6′ [*x x x l*]*a-áš-šú*
7′ [*x x x x*]*x-šú-nu*
8′ [*x x x x x x*]-*ni*
9′ [*x x x x x x*]-*u*
rest broken away

CT 53 448
(Beginning destroyed)
2 […] of the king [… w]ill [not] release us […]
4 [… …]…
5 [… y]ou *appealed to*
6 […] your […] gives *us*
7 […] I placed
8 [… he]alth
(Break)

r.2 [about *whom* I wrote to the ki]ng, [my] lord: "His […s] went […]
5 [… *who* g]ave counsel
6 [… th]ere is not
7 […] their/them […]
(Rest destroyed or too broken for translation)

144 6 *ú-še-si-*[*ib-u-ni*?]: perhaps a "Babylonian" form of *šēšubu* (cf. SAA 15 232:8). 7 According to PNA (1/I 54b s.v. Aduni-ilu), this letter dates from the reign of Esarhaddon, but the second attestation of CT 53 813:3 is now read as [^{m}]*a-du-ni*–[*ba-al*] in SAA 16 130. Thus, CT 53 423 could just as well be from the reign of Sargon II.
145 6 One might expect the writing *id-da-na-na-ši*, cf., e.g., *i*/*id-di-na-na-ši(-ni)* SAA 1 143:6′, r.5. Alternatively, "gives her".

146. – – –

K 13044

beginning broken away
1′ [*x x x x x*] ⌜*an*⌝ [*x x*]
2′ *an-nu-ti* TA *pa-*[*ni-x*]
3′ LUGAL *be-lí i-na-š*[*i* 0]
4′ É LUGAL *be-lí i-q*[*ab-bu-ni*]
5′ [L]Ú*.ARAD.M[EŠ *x x x x*]
rest broken away

CT 53 468

(Beginning destroyed)
1 [......] the king, my lord, take[s] these [...] from [...].
4 Whatever the king, my lord, sa[ys], the servants [...]
(Rest destroyed)

147. Royal Decision on the Division of Inheritance

K 13102

beginning broken away
1′ HA.L[A? *x x x x x x x*]
2′ *ina* UG[U *x x x x x x*]
3′ *a-na-k*[*u x x x x x*]

4′ UD-7-KÁM [*x x x x x*]
5′ *is-sa-*⌜*kan*⌝ [*x x x x x*]
6′ *ina* UGU-⌜*hi*⌝-*i*[*á x x x x*]
7′ ^{m}*aš-šur–mu-šal-l*[*im x x x x*]
8′ TA* MÍ-*šú* [*x x x x x*]
9′ UD-12-KÁM *i-*[*x x x x x*]
10′ *it-tal-ka* [*x x x x*]
11′ *un-qu ša* L[UGAL *i-si-si*?]
12′ *ú-de-e x*[*x x x x*]
e.13′ *am–mar ina* [ŠÀ-*bi*]
14′ *iš*!!-*šá-ṭar-ni x*[*x x x*]
15′ *ina* ŠU.2 DUMU.MEŠ-*šú i-*[*sa-kan*]
r.1 *a-na* NINDA.MEŠ *is-*[*sa-he-iš*?]
2 *ina* UGU DUMU.MEŠ-*šú ša* [*x x x*]
3 *ina* ŠÀ 3 DUMU.MEŠ-*šú* ⌜*a*?⌝-[*na x x*]
4 *ša i-ra-bi-ú-*[*ni x x x*]
5 *ina* TI.LA-*šú ki-i a*[*n-ni-i*]
6 *iq-ṭi-bi ma-a a*[*n-ni-u x x*]
7 *ma-a bé-ti* A.Š[À *a-na kas-pi*]
8 *la ta-da-na* [*x x x x*]
9 *ša ina* TI.LA-*šú* [*x x x x*]
10 *iš-ṭur-u-ni* [DUMU.MEŠ-*šú*]
11 *ina* A.MEŠ *ik-tar-*[*ru x x x*]
12 [*a-n*]*a* ⌜É?⌝ [*x x x x x*]
rest broken away

CT 53 486

(Beginning destroyed)
1 *the sha*[*re of* ......]
2 *on* [......]
3 I [......]
4 (On) the 7th day [*the king*] *gave* [*orders and sent a sealed document*] *to* m[e. *I summoned*] Aššur-mušall[im *the* ...] and his wife [......].
9 (On) the 12th day he [*and* ...] came t[o *me. He read*] the k[ing]'s sealed document [and] *p*[*laced*] all the utensils [and ...] that were written in [it] in the hands of his sons.

15 *For* (*eating*) bread *to*[*gether*],

r.2 *to* the sons of [*NN*],
3 from his three sons *who grew* [*up* ...]. When he was alive, he said (to them) as fo[llows]: "T[his is ...]. You may not sell my house and fie[ld for silver]." [His sons] cas[t] into water [*the document*] which he [...] wrote while still alive [and *altered* ......]

(Rest destroyed)

146 4 This type of use of *bēt* may be more indicative of the seventh century than the Sargon correspondence.
147 14 The tablet has *il-šá-ṭar-ni*, but reading *iš*!!-*šá-ṭar-ni* (*iššaṭ*a*rūni*) "(as much as) is written (in ...)", N prt. subj. of *šaṭāru*, makes good sense. Perhaps followed by A[D *x x*]. r.1 Or: *is-*[*sa-kan*] as in line 5. r.8 *taddana* is 2mp and must refer to the three sons.

148. We Are the King's Servants

K 14651
Obv. destroyed
Rev. beginning broken away
1′ *ina* ⸢ŠÀ-*bi-šú*⸣-*nu* [*x x x x*]
2′ *ú-ma-a an-nu-ri*[*g x x x*]
3′ *ša* É–AD-*šú* 50 L[Ú*$^{?}$.*x x x*]
4′ *na-ṣu-u-ni ma-a* [*x x x*]
5′ *ra-am-me-a li*[*l-li-ku-ni*$^{?}$]
6′ ⸢*ma*⸣-*a* LÚ*.ARAD.ME[Š *ša* LUGAL]
7′e [*a*]-*ni-ni mi-i-n*[*u ša* LUGAL]
rest broken away

CT 53 565
(Beginning destroyed)
r.1 *from* them [...].
2 Now then [...] of his paternal household are bringing 50 [...s], saying: "Release [...], let [*them come*].
6 We are the [king's] servants." Wha[t is that the king *our lord commands*?]
(Rest destroyed)

149. Fragment of a Letter Concerning a Person as a Pledge

K 14667
1 *a-na* [LUGAL *be-lí-ia*]
2 ⸢ARAD⸣-*k*[*a* ^{m}*x x x x x*]
rest broken away
Rev. beginning broken away
1′ [*x*]*x* ^{m}*k*[*i*$^{?}$-*x x x x x*]
2′ DUMU ^{m}*da-r*[*i–x x x x*]
3′ *šá-par-tu* ⸢*na*⸣ [*x x x x*]
4′ *pa-qi-di ni-*[*x x x x x*]
5′ *i-tu-bi*[*l x x x x*]
6′ AD-*šú* [*x x x x x*]
7′e LUGAL [*x x x x x*]
8′e *l*[*u x x x x x*]

CT 53 575
1 To [the king, my lord]: yo[ur] servant [NN].
(Break)
r.1 [...] N[N (...)], son of Dar[i-...] is assigned as a pledge [......]

5 brough[t ...]
6 his father [...]
7 the king [...]
8 *le*[*t* ......].

150. Fragment Referring to the City Gate

K 14802
beginning broken away
1′ [*x x*] ⸢*a*⸣-*na* [*x x x x x*]
2′ [*a*]*t-ta* LÚ*.[*x x x x*]
3′ [*ina* K]Á.GAL UR[U *x x x x*]
4′ *an-nu-te liš*$^{?}$-*ṭ*[*ur ina* UGU$^{?}$]
5′ *ša* LUGAL *a-n*[*a x x x x*]
6′ *iq-bu-ni x*[*x x x x*]
7′ [*l*]*i-li-k*[*a x x x x*]
8′ [*ina*$^{?}$ *p*]*a-an* KÁ.[GAL *x x x x*]
rest broken away

CT 53 590
(Beginning destroyed)
1 [...] to [...]
2 [y]ou (*and*) the [...].
3 *Let him wri*[*te down*] these [... at the] city [g]ate [of GN].
4 [*Concerning*] *what* the king said t[o ...]
7 [... sho]uld com[e ...]
8 [be]fore the city gate [of GN ...]
(Rest destroyed)

149 r.2 The most common Dari names are Dari-Bel and Dari-šarru. r.3 The topic of "pledge" is common in documents, but rarely mentioned elsewhere.

151. ---

K 15310

beginning broken away

1′ [*x x x x*] ⸢*a*⸣ *šar* ⸢*a*⸣-[*na* UGU$^{?}$]
2′ [*x x x*]-*nu* LÚ*.DUMU–*šip*-[*ri*]
3′ [*ša* LU]GAL EN *iš-pu*[*r-an-ni*]

4′ [*ma-a x* LÚ*$^{?}$.GA]L$^{?}$.MEŠ *an-nu-t*[*e* 0$^{?}$]
5′ [*a-na* DUMU$^{?}$]–MAN *di-ni* [*x x*]
6′ [*x x x x*].MEŠ ^{m}*x*[*x x x x*]

rest broken away

CT 53 633

(Beginning destroyed)

1 […] … *C*[*oncerning* …]*nu*, the messeng[er about whom the ki]ng, my lord, wrote [to me]:

4 "Give these [*x magna*]*tes* [*to the*] *crown* [*prince*]

6 […]s *of* N[N …]

(Rest destroyed)

152. ---

K 15360

lines 1-4 obliterated

5 [*x x x x x x-r*]*i*-⸢*ia*⸣ *ina* ⸢UGU⸣ *man-nu*
6 [*x x x x x x x*] *ù*
7 [*x x x x ú-šad*]-*ba-ba-áš-šú*
8 [*x x x x x x-r*]*i-ia a-na* É.GAL
9 [*x x x x x x-k*]*a-áš-šú*
10 [*x x x x x x x x*] *a-du*

rest broken away

Rev. beginning broken away

1′ [*x x x x x x x x*]*x š*[*u*]
2′ [*x x x x x x x x*] *i* [0]
3′ [*x x x x x x x x*]*x-a-te*
4′ [*x x x x x x x*]*x* ⸢*e*⸣ *ki*
5′ [*x x x x x d*]*u* ANŠE.KUR.⸢RA.MEŠ⸣
6′ [*x x x x ma-h*]*ir-u-ni*
7′ [*x x x x x-m*]*a u*[*r*]-*ta-mu-u-ni*
8′ [*x x x x x-l*]*i* ⸢*li*⸣-*lik-a-ni*
9′ [*a-na* LUGAL *be-lí-ia*$^{?}$] *a-sa-pa-ra*
10′ [*la* LÚ*.ARAD *ša*$^{?}$ LUG]AL *a-na-ku-u*
11′ [*x x x x x x*]*x* LÚ*.GA[L–*x*]
12′ [*x x x x x x x x x*]

CT 53 647

(Beginning obliterated)

5 […] to whom my […]
6 [……] and
7 [… *I* inc]ite him
8 […] my […] to the palace
9 [……] him

(Break)

r.5 […… *man*]*y* horses
6 […… acc]eptable
7 [……] have *left* me
8 [……] should come to me
9 I have written [*to the king, my lord*].
10 Am I [*not a servant* of the ki]ng?
11 [……] the chi[ef …]
12 [……].

151 2 Or: […]nu (and) the messeng[er]". 4f The interpretation is conjectural. 5 Or: "legal case".
152 5, 8 …-*r*]*i-ia* (e.g., *ṣe-he-ri-ia* or LÚ.A–*šip-r*]*i-ia* "my messenger") must refer to the same person(s). 10 Perhaps "until" or *ma*]-*a-du* "many" unless a plural stative form. r.6 If "horses [… that have been rece]ived" was meant, we would expect *mahrūni*.

153. Fragment Mentioning a Bel-ibni

Sm 2192

beginning broken away

1′ [*x x x*]*x* ⸢*x x*⸣ [*x x x x*]
2′ [*x x* ^{m}*di-d*]*i-i ù* $^{m⸢d⸣}$*x*[*x x x*]
3′ [*x x x š*]*a* LÚ*.*um-ma-ni* DUMU [*x x*]
4′ [*x x ú-sa-a*]*h-hi-ru-u-ni* [*x x*]
5′ [*x x x x*]*x-u-ni ú-se-r*[*i*$^{?}$*-x x*]
6′ [*x x* ^{m}]⸢^{d}EN⸣–*ib-ni si-*[*x x x*]
7′ [*ina* UGU]-*hi-ni is-sa-*[*kan*$^{?}$ *x x x*]
8′ [*x x x* T]A* *bu-*[*x x x x x*]
9′ [*x x x x*]*x x*[*x x x x x*]

rest broken away

Rev. completely broken away

CT 53 861

(Beginning destroyed)

2 [... Did]î and N[N]
3 [... *w*]*hom the scholars* (*and*) son of [...]
4 [... *ret*]*urned* [...]
5 [...] ... ...[...]
6 [...] Bel-ibni *pla*[*ced ... again*]*st* us [...]
8 [... *fr*]*om* ...[...]

(Rest destroyed)

154. Two Private Letters on One Tablet

BM 103016

1 IM ^{md}ME.ME–KA[R]-⸢*ir*⸣
2 *a-na* ^{m}SU-*a-a* PAB-*ia*
3 *ak-tar-rab-ka*
4 *ina* IGI ^{d}NIN.LÍL
5 *ina* UGU *a-bé-e-te*
6 ⸢*ša*⸣ *áš-pur-ka-a-ni*
7 *lu har-da-at*
8 *mi-nu ah–hur*
9 *a-bu-tú ši-i'–ši-i'*
10 *lu-u har-da-at*
11 *a-*[*n*]*a-*⸢*ku*⸣ *a-di* 10 UD.MEŠ
12 *ina* IGI-*ka a-na-ku*
13 NÍG.ŠID.MEŠ-⸢*ku*⸣-*nu*
14 *is-si-ni e-pu-uš*
r.1 *a-na* MÍ.ME-*ia*
2 NIN-*ia*
3 PAB-*ki* ^{md}ME–KAR-*ir*
4 *mi-i-nu ah–hur*
5 *ina* UGU DUMU.MÍ *ša áš-*⸢*pur*⸣-[*k*]*e-e-ni*
6 *lu-u ka-al-a*[*t*]
7 TA* É *lu la tu-*⸢*ṣa*⸣

8 *a-bu-tú ša* ^{m}*la*–ŠÀ-*bi*
9 *iq-ba-a-ni*
10 *ina* UGU ŠÀ-*bi-ia*

CT 53 974

1 A tablet of Gula-eṭir to Ribaya, my brother. I have blessed you before Mullissu.

5 Concerning the matter about which I wrote to you. It should be *watched over*.

8 What else? It is indeed the matter to be *watched over*. I shall be in your presence within 10 days. Do your (pl.) accounts with us.

(Second letter)

r.1 To *Me*ya, my sister, your brother Gula-eṭir.

r.4 What else?

5 Concerning *my* daughter about whom I wrote to you. Let her be detained, she should not go out of the house.

8 I have placed in my heart the word that La-libbi told me. I shall be *with* you in 10 days.

153 6 This Bel-ibni cannot be identified with certainty. 6f Or, perhaps "has insti[gated] a rebel[lion]", but so far *sīhu* does not appear in letters. Alternatively, read *is-sa-*[*ap-ra*$^{?}$ *x x*] "Bel-ibni *se*[*nt ... t*]*o* us [...]". 9 The copy suggests reading L]Ú.ERIM.[MEŠ.

154 Previous edition: Fales and Lanfranchi, Lettere no. 55, pp. 134f, 167f, 184. This tablet (BM 103016), which is in excellent condition and bears two letters to members of the sender's family in the same household, and which may concern the same matter, comes from Assur (Radner, StAT 1 p. 170 ad l. 4f). 9 Or, interpret *ši-i' ši-i'* as "Listen, listen!". r.1 Since no other names in this letter are Egyptian, the interpretation of the name as Egyptian Meia (PNA 2/II 747a) seems somewhat suspect. r.5-7, 15-16 The wording may indicate an affair which the family opposes. r.5, 15 The first-person singular suffix does not have to be written explicitly in logograms in NA.

11 *as-sa-kan-na*
12 *a-na-ku a-na* 10 UD.MEŠ
13 *ina* IGI-*ki a-na-ku*
14e *mi-nu ah–hur*
15e DUMU.MÍ ⸢LÚ⸣
16e *lu la t*[*a-mar*]

14 What else? *My* daughter should not s[ee] the man!

155. ---

K 20914
1 *a-na* LÚ*.*x*[*x x be-lí-ia*]
2 ARAD-*ka* ^{md}[*x x x x x*]
3 *lu-u* DI-*mu a*-[*na* LÚ*.*x x*]
4 *be-lí-ia* ⸢^{d}⸣[*x x x x*]
5 *a-na* LÚ.[*x x be-lí-ia*]
6 *lik-ru-b*[*u x x x x x*]
7 [*x x*]⸢*x x*⸣[*x x x x x*]
rest destroyed
Rev. uninscribed

K 20914
1 To the [..., my lord]: your servant [NN]. Good health t[o the ...], my lord! May [DN_1 and DN_2] bles[s] the [..., my lord]!

(Rest destroyed)

156. Fragment Mentioning the Chief of Trade

K 18514
beginning broken away
1′ *x x x x*]*x-an-ni x*[*x x x x*
2′ *x x x*] LÚ*.GAL–*ka-ri a*-[*x x x*
3′ *x x x*]*x ša a-na* UGU [*x x x*
4′ *x x x x*]-*nu-u-ni* [*x x x x*
e.5′ *x x x x*]-*e-a i*?-[*x x x*
6′ *x x x* E]N *x x*[*x x x*
Rev. destroyed

K 18514
(Beginning destroyed)
1 [...] *me* [...]
2 [...] the chief of trade [...]
3 [...] who *against* [...]
(Rest destroyed or too broken for translation)

157. Fragment of a Letter to the Palace Scribe

K 18872
beginning broken away
1′ *x x x x*] ⸢*a*⸣ *ak* [*x x x*
2′ *x x* LÚ.A.BA]–KUR *be-lí i*-[*x x*
3′ *x x x x*]-*ia ú-li* [*x x x*
rest uninscribed

K 18872
(Beginning destroyed)
2 [...] the [palace] scribe, my lord, [...]
3 [...] *set aside* [*for*] my [......].

155 A rare letter to an official and not to the king.
156 2 Given his potential importance, the chief of trade is probably somewhat under-represented in our sources, but he was active both in the east (SAA 19 94) and in the west (SAA 11 2 II 7 and SAA 19 38), occasionally leading military forces (SAA 4 94). For more on this official, see S. Yamada in Orient: Reports of the Society for Near Eastern Studies in Japan 40 (2005) 56f, 77-81, 84-85 and R. Mattila in Fs. Lanfranchi (2014) 405-407, 410f.
157 A fragment of a letter to the palace scribe (cf. SAA 10 130; SAA 16 48-49; SAA 19 13-14, 56, 123-124).

158. Day of the Disappearance of the Moon

K 19938
beginning broken away
1′ [*x x x*] *šá ša-x*[*x x x*]
2′ [*x x x*]*x* LUGAL *be-lí x*[*x x x*]
3′ [*x x* U]D.NÁ.ÀM *šu-*[*x x x x*]
4′ [*x x*]*x-šu* DÙG.GA *x*[*x x x x*]
5′ [*x x x x*]*x* [*x x x x x x*]
rest broken away

K 19938
(Beginning destroyed)

2 [...] the king, my lord [...]
3 [... the d]ay of the disappearance of the moon [...]
4 his [...] is good [...]
(Rest destroyed)

159. Fragment Mentioning Belet-balaṭi

K 20911
beginning broken away
1′ *x x x x x x*]*x* ⸢*is*⸣*-se-niš*
2′ *x x x x x x*]*x e-da-na-a-te*
3′ *x x x x x x*] ⸢^{d}⸣*be-lit*–TIN
4′ *x x x x x x*]*x* ⸢*ina*⸣ UGU
rest broken away
Rev. broken away

K 20911
(Beginning destroyed)
1 [......] *also*
2 [...] single [...]s
3 [......] Belet-balaṭi
(Rest destroyed or too broken for translation)

160. Setting to Work

Rm 2,16
beginning broken away
1′ [*x x*]*x-tú* [*x x x x*]
2′ ⸢*a*$^{?}$⸣*-na dul-*[*li x x x*]
3′ *da-a-*[*na*$^{?}$ *x x x*]
4′ *iṣ-ṣa-b*[*at*$^{?}$ *x x x*]
5′ *nu-qar-ra-*[*ab*$^{?}$ *x x x*]

r.1 *ha-ra-ma-*[*ma x x x*]
2 UZU.Á.2*-ni* [*x x x*]
3 *ni-šak-kan* ⸢*né*⸣*-*[*pa-áš*]
rest uninscribed

ABL 1088
(Beginning destroyed)

2 *for the* wo[rk ...]
3 *mu*[*ch* ...]
4 *seiz*[*ed* ...]
5 we will *brin*[*g* ...]
r.1 Thereaf[ter ...] we shall *set* [*to work*] *and* [*do it*].

158 [1] Or:]-*šá ša x*[*x*, e.g., "her/its [...] which".
159 [2] A feminine noun is required, cf. "single doors" in SAA 1 203 r.1. [3] Usually this divine name is written as ^{d}*be-lit*–TI.LA.
160 Originally, probably a small tablet. [1] E.g., [LÚ*.*qur-b*]*u-tú*. [3] Less likely *ṭa-a-*[*ba*$^{?}$. [4] An imperative *iṣ-ṣa* and the present tense *iz-za-x*[are also possible. [r.2f] Literally, "we will put our arms"; perhaps restore [*ina* UGU *dul-li*$^{?}$] SAA 5 294:2′ and 13 155:4 or similar (cf. SAA 13 40:9, 15f and 16 143 r.10′).

161. ---

Rm 558

1 [*a-na* LU]GAL *be-lí-*[*ia*]
2 [ARAD-*ka* ^{m}*x x x x x*]
rest of obverse broken away
Rev. beginning broken away
1′ [*x x*]*x* ⸢*am*$^{?}$⸣ *x*[*x x x*]
2′ [*x*] ⸢*ú*⸣-*rad-du-*[*u-ni*$^{?}$]
3′ [*a-n*]*a*$^{?}$ *kaq-qa-ri x*[*x x*]
4′ [*x x*]*x-mu* A.MEŠ-*ma* L[Ú*$^{?}$.*x*]
5′ [*a-n*]*a*$^{?}$ É.GAL *a-š*[*ap-par*$^{?}$]
rest uninscribed

ABL 1181

1 [To the ki]ng, [my] lord: [your servant NN].
(Break)

r.2 [...] added
3 [*t*]*o* the *ground* [...]
4 [...]... I *shall s*[*end*] water *and* the [...-*official t*]*o* the palace.

162. Appealing to the King

K 4762
Obv. destroyed
Rev. beginning broken away
1′ [*x x x x x x*]-*ta-ab x*[*x x*]
2′ [*x x x x x x*] ŠÀ URU.Š[À–URU]
3′ [*x x x x x*] *u re-eh-t*[*i*]
4′ [*x x x x x*] ⸢NUN$^{?}$⸣ *at-ti-d*[*i*$^{?}$*-in*]
5′ [*x x x x x*]-*ma*$^{?}$ *it-ta-šu-*⸢*u*$^{?}$⸣-*n*[*i*$^{?}$]
6′ [*x x x x x*] URU.⸢*na*$^{?}$⸣-*ṣir*
7′ [*x x x x*]-*bi-rat* AN-*e*

8′ [*x x x* $^{m?}$]*gab*$^{!}$-*bar i-da-bu-ub*
9′ [*ma-a ni-il*]-*lik* LUGAL *ni-hu-ru*
10′ [*x x x x*].MEŠ-*ni i-ba-áš*

11′ [*x x x x*] *ár-hiš ana-ku* TA* LUGAL
12′ [*x x ina* UG]U$^{?}$-*hi la ú-ra-me-šú-n*[*u*]
13′ [*x x x x x*] ⸢*x x x*⸣ *še*$^{?}$ [*x*]
rest broken away

ABL 1306
(Obverse destroyed)
(Break)

r.1 [......] ... [...]
2 [...... i]n/[fr]om the In[ner City]
3 [......] and the res[t]
4 [...] I *gav*[*e* ...]...
5 [......] have been taken *to m*[*e*]
6 [......] the town of *Naṣ*ir
7 [... the] ...*s* of heaven
8 [...] Gabbaru says: "[We shall g]o and appeal to the king (and then) [...]s will come to shame."
11 [... May] I quickly [...] *with* the king.
12 *I* did not *leave* the[m *because*] *of it.*
13 [......] ...
(Rest destroyed)

161 r.4 [*šu*]*l-mu* is unlikely; perhaps a plural stative like [*ka*]*r-mu* "[blo]cked; [del]ayed".

162 8 See coll. r.5 The form *it-ta-šu-*⸢*u*$^{?}$⸣-*n*[*i*$^{?}$] is a Babylonianism. r.6 The reading of the GN is uncertain; no Naṣir(u) is known from other sources. r.7 Probably a D stem participle. r.8 Although the name Gabbāru is well attested (PNA 1/II 411), the interpretation is not certain, and the name may be Sē'-gabbāri (PNA 3/I 1100a).

163. Harvesters Requested

K 1075

1 IM ^{m}[*x x x (x)*]
2 *a-na* ^{m}[*x x x (x)*]
3 *ul-t*[*u at-ta ṭup-p*]*i*
4 *ta-šá-m*[*a-a' ṭè-en-ga*]
5 *ina* UGU-*hi-i*[*a šup-ra*]
6 LÚ.*e-ṣi-du-*[*u-a*]
7 *gab-bi it-tal-*[*ku*]
8 ⸢*ù*⸣ *at-*⸢*ta*⸣ [*x (x)*]
rest broken away

Rev. beginning broken away
1′ *x x x*[*x (x)*]
2′ LÚ-*te* EN *šá e*[*n-na*]
3′ *e-te-ri a-di šá* [*en-na*]
4′ *i-ba-áš-šú im-mi-*[*du*]
5′ *ki-i ra-man-ka*
6′ *ta-ap-ta-na-ra-*[*as*]
7′ ⸢*ha*⸣*-an-ṭiš* LÚ.*e-ṣi-d*[*u*]
8′ *šup-ra la ta-k*[*a-la*]
rest (three lines) uninscribed

CT 54 7

1 A tablet of [NN] to [NN].

3 Onc[e you] hea[r] my [tablet, send your report] to m[e].

5 All [my] harvesters [are] gone, but you [...]

(Break)

r.2 Until n[ow], menfolk have increased so (much) that they have become really many by [now].

5 You are constantly making decisio[ns] on your own.

7 Send the harvester(s) quickly to me, do not de[tain] (them).

164. ---

K 1901 (+) K 7545

beginning broken away
1′ [*x x x x x x x-h*]*i-š*[*ú x (x)*]
2′ *x*[*x x x x x x x*]*-hi al-si*

3′ *ù x*[*x x x x x x a*]*-na-ku ki-n*[*ak*?]
4′ *um-ma* ^{m}*x*[*x x x x x*]*x-ru-ma la-a*
5′ *i-nam-din* [*x x x it-t*]*i-šú ir-ri-šú-ma*
6′ *a-di bal-*[*ṭa-ku x x x*]*x ul am-mar*

7′ ^{md}U.GUR–ŠE[Š-*ir x x x*]*x a-na be-lí-iá*
8′ *ki-i aq-*[*bu-ú um-ma m*]*a-la e-mu-qu*
9′ *šá* 1.*en* GIŠ.*hal-*[*li-ma-a*]*-ni lid-di-nam-ma*
10′ *a-na-ku u* LÚ.[*x x x*]*x-šú-šú it-ti*
11′ *be-lí-ia ni-*[*il-lik i*]*q-ta-ba-a*
12′ *um-ma be-lí* [*x x x*] ⸢*x x x*⸣*x-ma*
13′ *lu-uh-hi-s*[*am*?*-ma x x x x x*]
14′ PI.2.MEŠ [*x x x x x x*]
15′ *al-ta-*[*x x x x x x x*]

CT 54 33

(Beginning destroyed)

1 [......] *h*[*im* ...]

2 [......] I *read* [*on i*]*t*

3 ["]But [......] I *am loy*[*al*].

4 "N[N] should not *sell any* [...].

5 ["]They are cultivating [... wit]h him, but as long as [I] li[ve], I will not see [*any* ...].

7 Nergal-*naṣ*[*ir is* ...]. When I sa[id] to my lord, "Let him give me as many troops as a ra[f]t (holds), so I and his [...] can [go] with my lord", he said to me:

12 "My lord [......], *so*

13 "Let me retrea[t and ......]"

14 ears [......]

15 I have *s*[*ent* ......]

163 5 Or, read [*šuk-na*], but the most common meaning of *ṭēmu šakānu*, "to give orders", may not work here because the letter seems to be from a superior to an inferior. r.3 *e-te-ri* is NB pf. of *atāru,* with initial *ē*- instead of the more common *ī*-, cf. *e-te-er* Sumer 6 132:2 beside *i-te-er* ibid. 18 (CAD A/2 489a). 4 *im-mi-*[*du*] is prt. sg. 3 subj. of *mâdu (ma'ādu),* with assimilation *m' > mm,* cf. the spellings *im-i-du* listed in CAD M/1 26b. *ibašši* 'there is' has a reinforcing adverbial meaning in NA/NB.

164 7 Or: Nergal-naṣir-[...], see PNA 2/I 941.

16′ *ki-i* [*x x x x x x x*]
e.17′ *ki*$^{?}$*-r*[*i*$^{?}$ *x x x x x x*]
18′ *at* [*x x x x x x x x*]
19′ *x*[*x x x x x x x x x*]
r.1 [*a*]*-šar ta-*[*x x x x x*]
2 É*-ka-a šá* [*x x x x x*]
3 LÚ.NUN NUNDUN$^{?}$ GA [*x x x x x*]
4 *pa-ni a-mat šá be-l*[*í x x x x*]
5 *it-ti* GIŠ.[*x x x x x*]

6 *a-du-ú a-n*[*a x x x x*]
7 *liq-bi-ma* [*x x x m*]*a-la*
8 *pa-ni be-l*[*í-ia x x-n*]*im-ma*
9 *it-ti* [*x x x x*] *a-na-ku*
10 *ù* LÚ.[*x x x x*]*-ši-ib-šú*

11 *ši-hu u* [*x x x x*]*-a ṣi-bu-tu*
12 *šá be-l*[*í-ia x x x-n*]*i be-lí-iá*
13 *la* [*x x x x x x i*]*t-ti* ERIM.MEŠ
14 *šá* [*x x x x x x*]*-me*
15 [*x x x x x x x x-t*]*e*$^{?}$*-eb*
16 [*x x x x x x x x*]*-bi*

s.1 *la at-ta-šab a-na* UGU-[*hi x x x x x x*]
2 ⌜*x x*⌝*-nu-šá e-gir*$_{8}$*-ta-a a-na be-lí-ia* [*x x x x x*]

16 *when* [……]
17 … [……]
(Break)
r.1 [w]here *you* [……]
2 Is it your house *which* [……]?
3 a nobleman with … *beard* [……]
4 *before the word* of [my] lor[d ……]
5 with [……]
6 May [*my lord*] now say t[o …]
7 [a]ll the […] in the presence of [my] lord […]…
9 *with* […] I
10 and the [… *sett*]*led* him.
11 Rebellion and *my* […], the objective
12 of [my] lord […] my lord
13 *not* […… *w*]*ith* the men
14 *who* [……]
15 [……] …
16 [……] I did not settle [*ther*]*e*.
s.1 *Concerning* [……]
2 … my *letter* to my lord [……]

165. – – –

K 1978
beginning broken away
1′ [*x x*]*x x*[*x x x x x*]
2′ [*x* GA]BA.RI$^{!}$*-ka* [*x x x*]
3′ [*x-t*]*ir-ma* UR-[*x x x x*]
4′ [*x*]*x-ti šá it-t*[*i x x x x*]
5′ ⌜*i*⌝*-mu-ru áš-šá x*[*x x x x*]
6′ [*u*]*l ta-ki-is* A[D *x x x x*]

7′ *ki-ma*$^{?}$ *a'*–KUG.UD *šá* [*x x x x*]
8′ *ut-tir* ^{m}*na-di*[*n–x x x x*]
9′ *la–pa-ni* ^{m}*k*[*i-x x x x*]

10′ *áš-šá-a ú-x*[*x x x x*]
11′ *ù en-n*[*a x x x x x x*]
e.12′ *ki-i x*[*x x x x x x*]
13′ *um-m*[*a x x x x x x x*]

r.1 *x x*[*x x x x x x x x*]

2 *áš-*⌜*šá-a*⌝ [*x x x x*]

CT 54 48
(Beginning destroyed)
2 […] your [an]swer […]
3 […]… and …[……]
4 […]… who saw […] wit[h …]
5 *because* […]
6 *you* did [n]ot cut [……].
7 *If* he brings back […] *for the* silver *of* […]
8 Nadi[n-…]
9 […] from [NN].
10 *Since* [……]
11 and no[w ……]
12 *when* […]
13 saying: "[……]
r.1 [……]

2 *Since* ⌜…⌝

r.8 E.g., *an-n*]*im-ma* or KUR.N]IM.MA. r.11 In NB, though "rebellion" is written as *sīhu*.
165 2 See coll. 7 This line may have been misunderstood. 10, r.2 Alternatively, "I took".

3 KASKAL.2 *a-n*[*a x x x x*]
4 ⸢*u*⸣ *al-*⸢*kám-ma*⸣ [*x x x x*]
5 [KUG].UD *ki-i bu*$^{?}$*-di*$^{?}$ [*x x*]
6 [*x x*]*x* 2 MA.NA GÍN *x*[*x x*]
7 [*x*] ⸢*x x*⸣ TA *x* (*x*) ⸢RI⸣ [*x x x*]
8 [*x x*]*x* UGU-*hi x*[*x x x*]
9 [*x x* (*x*) L]Ú.NIGIR
10 [*x x* (*x*)]*x* MI *x*[*x x x*]
11 [*x x x*]*x* (*x*) [*x x x x x*]
rest broken away
s.1 ^{m}*še-l*[*i-bu x x x x x x x*]
2 *i-šá-aʾ-*[*al*$^{?}$ *x x x x x x x*]

3 road t[o …]
4 but come and […]
5 [silv]er *when* … […]
6 […] 2 minas and a shekel […]
7 […] … […]
8 […] *on* […]
9 […] a herald
(Break)
s.1 Šel[ebu ……]
2 *is aski*[*ng* ……]

166. – – –

K 5383
beginning broken away
1′ [*x x x x*]*x* [*x x*] *x*[*x x x*]
2′ [*x x x*] ⸢*x x*⸣ *a-na* LUGAL [*x x*]
3′ [*x x x*]-⸢*x*⸣-*ia a-na x*[*x x x*]
4′ [*x x x*] $^{md+}$AG–[*x*]*x* [*x x x x*]
5′ [^{md}*x*-K]AR-*ir* ⸢LÚ⸣.*x*[*x x x x*]
6′ [*x x x*] *šá* LUGAL [E]N-*a* [*x x x*]
7′ [*x x x*]-*ri šá* LUGAL *be-*[*lí-x x*]

8′ [*x x x* A]NŠE.KU[R.RA *x x*]
9′ [*x x x*]-⸢*ti*⸣ [*x x x x*]
10′ [*x x x*]*x* [*x x x x x*]
rest broken away
Rev. broken away

CT 54 77
(Beginning destroyed)

2 [……] to the king […]
3 [(…)] my […] to […]
4 […] Nabû-[…, …]
5 [DN-e]ṭir, the […]
6 […] *whom* the king, my [lo]rd […]
7 […] of the king, [my] lo[rd …]
8 […] hor[se(s) …]
(Rest destroyed)

167. NN Should Not Kill Me

K 5403
Obv. completely broken away
r. 1 [*x x x*]-*ma a-na* ŠÀ IGI.2 *šá* LUGAL *x*[*x x*]
2 [*x x i-d*]*u-kan-ni um-ma šá la* LUGAL [*x x*]
3 [*x x x*] ⸢*x x*⸣ *la i-du-kan-ni* [*x x*]
4 [*x x x x p*]*a-an* LUGAL ⸢*na*⸣-[*x x*]
5 [*x x x x x x x x*] ⸢*x x*⸣ [*x x x x*]
rest broken away

CT 54 88
(Beginning destroyed)
r.1 […] *in* the eyes of the king […]
2 [… will k]ill me, saying: "Without the king […]
3 […] … should not kill me […]
4 [… *bef*]*ore* the king […]
(Rest destroyed)

r.3 Possibly the idiom *harrānu ana šēpe šakānu.* r.5 *budê*-confection is possible, but not necessarily favored by the context.

168. – – –

K 5405 + K 7358

beginning broken away

1′ [*x x x x x x*] ⸢*x x*⸣
2′ [*x x x x x a*]*l-ta-ra-pi*
3′ [*x x x li*]*l-li-kám-ma*
4′ [*x x x*] ⸢*x*⸣ *šá a-ba-ku*
5′ [*x x x*] LÚ.*ki-it-ki-te-e*
6′ [*i-na* ŠÀ]*-bi ú-še-rib-ú-in-nu*
7′ [*x x x u*]*l ú-me-il-li*
8′ [*x x x*] LUGAL *na-*⸢*x*⸣

r.1 [*x x x x x x*]*-ra*
2 [*x x x x*]*-ni*
3 [*x x x x a*]*-ga-a*
4 [*x x x x*]*-ru*
5 [*x x x*] *ú-ba-ru-ti-iá*
6 [*x x x*]*-a iq-bu-ú*
7 [*x x*]*x* [*x x*] *mam-ma*

8 [*x x x*] *x*[*x x*]*-na-ti-iá*
9 [*x a*?]*-di* LÚ.EN.NAM LUGA[L *b*]*e-lí-a*
10 [*x x li*]*p-qí-du u mam-ma di-n*[*a*? *x x*]

11 [*x x*] *i-pu-uš* LUGAL *be-lí-*[*x x*]
12 [*x x*]*x-di-ia la i-*[*x x*]
13 [*x x*] ⸢*i-ṣu* LUGAL⸣ *b*[*e-lí-x x*]

rest broken away

CT 54 90

(Beginning destroyed)

2 [I] have burnt [......]
3 [let ...] come and
4 [...] *what to* lead away
5 [...] the craftsmen [...] made me enter [the]re.
7 *I* did [n]ot *fill* [...]
8 [...] the king ...
r.1 [......]
2 [......]
3 [... t]his [...]
4 [......]
5 [...] my *foreign guests*
6 [...] said
7 [...] anybody [...].
8 May the kin[g], my [l]ord, [*and* ...] appoint my [...]s [*together wi*]*th* the governor so that somebody settles [...] *cas*[*e*].
11 May the king, [*my*] lord not [...] my [...]...
13 [...] *are few*. The king, [*my*] l[ord ...]

(Rest destroyed)

169. – – –

K 5501

Obv. completely broken away
Rev. beginning broken away

1′ [*x x*] ⸢*x x* d?⸣[*x x x*]
2′ [*x x*] ⸢md⸣30–*bul-li*[*ṭ x x*]
3′ [*x x*] LÚ.DUMU–*šip-ri-šú x*[*x x*]
4′ [*x x*]*x* LUGAL *it-ti* [*x x x*]

rest uninscribed

CT 54 121

(Beginning destroyed)

r.2 [...] Sîn-bulli[ṭ ...]
3 [...] his messenger [...]
4 [...] the king *with* [...]

168 Join by M. Dietrich (--.11.1965). r.5 Or: "my residency". r.11 [*li*]*-i-pu-uš* is possible. r.13 As the top and the left side of the tablet are destroyed, this may not be the last line of the letter.

169 r.4 Alternatively, a verbal form in the perfect: "the king [...]ed".

170. ---

K 5520

beginning broken away
1′ [*x x*] ⸢*a-na-kan*⸣-[*na x x x x x*]
2′ [*x x*].KI *a-na x*[*x x x x x x*]
3′ [*x x*]-*ri* ^{md}AMAR.UTU–[*x x x x x x*]
4′ [*x x*] 3-*me* ANŠ[E.KUR.RA.MEŠ *x x x*]
5′ [^{m}*x*]*x*–^{d}U.GUR LÚ.*q*[*í-i-pi x x x x*]
6′ [*x x x*]*x a-lik* [*x x x x x*]
7′ [*x x x*]*x ri x*[*x x x x x x*]
8′ [*x x x*]*x šu* [*x x x x x x*]
9′ [*x x x*]⸢*x x*⸣[*x x x x x x*]
rest broken away

CT 54 127

(Beginning destroyed)
1 [...] here [......]
2 [...] to [......]
3 [...] Marduk-[... ...]
4 [...] 300 ho[rses ...]
5 [...]-Nergal, the de[legate ...]
6 [...] go [......]
(Rest destroyed or too broken for translation)

171. ---

K 5582

beginning broken away
1′ *x*[*x x x x x x x x x*]
2′ *x*[*x x x x x x x x x*]
3′ *na*-[*x x x x x x*]
4′ ⸢*ši-pir*⸣-[*ti x x x x x x*]
5′ ⸢*u*⸣ *x*[*x*] *šá* [*x x x x x*]
6′ *a-na x*[*x x x x x*]

7′ *ni-im-d*[*u-ud x x x x*]
8′ *it-t*[*i x x x x x*]
9′ *u en-n*[*a x x x x*]
10′ *šá* LUGAL *b*[*e-lí-ni x x x x*]

11′ *ši-pi*[*r-ti x x x x*]
12′ *šá* LUGA[L *x x x x*]
e.13′ *u ha-a*[*m x x x x*]
14′ ŠU.2 ^{m}[*x x x x x*]
r.1 *pi* ^{m}*x*[*x x x x x x*]

2 ^{d}AMAR.UTU *u* ^{d}[*zar-pa-ni-tum*?]
3 *li-pu-šu-m*[*a x x x x x*]
4 É.GAL ⸢AN⸣ [*x x x x x*]

5 *u tu-lah-h*[*i*?-*šú*? *x x x*]
6 *šá* LUGAL EN-[*i-ni x x x x*]
7 *ma* ⸢*x*⸣ *x*[*x x x x x*]
8 *šá* LUGAL *iq*-[*x x x x x*]

9 *nu-ṣal-l*[*a x x x x*]
10 *kap-da x*[*x x x x x x*]
11 *ha-an-ṭiš x*[*x x x x x*]

CT 54 140

(Beginning destroyed)

4 a lette[r ......]
5 *and* [...] of [......]
6 to [......]
7 we shall measu[re ......]
8 *wit*[*h* ......]
9 and now [...]
10 *which/who* the king, [our] l[ord ...]
11 the lett[er ...]
12 *of* the kin[g ......]
13 and gla[d ......]
14 the hand of [NN ...]
r.1 the *mouth* of [NN ...]
2 Let Marduk and [*Zarpanitu*] take action and [......]
4 the palace [......]
5 and (*where*) you *whisp*[*ered* ...]
6 *of* the king, [our] lord [...]
7 ... [......]
8 *what* the king *s*[*aid* ...]
9 we pray [to ......]
10 *are* planned [......]
11 quickly [......]

170 3-4 With so many horses (if the restoration is correct), this letter could be about Merodach-baladan.

171 r.2 Zarpanitu is the most likely restoration after Marduk, and according to some letters she clearly took an active role alongside Bel/Marduk (see, e.g., SAA 10 24 r.7f, 168 r.10-12).

12 *ina* ŠÀ-*bi x*[*x x x x x*]
13 LÚ.*šak-nu* [*x x x x x x*]
14 ⸢*x x x*⸣[*x x x x x x*]
rest broken away

12 in [......]
13 the prefect [......]
(Rest destroyed)

172. – – –

K 5807 + K 13106
beginning broken away
1′ [*x x x x*] ⸢*ak*?⸣ [*x x x x*]
2′ [*x x x*]*x a-šá-*[*x x x*]
3′ [*x x*]*-a a-na-k*[*u x x x*]
4′ [*x x*]*x a-na ṭe-e*[*m x x*]
5′ [*x a*]*l*?*-tap-ra šá iṣ-*[*x x*]
6′ [*x x*]*x* É *iš-pu-r*[*a x*]
7′ [*x x*]*x-ti šá* ^{d}EN *ú-bal-*[*laṭ*]
8′ [*x k*]*i-i ad-bu-ub*
9′ [*ul*] *i-man-gur um-ma x*[*x x*]
10′ [*x x i*?*-na*]*m-din ù* [*x x*]
11′ [*x x x x i*]*š-pu-*[*ra x*]
rest broken away
Rev. beginning broken away
1′ [*x x x x*] ⸢*ha*?⸣ [*x x x*]

2′ [*x x x a*]*l-kam-ma* [*x x*]
3′ [*x x x*]*x-ti a-na-k*[*u x x*]
4′ [*x x x x*] *la šú-ú* [*x x*]
5′ [*x x x x*] *u ú-še-*[*x x*]
6′ [*x x x x*] ^{m}*x*[*x x x*]
7′ [*x x x x*]*x*[*x x x*]
rest broken away

CT 54 169
(Beginning destroyed)

2 *I* ...[...]
3 I [*have* ...] *my* [...]
4 [...] to the *repo*[*rt of* ...] *I* have *written*. ...[...]
6 [...] *of the temple* wrote *to* [*me*]
7 [...]... *whom* Bel will *revi*[*ve*]
8 [... *wh*]*en* I spoke
9 he does [not] agree: "[...]
10 [... gi]ves and [...]
11 [... w]ro[te ...]
(Break)
r.2 [... c]ome and [...]
3 [...]... I [...]
4 [...]... he/it [...]
5 [...] ...[...]
6 [...] N[N]
(Rest destroyed)

173. Do Not Forsake Me in Their Hands

K 6147
beginning broken away
1′ [*x x x x x x x x x x*] ⸢*x x x*⸣
2′ [*x x x x x x x x b*]*e-lí-šú-nu* [*x x*]
3′ [LUGAL *be-lí-a ina* ŠU.2*-š*]*ú-nu la ú-maš-šar-an-ni*

4′ [*x x x x x* Š]À-*bi ša* LUGAL.MEŠ
5′ [*x x x x x*] *a-na-ku bal-ṭa-ku*
6′ [*x x x x x šu*]*-ú ù šu-nu*
7′ [*x x x x x x i*]*t-ta-šu-u*
other side destroyed

CT 54 172
(Beginning destroyed)

2 [......] their [l]ord [...]
3 [The king, my lord], should not forsake me in [th]eir [hands].
4 [...... *the mo*]*od* of kings
5 [......] I am alive
6 [...... h]e and they
7 [...... ha]ve *taken*
(Rest destroyed)

172 Join by M. Dietrich (--.11.1965). There may be more missing on the left than is indicated in the transliteration. 7 E.g., something like [LÚ.EN–*pi-q*]*i*?*-ti*, "[an offici]al", which is not exactly what one would expect.

174. ---

K 7425

beginning broken away

1′ [*x x x x x*]

2′ [*x x x x*]-*šú*

3′ [*x x x x*] ^{d}UTU

4′ [*x x x*] DINGIR.MEŠ

5′ [*x x i*]-*šá-as-si*

6′ [*x x-i*]*k-kan-ni*

7′ [*x x x ú-m*]*an-di*

8′ [*x x x x*.M]EŠ

rest broken away

CT 54 190

(Beginning destroyed)

2 [...] his/him [...]

3 [...] Šamaš

4 [...] gods

5 [*he*] *calls out* [*to* ...]

6 [*who ca*]*me*

7 [... I/he *noti*]*fied*

8 [... ...]s

(Rest destroyed)

175. ---

K 13050

beginning broken away

1′ [*x*.M]EŠ É [*x x x x x*]

2′ [*x x*]*x-nu uk*-⸢*x*⸣ [*x x x x x*]

3′ [*x x im-q*]*u-tu* [*x x x x*]

4′ [*x x x x*] A.ŠÀ.MEŠ *šá* [*x x x x*]

e.5′ [*x x x*] *mah-ru-tu* [*x x x x*]

6′ [*x x x x*]*x na-šá-a-ni* [*x x x x*]

r.1 [*x x x*] *i-nam-di-n*[*u x x x x*]

2 [*x x x*] 3-*lim* 10 *piš-k*[*i x x x x*]

3 [*x x x*].MEŠ-*ni ep-šá* [*x x x x*]

4 [*x a-na*] *pa-an* LUGAL *i*[*l-tap-ru x x*]

5 [*x x x*] *me u a*[*t-x x x x x*]

6 [*x x x x*] *šá i*-[*x x x x x*]

rest broken away

CT 54 242

(Beginning destroyed)

1 [...]s, a house [......]

2 [...] ... [......]

3 [...] he/they [fe]ll [...]

4 [...] the fields which [...]

5 the previous [......]

6 [...] were brought to me [...]

r.1 [...] they giv[e ...]

2 [...] 3,010 *wrongful demands* [...]

3 do [...]s! [...]

4 [...] w[rote t]o the king [...]

(Rest destroyed or too broken for translation)

176. Fragment Concerning the Palace Scribe

K 13051

beginning broken away

1′ [*x x x x x x x x x x*] *x*[*x*]

2′ [*x x x x x x x x x x*]-*bu*

rest broken away

Rev. beginning broken away

1′ [*x x x-n*]*a u a-na* UGU LUGAL [*x x*]

2′ [*x x x* ŠE]Š *šá ta-ra-man-ni* [*x x*]

CT 54 243

(Beginning destroyed)

r.1 [...] and to the king [...]

2 [... the broth]er you love [...]

174 [3] Or a PN [...]-Šamaš. [6] But orthographically [*ša*/*šá il-lik*^{i}]^{k}-*kan-ni* or [*ša*/*šá il-li-i*]*k-kan-ni* is suspect.

175 [2] E.g., [LÚ.*ša*]*k-nu*.

3′ [*x x x x*]*x* AD-*ú-a* AMA-*a ù* N[IN]-*a*
4′ [*x x x x*] *a-na* EN-*iá ta-at-tur*
5′ [*x x x i*]*l-li-ku a-na-ku šá ram-ni-iá*
6′ [*x x x x*] *it-mi-šum u a-na* UGU

7′ [*x x x i*]*ṭ-ru-ú u* NINDA.HI.A ZÍD.DA
8′ [*x x x x*]*x šá iš-šú-ú* LÚ.DUB.SAR–[KUR?]
9′ [*x x x ina*?] *pa-ni it-ta-ši u*[*m-ma*]

10′ [*x*]*x šá-kin* LÚ.DUB.SAR–É.[GAL]
11′ [*x*] *i-na-áš-šam-m*[*a*] ⸢*x*⸣ *x*[*x x*]
12′ [*x-h*]*a*? *ú-*[*x x x x*]
rest broken away

3 […] my father, mother and si[ster]
4 […] you returned to my lord
5 [… w]ent, I on my own
6 […] he swore to him, *but* they [*h*]*it* […].
7 Moreover, bread, flour […] which he took, the [*palace*] scribe *has taken* [*be*]*fore* […], saying: "[…] was placed.
10 The pa[lace] scribe will take […] an[d …]
(Rest destroyed or too broken for translation)

177. Bowls to the King

K 13152
beginning broken away
1′ [*x x x* LÚ.DUB.S]AR ᵐ[*x x x*]
2′ [*x x x x x*] *kap-pa-a-n*[*i*]
3′ [*x x x x x*] LUGAL *lu-še-bi-l*[*a*]
e.4′ [*x x x x x*] 1 MU.AN.NA
5′ [*x x x x x*] *i-pu-šú*
6′ [*x x x x x*]-*e ú-sa-*⸢*ka*⸣
r.1 [*x x x x x*] LUGAL *ú-ma-aṭ-ṭi*
2 [*x x x x x-b*]*i ma-a* LÚ.SA[G?]
3 [*x x x x x x*]-*ú-m*[*a x x*]
4 [*x x x x x x* L]UGAL *u* [*x x*]
rest broken away

CT 54 253
(Beginning destroyed)
1 [… scri]be (*and*) [NN ……]
2 The king should send […] bowls.
4 [……] one year
5 [……] *they* did
6 [……] I/he *strain*/s
r.1 [… *of*] the king *reduced*
2 [… sai]d: "A *eunu*[*ch*]
3 [……] … […]
4 […… the k]ing and […]
(Rest destroyed)

178. ---

K 13168
beginning broken away
1′ [*x*] ⸢*x x x x*⸣ *x*[*x x x x*]
2′ [*x*] *at-ta-ṣa-a* [*x x x x*]
3′ [*il*]-*ta-kan mam-ma i*[*na x x x x x*]
4′ [*x*] *it-ti-iq šá* [*x x x x*]
5′ [*x* L]Ú.*šak*?-*nu ù šá* [*x x x x*]
6′ [*x*]-*tu-ku um-*⸢*ma*⸣ *en-*[*na x x x*]
7′ [*x*] LUGAL *ul-te-en-ni* [*x x x x*]
8′ [*x x*] *ul gu*? *ʾa* [*x x x x*]
rest broken away

CT 54 255
(Beginning destroyed)

2 […] I came out. [He *p*]*laced* […].
3 Someone *fr*[*om* …]
4 passes […] *who* […]
5 […] the *prefect* and the […]
6 […]… saying, "no[w …]
7 […] the king has *changed* […]
(Rest destroyed or too broken for translation)

176 r.7 Or, *iṭ*]-*ṭe*$_4$-*ru-ú*, as CAD Ṭ 194a reads the first word.
177 2 Cf. SAA 13 50 r.3. 3 The beginning of the line may contain a metal, e.g., "[silver]" or "[copper]". Alternatively, it is not impossible that the king is the recipient of the bowls: "Let *me* send […] bowls [*to*] the king". 6 Possibly *me*]-*e ú-sa-ka* "I/he strain/s [wat]er". r.2 *mā* is an Assyrianism.
178 7 Or: "the king has repeated".

179. – – –

K 13822
Obv. broken away
Rev. beginning broken away
1′ [*x x x x*] ⸢*x x x x*⸣ [*x x*]
2′ [*x x x x*]*x ù ṭup-pi* ⸢*x*⸣ [*x x*]
3′ [LUGAL *be-l*]*í-a ki-i iš-ṭu-*[*ru*]
4′ [*x x x x*]*x* ^{m}*mar-du*[*k* 0$^{?}$]
5′ [*x x x x x*] *il-li-*[*ka* 0]
6′ [*x x x x x*]*x* LUGAL *lu-kal-*[*lim*]
7′ [*x x x x x*] LUGAL *li-*[*x x x*]
8′ [*x x x p*]*a-ni na-aṣ-b*[*i*$^{?}$*-x*]
9′ [*x x x x-t*]*i i-x*[*x x x*]
10′ [*x x x x x x*] *u* ^{d}UTU [*x x x*]
11′ [*x x x x x x*] É [*x x x*]
12′ [*x x x x x x x*]*x*[*x x x*]
rest broken away

CT 54 260
(Beginning destroyed)

r.2 […] and the tablet [… the king], my [lor]d wrot[e]
4 […] Mardu[ku]
5 [……] cam[e].
6 May the king sho[w *it* ……]
7 […] let the king […]
8 […] … […]
9 [……] … […]
10 [……] and Šamaš […]
(Rest destroyed or too broken for translation)

180. – – –

K 14142
beginning broken away
1′ [*x x x x x x x x x*]*x a*$^{?}$ [*x x x x x x*]
2′ [*x x x x x x p*]*a-an hu x*[*x x x x x*]
3′ [*x x x x x m*]*i te na a-k*[*an-na x x*]
4′ [*x x x x x x*] *áš-šap-pil sa*[*g*$^{?}$ *x x x x*]
5′ [*x x x x*] *nu iš kiš ia-*[*x x x*]
6′ [*x x x x t*]*a-na*[*m-s*]*u*$^{?}$*-ú* [*x x x x*]
7′ [*x x x x*]*x ti x*[*x x x x x x*]
8′ [*x x x x x x x x x x x x*]
rest broken away
Rev. beginning broken away
1′ [*x x x x x x x*]*x* ⸢*ú*⸣ [*x x x x x*]
2′ [*x x x x x*]*x-al* ⸢*ra*⸣*-*[*x x x x*]
3′ [*x x x x x*] ⸢*x*⸣ ANŠE.KUR.⸢RA⸣.M[EŠ *x x x x*]
4′ [*x x x x x*]*x* LUGAL-*ú-tú ina* ⸢KUR.*ha-za*⸣-[*x x x x*]
5′ [*x x x x x x x* ^{m}*k*]*u-ri-gal-z*[*u x x x x*]
6′ [*x x x x x x x x*] ⸢*x x dan x x x*⸣ [*x x*]
7′ [*x x x x x x*]*x-*⸢*i a*⸣*-nam-din-ú-ka* [*x x*]
8′ [*x x x x x x-k*]*a*$^{?}$*-a a-na ul-l*[*i*]*-t*[*i x x*]
9′ [*x x x x x x x x*]*-*⸢*ti*⸣ *ki-iṣ-ru* [*x x x*]
10′ [*x x x x x x x x x*] ⸢*mir*$^{?}$⸣ [*x x x*]
rest broken away

CT 54 265
(Obverse destroyed or too broken for translation)

r.3 [……] horses […]
4 [……] the kingship in the land of Haza[…]
5 […… K]urigalzu […]
6 [……] …… […]
7 [……] that I will give to you […]
8 […] *do* [*yo*]*ur* […] to *the f*[*a*]*r* […]?
9 [……] cohort […]
(Rest destroyed or too broken for translation)

179 r.6 Or, "let […] sho[w] *it* [to] the king"; the above-mentioned tablet may be the object of the clause.
180 r.5 The personal name Kurigalzu is rarely attested in NA-NB sources and, as in this case, mostly under rather cryptic circumstances (see PNA 2/I 640f).

181. – – –

K 14593
beginning broken away
1′ *[x x x x x x x x x x x x]* ⸢*di*⸣ *[x]*
2′ *[x x x x x x x x x x x ú]-še-ṣi*

3′ *[x x x x x x x x x x x x]*⸢*x x*⸣*-ti*

4′ *[x x x x x x x x x x x x]* $^{md+}$AG–*ú-še-zib*
5′ *[x x x x x x x x x x x x]x* URU.MEŠ
6′ *[x x x x x x x x x x x x]x*
7′ *[x x x x x x x x x x* $^{md+}$A]G–NUMUN–DÙ
rest broken away

Rev. beginning broken away
1′ *[x x x x x x x x x x x x]* ⸢*x*⸣ *[x x x x]*
2′ *[x x x x x x]-r[u] ta-mur-*⸢*ma x*⸣ *[x]*
3′ *[x x x x x r]u*$^?$ *iš-[x x x]* GÍN KUG.UD
4′ *[x x x x x]-ri [x x x i-hi]-ṭu-ma*
5′ *[x x x x x]* ^{d}PA *x[x x x x x x š]ú-nu*
6′ *[x x x x x]-din [x x x x x x x]-ru*
7′ *[x x x x x x x x x x x x]* ERIM.MEŠ
8′ *[x x x x x] ú-[x x x x x x x x]x*
9′ *[x x x x x]x[x x x x x]x-nu-šú*
10′ *[x x x x x x]x a-na* UGU-*hi [x x x]*
rest as far as preserved, uninscribed

CT 54 267
(Beginning destroyed)

2 [...... br]ought out

---

3 [......]

---

4 [......] Nabû-ušezib
5 [......] cities
6 [......]
7 [...... Na]bû-zeru-ibni
(Break)

r.2 [...] you saw and [...]
3 [......] ... [...] shekels of silver
4 [...... *did wr*]*ong* and
5 [......] Nabû [...... t]hey
6 [......]
7 [......] men
8 [......]
9 [......]... him
10 [......] to [...]

182. – – –

K 14639
beginning broken away
1′ *[x x x x x]* ⸢*x*⸣ *[x x x]*
2′ *[x x x x] i-ba-á[š-ši*$^?$*]*
3′ *[ki-i* LUGAL *b]e-lí-a ha-d[u]-ú*
4′ *[x x x-an]-na-ši*
5′ *[x x a-na pa-n]i*$^?$ LUGAL *i-tab-ku*

6′ *[x x x x] il-tap-ra-an-na-šú*
7′ *[x x e-te*$^?$*]-riš-an-na-ši*
8′ *[x x x x x]-ni-šú-ka*
9′ *[x x x x x x] ni-ma-ti*
10′ *[x x x x x x x-r]a*
11′ *[x x x x x x x]-ri*
rest broken away

CT 54 273
(Beginning destroyed)

2 [...] ther[e is].
3 [If the king], my [l]ord, wishes, [*let them* ...] us. They brought [...] in[to] the king['s *presen*]*ce*.
6 [...] wrote to us
7 [... *requ*]*ested* of us
8 [... *they* ...]... *to* you
9 [......] we will die
(Break)

181 Previous edition: de Vaan Bel-ibni 343f, but it is uncertain whether this is a fragment by Bel-ibni (PNA 2/II 904b s.v. Nabû-ušēzib, no. 5a).
182 [8] Perhaps something like *lu/ú-šak*]*-ni-šú-ka*, the latter option, e.g., "[*they* made ... su]bmit to you".

Rev. beginning broken away
1′ [*x x x x x x x x*]
2′ [*x x x x x x x x*]
3′ [*x x x x x x x x*]
4′ [*x x x x x x x-b*]*i*
5′ [*x x x x x x x x*]-*ma-at*
6′ [*x x x x x x x*]-*niš-ši*
7′ [*x x x x x x x*]–$^{d+}$AG
8′ [*x x x x x x x i*]*l-li-ku*
9′ [*x x x x x x x i*]*k-ta-ba-as*
10′ [*x x x x x x x*] *un-de-el-li*
11′ [*x x x x x x x* AD]-*ka u* AD–AD.ME[Š-*k*]*a*
12′ [*x x x x x x x x* L]UGAL *be-l*[*í-ia*]
13′ [*x x x x x x x x x*]*x šá* [*x x*]
rest broken away

r.6 [……] *her/it*
7 […… …]-Nabû
8 […… w]ent
9 [……] he *set foot*
10 [……] filled up
11 [……] your [father] and grandfathers
12 […… the k]ing, [my] lord
(Rest destroyed or too broken for translation)

183. – – –

K 14669
beginning broken away
1′ [*x x x x*]*x* [*x x x x*]
2′ [*x x x b*]*e-lí-i*[*a*]
3′ [*x x u*]*m-ma*
4′ [*x x* G]IŠ.MI LUGAL *be-lí-iá*

5′ [*x x*] *u ke-e-ni*
6′ [*x x*] LÚ.*kab-tu*
7′ [*x x i*]*t-ti-šú*
8′ [*x x x*] *a-na-ku*
9′ [*x x x*]*x*.MEŠ
10′ [*i-qab*]-*ba-a*
11′ [*x x p*]*a-ni*
12′ [*x x x*].MEŠ
13′ [*x x x x x*]

r.1 [*x x x x x*]
2 [*x x x x*]-*iá*
3 [*x x x x-n*]*u*
4 [*x x x*] É–AD-*iá*
5 [*x x x*]*x-ú-nu*
6 [*x x ṣ*]*a*$^{?}$ *li-iṣ-bat*
7 [*li*$^{?}$-*i*]*l-lik it-ti-šú-nu*
8 [*x x x*] *ki-i*
9 [*x x x x*] LUGAL EN-*iá*
10 [*x x x x*] *šá*
11 [*x x x x x*]-*lid*
12 [*x x x x x x*]*x*
rest broken away

CT 54 278
(Beginning destroyed)

2 […] m[y l]ord
3 […]: "[(…) under the pro]tection of the king, my lord
5 […] and righteous
6 […] an important person
7 [… w]ith him
8 […] I
9 […]s
10 [tel]ls me
11 [*in the pre*]*sence of* […]s
(Break)

r.2 my […]
3 [……]
4 […*s have* …] my paternal house.
6 May he seize […],
7 go (and) […] with them.
8 *If* [… of/to] the king, my lord
(Rest destroyed or too broken for translation)

r.6 Or, read, e.g., *ul*] *niš-ši* "we did not *take* […]".
183 Perhaps much more is missing from the left than the translation indicates. 5 This line may refer to the king.
r.6 Or, perhaps more likely -*i*]*á li-iṣ-bat*.

184. ---

K 15048
beginning broken away
1′ [*x x x*]*x mim x*[*x x x x*]
2′ [*x x* ŠE]Š-*a ih-ta-*[*x x x x*]
3′ [*x x x*]*x* DUMU.MEŠ [*x x x x*]
4′ [*x x*]*-nu i-da-*[*x x x x*]
5′ [*x ul*]*-tu* MU.MEŠ [*x x x x*]
6′ [*x ul-t*]*e-eš-mi al-*[*x x x x*]
7′ [*x x*]*-ti šá* LUGAL *x*[*x x x x*]
8′ [*x x x*]*x ki-i šu-*[*x x x x*]
9′ [*x x x r*]*am-ni-ia* [*x x x x*]
10′ [*x x* LUG]AL *i-na* ŠÀ-*b*[*i x x x*]
11′ [*x x in*]*a* ŠÀ-*bi* KUR–*aš-*[*šur*.KI *x x*]
12′ [*x x x*]*-na šá a-*[*x x x x*]
13′ [*x x x*]*x ti x*[*x x x x*]
rest broken away
Rev. completely broken away

CT 54 288
(Beginning destroyed)

2 [...] my [broth]er has [......]
3 [...] the sons [...]
4 [...] ... [...]
5 [... f]or years [...]
6 [... I inf]ormed (*and*) [...]
7 [...] *of* the king [......]
8 [...] *like* [...]
9 [... m]yself [...]
10 [... the ki]ng *in* [...]
11 [... i]n As[syria ...]
12 [*NN*] *who* [...]
(Rest destroyed or too broken for translation)

185. ---

K 15068
beginning broken away
1′ [*x x x x*] ⸢*x*⸣ [*x x x*]
2′ [*x x i*]*-kaš-ša-d*[*u x x*]
3′ [*x x x*]*-a-ti x x*[*x x x*]
4′ [*x x x*] *it-tan-nu* [*x x*]
5′ [*x x x*]-⸢*ti*⸣-*šú a-na* [*x x x*]
6′ [*x x x*]*x* LÚ.*ra-i-*[*ma-nu šá*?]
7′ [*x a-na*?]*-ku dib-bi* [*x x x*]
8′ [*x x x*] ⸢*x*⸣ *šá* KUR.*x*[*x x x x*]
9′ [*x x x x x*] ⸢*x*⸣ [*x x x x*]
rest broken away

CT 54 290
(Beginning destroyed)

2 [... they will] reach [...]
3 [...]s [...]
4 [...] they gave [...]
5 his [...] to [...]
6 [... *I a*]*m* a lo[ver of ...]. The words [...]
8 [...] *of* the land [...]
(Rest destroyed)

186. ---

K 15077
beginning broken away
1′ *x*[*x x x x x x*]
2′ ⸢É?⸣ [*x x x x x x*]
3′ *um-*[*ma x x x x x*]
4′ md+A[G?–*x x x x x*]
5′ *ù* [*x x x x x x*]
6′ *k*[*i-i x x x x x x*]
7′ [*x x x x x x x*]

CT 54 292
(Beginning destroyed)

3 "[......]
4 Na[bû-... ...]
5 and [......]
6 *wh*[*en* ......]

184 4 Possibly a form of *dabābu* or *dâku*. 6 This could be a hendiadys.
185 7 Perhaps restore [LUGAL? *a-na*]*-ku*.

e.8′ [*x x x x x x x*]
9′ *x*[*x x x x x x*]
10′ *šá* [*x x x x x x*]
11′ KUR [*x x x x x x*]
12′ *mìn-d*[*e-e-ma x x x*]

r.1 DAM-*s*[*u x x x x x*]
2 *lu-ú* DA[M *x x x x*]
3 DINGIR.MEŠ-*k*[*a ina* ŠU.2 *x x*]
4 *i-man-nu-*[*ú x x x x*]
5 *li-in-qu-*[*tu x x x*]
6 ŠÀ-*bu-ú šá* [*x x x x*]
7 [*x*]⸢*x x*⸣[*x x x x x*]
rest broken away

(Break)

10 *who* [......]
11 *the land* [*of* ......]
12 perh[aps ...]
r.1 hi[s] wife [......] or the wif[e *of* ...] yo[ur] gods will deliver [*her* into the hands of ...].
4 Let [...] *fal*[*l* ...]
6 just like that [...]
(Rest destroyed)

187. ---

K 15078
beginning broken away
1′ ⸢*x x*⸣ *x*[*x x x x x*]
2′ ERIM.MEŠ ⸢É⸣ [*x x x x x*]
3′ UN *šá* A[D-*šú x x x*]
4′ ^{m}*ra-a-nu x*[*x x x x x*]
5′ *ki-i la a-*[*x x x x x*]
6′ *um-ma* DUMU [*x x x x x*]
7′ É ^{m}ŠEŠ.M[EŠ-*šá-a x x*]
8′ *a-na in*$^{?}$ *x*[*x x x x x*]
9′ *i-tab-ba*[*k x x x x*]
10′ [*x x*] ⸢*x*⸣ [*x x x x x*]
rest broken away

CT 54 293
(Beginning destroyed)

2 the men of the house [*of* ......]
3 the *people* of [his] fat[her ...]
4 Ranu [......]
5 *whether I* not [......]
6 saying: "the son [*of* ......]
7 the house of Ahhe[šaya ...]
8 to ...[......]
9 pour[s ......]
(Rest destroyed)

188. ---

K 15127
beginning broken away
1′ [*x x x x x x*] *x*[*x x x*]
2′ [*x x x*] ZÍD 2-*me* 20 GÚ.[UN *x x x*]
3′ [*x k*]*it-ti* ŠE.BAR *šá* LÚ.*a-*[*x x*]
4′ [(*x*) *x m*]*a-a'-da as si* ⸢É$^{?}$⸣ [*x x*]
5′ [*ina*] ŠU.2-*šú-nu* LUGAL *be-lí l*[*i-x x*]
6′ [*x*]*x-tu-ma šú-ú šá a-n*[*a x x x*]

7′ [*x x*]*x e-reš x*[*x x x x x*]
8′ [*x x ú*]-*ṣu-ú* [*x x x x x*]
9′ [*x x x*]*x* [*x x x x x x x*]
rest broken away
Rev. completely broken away

CT 54 295
(Beginning destroyed)

2 [...] flour, 220 tale[nts ...].
3 [*In t*]*ruth*, the barley of the [...]
4 *I* ... much [...], *the house* [...]
5 let the king, my lord, [... into] their hands.
6 It is the [...]... who/which t[o ...]
7 [...] sow [...]
8 [... g]o(es) ou[t [...]
(Rest destroyed)

187 [2] Possibly ⸢É⸣–[AD-*šú*$^{?}$]; cf. the following line. [3] The singular UN is surprising.
188 [4] *as-si* is unlikely to be an Assyrianism, "I read", maybe the last sign is not ⸢É$^{?}$⸣.

189. ---

K 15357

beginning broken away

1′ [*x x x*]*x ri* ⌜*x*⌝ [*x x x*]
2′ [*x x x*]*x ù* [*x x x*]
3′ [*x x*.K]I-*a-a šá* [*x x x*]
4′ [*x x il*]-*du-du* [*x x x*]
5′ [*x x x*]*x* ERIM.M[EŠ *x x*]
6′ [*x x x*]*x*.MEŠ *x*[*x x x*]
7′ [*x x x*]*x* DUMU *šá* [*x x x*]
8′ [*x x* D]UMU *ri*-[*x x x*]
9′ [*x x x*]-*lak-ku*$^{?}$ [*x x x*]
e.10′ [*x x x*]*x* DUMU *š*[*á x x x*]
11′ [*x x x*] ⌜*x x*⌝ [*x x x*]
12′ [*x x x x x x x*]
13′ [*x x x x*]*x*[*x x*]
r.1 [*x x x*]*x du*-[*x x x x*]
2 [*x x x*]*x* UGU *x*[*x x x x*]
3 [*x x x*] *bir-ti* [*x x x x*]
4 [*x x i*]-*qab-bu*-[*ú x x x*]
5 [*x x x*]*x ha-ra*-[*x x x x*]
6 [*x x x*]*x ka šá x*[*x x x x*]
7 [*x x x*]*x-šú-nu gab-b*[*i x x*]
8 [*x x x*]*x*[*x x x x x*]

rest broken away

CT 54 309

(Beginning destroyed)

2 [...] and [...]
3 the *men* [of ...] who [...]
4 [... *dr*]*agged* [...]
5 [...] men [...]
6 [...]s [...]
7 [...] son of [...]
8 [... s]on [...]
9 [... *c*]*omes* [...]
10 [...] son o[f ...]

(Break)

r.3 [...] between [...]
4 [... s]ay [...]
5 [...] ... [...]
6 [...] ... [...]
7 [...] all their [......]

(Rest destroyed)

190. ---

K 15403

beginning broken away

1′ [*x x x x*] ⌜*x x*⌝ [*x x x*]
2′ [*x x ni-il*]-*te-mu-ú a-n*[*a* IGI$^{?}$]
e.3′ [LUGAL EN-*i-ni*] *ni-šap-p*[*a-ra*]

blank line

r.1 [LUGAL EN-*a-ni i*]-*di ki-i* $^{\text{md+}}$A[G–*x x*]
2 [*x x x x*]-*e-mu ù la* [*x x x x*]
3 [*x x x x*]*x bab-ba-nu*-⌜*ú*⌝ [*x x*]
4 [*x x x x*]-*ú a-ša*[*r x x x x*]
5 [*x x x x x*]⌜*x x*⌝ [*x x x x x*]

rest broken away

CT 54 315

(Beginning destroyed)

1 [*if* we h]ear [*any news*], we shall writ[e] t[o the king, our lord].

r.1 [The king, our lord, k]nows that Na[bû-...]
2 [... *ne*]*ws* and *non*-[......]
3 [...] good [...]
4 [......] wher[e ...]

(Rest destroyed)

189 9 For a possible *il*]-*lak-ku*, see, e.g., SAA 17 155 r.5, 9. r.5 E.g., *ha-ra*-[*bu*/*pu*. r.6 Perhaps "your [...] who" or *ka-šá* "to you".

191. Chaldeans in Calah

K 15406

beginning broken away

1′ [*x x* LÚ.*k*]*al*$^{?}$-⸢*di*$^{?}$⸣ *x*[*x x*]
2′ [*x x ma*]-*a*ʾ-*d*[*a x x*]
3′ [*x x* L]Ú.*kal-di* [*x x*]
4′ [*x x x i*]*na* URU.*kal-h*[*i x x*]
5′ [*x x x*] *ram-n*[*u x x*]
6′ [*x x x*]*x*[*x x x*]

rest broken away

CT 54 317

(Beginning destroyed)

1 [… *the Ch*]*aldeans* […]
2 [… m]an[y …]
3 […] the Chaldeans […]
4 [… i]n Cala[h …]
5 […] *on* [*their*] *ow*[*n*]

(Rest destroyed)

192. Fragment of a Letter about Blood *Money*

K 15615

beginning broken away

1′ *šá a*-⸢*na*⸣ U[GU *x x x x*]
2′ *i-dab-bu*-[*x x x x x*]
3′ *da-mu šá* L[Ú$^{?}$ *x x x x x*]
4′ *at-ta*-⸢*din*$^{?}$⸣ [*x x x x x*]
5′ *it-ta-din* [*x x x x x x*]
r.1 *i-na* KÁ ⸢*x x x x*⸣ [*x x x*]
2 *um-ma x*[*x x x x x x x*]
3 [*x*]*x* AN *x*[*x x x x x x*]

rest broken away

CT 54 318

(Beginning destroyed)

1 who is/are speak[ing …] again[st …].

3 I have *paid* the blood *money* for the […...]

5 he *gave* […...]

r.1 at the … gate […]

2 saying, "[……]

(Rest destroyed)

193. – – –

K 15625

beginning broken away

1′ [*x x x x x x*]*x x*[*x x x*]
2′ [*x x x x x* N]UN$^{?}$.KI [*x x x*]
3′ [*x x x x x*]*x la* [*x x x*]
4′ [*x x ul*$^{?}$ *id-b*]*u-ub* [*x x x*]
5′ [*x x x x*] ⸢*i*⸣-*na-as-s*[*a*$^{?}$-*ah x x*]
6′ [*x x* TIN.T]IR$^{?}$.KI *i-x*[*x x x*]
7′ [*x x x x*]*x* ^{d}UTU *i-x*[*x x x*]
8′ [*x x x x*] *a-mur*$^{?}$-*a*ʾ *l*[*a x x*]
9′ [*x x* KUR–*aš*]-*šur*.KI [*x x x x*]
10′ [*x x x x*]-*nu-šú*$^{?}$ [*x x x x*]

rest broken away

CT 54 319

(Beginning destroyed)

2 [… *E*]*ridu* […]
3 […] *not* […]
4 [… *did not* spe]ak […]
5 […] will *remo*[*ve* …]
6 [… *Baby*]*lon* […]
7 […] Šamaš […]
8 […] *I saw* […]
9 [… As]syria […]
10 […] *him*/*his* […]

(Rest destroyed)

192 4 However, if the reading is *at-ta-d*[*i*, then the predicate is more likely to be from *nadû* than from *nadānu* (cf. line 5).
193 2 Or: UD.KIB.N]UN$^{?}$.KI "*Sipp*]*ar*". 4 Or: *i-dab-b*]*u-ub*, etc. 6 Alternatively, read *x*]*x ki-i x*[*x*.

194. – – –

K 15643

beginning broken away
1′ [*x x x*] ⸢*x x x*⸣ [*x x x x x*]
2′ [*x x i*]*l-ta-ṭar x*[*x x x x x*]
3′ [*x x x*]*-ba-la a-n*[*a*? *x x x x x*]
4′ [*x x x*] *ba-lu-us-s*[*a x x x x*]
5′ [*x x x*] *um-ma am-ma-*[*ru x x x x*]
6′ [*x x x k*]*i-i* 1.*en x*[*x x x x x*]
7′ [*x x x x*]*x*.MEŠ-*šú* [*x x x x x x*]
rest broken away

CT 54 320

(Beginning destroyed)
2 [... he has] written [...]
3 [... *br*]*ings t*[*o* ...]
4 [...] *without he*[*r* ...]
5 [...] saying: "*I se*[*e* ...]
6 [... *a*]*s one* [...]
7 [...] his [...]s [......]
(Rest destroyed)

195. – – –

K 15687

beginning broken away
1′ [*x x x*] ⸢*x*⸣ [*x x x x x*]
2′ [*x* LU]GAL KUR–KÚR [*x x x x x*]
3′ [*x x*] *du làh x*[*x x x x x*]
4′ [*x* NU]MUN *i-ša*[*k-kan x x x x*]
5′ [*x x*] LUGAL *s*[*i-x x x x x*]
e.6′ [*x x*]*x* BAR *is-*[*x x x x x*]
r.1 [*x-n*]*a*? LUG[AL *x x x x x*]
2 [*x x*]*-da ina* U[GU *x x x x x*]
3 [*i-ša*]*l-lal-šú is-*[*x x x x x*]
4 [*x x x x*] ⸢*x*⸣ [*x x x x x*]
rest broken away

CT 54 322

(Beginning destroyed)
2 [... the k]ing [...] the enemy country [(...)]
3 [...] ... [......]
4 [...] will pl[ace] seed [......]
5 [...] the king [......]
6 [...] ... [......]
r.1 [...] the ki[ng, [......]
2 [...] *Concer*[*ning* ......]
3 [will ta]ke him captive [......]
(Rest destroyed)

196. – – –

K 15689

beginning broken away
1′ [*x x x x*] *š*[*ú*? *x x x x x*]
2′ [*x x x*] ⸢*nu*? *a*?⸣ É LÚ.[*x x x*]
3′ [*x x x*]*x* ERIM.MEŠ *a-g*[*a-nu-tu x*]
4′ [*x x x*] *i-di-ni ni x*[*x x x*]
5′ [*x x* U]ZU.SILIM *a-ga-a mur-*[*ru-ur x*]
6′ [*x x x*] *a-ki-i* KUG.GI 1 [GÚ.UN? *x x*]
7′ [*x x x x x*] *a-ka*[*n*?*-na x x x*]
rest broken away

CT 54 323

(Beginning destroyed)
2 [...] the house of the [...]
3 [...] th[ese] men [(...)]
4 [...] he *sold* [...]
5 [...] this 'well-being' is *chec*[*ked* ...]
6 [...] *like* gold of 1 [*talent* ...]
7 [......] *he*[*re* ...]
(Rest destroyed)

194 4 I.e., one might expect *ba-lu-uš-ša*.
195 The wording of this fragment may suggest that it is not a letter, but perhaps a query (SAA 4). 2 Or, "[... the k]ing of the enemy country".
196 5 UZU.SILIM = *šulmu* (CAD Š/3 247a); for this passage, cf. CAD M/2 223b.

197. Performing *Extispicy*

K 15693
beginning broken away
1′ ⸢*x x x*⸣-*ni* [*x x x x x*]
2′ *ni-ba-ru-ma* [*x x x x x*]
3′ *it-ta-šu-*⸢*ú*?⸣ [*x x x x x*]
4′ *ni-ma-at dib-b*[*i*? *x x x x*]
5′ *nu-šá-áš-mu-ú* [*x x x x x*]
6′ *nu-ul-t*[*e-bi-la x x x*]
7′ *šá* LÚ.[*x x x x x x x*]
8′ *nu-*[*x x x x x x x x x*]
rest broken away

CT 54 325
(Beginning destroyed)
1 [...... *that*] we *perform* [*the extispicy*] and [......]
3 they took [......]
4 we will die. The word[s ......]
5 we will inform [......]
6 we have dis[patched ......]
7 *of* the [......]
8 we [......]
(Rest destroyed)

198. Keeping the King's Watch

K 15704
beginning broken away
1′ [*x x x x*]*x x*[*x x x x x*]
2′ [LUGAL *be-l*]*í-ia* [*x x x x x*]
3′ [*x x x*]*x* LU[GAL *x x x x x*]
4′ [*x x x*]-*ia i-*[*x x x x x*]
5′ [*x x x-n*]*u* ARAD.M[EŠ *x x x x x*]
6′ [*x x x*]-*ia ni-*[*x x x x x*]
7′ [*x x* EN].NUN *šá* LU[GAL *x x x x x*]
8′ [*x x a-na*]*m-ṣar* [*x x x x x*]
rest broken away

CT 54 333
(Beginning destroyed)
2 [the king], my [lor]d [......]
3 [...] the ki[ng ......]
4 [he/they ...] my [...]
5 [...] the servants [......]
6 we [...] my [......]
7 [... I will ke]ep [the wa]tch of the king, [*my lord* ......]
(Rest destroyed)

199. – – –

K 15706 + K 21906
1 [*x x x*] *be-lí-i*[*a x x x x x*]
2 [*x be*]-*lí-ia-ma x*[*x x x x x*]
3 [*x x x*] *ia-šu be-lí* [*x x x x x*]
4 [*x ki-i*?] 1-*en pi-*⸢*i*⸣ *x*[*x x x x x*]
5 [*x x x*] ⸢*x*⸣ *x*[*x x x x x x*]
rest broken away
Rev. beginning broken away
1′ [*x x x x*]*x* ⸢*x x*⸣ [*x x x x x*]
2′ [*x x x*] *ù*? *a-na* UG[U *x x x x x*]

CT 54 335+
1 [...] m[y] lord [......]
2 [...] my [lo]rd [......]
3 [...] me, [my] lord [......]
4 [... *with*] one *accord* [......]
(Break)

r.2 [...] And concern[ing ......]

199 Join by J. Fincke (8.8.2003). eBL edition (https://www.ebl.lmu.de/fragmentarium/K.15706) accessed 17.7.2023. The first and last lines of the tablet may be partially preserved, although the left side may have contained writing. However, the attribution of the obverse and reverse is uncertain and they may have to be reversed. [3] Or (see eBL), -*ia šu-bat* "my [...], the seat of". [r.2] Alternatively, read -*ši-ma a-na* ... as in eBL.

3′ [*x x x*]*x ṭè-e-mi bab-ba-n*[*i-i x x x x*]
4′ [*x x x*] *ep-šú šu-tu-ma x*[*x x x x x*]
5′ [*x x x*]*x bab-ba-nu-ú* [*x x x x x*]
6′ [*x x x*] ⸢*it-ti*⸣ *x x*[*x x x x x*]
7′ [*x x x*]*x-tin* ^{m}*ṣil-la-a* [*x x x x x*]
8′ [*x x x*]*-kin mah-ri-i* [*x x x x x*]
9′ [*x x i*]*-ma-aq-qut pa-a*[*r*?*-x x x x*]

10′e [*x x*] ⸢*a*⸣*-lit-te mu-šeš-è*[*r-tu*? *x x*]
11′e [*x x*]*x* ⸢*x x x x*⸣ [*x x x*]
12′e [*x x x x x x x x x*]
13′e [*x x x b*]*e-lí a-n*[*a*] *x*[*x x x x*]
14′e [*x x x x*] *aq-ta-*[*bi x x x x x*]

3 […] excellent news [……]
4 […] made. It/he [……]
5 […] excellent [……]
6 […] with … [……]
7 […]… Ṣillaya [……]
8 […] earlier [……]
9 […] will fall …[……]
10 […] woman giving birth, who gives birth successf[ully …]
11 […] … […]
12 [……]
13 […] my [l]ord to [……]
14 […] I sai[d (……)]

200. – – –

K 15711
beginning broken away
1′ [*x x x*] ⸢*ba*?*-hu*?*-ma*?⸣ [*x x x*]
2′ [*x x id*?]*-di-na mìn-de-*⸢*e*⸣*-*[*ma x x*]
3′ [*x x x*]*x mi-nam-ma u*[*l*? *x x*]
4′ [*x x x i*]*d*?*-di-nu mim-ma* [*x x x*]
5′ [*x x x*]*-šu liq-bu-*[*ú* (*x x*)]
rest uninscribed
other side destroyed

CT 54 340
(Beginning destroyed)

2 [… *g*]*ave me*. Perhaps […]
3 […] Why [*did* …] *not* give […]?
4 *Whatever* […], let them speak [*to*] his […].

201. Fragment Mentioning the Puqudu

K 15717
beginning broken away
1′ [*x x x*]*-na ru-*[*x x x*]
2′ [*x x x*] LÚ.*pu-q*[*u-du x*]
3′ [*x x x*]*x-šú-ni x*[*x x x x*]
4′ [*x x x x*]
rest broken away

CT 54 345
(Beginning destroyed)
1 […] … […]
2 […] the Puq[udu …]
3 […]… […]
(Rest destroyed)

r.9-10 These lines may be a quotation from a literary source. Possibly negated *la*?] ⸢*a*⸣*-lit-te* "a woman [having trouble] giving birth". r.10-14 If it is correct that the top (or bottom) edge has a total of five lines, then the original was probably a large tablet. r.14 The predicate *aqtabi* may be the last word of the letter.

200 2f Usually *mindēma* is followed by *šarru bēlā iqabbi umma*, which is possible here.

202. ---

K 16109

beginning broken away
1′ [*x x x x*] ⌜*ul*$^{?}$⌝ [*x x x*]
2′ [*x x x*]*x-su-su x*[*x x x*]
3′ [*x x x*] *il-qé-e x*[*x x x*]
4′ [*x x x*]*x*.MEŠ *il-la*[*k-x x*]
5′ [*x x x x-á*]*š-šú mìn-de-*[*e-ma* LUGAL$^{?}$]
6′ [*be-lí-a*$^{?}$] ⌜*i*⌝*-qab-b*[*i x x x*]
rest broken away

CT 54 347

(Beginning destroyed)
2 [...]... [...]
3 Did he take [...]? [...]
4 [...]s will *com*[*e*]
5 [...] *him.* Perha[ps *the king, my lord*], will sa[y ...]
(Rest destroyed)

203. ---

K 16122

beginning broken away
1′ [*x x x x*] ⌜*x*⌝ [*x x x*]
2′ [*x x x x*]-⌜*i*⌝*a x*[*x x x*]
3′ [*x x x x*] *a-na* [*x x x*]
4′ [*x x x x*] URU.⌜*šá–a*⌝-[*me-le-e*]
5′ [*x x x x á*]*š-pu-ru* [*x x x x*]
6′ [*x x x* ^{m}LUGAL]*–lu–d*[*a-a-ru x*]
7′ [*x x x x x*] ⌜*x*⌝ [*x x x*]
rest broken away

CT 54 356

(Beginning destroyed)
3 [...] to [...]
4 [...] the town of Ša-a[mele]
5 [... I] sent [...]
6 [... Šarru]-lu-d[ari ...]
(Rest destroyed)

204. Hit on the Head

K 16129

beginning broken away
1′ [*x x x x x x x x x*] ⌜*x x x*⌝ [*x*]
2′ [*x x x x x x x x*.M]EŠ *ina* UD *a-g*[*a-a*]
3′ [*x x x x x x x x x*] *a-na-ṣa-ru*
4′ [*x x x x x x x x i*]*m-haṣ-ma* UGU*-iá*
5′ [*x x x x x x x x-b*]*u-uh hur-ba-šú*
6′ [*x x x x x x x x x*]*-a*$^{?}$ *i-nam-dan-ni-ma*
7′ [*x x x x x x x x x*] *a-na-ku*
8′ [*x x x x x x x x*]*x šu-ú* [*x x x*]
9′ [*x x x x x x x x*]*x*[*x x x x x*]
rest broken away

CT 54 360

(Beginning destroyed)
2 [......]. From th[is] day on, I am keeping the [......] watch
4 [...... he] hit me on the head
5 [... ...]... terror
6 [......] he will give me *my* [...] and
7 [......] I
8 [......] he [...]
(Rest destroyed)

202 [2] The sequence *-su-su* can be the end of a personal name. For example, "Did [...]*susu*, [...], take [...]? [4] One could even read ⌜MAN$^{?}$⌝.MEŠ *il-la*[*k-ú-ni*] "The kings are com[ing]/go[ing]".

203 [4] For the partially restored town, see SAA 21 131:12; SAA 22 19:13, 17, 20, 43 e.8; RINAP 3/1 1:43.

204 [5] Theoretically, *hurbaššu*, "lie it/him waste", is also possible.

205. ---

K 16136

Obv. illegible
Rev. beginning broken away
1′ [*x*] *x*[*x x x x x x x*]
2′ *ù ku*-[*x x x x x x x*]
3′ *i-ma-ah-h*[*ar x x x x x x*]
4′ É *be-lí-i*[*a x x x x x x*]
5′ *ap–pi-i*[*t-ti x x x x x x*]
6′ *i-r*[*a-x x x x x x x*]
s.1 [*x m*]*im-ma p*[*a*[?]-*x x*] LÚ.TÚG.K[A.KÉŠ *x x x*]

CT 54 367

(Beginning destroyed)

r.2 and [......]
3 he will *recei*[*ve* ......]
4 the house of m[y] lord [......]
5 accordi[ngly ......]
6 *lo*[*ves* ......]
s.1 [... *a*]*ny* [...] the ta[ilor ...]

206. ---

K 16139

beginning broken away
1′ [*x x x x x x*] *x*[*x x x x x x*]
2′ [*x x x x x*]*x x*[*x x x x x x*]
3′ [*x x x x iš*]-*pu-ra* [*x x x x x x*]
4′ [*x x x x x*] *ú-ṣu*-[*ú x x x x x*]
5′ [*x x x x x*]*x x*[*x x x x x x*]
6′ [*x x x x x*]*x x*[*x x x x x x*]
7′ [*x x x x x*]-*dan ú*-[*x x x x x x*]
8′ [*x x x x x*] *i x*[*x x x x x x x*]
9′ [*x x x* LUG]AL *be-lí-a iš-ku*[*n*]
10′ [*x x x x*]*x x i-nam-di-nu-nik*-[*ka*]
11′ [*x x x x*] *a-nam-di-na*
12′ [*x x a*[?]-*nam*]-*di-na*
13′ [*x x x x* U]D-5-KÁM *ul a-su-ba* [0[?]]
14′ [*x x x x* L]Ú.ARAD–É.GA[L]
15′ [*x x x x x*]*x x šá x*[*x*]
rest broken away
Rev. completely broken away

CT 54 369

(Beginning destroyed)

3 [... he wr]ote [......]
4 [...] go(es) ou[t ......]
(Break)

9 [The ki]ng, my lord, *pu*[*t* ...]
10 they will give [...] to you
11 I will give [...]
12 [*I* will gi]ve [...]
13 [... On] the 5th [da]y, I did not draw water
14 [......] a *builder*
(Rest destroyed or too broken for translation)

207. Fragment Mentioning the *Ritual* of Ištar of [...]

K 16603

beginning broken away
1′ [*x x x x*] ⸢*x x x*⸣ [*x x x x x*]
2′ [*x x x*]–SUM-*na e-ki*-⸢*x*⸣ [*x x x*]
3′ [*x x x d*]*ul-la* IŠ.TAR URU.[*x x x*]
4′ [*x x x x*] ⸢*x x*⸣ [*x x x x x*]
rest broken away

CT 54 386

(Beginning destroyed)

2 [...]-iddina ... [...]
3 [... the *r*]*itual* of Ištar of [...]
(Rest destroyed)

205 r.4 Presumably not a letter to the king.
206 9 Perhaps "[The ki]ng, my lord, *gav*[*e orders that*]". r.14 Lit. 'a palace servant'.
207 2 Perhaps a form of *ekēmu* "to take away", although the partially visible sign is not *mu*.

208. – – –

K 16608
beginning broken away
1′ [*x x x x x x x x i*]*i*$^{?}$*-ti-šú a-n*[*a x x x x*]
2′ [*x x x x x x x* LUG]AL EN-*a iš-k*[*u-nu x x x*]
3′ [*x x x x*]*x ù ú-še-b*[*i-la x x x x*]

4′ [*x x x x*]*x-tu-ú e-p*[*u-uš*$^{?}$ *x x x*]
5′ [*x* LUGAL EN]-*iá ad-din nu-x*[*x x x x x*]

6′ [*x x* LUGAL E]N-*iá pa-ni* [*x x x x x*]
7′ [*x x x x x*] *liš-kun n*[*a*$^{?}$*-x x x x x*]
8′ [*x x x x x x x*] *x*[*x x x x x x*]
rest broken away
Rev. completely broken away

CT 54 390
(Beginning destroyed)
1 [...... w]ith him to [...]
2 [...... the k]ing, my lord, *ga*[*ve orders* ...]
3 [... *which*] *I* [...*ed*] and sen[t ...]
4 *Did I d*[*o* ...]...? [*When*] I gave [... to the king], my [lord], [......].
6 May [*the god of* the king], my [lo]rd, *turn to* [......]
(Rest destroyed)

209. – – –

Sm 1220 + Sm 1221
beginning broken away
1′ ^{m}[*x x x x x x x x x*]
2′ *u* [*x x x x x x x x x*]
3′ [*x x x x x x x x x*]
4′ [*x x x x x x x x x*]
5′ *be-l*[*í x x x x x x x*]
6′ *u*[*l x x x x x x x x x*]
7′ *k*[*i-i x x x x x x x x*]
rest broken away
Rev. beginning broken away
1′ *x*[*x x x x x x x x x*]
2′ *ki-i* [*x x x x x x x x*]
3′ *ul i*[*š-pu-ru x x x x x*]
4′ *pi-i* $^{d+}$A[G$^{?}$ *x x x x x*]
5′ *im-haṣ bu-*[*x x x x x*]
6′ *i-hi-pi* [*x x x x x x*]
7′ *ú-maš-š*[*ar x x x x x x x*]
8′ [*x*] *x*[*x x x x x x x*]
rest broken away

CT 54 409
(Beginning destroyed)
1 [*NN* ......]
2 and [......]
(Break)
5 [*my*] lord [......]
(Break)

r.2 *when* [......]
3 [they/he] did not *w*[*rite* ......]
4 the *command* of Na[bû ......]
5 he struck [......]
6 he will break [......]
7 he abando[ns ......]
(Rest destroyed)

208 [3] Probably the conjunction *ù* links two verbs. [4] TU-*ú* as a form of *erēbu* is possible. [5] Perhaps read *ad-din-nu*. [7] Or: "let him give [orders]".
209 [r.7] Usually negated: "[let] him [not] forsa[ke me]" or similar.

210. – – –

Sm 1700
beginning broken away
e.1′ [*x x x x*] DINGIR.M[EŠ *x x x x*]

r.1 [*x x x*]*x-qa* DUMU.MÍ ⸢*x*⸣ [*x x x x*]
2 [*x x* $^{md+}$EN]–*ú-sa-ti* [*x x x x*]
3 [*x x* D]UMU ^{m}*kab-ti-*[*ia x x x x*]
4 [*x x*.M]EŠ ^{m}ŠEŠ.M[EŠ-*šá-a x x x*]
5 [*x x x*]-*r*[*a*$^{?}$ *x x x x x x*]
rest broken away

CT 54 420
(Beginning destroyed)
1 [...] gods [...]
r.1 [...]... daughter [...]
2 [... Bel]-usati [...]
3 [... s]on of Kabti[ya ...]
4 [x$^{?}$ *son*]s of Ahhe[šaya ...]
(Rest destroyed)

211. – – –

Sm 1800
beginning broken away
1′ [*x x x x x*] ⸢*x x*⸣ [*x x*]
2′ [*x x* BA]N$^{?}$ *šu-ú*
3′ [*x x x x-t*]*i šá* KUR.KUR *gab-bi*
4′ [*x x x x*]-*a sa-ad-ra*
5′ [*x x x*] *ra-ah-ṣa-ku*
6′ [*x x x* KAS]KAL.2 *ak-kil-li*
7′ [*x x x*] *i-šem-mu-ú*

r.1 [*x x x x x x x x x x*]
2 [*x x x x x x x x x*]-*ka*
3 [*x x x x x x x a*]*l-tap-ra*
4 [*x x x x x x x x*]-*pa-nu*
5 [*x x x x x x x x ip*$^{?}$-*t*]*a-làh*
6 [*x x x x x x x x*]*x*[*x*]
rest broken away

CT 54 423
(Beginning destroyed)
2 [......] he/it
3 [......] of all lands
4 *my* [...*s*] are *arrayed*
5 [...] I am confident [*but*] I was being held (back) [*on the* ro]ad
7 [...] will hear
(Break)

r.3 [I am] writing [......]
4 [......]...
5 [... *he* became] afraid
(Rest destroyed)

212. – – –

Rm 2,491
1 ⸢ŠAB$^{?}$⸣ LÚ.*x*[*x x x x x*]
2 LÚ.TUR.ME[Š *x x x x*]
3 DUMU ^{m}*x*[*x x x x x x*]
4 ^{md}AMAR.U[TU–*x x x x*]
5 ⸢*ka*⸣-*x*[*x x x x x x*]
rest broken away
Rev. beginning broken away
1′ [*x*]*x* [*x x x x x*]

CT 54 445
1 *A* jar, the [......]
2 the apprentices [*of NN*], son of [NN ...]
4 Mard[uk-...]
(Break)

210 r.1 If ⸢1/2⸣ *qa*, "1/2 litre", then this fragment may concern rations allocated to individuals. r.2 For the restoration, see Dietrich, AOAT 7 (1970) 62 n.3 and PNA 1/II 337a.
211 2 "a *bo*]*w*". 6 *ak-kil-li* is more likely an N stem form and probably not *ana killi*.
212 1 Or, ⸢SAG$^{?}$⸣.

2′ *i-ba-á*[*š-ši x x x x*]
3′ DUMU ^{m}*šu-m*[*a-a x x x*]
4′ *šu-ú i-nam-d*[*in x x x*]
5′ *a-na šú-man-ni ki-i* [*x x x*]
6′ *ù ia-a-šú zi-x*[*x x x x*]
7′ ⸢*x x x*⸣ [*x*] ⸢*ki-i šá ú*⸣-[*x x x*]
8′ [*x x x x*]*x* [*x x x x x*]
9′e [*x x x x x x x*]
10′e [*x x x x x x x*]
11′e [*u*]*l-li* URU [*x x x x*]
s.1 [*x x*] *i-za-zu*

r.2 There i[s ...]
3 son of Šum[aya ...]
4 he will giv[e ...]
5 for *names like* [...]
6 And, for myself [...]
7 ... *just as* [...]
(Break)
10 [I/he *did not g*]*o up*. The [*people of*] the town are standing [*there*].

213. Fragment about a Possible Quarrel

81-2-4,481
beginning broken away
1′ ⸢*šá* LUGAL *ki-i i*⸣-*p*[*u-šú*]
2′ *pi-i šá gab-bi x*[*x x a-di*]
3′ UGU UD-*me a-ga-a* [*it-ti-ia*]
4′ *ul id-bu-u*[*b x x x*]
5′ *šá* LUGAL *i-x*[*x x x x*]
6′ *ut-tir x*[*x x x x x x x*]
7′ ⸢*x x*⸣ *x*[*x x x x x x x x*]
rest broken away
Rev. beginning broken away
1′ *x*[*x x x x x x x x x x x*]
2′ *ul x*[*x x x x x x x x x*]
3′ *ki-i* É [*x x x x x x x x*]
4′ UGU AD-*k*[*a x x x x x x x x*]
5′ ^{m}*man-nu–ki-i–*[*x x x x x x x x*]
6′ *dan-nu-ti x*[*x x x x x x x x*]
7′ [*x x*] UGU *x*[*x x x x x x x x*]
8′ [*x x* LU]GA[L *x x x x x x x x*]
rest broken away

CT 54 477
(Beginning destroyed)
1 Having do[ne] the king's [...], he has not spoken [to me] about the whole matter [... un]til the present day.
4 *I returned* [...] *of* the king [......]
(Break)

r.2 *not* [......]
3 *since* the house [......]
4 [*aga*]*inst* yo[ur] father [......]
5 Mannu-ki-[..., ...] strong [...s ......]
7 [...] *on* [......]
8 [... the ki]n[g ......]
(Rest destroyed)

214. Fragment Mentioning Belet-balaṭi

81-2-4,497
beginning broken away
1′ [*x x x x x x*] ⸢*šu-a-tu na x*⸣ [*x x x x x x*]
2′ [*x x x x x x*] *a-na iá-a-tú ul* [*x x x x x x*]
3′ [*x x x x* LÚ].⸢A⸣–KIN $^{md+}$EN.LÍL–NU[MUN–*ib-ni x x*]

CT 54 479
(Beginning destroyed)
1 [...] that ...[... ...]
2 [......] *not* for *mine* [......]
3 [... the] messenger *of* Illil-*ze*[*ru-ibni* ...]

r.5 Orthographically, if interpreted correctly, *šú-man-ni* is a bit awkward. r.11f The interpretation of the end is a guess.

213 It is possible, but only a guess, that Mannu-ki-[...] (r.5) is the official with whom the writer has problems; see, e.g., Mannu-ki-Libbali's letter SAA 16 78. r.3f E.g., SAA 18 64:8 has *ana muhhi abīya* "on behalf of my father".

214 1 Because of the word *šuātu*, this may be a fragment of a query (i.e., an addition to SAA 4, although they are very schematic, or to SAA 8 or SAA 10). 2 The spelling *iá-a-tú* suggests a feminine form of a possessive pronoun of *yāʾu* "mine", but the preposition *ana* may make this interpretation uncertain. Perhaps "for *me*". 3 A person called Illil-zeru-ibni appears in SAA 10 110:8.

4′ [*x x x x x x*]-*a a-na nu-ru* DINGIR.M[EŠ *x x x*]
e.5′ [*x x x x x x*]*x-lik* ^{d}NIN–⸢TIN⸣ [*x x*]
rest broken away

4 [...] *my* [...] for light of the gods [...]
5 [......]... Belet-balaṭi [...]
(Rest destroyed)

215. ---

83-1-18,308
beginning broken away
1′ [*x x x x x*] ⸢*x*⸣ *x*[*x*] ⸢*x*⸣
2′ [*x x*]*x* ⸢*x*⸣ *nim-me* [*x x*]
e.3′ [*x*] LUGAL EN-*iá a-šap-p*[*ar*]
4′ [*x x*]*x a-šar ú-šú-uz-z*[*u*]
5′ [*x x x*]*x-du ul i*-DAN-⸢*x*⸣
r.1 [*x x x x*]-*iá lu-ú*
rest broken away

CT 54 522
(Beginning destroyed)
2 [...] I am sendi[ng] ... [... *to*] the king, my lord.
4 [...] where they stan[d]
5 [...] ... will not ...
r.1 my [...] should
(Rest destroyed)

216. ---

83-1-18,708
beginning broken away
1′ [*x x x x*]*x* ⸢*mi-ta-ku x x-lu*?⸣
2′ [*x x x x* LUGAL] EN-*ia ub-ba-lu*
3′ [*x x x x x x*]*x-la* UN.MEŠ KUR
4′ [*x x x x* EN.N]UN *šá* É–EN-*ia*
5′ [*x x x x x x*]-*ú gab-bu-ú*
6′ [*x x x x x* K]UG.UD *u* KUG.GI
7′ [*x x x x x ṣ*]*i-bu-ut-su*
8′ [*x x x x x* KU]R.KUR *gab-bi*
9′ [*x x x x x x x-š*]*u-nu*
10′ [*x x x x x x x x-k*]*i-ia*
11′ [*x x x x x x x x x*]*x*
rest broken away
Rev. beginning broken away
1′ [*x x x x x x x x x*]*x*
2′ [*x x x x x x*]*x* ⸢*ip*⸣-*qí-du*
3′ [*x x x x x* LU?.*k*]*i-ib-ra-a*
4′ [*x x x x x-š*]*u-nu ina* ŠÀ-*bi*
5′ [*x x x x x x*] *id-du-ku*
6′ [*x x x x x x*] ⸢*ú*⸣-*še-zi-bu*
7′ [*x x x x x*.M]EŠ *šá a-na* UGU
8′ [*x x x x x x*] KUR.NIM.MA.KI
9′ [*x x x x ina bi*?-*r*]*i-šú-nu*
10′ [*x x x x x x x x* LUG]AL [E]N-*ia*
11′ [*x x x x x x x x x x*]*x*
rest broken away

CT 54 530
(Beginning destroyed)
1 [...] I am dead [...]
2 [... *that*] *I* bring [*to* the king], my lord.
3 [... ...]... the local people
4 [... the gua]rd of the house of my lord
5 [...] *does/did all* [...]?
6 [... s]ilver and gold
7 [...] his [w]ish
8 [...] the whole [co]untry
(Break)

r.2 [......] appointed
3 [...... *people*] *of the* [*river b*]*ank*
4 [...] killed [t]heir [...] in
5 [......]
6 [......] *made escape*
7 [......]s *who to/against*
8 [......] Elam
9 [...... *betwe*]*en* them
10 [...... to the ki]ng, my [lo]rd
(Rest destroyed)

5 E.g., *i*]*l*?-*lik* "he w]ent". Belet-balaṭi "the Lady of Life" is celestially known as Vega. The spelling ^{d}NIN–TIN does not occur elsewhere in SAA.
215 5 The first two signs look like NU DU; perhaps "is/are not coming to ...".
216 2 Or, "they bring".

217. – – –

83-1-18,735

beginning broken away
1′ *dib-bi šá* DINGIR.ME[Š *šá x x x x a-na*]
2′ LUGAL EN-*iá ú-pah-hi*[*r-ú-ni* (*x x x*)]

3′ ⸢*na*⸣-*šú a-di la* LUGAL EN-*a* [*ú-ši-bu*]
4′ [1.*e*]*n* ŠÀ-*bu-šú-nu* KÁ *ul* [*uṣ-ṣu-ú*]

5′ [A.ME]Š *šá* PÚ.MEŠ *i-šat-t*[*u-ú šá* LUGAL]
6′ [EN]-*a iš-pur-an-ni a-n*[*a x x x x x*]
7′ [*na-d*]*a-nu u ma-ha-ra i*[*p-pu-šú* (*x x*)]
8′ [*a-n*]*a* ZI-*su-nu ina* KUR *šá* LUGA[L EN-*iá*]

9′ [*x x x*]*x* ⸢*a-na*⸣-*ku* [*x x x x x x*]
rest broken away

Rev. beginning broken away
1′ *x*[*x x x x x x x x x x x*]
2′ *x*[*x x x x x x x x x x x*]
3′ *x*[*x x x x x x x x x x x*]
4′ ᵐ*x*[*x x x x x x x x x x*]
5′ ŠU.2-*š*[*u x x x x x x x x x*]
6′ *u am–mì-*[*ni x x x x x x x x*]
7′ *x*[*x x x x x x x x x x x*]
rest broken away

CT 54 536

(Beginning destroyed)

[1] The divine oracles [which the *prophets*] collected [for] the king, my lord, [(...)] have been brought.

[3] Before the king, my lord, [ascended the throne] no [on]e of them [went out] of the gate, drin[king water] of the wells.

[5] [As to what the king], my [lord] wrote to me, fo[r their ... they] p[ractice se]lling and buying, [fo]r their lives [they ...] in the land of the kin[g, my lord].

[9] [...] I [......]

(Break)

[r.4] [NN ......]

[5] hi[s] *hand* [......]

[6] and wh[y ......]

(Rest destroyed)

218. – – –

83-1-18,804

beginning broken away
1′ ⸢*x*⸣ *qa* [*x x x x x x x x x x x*]
2′ ᵈAMAR.UTU [*x x x x x x x x x*]
3′ *a-na* AMA–LU[GAL? *x x x x x x x*]
4′ *ù a-na* ᵐ[*x x x x x x x x x*]
5′ *ú-ṣal-la a-na* [*x x x x x x*]

6′ *ina* ⸢*pa*⸣-*ni* LUGAL EN-[*ia x x x x x x*]
7′ *ù* LUGAL EN-⸢*a*⸣ [*x x x x x x x x*]
rest broken away

CT 54 542

(Beginning destroyed)

[1] ... [......]

[2] Marduk [......]

[3] I pray to the *qu*[*een*] mother, [......] and [NN ......].

[5] *To* [......]

[6] in the presence of the king, [my] lord ......]

[7] Moreover, the king, my lord [......]

(Rest destroyed)

217 [1] Alternatively, for example, "the things which the gods". [6] Or, *a-n*[*a-ku* (as in line 9) + a verb.

218 It is difficult to estimate whether there are really as many signs missing from the right side of the tablet as the transliteration indicates. [1-2] These lines may contain the standard blessing: "[May Nabû and] Marduk [bless the king, my lord!]" [3] If LU[GAL is correct, this is a more tilted variant of the sign than in lines 6 and 7.

219. Fragment Mentioning Babylon, Elam, and Bows

83-1-18,886

beginning broken away

1′ *x x x x x x*] ⸢*x x x*⸣
2′ *x x x x x x*] AD *hal-qu*
3′ *x x x x x x*] E.KI *i-hal-li-qu*
4′ *x x x x x x*] KUR.NIM.MA.⸢KI⸣

r.1 *x x x x x*] UGU-*hi*
2 *x x x x x*]*x-šú-nu*
3 *x x x x-m*]*a* 3-*me* GIŠ.BAN.MEŠ
4 *x x x x x*]*x it-ti*
5 *x x x x x*]*x-a-a lid-di-nu-nu*
6 *x x x ma-ṣar*]*-ti taṣ-ṣu-ru-ma*
7 *x x x x x x*] ⸢*x x x x*⸣

rest broken away

CT 54 553

(Beginning destroyed)

2 [......] *father*, a refugee
3 [...... *of*] Babylon *fled*
4 [......] Elam
r.1 [......] *on*
2 [......] them/they
3 [......] 300 bows
4 [......] with
5 [......] let them give me *my* [...]
6 [... that] you have kept the [watc]h and

(Rest destroyed or too broken for translation)

220. A Message from Bel

Bu 91-5-9,31

beginning broken away

1′ [*x x x x x x x x x x x x x x x*]*x-pa*
2′ [*x x x x x x x x x x x x x*]*x-su*
3′ [*x x x x x x x x x x x*] 1-*en šá dum-qa*
4′ [*x x x x x x*]*-ú a-di* UGU *šá en-na*
5′ [*x x x x x*]*-ti-ni šu-pa-li-ti*

6′ [*x x x x x x x x x*]*-di ul-tu* UGU *šá* $^{d+}$EN
7′ [*x x x x x x x x x x x*] *iš-pur-an-ni a-di* UGU
8′ [*šá en-na iq-ba-a u*]*m-ma a-na pa-an* LUGAL EN-*iá*
9′ [*x x x x x x*] ⸢*x x*⸣ *mah-ri-ti*
10′ [*x x x x x x x x x x*] *šu-ut-ti*
11′ [*x x x x x x x x x x x x x x x x*] ⸢*x x*⸣

rest broken away

Rev. beginning broken away

1′ [*x x x x x x x x-š*]*ú-n*[*u*] ⸢*x x x*⸣
2′ [*x x x x x x*] *ul ti-de-e*
3′ [*x x x x x x*] *a-na-ku*

rest uninscribed

CT 54 559

(Beginning destroyed)

3 [......] one *who* goodness
4 [......] up until now
5 [......] our lower [...]
6 [... ...]... Ever since that Bel [......, ...] wrote to me. [He told me] up until [now]: “[...] to the king my lord
9 [......] *previous* ... [...]
10 [...... *in a*] *dream*

(Break)

r.1 [...... *t*]*hei*[*r* ...] ...
2 [......] don’t you know
3 [*that* ......] I

219 [3] One should probably not rule out an]-*e*.KI interpretation. [r.3] Or: “300 bowmen”.
220 [6, 10] For Bel and a dream in the same context in a letter, see, e.g., SAA 10 361, possibly also SAA 19 149.

221. – – –

Bu 91-5-9,43
beginning broken away
1′ [*x*]*x* ⸢*ka*⸣ [*x*]
2′ [*l*]*u-ur-ri-k*[*u*]
3′ ⸢*ù*⸣ *lu-rab-bi-šu*
4′ ⸢*šá*⸣ *ina* ŠÀ-*bi a-mat*
5′ [*a*]*n-ni-ti*
6′ ⸢ŠÀ⸣-*ba-a*
7′ ⸢*li*⸣-*bal-li-ṭu*
8′ [*x x*]*x* 7 *šú-nu*
9′ [*x x-n*]*a*$^{?}$*-ku*
e.10′ [*x x x*]*x x-ta*

r.1 [*x x x*]*x at-*⸢*ta*⸣
2 [*x x x*]*x at-*⸢*ta*⸣
3 [*x x x*]*x* ⸢*ú*⸣*-ṣi*
4 [*x x x*]*x* ⸢*x-ta*$^{?}$⸣
5 [*x x i*]*l-tap-ra*
6 [*x x*]*-ni-im-*⸢*ma*⸣
7 [*x x*]*x* [*x*] ⸢*x*⸣
8 [*x x*]*x* ⸢*x*⸣[K]I$^{?}$*-a-a*
9 [*x*] ⸢GÚ⸣ [*x*]*x-tu*
10 [*x*] *a-n*[*a*] LUGAL ⸢EN⸣*-iá*
11 [*iš-p*]*u-ru u* LUG[AL EN-*a*]
rest broken away

CT 54 561
(Beginning destroyed)
1 [l]et them exte[nd] and enlarge [...], let them revive my heart with this word.
8 [...] they are seven
9 [...]...
10 [...] ...
r.1 [...] you
2 [...] you
3 [...] *went out*
4 [...] ...
5 [... has w]ritten
6 [...] ...
7 [......]
8 [... the ...]s
9 [...] *shore* [...]...
10 [... wro]te t[o] the king, my lord, *but* the ki[ng, my lord]
(Rest destroyed)

222. – – –

BM 134599 (1932-12-12,594)
beginning broken away
1′ [*x x x n*]*a*$^{?}$ *i*[*b*$^{?}$ *x x x x x*]
2′ [*x x x p*]*a-ni-ku-n*[*u x x x*]
3′ [*x x x x*] *nu ú x*[*x x x x*]
4′ [*x x x š*]*á* ^{m}NUMUN-⸢*ú*⸣-[*tu*$^{?}$ *x x x x*]
5′ [*x x x x*] *a-ha-me*[*š x x x x*]
6′ [*x x x x*]-⸢*i*⸣*-ni l*[*a x x x x*]
7′ [*x x x*.ME]Š$^{?}$ *ta r*[*u*$^{?}$ *x x x x*]
8′ [*x x x x*]*x i*[*l-x x x x*]
9′ [*x x x x*] ⸢*x*⸣ [*x x x x x*]
rest broken away

CT 54 593
(Beginning destroyed)
2 [... *b*]*efore* you (pl.) [...]
3 [...] ... [...]
4 [... *o*]*f* Zeru[*tu* ...]
5 [...] *one anoth*[*er* ...]
6 [...] our [...] *n*[*ot* ...]
(Rest destroyed or too broken for translation)

221 [6] E.g., [*ki-i pi-i an*]*-ni-im-ma*, "[in the same] way", if space permits.
222 [4] This attestation of a PN is not recorded in PNA.

223. ---

K 19998

beginning broken away

1′ *x x x*] ⸢*x x*⸣ [*x x x*
2′ *x x x*]*x ma-la x*[*x x x*
3′ *x x x*] *zi x*[*x x x x*
r.1 *x x*]*x* LUGAL *la i-qab-bi x*[*x x*
2 *x m*]*a-a'-du-ti ina* UGU BÀD [*x x*
3 *x x x*] *en še di mim-ma* ⸢LUGAL⸣ *x*[*x x*
4 *x x x*] ⸢*x x x*⸣ [*x x x*

rest broken away

K 19998

(Beginning destroyed)

2 [...] *all* [...]
3 [......]
r.1 [...] The king should not say [...]
2 [... m]any [...] on the wall [...]
3 [...] ... *anything* the king [...]

(Rest destroyed)

224. ---

K 20563

beginning broken away

1′ *x x x x*] *x* [*x x x x*
2′ *x x x x*]*x ina* ŠÀ-*bi* [*x x x x*
3′ *x x x x*]*x*–DINGIR A ^{m}SU[HUŠ–*x x x x*
4′ *x x x* G]I$^{?}$.*a-ma-te i-*[*x x x x*
5′ *x x x x*] *x x x* [*x x x x*

rest broken away

K 20563

(Beginning destroyed)

2 ...] in *the middle of* [...
3 ...]...-ilu, son of Ub[ru-...
4 ...]... the *rafts* ... [...

(Rest destroyed)

225. Fragment of a Private Letter about a Legal Case

TIM 11 29

beginning (1 or 2 lines) broken away

1′ [PAB$^{?}$]-⸢*ka*⸣
2′ ⸢*x x x*⸣–PAB$^{?}$
3′ ^{m}*lu*$^{?}$–*ba-la-aṭ*
4′ *ina* UGU-*ka i-la-ka*
5′ *a-na* ^{m}*šúm-ma–an-ni*
6′ *qi-bi* ^{m}*hur-u-a-ṣi*
r.1 ⸢*ka*$^{?}$⸣-*al*$^{!}$-*li-me-šú*
2 *de-e-nu*
3 *i-si-šu*
4 (*lid*$^{!}$)-*bu-bu*

rest as far as preserved, uninscribed

IM for study

1 [To NN, my *brother*]: your [*brother*] ...-*uṣur.*

3 *Lu*-balaṭ is coming to you. Say to Šumma-anni: "Show Hur-waṣi to him". He (should pl)ead a case with him.

224 4 Cf. SAA 18 85:10. Despite the appearance of the signs, this small fragment may be more NB than NA. Alternatively, *a-ma-te* "words", probably not "maids", since the word is usually written logographically (GÉME.MEŠ).

225 1, 4, 6, r.1 Because of the rather informal use of the 2nd person singular suffix and imperatives, we assume that the relationship between sender and recipient is that of equal "brother" and not necessarily of "lord" and "servant". 2 The drawn copy of the letter (TIM 11 29) may suggest that the first sign in the sender's name is KASKAL, but it is strange if the name appears without the mister-sign, although cf. r.4. r.4 An inadvertent omission of the first syllable may be the easiest way to explain this form. As, e.g., in SAA 15 159: 7′-8′, the form can be taken as singular. But see also TIM 11, p. 47, whose solution is to assume a third imperative in the sequence.

5. Neo-Assyrian Treaties and Loyalty Oaths
Additions to SAA II

FIG. 16. *Man eaten by vulture: illustrations of images, like editions of texts, vary in quality.*
Top: original, BM 124556. Middle: Layard's field drawing, Original Drawings III, NW VI. Bottom: engraving made for Layard, Monuments of Nineveh I, Pl. 18.

226. Treaty of Assurnasirpal II

VAT 10948 + VAT 11204 + VAT 12313

beginning broken away

1′ [*x x x x x*] AŠ$^{?}$ [*x x x x x x x x x*]

2′ [*x x x x*]-*na-ni x x* [*x x x x x*] *x* AN$^{?}$ [*x x x x x*]

3′ [*x x x x*] ^{m}AŠ–PAB–A MAN ⸢KUR⸣–*aš-š*[*ur* A G]ISKIM–⸢^{d}⸣[MAŠ MAN KUR–*aš-šur-ma*]

KAL 9, no. 68

(Beginning destroyed or too broken for translation)

3 [……] Assurnasirpal (II), king of Assy[ria, son of Tu]kulti-[Ninurta, likewise king of Assyria].

4′ [*a-de-e*$^{?}$ *š*]*á* ^{m}AŠ–PAB–[A MAN KUR–*aš-šur*] ⸢A GISKIM–^{d}⸣[MAŠ MAN KUR–*aš-šur-ma*]

5′ [*x x x x*]*x-ta-šú-ni* [*x x x x x x*] *x* [*x x x x x*] *x* [*x x*]

6′ [*x x x x*]*x* [(*x x x*)] *x* [*x x x*] *x* [*x x*]

4 [The *treaty* o]f Assurnasir[pal (II), king of Assyria], son of Tukulti-[Ninurta, likewise king of Assyria].

(Two lines too broken for translation)

7′ [DINGIR.MEŠ *a-ši-bu*]-⸢*ut*⸣ *e-lat qaq-*[*q*]*a-*[*ri* DINGIR.M]EŠ *a-ši-b*[*u-ut šap-la-a*]*t qaq-q*[*a-ri*]

8′ [*x x x* ^{d}É.A MAN] *ap-*⸢*si-i* DINGIR⸣.[MEŠ *a-ši*]-*bu-ut* BAR[AG.MEŠ *x x x š*]*a* UB.MEŠ

9′ [*x x x x x* DING]IR.MEŠ ⸢*am*⸣-*mar* [*ina ṭup*]-*pi an-ni-*[*i* MU-*šú-nu šá*]-⸢*aṭ*⸣-*ru*

10′ [*x x x x x x x x*] *x* [*da*]*n*$^{?}$-[*da*]*n*$^{?}$-*nu ina* GIŠ.TUKUL.MEŠ-[*šú e*]*z-zu-te*

11′ [*x x x x x x x x x*]*x-ku-nu* ⸢*li*⸣-[*x x x li-p*]*a-ra-'a-*⸢*ku*⸣*-nu*

12′ [*x x x x x x x x lim-ha-ṣ*]*u-*⸢*ku*⸣-*n*[*u*] *lis-su-hu-ku-nu* ⸢*x*⸣

13′ [*x x x x x x x x x*] ⸢*lu*⸣-*ṣa-mu-*⸢*ú*⸣ [*š*]*a* A.MEŠ ZI.ME[Š-*ku-nu*]

rest (about 1 or 2 lines) uninscribed

r.1 [*x x x-ku-n*]*u*$^{?}$ *ina ka-šu-*⸢*ši*⸣ *lu-ṣa-lu* ⸢*ar-ra*⸣*-ta*

7 [The gods dwell]ing above the ear[th, the god]s dwell[ing beneat]h the ear[th, … Ea, king of] the Abyss, the god[s, dwe]lling in the shri[nes … o]f the four regions, […… may] all the [go]ds [whose names are wr]itten [in] this [tab]let [……], [may …, *the str*]*on*[*ge*]*st one*, with [*his* f]ierce weapons [……] you, [… *you*, and c]ut you off, [may … …s strik]e you, uproot you,

13 [……] may they make [your] throats thirst [f]or water.

r.1 [*You*]*r* [*gods*] should fight with destructive weapon, and curse you [grim]ly with a painful curse.

---

226 Previous editions: Frahm, KAL 3 66 (only VAT 10948); Jakob, KAL 9 68. Importantly, Jakob (KAL 9, p. 126f) has already pointed out this fragment's close resemblance to the curses in Esarhaddon's Succession Treaty (see SAA 2 6, lines 453-478). 4 Jakob's restoration at the beginning is likely, but not certain. 12 At the end of the line, Jakob's copy shows the traces of a sign, but it may be ignored, although two or three more signs might have followed it (cf. line 13). 13 Syntactically, a comparable sentence is phrased differently in SAA 2 6 476f., where "your ghost(s)" is the subject.

2 [NÍG.GIG *ag-gi*]*š li-ru-ru-ku-nu* ^{d}U.DAR *reš-ti*
3 [*ina* MÈ *dan-ni* GIŠ.BAN-*k*]*u-nu lu-ša-bir x* [*x n*]*a-*⌜*ás-pan*⌝*-ta-ku-*⌜*nu*⌝ *liš-kun*
4 [*x x x l*]*u-šam-qit ina* K[I.TA KÚR *li*]*-ši-šib-ku-nu*
5 [*x x x*] GIŠ.MI UD.D[A *lu*]*-*⌜*uk*⌝*-ta-šid-ku-nu*

2 May Ištar, the foremost, smash [y]our [bow in the thick of battle], may she [m]assacre you [...], strike [...] down, and [have] you crouch un[der (your) enemy].
5 [... may] shade and daylight always chase you away.

---

6 [*x x x x x*] *x ri mi um*$^{?}$ [*x x x x x x*] *x x* ⌜MU$^{?}$⌝ NUMUN
7 [*x x e*]*ṭ-lu a-na ar-*[*da-ti*$^{?}$ *x x x x x x* D]Ù$^{?}$ A *ṣi-im-*[*x*]
8 [*x x* U]D$^{?}$ *eṭ-li x*[*x x x x x x x-k*]*u-nu*
9 [*x x*]*-uz um-mat-k*[*u-nu x x x x x x x lu-ha*]*l-liq*

6 [...] ... [......] seed
7 [... the yo]ung man *to* the *you*[ng *woman* ......] ...
8 [...] *of* the young man [...... y]ou,
9 [...] y[our] main force, [may *he* des]troy [*your* ......].

---

10 [*x x-t*]*u*$^{?}$ ⌜GAL⌝*-tu u*[*z*$^{?}$ *x x x x x x x tá*]*k*$^{?}$*-ku-nu*
11 [*x x* DÙ$^{?}$] ⌜A$^{?}$⌝ *ṣi-i*[*m x x x x x x x*] *x-um*
12 [*x x x x*] *x* [*x x x x x x x*] *x* [*x x*]
rest broken away

10 [*May*] the great (f.) [... ......] you,
11 [...] ... [......] ...
(Rest destroyed)

227. Fragment of Sennacherib's Succession Treaty

VAT 10470

KAL 3, no. 67

I′ beginning broken away
1′ [*x x x x x x x x x x x x x*]x-⌜*šá-ni*⌝

(Beginning destroyed)

2′ [*x x x x x x x x x x x x x*] ⌜KIMIN$^{?}$⌝
3′ [*x x x x x x x x x x x x x*]x
4′ [*x x x x x x x x x x x x x*]x
rest (one line) broken away

II′ beginning broken away
1′ [*šúm-ma me-me-ni a-n*]*a*$^{?}$ $^{m⌜d?⌝}$[30–PAB.MEŠ–SU MAN KUR–*aš-šur*$^{?}$]
2′ [^{m}*aš-šur*–PAB–AŠ$^{?}$ D]UMU–MAN *ša* ⌜É$^{?}$⌝–[UŠ-*te*]
3′ ⌜*ù re*⌝*-eh-te* DUMU.MEŠ-*šú* ⌜*ṣe-eh*⌝*-r*[*u-te si-hu*]
4′ *bar-tum ša du-a-ki-šú-nu ša* ⌜*mu*⌝*-a-ti-šú-*[*nu hul-lu-qi-šú-nu*$^{?}$]
5′ *a-na ka-na-šú-nu* [[*x x x*]] *i-q*[*ab-ba-ka-nu-ni*]

II 1 [If anyone] should s[peak] to you [of rebellion] or insurrection (with the purpose) of killing, assassinating, [and eliminating Sennacherib, king of Assyria, *Esarhaddon*], the crown [pr]ince d[esignate], and the rest of his youn[ger] sons, or if you should hea[r] it from the mouth of anyone, you shall come, repo[rt] and seize the perpetrators of

r.2-4 Cf. SAA 2 6 453f. r.7, 11 It may be too manipulative to read DÙ A as logograms but, apart from Assurbanipal, at least Nabû-bani-apli and Šamaš-bani-apli are also attested as personal names (see PNA). In this context, personal names are unlikely, but not impossible. r.9 For a possible restoration, see Jakob KAL 9, p. 127. r.10 It remains uncertain whether Gula should be restored in this line as "the great physician".

227 Previous edition: Frahm, KAL 3 67 (see his edition for further commentary on the fragment). The fragment comes from the lower part of a multi-column tablet, but its exact position within the tablet cannot be determined. The relationship of the fragment to no. 228 is uncertain (see ibid. pp. 130, 133). II 1-6 With minor differences this is the same wording as in the later SAA 2 6 130-135.

6′ *lu-u at-tu-nu pi-i me-me-ni ta-ša*[*m-ma-a-ni*]
7′ *la tal-lak-a-ni-ni la ta-qab-*[*ba-a-ni*]
8′ *e-pi-šá-nu-ti ša bar-ti ù* ERIM.MEŠ [EN–*hi-ṭi*]
9′ ⸢*la*⸣ *ta-ṣa-bat-a-ni-ni ina* UGU ^{md}30–[PAB.MEŠ–SU]
10′ MAN KUR–*aš-šur* EN-*ku-nu* ^{m}0 DU[MU$^{?}$–MAN *ša* É–UŠ-*te*$^{?}$]
e.11′ ⸢*ù*⸣ *re-eh-ti* ⸢DUMU⸣.MEŠ-*šú* *ṣ*[*e-eh-ru-te*]
12′ [*x x x x*] ⸢*x x*⸣ [*x x x x x x*]
rest broken away

insurrection and the [traitorous] troops (and) [bring them] to Sen[nacherib], king of Assyria, your lord, the cr[own prince designate], and the rest of his y[ounger] sons [......]

(Rest destroyed)

228. Another Fragment of Sennacherib's Succession Treaty

VAT 12007
1 [*šúm-ma lu-u* LÚ.*aš-šur*.K]I-*a-a lu-u da-gíl–pa-ni š*[*a* KUR–*aš-šur*.KI]
2 [*lu-u* LÚ.*ša–zi*]*q-ni lu-u* L[Ú.SAG 0$^{?}$]
3 [*a-na* ^{md}30–PA]B$^{?}$.MEŠ-⸢SU LUGAL KUR⸣–*aš-šur*.KI [*a-na*$^{?}$]
4 [^{m}*aš-šur*–PAB–AŠ$^{?}$ DUMU–M]AN ⸢*ša* É⸣–*re-du-t*[*e*] ⸢*ù*⸣ [*a-na*$^{?}$ *re-eh-te*]
5 [DUMU.MEŠ-*šú ṣe-eh-ru-t*]*e ṣi-*⸢*it*⸣ ŠÀ-*bi* [*ša* ^{md}30–PAB.MEŠ–SU]
6 [MAN KUR–*aš-šur*$^{?}$ *lu-u ina* A.Š]À *lu-u ina* ⸢ŠÀ⸣ URU [*e-ta-as-ru-šú-nu*]
7 [*si-hu bar-tum ina* U]GU-*hi-šú-*[*nu e-tap-šu*]
8 [*x x x x x x*] ⸢*x x x*⸣ [*x x x x x x*]
rest broken away

KAL 3, no. 68
1 [If an Assyr]ian or a vassal o[f Assyria, or a bea]rded (courtier) or a [eunuch besieges Sennac]herib, king of Assyria, [*Esarhaddon*, the cr]own [prince] designate and [the rest of his younge]r [sons], the offspring [of Sennacherib, *king of Assyria*, in count]ry or in town, [and carries out rebellion or insurrection aga]inst th[em ......]

(Rest destroyed)

229. The Tell Tayinat Treaty Tablet of Esarhaddon

Tell Tayinat, Ms. T
i (1) NA4.KIŠIB ^{d}*a-šur*4 LUGAL DINGIR.MEŠ
ii (2) EN KUR.KUR *ša* [*la šu-un-né-e*]
iii (3) [NA4].KIŠIB ⸢NUN-*e* GAL-*e*⸣ AD DINGIR.MEŠ
iv (4) *ša* ⸢*la pa*⸣-*qa-a-ri*

Lauinger, JCS 64 (2012), p. 88f.
i Seal of the god Aššur, king of the gods, lord of the lands – [not to be altered]; seal of the great ruler, father of the gods – not to be disputed.

II 7-9 See SAA 2 6 158-160. II 10 As Frahm points out, there is no personal name immediately after the mister-sign. This might suggest that the fragment is a draft (Frahm, KAL 3, p. 132). Alternatively, one could read *ana*, although it is only used in this corpus in SAA 2 2 and in 6 471.

228 Previous edition: Frahm, KAL 3 68 (see his edition for further commentary on the fragment). The relationship of the fragment to no. 227 is uncertain (see ibid. pp. 130, 133). 1-7 See SAA 2 6 162-166. 3 The copied sign is a good MEŠ; however, its appearance is more Babylonian than Assyrian. 3-4 Frahm's restored sequence of *lū ana* may seem superfluous. 4-5 Cf. *u rēhte mar'ē ṣīt libbi ša* RN in SAA 2 6 497, 516, 633B-C, see also no. 229 (below).

229 Previous edition: J. Lauinger, JCS 64 (2012) 88-89 (photos), 91-113 (transliteration and partial translation). The main differences between the Nimrud manuscripts of Esarhaddon's Succession Treaty (SAA 2 6) and the Tell Tayinat tablet have been outlined by Lauinger (2012) p. 113f. who also provides a commentary of the ms (ibid. pp. 113-22). It should be noted that collation of the original could still improve some of the readings on the obverse of the tablet.

I

1 (1) *a-de-e ša* ^{m}*aš-šur*–PAB–AŠ MAN KUR–*aš-šur*
2 (2) DUMU ^{md}30–PAB.MEŠ–SU MAN KUR–*aš-šur*
3 (3) TA LÚ.EN.NAM KUR.*ku-na-*⸢*li*⸣*-a*
4 (4) TA LÚ.2-*e* LÚ.GAL–É
5 (4) ⸢LÚ.A⸣.BA.MEŠ LÚ.DIB.PA.MEŠ LÚ.3.U$_{5}$.MEŠ
6 (4) LÚ.GAL–URU.MEŠ LÚ.*mu-tir–ṭè-me*
7 (4) LÚ.GAR-*nu*.MEŠ LÚ.GAL–*ki-ṣir*.MEŠ
8 (4) LÚ.EN–GIŠ.GIGIR.MEŠ LÚ.EN–*pet-hal-*⸢*la*⸣*-ti*
9 (4) LÚ.*zak-ku-e* LÚ.*kal-la-*⸢*ba-ni*⸣
10 (4) LÚ.⸢*um*⸣*-ma-a-ni* LÚ.⸢*a*⸣-[*ri-ti*?]
11 (4-5) LÚ.⸢*kit*⸣*-ki-tu-u* TA LÚ.ERIM.MEŠ [ŠU.2-*šú gab-bu*]
12 (5) ⸢TUR *u* GAL⸣ *mal ba-*[*šú-u*]

(Seal of Sennacherib)

13 (9) [*is*]-⸢*si*⸣*-šú-nu* ERIM.MEŠ-*šú-nu ša* EGIR *a-de-e*
14 (10, 6) *ina* [UD]-*me* ⸢*ṣa*⸣*-a-ti ib-ba-šu-ni* TA *na-pa-ah* ^{d}UTU-*ši*
15 (6-7) [*x*] *a-di e-reb* ^{d}UTU-*ši am-mar* ^{m}*aš-šur*–PAB–AŠ
16 (7-8) MAN KUR–*aš-šur* LUGAL-*u-tú* EN-*u-tú ina* UGU-*hi-šú-nu*
17 (8, 11) *up-pa-áš-u-ni ina* UGU ^{m}*aš-šur*–DÙ–A DUMU–MAN GAL-*u*
18 (11-12) *ša* É–UŠ-*te* DUMU ^{m}*aš-šur*–PAB–AŠ MAN KUR–*aš-šur*
19 (12) *ša* [*ina* UGU]-*hi-šú a-de-e is-si-ku-*(*nu*) *iš-kun-u-*[*ni*]

---

20 (13-14) [*ina* IGI MUL.SAG].⸢ME.GAR MUL⸣.*dil-bat* MUL.UDU.IDIM.SAG.[UŠ]
21 (14-15) ⸢MUL.UDU.IDIM.GUD.UD⸣ MUL.⸢*ṣal-bat-a-nu* MUL⸣.[GAG.SI.SÁ]

22 (16) [*ina* IGI ^{d}]*aš-šur* ⸢^{d}⸣*a-*⸢*num*⸣ ^{d}BAD ⸢^{d}⸣[É.A]
23 (17) ^{d}30 ^{d}⸢UTU⸣ ^{d}IM ^{d}MES ^{d}PA ^{d}[PA.TÚG?]
24 (19) ^{d}*še-ru-u-*⸢*a*⸣ ^{d}*be-let*–DINGIR.MEŠ DINGIR ⸢MEŠ? *a*?⸣-[*ši-bu-ti*]
25 (21-22) AN-*e* KI.⸢TIM⸣ DINGIR.MEŠ *ina* KUR–⸢*aš-šur*⸣ [DINGIR.MEŠ]
26 (22-23) ⸢KUR⸣–*šu-me-ri* ⸢*u*⸣ URI.KI ⸢DINGIR⸣.[MEŠ KUR.KUR]
27 (23) *ka-li-šú-*⸢*nu*⸣ [*ú*]-*dan-nin-*[*u-ni*]
28 (4) *iṣ-ba-tú* [*iš-ku-nu-ni*]

---

§ 1 Preamble

I 1 The treaty of Esarhaddon, king of Assyria, son of Sennacherib, king of Assyria, with the governor of Kunalia, with the deputy, the majordomo, the scribes, the chariot drivers, the third men, the village managers, the information officers, the prefects, the cohort commanders, the charioteers, the cavalrymen, the exempt, the outriders, the specialists, the *shi*[*eld bearers*], the craftsmen, (and) with [all] the men [of his hands], great and small, as many as there a[re] –

(Seal of Sennacherib)

[wi]th them and with the men who are born after the treaty in the [fu]ture, from the east [...] to the west, all those over whom Esarhaddon, king of Assyria, exercises kingship and lordship, concerning Assurbanipal, the great crown prince designate, the son of Esarhaddon, king of Assyria, [on] whose [be]half he established the treaty with you.

---

§ 2 Divine Witnesses

20 (which he) confirmed, made and [concluded in the presence of Ju]piter, Venus, Saturn, Mercury, Mars and [Sirius];
22 [in the presence of] Aššur, Anu, Illil, [Ea], Sîn, Šamaš, Adad, Marduk, Nabû, [Nusku, (Uraš, Nergal, Mullissu)], Šerua, Belet-ili, (Ištar of Nineveh, Ištar of Arbela), the gods d[welling in] heaven and earth, the gods of Assyria, [the gods] of Sumer and [Akka]d, all the god[s of the lands].

---

[23] Presumably Uraš, Nergal and Mullissu were omitted in ms T (ibid. p. 114).

§3 Adjuration

29 (25) *aš-šur* AD DINGIR.MEŠ EN KUR.⸢KUR⸣ [*ti-tam-ma*]

30 (26) ⸢^{d}*a*⸣-*num* ^{d}BAD ^{d}É.A ^{d}⸢30⸣ [^{d}UTU$^{?}$ MIN]

31 (28) ⸢^{d}⸣[PA ^{d}PA.TÚG] ^{d}IB ^{d}⸢U⸣.[GUR MIN]

32 (29) ⸢^{d}⸣NIN.L[ÍL ^{d}*še*]-⸢*ru*⸣-*u-a* ⸢^{d}⸣[*be-let*–DINGIR.MEŠ MIN]

33 (33) ^{d}15 ⸢*šá*⸣ ⸢URU⸣.[NINA].⸢KI⸣ ^{d}15 ⸢*ša arba*⸣-[*il* MIN]

34 (?) DINGIR.MEŠ ⸢*ka-li*⸣-*šú-nu šá* URU.[*kal-ha*$^{?}$ MIN]

35 (31) DINGIR.MEŠ ⸢*ka-li-šú*⸣-*nu šá* URU.ŠÀ–⸢URU⸣ [MIN]

36 (32) DINGIR.MEŠ DÙ-*šú-nu š*[*á* URU.NIN]A$^{?}$.KI MIN DINGIR.MEŠ ⸢DÙ⸣-[(*šú-nu šá*) URU.*kal-ha*$^{?}$ MIN]

37 (34?) ⸢*x x*⸣ [*x x x x*] ⸢*x x*⸣ [*x x*]

38 (35?) DINGIR.MEŠ [DÙ-*šú-nu šá* URU.*kàl-zi*$^{?}$ MIN]

(approximately 5 lines destroyed)

44′ (40A?) [DINGIR].⸢MEŠ⸣ [*x x x x x x x x x*]

45′ (40B?) ⸢DINGIR.MEŠ⸣ [*x x x x x x x x x*]

29 [Swear each individually] by Aššur, father of the gods, lord of the lands!
30 [Ditto] by Anu, Illil and Ea! [Ditto] by Sîn, [Šamaš, (Adad and Marduk)]!
31 [Ditto by Nabû, Nusku], Uraš and Ne[rgal]!
32 [Ditto] by Mulli[ssu, Še]rua and [Belet-ili]!
33 [Ditto] by Ištar of [Nineveh] and Ištar of Arbe[la]!
34 [Ditto] by all the gods of [*Calah*]!
35 [Ditto] by all the gods of the Inner C[ity]!
36 Ditto by all the gods o[f Ninev]eh! [Ditto] by all the gods [of *Calah*]!
37 [*Ditto by all the gods of Arbela*]!
38 [Ditto by all] the gods [of *Kilizi*]!

(Break)

44 [Ditto by all the god]s [of the lands; ditto by all] the gods [of heaven and earth! Ditto by all the gods of one's land and one's district]!

---

§4 Assurbanipal Designated Heir to Throne

46′ (41) *a-de-e* [*ša* ^{m}*aš-šur*–PAB–AŠ MAN KUR–*aš-šur ina* IGI DINGIR.MEŠ GAL.MEŠ]

47′ (42) *šá* AN-*e* [*u* KI.TIM *is-si-ku-nu iš-ku-nu-u-ni*]

48′ (43) *ša ina* U[GU *x x x x x x x x x x x x x*]

49′ (44?) *ša* ^{m}[*x x x x x x x x x x x x x x x x*]

50′ (45?) *ša* ⸢É$^{?}$⸣ [*x x x x x x x x x x x x x x x x*]

51′ (47?) *ina*$^{?}$ GIŠ$^{?}$.[GU.ZA *x x x x x x x x x x x x x*]

52′ (?) ⸢*x x*⸣ [*x x x x x x x x x x x x x x x x x*]

(approximately 9 lines destroyed)

46 (This is) the treaty [which Esarhaddon, king of Assyria, has concluded with you, in the presence of the great gods] of heaven [and earth], on be[half] of [Assurbanipal, the great crown prince designate, son of Esarhaddon, king of Assyria, your lord, whom he has named and appointed to the crown-princeship]:
51 [When Esarhaddon, king of Assyria, passes away, you will seat Assurbanipal, the great crown prince designate], upon [the royal throne, and he will exercise the kingship and lordship of Assyria over you. You shall protect him in country and in town, fall and die for him. You shall speak with him in the truth of your heart, give him sound advice loyally, and smooth his way in every respect].
(Break)

62′ (58) ⸢*te*⸣-[*na-a-ni tu-šá-an-na-a-ni šum-ma* ^{m}*aš-šur*–DÙ–A]
63′ (58) DUMU–[MAN GAL-*u šá* É–UŠ-*ti*]
64′ (59) *ša* ^{m}[*aš-šur*–PAB–AŠ MAN KUR–*aš-šur* EN-*ku-nu*]
65′ (60) ⸢*ú*⸣-*k*[*al-lim-*(*u*)-*ka-nu-ni ha-an-nu-um-ma la ta-da-gal-a-ni*]
66′ (61) LUGAL-*u-t*[*u* EN-*u-tu šá* KUR–*aš-šur*]
67′ (61) *ina* ⸢UGU-*hi*⸣-[*ku-nu la ú-pa-áš-u-ni*]

[62] You [shall neither change nor alter the word of Esarhaddon, king of Assyria, but serve this very Assurbanipal, the great crown] pri[nce designate], whom [Esarhaddon, king of Assyria, your lord], has pre[sented to you, and he shall exercise] the kingship [and dominion of Assyria] over [you].

---

§5 Obligation to Protect Heir

68′ (62) ⸢*šum-ma*⸣ [*x x x x x x x x x x x x x x x*]
69′ (?) ⸢*x*⸣ [*x x x x x x x x x x x x x x x*]
70′ (?) ⸢*x*⸣ [*x x x x x x x x x x x x x x x*]
71′ (?) ⸢*x*⸣ [*x x x x x x x x x x x x x x x*]
72′ (65-66) ⸢*la ta-na-ṣar-a-ni*⸣ [*ina* ŠÀ-*bi-šú tu-ta-ha-ṭa-a-ni*]
73′ (66-67) ⸢ŠU.2⸣-*ku*-⸢*nu*⸣ *ina* HUL-*t*[*i ina* ŠÀ-*bi-šú tu-bal-a-ni*]
74′ (67-68) [*ep-šú*] *bar-tú a-bu-tú l*[*a* DÙG.GA-*tú la* SIG$_5$-*tú*]
75′ (69) ⸢*te-pa-šá-niš-šú-ni*⸣ *ina* LUGAL-*t*[*i* KUR–*aš-šur tu-nak-ka-ra-šú-u-ni*]
76′ (69-70) ⸢TA⸣ ŠÀ-*bi* ŠEŠ.MEŠ-*šú* GAL.MEŠ ⸢TUR.MEŠ⸣ [*ina ku-mu-šú* GIŠ.GU.ZA]
77′ (70-71) KUR–*aš-šur*.KI? *t*[*u-šá-aṣ*]-*bat-a*-[*ni* LUGAL MAN-*ma*]
78′ (71) ⸢EN⸣ MAN-*ma ina* ⸢UGU⸣-*hi-ku-nu* ⸢*ta-šá-kan-a*⸣-[*ni*]
79′ (72) *a-na* ⸢LUGAL⸣ MAN-*ma* EN MAN-*ma ma*-[*mi*]-*tú ta-tam-ma-a-n*[*i*]

[68] You shall protect [Assurbanipal, the great crown prince designate, whom Esarhaddon, king of Assyria, has presented and ordered for you, and on behalf of whom he has confirmed and concluded (this) treaty with you; you shall not sin against him, nor bring] your hand [against him] with evil intent, nor revolt or do anything to him which is not [good and proper];

[75] [you shall not oust him] from the kingship [of Assyria] by [helping] one of his brothers, elder or younger, [to se]ize [the throne] of Assyria [in his stead], nor set [any other king or] any other lord over you, nor swear an oa[t]h to any other king or any other lord.

---

§6 Obligation to Report Opposition to Succession

80′ (73) ⸢*šum-ma at-tu*⸣-*nu* ⸢*a-bu-tú la x*⸣ (*x*)-⸢*tú la ba-ni-tú*⸣
(end of column I)

II
1 (74) *la ta-ri-is-su šá* [*e-peš* LUGAL-*te ina* UGU ^{m}*aš-šur*–DÙ–A]
2 (75) ⸢DUMU⸣–LUGAL (GAL) *šá* É–UŠ-*te* ⸢*la*⸣ [*tar-ṣa-tú-u-ni la ṭa-bat-u-ni*]
3 (76-77) *lu-u ina pi-i* ŠEŠ.⸢MEŠ⸣-[*šú* ŠEŠ.MEŠ AD.MEŠ-*šú* DUMU ŠEŠ.MEŠ AD.MEŠ-*šú qin-ni-šú* NUMUN É AD-*šú*]
4 (77-78) *lu-u ina pi*-⸢*i*⸣ [LÚ.GAL.MEŠ LÚ.NAM.MEŠ *lu-u ina pi-i* LÚ.*šá–ziq-ni*]
5 (78-79?) LÚ.S[AG *x x x x x x x x x x x x x x x*]
(rest broken away)

[80] If you [hear] any [*impro*]*per*, unsuitable or unseemly word concerning [the exercise of kingship which is] un[seemly and evil against Assurbanipal], the (great) crown prince designate, either from the mouth of [his] brothers, [his uncles, his cousins, his family (var. his people), members of his father's line]; or from the mouth of [magnates and governors, or from the mouth of the bearded courtiers] and the eu[nuchs, or from the mouth of the scholars or from the mouth of any human being at all, you shall not conceal it but come and report it to Assurbanipal, the great crown prince designate].

III

1 ⸢*x x x x x x x x x x x x x x x x*⸣
2 ⸢*x x x x x x x x x x x x x x*⸣
3 ⸢*x x x x x x x x x x x x x x*⸣
4 ⸢*x x x x x x x x x x x x x x*⸣
5 (178?) ⸢*ina* UGU ^{m}*aš-šur*–DÙ–A DUMU–MAN GAL⸣ [*šá* É–UŠ-*ti la tal-lak-a-ni-ni*]

§15 Obligation to Escape from Rebels

III 5 (178?) [You shall not make common cause with (any)one who may revolt against Assurbanipal, the great crown prince designate, son of Esarhaddon, king of Assyria, your lord, concerning whom he has concluded (this) treaty with you, but, should they seize you by force, you shall flee and come] to Assurbanipal, the great crown prince [designate].

---

6 [*x x x x x x x x x x x x x x x x*]
7 [*x x x x x x x x x x x x x x x x*]
8 [*x x x x x x x x x x x x x x x x*]
9 [*x x x x x x x x x x x x x x x x*]
10 [*x x x x x x x x x x x x x x x x*]
11 [*x x x x x x x x x x x x x x x x*]
12 [*x x x x x x x x x x x x x x x x*]

(rest broken away)

§16 Rejection of Rebellion

6 (180?) [You shall not, whether while *on a guard duty* ...... or on a day of rest, while residing within the land or while entering a *tax-collection point*, set in your mind an unfavorable thought against Assurbanipal, the great crown prince designate; you shall not revolt against him, nor make rebellion, nor do anything to him which is not good.]

(Break)

IV

1 (257) *la ta*-⸢*ta*⸣-*bak-a-ni* ⸢*gi*⸣-[*im*]-*lu* [*šá* ^{m}]*aš-šur*–DÙ–A
2 (258-59) DUMU–⸢LUGAL GAL⸣-*u šá* É–UŠ-*te la* ⸢*tu-tar-ra*⸣-*a-ni-ni*

§22 Action against Murderer of Assurbanipal

IV 1 [You shall wait for a woman pregnant by Esarhaddon, king of Assyria, (or) for the wife of Assurbanipal, the great crown prince designate (to give birth), and after (a son) is born, bring him up and set him on the throne

of Assyria, seize and slay the perpetrators of rebellion, destroy their name and their seed from the land, and] by shedding [blood for blood], avenge Assurbanipal, the great crown prince designate.

---

3 (259) ⸢*šum-ma*⸣ [*at*]-⸢*tu-nu* ^{m}⸣[*aš*]-⸢*šur*⸣–DÙ–[A DUMU]–MAN GAL *šá* É–UŠ-*te*
4 (261-62) ⸢DUMU⸣ [^{m}*aš-šur*–PAB]–AŠ MAN KUR–*aš-šur* [EN-*ku*]-*nu šam-mu šá mu-a*-⸢*ti-šú*⸣
5 (262-63) ⸢*tu-šá-kal*⸣-[*a*]-⸢*šú*⸣-*u-ni* ⸢*ta*⸣-[*šá*]-⸢*qi-a-šú*⸣-*ú-ni*
6 (263-64) [*ta-pa-šá-šá-šú-u-ni kiš-pi*] ⸢*te-pa*⸣-*šá-niš-šú-u-ni*
7 (264-65) [DINGIR.MEŠ *u* ^{d}IŠ.TAR *is-si-šú tu-šá-za*]-*na-a-ni*

§23 Prohibition against Killing Assurbanipal

3 You shall not give [As]surbani[pal], the great crown [prince] designate, son of [Esarha]ddon, king of Assyria, yo[ur lord], a deadly drug to eat or to drink, [nor anoint him with it], nor practice [witchcraft] against him, [nor make gods and goddesses ang]ry [with him].

---

§24 Action in Favor of Assurbanipal's Brothers

8 (266) [*šum-ma at-tu-nu*] ⸢*a*⸣-*na* ^{m}*aš-šur*–[DÙ]–A
9 (266) [DUMU–MAN GAL-*u*] ⸢*šá* É–UŠ⸣-*te*
10 (267) [DUMU ^{m}*aš-šur*–PAB–AŠ MAN KUR–*aš-šur* EN]-*ku-nu*
11 (268) [*ki-i nap-šá-te-ku-nu la tar-'a-ma-a*]-*ni*

(rest broken away)

[8] [You shall love] Assur[bani]pal, [the great crown prince] designate, [son of Esarhaddon, king of Assyria], your [lord, like yourselves].

(Break)

Reverse

V

---

§29 Injunction against Fomenting Strife between Prince and His Brothers

1 (344) *at-tu-nu ta-šam*[!]*-ma-a-*⸢*ni la*⸣ DÙG.GA-⸢*tú*⸣ *šá* ŠEŠ.MEŠ-*šú*
2 (345-46) *ina* IGI-*šú ta-qab-ba-a-ni* ⸢TA IGI⸣ ŠEŠ.⸢MEŠ⸣-*šú*
3 (346-47) *ta-par-ra-sa-šú-u-ni šum-ma qa-bi-a-*⸢*nu*⸣-*ti*
4 (347-48) *šá a-bu-tú an-ni-tú iq-ba-ka-nu-u-ni*
5 (348-49) *tu-ra-ma-šú-u-ni šum-ma la tal-lak-*⸢*a-ni-ni*⸣
6 (349-50) *a-na* ^{m}*aš-šur*–DÙ–A DUMU–MAN GAL-*u šá* É–UŠ-*te*
7 (350-51) *la ta-qab-ba-a-ni ma-a* AD-*ka a-de-e*
8 (351-52) *ina* UGU-*hi is-si-ni is-sa-kan ú-tam-ma-na-a-ši*

V 1 [If someone involves you in a plot, be it one of his brothers, his uncles, his relations, a member of his father's line, a eunuch or a bearded (courtier), an Assyrian or a foreigner, or any human being at all, saying: "Slander his brothers, sons by his own mother, before him, make it come to a fight between them, and divide his brothers, sons of his own mother, from him"], you shall not obey nor speak evil about his brothers in his presence, nor divide him from his brothers; you shall not let those who speak such things go free but shall come and report to Assurbanipal, the great crown prince designate as follows: "Your father imposed a treaty on us and made us swear an oath concerning it."

---

§30 Response to Attempts to Foment Strife

9 (353) *šum-ma ta-da-ga-la a-na* ^{m}*aš-šur*–DÙ–A DUMU–MAN
10 (353-54) GAL-*u šá* É–UŠ-*te* ŠEŠ.MEŠ-*šú la pal-hu-uš*
11 (354-55) *la kan-šu-uš* EN.NUN-*šú la i-na-ṣu-ru at-tu-*⸢*nu*⸣
12 (356) *ki ra-ma-ni-ku-nu ṣa-a-li la ta-ga-ra-šú-nu-ni*
13 (357) *pu-luh-tú* NÍG.BA.MEŠ-*te ina* ŠÀ-⸢*bi*⸣-*šú-nu*
14 (358) *la tu-še-rab-a-ni ma-a* AD-⸢*ku-nu*⸣ *ina* ŠÀ-*bi*
15 (358-59) *a-de-e is-sa-ṭar is-sa-kan ú-*⸢*tam*⸣-*ma-na-a-ši*

[9] You will not look at Assurbanipal, the great crown prince designate, or his brothers without reverence or submission. If someone does not protect him, you will fight them as if fighting for yourselves. You will bring frightful terror into their hearts, saying: "Your (pl.) father wrote (this) in the treaty, he established it, and he has made us swear (it)."

[353-59] Interestingly, the Tell Tayinat ms has twice the same section (§ 30 and § 30a) with only minor orthographic variations and a different line division (ibid. p. 116). [354-55, 357-58] The Tell Tayinat ms restores all the previously missing signs of these lines.

16 (353) *šum-ma ta-da-ga-la a-na* (^{m})*aš-šur–*[[*x*]]–DÙ–A
17 (353-54) DUMU–LUGAL GAL-*u šá* É–UŠ-*ti* ŠEŠ.MEŠ-[[*x*]]-*šú*
18 (354-55) ⸢*la pal-hu-uš la*⸣ *kan-šú-*⸢*uš*⸣ EN.NUN-*šú la i-na-ṣu-*[*r*]*u*
19 (355-56) *at-tu-nu ki* ⸢*ra*⸣-[*ma*]-⸢*ni*$^{!}$⸣-*k*[*u*$^{!}$-*n*]*u*$^{!}$ *ṣa-a-li*
20 (356-57) *la ta-ga-ra-šú-nu-ni pu-*⸢*luh-tú*⸣ NÍG.BA.MEŠ-*te*⸣
21 (357-58) *ina* ŠÀ-*bi-šú-nu la tu-še-rab-a-*⸢*ni*⸣
22 (358-59) *ma-a* AD-*ku-nu ina* ŠÀ *a-de-e is-sa-ṭar*
23 (359) *is-sa-kan ú-tam-ma-na-a-ši*

§30a [16] You will not look at Assurbanipal, the great crown prince designate, or his brothers without reverence or submission. If someone does not protect him, you will fight them as if fighting for y[ou]rse[lv]es. You will bring frightful terror into their hearts, saying: "Your (pl.) father wrote (this) in the treaty, he established it, and he has made us swear it."

---

24 (360) *šum-ma at-tu-nu ki-ma* (^{m})*aš-šur–*PAB–AŠ MAN KUR–*aš-šur*.KI
25 (360-61) EN-*ku-nu a-na šim-ti it-ta-lak*
26 (361-62) ^{m}*aš-šur–*DÙ–A DUMU–MAN GAL-*u šá* É–UŠ-*ti*
27 (362) *ina* GIŠ.GU.ZA LUGAL-*ti it-tu-šib*
28 (363) *a-bu-tú la* DÙG.GA-*tú šá* ⸢ŠEŠ.MEŠ⸣-*šú* DUMU AMA-*šú*
29 (364) *ina* IGI ŠEŠ-*šú-nu ta-qab-ba-a-ni* ⸢*tu-šá*⸣-*an-za-ra-ni*
30 (365) *ma* ŠU.2-*ka ina* HUL-*ti ina* ŠÀ-*bi-šú-nu ú-bil*

31 (366-67) *šum-ma* TA IGI ^{m}*aš-šur–*DÙ–A DUMU–MAN GAL *šá* É–UŠ-*ti*
32 (367-68) *tu-nak-kar-a-šá-nu-u-ni di-ib-bi-šú-nu*
33 (368-69) ⸢*la* SIG$_{5}$.MEŠ *ina* IGI⸣ ŠEŠ-*šú-nu ta-qa-ba-a-ni*
34 (369-70) *ma-za-su šá* ^{m}*aš-šur–*PAB–AŠ MAN KUR–*aš-šur* AD-*šú-nu u-kal-lim-u-šá-nu-*⸢*ni*⸣
35 (370-71) *ina* IGI ^{m}*aš-šur–*DÙ–A DUMU–MAN GAL-*u šá* ⸢É⸣–UŠ-*te ta-qab-ba-a-ni*
36 (372) TA ŠÀ *ma-za-*⸢*sú*⸣-*šú-nu ú-na-*⸢*kar*⸣-*u-šá-nu-ni*

§31 Injunction against Fomenting Strife after Assurbanipal's Accession

[24] When Esarhaddon, king of Assyria, your lord, passes away and Assurbanipal, the great crown prince designate, ascends the royal throne, you shall not say any evil word about his brothers, sons of his own mother, before their brother nor try to make them *accursed* (saying): "Bring your hand against them for an evil deed." You shall not alienate them from Assurbanipal, the great crown prince designate, nor shall you say any evil word about them in the presence of their brother.
(As for) the positions which Esarhaddon, king of Assyria, their father, assigned them, you shall not speak in the presence of Assurbanipal, the great crown prince designate, (trying to make him) remove them from their positions.

§32 Prohibition against Invalidation of Oath

37 (373) *šum-ma at-tu-nu sar-⸢bu*?⸣ [*ša ina* UGU DINGIR].⸢MEŠ⸣ *šá* UKKIN
38 (374) *lu pa-né-ku-nu lu* ŠU.2-*ku-⸢nu*⸣ [(*x*) *x x x*]-⸢*ku*⸣-*nu*
39 (375-76) *ta-pa-šá-šá-ni ina si-qi-ku-nu* ⸢*ta*⸣-[*rak-kas-a-ni*]
40 (376) *šá ma-mit pa-šá-ri*! *te*-⸢*pa*⸣-[*šá-a-ni*]

[37] You shall not smear your face, your hands, and your [throat] with … [*against* the god]s of the assembly, nor [tie] it in your *lap*, nor d[o] anything to undo the oath.

---

§33 Prohibition against Undoing the Oath

41 (377) *šum-ma at-tu-nu tur-tu tu-tar-ra-a-ni*
42 (378-79) *ma-mit ta-pa-šar-a-ni ši-in-ga-ti* ⸢*me*⸣-*me-né*
43 (379) *šá tur-ti tur-ri ma-mit pa-ša-ri ta-ha-sa-sa-ni-ni*
44 (380) ⸢*te*⸣-*ep-pa-šá-a-ni ta-mì-tú an-ni-tú a-na* ^{m}*aš-šur*–DÙ–⸢A⸣
45 (380-81) DUMU–MAN GAL-*u šá* É–UŠ-*te* DUMU ^{m}*aš-šur*–PAB–AŠ MAN KUR–*aš-šur*
46 (381-82) EN-*ku-nu* TA UD-*me an-ni-e a-di šá* EGIR *a-de-e*
47 (383-84) *ib-ba-šú-u-ni at-tu-nu* DUMU.⸢MEŠ⸣-*ku-nu* (*ša*) *a-na* UD-*me*
48 (384) *ṣa-a-ti ib-ba-šú-u-ni ta-ʾa-ku-nu*

[41] You shall not try to revoke or undo (this) oath … […]; you shall neither think of nor perform a ritual to revoke or undo this oath.

You and your sons to be born in the future will be bound by this oath concerning Assurbanipal, the great crown prince designate, son of Esarhaddon, king of Assyria, your lord, from this day on until what(ever) comes after this treaty.

---

§34 Attitude toward Swearing the Oath

49 (385) *šum-ma at-tu-⸢nu*⸣ *ki ina kaq-qar ta-mì-ti*
50 (385-86) ⸢*an*⸣-*ni-ti ta-za-za*-⸢*a*⸣-*ni ta-mì-tú šá* ⸢*da*⸣-*bab-ti*
51 (386-87) ⸢*šap*⸣-*ti ta-tam-ma-ni ina* ⸢*gu*⸣-*mur-ti* ŠÀ-*ku-nu*
52 (387) *la* ⸢*ta-tam-ma*⸣-*a-ni a-na* [DUMU.MEŠ]-*ku-nu*
53 (387-88) *šá* EGIR *a-de-e ib-ba-áš*-⸢*šú*⸣-[*u*]-⸢*ni*⸣
54 (388-89) *la tu-šal-ma-da-a-ni šum-ma at-tu-nu*
55 (389-90) GIG *la* SIKIL *ina* UGU *ra-ma-ni-ku*-⸢*nu*⸣ *ta-šá-kan-a*-⸢*ni*⸣
56 (390-91) *ina* ŠÀ *a-de-e šá* ^{m}*aš-šur*–PAB–AŠ MAN KUR–*aš-šur šá ina* UGU ^{m}*aš-šur*–DÙ–A
57 (391-92) DUMU–MAN GAL *šá* É–UŠ-*te la te-er-rab-a-ni*

[49] While you stand on the place of this oath, you shall not swear this oath with your lips only but shall swear it wholeheartedly; you shall teach it to your [sons] to be born after this treaty; you shall not feign incurable illness but take part in this treaty of Esarhaddon, king of Assyria, concerning Assurbanipal, the great crown prince designate.

---

58 (393) *a-na* EGIR UD-*me a-na* UD-*me ṣa-a-ti aš-šur* DINGIR-*ku-nu*
59 (394) ^{m}*aš-šur*–DÙ–A DUMU–MAN GAL *šá* É–UŠ-*te* ⸢EN⸣-*ku-nu*
60 (395-96) ⸢DUMU⸣.MEŠ-*ku-nu* DUMU.DUMU.MEŠ-*ku-nu a*-⸢*na* DUMU⸣.MEŠ-*šú* ⸢*lip*⸣-*lu-hu*

In the future and forever Aššur will be your god, and Assurbanipal, the great crown prince designate, will be your lord. May your sons and your grandsons fear him.

---

[373] Other mss omit *at-tu-nu* (ibid. 116). [378] ⸢*me*⸣-*me-ni* is not preserved in other mss (ibid. p. 116).

§35 Obligation to Guard the Treaty Document

61 (397) *šá ma-mit ṭup-pi an-ni-e e-nu-u e-gu-u* ⌜*i-haṭ-ṭu*⌝

62 (398-99) *i-pa-sa-su* AD EN *a*$^{!}$*-de-e* DINGIR.MEŠ GAL.MEŠ ⌜*e-te*⌝*-qu*

63 (399-400) *i-par-ra-ṣu ma-mit-su-un gab-ba-šú-nu* ⌜*ṭup-pi*⌝

64 (400-1) *a-de-e an-ni-e ṭup-pi aš-šur* MAN ⌜DINGIR⌝.MEŠ *u* DINGIR.⌜MEŠ⌝

65 (401-2) ⌜GAL⌝.MEŠ ⌜EN⌝.(MEŠ)*-iá ú-na-kar-u-ma ṣa-lam* ^{m}*aš-šur*–PAB–⌜AŠ⌝

66 (402-3) MAN KUR–*aš-šur* ⌜*ṣa*⌝*-lam* ^{m}*aš-šur*–DÙ–A DUMU–⌜MAN⌝ GAL *ša* É–UŠ-⌜*te*⌝

67 (404) *lu ṣa-lam* ⌜ŠEŠ.MEŠ⌝*-šú* DUMU.UŠ.MEŠ*-šú ša* ⌜*ina* UGU*-hi*⌝*-[šu]*

68 (404-5) *ú-na-kar-u-ni* NA$_4$.KIŠIB (NUN) GAL*-e an-ni-e*

69 (405-6) *šá a-de-e šá* ^{m}*aš-šur*–DÙ–A DUMU–MAN GAL *šá* É–UŠ*-te*

70 (406?) DUMU ^{m}*aš-šur*–PAB–AŠ MAN KUR–*aš-šur* EN*-ku-nu ina* ŠÀ *šá-ṭir-u-ni*

71 (407-8) *ina* NA$_4$.KIŠIB *šá aš-šur* LUGAL DINGIR.MEŠ *ka-nik-u-ni*

72 (408-9) *ina* IGI*-ku-nu šá-kín-u-ni ki* DINGIR*-ku-nu la ta-na-*⌜*ṣar*⌝*-a-ni*

[———————————————]

61 Whoever changes, neglects, violates, or voids the oath of this tablet (and) transgresses against the father, the lord, (and) the treaty of the great gods(?) (and) breaks their entire oath, or whoever discards this treaty tablet, a tablet of Aššur, king of the gods, and the great gods, my lords, or whoever removes the statue of Esarhaddon, king of Assyria, the statue of Assurbanipal, the great crown prince designate, or the statue(s) of his brothers (and) his sons *which are over him* – you will guard like your god this sealed tablet of the great ruler on which is written the treaty of Assurbanipal, the great crown prince designate, the son of Esarhaddon, king of Assyria, your lord, which is sealed with the seal of Aššur, king of the gods, and which is set up before you.

[———————————————]

§36 Injunction against Destroying the Document

73 (410) *šum-ma at-tu-nu tu-na-kar-a-ni ina* ^{d}GIŠ.BAR

74 (411) ⌜*ta*⌝*-pa-qid-da-a-ni a-na* A.MEŠ *ta-na-da-a-ni*

75 (412) *ina ep-*⌜*ri*⌝ *ta-kàt-ta-ma-a-ni ina mim-ma*

76 (412-13) *ši-pir* ⌜*ni-kil-ti*⌝ *ta-bat-a-ni tu-hal-la-qa-a-ni*

77 (413) *ta-sa-*⌜*pa*⌝*-na-a-ni*

73 If you should remove it, consign it to the fire, throw it into the water, cover it in the earth or destroy it by any cunning device, annihilate or deface it,

---

§37-56 Standard Curse Section

78 (414) ^{d}*aš-šur* MAN DINGIR.MEŠ ⌜*mu*⌝*-šim* NAM.MEŠ

79 (414-15) *ši-mat* MÍ.HUL$^{!}$ *la* DÙG.GA*-ti li-ši-im-ku-nu*

78 May Aššur, king of the gods, who decrees the fates, decree an evil and unpleasant fate for you.

---

80 (417) ^{d}⌜NIN⌝.LÍL *hi-ir-tú na-ram-ta-šú*

81 (417-18) *a-*⌜*ma*⌝*-ti-ku-nu li-*⌜*lam*⌝*-mì-in*

82 (418) *a-a i-ṣi-ba-ta a-bu-tú-ku-nu*

80 May Mullissu, his beloved wife, make your words evil, may she not intercede for you.

---

83 (418A) ^{d}⸢*a*⸣-*num* MAN DINGIR.(MEŠ) GIG *ta*-⸢*ni*⸣-*hu* 84 (418A-B) *di*-⸢*ʾu*⸣-*u di-lip-tú ni-sa-tú la* DÙG.⸢GA UZU⸣ 85 (418B-C) ⸢UGU⸣ *nap-har* É.MEŠ-*ku-nu* ⸢*li*⸣-[*šá-az-nin*]	§38A 83 May Anu, king of the gods, let disease, exhaustion, malaria, sleeplessness, worries and ill health [rain] upon all your houses.
86 (419) ^{d}30 *na-nar* AN-[*e u* KI.TIM *ina* SAHAR.ŠUB-*bu*] 87 (420) *li-hal-lip-ku-nu* [*ina* IGI DINGIR.MEŠ *u*] ⸢LUGAL⸣ 88 (420-21) *e*-⸢*re*⸣-*eb-ku-nu* [*a-a iq-bi*] ⸢GIM! *šér-re*⸣-*me* 89 (421) ⸢MAŠ⸣.DÀ ⸢EDIN *ru-up*⸣-*da*	§39 86 May Sîn, the brightness of heaven [and earth], clothe you [with leprosy and forbid] your entering [into the presence of the gods or] king. Roam the desert like the wild-ass and the gazelle!

FIG. 17. *Wild asses in the desert.*
BM 124882.

COURTESY TRUSTEES OF THE BRITISH MUSEUM

90 (422) ⸢*x x x x x*⸣ [*x*] ⸢*x x x x x x x*⸣ (rest broken away, approximately 8 lines)	§40 90 [May Šamaš, the light of heaven and earth, not judge you justly. May he remove your eyesight. Walk about in darkness]!
VI 1 (431) ^{d}SAG.ME.[GAR EN] ⸢DINGIR⸣.MEŠ MAH *e-rab* ^{d}⸢EN⸣ 2 (431-32) *ina* É.*sag-gíl* ⸢*a*⸣-*a ú*!!-*kal-lim-ku*-⸢*nu*⸣ 3 (432) *ma li*-⸢*hal*⸣-*li-qa nap-šat-ku*-⸢*un*⸣	§43 VI 1 May Jupit[er], exalted [lord] of the gods, not show you the entrance of Bel in Esangil; may he destroy your life.
4 (433) ^{d}AMAR.UTU ⸢DUMU.UŠ⸣ *reš-tu-ú hi*-⸢*ṭu*⸣ 5 (433) ⸢*kab*⸣-*tú* ⸢*ma*⸣-*mit la pa*-⸢*šá*⸣-*a-ri* 6 (434) *a-na* ⸢*šim*⸣-*ti-ku-nu* ⸢*li*⸣-*ši-im*	§44 4 May Marduk, the eldest son, decree a heavy punishment and an indissoluble curse for your fate.
7 (435) ^{d}NUMUN–DÙ-*tú na*-⸢*di*⸣-*na-at* MU *u* NUMUN 8 (435-36) MU-*ku-nu* NUMUN-*a-ku*-[*n*]*u ina* KUR *li-hal-liq-qi*	§45 7 May Zarpanitu, who grants name and seed, destroy your name and your seed from the land.

9 (437) d*be-let*–DINGIR.MEŠ EN-⸢*lat*⸣ *nab-ni-ti ta-lit-tú*
10 (437-38) *ina* KUR-*ku-nu lip-ru-*⸢*us*⸣ *ik-kil* TUR.DIŠ
11 (438-39) *u la-ke-e ina* SILA *re-*⸢*bi*⸣*-ti li*!!*-iz-za-ma-a*
12 (439) *ta-ret-ku-un*

§46 [9] May Belet-ili, the lady of creation, cut off birth from your land; may she deprive your nurses of the cries of little children in the streets and squares.

---

13 (440) dIM GÚ.⸢GAL⸣ [AN]-*e* KI.TIM A.AN *šam-ut-e*
14 (440-41) *ina* KUR-*ku-nu* ⸢*lip-ru*⸣*-us ta-me-ra-a-ti-ku-nu*
15 (441) *li-iz-za-am-*[*m*]*a-a a-*⸢*na*⸣ *la* DÙG.GA
16 (442) *ina ri-ih-ṣi* ⸢*dan*⸣-[*ni*] ⸢KUR⸣-*ku-*⸢*nu*⸣ *li-ir-hi-iṣ*
17 (442-43) BURU$_5$ *mu-ṣa-hi-ir* [KUR BUR]U$_{14}$-[*k*]*u-nu li-kul*
18 (443-44) *ik-kil* NA$_4$.UR$_5$ *u* [NINDU *ina* É.MEŠ-*ku-nu*] ⸢*a-a ib-ši*⸣
19 (444-45) ŠE.PAD.MEŠ ⸢*a-na ṭe-a-ni*⸣ *lu tah-*[*li*]*-qa-ku-nu*
20 (445-46) *ku-um* ŠE.PAD.MEŠ *eṣ-mat-tú-ku-n*[*u*] DUMU.MEŠ-*ku-nu*
21 (446) DUMU.MÍ.MEŠ-*e-ku-nu li-ṭ*[*e*]*-e-nu*
22 (446-47) *ki-ṣir šá* ŠU.SI.MEŠ-*e-ku-nu ina l*[*e*]*-e-ši*
23 (447) ⸢*lu*⸣ *la i-ṭa-bu qa-qa-*⸢*a*⸣*-nu*
24 (447) TA ŠÀ *a-ṣu-da-a-ti-ku-*⸢*nu*⸣ NÍG.SILA$_{11}$.GA
25 (448) *le-kul* ⸢AMA⸣ UGU DUMU.MÍ-*ti-*⸢*šá*⸣ KÁ-*šá*
26 (448-49) *le-di-il ina bu-ri-ku-nu* ⸢UZU⸣ DUMU.MEŠ-*ku-nu*
27 (449-50) *ak-la ina bu-bu-u-*⸢*ti hu-šah*⸣*-hi*
28 (450) LÚ UZU LÚ *le-kul* LÚ KUŠ LÚ
29 (451) *li-la-biš* UZU.M[EŠ]-*ku-nu* [U]R.KU.MEŠ
30 (451-52) ŠAH.MEŠ *le-ku-*⸢*lu*⸣ *e-*⸢*ṭam*⸣*-ma-ku-*⸢*nu*⸣
31 (452) *pa-qi-du na-*⸢*aq*⸣ ((TA)) A *a-a ir-*⸢*ši*⸣

§47 [13] May Adad, the canal inspector of [heaven] and earth, cut off rain from your land and deprive your fields of grain, may he submerge your land with a great flood; may the locust who diminishes [the land] devour you[r harve]st; may the sound of mill or [oven] be lacking [from your houses], may the grain for grinding dis[app]ear from you; instead of grain may your sons and your daughters grind your bones; may not (even) your (first) finger-joint dip in the dough, may the *qāqānu*-worm eat up the dough from your bowls. May a mother bar the door to her daughter. In your hunger eat the flesh of your sons! In want and famine may one man eat the flesh of another; may one man clothe himself in another's skin; may dogs and swine eat your flesh; may your ghost have nobody to take care of the pouring of libations to him.

---

32 (453) dIŠ.TAR *be-let* ⸢MURUB$_4$⸣ MÈ *ina* MÈ *dan-ni*
33 (453-54) GIŠ.BAN-*ku-nu liš-*⸢*bir i*⸣*-di-ku-nu lik-si*
34 (454) *ina* KI.TA ⸢LÚ⸣.[KÚR-*ku*]-⸢*nu*⸣ *lu li-še-šib-ku-nu*

§48 [32] May Ištar, lady of battle and war, smash your bow in the thick of battle, may she bind your arms, and have you crouch under [yo]ur [enemy].

---

35 (455) ᵈU.GUR *qar-⸢rad⸣* DINGIR *ina* ⸢GÌR⸣*-šú la ga-mì-li* 36 (455-56) *nap-šat-ku-nu li-bal-li šag-gaš-tú* 37 (456) NAM.ÚŠ.MEŠ *ina* ŠÀ*-bi-ku-⸢nu⸣ [liš]-⸢kun⸣*	§49 [35] May Nergal, hero of the gods, extinguish your life with his merciless sword, and [s]end slaughter and pestilence among you.
38 (457-58) ᵈ⸢NIN⸣.LÍL *a-ši-bát* NINA.⸢KI GÍR⸣ *ha-an-ṭu* 39 (458) *it-ti-ku-nu li-ir-ku-us*	§50 [38] May Mullissu, who dwells in Nineveh, tie a flaming sword at your side.
40 (459-60) ᵈ15 *a-ši-bát* URU.*arba-ìl* ARHUŠ$_4$ *⸢gim⸣-lu a-a i-šá-kan* UGU*-ku-un*	§51 [40] May Ištar, who dwells in Arbela, not show you mercy and compassion.
41 (461) ᵈ*gu-la a-zu-gal-⸢la-tú⸣* GAL*-tú* ⸢GIG⸣ *ta-né-hu ina* ŠÀ*-bi-ku-nu* 42 (462) *si-mu la-zu ina zu-u'-r[i$^{!?}$]-⸢ku⸣-nu li-šab-[š]i* ÚŠ.MEŠ *šar-ku* 43 (463) *ki-ma* A.MEŠ *ru-[u]n-ka*	§52 [41] May Gula, the great physician, put sickness and weariness in your hearts and an unhealing wound in your body. Bathe in blood and pus as if in water!
44 (466) ᵈ*a-ra-miš* EN–URU KUR.SI EN–URU KUR.⸢*az-a-i*$^?$⸣ A.MEŠ SIG$_7$.MEŠ *li-mal-li-⸢ku-nu⸣*	§54 [44] May Aramiš, lord of the city and land of Qarne (and) lord of the city and land of Aza'i, fill you with green water.

[456] *-bi-* is to be added to Lauinger's edition. [464f] Two lines omitted from the present manuscript (ibid. p. 119). [466A and B] These three lines are not known from other manuscripts (ibid. p. 119).

FIG. 18. *Man-eating lion: seal-impressions from Ishtar Temple, Nineveh.*
BM 122108+.

45 ^{d}IM ^{d}((DIŠ))*ša-la šá* URU.*kur-ba-ìl si-*⸢*ih-lu*⸣ UZU.ME
46 ⸢*la*⸣ DÙG.⸢GA⸣ *ina* ⸢*zu*⸣*-mur* KUR-*ku-*⸢*nu*⸣ *li-šab-ši*

§54A [45] May Adad (and) Šala of Kurba'il create piercing pain and ill health everywhere in your land.

---

47 ^{d}*šar-rat–a-am-qár-*⸢*ru*⸣*-u-*⸢*na*⸣ TA ŠÀ-*ku-*[*n*]*u li-šá-hi-ha tul-t*[*u*]

§54B [47] May Šarrat-Ekron make a worm fall from your insides.

---

48 (467) ^{d}*ba-a-a-ti*$^{!!}$–DINGIR (^{d})*a-na-an-ti–*⸢^{d}⸣*ba-a-a-ti–*DINGIR
49 (468) *ina* ŠU.2 UR.MAH *a-ki-li lim*$^{!}$*-nu-ku-nu*

§54C [48] May Bethel (and) Anath-Bethel hand you over to the paws of a man-eating lion.

---

50 (469-70) ^{d}*ku-bába* ^{d}*kar-hu-ha šá* URU.*gar-*⸢*ga*⸣*-miš ri*$^{!?}$*-im-ṭu*
51 (470-71) *dan-nu ina* ŠÀ-*ku-nu liš-kun* ⸢ÚŠ⸣.MEŠ-*ku-nu ki-m*[*a t*]*i-ki ina qaq-qar lit-tu-tuk*$^{!}$

§55 [50] May Kubaba (and) Karhuha of Carchemish put a serious *venereal* disease within you; may your blood drip to the ground like raindrops.

---

52 (472) DINGIR.MEŠ GAL.MEŠ *šá* AN-*e* ⸢KI⸣.TIM *a-ši-bu-te*
53 (472-73) *kib-ra-a-ti ma-la ina* ⸢*ṭup*⸣*-pi an-ni-e*
54 (473-74) MU-*šú-*(*nu*) *zak-ru lim-ha-*⸢*ṣu*⸣*-ku-u-nu*
55 (474-75) *li-kal-mu-ku-nu a-ra-*⸢*tú*⸣ *ma-ru-uš-tú*
56 (475-76) *ag-giš li-ru-ru-ku-*⸢*nu*⸣ *e-liš ina* TI.LA.MEŠ

§56 [52] May all the great gods of heaven and earth who inhabit the universe and are mentioned by name in this tablet, strike you, look at you in anger and curse you grimly with a painful curse.

57 (476-77) *li-sa-hu-u-ku-nu šap-liš ina* KI.TIM *e-*⸢*ṭam*⸣*-ma-ku-nu*
58 (477-78) A.MEŠ *li-za-mu-u* GIŠ.⸢MI⸣ [*u*] Ú.DA *lik-ta-še-du-ku-nu*
59 (478-79) *a-na pu-uz-ri šá-ha-ti* ⸢*la*⸣ *ta-nem-mì-da*
60 (479-80) ⸢NINDA.MEŠ⸣ *u* A.MEŠ *li-zi-bu-*⸢*ku*⸣*-nu* ⸢*su-un-qu hu-šah-hu*⸣
61 (480-81) *bu-bu-tú mu-ta-nu ina* IGI-⸢*ku*⸣*-nu a-a ip-pi-ṭir*

[57] Above, may they take possession of your life; below, in the netherworld, may your ghost be deprived of water. May shade [and] daylight always chase you away, and may you not find refuge in a hidden corner. May food and water abandon you; may want and famine, hunger and plague never be removed from you.

62 (481-82) ⸢*si-si*⸣ *šá ar-da-ti-ku-n*[*u*] ⸢*mat-nat šá* LÚ.GURUŠ-*ku-nu*⸣
63 (482) *ina ni-ṭil* IGI.2.MEŠ-*ku-nu* UR.KU.MEŠ ŠAH.MEŠ
64 (483) *ina* ⸢*re*⸣*-bit* URU.*aš-šur* ⸢*li*⸣*-in-da-šá-ru*
65 (483-84) LÚ.ÚŠ.MEŠ-*ku-*⸢*nu* KI⸣.TIM *a-a* ⸢*im*⸣*-hur ina kar-ši* UR.KU.MEŠ
66 (484-85) ŠAH.MEŠ *lu na-*⸢*aq*$^{!!}$⸣*-bar-ku-n*[*u*] UD-*me*.MEŠ-*ku-*⸢*nu*⸣ *lu e-ṭu-u*

[62] Before your very eyes may dogs and swine drag the *teats* of your young women and the *penises* of your young men to and fro in the squares of Assur; may the earth not receive your corpses but may your burial place be in the belly of a dog or a pig.

67 (485) MU.MEŠ-*ku-nu lu ek-*⸢*la*⸣ *ek-le-ti*
68 (486) *la na-ma-ri a-na* ⸢*šim*⸣*-ti-ku-nu li-ši-mu*
69 (487) *ina ta-né-hi di-lip-ti n*[*a*]*-piš-ti-ku-nu* ⸢*liq-ti*⸣

[67] May your days be dark and your years dim, may darkness which is not to be brightened be declared as your fate. May your life end in exhaustion and sleeplessness.

70 (488) U$_4$.NÁ.ÀM *a-bu-bu la mah-ru ul-tú* KI.TIM
71 (489) *li-la-am-ma na-aš-pan-ta-*⸢*ku*⸣*-nu liš-*[[*x*]]*-kun*
72 (489-90) *mim-ma* DÙG.GA *lu ik-kib-ku-nu mim-ma* GIG *lu ši-mat-ku-nu*
73 (490) *qi-i-ru ku-up-ru lu* ⸢*ma*⸣*-ka-la-ku-nu*
74 (491) KÀŠ.ANŠE.(NITÁ) *lu maš-qit-ku-nu nap-ṭu lu pi-iš-šat-ku-nu*
75 (492) *e-la-pu-u šá* ÍD *lu tak-ti-im-ku-nu*
76 (493) *še-e-du ú-tuk-ku* ⸢MÁŠKIM *lem*⸣*-nu* É*-ku-nu li-hi-ru*

70 May an irresistible flood come up from the earth and devastate you; may anything good be forbidden to you, anything ill be your share; may tar and pitch be your food; may urine of an ass be your drink, may naphtha be your ointment, may duckweed be your covering. May demon, devil and evil spirit select your houses.

---

§57 Vow of Allegiance to Assurbanipal

77 (494) DINGIR.MEŠ *an-nu-ti lid-gu-lu šum-ma a-né-ni*
78 (494-95) *ina* UGU ^{m}*aš-šur*–PAB–AŠ MAN KUR–*aš-šur ù* ^{m}*aš-šur*–DÙ–A DUMU–MAN ⸢GAL*-u*⸣
79 (495-96) *šá* É–UŠ*-te u* ŠEŠ.MEŠ*-šú* DUMU AMA-[*šú*]
80 (496) *šá* ^{m}*aš-šur*–DÙ–A DUMU–MAN GAL*-u šá* É–UŠ-⸢*te*⸣
81 (497) *u re-eh-ti* DUMU.MEŠ *ṣi-it–lib-bi šá* ^{m}*aš-šur*–[PAB]–AŠ
82 (497-98) ⸢MAN KUR–*aš-šur si-hu*⸣ *bar-tú né-ep-pa-áš-u-*⸢*ni*⸣
83 (498-99) [*pi-i-ni* TA LÚ.KÚ]R*-šú ni-ša-kan-u-*⸢*ni*⸣

77 May these gods be our witnesses: we will not make rebellion or insurrection against Esarhaddon, king of Assyria, against Assurbanipal, the great crown prince designate, against his brothers, sons by the same mother as Assurbanipal, the great crown prince designate, and the rest of the offspring of Esar[ha]ddon, king of Assyria, or make [common] cause [with] his [ene]my.

84 (499-500) ⸢*šum-ma*⸣ [*mu-šam-hi*]*-ṣu-u-te mu-šad-bi-bu-*⸢*ti*⸣
85 (500-1) ⸢*li-ih*⸣-[*šu ša*] *a-mat* HUL.⸢TIM⸣
86 (501-2) ⸢*la* DÙG.GA⸣ [*la*] ⸢*ba*⸣*-ni-tú da-bab sur-ra-*⸢*a*⸣*-te*
87 (502-3) ⸢*la ki-na-a-te*⸣ [*šá ina* UG]U ^{m}*aš-šur*–DÙ–A DUMU–MAN ⸢GAL⸣*-u*
88 (503-4) ⸢*šá*⸣ É–UŠ*-te u* ⸢ŠEŠ⸣.[MEŠ]*-šú* DUMU ⸢AMA⸣*-šú*
89 (504-5) ⸢*šá*⸣ ^{m}*aš-šur*–DÙ–A DUMU–MAN GAL*-u šá* [É–UŠ*-te ni-šam*]*-mu-u-ni*
90 (505-6) [*nu*]*-pa-za-*⸢*ar*⸣*-u-ni a-*[*na* ^{m}*aš-šur*–DÙ–A DUMU]–MAN GAL*-u*
91 (506-7) [*šá* É–UŠ*-t*]*e* EN*-in-*⸢*ni*⸣ [*la ni-qa*]*-bu-u-ni*

84 Should [we hea]r of [instig]ation to armed rebellion, agitation or malicious whisp[ers], evil, [un]seemly things, or treacherous, disloyal talk against Assurbanipal, the great crown prince designate, and against his brother[s] by the same mother as Assurbanipal, the great crown prince [designate, we] will not conceal it but [will rep]ort it t[o Assurbanipal], the great crown [prince designa]te, our lord.

92 (507-8) [UD*-me am-mar*] *a-né-ni* [DUMU.MEŠ*-ni* DUMU].⸢DUMU⸣.MEŠ*-ni*
93 (508) [*bal-ṭa-a-ni-ni* ^{m}*aš-šur*–DÙ–A DUMU–MAN] GAL*-u*
(rest broken away, approximately 4 to 5 lines destroyed)

92 [As long as] we, [our sons (and)] our [grands]ons [are alive, Assurbanipal], the great [crown prince designate, shall be our king and our lord, and we will not set any other king or prince over us, our sons or our grandsons. May all the gods mentioned by name (in this treaty) hold us, our seed and our seed's seed accountable (for this vow)].

VII

§58-106 Ceremonial Curse Section

1 (513) ⸢*šum*⸣-*ma at-tu-nu ina* ŠÀ ⸢*a-de*⸣-[*e an-nu-te šá* ^{m}*aš-šur*–PAB–AŠ]
2 (513-14) ⸢MAN⸣ KUR–*aš-šur ina* UGU ^{m}*aš-šur*–DÙ–A ⸢DUMU⸣–[MAN GAL-*u šá*] ⸢É⸣-UŠ-⸢*te*⸣
3 (515) ⸢*ù*⸣ ŠEŠ.MEŠ-*šú* DUMU ⸢AMA⸣-[*šú šá* ^{m}*aš-šur*–DÙ–A]
4 (515-16) ⸢DUMU⸣–MAN GAL-*u šá* É–UŠ-⸢*te u*⸣ [*re*]-⸢*eh-ti* DUMU⸣.[MEŠ]
5 (516-17) ⸢*ṣi*⸣-*it*–ŠÀ-*bi šá* ^{m}*aš-šur*–[PAB]–⸢AŠ⸣ MAN ⸢KUR⸣–[*aš-šur*] ⸢EN⸣-[*ku*]-⸢*nu*⸣
6 (517) ((⸢*a*⸣-*de-e*)) *is-si-ku-*[*nu*] ⸢*iš-kun*⸣-*u-ni*
7 (517-18) ⸢*ta-ha-ṭa-a-ni*⸣ ^{d}[*aš-šur* AD] DINGIR.MEŠ ⸢GAL⸣.MEŠ
8 (518) [*ina*] GIŠ.TUKUL.MEŠ-*šú* ⸢*e*⸣-[*zu*]-*ti li*-⸢*šam*⸣-*qit-ku-nu*

VII 1 If you should sin against [this] treaty [which Esarhaddon], king of Assyria, has concluded with yo[u] concerning Assurbanipal, [the great crown] prince designate, and concerning his brothers, sons by [the same] mother [as Assurbanipal], the great crown prince designate, and the [re]st of the offspring of Esar[ha]ddon, king of [Assyria, yo]ur lord.
7 May [Aššur, father] of the gods, strike you down [with] his fierce weapons.

---

9 (519) ⸢^{d}⸣IGI.DU EN *a-šá-*⸢*re*⸣-*du* UZU.MEŠ-*ku-nu*
10 (520) ⸢TI$_{8}$⸣.MUŠEN *zi-i-bu li-šá-kil*

§59 9 May Palil, the foremost lord, let eagles and vultures eat your flesh.

---

11 (521-22) ⸢^{d}⸣É.A MAN ZU.AB EN IDIM A.⸢MEŠ⸣ *la ba-la-ṭi liš-*(*te*)-*šir*$_{4}$-*ku-nu*
12 (522) ⸢*a*⸣-*ga-nu-til-la-a* ⸢*li*⸣-*mal-li-ku-nu*

§60 11 May Ea, king of the Abyss, lord of the springs, give you deadly water to drink, and fill you with dropsy.

---

13 (523) ⸢DINGIR⸣.MEŠ GAL.MEŠ *šá* AN-⸢*e*⸣ KI.TIM A.MEŠ *u* Ì.GIŠ
14 (523) ⸢*a*⸣-*na* NÍG.GIG-*ku-nu* ⸢*liš*⸣-*ku-nu*

§61 13 May the great gods of heaven and earth *turn* water (and) oil into a *curse* for you.

---

15 (524) ⸢^{d}⸣GIŠ.BAR *na-din ma-ka-*⸢*li a*⸣-*na* DINGIR.MEŠ GAL.MEŠ
16 (525) ⸢MU⸣.MEŠ-*ku-nu* NUMUN.MEŠ-⸢*ku*⸣-*nu ina* ^{d}GIŠ.BAR *liq-mu*

§62 15 May Girra, who gives food to small and great, burn up your name and your seed.

---

17 (526) KIMIN DINGIR.MEŠ *ma-la ina ṭup-*⸢*pi*⸣ *a-*⸢*de-e*⸣ *an-ni-e*
18 (526-27) ⸢MU⸣-*šú-nu* ⸢*zak-ru am-mar* SIG$_{4}$⸣ *kaq-*⸢*qu*⸣-*ru*
19 (527-28) ⸢*lu-si-qu-ni-ku-nu*⸣ *kaq-qar-ku-nu* ⸢*ki*⸣-[*i*] ⸢AN.BAR⸣
20 (528-29) *le-pu-šu me-me-*⸢*ni ina* ŠÀ-*bi*⸣ *lu* ⸢*la i*⸣-*par-ru-ʾa*

§63 17 Ditto, may all the gods that are mentioned by name in this treaty tablet make the ground as narrow as a brick for you. May they make your ground like iron (so that) nothing can sprout from it.

---

21 (530) *ki-i šá* ⸢TA ŠÀ AN⸣-[*e*] *šá* ZABAR ⸢A.AN⸣
22 (530-31) *la i-za-nun-a-ni ki-i ha-an-ni-e*
23 (531-32) ⸢A.AN⸣ *na-al-šu ina* A.ŠÀ.[M]EŠ-*ku-nu ta-me-ra-te-*[*ku*]-⸢*nu*⸣
24 (532) *lu la il-lak ku-um* A.AN
25 (533) ⸢*pe*⸣-*ʾe-na-a-ti* ⸢*ina*⸣ KUR-*ku-nu li-iz-nu-na*

§64 21 Just as rain does not fall from a brazen heaven so may rain and dew not come upon your fields and [yo]ur meadows; instead of dew may burning coals rain on your land.

---

26 (534-35) ⸢*ki*⸣-*i šá* AN.NA [*ina*] IGI IZI *la i-za-zu-u-*⸢*ni*⸣ *at-*⸢*tu*⸣-*nu* 27 (535) [*ina*] IGI LÚ.KÚR-*ku-nu* ⸢*la*⸣ *ta-za-a-za* DUMU.MEŠ-*ku-*⸢*nu*⸣ 28 (536) [DU]MU.MÍ.MEŠ-*ku-*(*nu*) *ina* ŠU.2-⸢*ku*⸣-*nu la ta-ṣab-ba-ta*	§65 [26] Just as lead does not stand up before a fire, so may you not stand before your enemy (or) take your sons and your [dau]ghters in your hands.
29 (537-38) ⸢*ki*⸣-*i šá* NUMUN *ša* ANŠE.*ku-*⸢*din*⸣-[*ni*] *la-áš-šu-u-ni* MU-*ku-nu* 30 (538) ⸢NUMUN⸣-*ku-nu* NUMUN *šá* ŠEŠ.[M]EŠ-*ku-nu* DUMU.MEŠ-*ku-nu* 31 (539) ⸢DUMU.MÍ⸣.MEŠ-*ku-nu* TA ⸢KUR⸣ *li-ih-li-iq*	§66 [29] Just as a mule has no offspring, may your name, your seed, and the seed of your sons and your daughters disappear from the land.
32 (540) ⸢*ki-i šá* SI⸣ [*šá x x*]-*ni* NUMUN *u sík-kit* KAŠ 33 (541) *ina* ŠÀ-*bi* [*šak-nu*]-*ni* ⸢*ki*⸣-*i šá* NUMUN.MEŠ-*ni an-nu-te* 34 (541-42) ⸢*la i-par*⸣-[*ru*]-⸢*u'*⸣-*u-ni-*⸢*ni*⸣ *u sik-kit* KAŠ 35 (542) [*a*]-⸢*na*? *x-x*⸣-*ni-šá la* ⸢*ta*⸣-*sa-har-u-ni* 36 (543) ⸢MU⸣-*ku-nu* NUMUN-*ku-nu* NUMUN *šá* ŠEŠ.MEŠ-*ku-nu* DUMU.MEŠ-*ku-nu* 37 (544) ⸢*ina*⸣ UGU *pa-ni šá kaq-qi-ri li-ih-li-iq*	§67 [32] Just as a shoot is [...], (and) seed(s) and the *yeast* of beer are [placed] within, and just as these seeds do not sprout, and the *yeast* of beer does not turn [t]o its ..., may your name, your seed, and the seed of your brothers and your sons disappear from the face of the earth.
38 (545) ⸢^{d}⸣UTU *ina* GIŠ.APIN *šá* AN.BAR ⸢URU⸣-*ku-nu* KUR-*ku-nu* 39 (545-46) ⸢*na*⸣-*gi-ku-nu lu-šá-bal-kit*	§68 [38] May Šamaš with an iron plough overturn your city and your district.
40 (547) KIMIN.KIMIN *ki-i šá* U$_8$ *an-*⸢*ni*⸣-*ti* 41 (547-48) ⸢*šal*⸣-*qa-at-u-ni* UZU *šá* DUMU-*šá ina* KA-*šá* 42 (548-49) ⸢*šá*⸣-*kín-u-ni ki-i ha-an-ni-i* ⸢UZU⸣.MEŠ 43 (549-50) ⸢*šá*⸣ DUMU.MEŠ-*ku-nu* DUMU.MÍ.MEŠ-*ku-*(*nu*) *ina bu-*⸢*ri*⸣-*ku-nu li*?-(*šá*)-*kil*?-*ku-*⸢*nu*⸣	§69 [40] Ditto, ditto; just as this ewe has been cut open and the flesh of her young has been placed in her mouth, may they make you eat in your hunger the flesh of your sons and your daughters.
44 (551) *ki-i šá kab-su kab-su-tú* UDU.NIM ⸢MÍ⸣.NIM-*tú* 45 (551-52) ⸢*šal*⸣-*qu-u-ni ir-ri-šú-nu* TA GÌR.2-⸢*šú*⸣-*nu* 46 (552-53) ⸢*kar*⸣-*ku-u-ni ir-ri šá* DUMU.MEŠ-⸢*ku*⸣-*nu* 47 (553-54) ⸢DUMU⸣.MÍ.MEŠ-*ku-*(*nu*) TA GÌR.2.MEŠ-*ku-nu* ⸢*li*⸣-*kar-ka*	§70 [44] Just as young sheep and ewes and male and female spring lambs are slit open and their entrails rolled down over their feet, so may the entrails of your sons and your daughters roll down over your feet.

[552] After *kar-ku-u-ni*, most other manuscripts have *ir-ri-ku-nu* (line 553).

FIG. 19. *Vulture carrying entrails.* BM 118907.

48 (555) [*ki-i*] ⸢*šá*⸣ MUŠ ⸢d⸣NIN.KILIM *ina* ŠÀ [1]-*et hu-re-te*
49 (556) ⸢*la*⸣ *e-rab-u-*⸢*ni*⸣ *la i-rab-*⸢*bi*⸣*-ṣu-u-ni*
50 (557) [*ina*] UGU (*na-kas*) ZI.MEŠ ⸢*šá*⸣ *a-hi-iš id-*⸢*da*⸣*-bu-ub-u-ni*
51 (558) ⸢*at*⸣*-tu-nu* MÍ.MEŠ-⸢*ku*⸣*-nu ina* ŠÀ 1-*en* É *la te-ra-ba*
52 (559) ⸢*ina*⸣ UGU 1-*et* GIŠ.⸢NÁ⸣ *la ta-*⸢*tal*⸣*-la ina* UGU *na-kas*
53 (559) ⸢ZI⸣.MEŠ *šá a-*⸢*he*⸣*-iš du-*⸢*ub*⸣*-ba*

§71 48 [Just] as a snake and a mongoose do not enter the [sa]me hole to lie there together but think only of cutting each other's throat, so may you and your women not enter the same room to lie down in the same bed; think only of cutting each other's throats!

---

54 (560-61) *ki-i šá* NINDA.MEŠ ⸢GEŠTIN⸣ *ina* (ŠÀ) *ir-ri-ku-nu e-*⸢*rab-u*⸣*-ni ta-mì-tú*
55 (561-62) ⸢*an-ni-tú ina* ŠÀ *ir-ri*⸣*-ku-nu ir-ri šá* DUMU.MEŠ-*ku-*⸢*nu* DUMU⸣.[MÍ].⸢MEŠ⸣*-ku-nu lu-še-ri-*⸢*bu*⸣

§72 54 Just as bread and wine enter into the intestines, [so] may they (= the gods) make this oath enter into your intestines and into those of your sons and your daugh[ter]s.

---

56 (563-64) *ki-i šá* ⸢A.MEŠ⸣ *ina* ⸢ŠÀ⸣ *tak-ku-si ta-nap!-pa-ha-a-ni a-na* ⸢*ka-šú*⸣*-*[*nu*]
57 (564-65) [MÍ].⸢MEŠ-*ku-nu* DUMU.MEŠ⸣*-ku-nu* DUMU.MÍ.MEŠ-*ku-nu li-pu-hu-ku-nu*
58 (565-66) ⸢ÍD.MEŠ-*ku-nu* IGI.2⸣.[MEŠ]-*ku-nu* A.MEŠ-*ši-na a-na qí-niš* ⸢*lu*⸣*-sa-hi-ra*

§73 56 Just as you blow water out of a tube, may they blow out you, your [wom]e[n], your sons and your daughters; may your streams and your springs make their waters flow backwards.

---

59 (567) [N]INDA.MEŠ *ina pi-*⸢*it*⸣*-ti* KUG.GI *ina* KUR-*ku-nu* ⸢*lil*⸣*-qú*

§74 59 May they take [b]read away from your land in the same manner as gold.

---

60 (568) KIMIN.KIMIN ⸢*ki-i*⸣ *šá* ⸢LÀL⸣ *ma-ti-qu-u-ni* ÚŠ.MEŠ *šá* ⸢MÍ⸣.MEŠ-*ku-nu*
61 (569) DUMU.MEŠ-*ku-nu* DUMU.⸢MÍ⸣.MEŠ-*ku-nu ina pi-i-ku-nu li-im-ti-iq*

§75 60 Ditto, ditto; just as honey is sweet, so may the blood of your women, your sons and your daughters be sweet in your mouth.

---

62 (570) *ki-i šá šá-aṣ-*⸢*bu*⸣*-ti tul-tú ta-kul-u-ni*
63 (571) *ina bal-ṭu-ti-ku-n*[*u*] UZU.MEŠ-*ku-nu* UZU.MEŠ *šá* M[Í].MEŠ-*ku-nu*
64 (572) ⸢DUMU⸣.MEŠ-*ku-nu* DUMU.M[Í.M]EŠ-*ku-nu tu-es-su lu* ⸢*ta*⸣*-kul*

§76 [62] Just as a worm eats provisions, so may the worm eat, while you are (still) alive, your own flesh and the flesh of your wives, your sons and your daughters.

---

65 (573-74) GIŠ.⸢BAN⸣-*ku-nu liš-*⸢*bi-ru*⸣ *ina* KI.TA LÚ.KÚR-*ku-nu lu-še-ši-*[*bu*]*-ku-nu*
66 (574-75) GIŠ.BAN *ina* ŠU.2-*ku-nu lu-*⸢*šá*⸣*-bal-ki-tú* GIŠ.GIGIR.MEŠ-*ku-nu a-na qí-niš* ⸢*lu-šá-di-lu*⸣

§77 [65] May they (= all the gods) break your bow and subje[ct] you to your enemy; may they turn over the bow in your hands and make your chariots run backwards.

---

67 (576-77) *ki-i šá a-a-lu kaš-šu-*⸢*du*⸣*-u-ni de-*⸢*ku*⸣*-u-ni a-na ka-a-šú-nu*
68 (577-78) ŠEŠ.MEŠ-*ku-nu* ⸢DUMU⸣.MEŠ-*ku-*⸢*nu*⸣ *lu-kaš-ši-du li-du-ku-ku-nu*

§78 [67] Just as a stag is pursued and killed, so may you, your brothers and your sons be pursued and killed.

FIG. 20. *Stag and net.*
BM 124871.

69 (579-80) *ki-i šá bur-⸢di⸣ šá-hi la ⸢ta⸣-da-gal-u-ni ina bé-eš-ka-ni-šá*
70 (580-81) *la ta-sa-har-⸢u-ni at⸣-tu-⸢nu⸣* (*ina* UGU) MÍ.MEŠ-*ku-nu* DUMU.MEŠ-*ku-nu*
71 (581) *a-na* ⸢É⸣.[MEŠ]-⸢*ku*⸣-*nu la ta-sa-hu-ra*

§79 [69] Just as a caterpillar does not see and does not return to its cocoon, so may you not return (to) your women, your sons, and to your house[s].

---

72 (582) ⸢KIMIN⸣.KIMIN *ki-i šá* MUŠEN *ina* ⸢*du-ba*⸣-*qi*
73 (582-83) *i-sa-pak-u-ni a-na ka-šú-nu* ŠEŠ.MEŠ-*ku-nu*
74 (583-84) DUMU.MEŠ-*ku-nu ina* ŠU.2 LÚ.KÚR-*ku-nu liš-ka-nu-ku-nu*

§80 [72] Ditto, ditto; just as a bird is caught by a trap, so may they deliver you, your brothers and your sons into the hands of your enemy.

---

75 (585-86) UZU.MEŠ-*ku-nu* UZU.MEŠ *šá* [ŠEŠ?].MEŠ-*ku-nu* MÍ.MEŠ-*ku-nu* DUMU.MEŠ-*ku-nu*
76 (586-87) *ki qi-i-ri ku-u*[*p*]-*ri*!! *nap-ṭi lu-ṣal-li-mu*

§81 [75] May they make your flesh and the flesh of your [*brother*]s, your women and your sons as black as bitumen, pitch and naphtha.

---

77 (588-89) *ki-i šá ha-⸢e-pa-ru⸣-u*[*š*]-*hi ú-ma-mu ina kip-pi i-sa-pa-ku-u-ni*
78 (589-90) *at-tu-nu* ŠEŠ.MEŠ-*ku-nu* ⸢DUMU⸣.MEŠ-*ku-nu ina* ŠU.2 LÚ.KÚR-*ku-nu na-ṣa-bi-ta*

§82 [77] Just as a … beast is caught in a snare, may you, your brothers and your sons be seized by the hand of your enemy.

---

79 (591-92) UZU.MEŠ-*ku-nu* UZU.MEŠ *šá* ŠEŠ.MEŠ-*ku-nu* DUMU.MEŠ-*ku-nu*
80 (592-93) DUMU.MÍ.MEŠ-*ku-nu ki-i* ⸢UZU⸣ *šá hur-ba-bil-li lig-mu-ru*

§83 [79] May your flesh and the flesh of your brothers, your sons and your daughters be wasted like the flesh of a chameleon.

---

81 (594-95) *ki-i šá ina* ⸢ŠÀ *ka*⸣-*ma-*⸢*ni*⸣ [*šá*] LÀL HABRUD.MEŠ *pa-lu-za-a-*⸢*ni*⸣
82 (596-97) *ki-i ha-an-ni-e* UZU.⸢MEŠ⸣-*ku-nu* UZU.MEŠ *šá* ŠEŠ.MEŠ-⸢*ku*⸣-*nu*
83 (597-98) DUMU.MEŠ-*ku-nu* DUMU.⸢MÍ.MEŠ⸣-*ku-*⸢*nu ina*⸣ *bal-ṭu-ti-ku-nu* ⸢HABRUD⸣.MEŠ *lu pa-*⸢*lu-za*⸣

§84 [81] Just as the honeycomb is pierced with holes, so may they pierce your flesh, the flesh of your brothers, your sons and your daughters with holes while you are alive.

---

84 (599) *ki-*[*i šá*] ⸢BURU$_5$.MEŠ⸣ NUMUN *bar*!!-*mu kal-ma-tú mu-nu*
85 (600) [(*a-ki-lu*) URU.MEŠ]-*ku-nu* KUR-*ku-nu* A.ŠÀ.MEŠ-*ku-nu lu-*⸢*šá*⸣-*ki-lu*

§85 [84] May they cause your [towns], your land and your fields to be devoured just [as with] locusts, …, lice, caterpillars [(and other field pests)].

---

86 (601) *ki-i zu-um-bi ina* ŠU.2 LÚ.KÚR-*ku-nu le-pa-šu-ku-nu*
87 (602) ⸢LÚ⸣.KÚR-*ku-nu li-im-ri-iṣ-ku-nu*

§86 [86] May they make you like a fly in the hand of your enemy, and may your enemy squash you.

---

88 (603) [*ki-i šá*] ⸢*pi*⸣-*is-pi-su an-ni-ú*
89 (603-4) [*bé*]-*ʾi-šu-u-ni* ⸢*ki*⸣-*i ha-an-ni-e*
90 (604) *ina* IGI DINGIR.MEŠ ⸢*u* LUGAL⸣ *u a-me-lu-te*
91 (605) ⸢*ni-piš-ku-nu*⸣ [*lib*]-⸢*ʾi-i*⸣-*šu*

§87 [88] [Just as] this bug [st]inks, just so [may] your breath [s]tink before gods and king and mankind.

VIII

1 (606) [*a*]-*n*[*a* *ka-na-šú-nu* MÍ.MEŠ-*ku-nu* ŠEŠ.MEŠ-*ku-nu*]
2 (606-7) DUMU.MEŠ-*ku-nu ina pi-til-*[*ti li-ih-na-qu-ku-nu*]

§88 VIII 1 [May they strangle you, your women, your brothers] and your sons with a cor[d].

---

3 (608) *ki-i šá ṣa-lam šá* DU[H.LÀL *ina* IZI *iš-šar-rap-u-ni*]
4 (609) ⸢*šá*⸣ IM *ina* A.MEŠ *im-ma-ha-*⸢*ah-hu-u-ni*⸣
5 (610) [*ki*]-*i ha-an-ni-e la-an-ku-nu ina* ^{d}GIŠ.BAR *liq-*⸢*mu*⸣-[*u*]
6 (611) [*ina*] A.MEŠ *li-ṭa-bu-*[*u*]

§89 3 Just as an image of w[ax is burnt in the fire] and one of clay dissolved in water, so may your figure be burnt in the fire and sunk [in] water.

---

7 (612-13) ⸢*ki*⸣-*i šá* GIŠ.GIGIR *a-*⸢*di*⸣ *sa-se-šá ina* ÚŠ.MEŠ ⸢*ra*⸣-[*ah-sa-tu-u-ni*]
8 (613-14) ⸢*ki*⸣-*i ha-an-ni-e* GIŠ.GIGIR.MEŠ-*ku-*[*nu*]
9 (614-15) ⸢*ina*⸣ MÚRU LÚ.KÚR-*ku-*(*nu*) *ina* ÚŠ.MEŠ *šá ra-ma-ni-ku-*⸢*nu li*⸣-[*ra-ah-ṣa*]

§90 7 Just as (this) chariot is dr[enched] with blood up to its base-board, so may yo[ur] chariots [be drenched] with your own blood in the midst of yo(ur) enemy.

---

10 (616) *ki-i pi-laq-qi lu-šá-aṣ-bir-ku-*⸢*nu*⸣
11 (617) ⸢*ki*⸣-*i* MÍ *ina* IGI LÚ.KÚR-*ku-nu le-pa-šú-*⸢*ku*⸣-[*nu*]

§91 10 May they (= all the gods) spin you around like a spindle-whorl, may they make you like a woman before your enemy.

---

12 (618) ⸢KIMIN⸣.KIMIN *a-na ka-a-šú-nu* ŠEŠ.MEŠ-*ku-*⸢*nu*⸣
13 (618-19) DUMU.MEŠ-*ku-nu ki-i al-lu-*⸢*ti*⸣
14 (619-20) [*a*]-*na qí-in-niš lu-šá-di-lu-ku-*⸢*nu*⸣

§92 12 Ditto, ditto; they (= all the gods) make you, your brothers and your sons go backward like a crab.

---

15 (621) *ki-i* IZI *la* DÙG.GA-*tú la* SIG$_{5}$-*tú lu-šal-bu-ku-*[*nu*]

§93 15 May they make evil and wicked things surround you like fire.

---

16 (622) *ki-i šá* Ì.MEŠ *ina* ŠÀ-*bi* UZU.MEŠ *e-rab-u-ni*
17 (623) ⸢*ta*⸣-*mì-tú an-ni-tú ina* ŠÀ$^{!}$-*bi* UZU.MEŠ-*ku-nu*
18 (624-25) ⸢UZU⸣.MEŠ *šá* DUMU.MEŠ-*ku-nu lu-še-ri-bu*

§94 16 Just as oil enters (your) flesh, so may they cause this oath to enter into your flesh and the flesh of your sons.

---

19 (626) *ki-i šá a-*⸢*ra*⸣-*ru a-na* ^{d}EN *ih-ṭu-u-ni*
20 (627) ⸢*kap*⸣-*pi šá* Á.MEŠ-*šú-nu* GÌR.2.MEŠ-*šú-nu*
21 (627-28) ⸢*ú*⸣-*bá-ti-qu-u-ni* IGI.MEŠ-*šú-nu*
22 (628-29) ⸢*ú*⸣-*ga-lil-u-ni ki-i ha-an-ni-e*
23 (629-30) ⸢*lig*⸣-*ma-ru-ku-nu ki-i* ⸢GI⸣.AMBAR.MEŠ *ina* A.MEŠ
24 (630-31) ⸢*lu*⸣-*ni-šú-u-ku-nu ki-i* GI.MEŠ *ina rik-si*
25 (631) ⸢LÚ⸣.KÚR-*ku-nu li-šá-lip-ku-nu*

§95 19 Just as the *Cursers* sinned against Bel and he cut off their hands and feet and blinded their eyes, so may they annihilate you, and make you sway like reeds in water; may your enemy pull you out like reeds from a bundle.

---

26 (632) ⸢*šum-ma*⸣ *at-tu-nu* ^{m}*aš-šur*–PAB–AŠ MAN KUR–*aš-šur*
27 (633) ⸢*ù*⸣ ^{m}*aš-šur*–DÙ–A DUMU–MAN GAL-*u* ⸢*šá* É⸣–UŠ-*te*
28 (633B-C) ⸢*ù*⸣ *re-eh-ti* DUMU.MEŠ *ṣi-it*–ŠÀ-*bi*
29 (633C-34) ⸢*šá*⸣ ^{m}*aš-šur*–PAB–AŠ ⸢MAN KUR–*aš-šur tu-ram*⸣-*ma-a-ni*
30 (634-35) *a-na* ZAG ⸢GÙB⸣ *tal-lak-a-ni šá a-na* ZAG
31 (635) *il-lak-u-ni* GÍR.MEŠ *le-ku-la-šu*
32 (636) [*š*]*á a-na* GÙB *il-lak-u-ni* GÍR.MEŠ-*me le-ku-la-š*[*u*]

§96 [26] If you should forsake Esarhaddon, king of Assyria, Assurbanipal, the great crown prince designate, and the other sons, the offspring of Esarhaddon, king of Assyria, going to the south or to the north, may iron swords consume him who goes to the south and may iron swords likewise consume hi[m w]ho goes to the north;

---

33 (636A-B) ⸢*a*⸣-*na ka-a-šú-nu* DUMU.MEŠ-*ku-nu* DUMU.MÍ.MEŠ-*ku-nu*
34 (636C) [*k*]*i-i* UDU.NIM *ga-*⸢*de*⸣-*e li-qi-lu-ku-nu*

§96A [33] may they burn you, your sons, and your daughters [l]ike a spring lamb or kid.

---

35 (637) *ki-i šá ki-il-lu šá su-ʾe-e an-*⸢*nu*⸣-[*te*]
36 (637-38) ⸢*i*⸣-*hal-la-lu-u-ni at-tu-*⸢*nu* MÍ.MEŠ⸣-*ku-nu*
37 (638-39) ⸢DUMU⸣.MEŠ-*ku-nu* DUMU.MÍ.MEŠ-*ku-nu la ta-nu-ha*
38 (639-40) ⸢*la*⸣ *ta-ṣa-la-la eṣ-mat-*⸢*e*⸣-*ku-nu*
39 (640) ⸢*a*⸣-*na a-he-iš lu la i-qar-ri-ba*

§97 [35] Just as the noise of the[se] doves is persistent, so may you, your women, your sons and your daughters have no rest or sleep and may your bones never come together.

---

40 (641) *ki-i šá lib-bu šá hup-*⟨*pi*⟩ *ra-*⸢*qu*⸣-*u-ni*
41 (642) *ki ha-an-ni-e lib-ba-ku-nu li-ri-iq*

§98 [40] Just as the inside of a hole is empty, may your inside be empty.

---

42 (643) KIMIN.KIMIN *ki-i* LÚ.KÚR-*ku-nu ú-pa-tah-u-*⸢*ka*⸣-[*nu-ni*]
43 (644) ⸢LÀL⸣ Ì.MEŠ *zi-iʾ-za-ru-ʾu* ÚŠ.MEŠ GIŠ.ERIN
44 (645) *a-na šá-kan* ⸢*pi-it*⸣-*hi-ku-nu li-ih-liq-qi*

§99 [42] Ditto, ditto; when your enemy pierces you, may there be no honey, oil, ginger or cedar-resin available to place on your wound.

---

45 (646-47) *ki-i šá mar-tú mar-rat-u-ni* ⸢*at-tu-nu*⸣
46 (647) [MÍ].MEŠ-*ku-nu* DUMU.MEŠ-*ku-nu* DUMU.MÍ.MEŠ-*ku-nu*
47 (648) [*ina*] UGU *a-he-iš lu mar-ra-ku-nu*

§100 [45] Just as gall is bitter, so may you, your women, your sons and your daughters be bitter towards each other.

[636C] *li-qi-lu-ku-nu* is not preserved in the other extant manuscripts.

48 (649) ⌜^{d}⌝UTU *hu-ha-*⌜*ru*⌝ *šá* ZABAR *ina* UGU-*hi-ku-nu*
49 (649-50) ⌜DUMU⌝.MEŠ-*ku-nu li-is-hu-up ina giš-par-ri*
50 (650-51) ⌜*la*⌝ *na-par-šu-di li-di-ku-nu a-a ú-še-ṣi*
51 (651) ⌜*nap*⌝*-šat-ku-un*

§101 [48] May Šamaš clamp a bronze bird trap over you and your sons; may he cast you into a trap from which there is no escape, and never let you out alive.

---

52 (652) *ki-i šá na-a-du an-ni-tú šal-qa-tu-u-ni*
53 (652-53) A.MEŠ-*šá ṣa-pa-hu-u-ni ina kaq-qar ṣu-ma-mì-ti lap-*⌜*lap*⌝*-[tu]*
54 (654-55) *na-da-ku-nu lu ta-hi-bi ina ṣu-um me-e* ⌜*mu*⌝*-[u-ta]*

§102 [52] Just as this waterskin is split and its water runs out, so may your waterskin break in a place of severe thirst; d[ie] of thirst!

---

55 (656) KI.MIN KI.MIN *ki-i šá* KUŠ.⌜E⌝.SIR *an-ni-tú bat-qa-tu-u-*⌜*ni*⌝
56 (657) *ina kaq-qar pu-qut-ti ga-zi-ri* KUŠ.E.SIR-*ku-nu*
57 (658) *lib-tu*$^{!}$*-qu ina* UGU ŠÀ-*bi-ku-nu piš-la*

§103 [55] Ditto, ditto; just as these shoes are pierced, so may your shoes be pierced in a region of brier and *sharp stones*; crawl on your bellies!

---

58 (659) ^{d}EN.LÍL EN GIŠ.⌜GU⌝.ZA-*e* GIŠ.⌜GU⌝.ZA-*ku-nu lu-šá-bal-kit*

§104 [58] May Illil, lord of the throne, overthrow your throne.

---

59 (660-61) ⌜^{d}AG⌝ *na-ši ṭup-pi* NAM.MEŠ DINGIR.MEŠ MU-*ku-nu*
60 (661) *lip-šiṭ* NUMUN-*ku-nu ina* KUR *li-hal-líq*

§105 [59] May Nabû, bearer of the tablet of fates of the gods, erase your name, and destroy your seed from the land.

---

61 (662) GIŠ.IG *ina* IGI-*e-ku-nu lu-šar-hi-ṣu*
62 (663) GIŠ.IG.MEŠ-*e-ku-nu lu la i-pat-ti-a*

§106 [61] May they (= all the great gods) cause the door to be soaked (in blood?) before your eyes. May your doors not open.

---

§107 Date and Colophon

63 (664) ITI.GUD.SI.SÁ UD-⌜16⌝[+$x^{?}$].KÁM
64 (665) *lim-mu* ^{md}AG–EN–PAB
65 (665) LÚ.GAR–KUR URU.BÀD–LUGAL-*uk-ka*
66 (666) ⌜*a-de-e*⌝ *ina* UGU ^{m}*aš-šur*–DÙ–DUMU.UŠ
67 (667) DUMU–LUGAL GAL-*u šá* É–*re-du-ti*
68 (667-68) *ša* KUR–*aš-šur* ⌜*ù*⌝ ^{md}GIŠ.NU$_{11}$–MU–GI.NA
69 (669) DUMU–LUGAL *ša* É–*re-du-ti*
70 (669) *ša* KÁ.DINGIR.RA.KI
71 (670) ⌜*ša*⌝*-ak-nu*

[63] 1*6*th day of Iyyar (II), eponymy of Nabû-belu-uṣur, governor of Dur-Šarrukku. The treaty concluded on behalf of Assurbanipal, the great crown prince designate of Assyria, and Šamaš-šumu-ukin, the crown prince designate of Babylon.

6. Court Poetry and Literary Miscellanea
Additions to SAA III

FIG. 21. *Prisoner wearing Teumman's head.*
BM 124802b.

230. Syncretic Hymn to Ninurta

	VAT 9739	KAR 102
	beginning broken away	(Beginning destroyed)
1′	*[x x x]* ⸢*ni*⸣ *ma ru r[u x x x]*	1 […] … […],
2′	*[x x x]*.MEŠ-*e ta-na-ta-k[a*? *x x x]*	2 […]s, yo[ur] praise […],
3′	⸢UKKIN⸣ DINGIR.MEŠ ⸢GAL⸣.MEŠ *ú-šar-*⸢*bi*⸣*-[ka x x]*	3 the assembly of the great gods has praised [you …],
4′	^{d}NIN.URTA *qar-ra-du ta-[x x x]*	4 Ninurta, warrior, you […],
5′	*ha-mim ina kiš-šú-ti-šú-nu ta-x[x x x]*	5 gatherer, in their might you […],
6′	*tal-*⸢*qi*⸣*-ma par-ṣi-šú-nu ta-x[x x x x]*	6 you have taken their rites and you […],
7′	LUGAL-*ú-tum šá* EN-*e qa-tuk-k[a paq-da-at]*	7 kingship of lords [is entrusted] in yo[ur] hand,
8′	*be-lum ru-ub-ta-ka a-bu-bu [la ma-har*?*]*	8 lord, your rage is [*irresistible*] flood,
9′	*qar-ra-du šá* DINGIR.MEŠ *šá-qa-ta be-[lum*? 0?]	9 hero of the gods, you are exalted, *lo[rd]*,
10′	*be-lum pa-nu-ka* ^{d}*šam-šu qim-mat-ka* ^{d}[NISABA]	10 lord, your face is Šamaš, your locks [Nisaba],
11′	IGI.2.MEŠ-*ka be-lum* $^{d+}$EN.LÍL *u* ^{d}[NIN.LÍL]	11 your eyes, lord, are Enlil and [Ninlil],
12′	^{d}LAMA-*át* IGI.2.MEŠ-*ka* ^{d}*gu-la* ^{d}*be-let–ì-lí* [0?]	12 the pupils of your eyes are Gula (and) Belet-ili,
13′	SIG7–IGI.2.MEŠ-*ka be-lum maš-še-e* ^{d}30 [*u* ^{d}UTU]	13 your eyebrows, lord, are the twins, Sîn [and Šamaš],
14′	*a-gap-pi* IGI.2.MEŠ-*ka ša-ru-ur* ^{d}*šam-ši ša [x x x]*	14 your eyelashes are the radiance of the sun who […],
15′	*ši-kín* KA-*ka be-lum* ^{d}IŠ.TAR MUL.MEŠ [0?]	15 your mouth's shape, lord, is Ištar of the stars,
16′	^{d}*a-nu-um u an-tum* NUNDUN.2-*ka qí-bit-ka* [^{d}PA.TÚG?]	16 Anu and Antu are your lips, your speech is [*Nusku*],
17′	*mul-ta-bil-ta-ka* ^{d}PA.BÍL.SAG *šá e-la-an x[x x x]*	17 your *tongue* is Pabilsag (Sagittarius), who […] on high,

230 KAR 328 (VAT 11586, not edited here), a small fragment with seven partially preserved lines, has often been given the status of a join to KAR 102, but if this is the case, it can at most be an indirect join. The reverse of STT 118 provides parallels to the text, but it is not a duplicate of KAR 102. Previous editions: Ebeling, MVAeG 23/I (1918) 47-49; Annus Ninurta 205f; translations: Foster Muses, 713f.; von Soden, SAHG, 258f.; Seux Hymnes 131-33 (with notes); Pongratz-Leisten, "Imperial Allegories: Divine Agency and Monstrous Bodies in Mesopotamia's Body Description Texts," in B. Pongratz-Leisten and K. Sonik (eds.), *The Materiality of Divine Agency* (Boston and Berlin 2015) 122-23 (translation and discussion). [2] Or, *ta-na-ta-š[u*, already so since Ebeling (1918) 47. [3] ⸢UKKIN⸣ is taken from Annus Ninurta 205. [7] For the restoration, see Seux Hymnes 131, n.5. [9] Alternatively, *šá-qa-ta be-[lut-ka]* "exalted is [your] lo[rdship]", especially as the repetition of *bēlu* (see line 10) may seem questionable. [10] The spelling ^{d}*šam-šu* (perhaps an odd choice in this context, but cf. line 14) also justifies the interpretation "the Sun". [12, 15] Curiously, these two lines are written quite densely, but apparently not until the right edge of the tablet. [13] CAD M/1 328a records this line s.v. *massû* "leader", referring to the examples given in Tallqvist Götterepitheta p. 130. [16] After *qí-bit-ka*, however, Ebeling's copy shows the beginning of a Winkelhaken.

18′	AN-*e* KA-*ka be-lum kip-pat* AN-*e* KI-*ti šu-bat* DINGIR.[MEŠ GAL.MEŠ]	[18] the palate (lit. 'heaven') of your mouth, lord, is the circumference of heaven and earth, the dwelling place of the [great] god[s],
19′	ZÚ.MEŠ-*ka* ^{d}7.BI *mu-šam-qí-tu lem-nu* [*x x x*]	[19] your teeth are the Seven Gods, who bring the evil [...] to fall,
20′	*ṭé-eh* TE.MEŠ-*ka be-lum ṣi-it* MUL.MEŠ *na*[*m*$^{!}$-*ru-ti*]	[20] *next to* your cheeks, lord, is the rising of br[ight] stars,
21′	PI.2.MEŠ-*ka* ^{d}É.A ^{d}*dam-ki-na* NUN.ME *né-me-*⸢*qí*⸣ [*x x x*]	[21] your ears are Ea (and) Damkina, sages of wisdom [...],
22′	SAG.DU-*ka* ^{d}IM *šá* AN-*ú* KI.TIM GIM *kiš-kat-te-*⸢*e*⸣ [*x x x*]	[22] your head is Adad, who [*makes*] heaven and earth [...] like a kiln,
23′	SAG.KI-*ka* ^{d}*ša-la* [*hi*]-*ir-tu na-ra-am-tú mu-ṭib-*[*bat ka-bat-ti* ^{d}IM]	[23] your forehead is Šala, beloved wife, who makes [Adad's heart feel happy],
24′	GÚ-*ka* ^{d}AMAR.UTU DI.KUD AN-*e* [*u* KI.TIM] *a-bu-ub* [*x x x*]	[24] your neck is Marduk, judge of heaven, [and the netherworld], deluge [...],
25′	*nap-šat-ka* ^{d}*zar-pa-ni-tum ba-n*[*a-at* U]N.MEŠ *šá-*⸢*ri*$^{?}$⸣-*k*[*at*$^{?}$ TI.LA$^{?}$]	[25] your throat is Zarpanitu, creat[ress of pe]ople, *who grant*[*s life*],
26′	GABA-*ka* ^{d}PA *ba-ru-ú x*[*x x*]*x a-*[*x x x*]	[26] your chest is Šullat, who examines [......],
27′	MAŠ.SILÀ.MEŠ-*ka* ^{d}LUGAL *šá-kín h*[*i-iṣ-bi m*]*u-šá-az-*[*nin nu-uh-ši*]	[27] your shoulders are Haniš, who establishes y[ield], pours out [abundance],
28′	[Z]AG-*ka* ^{d}UTU.U$_{18}$$^{!}$.LU *bi-x*[*x x á*]*š*$^{?}$ *a-*[*x x x x*]	[28] your [rig]ht side is Uta'ulu [......],
29′	[KA]B-*ka* ^{d}NIN.PAB.NÌGIN.GAR.R[A *x x*]-*lu mu-x*[*x x x*]	[29] your [left si]de is Ninpanigarr[a, ...] ...[...],
30′	[Š]U.SI.MEŠ KIŠIB.MEŠ-*ka šá-q*[*u-ú*$^{?}$ *x a-g*]*e-e* [*x x x x*]	[30] [the f]ingers of your hands are *tal*[*l* ...]... [...],
31′	[UM]BIN.MEŠ-*ka be-lum* MU[L (*x x*) *n*]*a*$^{?}$-*bu-ú* [*x x x x*]	[31] your [na]ils, lord, are [the b]right sta[r ...],
32′	[*x x*]*x*.MEŠ-*ka* ^{d}*da-gan šá x*[*x x x x x x x x*]	[32] your [...]s are Dagan, *who* [......],
33′	[*x*]*x ina* GÌR.2.M[EŠ-*ka x x x x x x x x*]	[33] [...] *in* [*your*] feet [......],
34′	[L]I.DUR-*ka be-lu*[*m x x x x x x x x x*]	[34] your [n]avel, lord, is [......],
35′	[*x x*]*x-ka* ^{d}*z*[*a-ba*$_4$-*ba*$_4$ *x x x x x x x*]	[35] your [...] is Z[ababa, ...],
	rest broken away	(Rest destroyed)
B	other side destroyed	

[18] For the beginning of the line, see CAD Š/1 348b. [22] Or, consider GIM *kiš-kat-te-*⸢*e*⸣ as "like a craftsman/smith". [23] The restoration was already suggested by Ebeling (1918) 48. [26-29, 31] Cf. STT 118 rev. [27] The divine name is read as ^{d}LUGAL.NÍG.HAR in CAD N/1 119b. For the restoration, see Seux Hymnes p. 133, n. 27. [29] For the reading of [KAB]-*ka*, see ibid. p. 133, n.29. [30] The reading [*a-g*]*e-e* suggests a "[cro]wn/[tia]ra", but this is uncertain. [33] Possibly either GÌR.2.M[EŠ-*ka* or GÌR.2-*k*[*a*.

231. Praise to Ištar, Dream by Šerua

K 537/8; Gr. Nr. 21506d (Ass. Photo S. 6553)

1 *ṣa-bi-ta-at a-b*[*u*]*-tú* ⸢*e*⸣*-la-*⸢*a-ta*⸣ *ina* ⸢BARAG$^{?}$⸣
2 *šur-ba-a-*⸢*ta ina* É⸣ *mi-il-ki*
3 *pa-qi-da-at* ^{d}*a-nun-na-ki šá-qa-ta be-lut-sa*
4 ^{d}INNIN$^{!!}$ *ša* AN-*e lu-na-ʾi-id la-az-mur*

blank space of 4 lines

5 *ina tar-ṣi* ^{m}TUKUL–A–É.ŠÁR.RA LUGAL KUR–*aš-šur*.KI
6 [LUGAL$^{?}$] *ha-as-su* ^{d}UZU-*ú-a ina šat mu-ši*
7 [*ú-š*]*ab-ri-šú-ma* MU.MEŠ *an-nu-ti*
r.1 [*ana* KUR.*di-maš-q*]*a*$^{?}$ *ina* UGU-*hi it-*[*ta-lak*$^{?}$]
2 [ITI.*x* UD]-⸢5⸣-KÁM *lim-mu* ^{m}*aš-šur*–KALAG-*i*[*n-an-ni*]
3 [L]Ú.GAR.KUR KUR–*za-mu-a*
rest uninscribed

LKA 36

1 Let me praise by singing Ištar of heaven, the one who intercedes, exalted in the *sanctuary*, the greatest in the house of counsel, the one who takes care of Anunnaki, whose lordship is sublime.

(blank space of 4 lines)

5 In the time of Tiglath-pileser (III), king of Assyria, [*the*] circumspect [*king*], Šerua [ma]de him see these omens at night, and he w[*ent to Damasc*]*us* because of them.
r.2 [Month ...], 5th [day], eponym year of Aššur-da''i[nanni], governor of Mazamua.

232. Hymn to Nabû(?)

ND 2446

1 [*x x*] *ša*$^{?}$ DINGIR.MEŠ *man-nu e-la ka-a-ta ma-hi-ir* ⸢du$^{?}$⸣ [*x x x x x x x*]
2 [*x x x*]*x-ki*$^{?}$*-*⸢*in*$^{?}$⸣ *man-nu* ⸢*e-la*$^{?}$ *ka-a-ta*⸣ *ina* ⸢*mah*$^{?}$⸣*-x*[*x x x x x x x*]
3 [*x x x*] u KALAG.MEŠ *mu-za-ʾi-iz x*[*x x x x x x x*]
4 [*x x x*]*x* ⸢*x x*⸣ *tim*$^{?}$ *he-pu-u* É$^{?}$ ⸢*x x x x*⸣ *x*[*x x x x x x*]
5 [(*x x x*)] ⸢*x*⸣ *lu*$^{?}$ *x*[*x x x x x x x*]
6 [*x x x*]*x gi* ⸢*x x*⸣ *le-e-*⸢*ti*$^{?}$⸣ ⸢*šá*$^{?}$⸣ *x*[*x x x x x x x*]
7 [*x x*] ⸢*x x*⸣ LÚ.A ⸢*x x*⸣ *nap*$^{?}$ *na*$^{?}$*-kam-ti it-mu-n*[*in*$^{?}$ *x x x x x x x*]
8 [*x x*] *x*[*x x*]*x* AGA *ta-nit-ti-ka šum*$^{?}$*-ru* ⸢*x x x x x x x*⸣ [*x*] ⸢*x*⸣ [*x*]

ND 2446

1 [...] *of* the gods who is apart from you the one who accepts [......]?
2 [...] ... who is apart from you in ...[......]?
3 one who distributes *strong* [...]s [......],
4 [......] one who breaks the *house* [......],
5 [...] ... [......],
6 [......] *the cheek of* [......],
7 [...] ...... [......]
8 [...] the crown is your *furious* praise, ... [...],

231 Previous editions: Menzel Tempel 62*-63* (A. 776; transliteration); Helle, "The First Authors" (Ph.D. thesis, Aarhus University 2020) 329-30. 1 *e-la-a-ta* is understood as the feminine form of the adjective *elû* "high, exalted". 4 The text erroneously has ^{d}5.1.1 "Igigi", which is certainly influenced by the preceding Anunnaki. 6 Or, restore [MAN$^{?}$]. With UZU, this text provides an interesting variant spelling of the name Šerua. r.1 This line seems to describe the king's action in response to these nocturnal omens and, speculatively, we suggest combining the historical information from the eponym lists for the year 733 (Millard Eponyms pp. 45, 59, Pl. 12), i.e., for Tiglath-pileser's military campaign. If space permits, *a-na* should preferably be restored at the beginning. r.2f The eponym of the year 733. The importance of this date in a literary text has been stressed by May (SAAB 21 [2015] 100, n.105) and Helle op. cit. p. 329.

232 No previous editions. 7 The so-called LÚ could also be LUGAL.

9	[*x x*] ⸢*x x*⸣ *ki* LÚ *a-na* ⸢*x x x x*⸣ AN ⸢*x x x*⸣ *pal-hu-ú-ma*	[9] [...] man to ...... to *god* ... revere and
10	[*ú-na*]-ʾ*a-du zi-kir-ka šá x*[*x x*]*x* ⸢*tak x*⸣ *tir*$^{?}$ ⸢*x*⸣-*ma* ⸢*x x x*⸣ *te te ki*$^{?}$ ⸢*x x x x*⸣	[10] [pra]ise your name which ......
11	[*te*$^{?}$]-⸢*e*$^{?}$⸣-*pu-uš* GI–*ṭup-pi x*[*x x x*]-*bi pa-rak-ki ru-uš-ši-i* MUL *ur-pi-ti*$^{?}$	[11] [*you*] made the stylus *of* [...], red *dais*, the star of a cloud,
12	*gis-kim* SIG$_5$ GÚ DINGIR KUG.GI *x*[*x x*]*x a-na* HAR$^{!}$ ŠU *ru*-⸢*uš-ši-i*⸣ ŠU [*x*]*x* EN *si-ma-ni*	[12] good sign *is* a golden necklace of a god [...] for a red hand-ring, hand *of* [...], lord of the time,
13	⸢*qa*$^{?}$⸣-*ti-ia ud*$^{?}$-*du*-⸢*x x x x*⸣ *e-nu-ti*$^{?}$ É ⸢*x*⸣ *bi*$^{?}$ ⸢*i ṣir*⸣-*ta ap-ti-ha*$^{?}$	[13] my hands *are* ..., ... *of lordship*, I *blocked* the supreme ...
r.1	⸢*za x*⸣ *ta šu te*$^{?}$ *lal* ⸢*x*⸣ *mu*$^{?}$ ⸢*x x x x x*⸣ *ru-ṣa taš-kun-nim-ma šur-ka-a-na*	[r.1] ...... you placed *me* ... and ...
2	*ina*$^{?}$ *ul-la-ta*$^{?}$ *qi-lu*$^{?}$ ⸢*at*$^{?}$⸣ *pur*$^{?}$ ⸢*x x x*⸣ *a šu ru uš* ⸢*x x x*⸣ *ag dal ta*$^{?}$	[2] ......
3	*ka-a-ta a-ta-ha-ar-ka-ma na-piš-ta-šu šu-ṭi-ip i-na kak-ki*	[3] I keep petitioning you, save his life, with a weapon
4	EME *šah-šah-hi-ia* ⸢*x*⸣ *eš*-⸢*šìr*$^{?}$⸣-*ma* ⸢*x x x*⸣ EME-*ia ga-a-ṣi*$^{?}$	[4] *you* ... the tongue of my slanderer and ... my tongue (*with*) *gypsum*,
5	*an-na ki-na šá-ra-kim-ma* UDU$^{?}$.NITÁ$^{?}$ DÙG$^{?}$ NU KUD GÁ-*ma* BA-*eš*	[5] he set up and presented a *good*, un-slaughtered *ram* (*for*) granting a firm positive answer.

---

crosswise in lower part of rev.

6	[*x x x x x*] 10 *aš-šur*	[6] [......] 10, Aššur
7	[*x x x x x*] 10 EN	[7] [......] 10, Bel
8	[*x x x x x*] 10 ^{d}PA	[8] [......] 10, Nabû
9	[*x x x x x*] 1 ^{d}15 NINA	[9] [......] 1, Ištar of Nineveh
10	[*x x x x x*] 1 ^{d}15 *arba-ìl*	[10] [......] 1, Ištar of Arbela
11	[*x x x x x*] 1 ^{d}MAŠ	[11] [......] 1, Ninurta
12	[*x x x x x*] 1 ^{d}PA URU.NINA	[12] [......] 1, Nabû of Nineveh
13	[*x x x x x*] 1 ^{d}PA URU.*kal-ha*	[13] [......] 1, Nabû of Calah
14	[*x x x x x*] 1 ^{d}PA URU.BÀD–MAN–GIN	[14] [......] 1, Nabû of Dur-Šarruken
15	[*x x x x x*] 1 ^{d}30 URU.:.	[15] [......] 1, Sîn of ditto
16	[*x x x x x*] 1 ^{d}30 URU.KASKAL	[16] [......] 1, Sîn of Harran
17	[*x x x x x*] 1 ^{d}EN *kur-ba-*(*ìl*)	[17] [......] 1, Bel of Kurba(il)
18	[*x x x x x*] 1 ^{d}U.GUR *tar-bi-ṣi*	[18] [......] 1, Nergal of Tarbiṣu
19	[*x x x x x*] 1 ^{d}*be-lit*–TI.LA	[19] [......] *1*, Belet-balaṭi
20	[*x x x x x*] 2 ^{d}UTU *sip-par*	[20] [......] 2, Šamaš of Sippar
21	[*x x x x x*] 2 ^{d}U.GUR GÚ.DU$_8$.A	[21] [......] 2, Nergal of Cutha
22	[*x x x x x*] 2 ^{d}*za-ba*$_4$-*ba*$_4$	[22] [......] 2, Zababa
23	[*x x x x x*] ⸢2$^{?}$⸣ ^{d}BE EN.LIL.KI	[23] [......] 2, Enlil of Nippur
24	[*x x x x x x*] ^{d}*be-lit*–TI.LA	[24] [......] Belet-balaṭi
25	[*x x x x x x*]*x x x zi x x*	[25] [......] ...
26	[*x x x x x x*]⸢*x x*⸣[*x x*	[26] [......] ... [...]
	rest destroyed	(Rest destroyed or too broken for translation)

[13] E.g., *ud-du-uš*, "to renew". Or, *bi*$^{?}$ ⸢*i*⸣ as ⸢*tum*$^{?}$⸣. [r.4] Two verbs with rather opposite meanings are expected, the latter perhaps "to purify" or "to wash". [r.6-24] In this list (of offerings?), the minor gods are conspicuous by their absence. However, the major gods are listed with many of their main manifestations.

FIG. 22. *Ashurnasirpal II defeating Carchemish.*
Original Drawings III, NW 29-30.

233. Assurnasirpal II's Victories in the West

VAT 10047 (Ass 21548a, Ass. Photo S. 6799)	LKA 64
1 ⌜*a*⌝-*za-mu-ru* MAN *kib-ra-te e-tel* DINGIR.MEŠ-*n*[*i*] 2 *lu-na-ʾi-di* 3 *ša* ᵈBE *a-šib* É.ŠÁR.RA *lu-šá-ri-ih* DINGIR-*ut-su*	[1] I shall sing (the song of) the king of the world and praise the prince of the gods, [3] I shall glorify the divinity of Enlil, dwelling in Ešarra,

233 Previous edition: Bach, UF 49 (2018) 1-28 (see Bach's edition for the previous scholarship on the tablet).

4 ^{m}*aš-šur*–PAB–A *tam-tal-ku hi-ši-ih-tú* DINGIR.MEŠ GAL.MEŠ
5 A ^{m}TUKUL–MAŠ MAN *ta-na-da-te šur-ru-uh*
6 *ul-we-e* MURUB4-*šú* MAN *ba-a-a-ri ut-ta-ʾi-bu kàl ma-li-ki*
7 *iṣ-ṣi-mid* TA* URU.*kal-hi* KUR *dan-na-nu*
8 *iṣ-ṣa-bat ana* KASKAL

9 *a-na* DÙ-*uš ta-ha-zi-šú* URU.*gar-ga-mis*
10 *is-si-ni-qi ša* KUR.*hat-ti*
11 *a-na da-na-ni* EN-*te-ia nam-ku-ru*
12 É.GAL-*i-šú áš-lu-la*
13 *ṣal-mu bu-na-ni-ia ma-aq-ru a-na* É.KUR-*šú ú-šar-ri-ha*
14 KUR.*ku-mu-ha-a-a pa-te-na-a-a me-*⸢*lam-mì*⸣ *sah-pu-šú-nu*
15 [GIŠ].*gup-ni nam-ku-ru* GIŠ.KAL *uq-*⸢*nu*?⸣
16 *a*[*t*]*-ta-har*

17 DUMU.MÍ–MAN [*pa-t*]*e-na-a-a a-na ha-de-*⸢*e*⸣
18 [*n*]*a-a*[*d*?*-nu*]*-ni-ka*
19 *kàl* [*kib*?]*-ra-te* DU.DU-*ka a-na* KUR-*e ha-*⸢*ma-na*?⸣
20 *e-ta-ta-li*
e.21 *ú-še*?*-p*[*iš*?] ⸢SISKUR⸣.MEŠ KUG.[MEŠ-*te*] *a-na*
22 [*x*] ⸢*x x*⸣ [*x x x*] ⸢*x*⸣ *a-na* [*x x x*]
r.1 [*x x*] ⸢*x x*⸣ [*x x x x x x x x*]
2 [*x x q*]*é*?*-reb* K[UR.*x x x x x x x*]
3 [*x x x*]*x i-*[*x x x x x x x x x*]
4 [*x x*] *is x*[*x x x x x x x x x*]
5 [*x*] KUR.*ha-r*[*a-x x x x x x*]
6 SISKUR.MEŠ [KUG.MEŠ-*t*]*e x*[*x x x x*]
7 [GI]Š.ÙR.MEŠ *ere*-IGI ⸢TA*?⸣ *ha-ma-n*[*a* 0?]?
8 [*x x* GI]Š.⸢*gup-ni*⸣ *a-na* É.ŠÁR.[RA 0]
9 [*x x x x x*] ⸢*x x*⸣ [*x x x x x*]
10 [*x x*] *ù* ⸢^{d}UTU⸣ [*x x x x x*]

4 Assurnasirpal, the *circumspect*, required by the great gods, son of Tukulti-Ninurta, the king of praises, is splendid,

6 (with) his battle axe, the king of huntsmen *knocked down* all the western rulers,

7 he harnessed (*his chariot* and) from Calah, (his) *powerful palace*, he took to a military campaign.

9 He *repeatedly took* the city of Carchemish of the land Hatti to do battle with him,

11 *by force* of my lordship, I plundered the possessions of his temple,

13 a precious statue of my likeness I made glorious to his temple,

14 my radiance overwhelmed the people of Commagene and Patinu,

15 I received trees, (their) possessions, ebony, lapis lazuli.

17 The daughter*s* of the [Pat]inean king were *gi*[*ven*] to you for joy.

19 *I* kept marching to all [corn]ers (of the world) and going up to Mount Amanus,

21 *I had mad*[*e*] pure offerings for

22 [......] to [...]

r.1 [......]

2 [... *i*]*n* [......]

3 [......]

4 [......]

5 [...] the land of Har[a... ...]

6 [pur]e offerings [...], roofbeams of cedar from (Mount) Aman[us, ...] tree trunks for Ešar[ra]

9 [......]

10 [...] and Šamaš [......]

4 For the royal epithet, cf. SAA 3 2 r.10. Bach emends the word and reads (ibid. p. 6) ⸢*mu*⸣*-ut-tal-ku*, i.e., *muntalku*. CAD P 190a takes it as *par-ri-ku*. 7 Alternatively, perhaps read ⸢*ana*⸣ KUR.*lab-na-nu*, since KUR *dan-na-nu* is grammatically somewhat unsatisfactory. 11 If considering the text as it is, Bach's "to strengthen" is better, but there may be some doubt as to whether this was the nuance sought. 14 We interpret "my radiance", and not just "radiance/*melammu*", because of what was said in the previous line. 15 Bach reads [*i-šu*]*-ṭú-ni*, "They [dragg]ed forth", but it would be somewhat abrupt to have a 3rd person masculine plural predicate here, despite the suffix of the previous word. 16 Ebeling's copy shows *i-ta-har*, but immediately after *i* there is a hatched (broken) area. 19 Cf. CAD A/1 324b. Alternatively, one could read *kaq-*[*qa*?]*-ra-te*. 19-21 The verbal forms do not distinguish between the 1st and 3rd person singular. 21 Bach: [3]-*ú*^{kam} UDU.SISKUR^{meš}. r.2 Bach: *-ma kal* KUR[$^{meš?}$ r.7 It is surprising, probably a slip, that there is no KUR before *ha-ma-n*[*a*?]. r.8 Or, read, e.g., [*ša iš/il-d*]*a-*⸢*du-ni*⸣ "[*which he* to]wed to Ešar[ra]"; for this alternative, see, e.g., SAA 1 63, 102; SAA 5 8 and 127. r.10 Bach restores [^{d}XXX] "Sîn" and gives good reasons (ibid. 14), but since we cannot exclude "[Aššur]" we prefer to leave it open.

11	TU-*bu a-na* É.ŠÁR.RA ⌜*qa*?⌝-[*x x*]*x*	11 entered Ešarra ...[...]
12	*ina ni-iš* IGI.MEŠ-*šú*	12 *with his* glance, my beloved ruler, Assurnasirpal, the *representative*.
13	*ma-al-ku na-ra-ma* ŠÀ-*bi-ia* ^{m}*aš-šur*–PAB–A	
14	*šá-ga-na-ku*	
	blank space of 3 lines	
15	[TA*? K]A ^{m}*su-ku-a-a šá-ṭí-ir*	15 Written [by dicta]tion [*from*] Sukkaya.
	rest uninscribed	

r.14 The interpretation "governor" for *šakkanakku* may seem too modest in this context (cf. SAA 3 1 r.8′). r.15 See Hunger Kolophone no. 262 (referred to in PNA 3/I 1156a, cf. CAD P 466a). If we take the dictation interpretation seriously (PNA loc. cit., on the other hand, following Hunger, says "written upon the order of PN"), this could explain why the text has so many errors: missing signs, words, and erroneous replacements (e.g., the end of line 7 is odd). The restored beginning seems uncertain and could also be [*ša*/*a-na*/*i-na*/GIM?].

COURTESY TRUSTEES OF THE BRITISH MUSEUM

FIG. 23. *Princess and furniture delivered as gift to Ashurnasirpal II.* BM 118800.

234. The Hunter and the Asses

VAT 13833

1 *[la-a-i]ṭ a-a-bi da-a-iš na-ki-ri-i-šu*
2 *[še-'i]-⸢i⸣ i-me-ri* KUR-*i da-li-hi bu-lu* EDIN
3 *[eṭ-lu š]a* ^{d}*a-aš-šur tuk-lat-su* ^{d}IM *re-ṣu-šu*
4 *[a-l]i-ik a-na pa-ni-šu a-ša-red* DINGIR.MEŠ ^{d}⸢MAŠ⸣
5 *ba-a-a-ru a-na i-me-ri i-ka-pu-da qab-⸢lu⸣*
6 *a-na qi-it na-piš-ti-šu-nu ú-sa-ha-na pa-tar-⸢šu⸣*
7 *i-iš-mu-ú i-me-re-⸢e⸣ i-da-ku-ku ina re-e-⸢ši⸣*
8 *pu-lu-uh-tu šá ba-a-a-ri e-li-šu-nu la tab-kàt*
9 *i-ma-ha-ru te-šu-ú a-a-ú šá i-se-ni-qa-a-na-ši*
10 *šá qe-re-eb-ni la i-mu-ru ú-pa-ra-du pu-hu-ur-⸢ne⸣*
11 *a-ni-nu ⸢ú⸣-zu-ba-a-ni ina ki-is* KUR-*i šá-qu-ti*
12 *i–ma-si-ri šá ša-du-e šu-pa-ta-ni ma-a ra-ma-at*
13 *šá-a-ra šá ba-a-a-ri li-šá-i ki-pa-su-ma*
14 *ši-⸢da*$^{!}$*⸣-at qa-al-ti-šú e li-il-li-ka šá* DA *pu-hu-ru-ti*
15 *iš-me-e ba-a-a-ru šá bu-lu* KUR-*i da-ba-bu*
16 *šá-an-su-ku ṭè-šú-nu si-qi-ri-šú-nu pi-it-ru-du*
17 *ma-a* PEL *ši-ir-'a-an-šú-nu zi-ka-ru ma-a la mal-du*
18 *a-na qu-ra-de-e šá e-li ⸢šad-di*$^{!}$*⸣ a-bu-tu-ú i-zaq-qa-ar*
19 *ni-i-li-ik šá bu-li šad-di š[a]-ga-al-ta-šú-nu ni-iš-kun*
20 *i–ka-ki-i-ni-i šá sa-ha-an ⸢da⸣-mi-šú-nu ni-qí*
21 *a-di e-ni šam-me-šu il-tap-pa-ta pu-ha-di*
22 *il-ta-mar ki-ma* ^{d}IM ^{d}*šá-maš i-ṣi-mì-di ma-ši-r[i]*

LKA 62

1 [Curbe]r of enemies, trampler of his foes,
2 [seeke]r of mountain asses, vexer of steppe herds,
3 [a man w]hose trust is Aššur, whose help is Adad,
4 (and) whose [va]nguard is Ninurta, foremost of the gods,
5 the Hunter plans battle against the asses
6 and heats up his sword to end their lives.
7 The asses heard it, but they gambol ahead of it;
8 fear of the Hunter is not poured upon them.
9 They face the turmoil saying, "Who could approach us?
10 Who, having not seen our midst, could scare our host?
11 We are deposited in the purse of high mountains,
12 our dwelling place lies in the mountain enclosure.
13 May its circle make the hunter's empty words fly away,
14 may the range of his bow not reach (our) throng!"
15 The Hunter heard the talk of the mountain herd:
16 "Their mind is foul, their words are confused,
17 their muscles are weak, they were not born men!"
18 He utters the order to ascend the mountain to the heroes:
19 "Let's go and massacre the mountain herd!
20 Let's shed their blood with our hot weapons!"
21 He kept "touching" lambs until the source of his pasture;
22 He roared like Adad; Šamaš hitched the chariots;

234 Previous editions: Ebeling, Or. 18 (1949) 30-39; Edzard, Fs. Grayson (2004) 81-87; Pongratz-Leisten, SANER 6 (2015) 252-54, 468-75; Fink and Parpola, ZA 109 (2019) 177-88; for a discussion, see also Finn, SANER 16 (2017) 35-36, 150-54. On the dating of the text to the reign of Shalmaneser III, see Fink and Parpola, p. 182f.

r.1	*har-ra-an še-lal-ti* UD-*me ir-ti-di* [*ina mu-ši-ti*]	r.1 he marched the journey of three days [in a night].
2	*a-du la* ^{d}*šá-maš na-ba-hu i–bi-ru-šu-nu an-qu-lu*	2 While the sun didn't rise, a fiery glow was amidst them.
3	*ú-šar-ri-ṭi* ŠÀ-*bi a-ra-ti ú-na-pi-il la-ku-ti*	3 He slashed the wombs of the pregnant, ripped out babies;
4	*ša da-nu-ti-šú-nu ú-na-ki-is ki-šá-da-ti*	4 of their strongest, he cut the necks;
5	*qu-tu-ru ma-ti-šú-nu* ERIM.MEŠ-*šú-nu i-te*$^{!}$*-di-il*	5 the smoke of their land shut off their troops.
6	*ša a-na aš-šur i-ha-ṭu-ú i-mì-i kar-mì-iš*	6 The one who sins against Aššur, turns into ruin!
7	*la-za-mu-ru li-it aš-šur da-a'-na ša i-tal-la-ka a-na šal-m*[*e*]	7 Let me sing the victory of Aššur-mighty, who keeps going to battl[e],
8	*il-la-ta kib-ra-ti i-sa-at-ka-na li-i-t*[*ú*$^{!}$]	8 and keeps achieving victory over worldwide coalitions.
9	*li-iš-me ma-hi-ru-u a-na ar-ki-i lu-šá-an-*[*ni*]	9 Let the first one hear and te[ll] the later ones!

10	*a-na an-tum be-el-ti k*[*aq*]*-qí-ri* GAL-*t*[*u*$_4$]	10 To the goddess, the lady of the great land,
11	*a-na* ^{d}15 *a-ši-bat* [0] *qer-bi ir-kal-li*	11 to Ištar who dwells in the midst of Irkallu,
12	*áš-ri-gi-in-gal be-el-ti kaq-qí-ri* GAL-*tu*$_4$	12 Ašri-gingal, the lady of the great land,
13	*a-na* ^{d}15 *a-ši-bat qer-bi ir-kal-li*	13 to Ištar who dwells in the midst of Irkallu,
14	É *ir-kal-li šá a-li-ku-tu-šú la ta-a-a-r*[*u*]	14 the house of Irkallu, whose travellers do not return,
15	*aš-ru nu-ru la šá-kín* UN.MEŠ-⸢*šu*⸣	15 the place (where) light is not given to its people,
16	*aš-ru mi-tu-su sah-hu-pu ina ep-ri*	16 the place whose dead are covered with dust,
17	Á *ek-le-tú* MUL *ul ú-ṣa-a*	17 the dark side (where) no star comes out,
18	DUMU.MÍ ^{d}30 *ú-zu-un-šá ip-te-ma*	18 the daughter of Sîn put her mind to,
19	*ip-te-ma ú-za-an-šá ú-šá-áš-kín*	19 put her mind to (and) paid attention,
20	*šá a-li-ku-ú-tú-šá la ta-a-ru-ú*	20 that her travellers do not return.

235. Assurbanipal's Exploits in Elam

	K 2998 + 81-2-4,385 + K 3102 + 82-3-23,40	ABL 1007 + CT 54 55 + CT 54 490
	beginning broken away	(Beginning destroyed)
1′	[*x x x x x x x x x x*]*x* ⸢m⸣AN.ŠÁR–DÙ–DUMU.⸢UŠ⸣ [LU]GAL [GAL LUGAL]	1 Assurbanipal, [great ki]ng, [mighty king, king of the world, king] of Assyria, king of the [four] quarters, [......]
2′	[*dan-ni* LUGAL ŠÚ LUGAL] KUR–AN.ŠÁR LUGAL *kib-ra-a-ta* [*er-bet-ti*]	
3′	[*x x x x x x x x x*]*x* ^{d}AMAR.UTU *a-na* NUMUN *mi-i ba-x*[*x x x*]	3 [......] Marduk, to the seed of ... [...]

235 Fincke (1.12.2005) combined two pieces that Dietrich had joined in 1965. Topically, see SAA 3 20-22 (for no. 20, see also Hämeen-Anttila, SAAB 1, pp. 13-16). 1f Since these lines have Assurbanipal's epithets, they are probably not preceded by many lines. 3 It is difficult to understand *mi-i* here: is a sign missing?

4′	[*x x x x x x x* ^{m}A]N.ŠÁR–DÙ–DUMU.UŠ NUMUN *šá* ^{d}AMAR.UTU [*x x*]	4 [...... A]ssurbanipal, the offspring whom Marduk [...... l]ove, to the *true* king
5′	[*x x x x x x x i-r*]*a-mu-uš a-na* LUGAL *ki-na-*⸢*a*⸣-[*ta*$^{?}$]	
6′	[*x x x x x x x x x*]*x* ^{d}*zar-pa-ni-ti šar-rat* KUG-[*tú*]	6 [......] Zarpanitu, the holy queen.
7′	[*x x x x x x x x x*]*x aṣ-ṣa-bat la a-ma-a-ta* [0]	7 [......] I grasped [...] that I will not die.
8′	[*x x x x x x x x x*] A AN.ŠÁR ^{d}UTU ^{d}AMAR.UTU NUMUN-*ú-ka*	8 [......] son of Aššur, Šamaš (*and*) Marduk, your *progeny*,
9′	[*x x x x x x x x x*] *ze-ri-ka pi-ir-i-ka* [0]	9 [...... *of*] your seed, your offspring,
10′	[*x x x x x x x x x*] *i-ra-ʾa-mu-ú* EN LUGAL.MEŠ	10 [......] they love the lord of the kings,
11′	[*x x x x x x x x á*]*š-šá* GIŠ.BAN *a-na* ŠÀ-*bi-ku-nu* [*x*]	11 [...... *b*]*ecause of* the bow to your *hearts*
12′	[*x x x*]*x* ⸢*na*⸣ [*x x x x*]*x* KUR-*šú it-ta-na-an-biṭ is-pu-*[*x*]	12 [......] his country keeps shining brightly ...[...]
13′	[*x x x*]-*ka x*[*x x x x*]*x-am-ma* GÌR.2-*ka iṣ-ṣa-ab-bat* [0$^{?}$]	13 *your* [... ... ...]... and grasps your feet
14′	[*x x x*]*x ta-šak-x*[*x x*]-*niš-šú* EN LUGAL.MEŠ *i-na* ŠÀ [*x x*]	14 [...] you *pla*[*ce*] for him, lord of the kings, in [...]
15′	[*x x x*] ^{d}AMAR.UTU *i-*[*x x*]⸢*x-ku-nu*⸣-*šú i-na* ŠÀ-*bi šá ni-x*[*x x*]	15 [...] Marduk [...] you (pl.) *within those who* ...[...]
16′	[*x x x*]*x-ku-nu-šú i x*[*x x x*] É *ku hu ṣa an na x*[*x x*]	16 [...] you (pl.) [...] ...... [...]
17′	[*x x x*]*x-ki* MUL(.)MAŠ(.)HAL$^{?}$ *x*[*x x x*]*x* AN-*e ul i-x*[*x x*]	17 [...] the ... star [...] of heaven *does* not ...[...]
18′	[*x x x*] UD-*mu-us-su* [*x x x*]*x ir-ru-ub-ma ši-x*[*x x x*]	18 [...] *it* daily enters [...] and ...[...]
19′	[*x x x*]-*šú i-dab-b*[*u-ub x x x-n*]*u zi-i-mu šá* ^{d}[*x x*]	19 spea[ks] his [..., ...] the countenance of [DN],
20′	[*x x x*].MEŠ *kib-ra-tu*[*m x x x x*]-⸢*hu*⸣-*ú-ka* ⸢*qar*⸣-*r*[*ad* (*x*)]	20 [...]s of [the four] quarters [...] your [...], hero,
21′	[*x x x*]-⸢*šad*$^{?}$⸣-*ba-bu z*[*i*$^{?}$ *x x x x x*] *šá* ^{d}AMAR.UTU EN DINGIR.ME[Š 0$^{?}$]	21 [*who i*]*ncites* [......] of Marduk, lord of the god[s],
22′	[*x x x*]*x ta-dab-bu-ba* [*x x x x*] MU *šá* ^{d}U.GUR *qar-r*[*ad*]	22 [...] you are saying [...] the *name* of Nergal, her[o of the gods, *you*] are saying [...] crown of Marduk, king of the god[s],
23′	[DINGIR.MEŠ *x*]-⸢*dab*⸣-*bu-ba-aʾ* [*x x x x*] ⸢*a*⸣-*ga-a* ^{d}AMAR.UTU LUGAL DINGIR.[MEŠ]	
24′	[*x x x*]-⸢*bu-ku*⸣-*nu-šú* KUR–URI.[KI *x x x*] É-*šú ta-ki-il-lim x*[*x* (*x*)]	24 [...] *you*, Babylonia [...] his house, the one who trusts the god [...]
25′	[*x x x*] ⸢*gab*$^{?}$ *ri*$^{?}$ *na*$^{?}$ *hi*$^{?}$⸣ *ši-i x*[*x x x x x*]*x* KUR.KUR *gab-bi-šú-nu* [(*x*)]	25 [...] ...... [......] all their lands
26′	[*x x x x*] ⸢*x x*⸣ [*x x x x x x ka*]-*a-a-nu* EN LUGAL.[MEŠ]	26 [...... con]stantly lord of the king[s].
27′	[*x x x x x x x x x*] ⸢*x*⸣ [*x x x x x*]*x-iš ina* [*x x*]	27 [......]*ly* in [...]

4-5 Possibly listing more gods than just Marduk, though cf. *i-r*]*a-mu-uš* with line 10. 12 If there is a verb at the end, then, e.g., *sapāhu* "to scatter" and *sapānu* "to flatten" are possible. 13 Unless there is a form of *alāku* at the beginning. As such, *iṣ-ṣa-ab-bat* looks like a Gt prs form, but it can be interpreted as a normal G form *iṣabbat*. 17 KI as *itti* "with" or a post-determinative is not excluded. 22 Or, *šu*]-*mu*. 24 *ta-ki-il-lim* is taken as the sandhi spelling for *tākil ili*. 24, r.5f I.e., Babylonia = Akkad.

28′ [*x x x x x x x x*] ⌜*na*⌝-*ki-ri i-n*[*a x x x x*]
29′ [*x x x x x x x x x*]-*ú ina* ŠÀ-*bi* ^{d}[*x x x x*]
30′ [*x x x x x x x-g*]*a*$^{?}$-*at* GÌR.2-*šú la me-sa-a*[*t*$^{?}$ *x x x*]
31′ [*x x x x x x x*] *ina na-as-pan-du šá* ^{d}*ši-ma-a-l*[*i-a*]
32′ [*x x x x x x a*]-*na* ŠÀ-*bi it-tal-ka* EN LUGAL.ME[Š]
33′ [*x x x x x x x*] *a-ga-a ma-gar-ra-ka i-na da-am*
34′ [*x x x x x x x*]-*tu-šá en-na* 2-*ta* MU.AN.NA.MEŠ
35′ [*x x x x x x*] *ina da-am tal-lak* MU.AN.NA *a-ga-a*
36′ [*x x x x x x x*]-*pi dáb-du-šú-nu ta-šak-kan*
37′ [*x x x x x x* NUMU]N–*ha-al-gat-e in-da-ra-a-a*
38′ [*x x x x x x x*]-*nu* KI.MIN *ul-tu* UGU-*hi i-na* GIŠ.GU.ZA
39′ [*x x x x x x t*]*u-uš-šab-ma kiš-šú-tú šá ṣal-mat*–SAG.DU
40′ [*ta-be-el*$^{?}$] ^{m}AN.ŠÁR–*ba-an*–DUMU.UŠ EN LUGAL.MEŠ

[28] [......] the enemy in [...]
[29] [......] *against god* [...]
[30] [... *his* ...]..., his unwashed feet [...],
[31] [......] with the destruction of Šimal[i'a]
[32] [......] went there, lord of the king[s]
[33] [...] this [...], your wheel in the blood of
[34] [......]... now *for* two years
[35] [......] you *wade* in blood. This year
[36] [......] you will bring about their defeat
[37] [...... the see]d of Halgatê, the Indareans
[38] [......] ditto, ever since [you] sit on the throne [......] and [*rule*] the totality of the black-headed people, Assurbanipal, lord of the kings.

41′ [^{m}AN.ŠÁR–DÙ–DUMU.UŠ$^{?}$ *šá* LÚ.*in-d*]*a-ra-a-a ma-áš-ki-šú-nu*
42′ [*x x tu-ka-a-ṣ*]*a*$^{?}$ ⌜*um*⌝-*ma* ARAD.MEŠ-*ka a-ni-ni*
43′ [*um-ma ina* ŠÀ$^{?}$] ⌜É⌝-*ka la ta-ha-aṭ-ṭi* EN LUGAL.MEŠ
44′ [*x x x x x*]*x i-šap-pa-ru-nik-ka um-m*[*a*]
45′ [*x x x x*]-*ka la ta-hi-iṭ* EN LUGAL.M[EŠ]

[41] [*Assurbanipal*, you will *fla*]*y* the skin [of the Ind]areans, (who are) saying, "we are your servants, *you* do not sin [in] your house, lord of the kings."

[44] [*The* ...] write to you, saying: "you did not *examine* your [...], lord of the kings."

[28] Possibly, "the enemy [land]" or "the enemies". [29] Or, e.g., *ina* ŠÀ-*bi* DINGIR[(.MEŠ) *x x*]. [30] An obvious insult. Or, *la pár*$^{?}$-*sa-a*[*t*$^{?}$, but it seems forced to read *pár*-, and this is certainly not the typical *ašar šēpu parsat* "in a secluded place" clause of many rituals. [32] Perhaps better *i*]-*na* ŠÀ-*bi*; cf. SAA 1 41 r.2. [39] The most likely restorations are [KUR–AN.ŠÁR], [LUGAL-*ti-ka*] and [LUGAL-*ú-ti*]. [40] Space for more than four signs at the beginning, but a longer gap between the words can be expected. [41] At the beginning, space may be a problem for the proposed restoration. [43] Is *la ta-ha-aṭ-ṭi* a mistake for *la ni-ha-aṭ-ṭi*?

FIG. 24. *Sack of Susa, with statue of bull transported on cart.* BM 124946.

46′ [*x x*]⸢*x*⸣-*ma-ka iq-tab-bu-ka-a-ma um-m*[*a*]
47′ [^{m}*x x*] ⸢*x áš*$^{?}$ *x*⸣ DUMU-*ú-a šu-ú am–mì-ni-i ki-i* KUR *x*[*x*]
48′ [*x x*]*x ta-ṣar-ra-hu-ú-ma tu-maš-ša*[*r* (*x*)]
49′ [*x x*]*x-i hi-iṭ*⸣-*ṭi a-di* UGU *šá* ŠÀ-*ba-šú i-na* KUR-*k*[*a*]
50′ [*x x*]*x-le-e tu-ka-aṣ-ṣu ú-kan-m*[*a*]
51′ [*i-n*]*a* IGI EN LUGAL.MEŠ *i-ba-áš-ši-i a-na mu-*[*ti*$^{?}$]
52′ [*x x*]*x* ⸢*x*⸣ UD-*mu-im-ma za-qí-qí šá* ^{d}AMA[R.UTU]
r.1 [*x x x x t*]*u-šar-ba-ba ù ta-x*[*x x x*]-*li-n*[*i*]
2 [*x x x*] ⸢*a-na*⸣ *ram-ni-i-ka ma-x*[*x x* E]N LUGAL.M[EŠ]

46 Your […]… said to you: "[NN], is my son, why do you *flare up but abandon* [(…)] *when a land* […]?"
49 […] *my crime* until his *wish* in yo[ur] land
50 *I* will establish [the …]…s [that] you *flay but* are there (people) for *de*[*ath* i]n the presence of the lord of the kings?
52 […] *on* the same day ghosts *which* Ma[rduk]
r.1 [… y]ou *relax* and …[…]…
2 […] to yourself …[…, lo]rd of the kings.

---

3 [^{m}AN.ŠÁR–DÙ–DUMU.UŠ$^{?}$] *a-na* URU.*šu-šá-an* TU-*ma* ⸢UD⸣-20-KÁM *šá* ITI.SI[G$_4$]
4 [*x x x x x*]*x a-na* É–DINGIR *i-*⸢*šal*⸣-[*la*]*l* ŠÀ-*bu-ú šá*
5 [*x x x x* KUR.NI]M.MA.KI *i-mat a-na* É.KUR.MEŠ *šá* KUR–URI.KI
6 [*x x x x* É.KUR-*r*]*a*$^{?}$-*at* KUR–URI.KI [*šá i*]*š-lu-lu*
7 [*x x x x x x* ^{d}*i*]*l-te-e-ru* [*ù*] ^{d}*na-na-a*
8 [*x x x x x x x x*]*x-šú a-n*[*a x x l*]*ib-ba* URU *ab-bi-šú*
9 [*x x x x x x x p*]*a-ni-šú x*[*x x* N]A$_4$.AN.ZA.GUL$^{!}$
10 [*x x x x x x x x*] ⸢*ul tu*⸣-*qar-rib pa-ni-ka*
11 [*x x x x x x x x*] *dul-la-šá e-pu-uš*

3 [*Assurbanipal*] will enter Susa and, on the 20th day of Siv[an] (III), he will carry off [……] to the temple. *In the same way*, [… the *king* of E]lam will die, to the temples of Babylonia
6 […… the temp]les of Babylonia [which he] had plundered
7 […… I]lteru [and] Nanaya,
8 [……] his […] *t*[*o* … *i*]*n* the city of his fathers,
9 […… *b*]*efore* him […] a … stone vessel
10 [……] you *did not present*, your *face*
11 [……] did *her* work.

---

12 [EN LUGAL.MEŠ LÚ.SAG.MEŠ-*šú ina* GI]Š.GU.ZA *šá* KUR.⸢KUR *gab*⸣-*bi lu-še-eš-šib*
13 [*x x x x x x x x*]*x ina* ŠÀ-*bi šu-uz-ziz* ^{md}AMAR.UTU–LUGAL–PAB
14 [*x x x x x x* LÚ.*ša*]*k-nu šá* LÚ.SAG.MEŠ *ina* UGU URU.*šu-šá-an*
15 [URU.*x x x x r*]*u-ub-bi-iš a-na* $^{md+}$EN–ŠUR DUMU ^{m}*i-ba-a*
16 [*ina* UGU URU.*hi-da*]-*lu ru-ub-bi-iš* ^{md}AMAR.⸢UTU⸣–LUGAL–PAB
17 [LÚ.*x x ina* UGU URU.*t*]*a-mu-ú-nu* URU.*ki-il-ta-a-ta*
18 [URU.*x x x x x*]-*e ru-ub-bi-iš* ^{m}*mil-ki-i–*ÁG-*am*
19 [LÚ.GAL–KA.KÉŠ *i-n*]*a* UGU URU KUR.*a-ra-šú* É–URU.*bu-ur-nak-ka*

12 May [the lord of the kings] settle [his eunuchs on] the throne of all lands.

13 [……] station there! Promote Marduk-šarru-uṣur […… *and* the gov]ernor of eunuchs to be in charge over Susa [and …]; Bel-eṭir, son of Ibâ, [over Hida]lu; Marduk-šarru-uṣur, [the … over the cities of T]amunu, Kiltata, [and …]e; Milki-ramu, [chief tailor], over the land Arašu, Bit-Bu(r)nakka [and the city of …]šu; one of your eunuchs of [… also ove]r Hilmu and Pillat. [NN], governor, to the throne of the Indareans, [ditto].

49 Or, an anomalous *i-hi-iṭ-ṭi* "he sins/commits a crime" instead of the expected *i-ha-aṭ-ṭi*. 52 In connection with the *destruction* of Elam, "ghosts" appear in Assurbanipal's royal inscriptions. r.4 *libbū ša* often means "just like that". r.9 See coll. r.13, 16 On Marduk-šarru-uṣur, see PNA 2/II 729. r.15-20 SAA 3 29-30 convey the Assyrian feelings towards Bel-eṭir, son of Iba, after his rebellion against Assurbanipal (see, e.g., Frame Babylonia (17; 118, n. 87; 156, n. 107). The translation here follows that of CAD R 45b. r.17 As far as we know, Kiltata and Tamunu are thus far hapax GNs. r.19 This attestation and other GNs of the text are not listed in Bagg RGTC 7/3/1 but cf. pp. 124-25 s.v. Bīt-Bunakku.

20 [URU.*x x x x*]-*šú ru-ub-bi-iš* 1+*en* LÚ.SAG-*ka šá*
21 [*x x x i-na* UG]U URU.*hi-li-im ù* URU.*pi-il-la-at* KI.MIN
22 [^{m}*x x x x x* L]Ú.EN.NAM *i-na* UGU GIŠ.GU.ZA *šá in-da-ra-a-a*
23 [KI.MIN *x x x u*]*n-qa* LUGAL ŠÚ ^{m}AN.ŠÁR–DÙ–DUMU.UŠ LUGAL *dan-nu*
24 [*x x x x x*]*x*-⸢*ki*⸣ *lu-uš-ši-i-ma* 11-*lim* GIŠ.BAN.MEŠ
25 [*x x x x x x x*] ⸢*x*⸣ *nu-ra-ab-bi* ⸢É *x x x x*⸣
26 [*x x x x x x x x x*] ⸢*pa-an un*⸣-[*x x x x x x x*]

4 lines broken away

31 [*x x x x*] ⸢*x*⸣ [*x x x x x x x x x x x x x x x x*]
32 [*x x x x*] ⸢*x a*⸣ [*x x x x x x x x x x x x*] ⸢*x*⸣ *ši* [*x*]
33 [*x x x x*] ⸢*x im x*⸣[*x x x x x x x x x t*]*u*?-*šá-ka-al* [0]
34 [*x x x x*]*x* ⸢*i-ri-šú*⸣ [*x x x x x x*]⸢*x*⸣-*bi it-ma-a* [0]
35 [(*x um-ma*) ^{m}AN.ŠÁR]–⸢*ba-an*–DUMU.UŠ⸣ [*x x x x-t*]*a*?-*lu-ú-a* [0]
36 [*x x x x*] ⸢*x x šur* ^{m}AN⸣.[ŠÁR–DÙ–A? *x x*]*x-a-a-di ul-t*[*u*?]
37 [*x x x x*]*x*-⸢*ru a-na* URU⸣.*x*[*x x x x*]-*šá-da bi-ri-i-nu*
38 [*x x x x*]-⸢*nu-ma a-na pa-an* [^{m}AN.ŠÁR–D]Ù–A LUGAL ŠÚ *li-qi-nu*
39 [*x x x x*]-⸢*ti i-na x*⸣ [*x x x*]*x* DUMU ^{m}*i-ba-a šu-zib-in*-⸢*ni*⸣
40 [*x x x x*]-⸢*x-a* EN LUGAL⸣.[MEŠ *x š*]*al la ik-kal*
41 [*x x x x*] ⸢*man-nu šá i-ra*⸣-[*x x*]*x-ka ri-mu-ú-tú* SIG₅ *li-ri-man-ni*
42 [*x x x x*]*x*-⸢*šá i-ba-áš-ši*⸣ [*x x*] *ra-a'-i-ma-ni-ka*
43 [*x x x x k*]*i*-⸢*i ka-a*?-*re*?-*e*? *uš-ab*⸣ NAG LUGAL KUR.KUR *re-e-mu*
44 [*x x x x x x*]*x* ⸢ŠÀ-*bi x x-ni*⸣ *a-ga-a* EN LUGAL.MEŠ
45 [*x x x x x x*] ⸢*x x x*⸣ [*x x x*] ⸢*x a' it*⸣-*ta-na* ⸢*it*⸣-*ta*-⸢*x*⸣-*šú*
46 [*x x x x x x x x*] ⸢*x*⸣ [*x x x x*] ⸢*x x x-a-ma*? *lu*⸣-*uš-mu* EN LUGAL.MEŠ
47 [*x x x x x x x x x x x x*] ⸢*x x x x x x x x*⸣ GABA *he-pí*
48 [*x x x x x x x x x x x*] ⸢*ina*? EDIN?-*šú x x* EN⸣ LUGAL.[MEŠ]
49 [*x x x x x x x x*] ⸢*šá*⸣ [*x x*] LUGAL ⸢ŠÚ *li-pu-uš x x*⸣ [*x x*]

23 [... the s]eal of the king of the world, Assurbanipal, the mighty king,
24 [...]... let me summon 11,000 archers
25 [......] we *raised where* ...
26 [......] *before* [......]

(Break of 4 lines)

31 [......]
32 [......]
33 [...... *y*]*ou* feed
34 [...] they rejoice [......] swearing [...]:
35 "[(...) Assur]banipal, [(...)] *my* [...]...
36 [...] ... As[*surbanipal* ...] ... *fro*[*m*]
37 [...] ... *to* the town of [...]šada between us,
38 [...]... take *me* to the presence of [Assurba]nipal, king of the world!

39 [...] in [...], son of Ibâ, rescue me!
40 [...] the lord of the king[s ...] *does not* [*slan*]*der me.*
41 [...] anyone who lo[ve]s you, should grant me a beautiful gift,
42 [...] *exists* [...] your lover(s),
43 [... *li*]*ke a storehouse, sits and drinks*, the king of the lands, mercy
44 [......] *in* ... the crown of the lord of the kings,
45 [......] he gave me, he gave him,
46 [......] may *I* hear [...]..., the lord of the kings.
47 [......] ...... *breast* is [...] broken,
48 [......] *in its open country*, the lord of the king[s],
49 [......] let the king of the world *perform*

r.21 Interestingly, "ditto" replaces the repeated verbal form *rubbiš*. r.24 Lit. "bows". r.26 Or, e.g., *pa-an* UN.[MEŠ? r.36 ...]ayadi may be a GN. r.37 If *-šá-da* is still part of a GN, which is doubtful, then it is an unknown place name to us. End, alternatively, "our extispicy". r.38 *li-qi-nu* may contain a mistake resulting from the end of the previous line. r.39 CAD Š/3 208a suggests a PN at the end of the line together with the next line. r.40 Our guess is that the beginning of the line contained *kar-ṣi*]-⸢*ia*?⸣. It is difficult to decide whether the so-called *šal* and *la* belonged together or not, but there is quite a long gap between the two signs.

50 [*x x x x x x x*] ⸢*x x x*⸣ $^{d+}$EN ⸢*i-qa*$^{?}$*-ba*$^{?}$ *um-ma*⸣ [*x x x x*]
51 [*x x x x x x x x x*]*-me*$^{?}$*-ni* ^{m}AN.ŠÁR–DÙ–A LUGAL Š[Ú *x x x x*]
52 [*x x x x x x x x x i*]*n-da-ra-a-a* ⸢*bi*$^{?}$⸣ [*x x x x x*]
rest broken away or uninscribed

[......]
50 [......] ... Bel tells me: "[...]
51 [......] ... Assurbanipal, king of the wor[ld ...]
52 [...... the I]ndareans [...]
(Rest destroyed or uninscribed)

236. Fragment of a Praise to Assurbanipal(?)

83-1-18,696
beginning broken away
1′ ^{m}⸢^{d}⸣[*x x x x x x x x x*]
2′ *a-na* ^{m}*x*[*x x x x x x x x*]
3′ *ù* ^{d}[*x x x x x x x x*]
4′ *ù* ^{d}AMA[R.UTU *x x x x x x x*]
5′ *dan-nu* ^{md}[*x x x x x x x*]
6′ *ù* ^{d}*zar-pa-*[*ni-tum x x x x x*]

7′ ^{d}AMAR.UTU ⸢*ù*⸣ [*x x x x x x x*]
8′ *kiš-šu-t*[*ú x x x x x x x*]
9′ ^{d}*a-num* [*x x x x x x x*]
10′ *lu-dan-ni-*[*in x x x x x x*]
11′ AN.ŠÁR ^{d}*x*[*x x x x x x x x*]
12′ *bi-ri*[*t x x x x x x*]
13′ *a-na* LUGAL *ki*[*š-šat x x x x x*]

14′ UR.MAH.ME[Š *x x x x x x*]
15′ *kak-ki-šú-nu u* [*x x x x x x*]
16′ MUŠ.MEŠ *x*[*x x x x x x*]
17′ *z*[*i*$^{?}$*-x x x x x x x x x*]
rest broken away
beginning broken away
r.1′ *x*[*x x x x x x x x x x*]
2′ *x*[*x x x x x x x x x x*]
3′ *x*[*x x x x x x x x x x*]
4′ ^{m}[*x x x x x x x x x x*]
5′ *x*[*x x x x x x x x x x*]
6′ *i-*[*x x x x x x x x x*]
7′ *mu-x*[*x x x x x x x x x*]
8′ *li-*[*x x x x x x x x x*]
9′ *pu-ut x*[*x x x x x x x x*]
10′ *ina ṣi-*[*x x x x x x x x*]
11′ LUGAL *ki*[*š-šat x x x x x x x*]
12′ EN LUGAL.M[EŠ *x x x x x x x*]

CT 54 529
(Beginning destroyed)
1 [NN ......]
2 to [NN ......]
3 and [*DN* ......]
4 and Ma[rduk ......]
5 mighty, [NN ......]
6 and Zarpa[nitu ......]
7 Marduk and [......]
8 dominance [......]
9 Anu [......]
10 let [...] strength[en ......]
11 Aššur, [DN ......]
12 betwe[en ......]
13 to the king of the uni[verse ......].

---

14 The lions [......]
15 their weapons *and* [......]
16 the snakes [......]
17 [......]
(Break)
r.1 [......]
2 [......]
3 [......]
4 [NN ......]
5 [......]
6 [......]
7 ...[......]
8 [......]
9 *responsibility* [......]
10 *in* [......]
11 the king of the uni[verse ......]
12 lord of the kings [......]

r.51 Possibly *am*]*-me-ni* "[W]hy?"
236 1, 5 The PN could well be ^{m}AN.[ŠÁR–DÙ–DUMU.UŠ as in no. 235. 10 The subject is uncertain and may be plural.

13′ *ù* LUG[AL *x x x x x x x x*]
14′ 2-*me* ^{m}[*x x x x x x x x*]
15′ *i-la-*[*x x x x x x x x x*]
16′ *ki-*⸢*i*⸣ [*x x x x x x x x x*]
17′ *a-n*[*a x x x x x x x x x*]
rest broken away

13 and the ki[ng ......]
14 200, [NN ......]
15 *dee*[*ms* ......]
16 *when* [......]
17 t[o ......]
(Rest destroyed)

237. Omen for Assurbanipal Concerning Elam

Rm 2,455 — CT 35 pls. 37f

1 [*x x*] :. *ù šu-šu-riš* GAR *x*[*x x x x x x x x x x*]
2 [*x x* KUR.NI]M.MA.KI *a-na* [*x x x x x x x x x x*]
3 [*x x x*]*x ú-sap-pu-ma x*[*x x x x x x x*]*x* [*x x x x*]
4 [*x x x*] ⸢*x x*⸣ [*x x x x x x x x*] KI-⸢*šú*⸣

1 [...] and *places* in a *straightforward* manner [......]
2 [... E]lam to [......]
3 [...] beseech*es* and [......]
4 [......] with him.

---

5 [*x x x x x x x x x x x x x*] ⸢*šub-bi-ma*⸣
6 [*x x x x x x x x x x x x x*]*-mi-i*
7 [*x x x x x x x x x x x x x*]*-su-ma*
8 [*x x x x x x x x x x x x x*] IGI-*šú*

5 [......] *fill with* [...] and
6 [......]...
7 [......]... and
8 [......] *before* him.

---

9 [*x x x x x x x x x x x x x*]*-ši*
10 [*x x x x x x x x x x x x x x*]*x-šú-nu it-tar-ru-šú-ma*
11 [*x x x x x x x x x x x x x x-n*]*u* UGU-*šú-un*

9 [......]
10 [......] their [...] shook it/him and
11 [......] *on* them.

---

12 [*x x x x x x x x x x x x x x*] *šá* 150-*šú* UR$_5$ ŠU.SI *eṣ-ret*
13 [*x x x x x x x x x x x x x*] KUR.NIM.MA.KI
14 [*x x x x x x x x x x x x x*]*x-su-ma*
15 [*x x x x x x x x x x x x x*] UGU-*šú-un*

12 [......] of its *left side* a drawing of sixty was drawn.
13 [......] Elam
14 [......]... and
15 [......] *on* them.

---

16 [*x x x x x x x x x x*] ⸢*x x-qa*$^{?}$*-qu*⸣ DINGIR.MEŠ GAL.MEŠ
17 [*x x x x x x x x x x*]*-nu-ma*
18 [*x x x x x x x x ba-ru*$^{?}$*-t*]*i* DUG$_4$*-ú*
19 [*x x x x x x x x x x*] BAL-*qí*
20 [*x x x x x x x x x x*] *qí-bi-ti*
21 [*x x x x x x x x x x*] *qí-bi-t*[*i*]

16 [......] ..., the great gods
17 [......]... and [......] they recite [... *from extispicy ome*]*ns*
19 [......] pours a libation [of ...],
20 [......] my *prayer*
21 [...... my] *prayer*.

---

237 Previous editions: Bauer Asb pp. 85-87; Pongratz-Leisten, "The King at the Crossroads between Divination and Cosmology," in Lenzi and Stökl (eds.), *Divination, Politics, and Ancient Near Eastern Empires* (2014), 44f (a translation of the reverse) and id. SANER 6 (2015) 374f, 476 (a translation and transliteration of the reverse); cf. Weidner, AfO 8 (1932-33) 175, n.3. [14] Possibly the same word as in line 7. [19] Or, e.g., "performs [a sheep offering]". [20] Or, "[at] the command [of]". [21] Of course, it cannot be excluded that the last word of the obverse is *qí-bi-m*[*a*$^{?}$] "Say [*to*".

r.1 [BÀ? *šá* ^{m}AN.ŠÁR–DÙ]–A LUGAL *dan-nu* NUN *na-a'-du šá* ^{d}15 *be-let* MÈ Á ER[IM.HI.A-*šú*]
2 [*šá* SAG.DU ^{m}*te-um-man* LUGAL KUR.NIM.M]A.KI *ina qé-reb tam-ha-ru* KUD-*su-ma* DUMU $^{md+}$EN—BA-*š*[*á*]
3 [*x x x x x x*]*x-tu-uk*? LÚ.*e-la-mi-i ina* GÚ-*šú i-lu-lu-ma* ^{m}AN.ŠÁR–DÙ–A
4 [*x x x i-tu-ra*?] ⸢*a*⸣-*na* NINA.KI URU *be-lu-ti-šú ha-diš i-riš-šú i-te-ep-pu-šú ni-gu-ti*

r.1 [*Omen for* Assurbani]pal, strong king, reverent prince, at the side of whose a[rmy] Ištar, the lady of battle, (marches), [who] cut off [the head of Teumman, king of Ela]m, in the midst of battle and the son of Bel-iqiš[a], 3 [......]... of the Elamite they hung around his neck, and Assurbanipal 4 [... *and returned*] to Nineveh, city of his lordship. They were exulting joyfully and made merry.

---

5 [^{m}*tam-mar-ít x x x x*]*x-ru šá* ^{m}*um-man-i-gaš* LUGAL KUR.NIM.MA.KI *ina* IGI ^{m}AN.ŠÁR–DÙ–A LUGAL ŠÚ
6 [*x x x x x x*] ⸢*i*⸣-*duk-ma i-na* GIŠ.GU.ZA-*šú ú-šib* ^{m}AN.ŠÁR–DÙ–A LUGAL ŠÚ *a-na a-mat*
7 [*šá* ^{d}15? ^{m}*tam-mar-í*]*t* LUGAL KUR.NIM.MA.KI *u ga-du rab-ban-na-ti-šú*
8 [*x x x x* NIN]A.KI URU *be-lu-ti-šú ina* IGI-*šú it-tan-ga-ra-ár-ru*

5 [Tammaritu (...)] killed [...]... *of* Ummanigaš, king of Elam, [......] before Assurbanipal, king of the world, and he sat on his throne. Assurbanipal, king of the world, at the command of [*Ištar*, Tammari]tu, king of Elam, together with his *magnates* rolled before him [... *in* Nine]veh, city of his lordship.

---

9 [^{m}AN.ŠÁR–DÙ–A? *šá* AN.ŠÁR *u*?] ⸢^{d}⸣15 *i-ram-mu-šú-ma i-na mi-gir* ŠÀ-*bi-šú-nu it-tar-ru-šú-ma* ^{m}*tam-mar-ít*
10 [*x x x x x r*]*i-ṣu-ti* ^{m}GIŠ.NU$_{11}$–MU–GI.NA *ṣu-um-mu-ru šu-ú* LÚ.HAL-*šú u rab-ban-na-ti-šú*
11 [(*x x*) *il-li-ku-ni*]*m-ma ú-na-áš-šá-qu* GÌR.2-*šú* ^{m}*tam-mar-ít u* LÚ.HAL-*šú* IGI-*šú ú-kan-nu a-ha-meš*

9 [*Assurbanipal whom Aššur and*] Ištar love, and they lead him with their full content, but Tammaritu [... who] had sought Šamaš-šumu-ukin's aid, he, his diviner and *magnates* [went] and kissed his feet, 11 Tammaritu and his diviner accused each other in his presence.

---

12 [*x x x x x*] 15 *u* 150 NA UR BÀ-*ut* ^{m}AN.ŠÁR–DÙ–DUMU.UŠ LUGAL ŠÚ *šá* ^{d}UTU *u* ^{d}15 Á ERIM.HI.A-*šú* DU-*ku-ma*
13 [*x x x x x*] *qé-reb tam-ha-ru i-na-ru-ma iš-ku-nu* ŠI.ŠI-*šú-un*

12 [If ...] the right and left side of the station *are* ..., it is the omen of Assurbanipal, king of the world, at the side of whose army Šamaš and Ištar marched and killed [(...) his foes] in the midst of battle and brought about their defeat.

---

r.1, 3 Even up to ten or more signs may be missing at the beginning of these lines. r.3 The so-called *uk* does not seem entirely convincing; it almost looks like a badly written LUGAL. r.5 Orthographically, *mār šipri*, "messenger", ending in *ru* is possible but rare (e.g., SAA 17 62:5). If a PN, e.g., ^{m}*ku-dú*]*r-ru*, son of the Elamite king Umman-aldaše (for details see PNA 2/I 634, no. 25), or ^{m}*ú-b*]*a-ru* (mentioned in SAA 21 58), then to be translated "whom". r.8 For the verbal form, cf. SAA 9 1 i 10′. r.9 It would be strange if, after a "sectional" ruling, this line began with ["whom"]; cf. Pongratz-Leisten, loc. cit. Probably Aššur and Ištar, but note Šamaš and Ištar in r.12. r.12 That is, here NA stands for *manzāzu* "station". Instead of reading UR, one might think of reading TUKU? (cf., e.g., SAA 4 3 r.14) and translate "the right and left sides have a 'station'."

FIG. 25. *Decapitation of Teumman, Elamite king.*
BM 124801c.

14 [*x x x x x* U]ZU *ga-mir* ERIM-*ni ina* MU.SAG UR$_{5}$ *šá* 15 *it-taš-kan* BÀ-*ut* ^{m}GIŠ.NU$_{11}$–MU–GI.NA

15 [*x x x x x š*]*á*? *it-ti* ERIM-*ni* ^{m}AN.ŠÁR–DÙ–A *na-ram* DINGIR.MEŠ GAL.MEŠ MÈ DÙ-*šú-ma* BAD$_{5}$.BAD$_{5}$-*šú*

14 [If ...] in the lift of the head of the right lung there is an (entrails) omen (predicting) the annihilation of the army, it is an omen of Šamaš-šumu-ukin, [*the ... brother*, wh]o fought against the army of Assurbanipal, the beloved of the great gods, but was defeated.

r.15 The two most common negative definitions of Šamaš-šumu-ukin in Assurbanipal's royal inscriptions, [ŠEŠ NU GI.NA *š*]*á*?, "[the unfaithful brother wh]o," and [ŠEŠ *nak-ri š*]*á*?, "[the hostile brother wh]o," are both possible here, but the restoration could be something else.

16 [*x x x x x q*]*é-reb tam-ha-ru iṣ-ba-tu-nim-ma ina* IGI ^{m}AN.ŠÁR–DÙ–DUMU.UŠ LUGAL ŠÚ	16 They seized [... in the m]idst of battle and [...] before Assurbanipal, king of the world.
17 [*x x x x x*]*x* ^{m}GIŠ.NU$_{11}$–MU–GI.NA *la ṭa-ab-ti*	17 [*Omen of*] Šamaš-šumu-ukin, unfavorable.

---

18 [*x x x x ba-r*]*u-tu šaṭ-ru ina mah-ri-i* TA ŠÀ ÉŠ.QAR *ki-i as-su-ha ana* LUGAL *be-lí-iá*	18 [The *omens* from the *bār*]*ûtu* series that I previously extracted from the series for the king, my lord.
19 [*x x x x m*]*ah-ru-tu* LUGAL *be-lí li-mur an-na-a-ti* BÀ.MEŠ *šá* LUGAL *be-lí-iá*	19 May the king, my lord, have a look at [the e]arlier [*omens*]; these are the omens of the king, my lord.
20 [*šá* IGI] LUGAL *be-lí-iá mah-ru ana* ŠÀ ÉŠ.QAR *nu-še-rid* ⸢*x x*⸣ *šá* ⸢*a-na*?⸣ ^{m}*tam-mar-ít*	20 [Whatever] is acceptable [to] the king, my lord, we shall take it down into the series, ... *which* [...] to Tammaritu,
21 [*x x x x*] *ri-ṣu-ti šá* ^{m}GIŠ.NU$_{11}$–MU–GI.NA *il-la-ka a-l*[*ak x x x x x*]	21 comes [to] the aid of Šamaš-šumu-ukin, ...[......].
22e [*x x x ta*]*l-li-ku-ú-ni a-na* BÀ.MEŠ *šá* ^{m}*tam-mar-ít niš-ṭ*[*ur x x x x x*]	22 [*When* you] *went away*, we wro[te] to the omens of Tammaritu [......]
23e [*x x x x*]*x-ti* DINGIR.MEŠ-*ka li-pu-š*[*ú*] *x*[*x x x x x*]*x x*[*x x x x x x*]	23 [...] may your gods *take action* [......]

238. Fragment Praising Assurbanipal

83-1-18,777	CT 53 944
beginning broken away	(Beginning destroyed)
1′ [*x x x x x x x*] ⸢*x x x*⸣ [*x x x*]	
2′ [*x x x x x*]*x-a-e* KÁ.DINGIR.R[A.KI *x x*]	2 [......]... Babylon [...]
3′ [*x x x*] ^{m}AN.ŠÁR–DÙ–A LUGAL *kiš-šá-ti man-nu* [*x x x*]	3 [...] Assurbanipal, king of the world, who [...]?
4′ [*x x x* L]Ú.*gi-mir-a-a ni-iš-mu-u-ni* [*x x x*]	4 [... *that*] we heard the Cimmerians [...]
5′ [*x x x x*] GIŠ.ÙR.MEŠ KALAG.MEŠ ANŠ[E.KUR.RA.MEŠ?]	5 [......] heavy beams, *ho*[*rses*],
6′ [*x x x x*]*x ku-zip-pi ú-q*[*a-x x x x*]	6 [......] *will br*[*ing*] garments [...]
7′ [*x x x x x* A]N.ŠÁR E[N *x x x x x x*]	7 [...... A]ššur, [*great*] lo[rd, ...]
8′ [*x x x x x x*]*x* [*x x x x x x x x*]	
rest broken away	(Rest destroyed)
Rev. completely broken away	

238 According to SAA 21, p. XLI: This "looks like a fragment of a paean to Assurbanipal, cf. SAA 3 19-24".

239. Letters to Assurbanipal from his Son

K 4449 + K 10319

I beginning broken away; traces of one line

1′ *[x x x x x x x x x x x x]* ⸢*x x*⸣ *a-na* NUMUN-*[ka]*

2′ *[x x x x x x x x x x x x]x-ka a-na pi-ir-i-ka*

3′ *[x x x x x x x x x x x a-na] pi-ir-i-ka lid-di-nu-u*ʾ

4′ *[x x x x x x x x x x x x]-a-ma ṭa-ba šum-ka* EN LUGAL.MEŠ

5′ *[x x x x x x x x x x x x]* LUGAL-*ú-tu ù bé-lu-tu a-ga-a*

6′ *[x x x x x x x x x x x x t]a-le-ʾa-a ma-al-la at-me-ka*

7′ *[x x x x x x x x x x x x]* ⸢*x x x x*⸣*-ak-ka* EN LUGAL.MEŠ

8′ *[a-na* ^{m}AN.ŠÁR–DÙ–DUMU.UŠ *ra-i]m ki-na-a-ta* EN LUGAL.MEŠ

9′ *[qí-bi-ma i-na* UD.MEŠ-*ka šá* ^{d}AMAR.UTU *i-r]a-mu-ši-na-a-ta*

10′ *[x x x x x x x* AN]-*e ù* KI.TIM *it-ti*

11′ *[x x x x x x x x]x is-si-lim it-ti-ka*

12′ *[x x x x x x x x* KU]R.KUR *dan-nu ù it-ti*

13′ *[x x x x x* ^{md}GIŠ.N]U_{11}–MU–GI.NA

14′ *[x x x x x x pi-ir]-i-ka šá a-na* LUGAL-*ú-tú*

15′ *[x x x x x x ú-ša]m-di-du-uš it-ti-šú-ma*

16′ *[x x x x x x x x]* ⸢*da*⸣ *is i-na* ITI.BARAG

17′ *[x x x x x x x x]* ⸢GIŠ⸣.*nar-kab-tú* KUG.GI

18′ *[x x x x x x x x x]x a-na* TIN.TIR.KI

19′ *[x x x x x x x x p]a*$^{?}$*-an* AN.ŠÁR ^{d}UTU

20′ *[x x x x x x x an-d]a-har pa-an* ^{d}*a-nim*

21′ *[x x x x x x x x x x]x an-da-har*

22′ *[x x x x x x x x x x x] it-ta-du-uš*

23′ *[x x x x x x x x x x x x]x* GARZA *šá* $^{d+}$EN

24′ *[x x x x x x x x x x x x]x-pu-šú*

25′ *[x x x x x x x x x x-r]at* GAL-*ti*

26′ *[x x x x x x x x x x x] ù* GIŠ.ŠUR.MÌN

27′ *[x x x x x x x x x x x] i-na*

28′ *[x x x x x x x x x x* KUR.*la*$^{?}$*-a]b-na-an*

29′ *[x x x x x x x x x x x x x]x x[x (x)]*

rest broken away

AfO 18 382ff (= SAA 3 25) + CT 54 219

(Beginning destroyed)

I 1 [......] ... to [your] seed.

2 [......] your [...] to your offspring

3 [......] may they give [... to] your offspring!

4 [......] your illustrious name, lord of kings.

5 [......] this kingship and dominion

6 [......] you can accomplish whatever you say

7 [......]... to you, lord of kings.

---

8 [Say to Assurbanipal, lov]er of truth, lord of kings:

9 [During your days, which Marduk l]oves, [...... of heaven] and earth has made peace with [.......] with you.

12 [...... of] the lands are strong; and with

13 [...... Šama]š-šumu-ukin

14 [...... of] your [*offspri*]*ng*, who for kingship

15 [......] *dragged* him with him

16 [......]... in the month of Nisan

17 [......] a chariot of gold

18 [......]... to Babylon

19 [......] *before* Aššur and Šamaš

20 [......] I received, before Anu

21 [......] I received

22 [......] they cast him

23 [......] the ordinances of Bel

24 [......]...

25 [......] great

26 [......] and cypress

27 [......] in

28 [...... Le]banon

(Break)

239 Join, which adds further lines to both Columns II and r. I, by J. Fincke (29.11.2005).

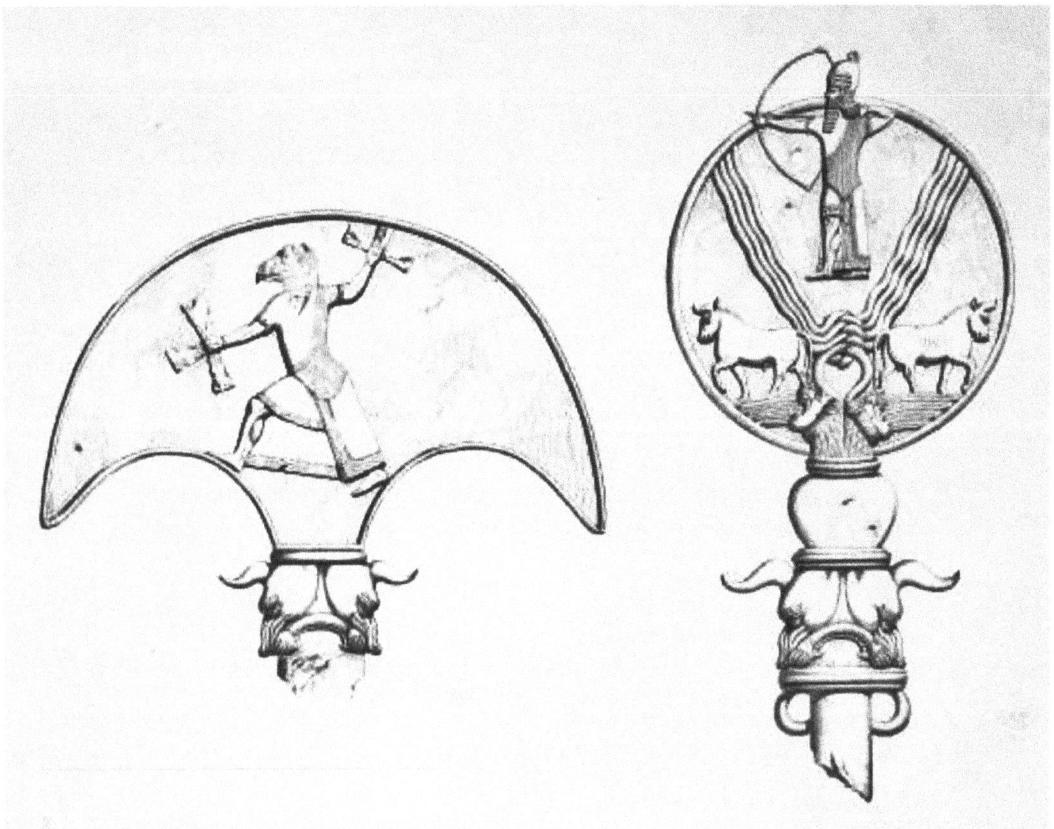

FIG. 26. *Divine standards accompanying Sargon at war.*
Botta and Flandin, Monument de Ninive II, Pl. 158.

II beginning broken away
1′ *an* x[x x x x x x x x x]
2′ ^{m}AN.ŠÁR–⌜DÙ–DUMU.UŠ⌝ [LUGAL *kib-ra-a-ti*]
3′ *er-bet-ti* LUGAL *kiš-š*[*a-ti qí-bi-ma um-ma*]
4′ *at-tu-ú-ka* ^{d}x[x x x x x]
5′ ^{d}IM *tuk-lat-ka ina pi-i* [x x x x]
6′ *šá da-na-ni-i-ka i-n*[*a im-ni-ka*]
7′ ^{d}UTU *il-lak i-na šu-*[*me-li-ka*]
8′ ^{d}15 *il-lak il-si* [x x x x]
9′ LÚ.*um-ma-ni-ka* ^{d}*a-nu-*[*ni-tum* x x]

10′ *ta-ha-zu at-ta qar-d*[*a*$^{?}$*-ta* x x x]
11′ *kul-la-si-na ta-bi-lu a-*[x x x]
12′ LÚ.*um-ma-ni-i-ka šá-kin šu-lu*[*m* x x]
13′ É 5 *ina* É 6 *ina* É 7 *lu-ṣ*[*u-*x x]
14′ *e-du lu-ṣa-am-ma lul-lik a-di ku-d*[*úr-ri*]

II 1 [Say to ......] Assurbanipal, [king of the] four [regions], king of the universe: [thus (speaks)] your own [...]:

5 Adad is your support; at the command of [..., the ...] of your might [.......].

7 [At your right] goes Šamaš, at your left goes Ištar. Anu[nitu] has called out [to the ...] of your army.

10 You are valiant *in* battle [......]

11 all of [which] you rule; [in ...... of] your army, there is peace [...].

13 May I emerge [...] the fifth house, in the sixth house, in the seventh house,

14 may I go out alone, and go as far as the bor[der]!

15′ *a-na* ^{m}AN.ŠÁR–DÙ–DUMU.UŠ LUGAL *kib-ra-a-[ti]*
16′ *er-bet-ti* LUGAL *[gít-m]a-la dan-nu qí-b[i-ma]*
17′ *um-ma ti-rik-ka šub-tú x[x x]*
18′ *li-ku-un* GIŠ.GU.ZA-*ka li-ri-[ku]*
19′ UD.MEŠ-*ka ši-ba-a lit-tu-tu* EN LUGAL.[MEŠ]
20′ *i-na* UD.MEŠ-*ka šá* ^{d}AMAR.UTU *i-ra-⌈mu⌉-ši-n[a-a-ta]*
21′ ^{d}SAG.ME.GAR *ina* AN-*e* KASKAL.MEŠ *kit-tú iṣ-ṣa-[bat]*
22′ ^{d}*ṣal-bat-a-nu* MUL-*ka i-na* AN-*e* [0]
23′ *zi-i-mu [i]t-tal-biš at-ta kiš-šu-t[ú x x]*
24′ *ki-i* UR.GAL [M]UL-*ka zi-i-mi* [0]
25′ *it-tal-biš* LUGAL KUR.KUR *kit-tim* AN.ŠÁR [0]
26′ *šá di-in kit-ti it-ta-ap-ha* [0]
27′ ⌈KÁ.GAL! AN-*e*⌉ *e-di-il-ti ta-ad-lu-x[x]*
28′ [*x x x x x x x x*] ⌈*x x x x x*⌉
29′ [*x x x x x x i*]*t-ta-x*[*x x x x*]
30′ [*x x x*]⌈*x*⌉-*ri* LÚ.*šar-ra-qa* L[Ú.*x x*]
31′ [*x x*]-*ma*? *bad-da-bat-tu ih-tal-liq* ⌈1⌉

32′ [*e-l*]*am*?-*ti* GIŠ.*pi-laq-qa ta-na-áš-ši-i-ma*
33′ [*mi-ṣ*]*ir* KUR.KUR *gab-bi ta-lam-ma-am-ma*
34′ [*x* (*x*) *i*]*t-ti-šú ul i-dab-bu-ub* EN LUGAL.MEŠ
35′ [*x x x*]*x* ^{m}AN.ŠÁR–DÙ–DUMU.UŠ LUGAL *dan-⌈nu liq-x⌉*

15 Say to Assurbanipal, king of the four regions, the [per]fect, mighty king:

17 thus (speaks your ..., [...] *seat*: May your throne be stable, may your days be long, enjoy old age, O lord of kings!

20 In your days, which Marduk loves, Jupiter has taken on courses of truth in the heavens, (while) Mars, your star, is clothed with a glitter in the heavens. As for you, total power [...].

24 Your star is clothed with a glitter like UR.GAL; the true king of the lands, Aššur, has shined forth *with* truthful judgement. You have [...ed] the closed gate of heavens [......]

28 [......]

29 [......]

30 [...]..., a thief, a [...] *is* [...] *fleeing* around.

31 *An* [*El*]*amite woman* brings (you) a spindle, and you *surround* [the bord]ers of all lands,

34 [...] does not talk to him, lord of the kings,

35 *may* [...] Assurbanipal, the mighty king, ...

Reverse

I 1 [*a-na* DUMU-*šú šá* ^{m}AN.ŠÁR–PAB]–SUM-*na* LUGAL *dan-nu*
2 [*x x x x x x x x x* K]Á.DINGIR.RA.KI
3 [*x x x x x x x x x* U]GU? *ki-i*
4 [*x x x x x x x x x* LU]GAL *ra-bu-ú*
5 [*x x x x x x x x x k*]*ib-ra-a-ta*
6 [*x x x x x x x* LUGAL] *dan-nu šá mi-hir-šú*
7 [*x x x x x x x x x* E]N LUGAL.MEŠ
8 [*x*]-*pi-ir-šú šá-lam ù an-⌈na-a x x⌉*
9 *a-na* DUMU–DUMU-*šú šá* ^{d}30–PAB.MEŠ–*r*[*í-ba*]
10 LUGAL *dan-nu* LUGAL KUR.KUR *šá li-pi-[is-su]*
11 *mu-ú-tú a-na* ^{m}AN.ŠÁR–*ba-an*–DUMU.U[Š]
12 *qi-b*[*i-m*]*a um-ma ap-lu-ú-ka u* [*x x x*]
13 *ina* UD.MEŠ-*ka ki-na-a-ta šá* ^{d}[AG]
14 *ù* ^{d}AMAR.UTU *i-ra-mu-ši-n*[*a-a-ta*]
15 ⌈*ṭuh-da*⌉ *ù meš-ru-ú ni-x*[*x x*]
16 É.[KU]R? ⌈*tu*⌉-*un-da-al-*[*li*]

r I 1 [Say to Esarha]ddon['s son], the mighty king, [...... B]abylon

3 [......] *when*

4 [......] great [ki]ng, [...... *king of the four* q]uarters [...... the] mighty [king], who [*has no*] equal, [...... lo]rd of the kings.

8 His ... well-being and this [......].

9 Say to Sennacherib's grandson, the mighty king, the king of the lands, who[se to]uch is death, to Assurbanipal: thus (speaks) your heir and [...]:

13 In your righteous days, which [Nabû] and Marduk love, you have filled the temple(s) with abundance and wealth ... [...].

II 29 [*i*]*t-ta-x* could be a noun, e.g., "omen[s]", or a verbal form "he has [...]ed". II 30 Perhaps something like [*i-na š*]*e*?-*ri* "[In the mo]rning". II 32f The reading [*e-l*]*am*?-*ti*, probably with no space for *mí* to precede it, is suggested by the partial assonance with *ta-lam-ma-am-ma* of the following line. r. I 4-7 Probably the whole passage contains only common epithets.

FIG. 27. *Elamite with spindle.*
Louvre Sb 2834.

17 *ina* KUR–AN.ŠÁR *i-ba-áš-ši* MU.[AN.NA]
18 *šá a-na* ZÍZ.A.AN ŠE.BAR *ma-hi-ri* [*x x x*]
19 *šá a-na* ⸢*x x*⸣.A.AN *ma-hi-ri x*[*x x x x*]

20 EN LUGAL.MEŠ ⸢*x x*⸣ *úr*$^{?}$ *a* [*x x x x*]
21 *a-na* ⸢*i*$^{?}$ *x*⸣ *a* ⸢*x*⸣ *qí-ba-a x*[*x x x x x*]
22 *si-il-me-ka li-ri-ku x*[*x x x x*]

[17] In the land of Assyria there have been y[ear(s)] when for wheat and barley the prices [......], when for ... the prices [......]
[20] Lord of kings ... [......]
[21] tell to ...... [......]
[22] May your peace be long lasting ... [......]

---

23 *a-na* ^{m}AN.ŠÁR–DÙ–DUMU.UŠ LUGAL ŠÚ LUGAL *k*[*ib*$^{!}$*-ra-a-ti*]
24 *e*[*r*]*-bet-ti a-na bi-nu-ut* AN.ŠÁ[R *ù*]
25 ^{d}UTU KU KAL *a-na na-ram* ⸢^{d}⸣[AMAR.UTU]
26 *ù* ^{d}*za*[*r*]*-pa-ni-ti a-na uz*$^{!}$-[*ni*]
27 *ra-pa-áš-ti a-na* ŠÀ-*bi r*[*u-ú-qí*]
28 *a-na le-ʾi-i a-na mul-t*[*e-ši-ru*$^{?}$]
29 *a-na mul-te-pi-šú a-na x*[*x x x*]
30 LUGAL *ki-na-a-ta šá giš-hu-r*[*i x x x*]

31 *um-ma mar-du-ú-ka šá x*[*x x x x*]
32 *li-šim* EN LUGAL.MEŠ [*x x x x*]
33 MU.AN.NA.MEŠ ⸢*biš*$^{?}$⸣*-te x*[*x x x x*]

[23] [Say] to Assurbanipal, king of the universe, the king of the four re[gions], to the ... creation of Aššur [and] Šamaš, to the beloved of Marduk and Zarpanitu, to the vast in understanding, to the fa[thomless] mind,
[28] to the competent, to the ord[erly], to the wizard, to the [...], to the king of righteousness who [...] designs:
[31] thus (speaks) your successor, who [......]:
[32] May the lord of kings decree [...]
[33] years of *slander* [......]

r. I 26, II 24 See coll.

34 *it-ta-ṣa-ar a-na* [*x x x x*]
35 *bu-kur-tú ud-*⸢*x*⸣ *x*[*x x x x*]
36 *ki-na-ta x*[*x x x x x x x*]
rest broken away
II beginning broken away; traces of two lines
1′ [*x x x x x x x x x x*]*-uš*
2′ [*x x x x x x x x x x*]*x-ti*
3′ [*x x x x x x x x x-b*]*u-ú*
4′ [*x x x x x x x x x*]*-tu* GARZA
5′ [*x x x x x x x x*] *pa-ni-ka*
6′ [*x x x x x x x x*]*-ku ṣi-ba-su*
7′ [*x x x x x x x x*]*-dan-an-ni*
8′ [*x x x x x x x x-q*]*u-na* EN LUGAL.MEŠ
9′ [*x x x x x x x x x*]*x-a-mu* AN.GAL
10′ [*x x x x x x x x x*]*x-ú a-na* ^{d}AMAR.UTU
11′ [*x x x x x x x x x*]*x id-dak-ka*
12′ [*x x x x x x x x š*]*á-la-nu-uš-šú*
13′ [*x x x x x x x x x*]*x* EN LUGAL.MEŠ
14′ [*x x x x x x x x*] *mi-iṣ-ri-*⸢*i*⸣*-šú*
15′ [*x x x x x x a-n*]*a* KUR–*na-ki-ri-ka*
16′ [*x x x x x x x x*]*x-ti-ka*
17′ [*x x x x x x x x u*]*l i-ka-su-ka*
18′ [*x x x x x x x x x*]*x ma-ṭú-ú-ma*
19′ [*x x x x x x x x x*] EN LUGAL.MEŠ
20′ [*x x x x x x x x x*]*-*⸢*ka*⸣*-ma*
21′ [*x x x x x x x x e-p*]*u-uš ù*
22′ [*x x x x x x x x x-s*]*u-lu hi-ri-i-ma*
23′ [*x x x x x x x x x x*]*x* URU-*šú a-ga-a*
24′ [*x x x x x x x x x* M]U.AN.NA$^{!}$.MEŠ
25′ [*x x x x x x x x x ta*]*-mah*$^{!}$*-har-šú-nu-tú*
26′ [*x x x x x x x x x x x*] ⸢*ik*⸣ [0]
rest broken away

34 he guarded for [......]
35 daughter [......]
36 righteousness [......]
(Break)

r. II 4 [......] ordinances
5 [......] *your face*
6 [......] his *grip*
7 [......]... me
8 [......] lord of kings
9 [......] *Ištaran*
10 [......] to Marduk
11 [......]... will *give* you
12 [......] apart from him
13 [......] lord of kings
14 [...... of] his boundary
15 [...... to] the land of your enemy
16 [......] your [...]
17 [......] they will [no]t bind you
18 [......]... are deficient
19 [......] lord of kings
20 [......] you
21 [...... do]es and
22 [......] dig [...]
23 [......] this city of his
24 [...... y]ears
25 [......] you will receive them
(Rest destroyed)

240. Fragment of Marduk Ordeal (Nineveh Version)

MGT 03
beginning broken away (for lines 1-38, see SAA 3 35 *and* 34)
1′ (39) [*ši-iz-bu ša ina* IGI ^{d}]⸢15 *šá* URU.*ni-nu-a i-hal-li*⸣*-pu-u-ni né-m*[*i-i*]*l* [*ši-i tu-ra-bu-šú-ni re-e-mu ina* UGU-*hi-šú ú-kal-lim ina* É–*ṣib-ta-te-šú tu-še-bal-áš-šú*]

MG 53

39 [The milk which] they milk [in front of] Ištar of Nineveh: (this is) because [she brought him up and showed him compassion. She sends him to his prisons.]

240 Previous edition (of this ms): MacGinnis et al., SAAB 28 (2022) 33-37. Restorations in square brackets are taken from SAA 3 35 and 34 (the Assur Version of the text). We have tried to follow the line division of the score transliteration (SAA 3 35), but it is clear that the manuscript deviates from the score, and as both the left and right edges of the tablet are missing, it is impossible to be sure how this ms began and ended the lines. [39] Here and in the following lines, the new piece confirms many earlier restorations, mainly based on SAA 3 34.

2′ (40) [*x ša ina si-qur-ri-te e-pi-šu-ni a-ki* DINGIR.MEŠ *e-si-ru-šu-ni i*]*h-ti-liq ina* ŠÀ-*bi e-te-li ma-a is–su-ri* ⸢*ú*⸣-*š*[*e-za-ab* TA* ŠÀ-*bi us-se-ri-du-ni-šú*]

[40] [The … which is done on the ziggurat: when the gods surrounded him, h]e fled and went up there, thinking: "Maybe I [shall be saved." They brought him down from there.]

3′ (41) [GIŠ.IG *bir-ri ša i-qa-bu-u-ni* DINGIR.MEŠ *šu-nu i-ta-as-ru-šú ina* É *e-tar-ba* GIŠ.I]G *ina pa-ni-*⸢*i*⸣*-šú e-te-di-il šú-nu hu-ur-ra-*⸢*a*⸣-[*ti ina* ŠÀ GIŠ.IG *up-tal-li-šú qa-ra-bu ina* ŠÀ-*bi up-pu-šú*]

[41] [The lattice door is so called (because when) the gods cornered him, he entered the building and] locked [the do]or before himself. [They bored] hole[s in the door and did battle through them.]

4′ (42) [*x x x x x x x x x x x x x x x x x x x x x x x x* E]N-*ú-ti-šú-nu a-na* EN–*hi-iṭ-ṭi ša* TA* ᵈE[N *i-zi-zu-u-ni i-du-ku-šú-ni*]

[42] [……] their [lord]ship (*was given*) to the criminal who [assisted] B[el and whom they killed.]

5′ (43) [EN.MEŠ *ú-ma-še ša ina* KÁ *ša* É.SAG.ÍL *i-za-z*]*u-ú-ni* LÚ.EN.NUN.MEŠ-*šú šu-nu ina* UG[U-*šú paq-du i-na-ṣu-ru-šu*]

[43] [The athletes who sta]nd [at the gate of Esaggil] are his guards: [they are appointed] ove[r him and guard him.]

6′ (44-45) [TÚG.*še-er-ʾi-i-tu ša ina* UGU-*hi-šú ša i-qa-bu-u-ni ma-a* A.MEŠ *šú-nu si-li-ʾa-a-te ši-na šu-ú*] *ina* ŠÀ *e-nu-ma e-liš ki-i an-ni-i iq-ṭi-bi k*[*i-i* AN-*e* KI.TIM *la ib-ba-nu-u-ni*]

[44] [The outfit which is on him and of which it is said: "That is water" – these are lies". (About) this], it is said in *Enuma Eliš* as follows: "W[hen heaven and earth were not

[41] Despite the spelling *šú-nu*, which is mostly used as a suffix, here it is an independent 3rd pl. m. pronoun. [44] *ki-i an-ni-i* does not appear in other manuscripts. After *iq-ṭi-bi*, *k*[*i-i* shows that the line division is not the same as in the score.

FIG. 28. *Ninurta pursuing Anzu.*
Ninurta Temple, Nimrud. Original Drawings I, 54.

7′ (45-46) [AN.ŠÁR *it-tab-ši ki-i* URU *u* É *ib-šu-u-ni šu-ú it-tab-ši* A.MEŠ *ša ina* UGU ^{d}*aš-šur šu-ú š*]*u-u-tú ša hi-ṭi-šu ina* ŠÀ *ka-dam-me e-si-i*[*p*]

created, Anšar came into being." (Only) when city and *temple* existed, he came into being. I]t is [the water which was over Aššur. T]hat (outfit) of his crime is gather[ed] in the storeroom.

8′ (47) [*la* A.MEŠ *la-biš ka-dam-mu x x x*]*-i ú-ba-du-du-šu ku-zip-p*[*i x x x x x x x* DUMU.MÍ ^{d}*a-nim id-du-x*]

47 [He is not clad in water]. They squander [the storeroom ...]. The garmen[t ...... the daughter of Anu. *They killed her.*]

9′ (48) [*x x x x x x x x x x x x x x*] ⸢*ú*⸣*-še-ṣu-u-ni* É*-su šu-ú ú-ba-*[*du-du me-še-e*ʾ*-tú-šu ši-i*]

48 [The *building from which*] they bring out [......], is his house; [they] squ[ander *on*. This is his *measurement*.]

10′ (49) [*x x x x x x x x x x x x š*]*a a-ki im–ma-la a-ki im–m*[*a-la ú-ka-x x x x x x* DINGIR.MEŠ AD.MEŠ*-šú šú-nu e-mu-ru-šú*]

49 [...... w]ho totally, utte[rly ...... are the gods, his fathers, seeing him].

11′ (50) [*da-ba-bu gab-bu ša ina* ŠÀ*-bi* LÚ.UŠ.KU.MEŠ *da-bi-bu-u-ni ša ha-ba-a-te ša i-ha-b*]*a-tu-šu-u-ni ša ú-šal-pa-tu-*⸢*ú*⸣*-*[*šu-ni šu-u* DINGIR.MEŠ AD.MEŠ*-šú šú-nu e-li-ú*]

50 [All the talk which they talk among the lamentation priests, and the acts of robbery which they comm]it and afflict him with [are the gods, his fathers, rising up.]

12′ (51-52) [*li-is-mu ša ina* ITI.GAN *ina* IGI ^{d}EN *ù ma-ha-za-a-ni gab-bu i-lab-bu-u-ni ša* ^{d}MAŠ *šu-ú ki-i*] ⸢^{d}*aš*⸣*-šur a-na* ^{d}NIN.URTA *ina* UGU *k*[*a-šá-di ša an-zi-i* ^{d}*qi-in-gu* ^{d}*a-sak-ku iš-pu-ru-ú-ni*]

51 [The race which they go round in front of Bel and all the cult centres in Kislev: this is of Ninurta.] 52 [When] Aššur [sent] (orders) to Ninurta for the d[efeat of Anzû, Qingu and Asakku, Nergal said before Aššur: "Anzû, Qingu and Asakku have been defeated."]

13′ (53-54) [^{d}U.GUR *ina* IGI ^{d}*aš-šur iq-ṭi-bi ma-a an-zu-u* ^{d}*qi-in-gu* ^{d}*a-sak-ku ka-áš-du*] ⸢AN⸣.ŠÁR *a-na* ^{d}U.GUR *i-sa-par m*[*a-a a-lik a-na* DINGIR.MEŠ*-ni gab-bu pa-si-ir ú-pa-sa-ar*]

53 Aššur wrote to Nergal: ["Go and give the good news to all the gods!" He gives the news, and they rejoice about it and go.]

14′ (54-55) [*šu-nu ina* UGU *i-ha-di-u il-lu-ku x x x x x x x x x x x x x-ki šu-ú x x x x* ^{d}*làh-mu a-ki ha*]*-*⸢*ri*⸣*-ip*! *šu-tu-u-ma* [*ma-ha-zu x x x x*]

55 [...... *is ..., the god Lahmu*] is the one *who* [*enters* the shrine as *f*]*irst* [...]

15′ (56-57) [*x x x x x x x x x x x*.MEŠ *ša na-gi-i x x x x x x x x x x ki la-a ina* UGU *x x*] ⸢KALAG.GA⸣ [*x x x x x x*]

rest broken away (for lines 57-72, see SAA 3 35 and 34)

56 [...... the ...s of the district ...... not on] *strong* [......]

47f The *badādu* D form *ú-ba-du-du* is new to the text. 48 For a further sequence belonging to this line, see SAAB 28 (2022) 36. 49 *a-ki im–ma-la a-ki im–m*[*a-la* is also new and the hitherto hapax *im–ma-la* is a variant of *a-na ma-la* "altogether, totally, utterly" (AEAD 59a s.v. *māla*). 55f For further sequences belonging to these lines, see SAAB 28 (2022) 36. 56f The placement and interpretation of KALAG.GA is only tentative.

241. Assyrians and Their Relations with Arameans

K 4525

beginning broken away

1′ [*x*] *šar x*[*x x x x x x x*]
2′ [*k*]*i-i it-ti* [*x x x x x x*]
3′ [*i*]*t-ti* É.GAL [*x x x x x x*]
4′ [L]Ú.*aš-šur*.KI-*a-a* LÚ.*nu-*[*kúr-ti*? *x x x x*]
5′ [SISKU]R.SISKUR?.MEŠ [*x x x x x x*]
6′ [*ù*?] *at-tu-nu* ŠÀ-*ba-k*[*u-nu lu* DÙG.GA-*ku-nu*?]
7′ [KI?] LÚ.*a-ra-me tal-l*[*a-ka*? *x x x x*]
8′ ⌜*x x*⌝ *mar*? *ú-šá-á*[*š*?-*x x x x x*]

r.1 *tal-bu-uš-ti tu-lab-ba-š*[*i*? *x x x*]
2 *ul-tu* LÚ.GAL.MEŠ *šá* KUR–*aš-šur*.KI [*x x x*]
3 LÚ.*ah-la-mu-ú šá se*!-*kep*!-*šú*!-*nu*! [*x x x*]
4 *di-ib-bi-i ki-i la i-le-*ʾ[*u-ú* 0?]
5 *ul i-na da-na-ni-ni ul x*[*x x x*]
6 $^{d+}$AG *ù* ^{d}AMAR.UTU *ki-*[*i pi-i an-ni-i*?]
7 *um-ma lu-ú* LUGAL-*ku-nu-*[*ma*? KI?]
8 *aš-šur*.KI-*a-a dib-bi* [DÙG.GA *du-ub-ba*?]
9 *um-ma* 3 MU.MEŠ *a-na* [*x x x*]
10 *ki-i ina* 1-*et* MU ⌜*i*?⌝-[*x x x x x x*]
11 *ki-i ina šá-ni-t*[*i x x x x x*]

rest broken away

ABL 1013

(Beginning destroyed)

2 [th]at with [……]
3 [w]ith the palace [……]
4 the Assyrians […] the *en*[*emies*]
5 [*sac*]*rifices* […].
6 [*And*] you (pl.) [*can be*] g[*lad*].
7 You g[*o … with*] the Aramean(s)
8 …… […]

r.1 You will dress (*them*) in clothing […].
2 Ever since the magnates of Assyria […]
3 the Ahlamû whose overthrow [*is* …]
4 *powerl*[*ess*] words,
5 not with our own strength, not […].
6 Nabû and Marduk (*say*) *as* [*follows*]: "Let your king [*speak kindly with*] the Assyrians:
9 "3 years *for* […] *if* in one year [……], *if* in the secon[d *year* ……]

(Rest destroyed)

242. Fragment of a Literary Text

K 8303

beginning broken away

1′ [*x x x x x-ṭ*]*i-rib* NÍG.NA
2′ [*x x x x x*] ARAD.MEŠ-*ka šu-*[*u*?]

blank space of one line

e.3′ [*x x x*.M]EŠ SIG₅.M[EŠ]
4′ [*x x*] *ú-rat ú-še-*[*x*]
5′ [*in*]-*da-na-ha-*[*ru*]
r.1 [*x a*]-*na* MU.AN.N[A]
2 [*x x x*]*x* ÁB.GUD.HI.A.MEŠ
3 [*x x*] ⌜*ú*⌝-*ra-hi-ṣa-na-ši*

CT 53 399

(Beginning destroyed)

1 [… *app*]*roached* […]. A censer
2 [……] he is [*one of*] your servants.

(blank space of one line)

3 [*They*] keep recei[ving] good […]s, [x] team(s of horses *and*) …[…].

r.1 [(…) *f*]*or a year*
2 […] he [*did not*] entrust cattle to us

241 There may be more signs missing on the right than indicated in the transliteration. [5] The reading [SI]SKUR is based on the edition of eBL (https://www.ebl.lmu.de/fragmentarium/K.4525), accessed 15.6.2023. However, the interpretation may not be entirely satisfactory. Alternatively, the two small tilted wedges could be interpreted as a word (or a verse) divider, and the line read as [*x*] ⌜*x*⌝-*kin*? : *meš*-[*x*. [8] E.g., *šakānu* Š, usually "to encourage" with *libbu*. [r.1] Cf. CAD T 93b. Or, read *tu-lab-ba-šú*. [r.3] See coll. The Ahlamû do not appear in letters but in omens and reports (SAA 4 and 8). The reading *se-kep-šú-nu* is taken from CAD S 72a. The problem with *se* is that it may have three verticals at the end. The eBL edition has (as drawn in ABL 1013) ÙZ *a-n*[*a*? at the end.

242 A fragment in NA script. [1] If the verb behaved like NA *qarābu*, the expected pf. form would be (X)X*q-ṭ*]*i-rib* with partial assimilation. Or: "pre]sented a censer", but this seems unlikely because of the word order. [2] Or: "th[ey] are your servants": *šu-*[*nu*].

4 [*x x x t*]*a-ra-ṣi*
5 [*x x x x x x*]*x-la*
6 [*x x x x x x x*]*x*
rest broken away

4 [… to *cl*]*ear up*
(Rest destroyed or too broken for translation)

243. Buying Equids

K 6609 + K 9899
beginning broken away
1′ *x x x x x x*] *ul i-na*[*m-din*]
2′ *x x x* ANŠE?].⸢NITÁ⸣.MEŠ ANŠE.*gam-ma*[*l*.MEŠ]
3′ *x x x*]*x i-*⸢*x*⸣*-tú a-na* É.GAL *ub-bal*
4′ *x x*]*-nu a-na kas-pi ú-tar*
5′ *i*]-⸢*nam*⸣*-di-nu šum-ma* LUGAL ANŠE.KUR.RA.MEŠ *ṣi-bi*
6′ *ina* Š]À*-bi* É.GAL *ki-i šá ana* LUGAL *mim-ma it-*⸢*x x*⸣*-ú? mah-ru-ti i-nam-*[*din*]
7′ *ina* U]GU*-hi-šú-nu* 1*-ú* ANŠE.KUR.[R]A *e-me-du*
Edge uninscribed
r.1 *x x x x*] *a-na* 2 LÚ.ERIM.[M]EŠ 1 ANŠE.⸢KUR.RA⸣ *e-me-du*
2 *x x x*] *a-na* 3 LÚ.ERIM.⸢MEŠ⸣ 1 ANŠE.KUR.RA *e-me-du*
3 *x x*.M]EŠ *ṣi-bi dan-nu-ti* ⸢*x*⸣2 MA.NA.TA.ÀM KUG.UD *i-nam-d*[*i-nu*]
4 *x x* M]A.NA.TA.ÀM K[UG].UD *i-nam-di-nu*
5 *x x x* M]A.NA.TA.ÀM ⸢KUG⸣.UD *i-nam-di-nu*
6 *x x x a*]*n-nu-ti* 1*-en dul-lu šá ina* IGI MAN *ma-hi-ru-u-ni le-pu-šú*
7 *x x x x x*]*x-nu* LÚ.⸢DUMU⸣*–kar-šá-a-ni* LÚ.ŠÁM.M[EŠ]
8 *x x x x x*] ⸢*x*⸣ *x*[*x* L]Ú.EN.NAM *ina* UGU*-hi-šú-nu x*[*x x x*]
rest broken away

K 6609+
(Beginning destroyed)
1 [……] *h*[*e*] does not *gi*[*ve*].
2 […] is bringing [*horses*, *don*]*keys*, came[ls *and* …]… to the palace.
4 […] *he* will *turn* […] *into* money (and)
5 *they* will [*s*]*ell* (*them*). If the king wishes horses,
6 [*i*]*n* the palace he will *gi*[*ve* …] to the king just as any former …
7 [(…)] *they* will *impose* [o]n them a single horse.
r.1 […] they *impose* 1 horse on 2 men.
2 […] they *impose* 1 horse on 3 men.
3 [… *if the king*] wishes *strong* […]s, [they] will pa[y] x+2 minas of silver each.
4 […] they will pay [x m]ina(s) of s[il]ver each.
5 […] they will pay [x m]ina(s) of silver each.
6 Let [*t*]*hese* […] perform a work that is acceptable to the king.
7 [……] the *mār-karšāni*, bought men
8 [……] the governor *to* them […]
(Rest destroyed)

4-5 Unless there is a verbal form in line 4 (such as "se[nd(s)]": *ú-še-*[*bal*]), followed by a foreign personal name?

243 See copy p. 295. Join by S. Parpola (--.7.1969). The text is partly in Babylonian, but the script is NA; this suggests the reign of Assurbanipal. The fragment is wide, but it is possible that it represents only a small part of a large tablet; the exact width of the tablet is somewhat uncertain. It may be a "normal" letter, a denunciation (cf. SAA 21, p. XLI), which would belong to Ch. 3. 1, 5-6, r.3-5 It is not entirely clear how *nadānu* is to be understood, i.e., "to give", "to pay" or "to sell"? 4, r.7 Perhaps not to be restored as [*i-nam-di*]*-nu* (cf. also line 7′). r.6 Or: *dan*]*nūti* "[the stro]ng (*one*)s" as in r.3. Or: "perform a ritual". r.7 Perhaps at the beginning ⸢*šú*?⸣*-nu*, "they are […]" or "their […]".

244. The Perfect One

K 10854		CT 54 223
	beginning broken away	(Beginning destroyed)
1′	[*x x x x*] ⌈*x*⌉ [*x x x x x x*]	
2′	[*x x x* LÚ].*um-ma-ni* [*x x x x x*]	2 [... the] *craftsmen* [......]
3′	[*x x x x*]⌈*x x x x*⌉[*x x x x x*]	(Break)
	four lines destroyed	
e.8	[*x x x x x x x x x*]*x*	
r.1	[*x x x x x*]*x*[*x x x x x*] ⌈*x*⌉	
2	[*x x x x x*]*x*[*x*] 1 *gi-it-*⌈*ma*⌉*-li* ⌈*at*?⌉*-t*[*a*]	r.2 [......] *yo*[*u*] are the perfect one,
3	[*x x x x x*]-⌈*ru*⌉ *x*[*x*].MEŠ ⌈*tu*⌉*-qa-a* GIM *mam-m*[*a*]	3 [......] like [*no*] one you are waiting for [...]s
4	[*x x x x x x x x x x x x x*]⌈*x*⌉[*x*]	
	rest broken away	(Rest destroyed)

244 2 Or: "scholars".

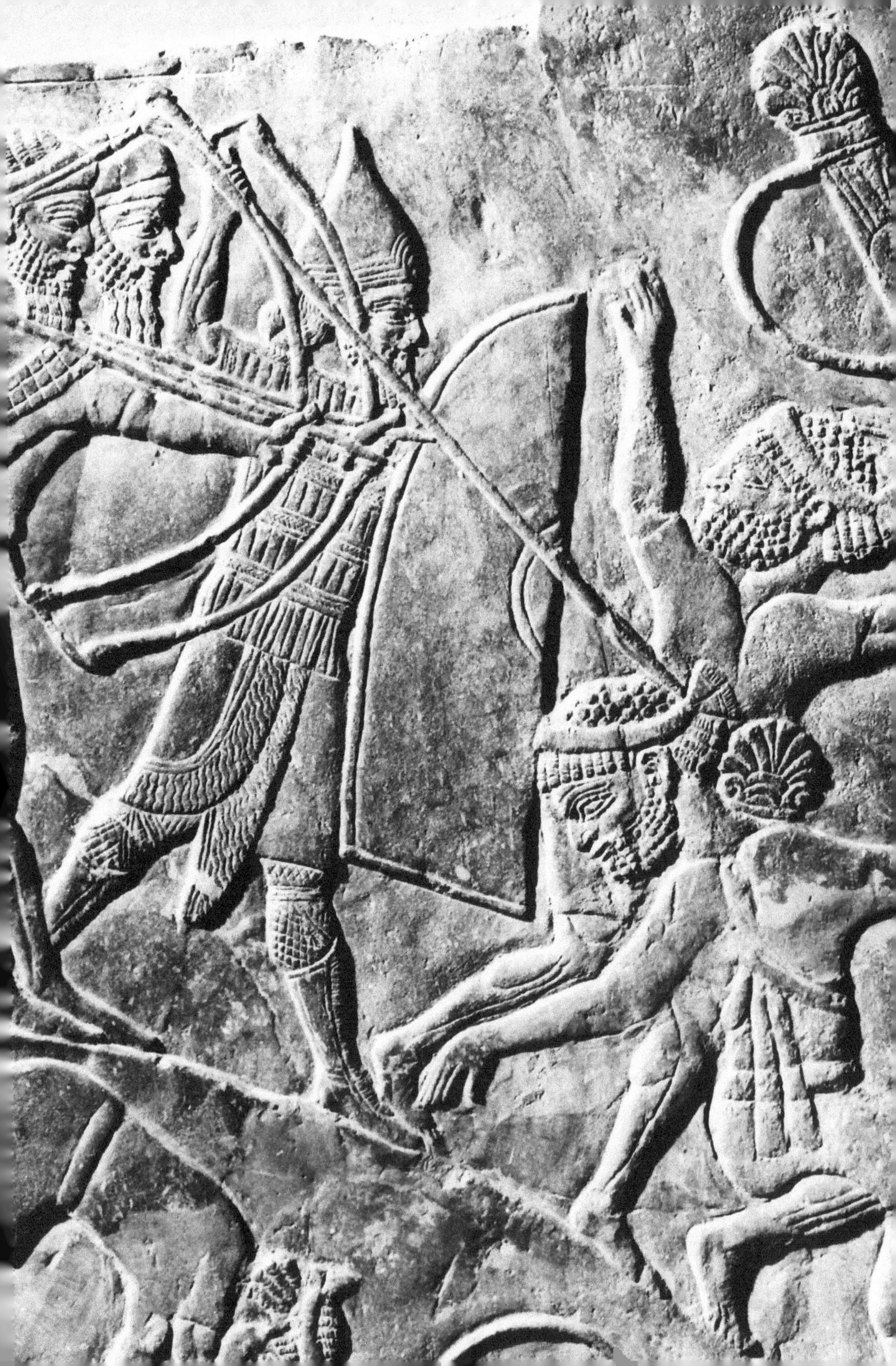

7. Queries to the Sungod
Additions to SAA IV

FIG. 29. *Ashurbanipal's army on the attack.*
BM 124801a.

245. Will Ursâ of Urarṭu ...?

Bu 91-5-9,62

Obv. completely broken away

Rev. beginning broken away

1′ ⸢*a*!⸣-*šal-ka* ^{d}UT[U *ki-i* TA UD-*me an-ni-e* UD-12-KAM *šá* ITI.BARAG]

2′ *a-di* UD-1-KÁM *šá* [ITI.*x x x x x x x x x x x x*]

3′ ^{m}*ur-sa-a* LU[GAL *šá* KUR.*ur-ár-ṭu a-di* LÚ.A.KAL.MEŠ-*šú*]

4′ TA *a-šar* [*áš-bu ur-ha* KASKAL *i-ṣab-ba-tu-nim-ma x x x*]

5′ *i-na x*[*x x x x x x x x x x x x x*]

rest broken away

s.1′ [ITI.B]ARAG UD-12-KÁM *ina* [*x x x x x*]

2′ [^{md}AM]AR.UTU–MU–PAB ^{m}*n*[*a-ṣi-ru* ^{m}*tab-ni-i*]

3′ [^{m}]⸢^{d}⸣PA–PAB.MEŠ–TI ^{md}*x*[*x x x x x*]

4′ [^{m}*x x x x x*] ⸢*x x*⸣ ^{md}*x*[*x x x x x*]

ADD 712

(Beginning destroyed)

r.1 I ask you, Šama[š, whether from this day, the 12th day of the month Nisan (I)], to the first day of [the month ..., ...], Ursâ, ki[ng of Urarṭu, together with his army, will take the road] from wherever [they are and *go to* ...]

5 *in* [......]

(Break)

s.1 [Month N]isan (I), 12th day. (Performed) in [......].

s.2 [M]arduk-šumu-uṣur, N[aṣiru, Tabnî], Nabû-ahhe-ballit, N[N, N]N, N[N].

246. Will Scythian and Cimmerian Troops Invade Šamaš-naṣir?

83-1-18,539 + Sm 1880

1 [^{d}UTU EN GAL-*ú š*]*á a-šal-l*[*u-ka a-na* GI.NA *a-pal-an-ni*]

2 [*x x x x x*]*x-si*!-⸢*x*⸣-*a*!-*a*! [*x x x x x x x x x x x*]

3 [*x x x x x m*]*i* [*x x x x x x x x x x*]

4 [*x x x x x*] URU.[*x x x x x x x x x x x*]

5 [*x x x x x l*]*u*?-*ú* [*x x x x x x x x x x*]

AGS 10 + PRT 79 (= SAA 4 36 + SAA 4 123)

1 [Šamaš, great lord, give me a firm positive answer to] what I am asking [you]!

2 [... the ...]si[]ean(s) [......]

3 [......]

4 [...] city [......]

5 [...] *or* [......]

245 Previous edition: Deller Zagros p. 113 (transliteration without restorations). The only queries in which the name of Ursâ (Rusâ) is preserved are SAA 4 18 and 19. The former was also performed in Nisan (I), and this fragment may be its duplicate or refer to the same occasion. r.1 See coll. r.1-4 These lines parallel those of SAA 4 18 r.5-7 and are also comparable with 19 r.7-9. r.2 The stipulated term in SAA 4 18 is from the ... th day of Nisan to the 1st day of Tammuz (IV). r.5 The sign following *i-na* is neither KUR nor URU. s.1 The date is not preserved in SAA 4 18 and 19. Usually the month and day date is followed by an eponym date, but see, e.g., SAA 4 185 s.1-4. s.2-3 The names of the diviners "Marduk-šumu-uṣur, Naṣiru, Tabnî, [......], Nabû-šallim, Balassu, Sukinu, [......], Kudurru and Kaṣiru, [......]" are preserved in SAA 4 18 as the performers of the extispicy.

246 Sm 1880 adds the beginning (five more lines) and the end (last line of the query) to SAA 4 36. 2 For collation, see SAA 4, p. 387b (no. 123).

6 [DINGIR]-*ut-ka* ⸢GAL⸣-*ti* ZU-*e* [*ina* SILIM-*tim ina* KA DINGIR-*ti-ka* GAL-*ti*]
7 ^{d}UTU EN GAL-*ú q*[*a-bi-i ku-un-i x x x x x*]
8 IGI-*ri* IGI-*ra* [ŠE.GA-*ú* ŠE.GA-*e*]

9 *e-zib šá* LÚ.A–*šip-ri* [*x x x x x x x x x x*]
10 *e-zib šá de-ni* UD-*mu* N[E-*i* GIM DÙG.GA GIM *ha-ṭu-ú*]
11 *e-zib šá ina* KI NE-[*i lu-ʾu-ú* MÁŠ MÁŠ-*ú*]
12 *e-zib šá* KI MÁŠ M[ÁŠ$^{?}$-*ú lu-ʾu-ú lu-ʾu-ú-tu* DIB.MEŠ-*ma ú-le-ʾu-ú*]
13 *e-zib ša* UDU.NITÁ DINGIR-[*ti-ka šá ana* MÁŠ MÁŠ-*ú* LAL-*ú ha-ṭu-ú*]
14 *e-zib šá* TAG-*it* [*pu-ut* UDU.NITÁ TÚG *gi-né-e-šú ar-šá-ti lab-šú*]
(rest broken away)

6 Does your great [divin]ity know it? Is it de[creed and confirmed in a favorable case, by the command of your great divinity], Šamaš, great lord? Will he who can see, see it [Will he who can hear, hear it]?

9 Disregard that the messenger [……].

10 Disregard the (formulation) of today's case, [be it good, be it faulty].

11 Disregard that [an unclean person has performed extispicy] in this place.

12 Disregard that [an unclean man or woman has come near] the place of the exti[spicy and made it unclean].

13 Disregard that the ram (offered) to [your] divi[nity for the performance of the extispicy is deficient or faulty].

14 Disregard that he who touches [the forehead of the sheep is dressed in his ordinary soiled garments]
(Break)

Rev. (beginning broken away)
1′ [*ú–lu ta-mit ina*] KA-[*ia ip-tar-ri-du lu-ú* ZI.MEŠ *lu-ú* BAR.MEŠ]
2′ [*a-šal*]-*ka* ^{d}[UTU EN GAL-*ú ki-i* LÚ.ERIM.MEŠ LÚ.*iš-ku-za-a-a* LÚ.ERIM.MEŠ]
3′ [L]Ú.*gi-mir-*[*ra-a-a* TA *né-ri-bi šá* URU.*x x x a-na* É–URU.*ha-am-ban*]
4′ È.MEŠ-⸢*nim*$^{?}$⸣-[*ma il-la-ku-ni a-na na-gi-i šá* URU.*x x ù na-gi-i*]
5′ *šá* URU.^{d}UTU–P[AB-*ir* ZI *ši-ih-ṭu šá* HUL-*tim ip-pu-šú* GAZ]
6′ GAZ-*ku i-ha*[*b-ba-tu i-šal-lá-lu ina* ŠÀ UDU.NITÁ NE-*i* GUB-*za-am-ma*]
7′ [*a*]*n-na* GI.[NA GIŠ.HUR.MEŠ SILIM.MEŠ UZU.MEŠ *ta-mit* SIG$_5$.MEŠ]
8′ [SILIM.M]EŠ *šá* SILIM-[*tim x x x x x x x x x x x x*]
(about 5 lines broken away)
9′ [UGU DINGIR-*ti-ka* GAL-*ti*] ^{d}UTU [EN GAL-*i lil-lik-ma* UR$_5$.ÚŠ *li-tap-pal*]

r.1 [or (that) the oracle query has become jumbled in my] mouth. [Let them be taken away and put aside!]

2 [I ask] you, [Šamaš, great lord, whether the troops of the *Scythians* (and) the troops of] the Cimmer[ians] will move out, [go to Bit-Hamban through the pass of …, make a hostile incursion to the district of … and the district] of the city Šamaš-n[aṣir ……], (and whether) they will kill, plu[nder, and loot].

6 [Be present in this ram, place (in it) a f]irm positive ans[wer, favorable designs, favorable, propi]tious [omens by the oracular command of your great divinity, and may I see (them)].
(Break)

9 [May (this query) go to your great divinity], O Šamaš, [great lord, and may an oracle be given as an answer].

247. Should Esarhaddon Send an Army to a Destination?

K 11492 (AGS 50) + Sm 412 + Sm 684

1 [^{d}UT]U EN GAL-*ú šá a-šal-lu-k*[*a an-na* GI.NA *a-pal-an-ni*]

2 [^{m}AN].ŠÁR–ŠEŠ–SUM-*na* LUGAL KUR–AN.ŠÁR *šá* ⸢TA⸣-*an-n*[*i* ERIM.MEŠ Á.KAL.MEŠ]

3 [*šá*] *i-na* Ú.*ur-ba-an-ni an-ni-*⸢*i*⸣ *šaṭ-ru-ma* ⸢*ina*⸣ [IGI DINGIR-*ti-ka* GAL-*ti šak-nu*]

4 [K]I ŠÀ-*ba-šú ub-lam a-na* KI[N-*š*]*ú-ma ti-iṣ-m*[*u-ru-ma* DINGIR-*ut-ka* GAL-*ti* ZU-*ú*]

5 [GI]M KA DINGIR-*ti-ka* GAL-*ti* ^{d}UTU EN GAL-*ú* EŠ.BAR-*ka* [*šal*]-*mu* EN–MU.⸢MU NE-*i*⸣ [^{m}AN.ŠÁR–ŠEŠ–SUM-*na* LUGAL KUR–AN.ŠÁR]

6 [*l*]*i-*⸢*iṣ-rim*⸣ *lik-*⸢*pid*⸣-*ma* ERIM.MEŠ Á.KAL.MEŠ *šu-nù-ti* KI [Š]À-*ba-šú ub-lam* [*liš-pur*]

7 [UGU DINGIR-*ti-ka* GAL]-⸢*ti*⸣ DÙG-*ab* GIM *ik-tap-du-ma il-tap-ru* ERIM.MEŠ Á.KAL.MEŠ ⸢*šu*⸣-*n*[*ù-ti*]

8 [KI ŠÀ-*ba-šú ub-lam*] DU-*ku-ú* LÚ.KÚR *šá ina* Ú.*ur-ba-an-ni an-ni-i šaṭ-ru-ma ina* IGI DINGIR-*ti-ka* GAL-*tú š*[*ak-nu*]

9 [*x x x x* Z]I-*bu ši-*⸢*ih*⸣-*ṭu šá* MÍ.HUL *ana* UGU-*hi-šú-ni i-šak-k*[*a-n*]*u*

10 [*šá* GAZ GAZ-*ku šá* DI]B DIB-*t*[*u š*]*á* SAR SAR-*tu ša* IR *i-šal-lá-lu*

11 [*x x x x x x x*]-*ú* DIN[GIR-*u*]*t-ka* GAL-*ti* ZU-*e*

12 [*x x x x x x x x x*] ER[IM.MEŠ] Á.KAL.MEŠ *šu-nù-ti*

13 [*x x x x x x i-na* Š]À-*bi* È.MEŠ-*ú*

14 [*x x x x x x x x x x*]*x* LÚ.KÚR IGI-*ru-ma* GAZ-*ku* SAR-*tu* TI-*ú*

15 [*x x x x x x x x x x*] DIB-*tu*

16 [*x x x x x x x x x x x*] ⸢*i*?-*na*? ŠÀ-*ba*?-*šú-un*⸣ *ia-ʾa-da-ru*

17 [GIŠ.TUKUL.MEŠ *šá x x x x x x x i-ma*]*r-ri-r*[*u*]

PRT 26 + CT 54 404 (= SAA 4 108+)

1 [Šam]aš, great lord, [give me a firm positive answer] to what I am asking y[ou]!

2 [Es]arhaddon, king of Assyria, who now is intent on send[ing to the destin]ation of his preference [the troops and armed forces wh]ich are written in this papyrus, and [placed before your great divinity, and (whom) your great divinity knows] —

5 in accor]dance with the command of your great divinity, Šam[aš], great lord, and your [favor]able decisions, should the subject of this query, [Esarhaddon, king of Assyria], strive and plan? [Should he send] these troops and armed forces to where he wishes? Is it pleasing [to your gre]at [divinity]?

7 If he, having planned, sends (them), will the[se] troops and armed forces go [*to where he wishes*]? Will the enemy whose name is written in this papyrus and p[laced] before your great divinity [...], (and) mount a dangerous attack against them?

10 [Will they kill what there is to kill, sei]ze what there is to seize, plunder what there is to plunder, loot what there is to loot?

11 Will they ......]? Does your great div[inity] know it?

12 [Will ......] these t[roops] and armed forces

13 [......] depart fr[om ......]

14 [......]? Will they see [...] of the enemy? Will they kill, plunder, take (away)?

15 [......] seize?

16 [......] Will they be afraid?

17 [Will they pre]vail [...]?

247 For the join, see von Soden, ZA 70 (1980) 148, who read lines 18-r.3 partly differently. 5 As in other queries with "the subject of this query", Esarhaddon's name and title are expected (already in Knudtzon, AGS 2, p. 147, line 1 and Klauber, PRT, p. 46). However, because of space limitations, the variants ^{m}*aš-šur*–PAB/ŠEŠ–AŠ/MU and KUR–*aš-šur* may be restored here instead of AN.ŠÁR, etc., in lines 2 and r.7.

18 [*e-zib šá di-in* UD NE GIM DÙG GIM LAL *e-zib šá* KU]G *lu-ʾu-ú* UDU SI[SKUR.SISKUR TAG.MEŠ *ú–l*]*u* ⸢*ana*?⸣ IGI ⸢SISKUR?⸣.-[SISKUR] G[IL]

[18] [Disregard the (formulation) of today's case, be it good, be it faulty. Disregard that a cle]an or an unclean person [has touched the sacrifici]al sheep, [or] bl[ocked] the way of the sacrif[icial sheep].

19 [*e-zib šá x x x x x x e-zib šá* KI MÁŠ? *l*]*u-ʾu-ú l*[*u-ʾu-ú-tu* DIB.MEŠ-*ma*] *ú-*[*le-ʾu-ú*]
e. uninscribed

[19] [Disregard that ...... Disregard that an un]clean man or w[oman has come near the place of the extispicy and] m[ade it unclean].

r.1 [*e-zib šá* UDU.NITÁ DINGIR-*ti-ka šá a-na* MÁŠ MÁŠ]-⸢*ú*⸣ LAL-*ú ha-ṭu-*[*ú*]

[r.1] [Disregard that the ram (offered) to your divinity for the performance of the extispi]cy is deficient or faulty.

2 [*e-zib šá* TAG-*it pu-ut* UDU.NITÁ TÚG *g*]*i-né-e-šú* ⸢*ár-šá*⸣*-a-ti lab-šú ina* MI Š[À].MUD ŠÀ.MUD IGI-[*ru*]
3 [*mim-ma lu-ʾu-ú* KÚ NAG-*ú* ŠEŠ-*šú mì*]-⸢*ih*⸣*-hu*! ZÍD.MAD.GÁ A.M[EŠ] *haṣ-bu u* IZI TAG.[MEŠ]

[2] [Disregard that he who touches the forehead of the sheep] is dressed in his [or]dinary soiled [garments], has seen f[e]ar and terror at night, [has eaten, drunk, or anointed himself with anything unclean], (or) has touched [the (libation) b]eer, the *maṣhatu*-flour, the water, the container, and the fire.

4 [*e-zib šá a-na-ku* DUMU LÚ.HAL ARAD-*ka* TÚG *gi-né-e-a ár-šá-ti lab-šá-k*]*u ina* MI ŠÀ.MUD ŠÀ.MUD IGI-*ru*
5 [*mim-ma lu-ʾu-ú* KÚ NAG ŠÉŠ-*šú ku-un qa-ti*] BAL-*ú uš-pe-el-lu*
6 [*ú–lu ta-mit i-na* KA-*ia ip-tar-ri-du lu-ú* ZI.MEŠ-*ha lu-ú bé*]-*e-ra*

[4] [Disregard that I, the haruspex, your servant, a]m [dressed in my ordinary soiled garments], have seen fear and terror at night, [have eaten, drunk, or anointed myself with anything unclean], (or) have changed or altered [the proceedings, or (that) the oracle query has become jumbled in my mouth].
[6] [Let them be taken out and pu]t aside!

7 [*a-šal-ka* ^{d}UTU EN GAL-*ú ki-i* EN–MU.MU] NE-[*i* ^{m}AN.ŠÁR–ŠEŠ–SUM-*na* LUGAL KUR–AN].ŠÁR
8 [LÚ.ERIM.MEŠ ANŠE.KUR.RA.MEŠ Á.KAL.MEŠ *šá*] *ina* Ú.*u*[*r-ba-an-ni an-ni-i šaṭ-ru-ma ina* IGI DINGIR-*ti-k*]*a* GAL-*tú* GAR-*ni*

[7] [I ask you, Šamaš, great lord, whether the subject of] this [query, Esarhaddon, king of Assy]ria, [should send the men, horses, and armed forces which are written] in [this document] and placed [before yo]ur great [divinity, to where he wishes, (whether) it is pleasing to your great] divinity,

9 [KI ŠÀ-*ba-šú ub-lam i-šap-pa-ru ina*] IGI DINGIR-[*ti-ka* GAL-*ti* DÙG.GA GIM *il-t*]*ap-ru-ma*
10 [DU-*ku* LÚ.KÚR *šá ina* Ú.*ur-ba-an*]-*ni an-nim-ma* [*šaṭ-ru-ma ina* IGI DINGIR-*ti-ka* GAL-*ti šak-nu*]
11 [*x x x x x* ZI-*bu ši-ih-ṭu šá* M]Í.HUL *ana* UGU-*š*[*ú-nu i-šak-ka-nu*]

[9] [(whether), if he se]nds them and [they go, the enemy who is written] in [this] pa[pyrus and placed before your great divinity], will [... mount] a dangerous [attack] against [them],

12 [*x x x šá* GA]Z GAZ-*ku šá* DI[B DIB-*tu šá* SAR SAR-*tu šá* IR *i-šal-lá-lu*]

[12] (and whether) they will kill [what there is to kil]l, [seize] what there is to se[ize, plunder what there is to plunder, and loot what there is to loot].

13 [BE GÍR 2-*m*]*a* GÍR 150 UGU GÍR 15 GAR MURUB$_4$ GÍR 150 [*x x x x x x x x x x x x x*]
14 [ŠÀ.NIGIN *x x*].MEŠ 15 ŠID-*šú-nu u sal*!*-hu ina* MURUB$_4$ [*x x x x x x x x x x x x x*]

[13] [The 'paths' are 2], the left 'path' is located over the right 'path.' The middle of the 'path,' on the left [......].

[18f] These lines were previously, before joining CT 54 404, read in SAA 4 108: [*ina* SILIM-*tim ina* KA DINGIR-*ti-ka* GAL-*ti* ^{d}UTU EN GAL-*ú qa-bi-i ku-un-i* IGI-*r*]*i* IGI-*mar* Š[E.GA-*ú* ŠE.GA-*e*] / [*e-zib šá ik-rib di-nim* UD NE-*i* GIM DÙG.GA *ha-ṭu-ú* KUG *lu-ʾu*]-*ú* [SISKUR.SISKUR TAG.MEŠ]. [19] For the suggested, unusual place of KI MÁŠ, see e.g., SAA 4 29:12′, 32 r.1 (restored). [r.3, 14] See coll.

15 [*x x x*] *ka-pí-iṣ* SAL.LA [NÍG.TAB] GÍR *šá* 150 1 D[U$_8$ *x x x x x x x x x x x*]
16 [*x x* MU]RUB$_4$ SUHUŠ-*sà zi-ri ha-si-si* GAR-*in* [*x x x x x x x x x x*]

17 $^{md+}$EN–DÙ-*uš* $^{md+}$EN–SILIM-*im* $^{m⸢d!+}$AG⸣–SILIM-[*im x x x x x x x x x*]
18 [U]GU DINGIR-*ti-ka* GAL-*ti* ^{d}UTU EN GAL-*ú* [*lil-lik-ma* KIN *li-tap-pal*]

14 [The coils of the colon ...] (and) are 15 in number and are damp. In the middle [......]
15 [......] is curled. The 'cavity' of [the 'crucible'] of the 'path' of the left is split in one place.
16 [......] The base of the [mid]dle ['finger' of the lung] is *twisted*. The 'ear' is present [......].
17 Bel-epuš, Bel-ušallim, Nabû-ušallim [......].
18 [May (this query) go] to your great divinity, O Šamaš, great lord, [and may an oracle be given as an answer].

248. Should Esarhaddon Carry Out a Plan Written on Papyrus?

K 11464 + 82-5-22,487

1 [^{d}UTU EN GAL-*ú šá a-šal-lu*]-*ka an-n*[*a* GI.N]A *a-pal-an-ni*
2 [*mim-ma šá i-na ni*]-*a-ri an*-[*ni-e*] *šaṭ-ṭa-ru-ú-ma*
3 [*i-na* IGI DINGIR-*ti-ka* GAL-*ti*] GAR-*un*
4 [^{md}*aš-šur*–ŠEŠ–SUM-*na* LUGAL KUR]–*aš-šur*.KI
5 [*ap–pi-it-ti li-pu*]-⸢*ú*⸣-*šú*
rest broken away
Rev. beginning broken away
1′ [*x x x x x x x x x x x x x šuk-nam-ma lu*]-⸢*mur*⸣
2′ [*x x x x x x x x x x x x x x*] ⸢SUHUŠ⸣ U IGI
3′ [*x x x x x x x x x x x x x x x x ina*] IGI *gíp-ši šá* 150 KIŠIB *at*$^{?}$-*ru* GAR
4′ [*x x x*] ⸢*x x x x x*⸣ [*x x x*] SILIM 2-*ma ina ku-kit-ti-šú-nu* GAR.MEŠ
5′ [*x x x x x* BE GIŠ].⸢TUKUL⸣ MÁŠ *ana* 150 ZI-*bi* [*x x*] ⸢DU⸣ U–MUR MURUB$_4$ SUHUŠ-*sà* BAR
6′ [*x x x* BE ŠÀ.NIGIN *x x x*] GUR.MEŠ 16 ŠID-*šú-nu* ŠÀ ⸢UDU⸣.NITÁ SILIM-*im* SI.LAL

AGS 134 + AGS 128 (= SAA 4 131 + SAA 4 181)

1 [Šamaš, great lord], give me a [fir]m positive ans[wer to what I am asking] you!
2 [Will Esarhaddon, king of] Assyria, [accom]plish [the things that] are written [in th]is papy[rus] and placed [before your great divinity]?
(Break)

r.1 [Be present in this ram, place (in it) a firm positive answer, favorable designs, favorable, propitious omens by the oracular command of your great divinity, and may I] see (them).
2 [......] faces the base of the 'finger.'
3 [...... in] front of the left 'mass' there is an additional vertebra.
4 [...]...... There are 2 'well-beings' placed in their ...
5 [... The 'wea]pon'-mark of the 'increment' is *ele*]*vated* to the left [...]. The base of the middle 'finger' of the lung is 'loose.'
6 [... The coils of the colon are ...] and turned. They are 16 in number. The heart of the [r]am is normal. Check-up.

r.15 Cf. Koch-Westenholz Liver Omens 273, 299. r.17 For collation, see SAA 4, p. 387b.

248 The small rejoined piece (82-5-22,487) does not add any more lines to the query, but it does add readings to lines r.5′-6′ (note also lines 1-2 and r.7′). 2 Restored as in SAA 4 131, which is different from SAA 4 181. r.4 Cf. Koch-Westenholz Liver Omens 351, n. 867.

7′ [UGU DINGIR-*ti-ka* GAL-*ti* ^{d}UTU EN GAL]-⌜*ú*⌝ *lil-lik-ma* UR$_5$.ÚŠ *li-tap-pal*

7 May (this query) go [to your great divinity, O Šamaš, gre]at [lord], and may an oracle be given as an answer.

249. Fragment Referring to the Troops of Assurbanipal

K 12213 + K 4720
beginning broken away
1′ ZI-*ib* ⌜KÚR⌝ [*x x* (*x*)]
2′ BE MÁŠ *ana ni-ri* [*x x* (*x*)]
3′ [*x*]*x* K]AR$^{?}$ [*x* (*x*)]
4′ BE NIN *zi-im* EZ[EN$^{?}$ 0$^{?}$]
5′ [0$^{?}$] ZI-*ib* IM
6′ BE AN.TA-*ti* EDIN MUR
7′ *šá* 15 *i-bir*
e.8′ *u* ŠÀ.NIGIN 16 [*x*]
9′ *it-ti a-ha-meš*
r.1 *i-te-lu-ú*
2 BE$^{?}$ UGU *u*$^{?}$ DUMU-*ti* TI-*qí*
3 1$^{?}$ na$^{?}$ tu IB$^{?}$ LÚ.A–KIN$^{?}$ [*x*] ⌜*x*⌝ [*x*]
4 ⌜*x*⌝ *u ud*$^{?}$ ⌜DU$_8$ GAR$^{?}$ *x*⌝ [*x*] U[GU$^{?}$ *x x*]
5 [BE] GAG.ZAG.GA K[UG$^{?}$ *x x* (*x*)]

---

6 LÚ.ERIM.MEŠ GAL$^{!}$ [ANŠE.KUR.RA.MEŠ$^{?}$]
7 ⌜*šá* ^{m}AN.ŠÁR–DÙ–A⌝ [LUGAL KUR–*aš*]
(rest broken away)

SAA 4 297+
(Beginning destroyed)
1 enemy attack [...].
2 The ‘increment’ [...] towards the ‘yoke.’
3 [...] is *atro*[*phied* ...].
4 If a lady has a *fest*[*ive*] appearance: attack of the wind.
6 The upper part extends beyond the surface of the right lung. The coils of the colon are 16 in number, and are of equal *height*.
r.2 ...... will take ...
3 ... the *messenger* [...]
4 ...... [...].
5 The breast-bone is *th*[*ick* ...].

---

6 The *great army* [*and horses*] of Assurbanipal, [king of Assyria]
(Rest destroyed)

250. Should Nabû-šarru-uṣur Be Appointed as Chief Eunuch?

K 1423 + K 8880
1 BE MURUB$_4$ N[A *pa-áš-ṭa x x x x*]
2 BE GÍR *k*[*a-pí-iṣ x x x x x*]
3 BE KALAG NU [GAR *x x x x x x*]
4 BE 150 Z[É *ṣa-mid x x x x x*]
5 BE ZÉ [*x x x x x x x x*]
6 ⌜BE U⌝ UGU ŠID.[MEŠ-*šú* TUR]
7 BE MÁŠ *ni-ri x*[*x x x*]

PRT 130+ (= SAA 4 299 + SAA 4 331)
1 The middle of the ‘sta[tion’ is effaced ......].
2 The ‘path’ is c[urled ......].
3 The ‘strength’ is ab[sent ......].
4 The left of the gall [bladder is attached ......].
5 The gall bladder [......].
6 The ‘finger’ is abnormally [small].
7 The ‘increment’ [...] the ‘yoke.’

249 2 Cf. Koch-Westenholz Liver Omens 280. 4-5 If understood correctly, these lines seem to criticise vanity. Note the playfulness of the writing with *zi-im* and ZI-*ib* IM. 6-r.1 See, e.g., SAA 4 317:11f. 8 The end could have [IGI], but space may be a problem for [IGI-*ti*], “[first extispicy]”. r.2 There are two or three horizontal wedges between *u* and DUMU. *martu*, “gall, bladder”, is possible, but it is always written with ZÉ in this corpus. r.6 ERIM GAL, without LÚ, would not be unusual (e.g., SAA 8 4 r.12, 103:10, 288:2). In the present passage, there may be some confusion between *ṣābu* “men” (LÚ.ERIM.MEŠ) and *ummānu* “army” (ERIM, ERIM-*ni*, ERIM.HI(.A)). The sign GAL is clear, possibly GAL$^{!}$.[MEŠ ANŠE.KUR.RA.MEŠ$^{?}$], and as drawn in SAA 4, p. 396, only the small size of the low final horizontal wedge is unexpected.

250 The combination of K 1423 and K 8880 produces a vertically complete tablet, although the upper right of the obverse and the lower right of the reverse are missing. 1 See Koch-Westenholz Liver Omens 82, 120. 2 Cf. ibid. 222, n. 590. 3 Cf. ibid. 322.

8 BE AN.TA-*ti* DU
9 BE U.SAG UGU SA-*ti*
10 BE U–MUR MURUB$_4$ SUHUŠ-*sà* BAR

11 BE GAG.ZAG.GA KUG
r.1 BE ŠÀ.NIGIN 150 Z[I.MEŠ]
2 *u* GUR.MEŠ ⸢24⸣ ŠID-*šú-nu*
blank line
3 TAG-*át*
4 ^{m}*dan-a* ^{m}*zi-zi-i* EN.ME$^{!}$–UMUŠ
5 ITI.AB UD-24-K[ÁM o$^{!}$]
6 ⸢*lim*⸣-*m*[*u* ^{m}*x x x x*]

7 ^{md}AG–LUGAL–ŠEŠ [LÚ.*x x x*]
8 *šá* ^{m}AN.ŠÁR–DÙ–DUMU.UŠ [MAN KUR–AN.ŠÁR]
9 ^{m}AN.ŠÁR–DÙ–DUMU.UŠ MA[N KUR–AN.ŠÁR]
10 *ana* UGU GAL–SAG-*ú*-[*ti lip-qid-su*]
11 GIM *ana* UGU KI.G[UB-*šú ip-taq-du*]
12 KA-*šú u* ŠÀ-*šú* [KI ^{m}AN.ŠÁR–DÙ–DUMU.UŠ (EN-*šú*)]
13 GAR-*a-an* [*x x x x x*]
s.1 *šá ina*$^{!}$ *bar*$^{!}$-*te paq*$^{!}$-*da*$^{!}$-⸢*a*$^{!}$-*ni*$^{!}$⸣ [*x x x*]

8 The upper part is *elevated.*

9 The 'cap' (rides) upon the 'outside.'

10 The base of the middle 'finger' of the lung is 'loose.'

11 The breast-bone is thick.

r.1 The coils of the colon are r[aised] and turned on the left (and) are *24* in number.

3 Unfavorable.

4 Dannaya (and) Zizî, reporters.

5 Month Tebet (X), 24th day, eponym year of [NN].

7 [Should] Assurbanipal, ki[ng of Assyria, appoint] Nabû-šarru-uṣur, [...] of Assurbanipal, [king of Assyria], to the office of Chief Eunuch?

11 If he [appoints him] to (this) posit[ion], will he in his speech and thoughts side [with Assurbanipal, (his lord)]?

13 [...] *which* were appointed in the rebellion [......].

251. A Blessing and a Report

K 10618
beginning broken away
1′ [*x x x x*] ⸢*id*$^{?}$⸣ [*x x x*]
2′ [^{md}EN$^{?}$]–⸢KASKAL⸣–KUR-*u-a* [*x x x*]
3′ [*x x x*]⸢*x*⸣ *x* DÙG.GA [*x x x*]
4′ [TA UD$^{?}$ *a*]*n-ni-i ṭu-ub* ŠÀ-*bi*
5′ [*ṭu-ub* UZU] *a-na* LUGAL *be-lí-iá*
6′ [*a-na da*]-*riš liš-ruk*
r.1 [BE U–MUR MURUB$_4$$^{?}$ 1]5 *it-bal-ši-ma*
2 [*ki-sit-ta-š*]*u*$^{?}$ TAG$_4$-*ib ina ṭu-ub-ba*-⸢*a*$^{?}$-*ti*$^{?}$⸣
3 [URU ZAG-M]U$^{?}$ *ana* KÚR SUM-*ma*

4 [*x x x*]*x* KUG.UD GABA$^{?}$.MEŠ [*x x*]
5 [*x x x*]*x*[*x x x x x*]
rest broken away

CT 54 220
(Beginning destroyed)

2 [*Bel*]-Harran-šadû'a [...]

3 [...]... good. May [DN] grant happiness [and physical well-being] to the king, my lord [*from* t]his [*day* until fore]ver!

r.1 [The right] side absorbs [*the 'middle finger' of the lung*], but leaves [*it*]*s* [*stump*].

2 *By means of friendship*, [*m*]*y* [*border town*] will be delivered to the enemy.

4 [...] silver, *breasts* [...]

(Rest destroyed)

r.4 See coll. s.1 For collation, see SAA 4, p. 388b (no. 331).

251 3 One could read ⸢*am*$^{!}$⸣–*mar* DÙG.GA, but this is suspect because of an Assyrianism (unless *am-mar*, "I will see") and a misplaced vertical wedge in *am*. r.1-2 See SAA 4 301:5, r.1-2. r.3 Restored after SAA 4 301:6.

252. Assurbanipal and a Dream

	K 4728 + K 8909	PRT 103+ (= SAA 4 316 + SAA 4 340)
1	BE SAG NA *zuq-qúr* NÍG.⸢TAB⸣ [15 *u* 150]	The top of the 'station' is pointed. If the 'cruci[ble'] is cu[rled] all over on the [right and left] upward, and the 'path' lies within it: in warfare, the weapons of the pr[ince will have no equal]. In a distant time, the prince's land will be ob[edient] to him.
2	*ana* AN.TA-*nu* TÉŠ.BI ⸢*kap*⸣-[*ṣa-at*]	
3	GÍR *ina* ŠÀ-*šú* GAR *ina* GIŠ.TUKUL ERIM ⸢NUN⸣ [GABA.RI NU TUKU-*ši*]	
4	*ina* UD SUD *šá* NUN KUR-*su ana* ⸢KA⸣-[*šú* TUŠ-*ab*]	
5	BE SILIM GÍR 15 ⸢ZÉ⸣ [BÙR ŠUB]–AŠ.[TE GAR.MEŠ]	The 'well-being', the 'path' on the right of the gall [bladder, and the 'base] of the throne' [are present].
6	BE 150 ZÉ [*ṣa-mid*]	The left of the gall bladder is [attached].
7	⸢BE⸣ [*ina*] SAG EDIN [ŠU.SI *x x x*]	[In the] top of the [...] surface of the ['finger' ...].
8	(traces of one line)	[......]
9	[BE AN].⸢TA⸣-*ti* DU *ha-si-si* GAR	[The upper pa]rt is *elevated.* The 'ear' is present.
10	[BE U]–⸢MUR⸣ MURUB$_4$ SUHUŠ-*sà* KÉŠ-*is*	The base of the middle ['finger' of the lu]ng is 'bound.'
11	[BE GAG].ZAG.GA KUG ŠÀ.NIGIN 14 ŠÀ UDU.NITÁ *šá-lim*	[The br]east-bone is thick. The coils of the colon are 14 in number. The heart of the ram is normal.
12	[BE *ina*] 15 NA BÙR ŠUB *šu-bat* 150 GÍR GAR-*át*	[In] the right side of the 'station' there is a hole. The left 'seat' of the 'path' is present.
13	[BE *ina*] 15 U BÙR ŠUB-*di ina* SAG EDIN 150 U	[In] the right side of the 'finger' there is a hole. In the top of the left surface of the 'finger' there is a 'weapon'-mark. It faces the top of the 'finger.'
14	⸢GIŠ⸣.TUKUL GAR-*ma* SAG U IGI	
15	⸢BE⸣ U.SAG MUR *pár-kiš* DU$_8$ ZI.GA ŠU	If the 'cap' of the lung is split crosswise: losses.
16	BE HAL NIGIN *ana* 15 U ŠUB-*di*	The ... has a hole on the right.
17	BE MÁŠ NIGIN BAR-*ma* DAR-*át*	The 'increment' ... is cut in the center.
18	[*x*]*x* 7 TAG.MEŠ *ina* ŠÀ	There are 7 unfavorable omens in this extispicy.
r.1	[MÁŠ].MI ⸢*šá*⸣ *am-ra-tu*	[The dre]am that was seen,
2	[*um*]-⸢*ma*⸣ DUG *šá* ^{d}*iš-tar arba-ìl*.KI	[in whi]ch a pot of Ištar of Arbela
3	[*ina* URU].⸢*zi*⸣-*ik-ku-ú*	[... *in* the city Z]ikkû —
4	[*x x x*]*x* ^{m}AN.ŠÁR–DÙ–A-*ú*	[*will*] Assurbanipal, [king of As]syria,
5	[MAN KUR–*aš*]-*šur bi-nù-ut* ŠU.2-*šú*	[...] a creation of his own hands
6	[*x x x*] 1 *ka* ⸢*am*? *maš*⸣	[...] ...?
7	[*x x x*] *ul* DÙG.GA	[...] Unfavorable.
8	[ITI.*x* UD-*x*-KÁM] *lim-mu* ^{m}AN.ŠÁR–BÀD–PAB	[Month ..., ...th day], eponym year of Aššur-duru-uṣur (652).
9	⸢*ina* ŠÀ!-*bi*⸣ [*x x e*]-⸢*tap*⸣-*šú* ^{m}*dan-a-a* LÚ.HAL	[Per]formed in [...]. Dannaya, haruspex;
10	^{md}ŠÚ–⸢MU⸣–[PAB] LÚ.EN–UMUŠ	Marduk-šu[mu-uṣur], reporter.

252 Together the two rejoined pieces form an almost complete tablet, although the readings of some of the destroyed signs cannot be restored. [1] Cf. Koch-Westenholz Liver Omens 121. [1-4] Cf. ibid. 295. [12] Cf. ibid. 87, 109, 214.
[r.9] There is probably not enough space in the break to restore [É.GAL GIBIL], "[the New Palace]", unless one reads ⸢É?⸣. instead of ⸢-*bi*⸣. [r.9, 11] For collations, see SAA 4, p. 388b, nos. 340 r.1 and 316 r.11 respectively.

11 DINGIR.MEŠ GAL.MEŠ DI$^{!}$.KUD.MEŠ
12 MAH.MEŠ *šur-bu-tu* ^{d}15 KUG
13 UD-*mu-us-su an-na šal-mu*
14 *šá* MÍ.SIG$_5$ *ana* LUGAL *be-lí-*⸢*iá*⸣
15 *li-tap-pa-lu-ma*
16 ŠÀ.SÈ.SÈ.KI-*ka*
17 *lu-šak-ši-du-*⸢*ka*⸣

11 May the great gods, august and exalted judges, and the pure Ištar daily give a favorable positive answer of good fortune to the king, my lord!

16 May they grant that you attain your goal!

253. Fragment Concerning an Extispicy in Year 651

K 396 + K 21929

1 [*x x x x x x*]*x* GIG *u* ŠUB.ŠUB-*u*[*t*]
2 [*x x x x x t*]*i* TI-*qí*
3 [*x x x x x* G]I.NA IGI.IGI-*e* KÚR *a-dak*
4 BE ⸢SAG⸣ NA DU$_8$ *u* ZÉ *šub-bat*
5 ERIM KÚR ŠÀ.SÈ.SÈ.KI-*šú* NU KUR-*ád*
6 BE GÍR 2-*ma* GÍR 15 UGU GÍR 150 GAR-*in*
7 NUN GIŠ.TUKUL.MEŠ-*šú* UGU GIŠ.TUKUL.MEŠ KÚR-*šú* Š[EŠ.MEŠ]
8 [*x x*]-⸢*ú*$^{?}$⸣ KALAG-*an* NUN NUN KUR-*su* DAGAL-[*eš*]
9 [KÚR$^{?}$] *a-dak u* ME.NI ⸢*dam*⸣-[*x*] ⸢*x*⸣ [*x x x*]
10 [ŠÀ UD]U$^{?}$ SILIM-*im an* [*x x x x x x x*]
11 [*x x*]*x* 15 ZÉ [*x x x x x x x*]
12 [ŠÀ UD]U$^{?}$ SILIM-*im* [*x x x x x x x*]
13 [*x* ED]IN U MURUB$_4$ *x*[*x x x x x x x*]
(rest broken away)

Rev. beginning broken away; traces of one line
1′ [*x x*]*x* ŠUB-*ma* [*x x x x x x*]
2′ ⸢*e*⸣-*zib šá ana* DU KASKAL UR$_5$-*tú* [*x x x* ŠÀ-*bi*]
3′ *šu-du-ru* NÍG.GIG [*ma-na-ah-ti šá* KASKAL]
4′ ŠUR-*an šá* È *iṣ*-[*x x x x x x*]
5′ ⸢*ú*⸣–*lu* NUN *a-a-lu* ⸢*x x x x*⸣ [*x x*]
(blank space of one line)
6′ ITI.NE UD-10-[KA]M *lim-mu* ^{m}UD-*gab* LÚ.NAM KASKAL.KI
7′ [^{m}*aš-šur*–KALAG]– LUGAL LÚ.KAŠ.LUL
8′ [^{m}*x x x*] LÚ.HAL ^{md}ŠÚ–MU–PAB ^{m}*dan-a* ⸢EN.MEŠ–UMUŠ⸣
9′ [o] *ina arba-ìl*.KI DÙ

PRT 110+ (= SAA 4 324+)

1 [If ……, …] will get ill and keep falling down.

2 [If …] will take [……].

3 [If … is fi]rm, I will defeat the enemy.

4 If the top of the 'station' is split and the gall bladder is flattened: the enemy's army will not achieve its enterprise.

6 If the 'paths' are two, and the right 'path' is located on the left 'path': the prince's weapons will pr[evail] over the enemy's weapons.

8 […] strengthening of the prince. The prince's country will expand.

9 I will defeat [*the enemy*], *and* the 'gate of the palace' [……].

10 [*The heart of the she*]*ep* is normal [……]

11 […] the right of the gall bladder [……].

12 [*The heart of the she*]*ep* is normal [……]

13 [(…)] the middle [sur]face of the 'finger' [……]

(Break)

r.2 Disregard that he is apprehensive (and) *troubled about* going to this campaign […]

4 ……[……]

5 or *the prince* [……] *help*.

6 Month Ab (V), 10th day, eponym year of Sagab, governor of Harran (651).

7 [Aššur-da''in]-šarru (was) cupbearer.

8 [NN] (was) haruspex; Marduk-šumu-uṣur (and) Dannaya, reporters.

9 Performed in Arbela.

253 2 For -*ti* TI-*qí*, see no. 249 r.2. 6-7 Cf. Koch-Westenholz Liver Omens 190. 9 Cf. ibid. 275. 10, 12 Despite the restoration, it is questionable whether the same phrase appears twice in this query. r.5 However, the blank space after this line is very narrow.

254. An Extispicy Fragment from Year 651

K 3791 + K 16276

1 BE SUHUŠ? [*x x x x x x*]
2 BE KI [*x x x x x x*]
3 ⸢*x*⸣ [*x x x x x x*]
4 BE ⸢*x x*⸣ [*x x x x x x*]
5 BE *šá*? *x*[*x x x x x x*]
6 BE *x*[*x x x x x x*]
7 BE KI [*x x x x x x*]
8 BE LÚ.ERIM.[MEŠ? *x x x x x x*]
9 *ur*-[*x x x x x x x x x x x*]
10 BE ŠÀ [*x x x x x x x x x x*]
11 BE KI.[TA-*tum*? *x x x x x x x*]
12 5 [TAG.MEŠ *x x x x x x x x x*]
13 ^{md}[*x x x x x x x x x x*]
(rest broken away?)

Rev. beginning broken away?
1′ *šá* GABA *x*[*x x*] *x*[*x x x*]
2′ *x*[*x x x x x x x x x x*]
3′ *a*-⸢*na*?⸣ [*x x x x x x x x*]

(blank space of one line)

4′ ITI.DU$_{6}$ UD-11-KÁM *lim-mu* ^{m}UD-[*gab*]
5′ ^{m}*aš-šur*–KALAG-*in*–LUGAL $^{m⌜d?⌝}$[*x x x*]
6′ [*i-na*] É–UŠ *e-tap*-[*šú*]
rest uninscribed

PRT 108+ (= SAA 4 327+)

(Beginning too broken for translation)

10 The inside of [......]
11 The lower [*part* ......]
12 There are 5 [unfavorable omens. ......]
(Break)

r.1 ...[......]
2 [......]
3 *t*[*o* ......]

4 Month Tishri (VII), 11th day, eponym year of Sa[gab] (651).
5 Aššur-da''in-šarru, [NN].
6 Perfor[med in] the Succession Palace.

255. Fragment of a Report Containing Blessings

K 4766 + 82-5-22,70 + K 14308

1 BE [N]A GÍD.DA [*x x x x*]
2 BE GÍR DAG.MEŠ-*š*[*ú ka-šid*]
3 BE KALAG GAR GÍR 150 Z[É *x x*]
4 *ù* [Š]À.NIGIN 16 *ina* UR$_{5}$.[ÚŠ-*ka*]
5 SI[LIM-*ti*]*m* 2 IZI.GAR GAR.M[EŠ *x*]
6 BE [*ina* UGU] MÁŠ GIŠ.TUKUL GAR-*ma* TA [15 *ana* 150 *te-bi*]
7 [ERIM-*ni hi-i*]*m-ṣa-a-ti* KÚR [KÚ]
8 [*x x x*] ⸢*x*⸣ *ban du* [*x*]
9 [*x x x x*]*x-ti* [*x x*]
10 [*x x x x* G]UR? [*x x x*]
rest broken away

CT 54 69+ (= SAA 4 341+)

1 The ['sta]tion' is long [...].
2 The 'path' [reaches] its 'seats.'
3 The 'strength' is present. The 'path' on the left of the gall [bladder]
4 and the coils of the colon are 16 in number. In [your] fa[vorab]le ext[ispicy] there are two *niphu*s.
6 If [over] the 'increment' there is a 'weapon'-mark and [it rises] from [right to left: my army will take] the enemy's [bo]oty.

(Break)

254 Unfortunately, K 16276 only contains the line beginnings on the obverse, but at least it confirms that r.6′ is the last line of the query. 8 This may have been read in error, as the sequence is not expected.

255 1 Cf. Koch-Westenholz Liver Omens 81, 97. 2 Cf. ibid. 222. 3 Cf. ibid. 322.

Rev. beginning broken away; traces of one line
1′ *i-rab-b*[*i x x x x x x*]
blank space of one line
2′ ITI.KIN UD-17-KÁM* *lim-m*[*e* ^{m}*x x x x*]
blank space of two lines
3′ ^{d}UTU *u* ^{d}IM DI.KU[D.MEŠ MAH.MEŠ$^{?}$]
4′ *lu-*⸢*ú*$^{!}$⸣*-du-ma an-n*[*a* GI.NA$^{?}$]
5′ *a-na* ⸢LUGAL$^{!}$⸣ *be-lí-iá li-d*[*i-nu*]
6′ ŠÀ.SÈ.SÈ.KI-*k*[*a*]
7′ *lu-*⸢*šak*⸣*-ši-du-*⸢*ú*$^{!}$⸣-[*ka*]
8′ *ṭu-ub* ŠÀ *u ṭu-ub* UZU.[MEŠ]
9′ *šá da-ra-a-t*[*i* 0]
10′ *a-na* [LU]GAL *be-lí-iá* [*li-qí-šú*]

r.1 will *increas*[*e* ......].

2 Month Elul (VI), 17th day, eponym ye[ar of NN].

3 By Šamaš and Adad, [*exalted*] judg[es], may they gra[nt] a [*firm*] positive answ[er] to the king, my lord!
6 May they make [you] attain yo[ur] goal and [bestow] eternal happiness and health upon [the ki]ng, my lord!

256. Fragment of a Query(?)

K 12255
beginning broken away
1′ [*x x x x* T]A ITI.BARAG UD-[*x*-KÁM *x x x x*]
2′ [*x x x x*]*x-ta-bu-ni*[*m-ma x x x x x*]
3′ [*x x x x*] ITI.DIRI.ŠE *šá* M[U.AN.NA]
4′ [*x x x t*]*i*$^{?}$ *hi ni me*$^{?}$ [*x x x x x x*]
5′ [*x x x x*] *ri bi x*[*x x x x x x*]
6′ [*x x x x x*]*x-ta-x*[*x x x x x x*]
7′ [*x x x x* ERI]M$^{?}$.MEŠ [*x x x x x x*]
8′ [*x x x x x*] *x*[*x x x x x*]
rest broken away

CT 54 231
(Beginning destroyed)
1 [... fr]om the month Nisan (I), [...th] day [......]
2 [...] ... [...]
3 [...] intercalary Adar (XII/2) of [*this*] y[ear]
(Rest too broken for translation)

257. Fragment of a Query(?) Mentioning Assurbanipal

K 15413
beginning broken away
1′ [*ina*$^{?}$] ⸢IGI *an*⸣*-n*[*i-x x x x*]
2′ [^{m}]⸢^{d}⸣*aš-šur*–DÙ–A DUMU–[LUGAL *x x*]
e Uninscribed
r.1 [*ina* U]GU LÚ.ERIM.ME[Š *x x x*]
2 [*x x x*].KI *x*[*x x x x x*]
rest broken away

CT 53 670
(Beginning destroyed)
1 *before* thi[s ......]
2 Assurbanipal, the [crown] prince [...]
r.1 [*Concer*]*ning the men* [......]
(Rest destroyed)

[r.2-4,10] Cf. Borger Ein Brief p. 56. [r.4] See coll. Borger reads the verbal form as *lu-*⸢*rad*⸣*-du-ma*, which is a viable alternative. [r.5, 7] See coll.

256 [2] Or, perhaps read *ta-bu* NI[M.MA.KI "*rise* of Ela[m]". [4] Possibly the beginning as *an-ni-t*]*i*, but this line may contain a foreign PN (or a GN). Note, e.g., Hinni-immī (PNA 2/I 473a) which, however, is impossible in this case. [5] E.g., *ú*/*ul-še*/*te*]*-ri-bi*.

258. Fragment of a Query Mentioning Mullissu, the Troops of Assurbanipal, and Adad

Sm 1954

beginning broken away

1′ [*x x x x x x x*] LUGAL Š[U? *x x x*]

2′ [BE MURUB$_4$-*tum*] SUHUŠ-*sà* BAR 150 [MUR SILIM-*im*?]

3′ [*x x x*]*x* ^{d}NIN.LÍL [*x x x*]

4′ [*x x* Š]UB-*ú* KALAG [*x x x*]

5′ [*x x x*]*x u* DU$_8$ KUG ŠÀ-*b*[*a*? *x x x*]

6′ [*x x x*] SIG$_5$ ŠÀ UDU.NI[TÁ *šá-lim x*]

7′ [LÚ.ERIM.MEŠ A]NŠE.KUR.RA.M[EŠ *ù e-mu-qí*]

8′ [*šá* ^{md}*aš-šur*–DÙ?]–A? LUGAL KUR–*aš-šu*[*r*.KI *x x x*]

9′ [*x x x*]*x ša*[*k x x x x x*]

rest broken away

Rev. beginning broken away

1′ [*x x x x*]*x*[*x x x x*]

2′ [*x x*]*x* LUGAL *be-lí-*[*iá x x*]

blank space of four lines

3′ [^{d}UTU *u*] ^{d}IM DINGIR.[MEŠ? *x x*]

4′ [*x x*]*x*.MEŠ *ina* A[N-*e x x*]

5′ [*x x* S]È.SÈ.KI-[*ka* 0?]

6′ [*lu-šak-š*]*i-d*[*u-ka*]

CT 54 430

(Beginning destroyed)

1 [......] the king *ha*[*nd* ...]

2 The base of [the middle part] is 'loose'. The left [*of the lung is normal*].

3 [...] Mullissu [...]

4 [... *th*]*ere are* [...]. The 'strength' [is ...].

5 [...] *and* a fissure. *Pure of heart* [...]

6 [...] *favorable*. The heart of the ra[m is normal (...)]

---

7 [The men], horses [and army *of Assurbani*]*pal*, king of Assyria [......]

(Break)

r.2 [...] the king, my lord [...].

3 [*May* Šamaš and] Adad, the god[*s of* ..., ...]s in hea[ven *and earth* ...].

5 [May they make you at]ta[in your w]ishes.

259. ---

Ki 1904-10-9,320

beginning broken away

1′ [*x x*]*x x*[*x x x x x*

2′ [*x x*]*x i x*[*x x x x x*

3′ [*x x*]*x* É? *gab-*[*x x x x*

4′ [*lu*]-⌜*ú*⌝ LÚ.G[AL?–*x x x*

5′ [*lu*]-⌜*ú*⌝ LÚ.*x*[*x x x x*

6′ [*x*] *kit ni* [*x x x x*

7′ [*l*]*u-ú* GAR-[*nu-šú x x*

8′ *lu-ú x*[*x x x x x*

rest broken away

ADD 1217

(Beginning destroyed)

3 [...] the *who*[*le*] *house* [......]

4 [whet]her the *ch*[*ief* ...]

5 [o]r the [...]

6 [*or*] ... [......]

7 [o]r [his] prefe[ct ...]

8 or [......]

(Rest destroyed)

258 2 The uncertain restoration is based on SAA 4 168 r.4′. 3 Mullissu does not appear in SAA 4. 4 Presumably restore [NU GAR-*in*] "[is absent]" or [GAR-*in*] "[is present]" or [SILIM GAR] "[and 'well-being' are present]", but there are other possibilities, as well. 6 Or: [... un]favorable". r.3 In SAA 4, Adad appears only together with Šamaš in no. 341 r.3 (see no. 255 above). r.4 Perhaps it is not impossible to read [DI.K]UD?.MEŠ, but at least UB.MEŠ and B]AN?.MEŠ are also possible. r.5 We do not expect anything after *-ka*.

259 This fragment may be an insurrection query or a legal transaction.

260. Šamaš-šumu-ukin and Extispicy Omens

K 8729

obverse totally broken away

r.1′ [*x x x* ^{md}GIŠ.NU$_{11}$]–⸢MU⸣–GI.NA [*x x x*

2′ BE-*m*[*a* EME UDU.N]ÍTA TÉŠ.BI *na-šik u x*[*x x x*
3′ *šá ina ri-ti* DINGIR DU-*ku-ma* [*x x x*
4′ *iš-šak-nu-ma* LÚ.HAL-*šú ina* U[D *x x x*
5′ *ú-šá-an-na-a ba-ru-t*[*u x x x x*

6′ BÀ.MEŠ *šá* LUGAL.MEŠ *šá ina ba-*[*x x x*
7′ *ul-te-bi-la-šú* LUGAL.ME[Š *x x x*
8′ LUGAL *be-lí li-mur-ma šá x*[*x x x*
9′ *ni-pu-šú um-ma a-m*[*u-ut*$^{?}$ *x x x*
10′e [*x*]*x*.⸢KUR$^{?}$⸣.MEŠ *šá ina* ŠÀ-*b*[*i x x x*
11′e [*x x x x x*] ⸢*x*⸣ [*x x x x*

K 8729

(Beginning destroyed)

r.1 [... Šamaš]-šumu-ukin [......].

---

2 If [the tongue of the she]ep is bitten all over *and* [......]
3 *which* go for the *divine* pasture [......] have been placed, and his haruspex changes [...... *to*]*da*[*y*]. An extispi[cy ......].

---

6 The omens of the kings *which* in [......], *I* have sent it [*to the king*].
7 Let the king, my lord, have a look [*what*] the kings [......] and *what* [......] *we shall do*, saying: the *li*[*ver omen of* ......]
10 [...]s which *are* in [......]
(Rest destroyed)

261. Unfavorable Omens in the Extispicy

K 3162

beginning broken away

1′ *x*[*x x x x x x x*]
2′ ^{m}⸢$^{d?}$⸣[*x x x x x x*]
3′ *ta-x*[*x x x x bi*$^{?}$-*r*]*i*
4′ *ú-šab-*[*x x x x x*]-*a*
5′ *ina* MÁŠ *iš-š*[*ak*$^{?}$-*x x x x*]
6′ *šá ina* MÁŠ *iš-š*[*ak-nu x x*]

7′ *ši-ik-nu ú-šá-x*[*x x x x*]
8′ *ina* UGU ŠÀ-*šú x*[*x x x x*] ⸢*x*⸣
9′ *šam-mu ana* NAG-*e la* DÙG.GA

r.1 5 TAG.MEŠ *ina* ŠÀ *ul* DÙG.G[A]

blank space of two lines

CT 54 58

(Beginning destroyed)

2 [NN ...]
3 [... *in extispi*]*cy*
4 ... [...]
5 *will be* pl[aced] in extispicy. [...]
6 which *will be* plac[ed] in extispicy [*is* ...].
7 The *appearance* ...[...]
8 *upon* it [...]
9 the drug is not good for drinking.
r.1 There are 5 unfavorable omens in the extispicy. It is unfavorable.

260 For this edition it was useful to consult the eBL edition (https://www.ebl.lmu.de/fragmentarium/K.8729), accessed 13.6.2023. It is unclear how many signs are missing from the right edge of the tablet. r.2 The sign(s) at the end could also be read as *u*[*l* or U[GU. r.4 Alternatively, the end could be read as *ina* K[I "in a [...] pla[ce". r.6 Assuming that 'omens', which are then sent to the king, is the main word here and not 'kings'. Perhaps *ina ba-*[*ri-ti*? r.9 *ni-bu-šú*, "his/its naming" is also possible. Or read *a-n*[*a-ku* instead of *a-m*[*u-tu*. r.10 Unless the beginning is to be read [*x*]*x* ⸢LUGAL$^{?}$⸣.MEŠ "the kings who are in".

261 Most of the reverse has been erased, but it is still relatively legible. 8 Perhaps *i*[*b-*: it looks different from what was drawn by Dietrich.

2 DINGIR.[[MEŠ GAL.MEŠ DINGIR.MEŠ EŠ. BAR]]
3 DI-[[*mu a-na* LUGAL *be-lí-iá*]]
4 *il*-[[*tap-ru-ú-ni*]]
5 [[*ši-ik-ni šá* UZU?.MEŠ *x*]]
6 [*x*] [[*x x* LUGAL EN *x*]] HUL
7 [*x x x x x x*] [[*šú*]]
rest broken away

2 The great gods, the gods of decision, have greeted the king, my lord.

5 The appearance of *flesh is* […]
6 […] the king, my lord, *bad* […]
(Rest destroyed)

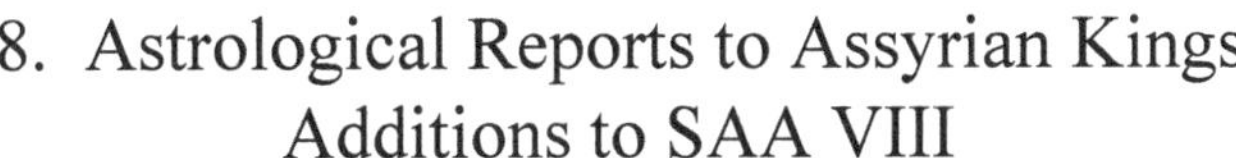

8. Astrological Reports to Assyrian Kings
Additions to SAA VIII

FIG. 30. *Sun, moon and stars carved as witnesses on Babylonian kudurru grant of Nebuchadnezzar I, c. 1100 BC.*
BM 90858.

262. Hemerology for the 1st of Nisan

	K 115	SAA 8 38
1	[1 *ina* ITI.BARAG UD-1-KÁM *li-te-lil l*]*i-te-bi-*⸢*ib*⸣	[1] [In Nisan (I), the first day, he should cleanse and] purify himself.
2	[NA$_4$.ZA.GÌN.DURU$_5$ *ina*] Ì.GIŠ *hal-ṣi* T[U$_5$]	[2] You s[oak *zagindurû* stone in] filtered oil, [you put *maštakal* plant in]to [beer and oil]. He rubs himself repeatedly.
3	[Ú.IN.NU.UŠ *ina*] Š[À KAŠ Ì.GIŠ ŠUB-*di*] *it-ta-nap-ša-*⸢*áš*⸣	
4	[*x* K]UŠ.*še-ni* [GADA *liš-kun* TÚG *eš*]-⸢*ši lil-la-biš*⸣	[4] [(...) he should put on linen] sandals and dress [in a n]ew [garment].
5	NA$_4$.ZA.GÌN.DURU$_5$ [*ina* TÚG.SÍG-*ka*] HÉ.[KÉŠ-*a*]*s*	[5] You [bin]d *zagindurû* stone [in yo]ur [hem, you go] to the house of a [fowler and (buy) two] doves, [male and fem]ale.
6	*a-na* É L[Ú.MUŠEN.DÙ DU-*ma* 2 T]U.MUŠEN.[MEŠ NITA *u* M]Í	
7	*ina* IGI ^{d}UT[U *ta-da-an-ši*]-*na-ti k*[*i-ma* DINGIR ÁŠ KUR$^{?}$]	[7] [You convict th]em before Šamaš. [He will obtain his *desire*] li[ke a god].
8	^{d}⸢UTU⸣ DI.[KUD AN-*e u* K]I.TIM *a*[*t-ta-ma*]	[8] (You say) "Šamaš, you are the ju[dge of heaven and] earth, un[clench for me the s]tro[ng *fists* of god or goddess, k]ing, magnate or nobleman!"
9	[*up-ni*$^{?}$ *d*]*an-n*[*a-ti*$^{?}$ *šá* DINGIR *u* ^{d}15 LU]GAL IDIM *u* NUN *š*[*up-ṭi-ra*]	
10	[NITA *ana* ^{d}UTU.È MÍ] *ana* ^{d}UTU.ŠÚ.A ⸢*ú*⸣-[*maš-šar*]	[10] He [releases the male (dove) to the east, the female] to the west.
11	⸢KU$_6$$^{?}$⸣ [*ta-bar-ma* Ú]H-*su a-na* ⸢KA⸣ [KU$_6$ ŠUB-*di*]	[11] [You catch] a fish [and put] his [spi]ttle in the mouth [of the fish; (and say)] "Fish, [carry off my] s[in, fi]sh, un[do] the curse! [Let it go down to the *a*]*ps*[*û*]!"
12	KU$_6$ *á*[*r-ni ta-bal* K]U$_6$ *ma-mit* D[U$_8$ *a-na* Z]U.A[B *šu-ri-di*]	
13	NÍG.NA ŠEM.LI *ina* IGI ^{d}UTU [GAR-*an* KAŠ.S]AG B[AL-*qí*]	[13] [You set up] a censer of juniper before Šamaš, pour a liba[tion of bee]r, pour a liba[tion] of milk to the right and left of his door.
14e	GA ZAG *u* KAB *ša* KÁ-⸢*šú*⸣ BAL-[*qí*]	
r.1	NINDA ZÍZ.ÀM UZU GUD UDU KÚ KAŠ ZÍZ.ÀM NA[G]	[r.1] He may eat emmer bread, beef and mutton, and dri[nk] emmer beer; when he says something, god, king, magnate and nobleman will be entirely favorable.
2	DINGIR LUGAL IDIM *u* NUN *e-ma* DUG$_4$.GA-*u ka-liš ma-gir*	
3	*e-ma* DU-*ku ki-ma* DINGIR *ni-iz-mat* ŠÀ-*šú* KUR-*ád*	[3] Wherever he goes, he will obtain his heart's desire like a god; he will shine like the sun; his dreams will be good; he will live long.
4	*ki-ma* ^{d}UTU ZALÁG-*ir* MÁŠ.MI.⸢MEŠ⸣-*šú* SIG$_5$.MEŠ TI.LA *ut-tar*	

262 See copy p. 294. Previous edition: SAA 8 38. This edition, which improves lines 1-13, r.2-6, is based on A. Livingstone, "On the Organized Release of Doves to Secure Compliance of a Higher Authority," in Fs. Lambert (2000) 380-81. [7] See Livingstone, p. 382. [11-12] Cf. BAM 318 iv 19-20 with a slightly different order. See Schwemer, JCS 65 (2013) 198, commenting on BAM 318 iv 19.

5 *ina* ⸢KISAL *a*⸣-*šar* ANŠE.KUR.RA GUB-*zu* GI.DU$_8$ KÉŠ-*as* 6 ÉN UD.BI (UD).KALAG.BI KIN.NAM ŠID-*nu*	5 You set up a portable altar in the courtyard, where the horses stand, you recite the incantation "Ud-bi (ud)-kalag-bi kin-nam".
7 *ša* ^{md}15–MU–KAM-*eš*	7 From Issar-šumu-ereš.

263. Akkad and Jupiter in Sivan (III)

K 5384	CT 54 78
1 [1 *x x x* Í]L$^?$-*ma* ^{d}[*x x x x x*	1 [If ... *carr*]*ies* [...] and [DN ......].
2 [GISKIM$^?$.M]EŠ *šá* KUR–URI.KI *pa-n*[*i-x x x*	2 [The] *prev*[*ious sign*]s concerning Akkad [......].
3 [*x x*] LUGAL KUR.KUR *be-lí-ia x*[*x x x* 4 [*x x*]*x* LÚ.GÚ.EN.NA *u* ^{m}⸢$^{d?}$⸣[*x x x x* 5 [IGI.2-*ia*$^?$] ⸢*šak*$^?$⸣-*na ana* LUGAL *be-lí*-[*ia*$^?$ *x x x* 6 [*x x x*]*x uṣ-ṣa-a ana* LUGAL [*x x x x* 7 [*x x x x*]-⸢*ú*⸣ *iš-x*[*x x x x x* 8 [*x x x x*] ⸢*x x*⸣ [*x x x x x* rest broken away Rev. beginning broken away 1′ [*x x x x x x x x*]*x* ⸢KUR–URI.KI⸣ *x*[*x x x x*] 2′ [*x x x x x x x*]*x*.ME *ka-tu-ú* ⸢*x*⸣ [*x x x*]	3 [...] the king of the lands, my lord, [......] 4 [...] the *šandabakku* and [NN (...)] 5 [*I am*] *devoted* to the king, [*my*] lord [......] 6 [...] *comes* out, for the king [......] 7 [......] ... [......] (Break) r.1 [......] Akkad [...] 2 [......]s are destitute [...]
3′ [1 MUL.SAG.ME.GAR *ina* ITI.SIG$_4$ *b*]*a-ìl zi-mu-šú* SA$_5$.MEŠ [*x x x*] 4′ [DINGIR.MEŠ *ze-nu-ti* KI KUR]–URI.KI.ME *i-šal-li*-[*mu* A.KAL.MEŠ] 5′ [*sad-ru-ti ina* KUR–UR]I.KI GÁL.MEŠ ŠE-*im u* ŠE.GI[Š.Ì *i-ma-id-ma*] 6′ [DINGIR.MEŠ *ina* AN]-⸢*e*⸣ *ana man-zal-ti-šú-nu* GUB.ME[Š 0] 7′ [BARAG.MEŠ-*šú-nu*] *ṭuh-di* I[GI.MEŠ 0]	3 [If Jupiter] is [br]ight in Sivan (III) and its features are red [...], 4 [angry gods] will be reconci[led] with Akkad; there will be [regular floods in Akka]d; barley and ses[ame will increase, and the gods in the sk]y will stand in their (appropriate) positions; [their shrines] will s[ee] wealth.
8′ [*ša* ^{m}*x x x x x*]	8 [From NN].

r.6 See Livingstone, p. 386f.

263 1 One might think of "[If Auriga carr]ies [radiance]"; cf. SAA 8 115 r.4 and 170 r.1. r.3 For the end, cf. SAA 8 115:4. r.3-7 These lines may have been quoted in part from SAA 8 115:1-10, a report by Bulluṭu which gives a longer description of Jupiter in Sivan.

264. Eclipse of the Sun

K 1309 + 83-1-18,301

1 1 20 KUR-*ma šá-ru-ru-šú e-*⸢*ṭú*⸣*-ú* LU[GAL *x x*]
2 GIŠ.TUKUL *il-lap-*[*pat x x x*]

3 1 20 KUR-*ma* KAB-*šú* ⸢*x x*⸣ LUGAL KUR [*x x x*]
4 *ul* ⸢*il*?⸣-[*x*] ⸢*x i x*⸣ *x*[*x x x*]
rest broken away
Rev. beginning broken away
1′ *ana* LUGAL DI-*mu ana* ⸢KÚR?⸣ ÚŠ [0?]

2′ AN.MI EŠ.BAR *šá* ⸢^{d}⸣UTU *pi-i* [*um-ma-ni šu-ú*?]
3′ *ina* GIŠ.LI.U$_5$.UM LUGAL KUR?.*x*[*x šá-ṭi-ir*?]

4′ *šá* ^{md}U.GUR–KAR-*ir*

RMA 181A + RMA 277S (= SAA 8 280 + SAA 8 286)

1 If the sun rises and its radiance is dark: the ki[ng of ...] will be affec[ted] by a weapon [...].

3 If the sun rises and its left side *is* ...: the king of [...] *will* not [......].

(Break)

r.1 For the king, well-being; for the *enemy*, death.

---

2 The (interpretation of the) eclipse, decision for the sun, [*it is*] (*from*) the oral tradition [*of the masters, written*] on a writing-board of the king of [*all*] *land*[*s*].

---

4 From Nergal-eṭir.

265. Regulus Near Moon

K 4708 + K 5712 + K 10298

1 GISKIM *šá a-na* LUGAL *lem-né-ti a-na* KUR *dam-qat*!
2 GISKIM *šá a-na* KUR *dam-qa-ti a-na* LUGAL *lem-n*[*é-et*]

---

3 *i-na mi-ni-i lu-mur* LUGAL *i-qab-bi-ma*

---

4 1 MUL.LUGAL *ana* IGI 30 TE-*ma* GUB UD.MEŠ NUN TIL.MEŠ
5 *a-mat te-še-e*! *ina* KUR DU$_8$-*ár ana* KUR SIG$_5$

RMA 199+ (= SAA 8 283+)

1 A sign which is unfavorable for the king is favorable for the land; a sign which is favorable for the land is unfav[orable] for the king.

---

3 The king will say, "From what shall I see (that)?"

---

4 If Regulus comes close to the front of the moon and stands there: the days of the ruler will come to an end; a confusing word will be solved in the land; for the land, favorable.

---

264 4 The so-called *il* does not look convincing and is quite different from the one in line 2. Or, read, e.g., *ul* ⸢*ga*?*-mi*?⸣-[*ir*]. The last partially visible sign is probably ⸢KUR⸣ or LU[GAL]. r.3 We would expect to read KUR.K[UR], but it looks as if KUR has been written over an erasure [[KUR?]].*x*[*x*], and the sign following begins with two horizontals.
265 1 This line is written on the top edge.

6	1 MUL.LUGAL *ana* UGU 30 [SI$_4$-*m*]*a* ⸢GUB⸣ LUGAL UD.MEŠ *ma-a'-du-tú* DIN-*uṭ*	[6] If Regulus [*comes close*] to the top of the moon and stands there: the king will live for many days; the land will not pros[per]; [for the *lan*]*d*, unfavorable.
7	KUR NU SI.[SÁ *ana* KU]R$^?$ HUL	
8	1 ŠU.SI *na$^?$-bah* x[*x x x x x x*] *na du$^?$*	[8] One finger, the rising of the [......]...
	blank space of 2 lines	
r.1	⸢1⸣ *ina* ITI.GUD MUL.[MUL *x x x x x x x*]	[r.1] If in Iyyar (II) the Pleia[des ......]
2	A.⸢ŠÀ$^?$⸣ [*x x x x x x x x x x x*]	[2] the *field* [......]
3	1 ⸢*x x*⸣ [*x x x x x x x x x x*]	(Break)
	about 6 lines broken away	
10e	*šá* ^{md}U.GUR–⸢KAR-*ir*⸣	[10] From Nergal-eṭir.

266. New Moon on 1st Day

	K 5723 + K 13012	RMA 56A + RMA 277N (= SAA 8 510 + SAA 8 475)
1	1 30 UD-1-KÁM [IGI$^?$ *x x x x x*]	[1] If the moon [*becomes visible*] on the 1st day: [......] a reign of [*long days* ......]
2	*pa-le-*⸢*e*⸣ [*x x x x x x x x*]	
3	GÌR.2 ⸢*šá$^?$*⸣ [*x x x x x x x*]	[3] The feet *of* [......]
4	⸢*x x x x x x x*⸣ [*x x x x x*]	[4] ...... [......]
5	[*x x x*] *ina* SU *šá* LUGAL [*x x x x*]	[5] [...] in the body of the king [...]
6	[*x x x*]-*ti* ŠÀ-*bi x* [*x x x x*]	[6] [...] *the mood of* [...]
7	[*x x i-s*]*in-ni ma-la ina* [*x x x*]	[7] [...] *any* [fes]tival in [...]
8	[*x x x*] LUGAL [*x x x x x*]	[8] [...] the king [...]
9	[*x x x*] KUR–MAR.TU.[KI *x x x x*]	[9] [...] the Westland [...]
Rev.	2 lines uninscribed	
1	*šá* $^{md+}$EN–*x*[*x x x*]	[r.1] From Bel-[...].

[7] The interpretation at the end seems a commonplace. Alternatively, e.g., [*ana* LUGAL N]U$^?$ HUL (cf. line 2), "[no]t bad [for the king]"; HUL in the final position could also mean that it should behave like a verb (cf. SAA 8 502:14) and not like a noun or an adjective (as it regularly does in this corpus). [r.1] Cf. SAA 8 275:6, also by Nergal-eṭir.

266 Despite K 5723 joining K 13012, many readings of this originally small tablet are still unknown.

267. Tablet of Urdu (798-VII-20)

Th 1905-4-9,257 (BM 98751)

beginning broken away

1′ [*x x x x*]-*bi-ti ul-lu-ti*
2′ [*x x x x*-*ṭ*]*u*$^{?}$-*ti ul-lu-ti*
3′ [*x x x x*]*x*-*a-ti ul-la-ti*
4′ [*x x x mu-d*]*e-e a-ma-ti ina* KUR *a-šib*
5′ [*x x* ^{m}*x*]*x*-*zi*–MU–PAB DUMU-*šú i-še-er*
6′ [*x x x x*]*x a-ba-at*
7′ [*x x x x*]-*ma* AN.MI 30 IGI
8′ [*x x x x x x x x x*]-*qa*$^{?}$-*bu*
9′ [*x x x x x x x x i*]-*paṭ-ṭar*
10′ [*x x x x x x x x x*] ⌜*x*⌝ [*x*]

r.1 [*x x x x x x x x x*] ⌜*x*⌝-*šú*$^{?}$
2 [*x x x x x x x x x*] SAG
3 [*x x x x x x x x x*]*x*-*at*
4 [*x x x x*]-*tú at-ta qa*-BE
5 [*x x x x*]*x*-*bar i-dam-mi*
6 [*x x x x*] *ki-ma la-a*
7 [*x x x x*] *li-hi-ir*
8 [*x x x x*] *li-hi-ir*

---

9 [*ṭup-p*]*i* ^{m}*ur-di* LÚ.A.BA [0]
10 [ITI].DU$_{6}$! UD-20-KÁM *lim-me* ^{m}*mu-tak-kil*–^{d}AMAR.UTU

ABL 1406

(Beginning destroyed)

1 [...] former [...]...
2 [...] former [...]...*s*
3 [...] former [...]...s
4 [...... educa]ted in matters, living in the land,
5 [......]*zi*-šumu-uṣur, his son, will *prosper*.
6 [......] the word of
7 [......] *and* the lunar eclipse *was* seen.
8 [...... ...]...
9 [...... will] *release*

r.1 [......]
2 [......] head
3 [......]...
4 [......] you ...
5 [......] ... has *convulsions*
6 [......] if not,
7 may [...] choose [...],
8 may [...] choose [...].

---

9 [Table]t of Urdu, scribe. [Month] of Tishri (VII), 20th day, eponym year of Mutakkil-Marduk (798).

268. Fragment of a Report

Bu 91-5-9,236

beginning broken away

1′ [*x x x x* G]AL.M[EŠ$^{?}$ *x x x x x*]

2′ [*x x x x*]*x* ŠUR ^{d}É.⌜A$^{?}$⌝ [*x x x x x*]
3′ [*x x x x*]*x*-*ú iš*-*x*[*x x x x x*]

4′ [*x x x* S]I.SÁ-*ma kit-tú u* [*mi-šá-ru ina* KUR-*šú* GÁL$^{?}$]

CT 54 575

(Beginning destroyed)

1 [...*g*]*reat* [...*s* ...]

---

2 [...] ... E*a* [...]
3 [...] ... [...]
4 [... will p]rosper, and [*there will be*] truth and [*justice in the land*].

---

267 Unfortunately, the fragmentary tablet does not provide any context, but it is worth publishing because it dates from the reign of Adad-nerari III, which is under-represented among the finds of the NA period. 1 For *ul-lu-ti*, especially its occurrences with a singular *ūm*(*u*), see CAD U&W 83b. 8, r.4 It is difficult to know whether (-)*qa*$^{?}$-*bu* and *qa*-BE are related to *qabû* "to say" or not. r.2 Or, "the beginning". r.7-8 The spacing of these lines suggests that there were not many signs, perhaps only three, before *li-hi-ir*. Waterman (RCAE 2 482f) took it as *li-ṭí-ir* "let him spare". r.10 Mutakkil-Marduk, and not, e.g., Mutakkil-Aššur, see the references given in PNA 2/II 784a s.v. Mutakkil-Marduk, no. 2c.

268 2 ŠUR may represent a form of *zanānu*, but the preceding sign is not a good AN. 4 For the restoration, see, e.g., SAA 8 364 r.3.

5′ [x x x x] ⌜x x x⌝ [x x x x]
rest broken away

(Rest destroyed)

269. Fragment of a Report(?)

K 14657
beginning broken away
1′ [x x x] ⌜x⌝ [x x x x]
2′ [x x x] ⌜x x⌝ [x x x x]
3′ [x x x] ⌜x x⌝ [x x x x]
4′ [x x]x *ma?-a’-diš* [x x x x]
e.5′ [x x]x ⌜x x⌝ [x x x x]
r.1 ⌜É⌝ *š[á]-ru-ru na-[šú-ú?* x x]
2 *[ṭ]ùl-lum-ma-a’* x[x x x x]
3 *a-na be-lí-ia* ŠÀ-*bi* [x x x x]
4 ⌜x x⌝ *da* x[x x x x x]
rest broken away

CT 54 276
(Beginning destroyed)
4 [...] *very* [...]
5 [......]
r.1 *when it car[ries]* r[ad]iance [...] *is* [t]reacherous [...]
3 to my lord. *Mood* [...]
(Rest destroyed or too broken for translation)

270. Fragment Referring to the Stylus and Written Objects

K 11974
1 GI–*ṭup-pu* x[x x x
2 SIG₅-*iq* x[x x x
3 *še-bil-áš-*⌜*šú*⌝ [x x
4 *lu-sa-an-[niq* x x
5 *šaṭ-ṭar-*⌜*a*⌝*-[ni* x x x
6 *ú-[*x x x x
7 x[x x x x x
rest broken away
Rev. broken away

K 11974
1 Stylus [......]
2 is good [......]
3 send *it to* him [......
4 *I shall che[ck it out* ......]
5 are written [......]
(Rest destroyed)

269 4 But Dietrich's copy has *lu*, not *ma*. r.1 This line suggests that the fragment belongs to an astrological report. r.2 CAD Š/3 262a interprets the word here as *šulummû* "recovery(?)".

270 See copy p. 294. In fragments like this, there is a thin line between a(n anonymous) letter and a report. Thus, this fragment may be relevant to SAA 8 or SAA 10.

FIG. 31. *Magical clay figurine from South-West Palace, Nineveh.*
BM 124296.

271. Two Clay Figurines for a Ritual

K 1293

1 *ṣa-lam* LÚ.ÚŠ *šá* IM
2 TÚG SA5 TÚG.*til-le-e-šú*

3 MU4.MU4-*su* NU GIDIM *lem-nu*
4 *šá* IM TÚG UD-1-KÁM
5 *tu-*[*lab-ba-as*$^?$*-s*]*u*$^?$
6 *ṣu-de-*⌜*e*⌝
7 *ha-ṣi-in* URUDU
8 3 GÍN A.BÁR 3 GÍN URUDU

ABL 461

1 You shall clothe a clay figurine of a dead person with a red garment (and) its (appropriate) *equipment*.

3 You [shall *don*] an evil ghost's clay figurine with a garment for one day.

6 (*You provide them*$^?$ *with*) provisions, an *axe* of copper, 3 shekels of lead, 3 shekels of

271 Previous edition: Scurlock Magico-Medical Means p. 540f. (No. 230). According to her (ibid. p. 111, n.370), "No. 230 is not a set of instructions for the performance of a ritual, but a list of paraphernalia necessary for the performance of a ritual". 4 For the reading UD-1-KÁM, see CAD U&W 93f. s.v. *ūmakkal*.

9 4 ŠE KUG.UD

---

10 NU GIDIM *šá* ZÍD ŠE.IN.NU
11 *u* KÀŠ ANŠE

r.1 URUDU.ŠEN.TUR *šá* 7 GÍN
2 *ka-tam-mi* URUDU

---

rest uninscribed

copper, 4 grains of silver.

---

10 A figurine of a ghost (made) of *flour*, straw and donkey's urine.

r.1 A *tangussu*-pot, (weighing) 7 shekels (with) a copper lid.

---

272. Fragment Referring to Stones

K 5805
Obv. broken away
Rev. beginning broken away
1′ [*x x*]*x x*[*x x x x*]
2′ [*x* I]GI.2.ME[Š *x x x*]
3′ [*x* I]GI.2.MEŠ *ta-*[*x x x*]
4′ [*x*] 14 NITA ⸢*ù*⸣ [*x x x*]
5′ [N]A4.*hal-ta* [*x x x*]
6′ [*x*] ⸢*bar*?⸣*-te x*[*x x x*]
rest broken away

CT 54 168
(Beginning destroyed)

r.2 [e]ye-[*stone*]s [...]
3 you [... e]ye-[*stone*]s
4 [...] 14 male and [*female* ...]
5 *haltu*-stone [...]
6 [...] *rebellion* [...]
(Rest destroyed)

273. Fragment of a Ritual

K 7365
beginning broken away
r.1′ [*x x x x*] ⸢AN *x id*?⸣ *l*[*a-x x x x x x*]
2′ [*x x x i*]*ṭ-ṭah-ha-*⸢*an-ni*⸣ [*x x x x x x*]
3′ [*x x x x*]*-ti* DÙ*-ni-ni x*[*x x x x x x*]

4′ [*x x x x*].MEŠ *tu-rab-ba* LUGAL [*x x x x*]
5′ [*x x x x* K]UŠ MÍ.ÁŠ.QAR*-ma a-n*[*a x x x*]
6′ [*x x x x*] *nad-na ina* ŠU.2*-šú x*[*x x x x*]
7′ [*x x x*] ŠÀ GIŠ.ŠÚ.NAGA Ú.IN.N[U].U[Š *x x x*]
8′ [*x x x*]*x* MÍ.ÁŠ.QAR A.MEŠ–ŠU.[2 *x x x*]

CT 54 181
(Beginning destroyed)

r.2 [... *it*] came close to me [......]
3 [...] performed [*evi*]*l* [...] against me [...].

---

4 You *raise* [the ...]s, the king [...]
5 [... the s]kin of the same female kid *t*[*o* ...]
6 [...] were given, in his hands [...]
7 [... *i*]*n a wooden bath, maštakal*-soap-w[or]t [...]
8 [...] a female kid, the wash water of hand[s ...].

---

[9] Cf. SAA 10 296 r.10. [10] Or, read ŠÈ, "excrement", as by Scurlock, instead of ZÍD "flour". [r.1-2] CAD K 298a.

272 The tablet probably contained ritual instructions. [r.2f] Perhaps read [NA4.I]GI.MEŠ as, e.g., in SAA 10 348:11. Alternatively, the 'eyes' may be preceded by a number. [r.6] The interpretation is highly conjectural.

273 This fragment may be part of a war ritual (cf. r.12). [r.1-3] This section seems to deal with threats, probably against the king. DÙ*-ni-ni* may stand for *ē*/*īpušūninni*. The preceding word ending in *-ti*, e.g., may be the end of *lemutti*, *lemnūti* or *lemnēti*. [r.2] Alternatively, read *t*]*ú-ṭah-ha-*⸢*an-ni*⸣, as the use of *ṭah* may suggest a D stem form. [r.8] Perhaps only 1 MÍ.ÁŠ.QAR, rather than, e.g., UD]U.MÍ.ÁŠ.QAR (cf. r.5). Water for a hand-washing (rite), possibly with a personal suffix.

9′ [*x x x*]*-i-bi* [*x x x x x x*]
10′ [*x x x*]*-is* UGU KUŠ [*x x x x x x x*]
11′ [*x x x x*]*x-ri-ia šá* K[I? *x x x*]
12′ [*x x x x x*]*x ina* KUR–*na-ki-r*[*i x x x*]
13′ [*x x x x x*]*x* UZU MÍ.ÁŠ.QA[R *x x x*]
14′ [*x x x x x* P]I?.2 GAR-*an* [*x x x x*]
15′ [*x x x x x x*]*x* ⸢*gab*?⸣ *x*[*x x x x*]
16′ [*x x x x x x x x*]*x x*[*x x x x*]
rest broken away

9 [...]... [......]
10 [...]... on the skin [......]
11 [...] my [...]... which/who [...]
12 [......] in the enemy country [...]
13 [......] the meat of the female ki[d ...]
14 *you* place [...... *ea*]rs [...]
(Rest destroyed or too broken for translation)

274. Fragment Listing Plants

K 16132
beginning broken away
1′ [*x x x x x x x*]*x*[*x*]
2′ [*x x x x x*] ⸢Ú?.ŠEŠ⸣
3′ [*x x x x*]*x* ⸢ŠEM⸣.[*x*]*x* ⸢*nab bil an*?⸣
4′ [*x x x-t*]*u* Ú.*ha-šá-nu*
5′ [*x x x x x*] Ú.*qul-qul-la-nu*
6′ [*x x x x x*]*x-ti*
7′ [*x x x x x x*] ⸢*x x*⸣
rest broken away
Rev. beginning broken away
1′ [*x x x x x x*] ⸢*x*⸣
2′ [*x x x x x x*]*-te is me*
3′ [*x x x x x x*]-⸢*da*?⸣*-ak*
4′ [*x x x x x x*]*x tab-ku*
5′ [*x x x x x x*]
6′ [*x x x x x x x*]*-mar*
7′ [*x x x x x x x x*] *šá*
rest broken away

CT 54 363
(Beginning destroyed)

2 [......] myrrh,
3 [...] *aromatic plant* ...,
4 [...] thyme,
5 [......] *cassia*,
(Break)

r.4 [......] *stored grain*
(Rest destroyed)

r.9 *rību* "earthquake" cannot be excluded in this context. r.12 This line may indicate the purpose of the ritual. r.14 Or, e.g., "*you* pay [att]ention [to]".

274 This fragment lists plants and may not be a letter.

THE BRITISH MUSEUM

0 cm 1 2 3 4 5 10

9. Legal Transactions of the Royal Court of Nineveh
Additions to SAA VI and XIV

FIG. 32. *BM Rm 157 = Text 275.*

275. Ubaru Buys a Man (679-VIII-6)

Rm 157

1 NA4.KIŠIB ^{m}*gi-ru*–^{d}IM *be-lí* LÚ SUM-*nu*

2 ^{m}*ú*-PA-*ru it-ti* ^{m}*gi-ru*–^{d}IM
3 *ma-hi-ru i-pu-uš-ma* 5/6 MA.NA KUG.UD
4 *i-hi-iṭ-ma* ŠÁM ^{m}*a-a*–*i-da-a*
5 *a-na* ^{m}*gi-ru*–^{d}IM *id-din* KUG.UD *na-din*
6 ^{m}*a-a*–*i-da-*⸢*a za*⸣*-rip tur-ru u da-ba-bu*
7 *ia-a-a'-nu man-nu šá ina* EGIR.MÉŠ UD.MÉŠ
8 *lu-u* ŠEŠ-*šú lu-u* LÚ.*mam-ma-nu-šú*
9 ⸢*lu*⸣*-u* LÚ.*šá-kin*$^{[i]n}$-*šú šá* DUL$^{?}$.DU-*ma*
e.10 *a-na* UGU ^{m}⸢*a*⸣*-a*–*i-da-a i-da-bu-bu*
11 ⸢*sa*$^{?}$*-ri-it*⸣ 1 MA.NA 1/3 GÍN KUG.UD
r.1 ⸢*a-na*⸣ ^{m}*ú*-PA-*ru i-nam-din*

2 IGI ^{m}*am-bi-iá* $^{md+}$AG–*ú-še-*⸢*zib*⸣
3 IGI ^{m}SUM-*i*[*á*] ^{m}*za-ba-a-a*
4 IGI ^{m}*bi-*⸢*bé*⸣*-e-a* ^{m}*na-bu-ut-*⸢*te*$^{?}$⸣
5 IGI ^{m}*su*$^{?}$*-li-iá* ^{md}IM–DÙ-⸢*uš*⸣
6 IGI ^{md}EN–DÙ-*uš* LÚ.A.BA
7 ITI.APIN UD-6-KÁM* MU-2
8 ^{d}*aš-šur*(–PAB–AŠ) LUGAL KUR–*aš-šur*
9 IGI $^{md+}$AG–AŠ–PAB
eleven fingernail impressions

Fs. Kessler, p. 237

1 Seal of Gir-Adda, owner of the man being sold.

2 Ubaru settled the purchase price with Gir-Adda and weighed out 5/6 minas of silver, the price of Aya-idâ, and gave it to Gir-Adda. The *money* is paid. Aya-idâ is purchased. Any revocation or litigation is void.
7 Whoever in the future, whether his (= Gir-Adda's) brother or a relative of his or his prefect, comes forward and speaks against (the sale of) Aya-idâ, shall pay a *fine* of one mina and 1/3 shekels of silver to Ubaru.

r. 2 Witness(es) Ambiya, Nabû-ušezib,
3 Witness(es) Iddin-Ay[a], Zabaya,
4 Witness(es) Bibiya, Nabutu,
5 Witness(es) Suliya, Adad-epuš,
6 Witness Bel-epuš, scribe.
7 Month Marchesvan (VIII), 6th day, year 2 of Esar(haddon), the king of Assyria.
9 Witness Nabû-nadin-ahi.

276. Ubaru Buys a Woman (680-V-26)

K 3790

1 NA4.KIŠIB ^{m}*man-nu*–*ki*–ŠEŠ
2 *be-lí* MÍ *a-mil-ti* SUM-*nu*

(four fingernail impressions)

3 ½ MA.NA KUG.UD ^{m}*ú-bar-ru*
4 *i-hi-iṭ-ma* ŠÁM MÍ.*ši-i*–*dan-na-ti*
5 *a-na* ^{m}*man-nu*–*ki*–PAB SUM-⸢*in*⸣
6 [KUG.U]D ⸢*na*⸣*-din* M[Í.*ši-i*–*dan-na-ti*$^{?}$]

Fs. Kessler, p. 241

1 Seal of Mannu-ki-ahi, owner of the woman being sold.

(four fingernail impressions)

3 Ubaru weighed out half a mina of silver and gave the price of Ši-dannat to Mannu-ki-ahi. [The *money*] is paid. [Ši-dannat *is purchased*.]

275 Previous edition: Luukko and Van Buylaere, Fs. Kessler (2018) 236-40.
276 Previous edition: Luukko and Van Buylaere, Fs. Kessler (2018) 240-43.

	rest broken away	(Break)
Rev.	beginning broken away	
1′	*[x x] x [x x x x x] x*	r.1 (too fragmentary for translation)
2′	*[x x] x su [x] x [x x]*	
3′	*[i-na$^{?}$ ka-n]ak$^{?}$* DUB MU-⸢*tim*$^{?}$⸣	3 [(*Present*) *at the sea*]*ling of this document*:
4′	[IGI ^{m}*am-bi-iá*$^{?}$ ^{m}]⸢^{d}PA⸣–*ú-še-zib*	4 [Witness(es) *Ambiya*], Nabû-ušezib,
5′	I[GI ^{m}*x x*] *x* ^{m}*ab-da-ba-a-ni*	5 Wi[tness(es) ...], Abdabani,
6′	I[GI ^{m}*x*] *x x x* ^{md}30–*ia-a-bi*	6 Wi[tness(es) ...]..., Sîn-yabi,
7′	⸢IGI⸣ [^{m}*x x*] *x* ⸢^{md}PA$^{?}$⸣–*da-la-a*	7 Witness(es) [...], *Nabû*-dalâ,
8′	⸢IGI⸣ [^{m}]*x x x* ^{m}⸢*dan*⸣-*na-a-a*	8 Witness(es) ..., Dannaya and the scribe, writer of the document, Amel-Nabû.
9′	*ù* LÚ.A.BA *šá-ṭir ú-ìl-ti*	
10e	^{m}LÚ–^{d}PA ITI.NE UD-26-KÁM*	10 Month Abu (V), 26th day, year 1 (680) of Esarhaddon, king of Assyria.
11e	MU-1 ^{d}*aš-šur*–PAB–AŠ	
12e	LUGAL KUR–^{d}*aš-šur*.KI	
s.1	*[x x x]* ⸢*x*⸣ *x la*	s.1 [...] ....

277. *Ubaru* Buys a Man

Rm 162		Fs. Kessler, p. 244
1	[NA4.KIŠI]B$^{?}$ ^{m}*la–tu-ba-áš*-⸢*šá*⸣-*n*[*i* (*x x*)]	1 [*Sea*]*l* of La-tubašan[ni], [owner] of the man being sold.
2	[*be-lí*$^{?}$] LÚ *a-me-lu* SUM-*nu*	
	(six fingernail impressions)	(six fingernail impressions)
3	[*x x x* ^{m}*rém*$^{?}$]-⸢*a*⸣-*ni*–DINGIR.MEŠ *a-na* ^{m}⸢*ú*⸣-*bar-ru*	3 [... *Rem*]*anni*-ilani to Ubaru
4	*[x x x x x] x–eri*$^{!}$*-ba* KUG.UD ⸢*x x x*⸣	4 [...]-eriba silver ...
5	*[x x x x x]x ur* ⸢m⸣[*ú*$^{?}$*-bar*$^{?}$]-⸢*ru*⸣	(Break)
6	*[x x x x x]* ⸢*x x x*⸣ *[x x x x]*	
	rest broken away	
Rev.	beginning broken away	
1′	*[x x x x x x x]* ⸢*x x*⸣ *[x x x]*	
2′	*[x x x x x x x* ^{m}*ú]-bar-ru* ⸢*x x*⸣	r.2 [...U]baru ...
3′	*[x x x x x x x] ú šad* ⸢*x x*⸣	3 [......] ......
4′	[*i-na ka-nak*$^{?}$] DUB MU-*a-ti*	4 [(*Present*) *at the sealing of*] this document:
5′	[IGI$^{?}$ *x x x x x*]*x lu ki*$^{?}$ LÚ.DUMU–SIG5	5 [*Witness*(*es*) ...] ..., chariot fighter,
6′	*[x x x x x x x]*–AŠ$^{?}$ LÚ ⸢ARAD$^{?}$⸣ LUGAL	6 [......]-*iddina, servant of* the king,
7′	*[x x x x x x x i]q*$^{?}$*-bi ta*$^{?}$ ⸢*na x x is*$^{?}$⸣	7 [......] ......
8′	rest broken away	(Rest destroyed)

277 Previous edition: Luukko and Van Buylaere, Fs. Kessler (2018) 243-45.

278. Fragment with an Eponym Date (678)

K 14583

1 [*x x x*]*x* ⌜*ki la*⌝ [*x x x*]
rest broken away
Rev. beginning broken away
1′ [ITI.*x* UD-*x*]1-⌜KÁM⌝
2′ [*lim-mu* ^{md}U.GUR]–MAN–PAB LÚ*.GAL–KAŠ.LU[L]

CT 53 531

(Beginning destroyed)

r.2 [Eponym year of Nergal]-šarru-uṣur, chief cupbeare[r].

279. Crimes in Nuhub

K 1078

1 *a-bat* LUGAL *ina* UGU-*hi* ^{m}*aš-šur*-PAB
2 ARAD *šá* LÚ*.GAL.KUR URU.*nu-hu-ba-a-a*
3 *ša* ŠU.2 ^{m}*qu-u-a* LÚ*.*šá–ziq*[!]-*ni*

4 ^{m}*ez-bu* ARAD *šá* LÚ.GAL–A.BA
5 *ina* IGI-*šú* UDU.MEŠ-*šu i-ra-ʾa*
6 UDU.MEŠ-*šu* LÚ.GAR.KUR *it-ti-ši*

7 *šu-ú da-a-ni mi-ha-ar-šú*[!]
8 *ú-se-ri-bi ina* É-*šú i-ṣa-bat*
9 NÍG.GUB *ša* SIG4.MEŠ *i-sa-kan-šú*

10 GIŠ.*ha-ṭu* ⌜*x x*⌝ [*x x*]*x*-⌜*ka*[?]⌝
11 ^{m}SUHUŠ–URU.[ŠÀ–URU[?] *x x x x x*]
12 *i-si*-[*x x x x x x x*]
rest broken away

Rev. beginning broken away
1′ ŠE *x*[*x x x x x x x x*]
2′ *ina* ŠÀ-*bi* [*x x x x x x*]
3′ *ik-ta-r*[*a-ar x x x ma-a*[?]]

4′ *mu-ki-nu-te-šú* [*ina* IGI]
5′ LUGAL *šup*[!]-*ra mu-ki-nu*
6′ *ša is-si-šú ú-kan-nu-ni*
7′ ^{m}*bé-su-a-a* URU.ŠÀ–URU-*iá*
8′ *ba-ti-qu-šú a-ki* MAN
9′ *iq-bu-u-ni i-ki-bu-su-ni*

10′ ^{md}UTU–AD–PAB URU.*nu-uh-ba-iá*
11′ A.ŠÀ *šá* ^{m}U.GUR–MAŠ *ip-tu-ga*

12′ ^{m}U.GUR–MAŠ *ma-a a-ta-a*
13e A.ŠÀ *ta-pu-ga-ni*

ABL 307

1 A ‘king’s word’ concerning Aššur-naṣir, a servant of the prefect of the Nuhubeans, in custody of Quia, a bearded courtier.
4 Ezbu, a servant of the chief scribe, was shepherding his sheep in his presence, (when) the prefect took away his sheep.
7 He made his equal enter into his house by force and imprisoned (him there), setting up for him the builder’s hod.
10 *A* (*shepherd’s*) *staff* … […]…
11 Ubru-[*Libbali* ……]
12 … [……]
(Break)

r.1 *grain* [……]
2 there [……]
3 he thr[ew … and said]:
4 “Send his witnesses [into the presence of] the king!”
5 The witness, who testified with him, was Bessu’aya, a man from Assur, his informer, when he mentioned the king and trod (*the field*).
10 Šamaš-abu-uṣur, a Nuhubean, took by force the field of Nergal-ašared.
12 Nergal-ašared said: “Why did you appropriate my field?

279 It is difficult to determine whether this carefully crafted tablet is a real court order or simply a memorandum based on geography (in this case, Nuhub). Seven people are mentioned by name, the two most important by profession being the prefect of the Nuhubeans and the chief scribe. CAD quotes many lines of this difficult text with varying degrees of success. [2] LÚ*.GAR.KUR GN + a nisbe is a rare form, while LÚ*.GAR.KUR GN usually means “governor of GN”. [3, 7, r.5, s.2] See coll. [9] Or as in CAD K 496b: “he imposed the brick basket upon him”. [12] *i-si-*… may be a verbal form in the perfect tense or a preposition, *issi* “with”, with a suffix. [r.1] Possibly ŠE.NU[MUN “seed(s); sown field(s)”. [r.2] Or, e.g., “in/from/with”.

14e *ma-a ha-du-a-a*
15e *i-ka-bu-su*
s.1 *ma-a a-lik* 7-*šú* MAN *ina* UGU-*hi-iá m*[*u-hur*]
2 DUG$_4$.DUG$_4$ *an-ni-u* MAN *lu-ka-ni* LÚ*$^{!}$.[*x* (*x*)]

[14] He said: "They tread it at my pleasure! Go and ap[peal] to the king seven times because of me!" Let the king settle this case.

s.2 The [...].

280. Assurbanipal Clears Nabû-le'i of Charges Concerning His Status

BM 29391 (98-11-14,24)

1 [LÚ.GAL$^{?}$.MEŠ] ⌈*šá*⌉ AN.ŠÁR–DÙ–DUMU.UŠ LUGAL KUR–*aš-šur*.KI
2 [*šá ina*] GUB.BA-*šú-nu* $^{md+}$AG–DA *it-ti* ^{m}*šu-la-*⌈*a*⌉
3 ⌈*ù*⌉ $^{md+}$AG–SUM-*na di-i-ni id-bu-bu-ú-ma* (^{m})$^{d+}$AG–DA
4 [*i*]*z-ka-a u* LUGAL KUR–*aš-šur*.KI *ki-i pi-i an-ni-i*
5 [*d*]*i-i-ni ip-ru-su um-ma* $^{md+}$AG–DA ^{m}*za-kir* AD-*šú*
6 [*u*]*r-tab-biš u a-na* É.ZI.DA *ug-dal-lib-šú*
7 [^{m}]$^{d+}$AG–SUM-*na ul i-di* [[*x*]] MU-*šú ul iš-kun*
8 *ù a-na* DUMU *ul ú-tir-šú* ^{m}*šu-la-a u* $^{md+}$AG–S[UM-*na*]
9 [*ul*$^{?}$ *i*]*-tu-ru-nim-ma* $^{md+}$AG–SUM-*na a-na* AD-*šú* ⌈*x*(*x*)⌉
10 [*ta-a*$^{?}$]*-ri ù* LUGAL KUR–*aš-šur*.KI *i-qab-bi*
11 [*um-ma mi*]*m*$^{?}$-⌈*ma*⌉ *id-di-nu na-din*
12 [*x x x x*] URU *u* EDIN *ma-la ba-*[*šu-ú*]
r.1 [^{m}*za-kir a-n*]*a* DUMU-*šú ra-bi-i id-di-*[*nu*]

---

2 [*ina* IGI ^{m}*sa-si*]*-ia* LÚ.*ha-za-an šá* URU.*ni-ná-*⌈*a*⌉
3 [*ina* IGI ^{md}*x*–Š]EŠ.MEŠ–*šul-lim* LÚ.DUB.SAR ⌈*x x x*⌉
4 [*ina* IGI ^{m}]⌈^{d}⌉UTU–*ba-la-ṭu šá–pa-an–*É.GA[L]
5 *ina* [IGI ^{m}]^{d}AMAR.UTU–SU LÚ.PA *šá* LÚ.UMBISAG *ar-ma-a*

BM 29391 (98-11-14,24)

[1] [The *magnates*] of Assurbanipal, king of Assyria, [in whose] presence Nabû-le'i litigated against Šulâ and Nabû-iddina, and (in whose presence) Nabû-le'i was cleared.

[4] Furthermore, the king of Assyria decided the case as follows: His father Zakir raised Nabû-le'i and consecrated him at the Ezida temple. He did not know Nabû-iddina, did not recognize him as heir, and he did not make him into a son. Šulâ and Nabû-id[dina will not c]ome back (to litigate) and Nabû-iddina [will *return*] to his father.

[10] And the king of Assyria says: [*wh*]*atever* he gave is given, any [*property* in] city and countryside, that [Zakir] gave [t]o his eldest son.

---

r.2 [Before Sasi]ya, the mayor of Nineveh.

[3] [Before DN-a]hhe-šullim, ... scribe.

[4] [Before] Šamaš-balaṭu, palace supervisor.

[5] [Before] Marduk-eriba, overseer of the Aramaic scribe(s).

s.2 The profession mentioned at the end is a mystery, but it may have something to do with who wrote this tablet.

280 Previous edition: Waerzeggers Ezida 681f. 1, r.15 As the personnel of the witness list is quite variable, it is not certain that the word broken off is *rabûti* "magnates"; it could also be *rabrabāni* "the high-ranking officers". However, it should then be read [LÚ.GAL.GAL.MEŠ], for which there is not enough space. 7 Literally: "he did not place his name". 8 Or: "he did not turn him into a son". r.2 Known as Sasî in the NA sources. r.3 Most likely Nabû-ahhe-šullim, although none of the individuals listed in PNA 2/II 798a. End probably contains a specifying scribal definition. r.5 This Marduk-eriba is almost certainly the same individual who is also known as the palace scribe in the reign of Assurbanipal; see Luukko, SAAS 16 (2007) 246 (n.127), 249 (n.149) and 253. As far as we know, the professional title mentioned here is not known from the Assyrian sources.

6 *ina* IGI ^{m}KI.NE.NE-*a-a* LÚ.EN.NAM *šá* É–*eš-š*[*ú*]
7 *ina* IGI ^{md}AMAR.UTU–MU–ŠEŠ GAL–LÚ.HAL
8 *ina* IGI ^{m}*na-ṣi-ru* LÚ.HAL
9 *ina* IGI ^{m}*a-qar-a* LÚ.HAL
10 *ina* IGI ^{m}TIN.TIR.KI-*a-a* LÚ.SAG LÚ.DUB.SAR *šá* LUGAL TIN.TIR.KI
11 *ina* IGI $^{md+}$AG–GÁL-*ši* LÚ.HAL
12 *ina* IGI ^{m}TUK-*ši*–DINGIR LÚ.DUB.SAR
13 [*ina*] IGI ^{md}U.⸢GUR$^{?}$⸣–KAR-*ir* LÚ.DUB.SAR
14 [*ina* IGI] ^{m}*ú-bar-ru*–^{d}7.BI LÚ.DAM.QAR–LUGAL PAB *an*-⸢*nu-tu*⸣
15 [LÚ.GAL$^{?}$].MEŠ *šá* LUGAL KUR–*aš-šur*.KI ⸢*šá* $^{md+}$AG–DA *ina pa-ni-šú-nu*⸣ [*it-ti*]
16 [^{m}*šu-la-a*] *u* $^{md+}$AG–MU *id-bu*-⸢*bu-ú*⸣-*ma iz-ka*-⸢*a*⸣

6 Before Kanunayu, governor of the New Palace.
7 Before Marduk-šumu-uṣur, chief diviner.
8 Before Naṣiru, diviner.
9 Before Aqara, diviner.
10 Before the eunuch Babilayu, scribe of the king of Babylon.
11 Before Nabû-ušebsi, diviner.
12 Before Raši-ili, scribe.
13 Before *Nergal*-eṭir, scribe.
14 [Before] Ubar-Sebetti, royal merchant – all these are [*the magnates*] of the king of Assyria in whose presence Nabû-le'i litigated [against Šulâ] and Nabû-iddina, and (in whose presence) Nabû-le'i was cleared.

281. Mistreated by Bel-iddina and Amel-Šamaš

K 838
1 7 GUD.MEŠ
2 3 ANŠE.NITÁ.MEŠ
3 *ina* URU.*ku-tú-li*
4 *ha-ab-la-ku*
5 4 GUD.MEŠ
6 *ina* URU.*de-ri*
7 ^{m}LÚ–^{d}*šá-maš*
8 *ih-tab-la-ni*
9 1 GUD | *ina* ŠÀ 30 ANŠE.EDIN.ME[Š]
10 *i-ti-ši*
11 *la i-di-na*
12 1 LÚ.TUR *ku-um*!
13 *ig-ri ša* ANŠ[E (*x*)]
14 *i-ta*$^{?}$-⸢*na*$^{?}$⸣ [0$^{?}$]
15 [^{m}]EN–⸢MAŠ$^{?}$⸣ PAB$^{?}$ [*x x*]
16 ⸢*ina*⸣ *kás-pi i-ti-d*[*in*]
r.1 2 LÚ.T[UR$^{?}$.MEŠ-*ia*]
2 ^{m}EN–AŠ ⸢*i*⸣-*t*[*i-ši*]

ABL 449
1 I was deprived of 7 oxen (and) 3 donkeys in Kutullu. In Der, Amel-Šamaš took away from me *by force* 4 oxen. He (also) took one ox for 30 wild-asses without paying. He has *given me* a young boy instead of the wages *for a donk*[*ey*] and sol[d] Bel-*ašared*, *brother of* [...]. Bel-iddina has tak[en] 2 [of my] *ma*[*nservant*s].

r.6 Since Kanunayu, governor of the New Palace and eponym of 666, is well attested in NA sources (PNA 2/I 602), the NB writing ^{m}KI.NE.NE-*a-a* here obviously corresponds to the common NA ^{m}ITI.AB-*a-a*. r.7 Marduk-šumu-uṣur (PNA 2/II 733f) is one of the better known scholars under Esarhaddon and Assurbanipal. r.8-9 Naṣiru (PNA 2/II 934f) and Aqara (PNA 1/I 121 s.v. both Aqarâ and Aqar-Aia) performed many queries (SAA 4) under Marduk-šumu-uṣur for Esarhaddon and Assurbanipal. r.11 This individual may or may not have been attested in two Babylonian letters (cf. PNA 2/II 901f, nos. 8 and 10). r.12 Two well-attested Babylonian scholars of this name are known; this is probably the younger of the two, son of Nurzanu (PNA 3/I 1035, no. 3). r.13 It would be tempting, though uncertain, to regard *Nergal*-eṭir here as the "Babylonian astrologer of the family Gahal-Marduk" (PNA 2/II 945f) who sent many astrological reports to Esarhaddon, possibly also to Assurbanipal. r.14 Possibly the same person who is also known as "merchant" in Esarhaddon's reign (PNA 3/II 1369a, no. 3 s.v. Ubru-Sebetti).

281 The tablet is probably a court record or a statement for the court. 3 A hapax GN; see Bagg RGTC 7/2/1, p. 358f.
9 After GUD, the tablet has a tall vertical wedge, which Harper did not draw in his ABL copy. 9-11 Alternatively, e.g., "he took one *male* out of 30 wild-asses, but did not give it (back)". 12 See coll. 13 Or: "*for a hom*[*er of grain*]. 15 Presumably the name of the boy in line 12, but the signs are not as legible as in Harper's copy.

3 PAB *an-ni-ú*
4 *ša* ^{m}EN–AŠ
5 *ša* ^{m}LÚ–^{d}*šá-maš*
6 *ih-bi-lu-ni-ni*
rest uninscribed

[r.3] All this is what Bel-iddina and Amel-Šamaš have taken away from me *by force*.

282. – – –

Rm 2,560
beginning broken away
1′ [*x x x x x x x x*]*x-pi*

2′ [*x x x x x*]-*du-na-a-ši*
3′ [*x x x x i*]*t-ta-na-na-ši*
4′ [*x x x x x*]*x ina kas-pi*
5′ [*x x x la i*]*m-ma-gu-ru*
6′ [*ma-a* LÚ*.ARAD.MEŠ$^{?}$]-*ni ša* LUGAL *la ni-laq-qí*

7′ [*x x x* LÚ*.GA]L–URU.HAL.ṢU
8′ [*x x x x x*] *tak-lu*
9′ [*x x x x k*]*as-pi*
rest broken away
Rev. destroyed

CT 53 875
(Beginning destroyed)
[1] [......]...

---

[2] [... ...]... us
[3] [...] has given us
[4] [...] *for* money
[5] [... do not a]gree, [saying]: "We will not *acquire* [the *servant*]s of the king.

---

[7] [... the] fort [comman]der
[8] [......] reliable
[9] [...... m]oney
(Rest destroyed)

282 The purpose of this fragment with rulings is unclear. [1] *ka*]*s-pi* (cf. line 9′) or *ká*]*s-pi* seem to be excluded. [7f.] Cf. SAA 5 204:16-18.

FIG. 33. *Catching a wild ass.*
BM 124882.

283. Fragment of Legal Contract(?)

K 5603

beginning broken away

1′ KUG.UD ⌜*x*⌝ [*x x x x x*]

2′ 4 *u šá* DUMU *x*[*x x x x*]

3′ *ia-a-a'-n*[*u x x x*]

4′ *liš-me lu-ú* [*x x x x*]

e5′ *lu-u* LÚ.SA[G *x x x*]

r.1 *lu-u* LÚ.*šá-kin* [*x x x x*]

2 *mam-ma-nu-šú*? *x*[*x x x x*]

3 *a*-[*n*]*a* UGU-*h*[*i x x x*]

4 [*x x*] *nu* [*x x x x x*]

5 [*x*]*x*[*x x x x x*]

rest broken away

s.1 *ù ba*-[*x x x x x x x*]

2 *x*[*x x x x x x x*]

CT 54 148

(Beginning destroyed)

1 silver [......]

2 4 and *those of* the son *of* [...]

3 there is no [...]

4 let him hear whether [...]

5 or a eunu[ch ...]

r.1 or a prefect [...]

2 *his* relative [......]

3 *against* [...]

(Rest destroyed or too broken for translation)

283 This fragment may be an Assyrian-influenced legal contract and thus an addition to SAA 6 or SAA 14. [1] Perhaps KUG.UD *ina š*[*á x x x x*]. [2] Possibly DUMU ⌜m⌝[*x x x x*].

10. Imperial Administrative Records
Additions to SAA VII and XI

FIG. 34. *Female musicians at Ashurbanipal's court.*
Original Drawings V, 46

284. List of Professions and Promotions

Ki 1904-10-9,30
beginning broken away
1′ [*x x*]*x* ⸢*x x*⸣ [*x*] ⸢*x*⸣
2′ [LÚ].GAL–MU
3′ ⸢LÚ⸣.GAL–ANŠE.*ú-rat*
4′ LÚ.*šá*–IGI–KUR 2-*ú*
5′ 2 LÚ.GAL–⸢*ki*⸣-*ṣir qur*-ZAG
6′ 1 LÚ.:. LÚ.3-*šú*
7′ 6 LÚ.:. LÚ.*rak-su*.MEŠ
8′ 1 ⸢LÚ.2⸣-*u* LÚ.:. *qur*-ZAG
9′ 1 L[Ú.:. L]Ú.GAL–*ú-rat*
10′ [*x* LÚ.:.] *šá* MÍ– É.GAL
rest (4 lines) uninscribed
Rev. beginning broken away
1′ [^{m}*x x x*]-*e-me*
2′ [*a-na* L]Ú.*šá*–IGI–KUR-*ú-ti*
3′ [^{m}]*ah-ú*–*mil-ki*
4′ [*a*]-*na* LÚ.GAL–MU-*ú-ti*
rest uninscribed

RA 17 194
(Beginning destroyed)

2 chief cook;
3 team commander;
4 deputy palace supervisor;
5 2, cohort commander of the bodyguard;
6 1, ditto of 'third man';
7 6, ditto of the recruits;
8 1, deputy, ditto of the bodyguard;
9 1, [ditto of] the team commander;
10 [x, ditto] of the queen
(Break)

r.1 [...]*eme* [for] the position of the palace supervisor.
3 Ahi-milki [f]or the position of the chief cook.

285. List of People, Some with Professions

IM 3202
1 [*x x* ^{m}*k*]*i*?-*rib-tú*–*aš-šur*
2 [*x x* ^{m}]*rém-u-tú*
3 [*x x* ^{m}*m*]*an-nu*–*ki*–15–ZU
4 [*x x* ^{m}*h*]*a*?-*an*–*ṣa-ru-ru* 3.U5
5 [*x x*] ⸢^{m}⸣^{d}ŠÚ–KAM-*eš*
6 [*x x*] ⸢^{m}⸣DINGIR–*ia-di-i'*
7 [*x* ^{m}*x*]-*hi*–*aš-šur*
8 [*x x* ^{m}*x*]*x*–EN–PAB
r.1 [*x x x* ^{m}]*na-ni-i*
2 [*x x x*]–É.ŠÁR A ^{m}I–*aš-šur*
3 [*x x x* SU]M? ^{m}*šam-šá-ni*–DINGIR NINDA
4 [*x x* ^{m}]*aš-šur*–NUMUN–AŠ
5 [*x x* ^{m}]*ki-rib-tú*–*aš-šur*

TIM 11 36
1 [... K]iribtu-Aššur;
2 [...] Remutu;
3 [... M]annu-ki-Issar-le'i;
4 [... H]an-Ṣaruru, 'third man';
5 [...] Marduk-ereš;
6 [...] Il-yadi';
7 [... ...]*hi*-Aššur;
8 [... DN]-belu-uṣur;
r.1 [...] Nanî;
2 [... ...]-Ešarra, son of Na'di-Aššur;
3 [... ...]... Šamšanni-ilu, baker;
4 [...] Aššur-zeru-iddina;
5 [...] Kiribtu-Aššur;

284 Previous edition: Meek, RA 17 194 (copy).
285 See Radner, StAT 1 (1999) 139 on the provenance of the tablet.

6	[*x x*] ^{md}PA-*u-a* SIMUG	6 [...] Nabû'a, smith;
7	[*x*]*x* IGI *u ta šá a šá šá ma*	7 [...] ......

286. Survey of Female Singers, etc.

K 1473 + K 10447 + K 1944a + K 15604

ADD 827 + ADD 914 + ADD 1135 + CT 53 674 (= SAA 7 24+)

1	⸢3!6⸣ *ár-ma-a-*⸢*a*⸣*-*[*te x x x*]	1 36 Aramean [women, ...];
2	15! *ku-sa-a-a-t*[*e x x x*]	2 15 Kushite wom[en, ...];
3	7 *aš-šur-a!-a-te* GÉ[ME.MEŠ-*ši-na*?]	3 7 Assyrian women, m[aids *of theirs*];
4	4 *ši-ih-lu* P[AB *x x* (*x x*)]	4 4 *replacements*; in a[ll ...].
5	[*x*]3 MÍ.*ṣur!-ra-a-a-te* GÉ[ME]	5 [x+]3 Tyrian women (and) a ma[id];
6	[*x* MÍ].⸢*káš!*⸣*-šá-a-a-te* :.	6 [x] Kassite women, ditto;
7	[*x ši-i*]*h-lu* PAB 1⸢5?⸣ [0]	7 [x *repl*]*acement(s)*; in all 1*5*.
8	[*x x x x d*]*a-a-a-te* GÉM[E]	8 [x] women from [...]d (and) a mai[d];
9	[*x* M]Í.KUR.GAR.RA.MEŠ *ši-ih-lu* [0]	9 [x fem]ale Corybantes (and a) *replacement*;
10	⸢3⸣ *ár-pad-da-a-a-te* GÉ[ME]	10 3 women from Arpad (and) a ma[id];
11	1 *ši-ih-lu* PAB 5 2 GÉM[E.MEŠ]	11 1 *replacement*; in all, 5 (*women*), 2 mai[ds];
12	1 MÍ.*as!-d*[*u?-di*]*-tú* [*x x x*]	12 1 woman from Ash*d*[*od*, ...];
13	2 *hat-ta-a-*⸢*a-te?* GÉME⸣ [0?]	13 2 Hittite women (and a) maid.
14	PAB 94 [[*x*]] 4?6 GÉME.MEŠ-⸢*ši!-na!*⸣ [0]	14 In all, 94 (women and) 46 maids of theirs:
15	PAB! *ša* AD-*šú ša* A–MAN PAB 1-*me*-40	15 total, of the father of the crown prince; in all, 140.
	————	————
16	MÍ.*ši-ti–tab!-ni* 2! GÉME.MEŠ :.	16 The woman Šiti-tabni, 2 maids, *ditto*;
17	MÍ.*a-mat–e-mu-ni* 3 ⸢:.⸣	17 the woman Amat-Emuni, 3 ditto.
	————	————
18	8 MÍ.NAR!.GAL	18 8 female chief musicians;
19	3 MÍ.*ár-ma-a-a-te*	19 3 Aramean women;
20	11! MÍ.*hat-ta-a-*⸢*a-te!*⸣	20 11 Hittite women;
21	13 MÍ.*ṣur-ra-*[*a-a-te*]	21 13 Tyrian wo[men];
22	13 MÍ.KUR.GAR.R[A?.MEŠ]	22 13 female Cory[bantes];
23	4 MÍ.SAH?-[*x x x* (*x*)]	23 4 women from *Sah*[...];
e.24	9 MÍ.*kaš-šá-*[*a-a-te*]	24 9 Kassite women;
25	PAB 61 MÍ.NA[R.MEŠ]	25 in all, 61 female music[ians].
r.1	6 MÍ.*láh-hi-nat* [(*x x*)]	r.1 6 temple stewardesses [...];
2	6 MÍ.A.BA.MEŠ *ár-x*[*x x* (*x x*)]	2 6 female ... [...] scribes;

r.7 The final line may include abbreviations, logograms or mistakes, at least its segmentation is puzzling, e.g., IGI-*u* TA*? *šá* A $^{(m?)}$*šá-šá-ma*, "the previous [...] from/with that of the son of ..." would not make too much sense.

286 With a new join (K 15604), this is an updated version of SAA 7 24. 1-3, 5f, 12, 15f, 18, 20, r.3, 6, 8, 10 See coll. 4 The sum is at least 62, but if maids are also counted, then obviously even higher. 5 The number of Tyrian women is something between 3 and 9. 8 and 10 It is difficult to be certain, but is the latter line possibly an erroneous repetition? 14 The total of maids suggests that their number was relatively high for the first three groups (Aramean, Kushite and Assyrian women). For collation, see SAA 7, p. 254a (no. 24:16).

3 ⌜1$^{!}$⌝ MÍ.*an-dar-i-tú*
4 4 MÍ.*du-ra-a-a-te*
5 15 MÍ.SIMUG.MEŠ MÍ.GAR.U.U.MEŠ
6 1 MÍ.ŠU$^{!}$.I PAB 33
7 PAB 1-*me*-94 [[*x*]] 5$^{?}$2 GÉME.MEŠ
8 1$^{!}$ MÍ.*mu-raq*$^{!}$*-qí-tú* 0$^{!}$
9 2 GÉME.MEŠ-*šá*
10 PAB 1-*me*-5$^{!}$6 [*x x x*]

---

11 [*x x x x x x x*]⌜*x*⌝[*x x*]
12 [*x x x x x x x*] *zu* [*x*]
13 [*x x x x x x m*]*a*$^{?}$ *a* [*x*]
break, then uninscribed

3 1 woman-...;
4 4 women from Dor;
5 15 female smiths and stone-borers;
6 1 female barber; in all, 33.
7 Grand total: 194 (women) and 52 maids;
8 (also) 1 female *spice-bread baker*; her 2 maids;
10 in all, 156 [...].

(Rest destroyed or uninscribed)

r.10 Perhaps "156 [*women*]".

FIG. 35. *Sargon's officers at banquet.*
Botta and Flandin, Monument de Ninive I, Pl. 64.

287. Accounts from Ceremonial Banquet

	K 7702 + K 13029 + K 13198 + K 13752 + K 18554	ADD 834 + ADD 837 + ADD 849 + ADD 903 + SAA 7, copy p. 258 (= SAA 7 150 + SAA 7 179)
I	except for ends of two lines, completely destroyed	(Beginning destroyed)
II	upper part broken	
1′	[1] ⸢GAL–*ki*⸣-*ṣir* ⸢KAB⸣	II 1 [*1*], cohort commander of the left;
2′	[1] DIB–PA.MEŠ 3-*šú*.MEŠ :.	2 [*1*], chariot driver(s), 'third men' ditto, permanent;
3′	SAG$^{!}$.UŠ$^{!}$.MEŠ	
4′	⸢1⸣ 2 *qur*-ZAG GÌR.2 DU$_{8}$.MEŠ	4 *1*, 2 bodyguards of the *ša šēpi* guard, of the open-chariotry;
5′	⸢1⸣ DIB–PA A–MAN *ša*$^{!}$ KI-*šú*	5 *1*, chariot driver of the crown prince, (and) *his colleague*(*s*);
6′	[1] ⸢BANŠUR$^{?}$⸣ 2-*u* A–MAN	6 [*1*], second *table* of the crown prince;
7′	[*x* GAL–*ki*]-*ṣir*.MEŠ :.	7 [... coho]rt commanders, ditto;
8′	[0] 2$^{!}$ GIGIR$^{!}$ A–MAN DU$_{8}$.MEŠ :.	8 2, chariot-horse-trainer of the crown prince, of open chariots, ditto;
9′	⸢1⸣ [[*x*]]^{d}⸢*x*⸣–SUM–MU	9 1, *Nabû*-nadin-šumi;
10′	[0] 1 GAL–50.[MEŠ GIŠ$^{?}$].⸢GIGIR$^{!}$⸣.MEŠ	10 1, commanders-of-50 of the chariotry;
11′	[0] ^{d}ŠÚ–[*x x x*]*x*	11 Marduk-[...];
12′	[0] 6 NAR.MEŠ	12 6 singers of [...];
13′	[0] GAL–⸢SAG$^{!}$⸣	13 chief eunuch;
14′	⸢*x*⸣ NAM.MEŠ ⸢*x x-ni*$^{!}$⸣ SAG$^{!}$.MEŠ	14 [...], governors, [...], *eunuchs*;
15′	[0] 1 GAR-*nu*.MEŠ *ša* BAD-HAL	15 1, prefects of the cavalry;
16′	[*x*] ⸢SAG$^{!}$⸣.MEŠ BÙLUG.MEŠ	16 [...] eunuchs, trainees;
17′	[*x*] GAR-*nu*.MEŠ A–MAN	17 [...] prefects of the crown prince;
18′	[*x*] *šá*–IGI–SILA	18 [x], overseers of the streets;
19′	[*x*] GAL$^{!}$–50$^{!}$ 3-*šú*.MEŠ	19 [x], commanders-of-50 of the 'third men';
	slight space	
20′	[*x x*] ⸢*x x x*⸣ [*x x*]	(Break)
	rest broken away	
III	upper part broken	
	traces of two illegible lines	
3′	[*x x x*]*x*.⸢MEŠ⸣ *ša* 3-*šú*.MEŠ ⸢GÌR.2⸣	III 3 [...]s of the 'third men' of the *ša šēpi* guard;
4′	[PAB] ⸢7⸣ *ina*$^{!}$ ⸢EN$^{!}$.NUN$^{!}$⸣-*šú-nu*	4 [In all] 7, in their guards.
5′	(line erased or eroded)	
6′	⸢1$^{?}$⸣ 2-*u-te um-man*	6 *1*, deputies, scholars, diviners;
7′	LÚ.HAL.MEŠ	
8′	⸢1$^{?}$⸣ ^{m}30–MAN–PAB	8 *1*, Sîn-šarru-uṣur;
9′	[*x*] ^{md}⸢NIN⸣.GAL–AŠ	9 [...] Nikkal-iddin;
10′	⸢10$^{?}$⸣ [*ub-sa-*(*a*)]-*te qab-sa-te*	10 *10*, the central [*stables*];
11′	[1$^{?}$] *um*-⸢*man*⸣ [Š]U.2 MAN	11 [*1*], scholars in the service of the king;
12′	[1$^{?}$] ŠÀ–URU-*a-a*	12 [*1*], (ditto) from Assur;
13′	⸢1$^{?}$⸣ DUMU.MEŠ NINA.KI	13 *1*, (ditto) from Nineveh;

14′ ⸢4?⸣ DUMU.MEŠ URU.*arba-ìl*
15′ [PA]B 7 TÙR PAB 1 ⸢*x*⸣
16′ [PA]B 22 *ina* É.GAL
17′ [PA]B 85 *ga-ṣu-*⸢*te*⸣
18′ [*x*] SIPA?.MEŠ *la*? DÙG? GAL
19′ [*x*]7 *x*[*x*].M[EŠ] ⸢*x*⸣*-di-ni*
20′ [*x*]4! GIŠ.⸢IG?⸣.MEŠ *šaṭ-ru*
21′ 32! [U]DU?.MEŠ 1 KUŠ.SAL
remainder broken away

IV upper part broken
traces of two lines
1′ 1 [*x x x x x x*]
2′ 2 [*x x x x x x*]
3′ 1-*me*? [*x x x x x x*]
4′ PAB 4 [*x x x x x x*]
5′ 3 *x*[*x x x x x x*]
(three lines broken away)
9′ 1 KUŠ.S[AL? *x x x*]
10′ 1 AM [*x x x*]
11′ *ina* IGI KU[R? *x x x*]
12′ 1 GAL–*k*[*i-ṣir*? *x x x*]
13′ 2 TÚG.*me*?-[*x x x*]
remainder broken away

14 *4*, (ditto) from Arbela;
15 [Tot]al 7, the yard; total 1, ...;
16 [Tot]al 22, in the palace;
17 [Tot]al 85, *cuts* (*of meat*);
18 [x], *shepherds* ...;
19 [x]+7, [...]*s* ...;
20 [x]+4, inscribed *doors*;
21 32 [*s*]*heep*, 1 wineskin
(Break)

IV 1 1 [......]
2 2 [......]
3 *100* [......]
4 In all, 4[+x ......]
5 3 [......]
(Break)
9 1 *winesk*[*in* ...]
10 1 *wild bull* [...]
11 before the *pala*[*ce* ...]
12 1 *c*[*ohort*] *commander* [...]
13 2 [...] textiles
(Rest destroyed)

288. Royal Funeral

K 7856 + K 6323 + K 14241 + 80-7-19,122
I
1 *ú-nam-ba-a hi-ra-a-te*
2 *i-ta-nap-pa-la a-tap-pi*
3 *ša* GIŠ.MEŠ *u* GURUN DÙ-*šú-nu*
4 *ud-du-ru pa-nu-šú-un*
5 *ib-ka-a ṣi-*⸢*ba*⸣*-x*[*x x*]
6 *šá ina di-ši* ⸢*da?*⸣*-x*[*x x*]
7 *ú-šar-bi x*[*x x x*]
8 NA4.I.DIB.[MEŠ *x x x*]
9 *ut-ta-*[*na-ah x x x*]
10 *ut-tah-*[*ha-su x x*]
11 *i-x*[*x x x*]
about 11 lines missing

ADD 941 + ADD 978 + (= SAAB 1 12)

I 1 The ditches wailed, the canals respond, all trees and fruit, their faces darkened (i.e. mourned). *Bir*[*ds*] wept, that in the grass ...[...]

7 exalted [...]
8 the threshold[s ...]
9 sig[hed ...]
10 wai[led ...]
11 ...[......]
(Break)

287 III 17 This line may be important in specifying what is being counted, but usually *gaṣṣu* "chopped, severed, tripped", if interpreted correctly, is not used in such contexts. III 19 Not SI[PA].M[EŠ].

288 Previous editions: MacGinnis, SAAB 1 (1987) 1-13 (K 7856 + K 6823); Kwasman, Fs. Parpola (2009) 111-25 (K 7856 + K 6823 + 80-7-19,122 [ADD 978] + K 14241; a full edition with a copy). I 5 On the difficulty of restoring the last word, see ibid. 117f.

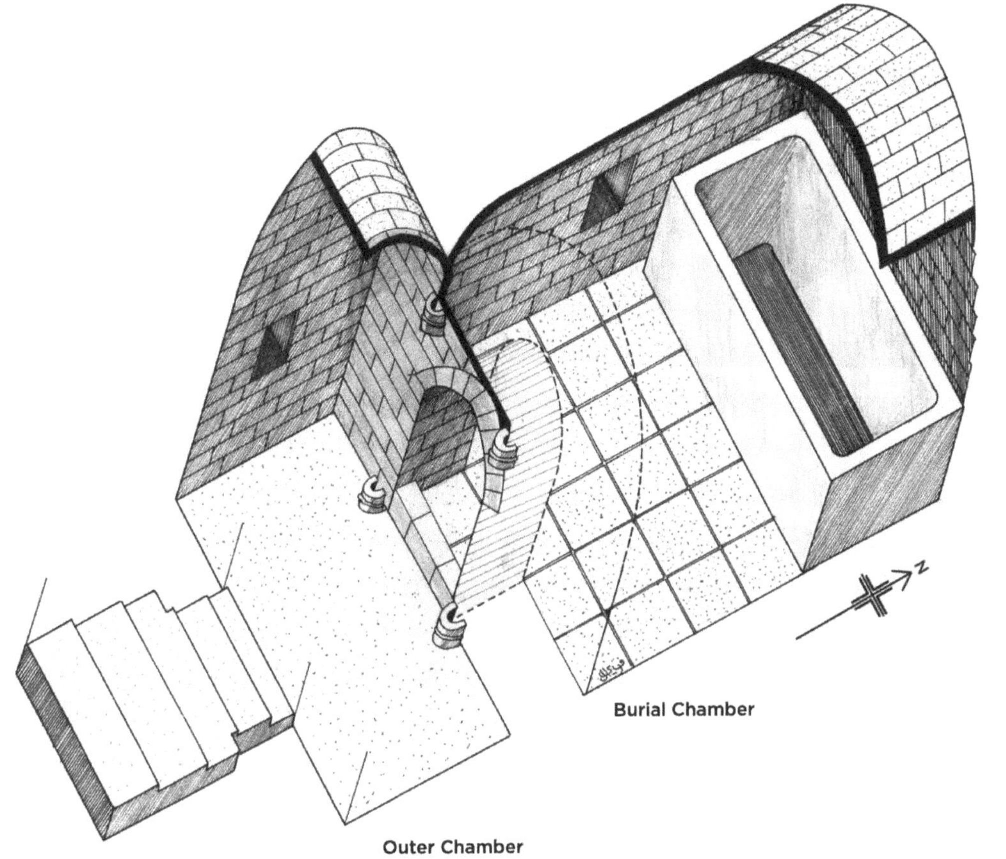

FIG. 36. *Isometric view of Royal Tomb II, Nimrud, with entrance from steps on left and coffin on right. Reign of Sargon II.*
Muzahim Mahmoud Hussein, Nimrud: The Queens' Tombs, Pl. 29 (Baghdad, Chicago 2016).

23	[x x x x x] ⌜x⌝	23 [......]
24	[*x x x x x* A]D$^{?}$-*u-a*	21 [...] my [*fat*]*her*
25	[*x x x x x x*]*x-u-ni*	(Rest destroyed or too broken for translation)
26	[*x x x x x x*]*x-a*	
	rest broken away	
II		
1	*dáp-pa-a*[*s-tú*]	II 1 1 blank[et]
2	ZAG MI DA *x*[*x x*]	2 *front* black ...[...]
3	⌜*x x x x*⌝ [*x* (*x*)]	(Break)
	about 12 lines missing	
16	[*x x x x*] *x*	16 [......]...
17	[*x x x*]*x* GÙN	17 [...] multi-coloured
18	[*x* (*x*) *x*]*x* SA$_5$	18 [...] red
19	[1 N]Á$^{!}$ ZÚ KUG.UD	19 [1 b]ed of ivory and silver
20	[1] NA$_5$:. :.	20 [1] chest ditto, ditto
21	⌜1⌝ GU.ZA GÌR.2 :. ⌜:.⌝	21 1 chair with feet ditto, ditto

22 ⸢1⸣ ŠIBIR ⸢:.⸣ [:.]
23 ⸢1 *ma*⸣-*k*[*a-su* :. :.]
24 [*x* (*x*) G]Ú.⸢ZI.MEŠ :.⸣
25 1 ⸢*kap*⸣-*pi* KUG.GI
26 2 *zer-re-tú* :.
27 2 *qa*-ZAG KUG.UD
28 10 ANŠE.KUR.⸢MEŠ⸣
29 30 GUD.MEŠ
30 3-*me* UDU.MEŠ
31 [PAB *a*]*n-ni-u* LUGAL KUR.URI
32 [1 GI]Š.NÁ URUDU *ša* GÌR.2.MEŠ
33 [1] TÚG.SÌG
34 [*x x*] ⸢*x x x x*⸣
rest broken away

III
1 [*x x x*]*x* DÙG.GA
2 [*x x x*]-*su*.HI.A
3 [*x x* (*x*)] :.
4 [*x x* (*x*) N]A$_4$.*šá-di-du*
5 [*x x* (*x*) *x*]*x* ⸢*x*⸣
6 [*x x x* KUG].⸢GI⸣
7 [*x x x x*]*x*
8 [*x x x* ANŠ]E.KUR
9 [*x x x*]*x* KUG.GI
10 [*x x x x*]*x*-⸢*tu*$^?$⸣-*me*
11 [*x x*] *qa* ⸢*x x x*⸣
12 [*x x*]*x-ni šá* [*x x*]
13 *x*[*x i*]*na* É.GAL [*x x*]
14 *ú*$^!$-*rab*$^!$-*bi*-⸢*i*$^?$⸣ [*x x*]
15 *a-na* 9-*a*-[*a x x*]
16 *a-na* ^{d}GIŠ.⸢NU$_{11}$⸣.[GAL]
17 ANŠE.KUR.MEŠ-*ma*$^?$ MÍ.K[UR.MEŠ]
18 *a-du-uk-m*[*a*]
19 *a-na qé-bé-r*[*i*]
20 *ad-din-šú-nu-ti*

---

21 1 *ṣa-lam man-za-si*
22 1 U.SAG NIM KUG.GI
23 4 BAR.DIB GÙN
24 4 *dam*$^!$-⸢*x x*⸣
25 4 KI.TA *h*[*al-pat*.MEŠ]
26 4 *na-ṣa*-[*bat*.MEŠ]
27 1 BAR.[DIB]
28 1 [*x x x x x*]
rest broken away

22 1 sceptre ditto, [ditto]
23 1 bo[wl ditto, ditto]
24 [... c]ups ditto
25 1 golden drinking bowl
26 2 chains ditto
27 2 silver cups
28 10 horses,
29 30 oxen (and)
30 300 sheep;
31 this is [the total] of the king of Akkad.
32 [1] bronze [b]ed with feet
33 [1] textile
34 [...] ...
(Rest destroyed)

III 1 [...] good
2 [... ...]...s
3 [...] ditto
4 [...] antimony
5 [... ...]...
6 [... *of gol*]*d*
7 [... ...]...
8 [...] horse
9 [......] gold
10 [... ...]...
11 [...] ...
12 [...]... *who* raised [....... i]n the palace.

15 9 tim[es ...] I slaughtered horses *and* ma[res] for Šam[aš] an[d] gave them to be buri[ed].

---

21 1 socle statue
22 1 Elamite gold mitre
23 4 multi-coloured robes
24 4 ... [...]
25 4 lower reinforced g[arments]
26 4 sash [holders]
27 1 *ro*[*be*]
28 1 [...]
(Rest destroyed)

IV		
1	1 GIŠ.GIGIR *tal-lul-tú* KUG.G[I]	IV 1 1 chariot with gold[en] trappings
2	1 *ša*–GIŠ.MI :.	2 1 umbrella ditto
3	1 GIŠ.TUKUL.DINGIR *duq-di*	3 1 almond-wood weapon
4	KA SUHUŠ KUG.GI	4 (of which) top and bottom gold
5	1 GIŠ.PA *mur-ra-nu* SA5 :.	5 1 red *murranu*-wood sceptre ditto
6	1 GIŠ.PA *duq-di* :.	6 1 almond-wood sceptre ditto
7	2 GIŠ.BAN.MEŠ *šuq-di* :.	7 2 almond-wood bows ditto
8	1 DUR.KIB :.	8 1 dur.kib ditto
9	1 *qu-un-di* URUDU :.	9 1 bronze *qundu* ditto
10	1 *šá*-KAR.SA :. :.	10 1 *šá*-kar-*sa* ditto, ditto
11	1 *šu-na-nu* SI *pu-šú-hi* :. ⸢:.⸣	11 1 tray *with a horn* (*in the shape*) *of a shrew* ditto, ditto
12	1 *šá–šá-da-di* KUG.U[D]	12 1 silv[er] processional carriage
13	1 *mi-lu-u šap-pa-*[*a-te*]	13 1 *milû for* contai[ners]
14	[*x x*] *x* ⸢*x x*⸣ [*x x x*]	14 […]… […]
	about 7 lines missing	(Break)
22	⸢2⸣ *x*[*x x x x x x*]	22 2 [……]
23	⸢1⸣ [*x x x x x x*]	23 1 [……]
	rest broken away	(Rest destroyed)
Rev.		
I′	beginning broken away	(Beginning destroyed)
1′	⸢1⸣ [*x x x*]	r. I′ 1 1 […]
2′	1 [*x x x*]	2 1 […]
3′	2 :. [*x x x*]	3 2 ditto […]
4′	16 U.SA[G.MEŠ]	4 16 mitr[es]
5′	5 *šik-na-*⸢*a*⸣*-*[*ni*]	5 5 *šiknu*-garmen[ts]
6′	15-*šú šá-har-rat* ⸢:.⸣	6 15 pairs of leggings ditto
7′	8-*šú* ⸢É–Á⸣.MEŠ :.	7 8 pairs of sleeves ditto
8′	6 *ṣip-rat*	8 6 *sashes*
9′	4-*šú* KUŠ.D[A].⸢E⸣.SÍR	9 4 pairs of shoes
10′	5 GÚ.LÁ [*x x*]*x* ⸢*x*⸣	10 5 cloaks […]
11′	5 *muk-lal*.[MEŠ]	11 5 shawls
12′	5 KI.TA–*hal-*[*pat*]	12 5 lower reinforced gar[ments]
13′	3 *ga-me-di* ⸢*x x*⸣	13 3 *gammidu*-garments …
14′	3 KI.TA–*hal-*[*pat*]	14 3 lower reinforced gar[ments]
15′	4 U.SAG BABBAR.MEŠ	15 4 white mitres
16′	4-*šú šá-har-rat* [SA5]	16 4 pairs of [*red*] *leggings*
17′	4-*šú* É–Á.MEŠ	17 4 pairs of sleeves
18′	4 *šik-na-n*[*i*]	18 4 *šiknu*-garments
II′	beginning broken away	(Beginning destroyed)
1′	[*x x x x x x*]*x*	r. II′ 1 [……]
2′	[*x x x x*]-⸢*x*⸣-*šú*	2 *his* […]…

r. I 12, 14 There is not much space at the end. Thus, *hal-*[*pat*] appears more likely than *hal-*[*pa-te*].

b

FIG. 37. *Objects in Royal Tomb II, Nimrud. Reign of Sargon II.*
Muzahim Mahmoud Hussein, Nimrud: The Queens' Tombs, Pl. 33b (Baghdad, Chicago 2016).

3′ [AD *b*]*a*-⸢*nu*⸣-*u-a*
4′ [*qé*]-⸢*reb*⸣ KI.MAH *šú-a-tú*
5′ *a-šar ni-ṣir-ti*
6′ *ina* Ì.GIŠ LUGAL-*ti*
7′ *ṭa-biš uš-ni-il-šú*
8′ NA$_4$.*a-ra-nu*
9′ *a-šar ta-aṣ-lil-*⸢*ti*⸣-*šú*
10′ *ina* URUDU *dan-ni*
11′ KÁ-*šá ak-nu-uk-ma*
12′ *ú-dan-ni-na ši-pat-*⸢*sa*⸣
13′ *ú-nu-ut* KUG.GI KUG.UD
14′ *mim-ma tar-si-it* KI.MAH
15′ *si-mat be-lu-ti-šú*
16′ *ša i-ram-mu*
17′ *ma-har* ^{d}UTU
18′ *ú-kal-lim-ma*
19′ ⸢*it*⸣-*ti* AD *ba-ni-ia*
20′ *a-na* KI.MAH GAR-*un*
21′ ⸢*qi*⸣-*šá-a-ti a-na mal-ki*
22′ ^{d}*a-nun-na-ki*
23′ *ú* DINGIR.MEŠ *a-ši-bu-ut* KI.⸢TIM⸣
24′ [*ú*]-*qa-a-a-iš*

[3] [Father], my begetter, I gently laid him in the [mi]dst of that tomb, a secret place, in royal oil. The stone coffin, his resting place – I sealed its opening with strong copper and secured the clay sealing.

[13] I displayed gold and silver objects, everything proper for a tomb, the emblems of his lordship, that he loved before Šamaš and I placed (them) in the tomb with my father, my begetter.

[21] I presented gifts to the *malki*, the Anunnaki and the gods residing in the netherworld.

289. Towns and Villages

K 16035		CT 53 720
1	[URU.*x x x*]*x*–^{d}ZA.B[A4.BA4]	1 [The town of ...]-Zab[aba together with its villag]es;
2	[*a-du* URU.Š]E.MEŠ-[*šú*]	
3	[URU.*x x x*]-*ki-ra*-[*x*]	3 [the town of ...]kira[... together with its vil]lages;
4	[*a-du* URU].ŠE.MEŠ-[*šú*]	
5	[URU.*x x x*]–APIN-⌜*a*⌝-[*a*?]	5 [the town of ...]... [together with] its [vil]lages;
6	[*a-du* UR]U.ŠE.MEŠ-*šú*	
7	[URU.*x x*]-*pa-áš*	7 [the town of ...]paš [together with] its [villages];
8	[*a-du* URU.ŠE.MEŠ]-*šú*	
9	[URU.*x x x x x*]	9 [the town of ... together with its villages];
10	[*a-du* URU.ŠE.MEŠ-*šú*]	
11	[URU.*x x x*]*x* [*x x*]	11 [the town of ... together with its vill]age[s];
12	[*a-du* URU].ŠE.[MEŠ-*šú*]	
13	[URU.*x x x*]*x* [*x x*]	13 [the town of ...]
	rest broken away	(Rest destroyed)
Rev.	uninscribed	

290. List of Chariot Troops

K 1995 + K 19290		ADD 852+ (= SAA 11 123+)
I	beginning broken away	(Beginning destroyed)
1′	[^{m}*x*] ⌜*x*–U.GUR?⌝	I 1 [...]-*Nergal*
2′	[^{m}*x*]-*ni*–GIŠ LÚ*. GIŠ.GIGIR	2 [... ...]ni-lešir, horse trainer;
3′	[*x x*]*x-at* UD-10-K[ÁM*]	3 [...]... 10th day [...]
4′	[(*x x*)] ^{m}10–*ki-in* LÚ*.*s*[*u*]	4 [...] Adad-ken, ho[rse trainer],
5′	⌜*ša*?⌝ [*x x x x*]	5 *of* [......]
6′	PAB 4 LÚ*.*su-sa-ni*	6 Total 4 horse trainers of the *zun*(*zurahu*).
7′	*šá* LÚ*.*zu*!-*un*!	
8′	PAB 8 *ša* ŠU.2 ^{m}PAB-*u-a*–IGI	8 Total 8, in the charge of Ahu'a-lamur, of the city of Halzu.
9′	*ša* URU.*hal-zi*	
10′	^{m}SUHUŠ–15 LÚ*. GIŠ.GIGIR	10 Ubur-Issar, horse trainer;
11′	^{m}*mu-še-zib*–DINGIR :	11 Mušezib-ilu, ditto.

289 Cf. SAA 11 12 (CT 53 236).

290 This join may not seem entirely convincing at first glance, but, e.g., the sign forms (LÚ*, GIŠ, GIGIR, *ki*, *ni*) match perfectly between the two pieces, and "horse trainers" feature in both. Moreover, the colour of the clay is the same, and the small fragment K 19290 sits well on the first column of the obverse of K 1995 (read in the BM, June 2014). Structurally, however, lines I 3-4 may cause a bit of a headache, but an abbreviated profession is probable (cf. lines I 12, 14). [I 7, II 2, 16, 18, r. I 2, II 5] Exclamation marks indicating collations correcting the ADD copy have been retained; see a copy of K 1995 in SAA 11, p. 208.

12′	^{m}*qu-qu-u-a su*	12 Ququa, horse trainer;
13′	^{md}UTU–PAB–AŠ	13 Šamaš-ahu-iddina.
14′	[^{m}]^{d}UTU–*šal-lim su*	14 Šamaš-šallim, horse trainer;
15′	^{m}*si-lim*–^{d}IM ⸢:⸣	15 Silim-Adad, ditto.
II	beginning broken away	(Break)
1′	[*x x*]*x*[*x x x*]	
2′	^{m}*za-ba*$^{!}$*-ba*$^{!}$–GAR	II 2 Zababa-iškun
3′	^{m}*za-an-du-ru*	3 Zanduru
4′	^{m}*su-sa-nu*	4 Susanu
5′	^{m}*man-nu–ki*–10	5 Mannu-ki-Adad
6′	^{m}*met-tú–a-dúr*	6 Metu-adur
7′	^{m}DUMU.UŠ–PAB	7 Aplu-uṣur
8′	^{m}*aš-šur–kal-lim-an-ni*	8 Aššur-kallimanni
9′	^{m}KÁ.DINGIR-*a-a*	9 Babilayu
10′	^{m}*gu-ru-du*	10 Gurrudu
11′	^{md}15–MU–GIN	11 Issar-šumu-kinni
12′	^{m}DÙG.GA–PAB.MEŠ	12 Ṭab-ahhe
13′	^{m}*gíd-gíd-da-nu*	13 Gidgiddanu
14′	^{m}*man-nu–ki*–PAB.MEŠ	14 Mannu-ki-ahhe
15′	^{md}UTU–AD–PAB	15 Šamaš-abu-uṣur
16′	^{m}GÌR.2–15–DIB$^{!}$-*bat*$^{!}$	16 Šep-Issar-aṣbat
e.17′	^{m}*la–tú-ba-šá-ni*–DINGIR	17 La-tubašanni-ili
18′	PAB 23$^{!}$	18 Total 23.
Rev. I		
1	^{md}PA–*taq-qin-an-ni*	r. I 1 Nabû-taqqinanni
2	*nu*$^{!}$*-u-a*	2 …
	stamp seal impression	(Stamp seal impression)
3	^{m}⸢*x x x*⸣ [	(Break)
	rest broken away	
II		
1	^{m}*lu*–TI.LA	r. II 1 Lu-balaṭ
2	LÚ*.*su-sa-nu ú-re-e*	2 horse trainer of the teams.
	one line erased	
3	^{m}*šá–aš-šur–a-ni-ni*	3 Ša-Aššur-aninu.
	blank space of about 5 lines	(blank space of about 5 lines)
4	[^{m}*x x x*]-*gab-bi*	4 [...]-gabbi,
5	[^{m}*x x*]–*dà-ri*$^{!}$	5 [...]-dari,
6	[^{m}*x x x x*]-*i*	6 [...]i
	rest broken away	(Rest destroyed)

291. Fragment of Sheep List(?)

83-118,858
beginning broken away
1′ *x x x*] ⸢*x x x*⸣
2′ *x x x*] *ir* ⸢*x*⸣
3′ *x x x*] 1-*lim*-2-*me* UDU.MEŠ
4′ *x*]-*šab-ši ba*$^{?}$-*i-ti*
5′ *x x*]-*i gab-bi-šú*
e.6′ ^{md}*x*]–U–PAB TA* ŠÀ-⸢*bi x x*⸣
7′ *x x*] ⸢*x x x*⸣ [*x x x*]
Rev. broken away

83-118,858
(Beginning destroyed)
3 [...] 1,200 sheep
4 [...]šabši, ...
5 [...] the *whole* [...]
6 [... DN]-belu-uṣur *from*
(Rest destroyed)

292. ---

K 19013
beginning broken away
1′ *x x*]*x* É ^{m}GÌR.2–⸢^{d}⸣[*x x x*
2′ *x x*] *ša* GAL–MU [*x x x*
blank line
3′ *x*]*x* LÚ*.ERIM.MEŠ *ša ú-hal-*⸢*li*⸣-[*qu-ni*
4′ *x* L]Ú*.*za-bíl*–[*x x x x*
5′ *x x x*] 22$^{?}$ [*x x x x x*
rest broken away

K 19013
1 [...] the house of Šep-[DN ...]
2 [...] *which* the chief cook [...]

3 [...] the men who *destro*[*yed* (...)]
4 [...] the [...] *carrier* [...]
(Rest destroyed)

293. ---

Sm 378
coating almost completely gone
r.1e [U]D-25-KÁM ŠU.2 ^{m}EN–PAB–PAB
2e LÚ*.*rak*-(*su*) PAB 4

Sm 378
(Except for the end, tablet destroyed)
1 25th [d]ay, in the charge of Bel-ahu-uṣur, recruit; in total, 4 (*persons*).

291 [4] Possibly a PN ending in -*mušabši*, -*ušabši* or -*šabši*.
292 [1] The first visible sign could be ⸢*ša*⸣. This Šep-[...] is not listed in PNA 3/II 1262f.
293 Originally a small horizontal tablet. [r.2] The objects enumerated are uncertain but it is easy to imagine, for example, a recruit accompanying a group of people.

294. List of Messengers

K 124

beginning broken away

1′ [^{md}NI]N.GAL–DÙ-*n*[*i*]
2′ [^{m}*ri*]-*mu-tu*
3′ [^{m}*s*]*a-ma-a*
4′ [^{m}*x*-Š]EŠ-*ia* A ^{m}*ha-a-a-hu*–ŠEŠ
5′ ^{m}NÍG.GUB A $^{md+}$AG–SIG$_5$–DINGIR.MEŠ
6′ ^{m}*hu-za-la* A ^{m}*šá-la-mu*
7′ ^{m}NÍG.GUB *ù* $^{md+}$AG–MU–*iš-kun*
8′ LÚ.A–KIN.MEŠ

ABL 627

(Beginning destroyed)

1 [Ni]kkal-tabni,
2 [Re]mutu,
3 [S]ama',
4 [...-*a*]*hiya*, son of Haya-ahu-uṣur,
5 Kudurru, son of Nabû-damqi-ilani,
6 Huzalu, son of Šalamu,
7 Kudurru and Nabû-šumu-iškun,
8 *are* messengers.

295. – – –

K 10859

1 [*x x x x x x x x x*]-*ti*
2 [*x x x x x x x x x*] LUGAL
3 [*x x x x x x x x*] ⸢É⸣.GA[L]
4 [*x x x x x x x x x*] LUGA[L]
5 [*x x x x x x x x x*] L[UGAL]
6 [*x x x x x x x x x*]*x* [*x x*]

rest broken away

Rev. beginning broken away

three lines blank

1′ [*x x x x x*]-*ši*? *lu*-⸢*ú*?⸣
2′ [*x x x x x* L]Ú.MAH *x*[*x x*]

blank space; in smaller script:

3′ [*x x x x* LÚ.GAL]–*mu-gi*
4′ [*x x x x x* ^{m}*aš*]-*šur–rém-a-ni*
5′ [*x x x x* ^{md}*šúm*?-*m*]*a*–DINGIR-*a-a*

CT 53 412

2 [......] the king
3 [...... the p]alace
4 [......] the kin[g]
5 [......] the k[ing]

(Break)

r.2 [...... e]missary

3 [... the *rab*] *mūgi*
4 [... Aš]šur-remanni
5 [... *Šumm*]*a*-ila'i

294 Previous edition: Vera Chamaza, AOAT 295 no. 51.
295 The nature of this fragment is uncertain: a letter, an administrative document or something else?

296. – – –

K 14616

beginning broken away

1′ [*x x x x x*] ⸢*ku*⸣-*m*[*u*$^{?}$ *x*]

2′ [*x x x x* AN]ŠE A.ŠÀ [*x x*]

3′ [*x x x x x*]-*ra-n*[*u x x*]

4′ [*x x x x x*] ⸢*ur*$^{?}$⸣ *x*[*x x*]

rest broken away

Rev. beginning broken away

1′ [*x x x x x x x*]*x* [*x*]

2′ [*x x* ^{m}*mu-tak*]-*kil–aš-šur*

3′ [*x x x x*]-*tú* KÚ [0]

rest uninscribed

CT 53 548

(Beginning destroyed)

1 [...] *in* [*his*] *stead*

2 [... x hect]ares of field [...]

(Break)

r.2 [... Mutak]kil-Aššur

3 *eats* [...]

296 This fragment is not necessarily from an administrative record. It could just as well be from a legal document.

11. Grants, Decrees and Gifts of the Neo-Assyrian Period
Additions to SAA XII

FIG. 38. *Confirmation of royal grant, with hand-modelled copy of seal-impression of Ashur-nadin-šumi, son of Sennacherib, as king of Babylon.*
BM 77611.

297. Fragment of Sennacherib's Donation

VAT 10530

beginning broken away

1′ [*x x x x x x x* NA$_4$$^?$].KIŠIB$^?$ [*x x x x x*]

2′ [NA$_4$.KIŠIB AN].⸢ŠÁR⸣ L[UGAL DINGIR.MEŠ]

3′ [NA$_4$.KIŠIB DINGIR *ru-bé*]-⸢*e*⸣ *ša* [*la pa-qa-ri*]

4′ [$^{md+}$EN.ZU-ŠEŠ.MEŠ-*eri-b*]*a* LUGAL ŠÚ LUGA[L KUR–*aš-šur*.KI NUN *mun-tal-ku*]

5′ [*mu-šak-lil pa-ra-a*]*ṣ* É.ŠÁR.RA [*ma-šu-ti*]

6′ [*ina bi-ri qí-bit* ^{d}]UTU [[*ù*]] ^{d}IM *mu-ša*[*r-bu-u šu-luh-hi-šú-un*]

7′ [*mu-tir* ^{d}LAMA É.ŠÁ]R.RA *la e-piš-ti* [[*ana*]] *áš-ri-*⸢*šú*⸣ [*a-na-ku*]

8′ [*i-nu-šu ul-tu ṣ*]*a-lam* AN.ŠÁR EN GAL-*e* EN-*ia* [[*i-pu-šu*]]

9′ [*ù ṣa-lam* DINGIR.MEŠ GA]L.MEŠ *i-pu-šu pa-ra-aṣ* É.ŠÁR.RA *ma-š*[*u-ti*]

10′ [*ina bi-ri qí-bit*] ⸢^{d}UTU⸣ *ù* ^{d}IM *ú-šak-li-lu*$^{!!}$

11′ [ ] [[*x x x x x*]]

blank space of about two lines

rest broken away

KAL 3, no. 63

(Beginning destroyed)

1 [……] *seal* […], [the seal of Aš]šur, k[ing of the gods; the seal of God the Kin]g, [not to be contested].

4 [I am Sennacherib], king of the world, kin[g of Assyria, circumspect monarch, the perfecter of the forgotten cul]t of Ešarra [according to the oracular command] of Šamaš and Adad, the enla[rger of their purificatory cult, the restorer of the protective deity of Eša]rra, which had ceased to function, to its place.

(unused seal space)

---

8 [At that time, after] I$^{!!}$ had made the [st]atue of Aššur, great lord, my lord, [and the statues of gre]at [gods], and perfected the forgo[tten] cult of Ešarra [according to the oracular command] of Šamaš and Adad.

(Rest destroyed)

298. Fragmentary Decree on the Offerings of the Aššur Temple

VAT 10922

Obv. completely destroyed

Rev. beginning broken away

1′ [*x x x x x x x*] ⸢*a*$^?$-*na*$^?$⸣ Ì.GI[Š$^?$ *x x x x x x*]

2′ [*x x x x x x x a*]*r-rat* HUL-*ti*[*m x x x x x x*]

3′ [*x x x x x x x ik-r*]*i-bi-ka i-še*[*m-mu-u*$^?$ *x x x x x*]

4′ [*x x x x* NUN EGIR-*ú ša pi-i dan-ni-te*$^?$ *šu*]-⸢*a-tú*⸣ *la ú-šam-*⸢*sak*⸣ [*ša* DUB *šu-a-tú*$^?$ *x x x x*]

KAL 3, no. 64

(Beginning destroyed)

r.1 [……] *to oil* [……]

2 [……] evil [c]urse [……]

3 [*DNs*] will he[ar] your [pra]yer [……]

4 […… a future prince] shall not cast aside [the wording of t]his [tablet. Whoever will … *this tablet*]

297 Previous edition: Frahm, KAL 3 63. Lines 2-7 duplicate SAA 12 86:1-4. 3 Unlike Frahm, but as in SAA 12 86:1, we restore DINGIR before *rubê*. 8-9 Text: "he had made …". 8-11 These lines partly summarize SAA 12 86:5-15.

298 Previous edition: Frahm, KAL 3 64. 4 Cf., e.g., SAA 12 9 r.6f. 6 For tentatively taking *ha-aš-ha-te* as *ha-aš-la-te*, see Frahm, KAL 3, p. 127.

5′ [*x x x x x x ez-zi-iš li-k*]*el*?*-mu-šu-ma ar-rat l*[*a*? *nap-šu-ri*? *li-ru-ru-šu x x x x*]

5 [... may *DNs* lo]ok at him [with wrath] and [curse him with] an i[rremovable] curse [......]

6′ [*x x x x x x x* G]IŠ.*za-ma-ru ha-aš-ha-te an x* [*x x x x x x*]

6 [......] fruit, *crushed grain* ... [......]

7′ [*x x x x x x x*] *x gi-nu-ú x* [*x x x x x x*]

7 [......] the regular offerings [......]

8′ [*x x x x x x x*] *x x x i-na* É–*aš-šur* ⸢*šá*⸣ [*x x x x x x*]

8 [......] in the Aššur temple *of* [......]

rest broken away

(Rest destroyed)

12. Assyrian Royal Rituals and Cultic Texts
Additions to SAA XX

FIG. 39. *Sheep and goats*.
BM 118882.

299. Fragment of a Royal Ritual with Stones and Sheep

	VAT 10113	KAL 12, no. 3 (= KAR 217)
I	beginning broken away	(Beginning destroyed)
1′	[*x x x x x x* 1] UDU 1 N[A$_4$ ^{d}*al-la-tum*]	i 1 [...... one] sheep, one st[one (for) Allatu],
2′	[1 UDU 1 NA$_4$] ⸢^{d}⸣EN–MAN [1 NA$_4$]	2 [one sheep, one stone] (for) Bel-šarru, [one stone] [(for) Daglanu], one stone (for) Siusa.
3′	[^{d}*da-ag-la-nu*] 1 NA$_4$ ^{d}*si-ú-sa*	
4′	[*aš-šur*? LUGAL *e-ma*]*r* ⸢1⸣ *me-se-ra* KUG.GI *i-ra-kas*	4 [The king sees *Aššur*], he ties a golden belt (around his waist).
5′	[^{d}NIN.LÍL? L]UGAL *e-mar* 1 *me-se-ra* KUG.GI *i-ra-kas*	5 [The k]ing sees [*Mullissu*], he ties a golden belt (around her waist).
6′	[^{d}*še-ru-i*]*a* LUGAL *e-mar* 1 TÚG.HI.A *ú-še-la*	6 The king sees [Šeru]a, he dedicates one garment.
7′	[^{d}P]A.TÚG LUGAL *e-mar* 1 TÚG.ÍB.LAL *ú-še-la*	7 The king sees [N]usku, he dedicates one *sash*.
8′	[^{d}M]AŠ LUGAL *e-mar* 1 NA$_4$ *ú-še-el-la*	8 The king sees [Ni]nurta, he dedicates one stone.
9′	[^{d}*kip-p*]*a-tum* LUGAL *e-mar* 1 NA$_4$ *ú-še-la*	9 The king sees [Kipp]atu, he dedicates one stone.
10′	[*a-di x x i-ṣ*]*a-li-ú-ni-ni* 1 UDU DÙ-*áš*	10 [While *they* are pu]tting [...], he sacrifices one sheep.
11′	[^{d}U.DAR–MU]L.MEŠ IGI-*mar* UDU.SISKUR.MEŠ	11 He sees [Ištar-of-Sta]rs, the king makes sacrifices [before he]r.
12′	[*i-na* IGI-*š*]*a* LUGAL DÙ-*áš*	
13′	[^{d}*ma-nu-g*]*al* LUGAL IGI-*mar*	13 The king sees [Manung]al, [he sacrifices one sheep].
14′	[1 UDU DÙ-*áš* ^{d}*x*]-*hi*?-*lal* IGI-*mar* 1 UDU *e-pa-áš*	14 He sees [...]..., he sacrifices one sheep.
15′	[*x x x x x x*] ⸢*ú*⸣-*še-el-la*	15 [...] he dedicates [...].
16′	[*x x x x x x x*]*x ša* LUGAL	16 [......] of the king
17′	[*x x x x x x x*]*x-še-be*.MEŠ	17 [......] ...s
18′	[*x x x x x x š*]*a* MAN *i*-⸢*x x*⸣ [*x*]	18 [...... o]f the king ...[...].
19′	[*x x x x x x x x x*] ⸢*x*⸣ [*x x x*]	(Rest destroyed or too broken for translation)
	rest broken away	

299 Previous editions: Schaudig, KAL 12 3 and id. NABU 2023/20 (corrected copy; earlier copy KAR 217); K. F. Müller, MVAeG 41/3 (1937) 47-49; see also Menzel Tempel 2, T 7, Nr. 6a and Panayotov, CDLN 2015:7. i 1-3 SAA 20 7 r.15-16; see also SAA 20 38 II 12-15, 42 II 33-34. i 10 Cf. SAA 20 7 II 27-28.

II beginning broken away
1′ [*x x x x x x x x x*]

2′ 1 N[A$_4$ *x x x x x x x x x*]
3′ [*x x x x x x x x x x x x x*]
4′ [*x x x x x x x x x x x x x*]
5′ [*x x x x x x x x x x x x x*]
6′ [*x x x x x x x x x x x x x*]
7′ [*x x x x x x x x x x x x x*]
8′ [*x x x x x x x x x x x x x*]
9′ 11 [NA$_4$.MEŠ *x x x x x x x x x*]
10′ 1 N[A$_4$*x x x x x x x x x x*]
11′ 1 N[A$_4$ *x x x x x x x x x*]
12′ 4 [NA$_4$.MEŠ *x x x x x x x x x*]

13′ *x*[*x x x x x x x x x*]
rest broken away

300. Fragment of a Royal Ritual

Bu 91-5-9,224
lines 1-2 broken away
3 [*x x x x x x x*] ⸢BE$^{?}$⸣ *u* ⸢*ia*$^{?}$⸣
4 [*x x x x x x x* UD]-9-KÁM
5 [*x x x x x x x*]*x-ti-ma*
6 [*x x x x x x x*]*x ba-a-a-*⸢*te*⸣
7 [*x x x x x x x*] ŠUB.MEŠ
8 [*x x x x x x*] LUGAL *e-ru-bu*
9 [*x x x x x*] ⸢*ù*⸣ MÍ.*še-ru-u-a*–KAR-*at*!
10 [*x x x x x*] ^{m}*kan-dàl-a-nu*
11 [*x x x x x*] ⸢*šá*⸣ URU UD-*me*
e.12 [*x x x* KUR.N]IM$^{?}$.KI
13 [*x x x x*]-*te šap*-⸢*x x x*⸣

r.1 [*x x x x x*] MAN KUR.NIM.KI
2 [*x x x x x*]
3 [*x x x x x* GIŠ].BANŠUR.MEŠ
4 [*x x x x x x x* D]U$_8$
5 [*x x x x x x x x*]*x-za*
6 [*x x x x x x x x x*]*x-lu*
7 [*x x x x x x x x x l*]*i*
8 [*x x x x x x x x x x*]*x*
rest (about 2 lines) broken away

CT 53 966
(Beginning destroyed)

4 [……] the 9th [day]
5 [……] …
6 [……] …
7 [……s] *will* fall
8 [……] enter [*the presence of*] the king
9 [……] and Šeru'a-eṭerat
10 [……] Kandalanu
11 [……] of the city. The day
12 […… *El*]*am*
13 [……] …
r.1 [……] king of Elam
2 [……]
3 [……] tables
4 […… will *re*]*lease*
5 [……]…
6 [……]…
(Rest destroyed)

II This broken column lists stones.
300 6 Reading [Bīt]-Ibâ(?) has been suggested (see Frame Babylonia 195). 10 On Kandalanu, see PNA 2/I 601a, no. 11 with previous literature.

GLOSSARY AND INDICES

Logograms and Their Readings

A → *mar'u, mê;* A.AN → *zunnu;* A.BÁR → *abāru;* A.KAL → *mīlu;* A—MAN → *mār šarri;* A.MEŠ → *mê;* A.MEŠ—ŠU → *mê qāti;* A.ŠÀ → *eqlu;* ÁB.GUD.HI.A → *sagullu;* AD → *abu;* AD—AD → *ab abi;* AGA → *agû;* AM → *rīmu;* AMA → *ummu;* AMA—LUGAL → *ummi šarri;* AN → *šamê;* AN.BAR → *parzillu;* AN.GAL → *Ištarān;* AN.MI → *attalû;* AN.NA → *annuku;* AN.ŠÁR → *Aššūr;* AN.ŠÁR—DÙ—A, AN.ŠÁR—DÙ—DUMU.UŠ → *Aššūr-bāni-apli;* AN.ŠÁR—ŠEŠ—SUM → *Aššūr-ahu-iddina;* AN.TA → *elēnu, elû B;* ANŠE → *imāru;* ANŠE.EDIN → *sirrimu;* ANŠE.KUR, ANŠE.KUR.RA → *sissû;* ANŠE.NITÁ → *imāru;* ARAD → *urdu;* ARHUŠ → *rēmu;* ÁŠ → *ṣibûtu;* Á → *ahu B;* Á.KAL → *emūqu;*

BA → *qiāšu;* BABBAR → *paṣû;* BAD—HAL → *pēthallu;* BÀD → *dūru;* BAD$_5$.BAD$_5$ → *dabdû;* BAL → *naqû;* BAN → *qassu;* BANŠUR → *paššūru;* BAR → *zâzu;* BAR.DIB → *kusītu;* BARAG → *parakku;* BÀ → *amūtu;* BE → *šumma, bēlu;* BULÙG → *tarbiu;* BUR → *naptunu;* BURU$_5$ → *erbiu;* BURU$_{14}$ → *ebūru;* BÙR → *šīlu;*

$^{d+}$AG → *Nabû;* $^{d+}$AG—ŠEŠ—SUM → *Nabû aha iddina;* $^{d+}$EN → *Bēl;* $^{d+}$EN.LÍL → *Illil;* ^{d}AMAR.UTU → *Marduk;* ^{d}AN.ŠÁR—ŠEŠ—SUM → *Aššūr-ahu-iddina;* ^{d}BAD → *Illil;* ^{d}EN → *Bēl;* ^{d}EN.LÍL → *Illil;* ^{d}EN—MAN → *Bēl-šarru;* ^{d}É.A → *Ea;* ^{d}GIŠ.BAR → *Girru;* ^{d}IB → *Uraš;* ^{d}IGI.DU → *Pālil;* ^{d}IM → *Adad;* ^{d}INNIN, ^{d}IŠ.TAR → *Issār;* ^{d}LAMA → *lamassu;* ^{d}LUGAL → *Šarru;* ^{d}LUGAL—GIŠ.ASÁL → *Bēl ṣarbi;* ^{d}MAŠ → *Inūrta;* ^{d}MES → *Marduk;* ^{d}NIN.GAL → *Nikkal;* ^{d}NIN.KILIM → *sikkû;* ^{d}NIN.LÍL → *Mullissu;* ^{d}NIN.TIN → *Bēlet balāṭi;* ^{d}NIN.URTA → *Inūrta;* ^{d}NUMUN—DÙ → *Zarpānītu;* ^{d}PA → *Nabû;* ^{d}PA.TÚG → *Nušku;* ^{d}SAG.ME.GAR → *Sagmegar;* ^{d}U.DAR → *Issār;* ^{d}U.DAR.MUL → *Issār kakkibī;* ^{d}U.GUR → *Nergal;* ^{d}UTU → *Šamaš, šanšu;* ^{d}UTU.È → *ṣīt šamši;* ^{d}UTU.ŠÚ.A → *erēb šamši;* ^{d}15 → *Issār;* ^{d}30 → *Sîn;* ^{d}30—ŠEŠ—SU → *Sîn-ahhē-rība;* ^{d}7.BI → *Sebetti;*

DAG → *šubtu;* DAGAL → *rapāšu;* DAM → *aššatu;* DAR → *šatāqu;* DI → *šulmu;* DI.KUD → *daiānu;* DIB → *etēqu, ṣabātu;* DIB—PA → *mukīl appāti;* DIN → *balāṭu;* DINGIR → *ilu, ilūtu;* DU → *alāku;* DU.DU → *alāku;* DÙ → *epāšu, epēšu, kalû;* DU$_8$ → *ša pattûti, paṭāru;* DUB → *ṭuppu;* DUG → *karputu;* DÙG, DÙG.GA → *ṭiābu;* DUG$_4$.DUG$_4$ → *dabābu;* DUG$_4$.GA → *qabû;* DUH.LÀL → *iškuru;* DUL.DU → *elû;* DUMU → *mār'u, mar'utu;* DUMU—DUMU → *mār mar'i;* DUMU—KÁ.DINGIR.RA.KI → *Bābili;* DUMU—LUGAL → *mār šarri;* DUMU—MAN → *mār šarri;* DUMU.MÍ → *mar'utu;* DUMU.MÍ—MAN → *mar'at šarri;* DUMU.UŠ → *aplu;*

E.KI → *Bābili;* EDIN → *ṣēru;* EGIR → *urki, urkīu;* EME → *lišānu;* EN → *bēl dāmi, bēl dēni, bēl hiṭṭi, bēlu, bēlūtu;* EN.ME—UMUŠ → *bēl ṭēmi;* EN—MU.MU → *bēl zakār šumi;* EN.NUN → *maṣṣartu;* EN—URU → *bēl āli;* ÉN → *šiptu;* ERIM → *ṣābu, ummānu;* ERIM.HI.A → *ṣābu;* EŠ.BAR → *purussû;* ÉŠ.QAR → *iškāru;* EZEN → *isinnu;* É → *Esaggil, bēt Aššūr, bēt ṣibitti, bēt rēdūti, bētu;* É—Á → *bēt ahi;* É—AD → *bēt abi;* É—DINGIR → *bēt ilāni, bēt ili;* É—EN → *bēt bēli;* É.GAL → *ēkallu;* É.KI.MAH → *kimahhu;* É.KUR → *ēkurru;* É.SAG.ÍL → *Esaggil;* É.SIG$_4$ → *igāru;* É.ŠÁR.RA → *Ešarra;* É—UŠ → *bēt rēdūti;* É.ZI.DA → *Ezida;* È → *aṣû, uṣû;*

GA → *zizibu;* GÁ → *šakānu;* GABA → *irtu;* GABA.RI → *mihru;* GADA → *kitû;* GAG.ZAG.GA → *kaskāsu;* GAL → *rabû;* GAL—É → *rab bēti;* GAL—LÚ.HAL → *rab bārê;* GAL—MU → *rab nuhatimmi;* GAL—NÍG.ŠID → *rab nikkassi;* GAL—SAG → *rab ša rēši, rab ša rēšūtu;* GAL—50 → *rab hanšā;* GÁL → *bašû;* GAR → *šakānu, šaknu;* GARZA → *parṣu;* GAZ → *duāku;* GEMÉ → *amtu;* GEŠTIN → *karānu;* GI → *amu, qanû, qarṭuppu;* GI.AMBAR → *appāru;* GI.DU$_8$ → *paṭīru;* GI.DUB.BA → *qarṭuppu;* GI.NA → *kuānu;* GIBIL.BI → *eššiš;* GIDIM → *eṭemmu;* GÍD.DA → *arāku;* GIG → *murṣu;* GIGIR → *mugirru;* GIM → *kî, kīma;* GÍN → *šiqlu;* GÍR → *patru;* GÌR.2 → *šēpu;* GISKIM → *ittu;* GIŠ → *iṣu;* GIŠ.APIN → *epinnu;* GIŠ.BAN → *qassu;* GIŠ.BANŠUR → *paššūru;* GIŠ.ERIN → *erēnu;* GIŠ.GIGIR → *mugirru;* GIŠ.GU.ZA → *kussiu, kussû;* GIŠ.HUR → *uṣurtu;* GIŠ.IG → *dassu;* GIŠ.KAL → *ušû;* GIŠ.LI.U$_5$.UM → *lē'u;* GIŠ.MÁR.DA → *martû;* GIŠ.MI → *ṣillu;* GIŠ.NÁ → *eršu;* GIŠ.PA → *haṭṭu;* GIŠ.SAR → *kiriu;* GIŠ—ŠU → *iṣ qāti;* GIŠ.ŠÚ.NAGA → *narmaku;* GIŠ.ŠUR.MÌN →

šurmēnu; GIŠ.TUKUL → *kakku;* GIŠ.TUKUL.DINGIR → *miṭṭu;* GIŠ.ÙR → *gušūru;* GÚ → *kišādu;* GU.ZA → *kussiu;* GUB → *uzuzzu;* GUB.BA → *mazzassu;* GÙB → *šumēlu;* GUD → *alpu;* GÙN → *birmu;* GUR → *tuāru;* GURUN → *inbu;* GÚ → *libānu;* GÚ.GAL → *gugallu;* GÚ.LÁ → *hullānu;* GÚ.UN → *biltu;* GÚ.ZI → *kāsu;*

HA.LA → *zittu;* HABRUD → *hurru;* HAL → *bārû;* HAR → *sabirru;* HÉ.KÉŠ → *rakāsu;* HUL → *lemuttu, lumnu;*

IDIM → *nagbu;* ÍD → *nāru;* IGI → *amāru, pānu;* IGI.DU → *ālik pāni;* IGI.IGI → *dabdû;* IGI.2 → *ēnu;* ÍL → *našû;* IM → *ṭuppu;* IM.GÍD.DA → *liginnu;* IR → *šalālu;* IŠ.TAR → *Ištār;* ITI → *urhu;* ITI.AB → *kanūnu;* ITI.APIN → *arahsamnu;* ITI.BARAG → *nisannu;* ITI.DIRI.ŠE → *addāru diri;* ITI.DU$_6$, ITI.DUL → *tašrītu;* ITI.GAN → *kislīmu;* ITI.GUD → *aiāru;* ITI.GUD.SI.SÁ → *aiāru;* ITI.KIN → *elūlu;* ITI.NE → *ābu;* ITI.SIG$_4$ → *simānu;* ITI.ŠE → *addāru;* ITI.ZÍZ → *šabāṭu;* IZI → *išātu;* IZI.GAR → *niphu;* Ì → *šamnu;* Ì.GIŠ → *šamnu;*

KA → *pû;* KAB → *šumēlu;* KAB.TÚG → *kaptukku;* KALAG → *da'ānu, danānu;* KALAG.GA → *dunnu;* KAR → *kāru;* KASKAL → *hūlu;* KASKAL—MAN → *hūl šarri;* KASKAL.2 → *hūlu;* KAŠ → *šikāru;* KAŠ.SAG → *šikāru;* KÀŠ → *šīnāti;* KÁ → *bābu;* KÁ.DINGIR.RA.KI → *Bābili;* KÁ.GAL → *abullu;* KÉŠ → *rakāsu;* KI → *erṣutu, itti;* KI.GUB → *manzāzu;* KI.MAH → *kimahhu;* KI.MIN → *šanīš;* KI.TA → *šapal, šaplû, šupālītu halluptu;* KI.TIM → *kaqquru;* KIN → *šapāru;* KISAL → *kisallu;* KIŠIB → *kunukku;* KUD → *nakāsu, parāsu;* KUG → *ellu;* KUG.GI → *hurāṣu;* KUG.UD → *ṣarpu;* KUR → *mātu, ēkallu, kašādu, šaddû;* KUR—AN.ŠÁR → *Māt Aššūr;* KUR.KUR → *mātu;* KUR.KÚR → *māt nakiri;* KUR.MAR.TU.KI → *Māt Amurrî;* KUR.NIM.KI → *Elamtu;* KUR.NIM.MA.KI → *Elamtu;* KUR—URI → *Urarṭu;* KUR—URI.KI → *Akkadû, Māt Akkadî, Urarṭu;* KÚR → *nakru;* KUŠ → *mašku;* KUŠ.DA.E.SÍR → *maš'ennu*?*;* KUŠ.E.SIR → *maš'ennu;* KUŠ.SAL → *ziqqu;* KÚ → *akālu;* KU$_6$ → *nūnu;*

LAL → *haṭû, rūṭu, ṣimittu;* LÀL → *dišpu;* LI.DUR → *abunnutu;* LUGAL → *šarru, šarrūtu;* LÚ → *amēlu;* LÚ.A → *mār šipri;* LÚ.A.BA → *ṭupšarru;* LÚ.A.BA—KUR → *ṭupšar ēkalli;* LÚ.A—KIN → *mār šipri;* LÚ.A—SIG$_5$ → *mār damqi;* LÚ.AD → *abu;* LÚ.ARAD → *urdu;* LÚ.ARAD—É.GAL → *urad ēkalli;* LÚ.DAM.QAR → *tamkāru;* LÚ.DIB—PA → *mukīl appāti;* LÚ.DUB.SAR → *ṭupšarru;* LÚ.DUB.SAR—É.GAL, LÚ.DUB.SAR—KUR → *ṭupšar ēkalli;* LÚ.DUMU → *mār šipri, mār karšāni;* LÚ.DUMU—DÙ → *mār banî;* LÚ.DUMU—KÁ.DINGIR → *Bābili;* LÚ.DUMU.SIG$_5$ → *mār damqi;* LÚ.EME → *ša lišāni;* LÚ.EN → *bēl piqitti, bēl-*[...]*;* LÚ.EN—GIGIR → *bēl mugirri;* LÚ.EN—KÚR → *bēl nakāri;* LÚ.EN.NAM → *pāhutu;* LÚ.EN.NUN → *maṣṣuru;* LÚ.EN—UMUŠ → *bēl ṭēmi;* LÚ.EN—URU → *bēl āli;* LÚ.ERIM → *ṣābu;* LÚ.GAL → *rabiu;* LÚ.GAL—A.BA → *rab ṭupšarri;* LÚ.GAL—ANŠE → *rab urāti;* LÚ.GAL—É → *rab bēti;* LÚ.GAL—(TÚG.)KA.KÉŠ → *rab kāṣiri;* LÚ.GAL—KAŠ.LUL → *rab šāqê;* LÚ.GAL—MU → *rab nuhatimmi;* LÚ.GAL—URU → *rab ālāni;* LÚ.GAL—URU.HAL.\U → *rab bīrti;* LÚ.GAR → *šaknu;* LÚ.GAL—50 → *rab hanšā;* LÚ.GAR.KUR → *šaknu;* LÚ.GIŠ.BAN → *ša qassi;* LÚ.GIŠ.DA → *a'lu;* LÚ.GIŠ.GIGIR → *susānu;* LÚ.GÚ.EN.NA → *šandabakku;* LÚ.GURUŠ → *eṭlu;* LÚ.IGI → *šību;* LÚ.IGI.DUB → *masennu;* LÚ.IGI.UM → *masennu;* LÚ.Ì.DU$_8$ → *atû;* LÚ.KAŠ.LUL → *šāqiu;* LÚ.KUG.DIM → *kuttimmu;* LÚ.KÚR → *nakru;* LÚ.MAH → *ṣīru;* LÚ.MAŠ.MAŠ → *āšipu;* LÚ.MUŠEN.DÙ → *ušandû;* LÚ.NAGAR → *naggāru;* LÚ.NAM → *pāhutu;* LÚ.NIGIR → *nāgiru;* LÚ.NUN → *rubû;* LÚ.PA → *ša huṭāri, uklu;* LÚ.SAG → *ša rēši;* LÚ.SANGA → *sangû;* LÚ.SIMUG—AN.BAR → *nappāh parzilli;* LÚ.SIMUG—URUDU → *nappāh erê;* LÚ.SIPA → *rā'iu;* LÚ.SIPA—MUŠEN → *rā'i iṣṣūri;* LÚ.SUKKAL → *sukkallu;* LÚ.ŠÁM → *ša šīmi;* LÚ.ŠÀ.TAM → *šatammu;* LÚ.TIN.TIR.KI → *Bābili;* LÚ.TÚG.KA.KÉŠ → *kāṣiru;* LÚ.TUR → *ṣehru, ṣuhāru;* LÚ.UGU → *ša muhhi* [...]*;* LÚ.UMBISAG → *ṭupšarru;* LÚ.UNUG.KI → *Uruk;* LÚ.UŠ → *rādiu;* LÚ.UŠ.BAR → *ušpāru;* LÚ.UŠ.KU → *kalû B;* LÚ.ZADIM—BAN → *sasin qassi;* LÚ.ZADIM—GAG.TI → *sasin uṣṣi;* LÚ.ÚŠ → *pagru;* LÚ.2 → *šaniu;* LÚ.3.U$_5$ → *tašlīšu;* LÚ.600—KUR → *nāgir ēkalli;*

MA.NA → *manû;* MA.NA.TA.ÀM → *manû;* MAH → *ṣīru;* MAN → *šaniu B, šarru;* MAŠ.DÀ → *ṣabītu;* MÁŠ → *ṣibtu, barû, bīru;* MAŠ.SILÀ → *naglabu;* MAŠKIM → *rābiṣu;* MÁŠ.MI → *šuttu;* ME.NI → *bāb ēkalli;* MÈ → *tāhāzu;* MI → *mūšu;* MÍ → *issu B;* MÍ.A.BA → *ṭupšarrutu;* MÍ.ANŠE.KUR → *atānu;* MÍ.ÁŠ.QAR → *unīqu;* MÍ—É.GAL → *sēgallu;* MÍ.GAR.U.U → *pallissu;* MÍ.HUL → *lemuttu;* MÍ.KUR → *atānu;* MÍ.KUR.GAR.RA → *kurgarrutu;* MÍ.NAR → *nuārtu;* MÍ.NAR.GAL → *nargallutu;* MÍ.NIM → *puhattu;* MÍ.SIG$_5$ → *de'iqtu;* MÍ.SIMUG → *nappāhtu;* MÍ.ŠU.I → *gallābtu;* MU → *šuātu, šumu;* MU—DINGIR → *nīš ili;* MU.AN.NA → *šattu;* MU.SAG → *nīš rēši;* MU$_4$.MU$_4$ → *labāšu*; MUL → *Dilibat, Ṣalbatānu, kakkabu, kakkubu;* MUL.LUGAL → *Šarru;* MUL.MUL → *Zappu;* MUL.SAG.ME.GAR → *Sagmegar;* MUL.UDU.IDIM.GUD.UD → *Šihṭu;* MUN → *ṭābtu;* MUR → *hašû;* MURUB$_4$ → *qablu, qablu C, qablû;* MURUB$_4$—URU → *qabsi āli;* MUŠ → *ṣerru;* MUŠEN → *iṣṣūru;*

NA → *manzāzu;* NAG → *šatû;* NAM → *šīmtu;* NAM.ÚŠ → *mūtānu;* NAR → *nuāru;* NÁ → *ṣalālu;* NA$_4$ → *abnu;* NA$_4$.I.DIB → *askupputu;* NA$_4$.KIŠIB → *kunukku;* NA$_4$.UR$_5$ → *arû B;* NA$_4$.ZA.GÌN.DURU$_5$ → *zagindurû;* NA$_5$ → *pitnu;* NE → *anniu;* NIGIN → *sahāru;* NÍG.BA → *qissu;* NÍG.GIG → *ikkibu, maruštu;* NÍG.GUB → *kudurru;* NÍG.NA → *nidnakku;* NÍG.SILA$_{11}$.GA → *lēšu;* NÍG.ŠID → *nikkassu;* NÍG.TAB → *naṣraptu;* NIM → *elû B;* NIN → *ahātu;* NINA, NINA.KI → *Nīnua;* NINDA, NINDA.HI.A → *kusāpu;* NINDU → *tinūru;* NITA → *zakkāru;* NU → *lā, ṣalmu;* NUMUN → *zar'u, zēru, zēr halgatê;* NUN → *rubû;* NUNDUN → *šaptu;* NUN.KI → *Eridu;* NUN.ME → *apkallu;*

PAB → *ahu, gimru;* PI.2 → *uznu;* PÚ → *būrtu;*

RI → *adannu;*

SA → *kīdītu;* SAG → *rēšāti, rēšu;* SAG.DU → *kaqqudu, qaqqadu;* SAG.KI → *pūtu;* SAG.UŠ → *kaiānu;* SAHAR.ŠUB → *saharšubbû;* SAL.LA → *ruqqu B;* SAR → *šaṭāru, habātu;* SA$_5$ → *siāmu;* SÈ.SÈ.KI → *ṣummirāti;* SI → *qarnu;* SI.SÁ → *ešēru;* SIG → *damāqu;* SIG$_4$ → *libittu;* SIG$_5$ → *damāqu;* SIG$_7$ → *urqu;* SIG$_7$.IGI → *šūr īni;* SIKIL → *elālu;* SILA → *sūqu;* SI.LAL → *piqittu;* SILIM → *šalāmu, šulmu;* SIMUG → *nappāhu;* SIPA → *rā'iu;* SISKUR, SISKUR.SISKUR → *niqiu;* SI$_4$ → *SI;* SU → *zumru;* SUD → *riāqu;* SUHUR → *ṭēhi;* SUHUŠ → *išdu;* SUM → *nadānu, tadānu;*

ŠAB → *šapputu;* ŠAH → *huzīru;* ŠÁM → *šīmu;* ŠÀ → *libbāti, libbu;* ŠÀ.MUD → *pirittu;* ŠÀ.NIGIN → *tīrāni;* ŠÀ.SÈ.SÈ.KI → *ṣummirāti;* ŠÀ—URU → *Libbi āli;* ŠE → *še'u, kissutu;* ŠE.BAR → *uṭṭutu;* ŠE.GA → *šemû;* ŠE.GIŠ.Ì → *šamaššammi;* ŠE.IN.NU → *tibnu;* ŠE.PAD → *kurummutu;* ŠÈG → *zunnu;* ŠEM.LI → *burāšu;* ŠEŠ → *ahu;* ŠEŠ.AD → *ah abi;* ŠÉŠ → *pašāšu;* ŠID → *manû B, minītu;* ŠU → *qātu;* ŠU.SI → *ubānu;* ŠU.2 → *qātu;* ŠUB → *nadû;* ŠUB.AŠ.TE → *nīd kussî;* ŠUB.ŠUB → *maqātu;* ŠUR → *zanānu;* ŠÚ → *kiššatu;*

TA → *inanna, issi/u;* TAG → *lapātu;* TAG_4 → *ezēbu;* TE → *lētu, ṭehû;* TÉŠ.BI → *ištēniš;* TI → *laqû;* TIL → *qatû;* TI.LA → *balāṭu;* TI_8.MUŠEN →*arû C;* TIN → *balāṭu;* TIN.TIR.KI → *Bābili;* TU → *erābu, erēbu;* TU.MUŠEN → *su''u;* TU_5 → *ramāku;* TÚG → *ṣubātu, šer'ītu, elītu;* TÚG.HI.A → *ṣubātu;* TÚG.IB → *nēbettu;* TÚG.ÍB.LAL → *nēbuhu;* TÚG.KUR.RA → *šuhattu;* TÚG.SÍG → *sissiktu;* TÚG.SÌG → *mihṣu, ṣubātu;* TUKU → *rašû;* TUR → *ṣahāru;* TUR.DIŠ → *lakû;* TÙR → *tarbāṣu;* TUŠ → *ašābu;*

U → *ubānu;* U.MUR → *ubān hašê;* U.SAG → *kubšu;* Ú → *hašānu, qulqulānu, urbānu;* Ú.IN.NU.UŠ → *martakal;* Ú.ŠEŠ → *murru;* U_8 → *agurrutu;* UB → *tubqu;* UD → *ūmu, ūmussu;* Ú.DA, UD.DA → *ṣētu;* UD.NÁ.ÀM → *ūm bubbuli;* UDU, UDU.HI.A → *immeru;* UDU.NIM → *hurāpu;* UDU.NITÁ → *iābilu;* UDU.SISKUR → *niqiu;* UGU → *muhhu;* ÚH → *ru'tu;* UKKIN → *puhru;* UNBIN → *ṣupru;* UN → *nīšī;* UNUG.KI → *Uruk;* UR.KU → *kalbu;* UR.MAH → *nēšu;* URI.KI → *Māt Akkadî;* URU → *ālu;* URU.BÀD—LUGAL → *Dūr-Šarrukku;* URU.BÀD—LUGAL.GIN, URU.BÀD—MAN—GIN → *Dūr-Šarrukīn;* URU.É → *Bīt Imbî;* URU.KASKAL → *Harrānu;* URU.NINA, URU.NINA.KI → *Nīnua;* URU.ŠÀ—URU → *Libbi āli;* URU.ŠE → *kapru;* URU.TIN.TIR.KI → *Bābili;* URUDU → *erû;* URUDU.ŠEN.TUR → *nangussu;* ÙR → *ūru;* UR_5 → *šû, šuātu;* UR_5.ÚŠ → *têrtu;* ÚŠ → *muātu, mūtānu;* ÚŠ.MEŠ →*dāmu;* UZU → *šīru;* UZU.Á.2 → *ahu B;* UZU.SILIM → *šulmu;*

ZABAR → *siparru;* ZAG → *imittu;* ZAG.MU → *pāṭu;* ZALÁG → *namāru;* ZÉ → *martu;* ZI → *napšutu, napištu, nasāhu, tabû, tību;* ZI.GA → *ṣītu;* ZÍD, ZÍD.DA → *qēmu;* ZÍD.MAD.GÁ → *maṣhutu;* ZÍZ.A.AN, ZÍZ.ÀM → *kunāšu;* ZU → *idû, la'û;* ZU.AB → *apsû;* ZÚ → *šinnu;*

1 → *issēn, issēnīu, issēt, līmu, meat;* 1.ŠU → *šūši;* 1.*en* → *issēn;* 1.*en-šu* → *iltēnšu;* 2 → *šaniu B, šina B, šinīšu, šitta, meat;* 3 → *šalšu, līmu, meat, tašlīšu;* 4 → *erbīšu, rabbu;* 7 → *seb'īšu;* 8 → *samān, samuntu;*

10 → *ešer, ešrāti;* 15 → *imittu;* 150 → *šumēlu;*

20 → *ešrā;*

30 → *šalāšā;*

40 → *arbā;*

50 → *hanšā;*

60 → *šeššā, šūši;*

70 → *seb'ā;*

80 → *samānā*

Glossary

a'lu "nomad": [LÚ.GIŠ.D]A.MEŠ 74:5,
abāku "to drive away, to send, to lead in": *a-ba-ku* 168:4, *a-bu-ku* 78 r. 7, *l*]*i-bu-kám-ma* 92 r. 5,
abālu "to bring": *nu-ul-t*[*e-bi-la* 197:6, *ub-lam* 247:4, 6, r. 9, *ub-lam*] 247:8, *ul-te-bi-la-šú* 260 r. 7, *ul-t*]*e-bi-la-áš-šú-nu-tú* 84:11,
aban hālti: [N]A₄.*hal-ta* 272 r. 5,
abāru "lead": A.BÁR 271:8,
abātu "to destroy, (N) to flee": *ta-bat-a-ni* 229 r. v 76,
abbūtu "intercession": *a-bu-tú-ku-nu* 229 r. v 82,
abnu "stone; hail; glass, gem": NA₄ 299 i 3, 8, 9, NA₄] 299 i 2, N[A₄ 299 i 1, ii 10, 11, N[A₄.MEŠ 299 ii 2, [NA₄.MEŠ 299 ii 9, 12,
abu "father": *ab-bi-šú* 236 r. 8, *a-bi-šu-ma* 72 r. 8, AD 29:3, 80:9, 120 r. 1, 219:2, 228:3, i 29, r. v 62, 288 r. ii 19, AD] 229 r. vii 7, A[D 165:6, A]D 34:9, [AD 288 r. ii 3, AD-*ka* 229 r. v 7, AD-*k*[*a* 213 r. 4, AD]-*ka* 182 r. 11, AD-*ku-nu* 229 r. v 14, 22, AD.MEŠ-*šú* 229 ii 3, 240:10, AD.MEŠ-*šú-nu* 84 r. 7, AD-*šú* 91:5, 120 r. 4, 280:5, 9, 286:15, A[D-*šú* 187:3, [AD-*šú* 149 r. 6, AD-*šú-nu* 229 r. v 34, A]D-*u-a* 288 i 24, AD-*ú-a* 176 r. 3, [L]Ú.AD.MEŠ-*e-a* 33:11,
ābu (Ab, name of the 5th month): ITI.NE 253 r. 7, 276 r. 10,
abūbu "deluge": *a-bu-bu* 229 r. vi 70, 230:8, *a-bu-ub* 230:24,
abullu "(city) gate": KÁ.GAL 24:2, 239 ii 27, KÁ.[GAL 150:8, K]Á.GAL 150:3,
abunnutu "umbilical cord": [L]I.DUR-*ka* 230:34,
abussu "storehouse": [*ub-sa-*(*a*)]-*te* 287 iii 9,
abutu "word, matter": *a-bat* 1:1, 120 r. 12, 279:1, *a-ba-at* 267:6, *a-bé-e-te* 154:5, *a-bu-tu-ú* 234:18, *a-bu-tú* 120 r. 18, 154:9, r. 8, 229 i 74, 80, r. v 4, 28, *a-bu-*[*tú* 5:6, *a-b*[*u*]-*tú* 231:1,
ab abi "grandfather": AD—AD.ME[Š-*k*]*a* 182 r. 11,
adanniš "very": *a—dan-niš* 113:c2, 6, 9, *a—dan-niš*] 121:5, *a—dan*]-*niš* 119:4, *a—*[*dan-niš*] 18:5, 114:6, 8, *a*]*—dan-*[*n*]*iš* 3:6, [*a—dan-niš* 119:4, 121:5, [*a—dan-niš*] 113:c9, [*a—d*]*an-niš* 18:4,
adāru "to be dark, gloomy, afraid": *ia-a-da-ru* 247:16, *šu-du-ru* 253 r. 3,
addāru (Adar, name of the 12th month): ITI.ŠE 17 r. 3,
addāru diri "intercalary Adar": ITI.DIRI.ŠE 256:3,
adê "treaty": *a-de-e* 120 r. 8, 128:7, 129:12, 229 i 1, 13, 19, 46, r. v 7, 15, 22, 46, 53, 56, 62, 64, 69, 717, viii 66, *a-de-*[*e* 229 r. vii 1, ((*a-de-e*)) 229 r. vii 6, [*a-de-e* 226:4,
adi "until, plus": *a-di* 11:15, 66 r. 6, 91:2, 93 r. 3, 116:3, 154:11, 163 r. 3, 164:6, 217:3, 220:4, 7, 229 i 15, r. v 46, 807, 234:21, 235:49, 239 ii 14, 245 r. 2, 3, *a-di*] 33:6, 213:2, *a-d*[*i*] 1 r. 13, *a*]-*di* 38:6, 168 r. 9, [*a-di* 299 i 10, *a-du* 1 r. 3, 33:4, 46 r. 2, 152:10, 234 r. 2, [*a-du* 289:2, 4, 6, 8, 10, 12,
adû "now": *a-du-ú* 29:8, 35:6, 69:11, 126:9, 164 r. 6, *a-du-ú*] 128 r. 12, *a-d*]*u-ú* 68 r. 4, 83:4, [*a-d*]*u-ú* 40:7,
agâ "this": *a-ga-a* 79 r. 5, 84 r. 14, 86:5, 93 r. 5, 196:5, 213:3, 235:23, 33, 35, r. 44, 239 i 5, r. ii 23, *a-g*[*a-a*] 204:2, *a*]-*ga-a* 168 r. 3,
agannû "this": *a-g*[*a-nu-tu* 196:3,
aganutillû "dropsy": *a-ga-nu-til-la-a* 229 r. vii 12,
agappu "wing": *a-gap-pi* 230:14,
agāru "to hire": *e-gu-ra-šu-nu-ni* 120 r. 17, *e-ta-ga-ra* 120 r. 11, 12, *i-gu-ru* 91:4,
aggiš "grimly": *ag-giš* 229 r. vi 56, *ag-gi*]*š* 226 r. 2,
agru "hireling": LÚ.*ag-ru* 120 r. 10, LÚ.*ag-ru-te* 120 r. 16, LÚ.*ag*]-*ru-ti-šú* 91 r. 8,
agû "crown, tiara": *a-g*]*e-e* 230:30, AGA 232:8,
agurrutu "ewe": U₈ 229 r. vii 40,
ahāiš "each other": *a-ha-meš* 126 r. 12, 237 r. 11, 248 e. 9, *a-ha-me*[*š* 88:4, 222:5, *a-he-iš* 229 r. vii 53, viii 39, 47, *a-hi-iš* 229 r. vii 50,
ahātu "sister": NIN 34:10, 249:4, N[IN]-*a* 176 r. 3, NIN-*ia* 154 r. 2,
ahāzu "to grasp, marry": *ih-haz* 86:5,
ahhūr "still": *ah—hur* 154:8, r. 4, 14,
ahu "brother": *a-h*[*u-šú* 20:3, PAB-*ia* 154:2, [PAB]-*ka* 225:1, PAB-*ki* 154 r. 3, PAB.MEŠ-*ka* 52:4, ŠEŠ 34:11, ŠE]Š 176 r. 2, ŠE]Š-*a* 184:2, ŠEŠ.MEŠ 229 ii 3, Š[EŠ.MEŠ] 253:7, ŠEŠ.MEŠ-*kunu* 229 r. vii 73, ŠEŠ.MEŠ-*ku-nu* 229 r. vii 36, 68, 78, 79, 82, viii 12, ŠEŠ.MEŠ-*ku-nu*] 229 r. viii 1, ŠEŠ.[M]EŠ-*ku-nu* 229 r. vii 30, [ŠEŠ].MEŠ-*ku-nu* 229 r. vii 75, ŠEŠ.MEŠ-*ni* 128:5, ŠEŠ.MEŠ-*n*[*i* 40:7, ŠEŠ.MEŠ-*šú* 128 r. 8, 229 i 76, r. v 1, 2, 10, 28, 67, vi 79, vii 3, ŠEŠ.MEŠ-[*šú* 229 ii 3, ŠEŠ.[MEŠ]-*šú* 229 r. vi 88, ŠEŠ-*šú* 131:2, 247 r. 3, 275:8, ŠEŠ-*šú-nu* 229 r. v 29, 33,
ahu B "arm, (pl.) army": Á 77 r. 1, 234 r. 17, 237 r. 1, 12, Á.MEŠ-*šú-nu* 229 r. viii 20, UZU.Á.2-*ni* 160 r. 2,
ah abi "uncle": ŠEŠ—AD-*iá* 71:4,
ai "may not": *a-a* 229 r. v 82, vi 2, 18, 31, 40, 61, 65, viii 50, [*a-a* 229 r. v 88,
aiābu "enemy": *a-a-bi* 234:1,
aiāka "where": *a-a-ka* 5:3, *a-a-k*[*a* 106 r. 5,
aiāru (Iyyar, name of the 2nd month): ITI.GUD 265 r. 1, ITI.GUD.SI.SÁ 229 r. viii 63,
aiāši "me": *a-a-ši* 120 r. 2, 9, *ia-a-ši* 19:12,

ia-a-ši] 56:4, *i*[*a-a-ši* 33:3,
aiu "what, which?": *a-a-ú* 234:9,
aiulu "stag": *a-a-lu* 229 r. vii 67, 253 r. 5,
akālu "to eat, consume; (Š) to feed; food": *ak-la* 229 r. vi 27, *ek-la* 229 r. vi 67, *e-ka-lu-u-ni* 1:6, *ik-kal* 235 r. 40, KÚ 247 r. 3, 5, 262 r. 1, 296 r. 3, [KÚ] 255:7, *le-kul* 229 r. vi 25, 28, *l*]*e-e-*[*k*]*u-la* 1 r. 12, *le-ku-la-šu* 229 r. viii 31, *le-ku-la-š*[*u*] 229 r. viii 32, *le-ku-lu* 229 r. vi 30, *li-kul* 229 r. vi 17, *li-šá-kil* 229 r. vii 10, *li-*(*šá*)*-kil-ku-nu* 229 r. vii 43, *lu-šá-ki-lu* 229 r. vii 85, *ta-kul* 229 r. vii 64, *ta-kul-u-ni* 229 r. vii 62, *tu-šá-kal-*[*a*]*-šú-u-ni* 229 iv 5, *t*]*u-šá-ka-al* 235 r. 33,
akanna "here": *a-kan-na* 37 r. 8, *a-ka*[*n-na* 196:7, *a-ka*[*n-na*] 132:9, *a-k*[*an-na* 180:3,
akê "how?": *a-ke-e* 120 r. 15, 121:8, 140 r. 11, *a-k*]*e-e* 11:14,
akī "as; as if; thus": *ak* 157:1, 172:1, *a-ki* 7:4, 32 r. 1, 105:5, 240:2, 10, 14, 279 r. 8, *a-ki-i* 196:6, *a-ki-*[*i* 133:15,
ākilu "man-eating": *a-ki-li* 229 r. vi 49, [(*a-ki-lu*) 229 r. vii 85,
alāku "to go, come": *a-lak-ka* 72 e. 9, *al-ka* 32 r. 3, 120:19, r. 3, 9, *a*]*l-kam-ma* 172 r. 2, *al-kám-ma* 165 r. 4, *al-la-kám-ma* 73:6, *al-lak-an-ni* 1 r. 13, *a-l*[*ak* 237 r. 21, *a-lik* 1:18, 21:5, 170:6, 278 s. 1, *a-*[*lik* 1 r. 2, *a*]*-lik* 21:8, *a-lik-ma* 31:9, [*a-l*]*i-ik* 234:4, *a-ta-lak* 72 r. 4, DU 248 r. 5, 250:8, 252:9, 253 r. 2, DU-*ku* 262 r. 3, [DU-*ku* 247 r. 10, DU-*ku-ma* 237 r. 12, 260 r. 3, DU-*ku-ú* 247:8, DU-*ma* 262:6, DU.DU-*ka* 233:19, *i-la-ka* 225:4, *il-lak* 122:1, 229 r. vii 24, 239 ii 7, 8, *il-*[*lak*] 25:4, *il-lak-u-ni* 229 r. viii 31, 32, *il-la-ka* 1 r. 8, 120 s. 1, 122:7, 139 s. 2, 237 r. 21, *il-la-k*[*a* 48 r. 2, *il-la-*[*ka*] 18:8, *il-l*[*a-ka* 72 e. 11, *il-la-kan-ni* 122:4, *il-la-ku-ni* 246 r. 4, *i*[*l-lik-u-ni*] 10:7, *il-li-*[*ka* 179 r. 5, *il-li-*[*ka*] 18:9, *il-l*[*i-ka* 31 r. 3, *il-l*]*i-ka* 61:4, *i*]*l-li-ka-ni* 129 r. 10, [*il-li*]*-ka-ni-ni* 1 r. 6, *il-l*]*i-ku* 66 r. 11, *il*]*-li-ku* 132:8, *i*]*l-li-ku* 176 r. 5, 182 r. 8, *i*[*l-li-ku-ni* 138:5, *il-li-ku-ni*]*m-ma* 237 r. 11, *il-li-ku-nu* 128:11, *il-lu-ku* 240:14, *it-tal-ka* 147:10, 235:32, *it-tal-k*[*a* 30 r. 7, *it*]*-tal-ka* 17 r. 2, [*it-ta*]*l-ka-ni* 60 r. 5, *it-tal-*[*ku*] 163:7, *it-ta*[*l-ku* 138:3, [*i*]*t-tal-ku* 138:5, [*it-t*]*al-ku-u-n*[*i* 9:13, [*it-ta*]*l-ku-ú-ni* 8:10, *it-t*[*al-x* 67 r. 1, *it-ta-lak* 10 r. 11, 229 r. v 25, *it-*[*ta-lak*] 231 r. 1, [*i*]*t-ta-lak* 70:13, *it-tal-lak* 22 r. 7, *it-*[*tan-al-lak*] 93 r. 3, *i-tal-ka* 4:3, *i-tal-ku* 64:1, 145 r. 4, *i-tal-la-ka* 234 r. 7, *la-al-lik* 120 s. 2, *lil-lik-ma* 246 r. 9, 248 r. 7, [*lil-lik-ma* 247 r. 18, *l*]*il-li-ka* 42:6, [*lil-li*]*-ka* 42 r. 1, *lil-l*]*i-kám-m*[*a* 118:1, *li*]*l-li-kám-ma* 168:3, *lil*]*-li-ku* 129:20, *li*[*l-li-ku-ni*] 148 r. 5, [*li-i*]*l-lik* 183 r. 7, *li-il-li-ka* 234:14, *li-lik-a-ni* 152 r. 8, [*l*]*i-li-k*[*a* 150:7, *lul-lik* 69:9, 239 ii 14, *lul-lik*] 31:2, [*lu*]*l-lik* 82:2, *ni-il*]*-lik* 162 r. 9, *ni-*[*il-lik* 164:11, *ni-i-li-ik* 234:19, *ni-il-lik-u-ni* 6:9, *tal-lak* 235:35, *tal-lak-a-ni* 229 r. viii 30, *tal-lak-a-ni-ni* 227 ii 7, 229 r. v 5, *tal-lak-a-ni-ni*] 229 iii 5, *tal-la-ka* 72 e. 10, *tal-l*[*a-ka* 241:7, *ta*[*l-li-ka* 85:9, *tal-li-ku* 33:9, *ta*]*l-li-ku-ú-ni* 237 r. 22, *ta-at-tal-ka* 21:19,
alālu "to hang": *i-lu-lu-ma* 237 r. 3,
āliku "goer, walker": *a-li-ku-tu-šú* 234 r. 14, *a-li-ku-ú-tú-šá* 234 r. 20,
ālik pāni "leader": IGI.DU 91 r. 10,
ālittu "pregnant": *a-lit-te* 199 r. 10,
alluttu "crab": *al-lu-ti* 229 r. viii 13,
alpu "ox": GUD 120 r. 8, 262 r. 1, 281:9, GUD.MEŠ 281:1, 5, 288 ii 29,
ālu "city, town": URU 212 r. 11, 228:6, 235 r. 8, 19, 237 r. 4, 8, 240:7, 280:12, 300:11, UR[U 83:9, 150:3, [URU 251 r. 3, URU-*ku-nu* 229 r. vii 38, URU.MEŠ 6:5, 8:9, 26 r. 4, 181:5, URU.MEŠ]-*ku-nu* 229 r. vii 85, URU.MEŠ-*ni* 60 r. 6, 62:5, URU-*šú* 239 r. ii 23,
amāru "to see, behold": *am-mar* 164:6, *am-ma-*[*ru* 194:5, *am-ma-ru-ni* 120:5, *a-ma*[*r*] 45:4, *a-mì-ru* 120:16, *am-ra-ku* 33:13, *am-ra-tu* 252 r. 1, *a-mur* 128 r. 2, *a-mur-a* 193:8, [*a-mur-ú-n*]*i* 105:6, *a-mu-ru-ni* 120 r. 18, *a-tam-mar* 81:3, *a-ta-mar* 120 r. 5, 129:15, *a-ta-mar-šú* 120 r. 6, *e-mar* 299 i 5, 6, 7, 8, 9, *e-ma*]*r* 299 i 4, *e-mu-*[*ru*] 52:4, *e-mu-ru* 240:10, *i-mu-ru* 165:5, 234:10, IGI-*mar* 299 i 11, 13, 14, IGI-*ra* 246:8, IGI-*ri* 246:8, IGI-*ru* 247 r. 4, IGI-*ru*] 247 r. 2, IGI-*ru-ma* 247:14, *le-mur* 22 r. 3, *li-mur* 237 r. 19, *li-mur-ma* 260 r. 8, *lu-mur* 265:3, *lu*]*-mur* 248 r. 1, [*lu-mur* 82 r. 3, *né-e-ta-m*[*ar* 6:11, *né-*[*mur-u-ni*] 12:4, *t*[*a-mar*] 154 r. 16, *ta-mar-u-ni* 1:9, 115 s. 1, *ta-ma*[*r-u-ni*] 7:7, *ta-mur-ma* 181 r. 2, *ta-mu-r*[*u* 134:1,
amatu "word, matter": *a-mat* 126 r. 13, 128:9, 12, 129:13, 164 r. 4, 221:4, 229 r. vi 85, 237 r. 6, 265:5, *a-ma-ti* 267:4, *a-ma-ti-ku-nu* 229 r. v 81,
amēlu "man": *a-me-lu* 277:2, LÚ 41:8, 154 r. 15, 229 r. vi 28, 232:9, 275:1, 277:2,
amēlūtu "mankind": *a-me-lu-te* 229 r. vii 90, LÚ-*te* 163 r. 2,
amīltu "woman": MÍ.*a-mil-ti* 276:2,
ammāka "there": *am-*[*m*]*a-ka* 120 e. 25,
am-mār see *mār,*
ammiu "that": *am-mu-ti* 1:4, *am-m*[*u-ti* 10 r. 7,
ammurig "then, at that time": *am-mu-rig* 120 s. 2,
amtu "maid, slave-girl": GEMÉ 286:13, GEM[É] 286:8, GE[MÉ] 286:5, 10, GEMÉ.MEŠ 286:16, r. 7, GEM[É.MEŠ] 286:11, GEMÉ.MEŠ-*šá* 286 r. 9, GEMÉ.MEŠ-*ši-na* 286:14, GE[MÉ.MEŠ-*ši-na*] 286:3,
amu "raft": G]I.*a-ma-te* 224:4,
amūtu "liver": *a-m*[*u-ut* 260 r. 9, [BÀ 237 r. 1, BÀ.MEŠ 237 r. 19, 22, 260 r. 6, BÀ-*ut* 237 r. 12, 14,
ana "to": *ana* 68:5, 88:4, 120:24, 232:12, 233:8, 237 r. 18, 20, 243:6, 247:9, 18, r. 11, 248 r. 5, 249:2, 250 r. 10, 11, 251 r. 3, 252:2, 4, 16, r. 14, 253 r. 2, 255:6, 261:9, 262:10, 263:5, 6, r. 6, 264 r. 1, 265:4, 5, 6, 7, [*ana* 231 r. 1, [[*ana*]] 297:7, *a-na* 1:1, 7, 15, 18, r. 15, 16, 2:3, 6:3, 8, 8:1, 3, 7, 9:3, 11, 9:3, 7, 16:7, 18:3, 4, r. 2, 19:2, 5, 9, 10, 14, 15, 19:1, 21:7, 9, 17, r. 1, 23:2, 25:2, 3, 26:1, 28:1, 3, 5, 29:2, 3, 4, 11, 30 r. 3, 31:3, 4, 6, 70, 10, 13, 31 e. 11, r. 5, 33:3, 8, 18, 36:3, 10, r. 8, 38:6, 39:4, 41:9, 43:5, 47:3, 6, 48:1, r. 1, 49:7, 51:3, 57:1, 65:5, 66 r. 7, 67:2, 8, r. 2, 69:9, 69:11, 14, 76:3, 7, 79 r. 2, 83:5, 6, 84:7, 85:5, 85:3, 88:1, 89 r. 3, 92 e. 1, r. 4, 94:4, 96:1, 3, 4, 96:1, 3, 98:2, 98:3, 100:1, 3, 102:3, 103:1, 3, 114:1, 3, 7, 9, r. 13, 115:3, 6, 7, 117:4, 5, 7, 118:2, 4, 119:3, 120:1, 2, 3, 6, 11, r. 1, 2, 9, 19, 21, 23, s. 1, 121:3, 123:10, 124:1, 3, 5, r. 4, 125:3, 126:2, 3, 9, 21, r. 1, 14, 127:2, 7, 128:12, 13, r. 7, 14, 129:16, r. 11, 131:3, 132:7, 8, 9, 133:10, 11, 135:3, 136:5, 6, 11, r. 7, 140:3, 14, 141:1, 4, 145 r. 2, 147 r. 1, 7, 149:1, 150:1, 152:8, 154:2, r. 1, 12, 155:1, 5, 156:3, 160:2, 163:2, 164:7, s. 1, 2, 166:2, 3, 167 r. 1, 170:2, 171:5,

172:4, 176 r. 1, 4, 6, 180 r. 8, 181 r. 10, 182:5, 185:5, 187:8, 192:1, 199 r. 2, 203:3, 212 r. 5, 214:2, 4, 216 r. 7, 218:3, 4, 5, 220:8, 225:5, 226 r. 7, 227 ii 5, 229 i 79, iv 8, r. v 6, 9, 16, 25, 44, 47, 52, 58, 60, 74, vi 6, 15, 19, 59, 68, vii 14, 15, 56, 58, 66, 67, 71, 73, viii 12, 19, 30, 32, 33, 39, 44, 232:9, 233:9, 11, 17, 19, 21, r. 8, 11, 234:4, 5, 6, 18, r. 6, 7, 9, 10, 11, 13, 235:3, 5, 11, 51, r. 2, 3, 4, 5, 15, 37, 38, 236:2, 13, 237:2, r. 4, 6, 20, 22, 239 i 1, 2, 14, 18, ii 15, r. i 9, 11, 18, 19, 21, 23, 24, 25, 26, 27, 28, 29, 34, ii 10, 240:4, 12, 13, 241 r. 9, 243:3, 4, r. 1, 2, 246:13, r. 3, 4, 247:4, r. 1, 251:5, 254 r. 3, 255 r. 5, 10, 261 r. 3, 262:6, 11, 265:1, 2, 269 r. 3, 275:5, e. 10, r. 1, 276:6, 277:3, 280:6, 8, 9, 288 iii 15, 19, r. ii 20, 21, 298 r. 1, *a-na*] 12:3, 30 r. 6, 31:1, 66 r. 1, 8, 121:4, 175 r. 4, 217:1, 239 i 3, *a-n*[*a* 10:6, 26:3, 27:4, 33 r. 15, 35:5, 40:8, 67 r. 4, 85:6, 104:3, 114 r. 3, 125:1, 129:14, r. 14, 138:4, 150:5, 164 r. 6, 165 r. 3, 188:6, 190:2, 194:3, 208:1, 217:6, 235 r. 8, 236 r. 17, 273 r. 5, *a-n*[*a*] 199 r. 13, 221 r. 10, *a-n*]*a* 33 r. 9, 86:7, 92 r. 8, 227 ii 1, 239 r. ii 15, 280 r. 1, *a-*[*na* 31 r. 7, 95:3, 105:4, 114:4, 147 r. 3, 151:1, 155:3, 229 r. vi 90, *a-*[*na*] 21:14, *a-*[*n*]*a* 40:1, 283 r. 3, *a*]*-na* 1 e. 19, 13:3, 71 r. 2, 235:32, 242 r. 1, [*a-na* 10:1, 12:1, 13:1, 18:1, 19:1, 21:11, 26 r. 7, 27:4, 45:5, 48:2, 56:4, 94:1, 98:1, 102:1, 105:7, 119:1, 6, 121:1, 128 r. 13, 129:8, 131:2, 133:13, 135:1, 136:1, 138:7, 140:1, 151:5, 152 r. 9, 161:1, 228:3, 4, 239 i 8, r. i 1, 251:6, 262:12, 284 r. 2, [*a-na*] 8 r. 5, 8:1, 21 r. 6, 27:1, 74 r. 4, 85:9, 94:1, 113:c1, 129:1, 135:5, 228:3, [*a-n*]*a* 29:2, 33:13, 44:2, 98:1, 101:1, 113:c3, 7, 137:4, 138:3, 147 r. 12, 161 r. 3, 5, 217:8, [*a*]*-na* 8:4, 229 r. vii 35, viii 14, 284 r. 4, [*a*]*-n*[*a* 229 r. viii 1,

anāhu "to be tired, exhausted" *ut-ta-*[*na-ah* 288 i 9,

anakanna "hitherto": *a-na-kan-*[*na* 170:1,

anāku "I": *ana-ku* 61:4, 162 r. 11, *ana-k*[*u* 54:6, *a-na-ku* 3:5, r. 1, 33:12, 71:5, 72 r. 4, 75 e. 10, 81:2, 86:4, 120:24, r. 10, 15, 129:10, 140:14, 154:12, r. 12, 13, 164:10, r. 9, 173:5, 176 r. 5, 183:8, 204:7, 217:9, 220 r. 3, 247 r. 4, *a-na-k*[*u* 101:3, 147:3, 172:3, r. 3, *a-na*]*-ku* 185:7, *a-n*[*a-ku* 3:3, 112 r. 3, *a-n*]*a-ku* 121:7, *a-*[*na-ku*] 105:5, *a-*[*na*]*-ku* 1 r. 13, *a-*[*n*]*a-ku* 154:11, *a*]*-na-ku* 164:3, [*a-na-ku*] 72 r. 8, 297:7, *a-na-ku-u* 140:20, 152 r. 10,

anīnu "we": *a-né-ni* 229 r. vi 77, 92, *a-ni-ni* 82 r. 3, 235:42, *a-n*]*i-ni* 12:11, [*a*]*-ni-ni* 148 r. 7, *a-ni-nu* 120:15, 123 r. 9, 234:11, *a-ni-*[*nu* 106 r. 3,

annāka "here": *an-na-ka* 120:24, *un-na-k*[*a*] 3:3,

anniš "hither": *an-ni-iš* 126 r. 6,

anniu "this": *an-na-a* 239 r. i 8, *an-na-a-ti* 237 r. 19, *a*]*n-na-ti* 1 r. 14, *an-nim-ma* 247 r. 10, *an-ni-e* 140 r. 18, 229 r. v 46, 61, 64, 68, vi 53, 717, 245 r. 1, *an-*[*ni-e*] 248:2, [*an-ni-e*] 52:6, *an-ni-i* 72 r. 6, 120 r. 1, 247:3, 8, r. 8, 280:4, *an-ni-i*] 241 r. 6, *an-ni-*[*i* 226:9, *an-ni*]*-i* 21:2, *an*]*-ni-i* 71 e. 14, *a*[*n-ni-i*] 147 r. 5, *a*]*n-ni-i* 251:4, *an-ni-ma* 52:5, *an-ni-te* 141 r. 2, *an-ni-ti* 120:23, r. 22, 140 r. 13, 229 r. v 50, 740, *an-n*]*i-ti* 120 r. 25, [*a*]*n-ni-ti* 221:5, *an-ni-tú* 1:8, 120:22, 229 r. v 4, 44, vii 55, viii 17, 52, 55, *a*]*n-ni-tú* 7:7, [*an*]*-ni-tú* 60 r. 3, *an-ni-u* 120:14, 278 s. 2, *a*[*n-ni-u* 147 r. 6, *a*]*n-ni-u* 288 ii 31, *an-ni-ú* 229 r. vii 88, 281 r. 3, *an-n*[*i-x* 257:1, *an-nute* 120 r. 16, *an-nu-te* 150:4, 229 r. vii 1, 33, *an-nu-t*[*e* 151:4, *an-nu-*[*te*] 229 r. viii 35, *an-nu-ti* 146:2, 229 r. vi 77, 231:7, *a*[*n-nu-ti*] 29:8, *a*]*n-nu-ti* 243 r. 6, *an-nu-tu* 129 r. 15, 280 r. 14, *ha-a*[*n-na*]*-ti* 1 r. 11, *ha-an-ni-e* 229 r. vii 22, 82, 89, viii 5, 8, 22, 41, *ha-an-ni-i* 1:10, 229 r. vii 42, *ha-an-nu-ti* 1:5, 5:8, *ha-an-nu-um-ma* 229 i 65, NE 247:18, NE-*i* 246 r. 6, 247:5, NE-[*i* 246:11, 247 r. 7, N[E-*i* 246:10,

annu "yes": *an-na* 232 r. 5, 246:1, 247:1, 252 r. 13, *an-n*[*a* 248:1, 255 r. 4, [*a*]*n-na* 246 r. 7,

annû "this": *an-nu-u* 120:3, *an-na-a-ta* 126 r. 1,

annuku "lead": AN.NA 229 r. vii 26,

annurig "now": *an-nu-ra* 26 r. 6, *an-nu-rig* 1:2, 14, r. 9, 22 r. 1, 109:2, 120 r. 6, 144:3, *an-nu-ri*[*g* 148 r. 2, [*an-nu-r*]*ig* 44:1, [*an-n*]*u-rig* 111 r. 4,

anqullu "reddish glow": *an-qu-lu* 234 r. 2,

anūtu "utensil": *a-nu-tú* 140:9, *a-nu-u-tú* 56:4, *ú-nu-ut* 287 r. ii 13,

AN.ZA.GUL (a stone, rdg. and mng. unkn.): N]A$_4$.AN.ZA.GUL 235 r. 9,

apālu "to answer; (Gtn) to echo, respond": *a-pal-an-ni* 248:1, *a-pal-an-ni*] 246:1, 247:1, *i-ta-nap-pa-la* 288 i 2, *li-tap-pal* 248 r. 7, *li-tap-pal*] 246 r. 9, 247 r. 18, *li-tap-pa-lu-ma* 252 r. 15,

apkallu "sage": NUN.ME 230:21,

aplu "heir": *ap-lu-ú-ka* 239 r. i 12, DUMU.NITA.MEŠ-*šú* 229 r. v 67, IBILA 229 r. vi 4,

appāru "reed": GI.AMBAR.MEŠ 229 r. viii 23,

apsû "abyss": *ap-si-i* 226:8, ZU.AB 229 r. vii 11, Z]U.A[B 262:12,

arahsamnu (Marchesvan, name of the 8th month): ITI.APIN 25:5, 275 r. 7,

arāku "to be long; (D) to lengthen": *ar-ra-ka-a-*[*ti* 93 r. 4, *a*]*-rak* 116:2, *a-ra-ku* 135:6, *a-r*]*a-ku* 136:3, GÍD.DA 255:1, GÍD.D[A 66 r. 10, GÍD.DA.MEŠ 120:2, *li-ri-ku* 239 r. i 22, *li-ri-*[*ku*] 239 ii 18, *lu-ur-ri-ku-ma* 127:4, [*l*]*u-ur-ri-k*[*u*] 221:2,

arāmu "to envelop, cover": *i-*[*ter-mu*] 128:14,

arānu "coffin, sarcophagus": NA$_4$.*a-ra-nu* 288 r. ii 8,

arāru "to curse": *a-ra-ru* 229 r. viii 19, *li-ru-ru-ku-nu* 226 r. 2, 229 r. vi 56, *li-ru-ru-šu* 298 r. 5,

arbā "forty": 40 287:15, 42 287 iii 20, 46 287:14,

ardatu "young woman": *ar-*[*da-ti* 226 r. 7, *ar-da-ti-ku-n*[*u*] 229 r. vi 62,

arhiš "quickly": *ár-hiš* 120 r. 5, 162 r. 11,

arītu see *ša-arīti,*

arki "after, behind" *ar-ki-šú* 126 r. 6, *ár-ki* 32:3,

arkû "second, junior, rear, later": *ar-ki-i* 234 r. 9,

arnu "guilt": *á*[*r-ni* 262:12,

arratu "curse": *a-ra-ti* 234 r. 3, *a-ra-tú* 229 r. vi 55, *ar-rat* 298 r. 5, *a*]*r-rat* 298 r. 2, *ar-ra-ta* 226 r. 1,

aršu "soiled, unclean": *ar-šá-ti* 246:14, *ár-šá-a-ti* 247 r. 2, *ár-šá-ti* 247 r. 4,

arû "to be pregnant": *e-te-ri* 163 r. 3,

arû B "handmill": NA$_4$.UR$_5$ 229 r. vi 18,

arû C "eagle": TI$_8$.MUŠEN 229 r. vii 10,

âru "(Gtn) "to guide, educate": *it-tar-ru-šú-ma* 237:10, r. 9,

askupputu "threshold": NA$_4$.I.DIB.[MEŠ 288 i 8,

asu "doctor, physician": *as-sa-ku* 73:4,

aṣābu "to add, increase; (D) to add to, multiply":

ú-ṣa-ba-ka 3 r. 2,

aṣû "to emerge": *at-ta-ṣa-a* 178:2, É.MEŠ-*nim-*[*ma* 246 r. 4, É.MEŠ-*ú* 247:13, *u*]*ṣ-ṣi* 12:7,

aṣūdu (a bowl for fruit and dough): *a-ṣu-da-a-ti-ku-nu* 229 r. vi 24,

ašābu "to sit, dwell": *a-ši-bu-te* 229 r. vi 52, *a-*[*ši-bu-ti*] 229 i 24, *at-ta-šab* 163 s. 1, TUŠ-*ab*] 252:4, *t*]*u-uš-šab-ma* 235:39, *ul-te-ši-*[*b*]*i* 32:6, [*ul-te*]*-ši-bu* 74:8, [*ú-ši-bu*] 217:3,

ašarēdu "foremost": *a-ša-red* 234:4, *a-šá-re-du* 229 r. vii 9,

āšipu "exorcist": [LÚ.MAŠ].MAŠ 115 r. 5,

ašru "place, site; (in st. constr.) where": *aš-ru* 234 r. 15, 16, *áš-ri* 33:8, *áš-ri-šú* 32:5, 297:7, *a-šar* 214 e. 4, 245 r. 4, 262 r. 5, 287 r. ii 5, 9, *a-ša*[*r* 190 r. 4, [*a*]*-šar* 80:4, 164 r. 1,

ašša "as soon as": *áš-šá* 165:5, *á*]*š-šá* 235:11,

aššatu "wife": DA[M 186 r. 2, DAM-*s*[*u* 186 r. 1,

aššu "because": *áš-šú* 72 e. 10,

atâ "why?": *a-ta-a* 5 r. 7, 6:6, 52:2, 56:1, 120:16, r. 26, 123 r. 5, 279 r. 12, *a-ta-a*] 5:4, *a-t*[*a*]*-a* 116:5, [*a-ta-a* 144:2,

atānu "mare": MÍ.ANŠE.KU[R.MEŠ] 60 r. 4, MÍ.K[UR.MEŠ] 288 iii 17,

atappu "canal" *a-tap-pi* 288 i 2,

atāru "to be additional": *at-ru* 248 r. 3,

atmû "utterance, saying": *at-me-ka* 239 i 6,

atta "you": *at-ta* 1:8, 31:11, 120:16, 163:3, 8, 221 r. 1, 2, 239 ii 10, 23, 267 r. 4, *at-t*[*a*] 244 r. 2, [*a*]*t-ta* 150:2,

attalû "eclipse": AN.MI 264 r. 2, 267:7,

attû "own": *at-tu-ka* 126:11, *at-tu-ú-ka* 239 ii 4,

attunu "you": *at-tu-nu* 227 ii 6, 229 i 80, r. v 1, 11, 19, 24, 37, 41, 47, 49, 54, 73, vii 1, 26, 51, 70, 78, viii 26, 36, 45, 241:6, *at-tu-nu*] 229 iv 8, [*at*]*-tu-nu* 229 iv 3,

atû "gate-guard": LÚ.Ì.DU$_8$ 116 r. 6,

azugallatu "chief woman physician": *a-zu-gal-la-tú* 229 r. vi 41,

ba'ālu "to be bright": *b*]*a-il* 263 r. 3,

ba'āru "to hunt, catch": [*ta-bar-ma*] 262:11,

ba'āšu "to be bad, smell foul": [*bé*]*-'i-šu-u-ni* 229 r. vii 89, [*lib*]*-'i-i-šu* 229 r. vii 91,

ba''û "to seek": *ú-ba-'u-u-ni* 1 r. 9,

babbanû "good": *bab-ba-n*[*i-i* 199 r. 3, *bab-ba-nu-ú* 128 r. 13, 190 r. 3, 199 r. 5,

bābu "gate, doorway": KÁ 137:5, 192 r. 1, 217:4, 240:5, KÁ-*šá* 229 r. vi 25, 287 r. ii 11, KÁ-*šú* 261 e. 14, KÁ–[*x* 44:7,

bāb ēkalli "gate of the palace": ME.NI 253:9,

baddudu "(D only) to squander, waste": *ú-ba-*[*du-du* 240:9, *ú-ba-du-du-šu* 240:8,

bagāru "mng. uncert.": *a-ba-gír* 120 e. 25,

bahû (mng. obscure): *ba-hu-ma* 200:1,

baiāru "hunter": *ba-a-a-ri* 233:6, 234:8, 13, *ba-a-a-ru* 234:5, 15,

baiātu "vigil": *ba-a-a-te* 300:6,

bakû "to weep": *ib-ka-a* 288 i 5,

balāṭu "life; to live; (D) to invigorate, revive": [*bal-ṭa-a-ni-ni* 229 r. vi 93, *bal-ṭa-ku* 173:5, *bal-*[*ṭa-ku* 164:6, *bal-ṭu* 91:3, 123 r. 2, *bal-ṭu-ti-ku-nu* 229 r. vii 83, *bal-ṭu-ti-ku-n*[*u*] 229 r. vii 63, *ba-la-ṭi* 229 r. vii 11, *ba-la-ṭ*[*i*] 87:4, DIN-*uṭ* 265:6, *li-bal-li-ṭu* 221:7, [TIN 135:6, TI.LA 262 r. 4, TI.LA] 230:25, TI.LA.MEŠ 229 r. vi 56, TI.LA-*šú* 147 r. 5, 9, *ú-bal-*[*laṭ*] 172:7,

balūt "without" *ba-lu-us-s*[*a* 194:4,

bānītu "creatress": *ba-ni-tú* 229 i 80, r. vi 86,

banû "to create": *ba-n*[*a-at* 230:25,

bānû "creator": *ba-ni-i* 39:5, *ba-ni-ia* 287 r. ii 19, *b*]*a-nu-u-a* 287 r. ii 3,

barmu "speckled": *bar-mu* 229 r. vii 84,

bārtu "rebellion": *bar-te* 249 s. 1, 272 r. 6, *bar-ti* 227 ii 8, *bar-tu* 33:7, *bar-tú* 229 i 74, r. vi 82, *bar-tum* 227 ii 4, 228:7,

barû "to examine, revise; (Š) to reveal": *ba-ru-ú* 230:26, MÁŠ-*ú* 246:13, MÁŠ-*ú*] 246:11, MÁŠ]-*ú* 247 r. 1, M[ÁŠ-*ú* 246:12, *ni-ba-ru-ma* 197:2, [*ú-š*]*ab-ri-šú-ma* 231:7,

bārû "haruspex, diviner": HAL 252:16, LÚ.HAL 247 r. 4, 252 r. 9, 253 r. 9, 280 r. 8, 9, 11, LÚ.HAL.MEŠ 287 iii 6, LÚ.HAL-*šú* 237 r. 10, 11, 260 r. 4,

bārûtu "extispicy": *ba-ru-t*]*i* 237:18, *ba-ru-t*[*u* 260 r. 5, *ba-r*]*u-tu* 237 r. 18,

bašû "to exist, (Š) to give birth, create, (N) to come about": *ba-šu-*[*ú* 33:9, *ba-*[*šu-ú*] 280:12, *ba-*[*šú-u*] 229 i 12, GÁL] 268:4, GÁL.MEŠ 263 r. 5, *ib-ba-šu-ni* 229 i 14, *ib-ba-šú-u-ni* 229 r. v 47, 48, *ib-ba-áš-šú-*[*u*]*-ni* 229 r. v 53, *ib-ši* 229 r. vi 18, *ib-šu-u-ni* 240:7, *it-tab-ši* 240:7, *i-ba-áš-ši* 21 r. 4, 42:8, 120 r. 18, 235 r. 42, 239 r. i 17, *i-ba-áš-*[*ši* 5:4, 75:3, *i-ba-á*[*š-ši* 212 r. 2, *i-ba-á*[*š-ši*] 182:2, *i-ba-*[*áš-ši* 35:8, *i-ba-áš-ši-i* 235:51, *i-ba-áš-šú* 33:15, 163 r. 4, *i-ba-áš-šú-ú* 71 e. 14, *i-ba-áš-šú-u-ni* 124 r. 1, *i-ba-šu-*[*ú* 33:10, [*i-ba-šú-u-ni* 21:6, *li-šab-ši* 229 r. vi 46, *li-šab-*[*š*]*i* 229 r. vi 42

bâšu "to be ashamed, come to shame": *i-ba-áš* 162 r. 10,

batāqu "to cut off, parcel out": *ba-taq-šú-nu* 37 r. 9, *bat-qa-tu-u-ni* 229 r. viii 55, *i*[*b-tu-qu-ni*] 66 r. 3, *lib-tu-qu* 229 r. viii 57, *ú-bá-ti-qu-u-ni* 229 r. viii 21,

bātiqu "informer": *ba-ti-qu-šú* 279 r. 8,

batqu "deficit, damage": *bat-qu* 37 r. 3, 140:13,

battibatti "around, about": *bad-da-bat-tu* 239 ii 31,

battu "side": *bat-ti* 120 r. 1,

bâtu "to pass the night, stay overnight": *ta-ba-a-t*[*a* 134:2,

baṭālu "to cease": *i-ba-ṭal-ú-ni* 116:4,

be'āšu see *ba'āšu,*

bēltu "lady, mistress": *be-el-ti* 234 r. 10, 12, *be-let* 229 r. vi 32, 237 r. 1, EN-*lat* 229 r. vi 9,

bēlu "lord": *be-li* 8:4, *be-lí* 6:4, 6, 9:5, 15:2, 5, 17:5, 22:5, r. 2, 42:2, 43 r. 1, 57:3, 62:4, 67:5, 100:4, 102:5, 106 r. 6, 111 r. 7, 112 r. 2, 117:7, 121:8, r. 6, 124:6, 130:8, 11, 141 r. 2, 146:3, 4, 157:2, 158:2, 164:12, 188:5, 199:3, 237 r. 19, 260 r. 8, 275:1, 276:2, *be-lí*] 33:5, 46:1, 49:5, 63:3, 121:6, *be-l*[*í* 35:3, 136 r. 10, 164 r. 4, 209:5, *be-l*[*í*] 15:4, 53 r. 5, *be*]*-lí* 61:2, *b*[*e-lí* 46:4, *b*[*e-lí*] 109 r. 1, *b*]*e-lí* 51:2, 58 r. 2, 199 r. 13, [*be-lí*] 19:6, 66:2, 277:2, *be-lí-a* 31:8, 37 r. 10, 69:13, 173:3, 206:9, *be-l*]*í-a* 179 r. 3, *b*]*e-lí-a* 168 r. 9, 182:3, [*be-lí-a*] 202:6, *be-lí-a-ni* 29:4, 7, [*be-lí-a-ni*] 29:9, *be-lí-i* 25 s. 1, *be-lí-ia* 6:1, 19:1, 26 r. 5, 8, 33:12, 13, 70:10, 93 r. 2, 97:1, 114:5, 121:1, 126 r. 13, 129:1, 7, r. 13, 155:4, 164:11, s. 2, 263:3, 269 r. 3, *be-lí-ia*] 28:1, 49 r. 2, 88:6, 94:1, 4, 98:1, 100:1, 103:1, 149:1, 152 r. 9, 155:1, 5, *be-lí-i*[*a* 68 r. 5, 199:1, 205:4, *be-lí-i*[*a*] 18:1, 129:4, *be-lí-*[*ia* 31:2, 263:5, *be-lí-*[*ia*] 9:1, 10:1, 3, 27:1, 114:1, 136:1, 161:1, *be-l*[*í-ia* 164 r. 8, 12, *be-l*[*í-ia*] 18:3, 26:1, 182 r. 12, *be-l*]*í-ia* 198:2, *be-l*]*í-i*[*a* 33:1, *be-*[*lí-ia*] 97:1, 117:4, *b*[*e-lí-ia*] 8:3, 95:1, 98:2, *b*]*e-lí-ia* 30 r. 1, *b*]*e-lí-i*[*a*] 183:2, [*be-lí-ia-a-ma*] 31:3, *be*]*-lí-ia-ma* 199:2, *be-li-iá* 47:6, 70:3, 5, 121:3, 4, 126 r. 14, 130 r. 4, 164:7, r. 12, 183:4, 237 r. 18, 19, 20, 251:5, 252 r. 14, 255 r. 5, 10, *be-lí-iá*]] 261 r. 3, *be-lí-*[*iá* 257 r. 2, *be-lí*]*-i-ni* 135:7, *be-*[*lí-i-ni* 38:7, *b*[*e-lí-i-ni* 30 r. 3, *be-lí-ni*] 135:1, *be-*[*lí-ni*] 29:2, *b*[*e-lí-ni* 171:9, [*be-lí-ni*] 135:4, *be-lí-šú-nu* 29:2, *b*]*e-lí-šú-nu* 173:2, *be-lí-*[*x* 30:5, 168 r. 11, *be-l*[*í-x* 83:1, *be-*[*lí-x* 166:7, *b*[*e-lí-x* 83:7, 92 r. 2, 168 r. 13, *be-lum* 230:8, 10, 11, 13, 15, 18, 20, 31, *be-lu*[*m* 230:34, *be-*[*lum* 230:9, BE-*ia* 20:1, BE-*i*[*a*] 12:1, 3, EN 74:2, 109 r. 3, 111 r. 6, 123 r. 7, 129:3, 136:1, 4, 151:3, 163 r. 2, 228:2, i 29, 78, 79, r. v 62, 709, 11, viii 58, 232:12, r. 7, 235:10, 14, 21, 26, 32, 40, 43, 45, 51, r. 40, 44, 46, 48, 236 r. 12, 239 i 4, 7, 8, ii 19, 34, r. i 20, 32, ii 8, 13, 19, 246:1, 7, r. 2, 247:1, 5, r. 7, 18, 248:1, r. 7, 261 r. 6, 297:8, EN] 229 r. vi 1, E[N 32:4, 238:7, E]N 156:5, 235 r. 2, 239 r. i 7, [EN 235 r. 12, 246 r. 9, EN-*a* 129:17, r. 15, 208:2, 217:3, 218:7, EN-*a*] 221 r. 11, [EN]-*a* 217:6, [E]N-*a* 166:6, EN-*a-ni* 190 r. 1, [EN-*a-ni*] 128 r. 15, EN-*a-nu* 39:7, EN-*e* 230:7, EN-*ia* 6:3, 18:5, 8, r. 2, 26:3, 43:5, 64 r. 4, 67 r. 2, 119:3, 6, 120:1, 2, 3, 6, 8, r. 23, 124:1, 3, 5, 140:3, 141:2, 216:2, 297:8, EN-*ia*] 19:2, 27:4, 28:3, 48:2, 66 r. 2, 95:3, 97:3, 98:3, 100:3, 101:1, 102:1, 103:3, 141:4, EN-*i*[*a* 44:2, EN-*i*[*a*] 13:3, EN-*i*]*a* 102:3, EN-[*ia* 218:6, EN-[*ia*] 8:1, 145 r. 2, EN]-*ia* 45:5, 119:1, E[N-*ia*] 18:6, 140:1, E]N-*ia* 46:6, E]N-*i*[*a*] 13:1, [EN-*ia*] 48:1, [E]N-*ia* 216 r. 10, EN-*iá* 8:3, 57:4, 109:3, 113:c8, 129:16, 176 r. 4, 183 r. 9, 214 e. 3, 217:2, 220:8, 221 r. 10, EN-*iá*] 114:3, 217:8, EN]-*iá* 208:5, E]N-*iá* 208:6, EN-*in-ni* 229 r. vi 91, EN-*i-ni*] 128 r. 14, 189 e. 3, EN-*i-n*[*i* 40:9, EN-[*i-ni* 171 r. 6, E]N-*i-ni* 39:1, EN-*ku-nu* 227 ii 10, 229 r. v 25, 46, 59, 70, EN-*ku-nu*] 229 i 64, EN-[*ku*]*-nu* 229 r. vii 5, EN]-*ku-nu* 229 iv 10, [EN-*ku*]*-nu* 229 iv 4, [EN.MEŠ 240:5, EN.(MEŠ)-*iá* 229 r. v 65, E]N-*šú* 68:7, (EN-*šú*)] 250 r. 12, EN-*šú-nu* 68:4, EN-*šú-n*[*u* 68 r. 2,

bêlu "to rule": *ta-bi-lu* 239 ii 11, [*ta-be-el*] 235:40,

bēlūtu "lordship": *be-lu-ti-šú* 237 r. 4, 8, 287 r. ii 15, *be-lut-sa* 231:3, *be-lut-ti-ka* 129:6, *bé-lu-tu* 239 i 5, EN-*te-ia* 233:11, EN-*u-tu* 229 i 66, EN-*u-tú* 229 i 16, E]N-*ú-ti-šú-nu* 240:4,

bēl āli "city lord": EN—URU 229 r. vi 44, LÚ.EN—URU.MEŠ 6:5,

bēl dāmi "avenger": EN—[*d*]*a-me* 120 r. 14,

bēl hiṭṭi "criminal": EN—*hi-iṭ-ṭi* 240:4, [EN—*hi-ṭi*] 227 ii 8,

bēl mugirri "chariot owner": LÚ.EN—GIGIR.MEŠ 229 i 8,

bēl nakāri "enemy": LÚ.EN—KÚR 37 r. 1,

bēl pēthalli "cavalry commander": LÚ.EN—*pet-hal-la-ti* 229 i 8,

bēl piqitti "official": LÚ.EN—*pi-qi-ta-te* 140:7, LÚ.EN—*pi-qit-ta-te* 58:2,

bēl ṭēmi "reporter": EN.ME—UMUŠ 250 r. 4, EN.MEŠ—UMUŠ 253 r. 9, LÚ.EN—UMUŠ 252 r. 10,

bēl zakār šumi "subject of the query": EN—MU.MU 247:5, EN—MU.MU] 247 r. 7,

bēl-[...]: LÚ.EN—*x* 20 r. 2, LÚ.E[N—*x* 21:9,

bêru "to put aside": *bé*]*-e-ra* 247 r. 6,

beškānu "cocoon": *bé-eš-ka-ni-šá* 229 r. vii 69,

bētu "house; (in st. constr.) where, what": *bé-et* 11:15, *bé*]*-et* 22:6, [*bé-et*] 12:4, *bé-ti* 147 r. 7, É 1 r. 13, 14:2, 22:8, 36:7, 44 r. 3, 57:6, 60:3, 84:2, 115:2, r. 2, 4, 115 e. 7, 120:9, 128:6, r. 11, 130 r. 8, 144:5, 146:4, 147 r. 12, 154 r. 7, 172:6, 175:1, 179 r. 11, 186:2, 187:2, 7, 188:4, 196:2, 205:4, 213 r. 3, 229 i 50, r. vii 51, 231:2, 232:4, 13, 234 r. 14, 235:16, r. 25, 239 ii 13, 240:3, 7, 259:3, 262:6, 269 r. 1, 291:1, É-*ka* 52:3, 235:43, É-*ka-a* 164 r. 2, É-*ku-nu* 229 r. vi 76, É-*ku-*[*nu* 130:6, É.MEŠ 47:2, 132:5, É.MEŠ-*ku-nu* 229 r. v 85, É.MEŠ-*ku-nu*] 229 r. vi 18, É.[MEŠ]-*ku-nu* 229 r. vii 71, [É.MEŠ-*šú-nu*] 32:9, É-*su* 240:9, É-*šú* 91 r. 5, 235:24, 279:8, É-*šú-nu* 126:11,

bēt abi "father's house": É—AD-[*ia* 80:11, É—AD-*iá* 183 r. 4, É—AD-*k*[*a* 29:4, É—AD-*šú* 148 r. 3, É—AD-*šú*] 229 ii 3,

bēt ahi "armlet, armpiece, sleeve": É—Á.MEŠ 287 r. i 7, 17,

bēt bēli "government": É—EN-*ia* 216:4, É—EN]-*šú* 129:10,

bēt ilāni: É—DINGIR.M[EŠ 75:7, É—DINGIR.[MEŠ 38:6,

bēt ili "temple": É—DINGIR 78 r. 7, 235 r. 4,

bēt kiṣri "linen closet": GIŠ.É—*ki-ṣir*.MEŠ 140 r. 6,

bēt rēdûti "Succession Palace": É.UŠ-*te* 229 r. vii 2, É—*re-du-t*[*e*] 228:4, É—*re-du-ti* 229 r. viii 67, 69, É—UŠ 254 r. 7, É—UŠ-*te* 229 i 18, ii 2, iv 2, 3, 9, r. v 6, 10, 35, 45, 57, 59, 66, 69, 80, vi 79, 88, vii 4, viii 27, É—UŠ-*te*] 227 ii 10, É—UŠ-*t*]*e* 229 r. vi 91, É—[UŠ-*te*] 227 ii 2, [É—UŠ-*te* 229 r. vi 89, É—UŠ-*ti* 229 iii 5, r. v 17, 26, 31, É—UŠ-*ti*] 229 i 63,

bētu eššu "new palace": É—*eš-š*[*ú*] 280 r. 6,

biādu "to stay overnight": *a-bi-ia-ad* 116 r. 5,

biltu "talent (weight); tax, tribute": GÚ.UN 3:1, 121 r. 4, GÚ.U]N 77 r. 7, GÚ.[UN 188:2, [GÚ.UN 196:6,

binūtu "form, creation": *bi-nu-ut* 239 r. i 24, *bi-nù-ut* 252 r. 5,

bīri "between": *bi-ri-i-nu* 235 r. 37, *i—bi-ru-šu-nu* 234 r. 2,

birmu "multi-coloured textile": *bi-ir-mu* 126:18, GÙN 288 ii 17, iii 23,

birru "lattice": *bir-ri* 240:3,

birti "between, through, in the midst of": *bir*]*-te* 22:9, *bir-ti* 189 r. 3, *bi-ri*[*t* 236:12, *bi-r*[*it* 36 r. 4,

bīru "extispicy": *bi-ri* 297:6, 10, *bi-r*]*i* 261:3, *bi-r*]*i-šú-nu* 216 r. 9,

bir kabti "nobleman": LÚ.*bir—kab-ti* 80:6,

bištu "obscenity, slander": *biš-te* 239 r. i 33,

bitqu "accusation, allegation": *bit-qi* 66 r. 3,

bubūtu "hunger": *bu-bu-tú* 229 r. vi 61, *bu-bu-u-ti* 229 r. vi 27,

būdu (mng. uncert.): *bu-di* 165 r. 5,

bukurtu "daughter": *bu-kur-tú* 239 r. i 35,

bullû "to extinguish": *li-bal-li* 229 r. vi 36,

būlu "cattle": *bu-li* 234:19, *bu-lu* 234:2, 15,

bunnannû "likeness": *bu-na-ni-ia* 233:13,

burāšu "juniper": ŠEM.LI 262:13,

burdi-šāhi "caterpillar": *bur-di—šá-hi* 230 r. vii 69,

būrtu "well": PÚ.MEŠ 217:5,

būru "well; calf": *bu-ri-ku-nu* 229 r. vi 26, 743,
buṭnu "pistaccio": GIŠ.*bu-ṭu-ni* 8:7,
daᾱnu "to be strong, (D) to strengthen; force": *da-aᴂna* 234 r. 7, *da-a-[na* 160:3, *da-a-ni* 279:7, KALAG-*an* 253:8, *ta-da-in* 120:23,
dabābtu "speech, talk": *da-bab-ti* 229 r. v 50,
dabābu "to talk, plot, contest; (Š) to incite, provoke": *ad-bu-bu* 33:19, *ad-bu-bu-[ni* 116 r. 2, *ad-bu-ub* 172:8, *da-bab* 229 r. vi 86, *da-ba-a-bi* 120 r. 18, *da-ba-ba* 128 r. 13, *da-ba-bu* 234:15, 275:6, [*da-ba-bu* 240:11, *da-bi-bu-u-ni* 240:11, *du-bu-ub-ma* 33:17, *du-ub-ba* 229 r. vii 53, *du-ub-ba*] 241 r. 8, DUG$_4$.DUG$_4$ 278 s. 2, *id-bu-bu-ú-ma* 280:3, r. 16, *id-bu-u[b* 213:4, *id-b]u-ub* 193:4, *id-da-bu-ub* 30 r. 8, *id-da-bu-ub-u-ni* 229 r. vii 50, *id-du-bu-ub* 11:9, *i-dab-bu-ub* 239 ii 34, *i-dab-b[u-ub* 235:19, *i-dab]-bu-u[b* 41:3, *i-dab-bu-[x* 192:2, *i-d]ab-bu-bu* 74:4, *i-da-ab-bu-bu-u-ni* 21 r. 3, *i-da-bu-bu* 120:8, 274 e. 10, *i-da-bu-b[u* 64 r. 5, [*i-d*]*a-bu-bu* 111 r. 9, *i-da-bu-bu-ni* 120 r. 23, *i-da-bu-ub* 120:22, 162 r. 8, [*i*]*-da-bu-ub* 120 e. 26, *lid-bu-ub* 120 r. 16, (*lid*)*-bu-bu* 225 r. 4, *ta-dab-bu-ba* 235:22, *ú-šad*]*-ba-ba-áš-šú* 152:7,
dabdû "defeat": BAD$_5$.BAD$_5$-*šú* 237 r. 15, *dáb-du-šú-nu* 235:36, IGI.IGI-*e* 253:3,
dagālu "to look; (Š) to show": *a-da-gal* 21 e. 10, *i-da-ga-lu-ni-ni* 120 r. 15, *id-gu-lu* 33:20, *lid-gu-lu* 229 r. vi 77, *ta-da-ga-la* 229 r. v 9, 16, *ta-da-gal-a-ni*] 229 i 65, *ta-da-gal-u-ni* 229 r. vii 69, *ul-ta-ad-g*]*i-lu* 82 r. 2,
dāgil pāni "subject": *da-gíl–pa-ni* 228:1,
daiāltu "excursion": *da*]*-a-a-la-te-šú* 11:10,
daiālu "courier, scout, spy": *da-ia-li* 22:3, LÚ.*da*]*-a-a-li* 121 r. 1, LÚ.[*d*]*a-a-a-li-ia* 10:8, [LÚ.*da-a*]*-a-li-ia* 10:4, LÚ.*da-a-a-lu* 120 r. 26,
daiānu "judge": DI.KUD 230:24, DI.[KUD 262:8, DI.KUD.MEŠ 252 r. 11, DI.KU[D.MEŠ 255 r. 3,
dakāku "to gambol": *i-da-ku-ku* 234:7,
dâku "to kill": *a-dak* 253:3, 9, *a-du-uk-m[a*] 288 iii 18, *da-ki-i[a* 79 r. 2, *di-ku* 138:6, *id-duk* 32:9, 78 r. 5, *i-dak-ka* 128 r. 5, *i-duk-ku-ni* 120:4, *i-du-ku-šú* 240:4, *li-du-uk* 41:4,
dalāhu "to disturb": *da-li-hi* 234:2,
dalālu "to praise": *d*]*ul-la* 207:3,
damāqu "to be good, beautiful, skilled, fortunate": *dam-qat* 265:1, *dam-qa-ti* 265:2, SIG 41:10, 232:12, SI[G] 43:3, SIG$_5$ 235 r. 41, 258:6, 265:5, SIG$_5$-*iq* 270:2, SIG$_5$.MEŠ 229 r. v 33, 262 r. 4, SIG$_5$.MEŠ] 246 r. 7, SIG$_5$.M[EŠ] 241 e. 3, SIG$_5$-*tú* 229 r. viii 15, SIG$_5$-*tú*] 229 i 74,
damû "to have convulsions": *i-dam-mi* 267 r. 5,
dāmu "blood, resin": *da-am* 235:33, 35, *da-mi-šú-nu* 234:20, *da-mu* 192:3, ÚŠ.MEŠ-*ku-nu* 229 r. vi 51,
danānu "to be strong": *d*]*an-n[a-ti* 262:9, *dan-ni* 120 r. 14, 22, 226 r. 3, 229 r. vi 32, 287 r. ii 10, *dan-[ni*] 229 r. vi 16, [*dan-ni* 235:2, *dan-ni-te* 298 r. 4, *dan-nu* 38:5, 229 r. vi 51, 235 r. 23, 236:5, 237 r. 1, 239 i 12, ii 16, 35, r. i 1, 6, 10, *dan-nu-ti* 213 r. 6, 243 r. 3, *da-nu-ti-šú-nu* 234 r. 4, *da-na-ni* 233:11, *da-na-ni-i-ka* 239 ii 6, *da-na-ni-ni* 241 r. 5, KALAG 250:3, 255:3, 258:4, KALAG.MEŠ 232:3, 238:5, *lu-dan-ni-[in* 236:10, *ú-dan-ni-na* 287 r. ii 12, [*ú*]*-dan-nin-[u-ni*] 229 i 27,
dandannu "strongest": [*da*]*n-[da*]*n-nu* 226:10,
dannānu "powerful": *dan-na-nu* 233:7,
dappastu "blanket": *dáp-pa-a[s-tú*] 288 ii 1,
dāriš "forever": *da*]*-riš* 251:6,
darû "everlasting": *da-ra-a-t[i* 255 r. 9, *da-ru-tu* 129:8,
dassu "door": GIŠ.IG 229 r. viii 61, GIŠ.I]G 240:3, [GIŠ.IG 240:3, GIŠ.IG.MEŠ 287 iii 19, GIŠ.IG.MEŠ-*e-ku-nu* 229 r. viii 62,
dātu "after": *i–da-at* 10 r. 7, *i–da-te* 121 r. 2,
deḍqtu "goodness": MÍ.SIG$_5$ 252 r. 14,
dēktu "defeat": *de-ek-[tú*] 15:6,
dekû "to raise, summon, mobilize": *i[d-de-ke* 138:6,
dēnu "judgment": *de-e-nu* 225 r. 2, *de-ni* 246:10, *i–de-en-[ni*] 7:4,
diānu "to judge, pass verdict" *ta-da-an-ši-[na-ti* 262: 7,
diāšu "to trample upon, tread down": *da-a-iš* 234:1,
di'u "headache, illness": *di-'u-u* 229 r. v 84,
dibbī "words": *dib-bi* 36:5, 185:7, 217:1, 241 r. 8, *dib-b[i* 197:4, *d*]*ib-bi* 72 r. 5, *dib-bi-ni* 33:21, *di-ib-bi-i* 241 r. 4, *di-ib-bi-šú* 120:12, *di-ib-bi-šú-nu* 229 r. v 32,
diliptu "sleeplessness": *di-lip-ti* 229 r. vi 69, *di-lip-tú* 229 r. v 84,
dinānu "substitute": *di-na-an* 31:2,
dišpu "honey": LÀL 229 r. vii 60, 81, viii 43,
dīšu "grass": *di-ši* 288 i 6.
duāku "to kill": *de*]*-e-ku* 80:9, *de-ku-u-ni* 229 r. vii 67, *du-a-ki-ia* 120:7, *du-a-ki-šú-nu* 227 ii 4, *duk-šu* 122:3, GAZ 133:14, 247:10, GAZ] 246 r. 5, GA]Z 247 r. 12, GAZ-*ku* 246 r. 6, 247:10, 14, r. 12, *id-du-ku* 216 r. 5, *id-[du-ku*] 75:4, *i-duk-ma* 237 r. 6, *i-du-kan-ni* 167 r. 3, *i-d*]*u-kan-ni* 167 r. 2, *la-du-ak-k[a*] 21:4, *li-du-ku-ku-nu* 229 r. vii 68,
dubāqu "trap": *du-ba-qi* 229 r. vii 72,
dullu "work, ritual, treatment": *dul-la-šá* 235 r. 11, *dul-[li* 160:2, *dul-li-šú-nu* 58 r. 1, *dul-lu* 11:16, 21:5, 43:4, 44 r. 3, 50:5, 140 r. 5, 243 r. 6, [*dul-lu*] 41 e. 11, *du$_6$-li* 120 r. 22,
dumqu "beauty, good luck": *dum-qa* 220:3,
dunnu "strength": KALAG.GA 240:15,
dunqu "fortune": *du-un-q[u* 29:5,
duqdu "almond": *duq-di* 288 iv 3, 6,
dūru "city wall": BÀD 16:4, 223 r. 2,
DUR.KIB (rdg. and mng. unkn.): DUR.KIB 288 iv 8,
ebāru "to cross": *e-tab-[r*]*u-ni* 22:4, *e-tab-ru-u-[ni*] 9:10,
ebēbu "(Dt) to clean o.s.": *l*]*i-te-bi-ib* 262:1,
ebēru "to cross": *e-bir* 139:4, *i-bir* 249:7, *šu-u*]*b-bi-ra* 78:3,
ebūru "harvest": BUR]U$_{14}$-[*k*]*u-nu* 229 r. vi 17, *e-bu-ru* 92 e. 2, r. 5,
edālu "to lock": *e-di-il-ti* 239 ii 27, *e-te-di-il* 240:3,
ēdānīu "single, lone (horse)": *e-da-na-a-te* 159:2,
edānu "term, deadline": [*e*]*-da-nu* 58 r. 1,
edēlu "to bar, close, lock": *i-d*]*i-lu* 76 r. 2, *i-te-di-il* 234 r. 5, *le-di-il* 229 r. vi 26,
ēdu "single, lone": *e-du* 239 ii 14,
egirtu "letter, document": *e*]*-gi-ra-ti* 72:6, *e-gir-ta-a* 163 s. 2, *e-gír*.MEŠ 120 s. 1, *e-gír-ti* 120 r. 19, 20, *e-gír-tu-šú* 120:11, *e-gír-tú* 1:8, 7:7,
egû "to disregard, neglect": *e-gu-u* 229 r. v 61,

ēkallu "palace": É.GAL 1 r. 14, 6:10, 11:13, 17:4, 84:7, 120:10, 143:2, 152:8, 161 r. 5, 171 r. 4, 241:3, 243:3, 6, 287 iii 15, 288 iii 13, É.GA[L] 295:3, É].GAL 11 r. 1, [É.GA]L 143:4, É.GAL-*i-šú* 233:12, É.GAL-*ka* 129:5, KUR 233:7,

ēkānu "where?": *e-k[a-nu]* 132:7,

ekletu "darkness": *ek-le-ti* 229 r. vi 67, *ek-le-tú* 234 r. 17,

ēkurru "temple": É.[KU]R 239 r. i 16, É.KUR.MEŠ 235 r. 5, É.KUR-*šú* 233:13,

ela "apart from, besides, except for": *e-la* 232:1, 2,

elālu "to be(come) pure": SIKIL 229 r. v 55,

elapû "algae, duckweed, seaweed": *e-la-pu-u* 229 r. vi 75,

elāti "(space) above": *e-lat* 226:7,

elēlu "to become pure": *li-te-lil* 262:1,

elēnu "upper part": AN.TA-*nu* 252:2, *e-la-an* 230:17,

eli "over, upon": *e-li-šu-nu* 234:8,

eliš "above, upward": *e-liš* 229 r. vi 56,

elītu "upper garment": TÚG.*e-la-a-ti* 126:16,

ellu "pure, holy": KUG 250:11, 252:11, r. 12, 258:5, KU]G 247:18, K[UG 249 r. 5, KUG.[MEŠ-*te*] 233 e. 19, [KUG.MEŠ-*t*]*e* 233 r. 6, KUG-[*tú*] 235:6,

elû "to go up, ascend; (D) to raise, lift, remove, set aside; (Š) to promote, set aside, donate": *e-la-a-ta* 231:1, *e-li* 234:18, *e-ta-ta-li* 233:20, *e-te-li* 240:2, *i-te-lu-ú* 249 r. 1, *li-la-am-ma* 229 r. vi 71, *lu-še-li* 42 r. 2, [*u*]*l-li* 212 r. 11, *ú-li* 157:3, *ul-te-lu-ú* 126 r. 11, *ú-še-el-la* 299 i 8, 15, *ú-še-la* 299 i 6, 7, 9,

elû B "upper": AN.TA-*ti* 249:6, 250:8, AN].TA-*ti* 252:9, NIM 288 iii 22,

elūlu (Elul, name of the 6th month): ITI.KIN 255 r. 2,

ēma "wherever": *e-ma* 262 r. 2, 3,

emēdu "to lean; to impose": *e-me-du* 243:7, r. 1, 2, *im-mi-[du]* 163 r. 4, *le-mid-a[n-ni]* 67 r. 5, *ta-nem-mì-da* 229 r. vi 59,

emû "to turn into, become": *i-mì-i* 234 r. 6,

emūqu "strength, (armed) forces, army": Á.KAL.MEŠ 247:6, 7, 12, r. 8, Á.KAL.MEŠ] 247:2, *e-mu-qi*] 258:7, *e-mu-qi-šú* 37 r. 2, *e-mu-qi-š[ú* 80:2, *e-mu-qu* 37 r. 5, 80:7, 126:7, 8, 9, 164:8, LÚ.Á.KAL.MEŠ-*šú*] 245 r. 3, LÚ.*e-mu-qi* 78:2, LÚ.*e-m*]*u-qi-šú* 78:5,

enāšu "to become weak; (D) to weaken": *lu-ni-šú-u-ku-nu* 229 r. viii 24,

enna "now": *en-na* 29:8, 30:6, 69:11, 91:2, 92 e. 2, 126 r. 12, 138:5, 220:4, 8, 235:34, *en-na*] 33:4, *en-n[a* 33 r. 16, 128 r. 12, 133:14, 165:11, 171:8, *en-[na* 178:6, *e[n-na]* 163 r. 2, [*en-na*] 163 r. 3,

enû "to alter, change": *e-nu-u* 229 r. v 61, *te-[na-a-ni* 229 i 62,

ēnu "eye; spring": *e-ni* 234:21, IGI.2 167 r. 1, [IGI.2-*ia*] 263:5, [I]GI.2-*ia* 22:9, IGI.2.MEŠ 8:6, I]GI.2.MEŠ 272 r. 3, I]GI.2.ME[Š 272 r. 2, IGI.2.MEŠ-*ka* 230:11, 12, 14, IGI.2.MEŠ-*ku-nu* 229 r. vi 63, IGI.2.[MEŠ]-*ku-nu* 229 r. vii 58,

enūtu "lordship": *e-nu-ti* 232:13,

epāšu "to do, make, perform; (D) to do, practice, exercise; (N) to be done": *e-pa-áš* 299 i 14, *e-pa-še* 8 r. 5, DÙ-*áš* 299 i 10, 12, 14, *ep-šá* 106 r. 3, 175 r. 3, *ep-šá-ak* 139 s. 3, *ep-šá-ku* 120:14, *ep-šú* 199 r. 4, [*ep-šú*] 229 i 74, *e-pa-š[u-u-ni]* 52:5, *e-peš* 133:13, [*e-peš* 229 ii 1, [*e-piš* 27:3, *e-pi-šu-ni* 240:2, *e-pu-šá-an-ni* 56:3, *e-pu-šu* 33:7, [*e-pu-šu*] 52:5, *e-pu-[šú]* 243 r. 6, *e-pu-uš* 154:14, 235 r. 11, *e-pu-u[š]* 21:6, *e-p[u-uš* 208:4, *e-p*]*u-uš* 239 r. ii 21, *e-tapšu*] 228:7, *e-tap-[šú]* 254 r. 7, *e*]*-tap-šú* 252 r. 9, *i-tap-šú* 120 r. 8, *i-pu-šu* 297:9, [[*i-pu-šu*]] 297:8, *i-pu-šú* 29:3, 176 e. 5, *i-p[u-šú]* 213:1, *le-pa-šu-ku-nu* 229 r. vii 86, *le-pa-šú-ku-[nu]* 229 r. viii 11, *le-e-pu-šú* 42 r. 1, *le-pu-šu* 229 r. vii 20, [*l*]*e-pu-[šu]* 44 r. 4, *le-[pu-šú]* 109 r. 2, *le-pu-uš* 11:14, 43 r. 3, *né-ep-pa-áš* 120:15, *né-pa-áš* 43:4, *né-[pa-áš]* 160 r. 3, *ni-pu-šú* 260 r. 9, *te-ep-pa-šá-a-ni* 229 r. v 44, *te-pa-[šá-a-ni]* 229 r. v 40, *te-pa-šá-niš-šú-ni* 229 i 75, *te-pa-šá-niš-šú-u-ni* 229 iv 6, [*te*]*-e-pu-uš* 232:11, *up-pa-áš-u-ni* 229 i 17, *ú-pa-áš-u-ni*] 229 i 67,

epēšu "to do, make, perform": DÙ-*ni-ni* 273 r. 3, DÙ-*šú-ma* 237 r. 15, DÙ-*uš* 233:9, *ip-pu-šú* 246 r. 5, *i[p-pu-šú* 217:7, *i-pu-uš* 168 r. 11, *i-pu-uš-ma* 275:3, *i-te-ep-pu-šú* 237 r. 4, *i-tep-šá-an-ni* 29:4, *li-pu-šu-m[a* 171 r. 3, *li-pu-š[ú]* 237 r. 23, *li-pu-uš* 129 r. 18, 235 r. 49, *li-p[u-uš]* 88:7, *li-pu*]*-ú-šú* 248:5, *mul-te-pi-šú* 239 r. i 29, *né-ep-pa-áš-u-ni* 229 r. vi 82, *ni-te-pu-uš* 30 r. 6, *te-pu-šá-an-na-ši* 29:6, *ú-še-p[iš]* 232 e. 21,

epinnu "plough": GIŠ.APIN 229 r. vii 38,

ēpišānu "maker, doer": *e-pi-šá-nu-ti* 227 ii 8,

epištu "ritual": *e-piš-ti* 297:7,

epru "dust": *ep-ri* 229 r. v 75, 234 r. 16,

eqlu "field": A.ŠÀ 46 r. 3, 265 r. 2, 279 r. 11, 13, 296:2, A.Š[À 147 r. 7, A.Š]À 228:6, A.ŠÀ.MEŠ 175:4, A.ŠÀ.MEŠ-*ku-nu* 229 r. vii 85, A.ŠÀ.[M]EŠ-*ku-nu* 229 r. vii 23,

erābu "to enter": *e-rab* 229 r. vi 1, *e-rab-uni* 229 r. viii 16, *e-rab-u-ni* 229 r. vii 49, 54, *e-re-eb-ku-nu* 229 r. v 88, *e-ru-bu* 300:8, [*e-ru*]*-bu-u-ni* 62:2, *e-tar-ba* 240:3, *e-ta-rab* 140 r. 2, *i-r[u-ub* 136 e. 8, *lu-še-ri-bu* 229 r. vii 55, viii 18, *te-ra-ba* 229 r. vii 51, *te-er-rab-a-ni* 229 r. v 57, TU-*ma* 235 r. 3, *tu-še-rab-a-ni* 229 r. v 14, 21, *ú-se-rib* 50:3, *ú-se-ri-bi* 279:8, see also *erēbu*,

erāšu "to request, desire": *e-ri-[iš* 73:5,

erbettu "four": *er-bet-ti* 239 ii 3, 16, *e[r]-bet-ti* 239 r. i 24, [*er-bet-ti*] 235:2,

erbišu "four times": 4-*šú* 287 r. i 9, 16, 17,

erbiu "locust": BURU$_5$ 229 r. vi 17, BURU$_5$.MEŠ 229 r. vii 84,

erēbu "to enter; (Š) to introduce": *e-reb* 229 i 15, *e-ter-ba* 65:5, *ir-ru-ub-ma* 235:18, *i-te-er-bu* 33 r. 6, TU-*bu* 233 r. 11, *tu-ul-te-rib-an-na-ši* 29:5, *ú-še-rib-ú-in-nu* 168:6, *ú*]*-še-ri-bu-uš* 91 r. 6, see also *erābu*,

erēb šamši "sunset, west": ^{d}UTU.ŠÚ.A 262:10,

erēnu "cedar": *ere*-IGI 233 r. 7, GIŠ.ERIN 229 r. viii 43,

erēšu "to request": *e-reš* 188:7, *e-re-ši* 32 r. 4, *e-te*]*-riš-an-na-ši* 182:7, *i-ri-šú* 235 r. 34, *ir-ri-šú-ma* 164:5,

erṣetu "ground, earth": KI-*ti* 230:18,

eršu "bed": GIŠ.NÁ 229 r. vii 52, GI]Š.NÁ 288 ii 32,

erû "copper": URUDU 271:7, 8, r. 2, 288 ii 32, iv 9, r. ii 10, URU]DU 77 r. 1,

esāpu "to gather, collect": *lu-si-pu-[šú-nu]* 139 s. 1,

esāru "to besiege, shut in": *e-si-ru-šu-ni* 240:2, [*e-ta-as-ru-šú-nu*] 228:6, *i-ta-as-ru-šú* 240:3,
eṣentu "bone": *eṣ-mat-e-ku-nu* 229 r. viii 38, *eṣ-mat-tú-ku-n*[*u*] 229 r. vi 20,
eṣēru "to draw": *eṣ-ret* 237:12,
ēṣidu "harvester": LÚ.*e-ṣi-d*[*u*] 163 r. 7, LÚ.*e-ṣi-du-*[*u-a*] 163:6,
eṣû "to be(come) scarce": *e-ṣa-na-ši* 108 r. 3,
ešer "ten": [10] 286 iii 10, 10 44:5, 7, 126 r. 12, 139:4, 154:11, r. 12, 175 r. 2, 232 r. 6, 7, 8, 286 iii 9, 288 ii 28,
ešēru "to be, go straight; (Š) to guide to": *eš-šìr-ma* 232 r. 4, *i-še-er* 267:5, *liš-*(*te*)*-šir₄-ku-nu* 229 r. vii 11, SI.[SÁ 265:7, S]I.SÁ-*ma* 268:4,
ešrā "twenty": 20 44:8, 120 r. 70, 188:2, 264:1, 3, 22 287 iii 15, 292:5, 23 289 e. ii 18, 24 250 r. 2,
eššiš "anew": GIBIL.BI 262 r. 6,
eššu "new": *eš*]-*ši* 262:4,
etāku "to be alert": *e-ti-ik* 120 r. 22, *et-ku* 1:10,
etēqu "to pass through, move on; (Š) to pass on": *e-te-qu* 229 r. v 62, DIB.MEŠ-*ma* 246:12, DIB.MEŠ-*ma*] 247:19, *it-ti-iq* 178:4, *lu-še-ti-q*[*u*] 115 r. 4, *ú-še-t*]*i-qa-an-ni-ma* 69:16,
eṭemmu "spirit, ghost": *e-ṭam-ma-ku-nu* 229 r. vi 30, 57, GIDIM 271:3, 10,
eṭēru "to save, spare": *in-ni-ṭ*[*ir* 32 r. 6,
eṭlu "young man": *eṭ-li* 226 r. 8, *e*]*ṭ-lu* 226 r. 7, [*eṭ-lu* 234:3, LÚ.GURUŠ-*ku-nu* 229 r. vi 62,
eṭû "to be dark": *e-ṭu-u* 229 r. vi 66, *e-ṭú-ú* 264:1,
ezābu "to leave, abandon; to save; (Š) to rescue, escape": *e-ta-az-bu-ni* 120:9, *li-zi-bu-ku-nu* 229 r. vi 60, *š*]*e-zib* 80:11, *ú-še-zi-bu* 216 r. 6, *šu-zib-in-ni* 235 r. 39, *ú-zu-ba-a-ni* 234:11,
ezēbu "to leave, disregard": *e-zib* 246:9, 10, 11, 12, 13, 14, 247:18, 19, r. 1, 253 r. 2, [*e-zib* 247:18, 19, r. 2, 4, TAG₄-*ib* 251 r. 2,
ezēzu "to be angry": *i-te-zi-*[*iz* 133:7,
ezziš "angrily": *ez-zi-iš* 298 r. 5,
ezzu "angry": *e-*[*zu*]*-ti* 229 r. vii 8, *e*]*z-zu-te* 226:10,
gabbu "all": *gab-ba-šú-nu* 229 r. v 63, *gab-bi* 29:6, 88:2, 163:7, 211:3, 213:2, 216:8, 235 r. 12, 239 ii 33, *gab-b*[*i* 189 r. 7, *gab-bi-šú* 291:5, *gab-bi-šú-nu* 120 r. 23, 235:25, *gab-bu* 120:10, 14, r. 14, 140:4, 18, 240:11, 12, *gab-bu*] 229 i 11, *gab-bu-ú* 216:5,
gadiu "male kid": *ga-de-e* 229 r. viii 34,
gadu "with": *ga-du* 237 r. 7,
gallābtu "female barber": MÍ.ŠU.I 286 r. 6,
gallubu "(D only) to shave, share, clip": *ug-dal-lib-šú* 280:6,
gallulu "to blind": *ú-ga-lil-u-ni* 229 r. viii 22,
galû "(Š) to exile": *l*[*i*]*-še-eg-la-a*[*n-na-šú*] 37 r. 13,
gamāru "to come to an end, finish; (D) to complete; to abolish": *gam-mur* 60:3, *ga-mir* 237 r. 14, *i*]*g-da*[*m-ru* 80:12, *lig-ma-ru-ku-nu* 229 r. viii 23, *lig-mu-ru* 229 r. vii 80, *nu-gam-m*[*a-ru-ni*] 60 r. 3, *ú*]*-gam-mu-ru* 122:6,
gāmilu "merciful": *ga-mì-li* 229 r. vi 35,
gammalu "camel": ANŠE.*gam-ma*[*l*.MEŠ] 243:2,
gammaru "annihilation": *ga-am-m*[*a-ru*] 33:10,
gammīdu "mangled garment": *ga-me-di* 288 r. i 13,
gammurtu "totality": *gu-mur-ti* 229 r. v 51,
garû "to turn hostile, start a fight": *ta-ga-ra-šú-nu-ni* 229 r. v 12, 20,
gaṣṣu "gypsum": *ga-a-ṣi* 232 r. 4,
gaṣṣu B "cruel": *ga-ṣu-te* 287 iii 16,
gazāru "to cut": *ga-zi-ri* 229 r. viii 56,
gīdu "sinew": *gi-di* 42:3, *g*]*i-di* 42:9, [*gi-di* 42:7, [*gi-d*]*i* 42 r. 2,
gimlu "compassion": *gim-lu* 229 r. vi 40, *gi-*[*im*]*-lu* 229 iv 1,
gimru "total": PAB 44:10, 60:5, 280 r. 14, 281:15, r. 3, 287:7, 11, 14, 15, e. 25, r. 6, 7, 10, 287 iii 14, iv 4, 290 i 6, 8, e. ii 18, 293 r. 2, P[AB 286:4, [PAB 288 ii 31, [PAB] 286 iii 4, [PA]B 286 iii 14, 15, 16,
ginû "ordinary; regular offering": *gi-né-e* 19:15, *gi-né-e-a* 247 r. 4, *gi-né-e-šú* 246:14, *g*]*i-né-e-šú* 247 r. 2, *gi-nu-ú* 298 r. 7,
gipšu "mass": *gíp-ši* 248 r. 3,
giskimmu "omen": *gis-kim* 232:12,
gišhurru "magic circle": *giš-hu-r*[*i* 239 r. i 30,
gišparru "trap, snare": *giš-par-ri* 229 r. viii 49,
gišru "bridge": *giš-ri* 10 r. 10,
gitmālu "perfect": [*gít-m*]*a-la* 239 ii 16, *gi-it-ma-li* 244 r. 2,
gugallu "canal inspector": GÚ.GAL 229 r. vi 13,
gupnu "tree (trunk)": GI]Š.*gup-ni* 233 r. 8, [GIŠ].*gup-ni* 233:15, GIŠ.*gu-up-ni* 8:7,
gušūru "log, roof-beam": GIŠ.ÙR.MEŠ 87:2, 238:5, GIŠ.Ù[R.MEŠ 98:4, [GI]Š.ÙR.MEŠ 233 r. 7,
habālu "to be indebted": *ha-ab-la-ku* 281:4, *ih-bi-lu-ni-ni* 281 r. 6, *ih-tab-la-ni* 281:8,
habātu "to plunder": [*ah-bu-tu* 72:6, [*hab*]*-tu-ni* 75:3, *ha-ba-a-te* 240:11, *i-ha*[*b-ba-tu* 246 r. 6, *i-ha-b*]*a-tu-šu-u-ni* 240:11, SAR-*tu* 247:10, 14, r. 12,
hadīš "joyfully": *ha-diš* 237 r. 4,
hadû "to be glad": *ha-de-e* 233:17, *ha-du-ni* 120:15, *ha-d*[*u*]*-ú* 182:3, *i-ha-di-u* 240:14,
hadûia "at my pleasure": *ha-du-a-a* 279 r. 14,
haeparušhi (an animal): *ha-e-pa-ru-u*[*š*]*-hi* 229 r. vii 77,
hakāmu "to understand, comprehend": *li-ih-kim* 120 r. 17, 25,
halālu "to slink, creep in": *i-hal-la-lu-u-ni* 229 r. viii 36,
halāpu "to clothe": *i-hal-li-pu-u-ni* 240:1, *li-hal-lip-ku-nu* 229 r. v 87,
halāqu "to disappear; (D) to cause to be lost": *ah-te-liq* 79 r. 3, *hal-qu* 219:2, *hul-lu-qi-šú-nu*] 227 ii 4, *i-hal-li-qu* 38:3, 219:3, *ih-li-qa* 92 r. 7, *i*[*h-li-qu* 80:9, *i*]*h-ti-liq* 240:2, *ih-tal-liq* 239 ii 31, *li-hal-li-qa* 229 r. vi 3, *li-hal-liq* 229 r. viii 60, *li-hal-liq-qi* 229 r. vi 8, *li-ih-li-iq* 229 r. vii 31, 37, *li-ih-liq-qi* 229 r. viii 44, *lu-ha*]*l-liq* 226 r. 9, *tah-*[*li*]*-qa-ku-nu* 229 r. vi 19, *tu-hal-la-qa-a-ni* 229 r. v 76, *ú-hal-li-*[*qu-ni* 292:3, *ul*]*-tah-li-qu* 91:10,
halāṣu "to press, squeeze": *hal-ṣi* 262:2,
hallimu "raft": GIŠ.*hal-*[*li-ma-a*]*-ni* 164:9,
halqu "fugitive, runaway": LÚ.*hal-qu* 38:2,
hamāmu "to gather": *ha-mim* 230:5,
hamāṭu "to glow": *ha-an-ṭu* 229 r. vi 38,
hamû "to immobilize, stun": *a-ha-ma-a-šú* 61:3, *ha-a*[*m* 170 e. 12, *i-ha-am-mu-ú* 133:12,
hanāqu "to strangle": *li-ih-na-qu-ku-nu*] 229 r. viii 2, *tah-ha-an-qu* 115:5,
hanniu see *anniu*,
hanšā "fifty": 50 80:5, 148 r. 3, 52 286 r. 7, 56

286 r. 10,
hanṭiš "quickly": *ha-an-ṭiš* 85:4, 163 r. 7, 171 r. 11, *ha-[an-ṭiš* 85:8, *h]a-an-ṭiš* 71 r. 3, [*ha-an-ṭiš*] 74 r. 5,
hapû "to break, destroy": *ih-te-pe* 32:10, *ta-hi-bi* 229 r. viii 54,
harābu "(Š)to lay waste": *ha-rib-ti* 78:6,
harādu "to watch (over), attend": *har-da-at* 154:7, 10,
harammāma "later": *ha-ra-ma-[ma* 160 r. 1,
harāpu "to be early, first": *ha*]*-ri-ip* 240:14,
harrānu "road, way, journey, business venture": *har-ra-an* 234 r. 1,
hasāsu "to remember": *ha-as-su* 231:6, *hu-us*]*-sa-am-ma* 84 r. 12, *hu-us-su* 120 r. 13, *ta-ha-sa-sa-ni-ni* 229 r. v 43,
hasīsu "ear": *ha-si-si* 247 r. 16, 252:9,
haṣānu "to shelter, prtotect": *ni-ha-ṣi-[ni*] 60 r. 6,
haṣbu (a container of earthenware, "pot"): *haṣ-bu* 247 r. 3,
haṣṣinnu "axe": *ha-ṣi-in* 271:7,
hašānu "thyme": Ú.*ha-šá-nu* 274:4,
hašhu "need": *ha-aš-ha-te* 298 r. 6,
hašû "lung": MUR 249:6, 252:15, [MUR 258:2,
hatannu "brother-in-law" LÚ.*ha-te-ni-šú* 123 r. 1,
haṭṭu "sceptre": GIŠ.*ha-ṭu* 279:10, GIŠ.PA 288 iv 5, 6,
haṭû "to make a mistake, sin": *ah-ṭi* 71:5, *ha-ṭu-ú*] 246:10, 13, *ha-ṭu-[ú*] 247 r. 1, *i-ha-ṭu-ú* 234 r. 6, *i-haṭ-ṭa-an-ni* 21:16, *i-haṭ-ṭu* 229 r. v 61, *ih-ṭu-u-ni* 229 r. viii 19, *ih-ṭu-ú* 126:2, LAL-*ú* 246:13, 247 r. 1, *ta-ha-aṭ-ṭi* 235:43, *ta-ha-ṭa-a-ni* 229 r. vii 7, *ta-ha-ṭa-a-ni*] 229 i 72,
hâṭu "to weigh": *i-hi-iṭ-ma* 275:4, 276:5, *i-hi*]*-ṭu-ma* 181 r. 4, *ta-hi-iṭ* 235:45,
hazannu "(police) superintendent, inspector": LÚ.*ha-za-an* 280 r. 2,
hepû "to break, destroy": *he-pu-u* 232:4, *ih-te-p[u-u* 126 r. 10, *i-hi-pi* 209 r. 6, *he-pí* 235 r. 47,
herû "to dig": *hi-ra-a-ma* 75 e. 9, *hi-ri-i-ma* 239 r. ii 22,
himṣāti "booty, spoils": *hi-i*]*m-ṣa-a-ti* 255:7,
hiāru "to choose": *li-hi-ir* 267 r. 7, 8, *li-hi-ru* 229 r. vi 76,
hirītu "canal": *hi-ra-a-te* 288 i 1,
hīrtu "wife, spouse": [*hi*]*-ir-tu* 230:23, *hi-ir-tú* 229 r. v 80, *hi-r[a-a-ti* 80:3,
hiṣbu "yield, abundance": *h[i-iṣ-bi* 230:27,
hišihtu "desire": *hi-ši-ih-tú* 233:4,
hiṭṭu "fault, crime, sin": *hi-iṭ-ṭi* 235:49, *hi-ṭa-a-ti* 126:1, *hi-ṭi-šu* 240:7, *hi-ṭu* 67 r. 5, 229 r. vi 4,
hubšû (mng. uncert.): *húb-še-e* 126:20,
hubtu "booty, captives": *hu-u[b-tu*] 52:3, *h*]*u-ub-tú* 72:5, LÚ.*hu-ub-te* 1:5, LÚ.*hu-ub-ti* 1:9, LÚ.*hu-ub-tu* 1:17, r. 6, 8, LÚ.*h[u-ub-tu*] 1:16,
huhāru "trap": *hu-ha-ru* 229 r. viii 48,
hullānu "cloak, wrap": GÚ.LÁ 288 r. i 10,
hūlu "road, way": *hu-li-ni* 6:7, KASKAL 233:8, 245 r. 4, 253 r. 2, KASKAL] 253 r. 3, KASKAL.MEŠ 239 ii 21, KASKAL.2 165 r. 3, KAS]KAL.2 211:6, KASKAL.2-*ku-nu* 12:7,
hūl šarri "king's road, highway": KASKAL—MAN 116 r. 4,
huppu "hole" *hup-(pi)* 229 r. viii 40,
hurāpu "male spring lamb": UDU.NIM 229 r. vii 44, viii 34,
hurāṣu "gold": KUG.GI 77 r. 7, 126:13, 14, 17, 20, 196:6, 216:6, 229 r. vii 59, 232:12, 239 i 17, 288 ii 25, iii 9, 22, iv 4, r. ii 13, 299 i 4, 5, KUG.G[I] 126:17, 288 iv 1, KUG.[GI 77 r. 10, KUG].GI 288 iii 6,
hurbabillu "chameleon": *hur-ba-bil-li* 229 r. vii 80,
hurbāšu "frost": *hur-ba-šú* 204:5,
hurru "hole, burrow": HABRUD.MEŠ 229 r. vii 81, 83,
hurrutu "hole": *hu-re-te* 229 r. vii 48,
hušahhu "famine": *hu-šah-hi* 229 r. vi 27, *hu-šah-hu* 229 r. vi 60,
huṭārtu "rod, sceptre": GIŠ.*hu-ṭar-ti* 120:23, GIŠ.*hu-ṭar-tu* 120:20, 22,
huzīru "pig": ŠAH.MEŠ 229 r. vi 30, 63, 66,
iābilu "ram": UDU.NITA 232 r. 5, UDU.NITÁ 246:13, 14, r. 6, 247 r. 1, 2, 248 r. 6, 252:11, UDU.NI[TÁ 258:6, UDU.N]ITÁ 260 r. 2, UDU.NITÁ.MEŠ 129:21,
iānu "is not": *ia-a-nu* 126:9, *ia-a-nu-ú* 129 r. 16, *ia-a-aɢnu* 275:7, *ia-a-aɢn[u* 283:3,
iāši "me": *ia-a-šú* 212 r. 6, *ia-šu* 199:3,
idu "side": *i-di-ku-nu* 229 r. vi 33,
idû "to know": *i-da-an-ni* 33:5, *i-di* 29:10, 33:6, 36:6, 138:7, 280:7, *i*]*-di* 190 r. 1, *ti-de-e* 220 r. 2, ZU-*e* 246:6, 247:11, ZU-*ú*] 247:4,
igāru "wall": É.SIG$_4$ 49:7, *i-ga-ru* 115:4,
igrī "wages": *ig-ri* 281:13,
ijû "mine": *iá-a-tú* 214:2,
ikkibu "abnomination, taboo": *ik-kib-ku-nu* 229 r. vi 72, NÍG.GIG 253 r. 3, [NÍG.GIG 226 r. 2,
ikkillu "noise, scream, cry, wail": *ik-kil* 229 r. vi 10, 18, *ki-il-lu* 229 r. viii 35,
ikku "temper, mood": *ik-ki-ia* 134:6,
ikribu "blessing": *ik-r*]*i-bi-ka* 298 r. 3,
ilku "state service, duty": *il-ku* 124:8,
illatu "band, host, confederation": *il-la-ta* 234 r. 8,
illūru "pink": GIŠ.*i[l-lu-ru* 77 r. 7,
iltēnšu "once, one time; firstly":
ilu "god": DINGIR 32:10, 41:10, 229 r. vi 35, 232:12, 260 r. 3, 262:7, 9, r. 2, 3, 297:3, DINGIR-*ku-nu* 229 r. v 58, 72, DINGIR.ME 74 r. 5, DINGIR.[MEŠ 261 r. 2, DINGIR.MEŠ 30:6, 42:1, 74 r. 3, 174:4, 228:1, 3, i 24, 25, 29, 34, 35, 36, 38, 45, 46, r. v 62, 64, 71, 78, 87, vi 1, 52, 77, vii 7, 13, 15, 17, 90, viii 59, 230:3, 9, 232:1, 233:4, 234:4, 237:16, r. 15, 240:2, 3, 10, 252 r. 11, 261 r. 2, 288 r. ii 23, 297:9, DINGIR.MEŠ] 297:2, DINGIR.ME[Š 114 r. 5, 6, 217:1, 235:21, DINGIR.M[EŠ 209 e. 1, 214:4, DINGIR.M]EŠ 226:7, DINGIR.(MEŠ) 229 r. v 83, DINGIR.[MEŠ 226:8, 229 i 26, 230:18, 257 r. 4, DINGIR.[MEŠ] 235:23, DINGIR].MEŠ 229 r. v 37, DING]IR.MEŠ 226:9, [DINGIR.MEŠ 226:7, 229 iv 7, 235:23, 263 r. 4, 6, [DINGIR.MEŠ] 229 i 25, [DINGIR].MEŠ 229 i 44, DINGIR.MEŠ-*ka* 120 r. 13, 237 r. 23, DINGIR.MEŠ-*k[a* 186 r. 3, DINGIR.MEŠ-*n[i*] 233:1,
ilūtu "divinity": DINGIR-*ti-ka* 246:6, r. 9, 247:3, 5, 7, 8, r. 1, 10, 18, 248:3, r. 7, DINGIR-*ti-k*]*a* 247 r. 8, DINGIR-[*ti-ka* 246:13, 247 r. 9, DINGIR-*ut-ka* 247:4, DIN[GIR-*u*]*t-ka* 247:11, [DINGIR]-*ut-ka* 246:6, DINGIR-*ut-su* 233:3,

imāru "donkey; homer, hectare": ANŠE 115 r. 1, 129:21, 271:11, ANŠ[E 281:13, AN]ŠE 296:2, ANŠE.(NITÁ) 229 r. vi 74, ANŠE.NITÁ.MEŠ 281:2, ANŠE].NITÁ.MEŠ 243:2,

imēru "ass, donkey": *i-me-re-e* 234:7, *i-me-ri* 234: 2, 5,

imittu "right side, south; shoulder": ZAG 229 r. viii, 261 e. 14, 288 ii 2, [Z]AG-*ka* 230:28, 15-*šú* 288 r. i 6,

immeru "sheep": UDU 115:6, 247:18, 262 r. 1, 299 i 1, 2, 10, 14, UD]U 253:10, 12, UDU.HI.A 19:13, UD]U.HI.A-*šú*-[*nu*] 7:14, UDU.MEŠ 19:18, 288 ii 30, 291:3, [U]DU.MEŠ 287 iii 20, UDU.MEŠ-*šu* 279:5, 6,

im-māla "once": *im—ma-la* 240:10, *im—m*[*a-la* 240:10,

ina "in": *ina* 1:3, 5, 6, 11, r. 7, 10, 11, 3:2, 4:4, 5:1, 2, 7, r. 2, 6, 10:4, 12:7, 14:2, r. 2, 17:4, 18:6, 20 r. 3, 20:13, 18, 19, r. 2, 21 e. 11, 26:4, r. 7, 31 r. 4, 31:5, 42:9, e. 11, r. 2, 43 r. 3, 44:3, 4, 5, 6, 7, 8, 9, 10, r. 3, 51:1, 54:3, 56:2, 57:4, 6, 59:6, 61:6, 61:1, 64:5, 65:7, 66:2, r. 4, 71:2, 77 r. 3, 77 r. 7, 80:5, 87:4, 92 r. 6, 93 r. 1, 98:5, 100:4, 104:1, 114 r. 14, 115 e. 7, r. 1, 3, 4, 120:5, 6, 7, 9, 10, 13, 14, 17, 20, 23, e. 25, r. 1, 4, 5, 10, 11, 12, 19, 20, 22, 24, s. 1, 2, 122 r. 4, 123:5, 11, r. 6, 124:6, 126 r. 15, 128 r. 3, 129:20, 130:12, 133:2, 5, 134:3, 140 r. 3, 4, 10, 12, 17, s. 1, 2, 142:5, 143:2, 144:1, 147:2, 6, e. 13, 15, r. 2, 3, 5, 9, 11, 148 r. 1, 150:4, 152:5, 154:4, 5, 12, r. 5, 10, 13, 159:4, 162 r. 12, 163:5, 171 r. 12, 173:3, 176 r. 9, 180 r. 4, 186 r. 3, 195 r. 2, 204:2, 216 r. 4, 9, 217:8, 218:6, 221:4, 223 r. 2, 224:2, 225:4, 226:10, r. 1, 4, 227 ii 9, 228:6, 7, 229 i 14, 16, 17, 25, 46, 48, 51, 67, 73, 75, 78, ii 1, 3, 4, iii 5, r. v 2, 8, 13, 14, 21, 22, 27, 29, 30, 33, 35, 37, 39, 49, 51, 55, 56, 67, 70, 71, 72, 73, 75, 86, vi 2, 8, 10, 11, 14, 16, 18, 22, 26, 27, 32, 34, 35, 37, 41, 42, 46, 49, 51, 53, 56, 57, 61, 63, 64, 65, 69, 78, 87, vii 1, 2, 16, 17, 20, 23, 25, 28, 33, 37, 38, 41, 43, 48, 51, 52, 54, 55, 56, 59, 61, 63, 65, 66, 69, 72, 74, 77, 78, 81, 83, 86, 90, viii 2, 3, 4, 5, 7, 9, 11, 16, 17, 23, 24, 48, 49, 53, 54, 56, 57, 60, 61, 66, 230:5, 33, 231:1, 2, 5, 6, r. 1, 232:2, r. 2, 233 r. 12, 234:7, 11, r. 16, 235:15, 27, 29, 31, 35, 38, 43, 49, r. 12, 13, 14, 17, 48, 236 r. 10, 237 r. 2, 3, 5, 8, 14, 16, 18, 239 ii 5, 13, 21, r. i 13, 17, 240:1, 2, 3, 5, 6, 7, 11, 12, 13, 14, 15, 241 r. 10, 11, 243:6, 7, r. 6, 8, 244 s. 1, 246:6, 11, r. 6, 247:3, 8, r. 2, 4, 8, 10, 14, 248 r. 4, 249 s. 1, 251 r. 2, 252:3, 4, 13, 18, r. 9, 255:4, 257 r. 5, 260 r. 3, 4, 6, 10, 261:5, 6, 8, r. 1, 262:1, 7, 13, r. 5, 263 r. 3, 5, 6, 264 r. 3, 265:5, r. 1, 266:5, 7, 267:4, 268:4, 273 r. 6, 12, 275:7, 279:1, 5, 8, r. 2, s. 1, 280 r. 5, 6, 7, 8, 9, 10, 11, 12, 15, 281:3, 6, 9, 16, 282:4, 287 iii 4, 15, iv 11, 288 i 6, r. ii 6, 10, *ina*] 11:12, 246 r. 1, 247 r. 9, 248 r. 3, 252:12, 13, 262:2, 3, 280:2, *in*]*a* 6:9, 184:11, *i*[*na* 105:3, 178:3, *i*]*na* 142:3, 191:4, 288 iii 13, (*ina* 229 r. vii 70, [*ina* 8:11, 8:4, 10, 11:8, 12:5, 15:5, 18:8, 20 r. 8, 33:20, 42:1, 4, 49:4, 58:2, 60 r. 6, 61:3, 66:1, r. 1, 67:3, 74:7, 80:3, 102:4, 109:3, 113:c4, 117:9, 11, 120 r. 25, 150:3, 8, 153:7, 226:9, r. 3, 229 i 19, 20, 22, 72, 76, r. v 87, 234 r. 1, 235 r. 16, 246:6, 252 r. 3, 255:6, 257 r. 1, 262:5, 279 r. 4, 280 r. 2, 3, 4, 14, 297:6, 10, [*ina*] 3:2, 25:5, 44:11, 111 r. 5, 124 r. 2, 188:5, 229 r. vii 8, 26, 27, 50, viii 6, 47, 252:7, 257:1, 280 r. 13, *i-na* 33:15, 36:9, r. 4, 38:4, 5, 73:8, r. 1, 81:3, 84:7, 126:16, r. 6, 8, 128:6, 9, 14, r. 1, 184:10, 192 r. 1, 232 r. 3, 235:14, 33, r. 21, 22, 39, 237 r. 6, 9, 239 i 9, 16, 27, ii 7, 20, 22, 241 r. 5, 245 r. 5, 247:3, 13, 16, r. 6, 248:2, 265:3, 298 r. 8, *i-na*] 93 r. 1, *i-n*[*a* 128:8, 235:28, 239 ii 6, *i-n*]*a* 81:7, 235 r. 19, *i-*[*na* 111 r. 8, [*i-na* 134:3, 168:6, 248:3, 276 r. 3, 277 r. 4, 299 i 12, [*i-na*] 254 r. 7, [*i-n*]*a* 75:4, 235:51,

inanna "now": TA-*an-n*[*i* 247:2,

inbu "fruit": GURUN 288 i 3,

innû "ours": *in-nu-u* 140:19,

inūšu "at that time": [*i-nu-šu* 297:8,

irkallu "netherworld": *ir-kal-li* 234 r. 11, 13, 14,

irrī "entrails, intestines": *ir-ri* 229 r. vii 46, 55, *ir-ri-ku-nu* 229 r. vii 54, 55, *ir-ri-šú-nu* 229 r. vii 45,

irtu "breast": GABA 235 r. 47, 254 r. 1, GABA-*ka* 230:26, GABA.MEŠ 251 r. 4, GABA-*šú-nu* 126:17,

isinnu "festival": EZ[EN 249:4, *i-s*]*in-ni* 266:7,

isītu "tower": *e-si-ti* 86:6, *i-si-tú* 16:3,

isqu "share, lot": *is-q*[*a-ti* 44:6,

issahēiš "together": *is-*[*sa-he-iš*] 147 r. 1,

issēn "one": [1-*en*] 72 r. 4, [1-*e*]*n* 1 r. 7, 1-*en* 36 r. 6, 120 r. 10, 11, 134:3, 140:19, r. 10, 13, s. 2, 199:4, 220:3, 229 r. vii 51, 243 r. 6, 1-*ma* 115:6, [1.*e*]*n* 217:4, 1.*en* 90:5, 128:8, 164:9, 194:6, 235 r. 20, 1.*e*]*n* 136 r. 5,

issēniš "also, in addition": *is-se-niš* 159:1,

issēnīu "single, individual": 1-*ú* 243:7,

issēt "one": [1]-*et* 229 r. vii 48, 1-*et* 5:6, 229 r. vii 52, 241 r. 10,

issi "with": *is*]-*se-e-šú* 21:6, [*is-se-i*]*a* 21 r. 3, *is-si-iá* 120 r. 23, *is-si-ka* 116 r. 1, *is-si-ku-nu* 229 i 47, *is-si-ku-*(*nu*) 229 i 19, *is-si-ku-*[*nu*] 229 r. vii 6, *is-si-ni* 120 r. 9, 154:14, 229 r. v 8, *is-si-*[*ni*] 60 r. 5, *is-si-šú* 120 r. 8, 229 iv 7, 279 r. 6, *is-si-šú-nu* 1 r. 4, [*is*]-*si-šú-nu* 229 i 13, *i-si-ia* 140 r. 1, *i-si-šu* 225 r. 3, *i-si-šú* 59:4, KI-*šú* 287 ii 5,

issi/u "with/from": TA 1 r. 6, 8, 11, 8:6, 11:13, 14, 14:4, r. 3, 64 r. 2, 66:6, 120:21, 24, e. 27, r. 16, 27, 143:3, 144:5, 146:2, 147:8, 154 r. 7, 162 r. 11, 165 r. 7, 229 i 3, 4, 11, 14, 76, r. v 2, 31, 36, 46, vi 24, 47, 83, 721, 31, 45, 47, 233:7, r. 7, 237 r. 18, 240:4, 245 r. 1, 4, 246 r. 3, 255:6, 291 e. 6, T[A 55:3, 110 r. 1, T[A] 55 r. 1, T]A 3:3, 8:7, 19:6, 24:2, 42:7, 153:8, 256:1, ((TA)) 229 r. vi 31, [TA 8:11, 10:6, 115 s. 1, 233 r. 15, 251:4, [TA] 14:2,

issu B "woman, wife": MÍ 229 r. viii 11, MÍ] 262:10, M]Í 262:6, MÍ.MEŠ 1 r. 5, 9, 11, MÍ.M[EŠ 1 r. 14, MÍ.MEŠ-*ku-nu* 229 r. vii 51, 60, 70, 75, viii 1, 36, M[Í].MEŠ-*ku-nu* 229 r. vii 63, [MÍ].MEŠ-*ku-nu* 229 r. vii 57, viii 46, MÍ-*šú* 147:8,

issurri "perhaps": *is—su-ri* 240:2, [*i—s*]*u-ri* 67 r. 6,

iṣṣūru "bird": MUŠEN 229 r. vii 72,

iṣu "tree, wood": GIŠ 10:12, GIŠ.MEŠ 288 i 3,

īṣu "slight, insignificant": *i-ṣu* 168 r. 13,

iṣ qāti "handcuffs": *iš-qa-*[*ti* 46:5, GIŠ—[ŠU].2.MEŠ 49 r. 3,

išātu "fire": IZI 229 r. vii 26, viii 3, 15, 247 r. 3,

išdu "foundation, base": SUHUŠ 127:7, 248 r. 2, 254:1, 288 iv 4, SUHUŠ-*sá* 247 r. 16, 248 r. 5, 250:10, 252:10, 258:2,

iškāru "assigned quota, impost; series": ÉŠ.QAR 237 r. 18, 20, *iš*-QAR 124 r. 4,

iškuru "wax": DU[H.LÀL 229 r. viii 3,

ištēniš "entirely": TÉŠ.BI 252:2, 260 r. 2,
itti "with": *it-ti* 29:9, 33:16, 40:10, 126 r. 12, 129:11, r. 15, 164:10, r. 5, 9, 169 r. 4, 199 r. 6, 219 r. 4, 237 r. 15, 239 i 10, 12, 241:2, 248 e. 9, 275:2, 280:2, 288 r. ii 19, *it-t[i* 165:4, 171:7, *i]t-ti* 164 r. 13, [*it-ti* 72 r. 5, [*it-ti*] 280 r. 15, [*i*]*t-ti* 241:3, *it-ti-ia* 70:9, [*it-ti-ia*] 213:3, *it-ti-iá* 71:6, *it-ti-ka* 239 i 11, *it-ti-ku-nu* 229 r. vi 39, *it-ti-ni* 37 r. 7, *it-ti-šú* 115:4, *it-t]i-šú* 164:5, *it*]-*ti-šú* 136:8, *i*]*t-ti-šú* 183:7, 208:1, 239 ii 34, [*it-ti-šú* 74 r. 7, *it-ti-šú-ma* 239 i 15, *it-ti-šú-nu* 40:6, 84 r. 4, 183 r. 7, *it-t*]*i-šú-nu* 84 r. 11, KI 246:11, 12, 247:6, 19, 254:2, 7, 263 r. 4, KI] 241 r. 7, K[I 273 r. 11, KI 247:8, r. 9, 250 r. 12, [KI] 241:7, [K]I 247:4, KI-*šú* 237:4, KI-*šú* 287 ii 5,
ittu "omen": GISKIM 265:1, 2, GISKIM.MEŠ 129 r. 9, [GISKIM.M]EŠ 263:2,
kabāsu "to tread upon, trample": *i-ka-bu-su* 279 r. 15, *i-ki-bu-su-ni* 279 r. 9, *i*]*k-ta-ba-as* 182 r. 9, *kab-su* 229 r. vii 44,
kabattu "mind, mood; liver": *ka-bat-ti* 127:6, 230:23, MÁŠ 246:11, 12, 13, 247:19, r. 1, 248 r. 5, 249:2, 250:7, 252:17, 255:6, 261:5, 6,
kabātu "to be weighty; (D) to honour": *kab-tú* 229 r. vi 5, *ta-ka-bit* 120:23,
kabsutu "young ewe": *kab-su-tú* 229 r. vii 44,
kabtu "important (person)": LÚ.*kab-tu* 183:6,
kadammu "storeroom": *ka-dam-mu* 240:8, *ka-da-*[*am-me*] 70:14,
kaiānu "constant": *ka*]-*a-a-nu* 235:26, SAG.UŠ.MEŠ 287 ii 3,
kakku "weapon": GIŠ].TUKUL 248 r. 5, GIŠ.TUKUL 252:3, 14, 255:6, 264:2, GIŠ.TUKUL.MEŠ 253:7, [GIŠ.TUKUL.MEŠ 247:17, GIŠ.TUKUL.MEŠ-*šú* 229 r. vii 8, 253:7, GIŠ.TUKUL.MEŠ-[*šú* 226:10, *i–ka-ki-i-ni-i* 234:20, *kak-ki* 232 r. 3, *kak-ki-šú-nu* 236:15,
kakkubu "star": MUL 120 r. 4, 232:11, 234 r. 17, MU[L 230:31, MUL-*ka* 239 ii 22, [M]UL-*ka* 239 ii 24, MUL.MEŠ 230:15, 20,
kalāma "all, whole, entire, everything": *ka-la-mu* 25 s. 2,
kalbu "dog": UR.KU 129:9, UR.KU.MEŠ 229 r. vi 63, 65, [U]R.KU.MEŠ 229 r. vi 29,
kališ "completely": *ka-liš* 262 r. 2,
kallāpu "outrider": LÚ.*kal-la-ba-ni* 229 i 9,
kallumu "to show": *ka-al-li-me-šú* 225 r. 1, *li-kal-mu-ku-nu* 229 r. vi 55, *lu-kal-*[*lim*] 179 r. 6, *ú-kal-lim-ma* 288 r. ii 18, *ú-k*[*al-lim-*(*u*)-*ka-nu-ni* 229 i 65, *ú-kal-lim-ku-nu* 229 r. vi 2, *ú-kal-lim-u-šá-nu-ni* 229 r. v 34, *ta-ki-il-lim* 235:24,
kalmatu "louse": *kal-ma-tú* 229 r. vii 84,
kalu "all": DÙ] 226 r. 11, D]Ù 226 r. 7, DÙ-*šú-nu* 229 i 36, 288 i 3, DÙ-[(*šú-nu* 229 i 36, [DÙ-*šú-nu* 229 i 38, *kal* 19:5, *kàl* 233:6, 19, *ka-li-šú-nu* 229 i 27, 34, 35,
kalû "to hold back": *ak-kil-li* 211:6, *ik-lu-ú* 137:3, *i*]*k-lu-ú* 84 r. 5, *ik-*[*ta-lu-ú*] 92 e. 2, *ka-al-a*[*t*] 154 r. 6, *ta-k*[*a-la*] 163 r. 8, [*ta-ka*]*l-la-šú* 144:4,
kalû B "chanter, lamentation priest": LÚ.UŠ.KU.MEŠ 240:11,
kamānu (a sweetened cake): *ka-ma-ni* 229 r. vii 81,
kammusu "to sit, live, stay": *kam-mu-sa* 1 r. 7, 12, *kam-mu-*[*su* 104:2,
kanāku "to seal": *ak-nu-uk-ma* 288 r. ii 11, *ka-nak*] 277 r. 4, *ka-n*]*ak* 276 r. 3, *ka-nik-u-ni* 229 r. v 71,
kanāšu "to bend, bow down, submit": *kan-šu-uš* 229 r. v 11, *kan-šú-uš* 229 r. v 18,
kanāšunu "you": *ka-na-šú-nu* 227 ii 5, 229 r. viii 1,
kannû "well-tended(?)": *ka-an-ni-i* 120 r. 4,
kânu "to be firm, true; (D) to confirm": *ku-un-i* 246:7, *ú-kan-m*[*a*] 235:50, *ú-kan-nu-ni* 279 r. 6, see also *kuānu,*
kanūnu (Kanun, name of the 10th month; a festival): ITI.AB 250 r. 5,
kapādu "to plan": *i-ka-pu-da* 234:5, *ik-tap-du-ma* 247:7, *lik-pid-ma* 247:6,
kapāru "to wipe, cleanse": *i-kap-pa-ru-ni* 140:10,
kapāṣu "to be curled": *ka-*[*pí-iṣ* 250:2, *ka-pí-ìṣ* 247 r. 15, *kap-*[*ṣa-at*] 252:2,
kapda "at once, fast": *kap-da* 171 r. 10,
kappu "drinking bowl; wing": *kap-pa-a-n*[*i*] 177:2, *kap-pi* 229 r. viii 20, 288 ii 25,
kapru "village": URU].ŠE.MEŠ-[*šú*] 289:4, URU].ŠE.[MEŠ-*šú*] 289:12, URU.ŠE.MEŠ-*šú*] 289:10, URU.ŠE.MEŠ]-*šú* 289:8, URU.Š]E.MEŠ-[*šú*] 289:2, UR]U.ŠE.MEŠ-*šú* 289:6,
kaptukku (mng. and rdg. uncert.): KAB.TÚG 77 r. 1,
kaqqudu "head": SAG.DU 237 r. 2,
kaqquru "earth, ground": *kaq-qar* 229 r. v 49, viii 53, 56, *kaq-qar-ku-nu* 229 r. vii 19, *kaq-qa-ri* 161 r. 3, *kaq-qi-ri* 229 r. vii 37, *kaq-qí-ri* 234 r. 12, *k*[*aq*]-*qí-ri* 234 r. 10, *kaq-qu-ru* 229 r. vii 18, KI.TIM 229 i 25, 47, r. v 86, vi 13, 52, 57, 65, 70, 713, 230:22, 239 i 10, 288 r. ii 23, KI.TIM] 230:24, K]I.TIM 262:8,
karābu "to bless": *ak-tar-rab-ka* 154:3, *lik-ru-bu* 121:5, 124:5, *lik-ru-b*[*u* 155:6, *lik-ru-b*[*u*] 135:4, *lik-*[*ru-bu*] 114:5, *l*]*ik-ru-bu* 119:6,
karāku "to gather": *kar-ku-u-ni* 229 r. vii 46, *li-kar-ka* 229 r. vii 47,
karānu "wine": GEŠTIN 229 r. vii 54,
karāru "to lay, throw, cast": *ik-tar-*[*ru* 147 r. 11, *ik-ta-r*[*a-ar* 279 r. 3, *i-ka*]*r-ra-ru-u-ni* 21:14, *i-ka-ru-*[*ru-ni* 117:3, *kar-ra* 42:4, *kar-ru-ni* 41 e. 10,
karmiš "to ruins": *kar-mì-iš* 234 r. 6,
karputu "vessel": DUG 252 r. 2,
karšu "stomach; mind": *kar-ši* 229 r. vi 65,
karû "to be short": *ka-ru-u*] 134:5, *tak-ta-ra-ma* 12:8,
kāru "quay, port, harbour, trade colony": K]AR 249:3,
kārû (mng. obscure): *ka-a-re-e* 235 r. 43,
kaskāsu "breast-bone": GAG.ZAG.GA 249 r. 5, 250:11, GAG].ZAG.GA 252:11,
kaspu "money": *kas-pi* 123:5, r. 6, 124 r. 2, 243:4, 282:4, *kas-pi*] 147 r. 7, *k*]*as-pi* 282:9, *kás-pi* 281:16,
kasû "to bind": *i-ka-su-ka* 239 r. ii 17, *lik-si* 229 r. vi 33,
kāsu "goblet, cup, chalice": G]Ú.ZI.MEŠ 288 ii 24,
kaṣāpu "to reckon(?)": *ú-ká*[*ṣ-ṣip* 136 r. 8,
kaṣāru "to tie, knot, organize, form": *i-ka-ṣ*[*a-ru-ni*] 140:13, *ik-ka-aṣ-ṣ*[*ar* 25:5,
kāṣiru "tailor": LÚ.TÚG.K[A.KÉŠ 204 s. 1,

LÚ.TÚG.KA.KÉŠ.MEŠ 140:12,

kâṣu "to flay": *tu-ka-aṣ-ṣu* 235:50, *tu-ka-a-ṣ]a* 235:42, *ú-ka-ṣa* 49:3,

kašādu "to reach, conquer, vanquish; (D) to chase away; (Š) to make reach": *a]k-ta-šad* 72:4, *i-kaš-šad* 133:14, *i]-kaš-ša-d[u* 185:2, *ka-áš-du]* 240:13, *ka-šid]* 255:2, *kaš-šu-du-u-ni* 229 r. vii 67, KUR-*ád* 253:5, 262 r. 3, *lik-ta-še-du-ku-nu* 229 r. vi 58, *lu-kaš-ši-du* 229 r. vii 68, *lu-šak-ši-du-ka* 252 r. 17, *[lu-šak-š]i-d[u-ka]* 257 r. 7, *lu-šak-ši-du-ú-[ka]* 255 r. 7, *lu]-uk-ta-šid-ku-nu* 226 r. 5, *ta-kaš-šá-du* 93 r. 1, *[ta-k]aš-šá-du* 93 r. 3,

kāšunu "you": *ka-a-šú-nu* 229 r. vii 67, viii 12, 33, *ka-šú-nu* 229 r. vii 73, *ka-šú-[nu]* 229 r. vii 56,

kašūšu "overpowering": *ka-šu-ši* 226 r. 1,

katammu "lid" *ka-tam-mi* 271 r. 2,

katāmu "to cover, hide": *i-ka-at-[tam]* 127 r. 1, *ta-kàt-ta-ma-a-ni* 229 r. v 75,

katāru "to wait": *ak-t[ar-ra]* 62:3,

kāti "you": *ka-a-ta* 232:1, 2, r. 3,

katû "destitute, poor": *ka-tu-ú* 263 r. 2,

kettu "truth; nevertheless": *ket-t[u* 114 r. 12, *ket-tu-u* 143:3, *ke-e-tu* 1 r. 5, 11:11, *ke-tú* 64 r. 4,

kî "as; if, whether": GIM 229 r. v 88, 230:22, 244 r. 3, 246:10, 247:7, 18, r. 9, 250 r. 11, [GI]M 247:5, *ki* 152 r. 4, 229 r. v 12, 19, 49, 72, vii 76, viii 41, 232:9, 10, 240:15, 277 r. 5, 278:1, *ki-i* 3:6, 11:7, 8, 17:6, 29:7, 30:2, r. 5, 32:5, 10, 32:15, 19, 20, 21, 35:7, 36:6, 40:10, 52:5, 6, 71:5, r. 1, 79 r. 4, 85:8, 93 r. 2, 4, 109 r. 1, 112 r. 3, 120:15, r. 14, 22, 126:7, r. 8, 12, 128:8, 11, r. 6, 7, 10, 14, 15, 129:15, r. 17, 130 r. 7, 133:13, 138:5, 140:17, 147 r. 5, 163 r. 5, 164:8, e. 16, 164 e. 12, r. 5, 179 r. 3, 183 r. 8, 184:8, 187:5, 190 r. 1, 209 r. 2, 212 r. 5, 7, 213:1, r. 3, 229 r. vii 21, 22, 26, 29, 32, 33, 40, 42, 44, 54, 56, 60, 62, 67, 69, 72, 77, 80, 81, 82, 86, 89, viii 3, 7, 8, 10, 11, 13, 15, 16, 19, 22, 23, 24, 35, 40, 42, 45, 52, 55, 235:47, 236 r. 16, 237 r. 18, 239 ii 24, r. i 3, 240: 7, 241 r. 4, 10, 11, 243: 6, 245 r. 1, 246 r. 2, 247 r. 7, 280:4, *ki-i]* 15:3, 37 r. 6, 80:1, 199:4, 240:12, *ki-[i* 229 r. vii 84, 241 r. 6, *ki-[i]* 229 r. vii 19, *ki]-i* 37 r. 10, 90 r. 7, 92 r. 9, *k[i-i* 186:6, 209:7, *k]i-i* 33 r. 5, 83:5, 86:6, 130 r. 6, 172:8, 194:6, 235 r. 43, *[ki-i* 21:2, 33:6, 71 e. 14, 93 r. 1, 133:8, 182:3, 229 iv 11, r. vii 88, *[ki-i]* 229 r. vii 48, *[ki]-i* 88:6, 229 r. viii 5, *[k]i-i* 229 r. viii 34, 241:2,

kibrāti "regions, horizons; the world": *kib-ra-a-ta* 235:2, *k]ib-ra-a-ta* 239 r. i 5, *kib-ra-a-ti* 229 r. vi 53, *kib-ra-a-ti]* 239 ii 2, *kib-ra-a-[ti]* 239 ii 15, *k[ib-ra-a-ti]* 239 r. i 23, *kib-ra-te* 233:1, *[kib]-ra-te* 233:19, *kib-ra-ti* 234 r. 8, *kib-ra-tu[m* 235:20,

kīdītu "outside": SA-*ti* 250:9,

kīma "when, after, if": *ki-ma* 21:19, 121:7, 229 r. v 24, vi 43, 234:22, 262 r. 3, 4, 267 r. 6, *ki-m[a* 229 r. vi 51, *k[i-ma* 262:7, *ki-ma-a* 165:7,

kimahhu "tomb, mausoleum": É—KI.MAH-*hi* 120:21, KI.MAH 288 r. ii 4, 14, 20, KI.[MAH 44:8,

kinṣu "lower leg, shin, shank": *ki]n-ṣi-ia* 113:c 4,

kīnu "true, faithful, loyal, righteous, just": *ki-na* 232 r. 5, *ki-na-a-ta* 239 i 8, r. i 13, 30, *ki-na-a-[ta]* 235:5, *ki-na-a-te* 229 r. vi 87, *ki-na-ta* 239 r. i 36, *ki-n[ak]* 164:3,

kippu "snare": *kip-pi* 229 r. vii 77,

kipputu "circle, disc, loop, circumference": *ki-pa-su-ma* 234:13, *kip-pat* 230:18,

kiriu "orchard, garden": GIŠ.SA[R 106 r. 2, GIŠ.S[AR 106 r. 6, GIŠ.[SAR.MEŠ 26 r. 4,

kīru (mng. uncert.): *ki-r[i* 163 e. 17,

kisallu "courtyard": KISAL 262 r. 5,

kisittu "stem, trunk, stump": *[ki-sit-ta-š]u* 251 r. 2,

kislīmu (Kislev, name of the 9rd month): ITI.GAN 120:17, 240:12,

kissutu "fodder": ŠE.*ki-is-su-tú* 1 r. 16,

kīsu "money bag, purse": *ki-is* 234:11,

kiṣru "cohort; joint": *ki-iṣ-ru* 180 r. 9, *ki-ṣir* 229 r. vi 22,

kišādu "neck": GÚ-*ka* 230:24, *ki-šá-da-ti* 234 r. 4,

kiškattû "craftsman; forge": *kiš-kat-te-e* 230:22,

kišpī "sorcery": *kiš-pi]* 229 iv 6,

kiššatu "world, universe": *ki[š-šat* 236:13, r. 11, *kiš-š[a-ti* 239 ii 3, *kiš-šá-ti* 238:3, ŠÚ 235:2, r. 23, 38, 49, 237 r. 5, 6, 12, 239 r. i 23, 297:4, Š[Ú 235 r. 51,

kiššūtu "hegemony": *kiš-šú-ti-šú-nu* 230:5, *kiš-šu-t[ú* 236:8, 239 ii 23, *kiš-šú-tú* 235:39,

kitkittû "quartermaster corps": LÚ.*kit-ki-tu-u* 229 i 11, LÚ.*ki-it-ki-te-e* 168:5,

kitpulu "intertwined": *kit-[pu-la* 77 r. 4, 9,

kittu "truth": *kit-ti* 239 ii 26, *k]it-ti* 188:3, *kit-tim* 239 ii 25, *kit-t]u* 84 r. 13, *kit-tú* 239 ii 21, 268:4,

kitû "flax, linen; tunic": GADA 262:4,

kuānu "to be firm, loyal, true; (D) to confirm, establish": GI.NA 246:1, 247:1, GI.NA] 255 r. 4, GI.N]A 248:1, GI.[NA 246 r. 7, G]I.NA 253:3, *ke-e-ni* 183:5, *ku-un* 247 r. 5, *li-kun* 115:6, *li-ku-un* 239 ii 18, *lu-ka-ni* 278 s. 2, *ú-kan-nu* 237 r. 11, see also *kânu,*

kubru "thickness": *ku-bur* 47:5,

kubšu "cap, mitre": U.SAG 250:9, 252:15, 288 iii 22, r. i 15, U.SA[G.MEŠ] 288 r. i 4,

kūdunu "mule": ANŠE.*ku-din-[ni]* 229 r. vii 29,

kudurru "boundary stone; carrying basket, forced labour": NÍG.GUB 279:9, *ku-d[úr-ri]* 239 ii 14,

kukittu (mng. uncert.): *ku-kit-ti-šú-nu* 248 r. 4,

kullatu "totality": *kul-la-si-na* 239 ii 11,

kullu "to hold; to steer": *ú-ka-lu-ma* 126:10,

kūmu "instead": *ku* 235:16, *ku-me* 140 r. 17, *ku-m[u* 296:1, *ku-mu-šú* 229 i 76, *ku-um* 123 r. 1, 229 r. vi 20, 724, 281:12,

kunāšu "emmer": ZÍZ.ÀM 262 r. 1, ZÍZ.A.AN 239 r. i 18,

kunukku "seal; vertebra": KIŠIB 248 r. 3, KIŠIB.MEŠ-*ka* 230:30, NA_4].KIŠIB 297:1, NA_4.KIŠIB 228:1, r. v 68, 71, 275:1, 276:1, [NA_4].KIŠIB 228:3, [NA_4.KIŠIB 297:2, 3, [NA_4.KIŠI]B 277:1,

kuppû "snow, ice": *ku-pu-ú* 15:3,

kupru "bitumen, pitch": *ku-u[p]-ri* 229 r. vii 76, *ku-up-ru* 229 r. vi 73,

kurgarrutu "female Corybant": MÍ.KUR.GAR.R[A.MEŠ] 286:22, M]Í.KUR.GAR.RA.MEŠ 286:9,

kurru "tanner's paste": *[kur]-ru* 8:8,

kurummutu "barley (ration)": ŠE.PAD.MEŠ 229 r. vi 19, 20,

kusāpu "bread": NINDA 262 r. 1, 285 r. 3, NINDA.HI.A 176 r. 7, NINDA.MEŠ 1:6, r. 15, 147 r. 1, 229 r. vi 60, 754, NINDA.M[EŠ 1 r. 12, [N]INDA.MEŠ

229 r. vii 59,

kusītu "robe": BAR.DIB 288 iii 23, BAR.[DIB] 288 iii 27,

kussiu "throne, seat": GIŠ.GU.ZA 229 r. v 27, 235:38, r. 22, GIŠ.GU.ZA] 229 i 76, GIŠ.[GU.ZA 229 i 51, GI]Š.GU.ZA 235 r. 12, GIŠ.GU.ZA-*e* 229 r. viii 58, GIŠ.GU.ZA-*ka* 21:13, 239 ii 18, GIŠ.GU.ZA-*ku-nu* 229 r. viii 58, GIŠ.GU.ZA-*šú* 237 r. 6, GU.ZA 288 ii 21,

kuttimmu "goldsmith": LÚ.KUG.DIM 126:15, LÚ.KUG.D[IM] 126:13, LÚ.KUG.DIM.MEŠ 128:6,

kuzippu "garment": *ku-zip-pi* 120 s. 1, 238:6, *ku-zip-p[i* 240:8,

lā "not": *la* 5:5, 6:5, 10 r. 8, 11:10, 17:9, 21:16, 22:2, 29:3, 30:4, 33:4, 36 r. 2, 7, 44:3, 47:4, 49 r. 1, 52:5, 60:2, 4, r. 3, 64 r. 3, 4, 65 r. 9, 10, 11, 85:9, 115 s. 2, 120:3, 11, 12, 14, r. 2, 10, 124 r. 2, 126:6, r. 13, 16, 128 r. 11, 134:2, 139:4, 144:2, 145:3, 147 r. 8, 154 r. 7, 16, 162 r. 12, 163 r. 8, 164 r. 13, s. 1, 167 r. 2, 3, 168 r. 12, 172 r. 4, 173:3, 187:5, 190 r. 2, 193:3, 217:3, 223 r. 1, 227 ii 7, 9, 228:4, 229 i 65, 67, 72, 74, 80, ii 1, 2, iii 5, iv 1, 2, 11, r. v 1, 5, 7, 10, 11, 12, 14, 18, 20, 21, 28, 33, 52, 54, 55, 57, 72, 79, 84, vi 5, 15, 23, 35, 46, 59, 68, 70, 86, 87, vii 11, 20, 22, 24, 26, 27, 28, 34, 35, 49, 51, 52, 69, 70, 71, viii 15, 37, 38, 39, 50, 62, 234: 8, 10, 17, r. 2, 14, 15, 20, 235:7, 30, 43, 45, r. 40, 237 r. 17, 241 r. 4, 261:9, 275 s. 1, 278:1, 281:11, 282:5, 6, 286 iii 17, 297:7, 298 r. 4, *la*] 116:3, *l*[*a* 193:8, 222:6, 229 i 74, 298 r. 5, *l*[*a*] 1 r. 8, *l*]*a* 45:2, [*la* 18:9, 31:11, 66 r. 7, 74 r. 2, 152 r. 10, 228:2, r. vi 91, 230: 8, 240: 8, 297: 3, [*la*] 14 r. 5, 41 e. 10, 93 r. 2, 229 r. vi 86, *la-a* 139 e. 22, s. 2, 164:4, 240:15, 267 r. 6, *la*-[*a*] 116:5, *l*]*a-a* 10:13, [*la-a* 21:14, 61:4, NU 232 r. 5, 250:3, 252:3, 253:5, 265:7, 271:3, 10, NU.M[EŠ 47:5,

la'û "to be able": [*i-la*]-*ú-ni* 109 r. 2, ZU-*u-ni* 105:6,

labāšu "to dress": *it-tal-biš* 239 ii 25, [*i*]*t-tal-biš* 239 ii 23, *lab-šá-k*]*u* 247 r. 4, *lab-šú* 247 r. 2, *lab-šú*] 246:14, *la-biš* 240:8, *li-la-biš* 229 r. vi 29, *lil-la-biš* 262:4, MU$_4$.MU$_4$-*su* 271:3, *tu*-[*lab-ba-as-s*]*u* 271:5, *tu-lab-ba-š*[*i* 241 r. 1,

labīru "old": *la-bi-ri* 126 r. 8, *la-bir*-[*te* 6:10, [*la-bi-ri*] 32:5,

labû "to go around, surround; (Š) to make surround": *is-si-bi* 50:1, *i-lab-bu-u-ni* 240:12, *lu-šal-bu-ku*-[*nu*] 229 r. viii 15,

lahāšu "to whisper": *tu-lah-h*[*i-šú* 171 r. 5,

lahhennutu "stewardess": MÍ.*láh-hi-nat* 286 r. 1,

lakû "baby, infant": *la-ke-e* 229 r. vi 11, *la-ku-ti* 234 r. 3, TUR.DIŠ 229 r. vi 10,

lamādu "to learn": *tu-šal-ma-da-a-ni* 229 r. v 54,

lamānu "to be bad, evil; (D) to make bad, worsen": *li-lam-mì-in* 229 r. v 81, see also *lemēnu,*

lamassu "protective spirit": ^{d}LAMA 297:7, ^{d}LAMA-*át* 230:12,

lamû "to surround": *ta-lam-ma-am-ma* 239 ii 33,

lānu "body, figure, stature": *la-an-ku-nu* 229 r. viii 5,

lapātu "to touch, affect; (Š) to r uin, destroy, defeat": *il-lap*-[*pat* 264:2, *il-tap-pa-ta* 234:21, TAG-*át* 250 r. 3, TAG-*it* 246:14, 247 r. 2, TAG.MEŠ 247:18, 252:18, 261 r. 1, TAG.[MEŠ] 247 r. 3, [TAG.MEŠ 254:12, *ú-šal-pa-tu-ú* 240:11,

laplaptu "parching thirst": *lap-lap*-[*tu*] 229 r. viii 53,

laptu "roasted barley": *la-ap-ti* 140:15,

laqû "to take, buy": *il-qé-e* 202:3, *il-qi* 64 r. 3, *lil-qú* 229 r. vii 59, *ni-laq-qí* 282:6, *tal-qi-ma* 230:6, TI-*qí* 249 r. 2, 253:2, TI-*ú* 247:14,

laššu "is not": *la-áš*-[*šu*] 21:18, *la-áš-šu-u-ni* 229 r. vii 29, *la-áš-šú* 140 r. 11, 14, 16, s. 1, *l*]*a-áš-šú* 145 r. 6, *la-áš*-[*šú-ni*] 21 r. 5,

la pān "from": *la-pa-an* 136 r. 6, *la—pa-ni* 165:9,

la-qāt "from the hands of": *la*—ŠU.2 30:5, 126 r. 11,

lâṭu "to confine, control": [*la-a-i*]*ṭ* 234:1,

lazāzu "to persist": *la-zu* 229 r. vi 42,

le'û "to be able": *i-le-'u-ú* 129 r. 17, *i-le*-[*u-ú* 241 r. 4, *i-l*]*e-u-ú* 133:2, *le-'i-i* 239 r. i 28, *t*]*a-le-'a-a* 239 i 6, *ú-le-'u-ú*] 246:12, *ú*-[*le-'u-ú*] 247:19, see also *la'û,*

le'u "writing-board": GIŠ.LI.U$_5$.UM 264 r. 3, GIŠ.LI.U$_5$.[UM] 67:3, GIŠ.LI.[U$_5$.UM] 67:9, r. 3,

lemēnu "to be bad, evil": *lem-né-ti* 265:1, *lem-n*[*é-et*] 265:2, *lem-nu* 229 r. vi 76, 230:19, 271:3, see also *lamānu,*

lemuttu "evil, misfortune": HUL-*ti* 229 r. v 30, HUL-*t*[*i* 229 i 73, HUL-*tim* 229 r. vi 85, 246 r. 5, HUL-*ti*[*m* 298 r. 2, MÍ.HUL 229 r. v 79, 247:9, M]Í.HUL 247 r. 11,

lēšu "dough": *l*[*e*]-*e-ši* 229 r. vi 22, NÍG.SILA$_{11}$.GA 229 r. vi 24,

lētu "cheek": *lit-su* 88:2, *li-it* 234 r. 7, TE.MEŠ-*ka* 230:20,

libānu "neck": GÚ 221 r. 9, 232:12, GÚ-*šú* 237 r. 3,

libbāti "anger": ŠÀ-*ba-t*[*a* 83:8,

libbu "heart": *l*]*ib-ba* 235 r. 8, *lib-ba-ku-nu* 229 r. viii 41, ŠÀ 1:11, 4:4, 8:7, 10:4, 11:13, 54:3, 62:1, 63 r. 2, 116:3, 120 r. 4, 19, 20, 22, 27, 136:4, 140 r. 12, 147 r. 3, 162 r. 2, 167 r. 1, 228:6, 229 r. v 22, 36, 56, 70, vi 24, 701, 21, 48, 51, 55, 56, 81, 235:14, 237 r. 18, 20, 240:6, 246 r. 6, 248 r. 6, 252:11, 18, 254:10, 255 r. 8, 258:6, 261 r. 1, 262:3, 273 r. 7, 281:9, ŠÀ] 78 r. 7, 235:43, Š[À 98:5, Š]À 60 r. 6, (ŠÀ) 229 r. vii 54, [ŠÀ 253:10, 12, ŠÀ-*b*[*a* 258:5, ŠÀ-*ba-k*[*u-nu* 241:6, ŠÀ-*ba-šú* 235:49, 247:4, 8, r. 9, [Š]À-*ba-šú* 247:6, ŠÀ-*ba-šú-un* 247:16, ŠÀ-*bi* 14 r. 3, 21 e. 11, 38:4, 42:7, 88:4, 92 r. 6, 8, 104:1, 120 r. 5, 25, 127:5, 133:5, 10, 139 s. 2, 171 r. 12, 184:11, 216 r. 4, 221:4, 224:2, 228:5, 229 i 76, r. v 14, vii 20, 33, viii 16, 17, 234 r. 3, 235:15, 29, 32, r. 13, 44, 239 r. i 27, 240:2, 11, 251:4, 252 r. 9, 266:6, 269 r. 3, 279 r. 2, 291 e. 6, ŠÀ-*bi*] 80:5, 134:3, 253 r. 2, ŠÀ-*b*[*i* 184:10, 260 r. 10, ŠÀ]-*bi* 9:10, 92 r. 3, 168:6, Š]À-*bi* 9:11, 173:4, 243:6, 247:13, [ŠÀ-*bi*] 146 e. 13, ŠÀ-*bi-ia* 33:15, 154 r. 10, 233 r. 13, ŠÀ-*bi-ku-nu* 229 r. vi 37, 41, viii 57, 235:11, ŠÀ-*bi-šú* 229 i 72, 73, ŠÀ-*bi-šú-nu* 75:4, 92 r. 4, 148 r. 1, 229 r. v 13, 21, 30, 237 r. 9, ŠÀ-*bi-šú-nu*] 128:8, ŠÀ-*bi-šú-n*[*u*] 140 r. 10, [ŠÀ-*bu* 113:c8, [ŠÀ]-*bu* 18:5, ŠÀ-*bu-šú-nu* 217:4, ŠÀ-*bu-ú* 186 r. 6, 235 r. 4, ŠÀ-*ku-nu* 229 r. v 51, vi 51, ŠÀ-*ku*-[*n*]*u* 229 r. vi 47, ŠÀ-*šú* 250 r. 12, 252:3, 261:8, 262 r. 3,

libittu "brick": SIG$_4$ 229 r. vii 18, SIG$_4$.MEŠ 279:9,

liginnu "one-column tablet": [I]M.GÍD.DA 54 e. 1,
lihšu "whisper": *li-ih-[šu* 229 r. vi 85,
limmu "eponym year": *lim-me* 267 r. 10, *lim-m[e* 255 r. 2, *lim-mu* 229 r. viii 64, 231 r. 2, 252 r. 8, 253 r. 7, 254 r. 4, *lim-m[u* 250 r. 6, *[lim-mu* 278:2,
līmu "thousand": 1-*lim* 291:3, 3-*lim* 175 r. 2, 11-*lim* 235 r. 24,
liptu "affliction, touch": *li-pi-[is-su]* 239 r. i 10,
lismu "race": *[li-is-mu* 240:12,
lišānu "tongue": EME 232 r. 4, 260 r. 2, EME-*ia* 232 r. 4,
littūtu "extreme old age": *lit-tu-tu* 239 ii 19,
lītu "victory, triumph": *le-e-ti* 232:6, *li-i-t[ú]* 234 r. 8,
lū "let, may, be it": *lu* 1:10, r. 7, 8, 12, 3:1, 6:3, 11 r. 2, 21:12, 97:3, 99:3, 103:3, 120:11, 12, r. 22, 124:3, 140 r. 8, 9, 141:4, 154:7, r. 7, 16, 229 r. v 38, 67, vi 19, 23, 34, 66, 67, 72, 73, 74, 75, vii 20, 24, 64, 83, viii 39, 47, 54, 62, 232:5, 241:6, 277 r. 5, *l[u* 112 r. 2, 149 r. 8, *l]u* 8 r. 2, *[lu* 12:3, 13:3, 18:3, 6, 19:2, 98:2, 102:3, 121:3, *[lu]* 8:9, 95:3, 140:3, *lu-u* 26:3, 28:3, 94:3, 98:3, 114:3, 154:10, r. 6, 155:3, 227 ii 6, 228:1, 2, 6, 229 ii 3, 4, 275:8, 9, 282 e. 5, r. 1, *l]u-u* 121 r. 4, *[lu-u* 8:3, 10:3, 27:4, 113:c10, 119:3, 228:2, *[l]u-u* 48:2, *lu-ú* 29:2, 30:3, 33:6, 186 r. 2, 215 r. 1, 241 r. 7, 246 r. 1, 247 r. 6, 283:4, 295 r. 1, *l]u-ú* 246:5, *[lu-ú* 131:3, *[lu]-ú* 259:4, 5, *[l]u-ú* 259:7,
lu''û "to defile, soil; defiled, polluted": *lu-'u-ú* 246:11, 12, 247:18, r. 3, 5, *l]u-'u-ú* 247:19, *lu-'u-ú-tu* 246:12, *l[u-'u-ú-tu* 247:19,
lumnu "bad luck, ill fate": HUL 261 r. 6, 265:7, HU]L-*nu* 129 r. 11, *lum-nu* 129 r. 9,
mā "thus": *ma* 11:6, 15:7, 52:2, 62:6, 171 r. 7, 229 r. v 30, vi 3, 230:1, 285 r. 7, *m]a* 286 r. 13, *[ma* 11:14, *ma-a* 1:13, 16, 6:4, 8:6, 8, 10:11, 12, 13, 11:6, 8, 9, 11, 13, 15, r. 2, 12:12, 19:11, 14, 21:2, 8, 10, 17, 18, 19, r. 1, 2, 6, 57:2, 67:6, 9, r. 3, 104:3, 116:5, r. 4, 117:8, 120:11, 12, 15, 16, 19, 20, 21, 22, 23, e. 26, r. 1, 2, 3, 4, 5, 6, 9, 12, 19, 128:13, 147 r. 6, 7, 148 r. 4, 6, 177 r. 2, 229 r. v 7, 14, 22, 234:12, 17, 240:2, 6, 13, 279 r. 12, 14, s. 1, *ma-a]* 279 r. 3, *ma-[a* 2:7, *ma-[a]* 12:10, *m[a-a]* 21 r. 7, *m]a-a* 22:1, 66 r. 10, *[ma-a* 8:12, 11:10, 12:7, 10, 19:13, 21:4, 5, 7, 12, r. 4, 52:7, 66:4, 116:1, 121:7, 151:4, 162 r. 9, 282:6, *[ma-a]* 143:3, *[ma]-a* 46:2, 56:1, 57:1, 60 r. 4, 143:2, *[m]a-a* 120 e. 27,
ma'ādu "to be much": *i-ma-id-ma]* 263 r. 5, *m]a-a'-da* 188:4, *m]a-a'-du-ti* 223 r. 2, *ma-a-da* 126:8, *ma-a-d[a* 33:2, *ma-a-[da* 3:6, *ma]-a-d[a* 191:2, *ma-a-du-te* 120:7, *ma-a-du-tú* 265:6, *[m]a-a-du-ú-ti* 33:17, *ma]-du-ni-i* 66:5,
ma'diš "much, greatly": *ma-a-diš* 269:4,
madādu "to measure": *ni-im-d[u-ud* 171:6, *ú-ša]m-di-du-uš* 239 i 15,
maddattu "tribute": *ma-da-a-[ti]* 66 r. 6, *ma-da-[ti]* 19:14,
magarru "wheel, chariot": *ma-gar-ra-ka* 235:33,
magāru "to agree": *am-ma-gúr* 120 r. 10, *im-ma-gar* 128 r. 3, *i]m-ma-gu-ru* 282:5, *i(m)-ma-g]u-ur* 18:9, *i-man-gur* 76:4, 172:9, *l[a-ma-gu-ru]* 140:21, *ma-gir* 262 r. 2,
mahāhu "to decompose, dissolve": *im-ma-ha-ah-hu-u-ni* 229 r. viii 4,
mahāru "to accept, receive; to turn to, implore": *ah-h[ur* 113:c4, *[a-m]a-har-[ka* 46:3, *a-mah-har-šú-nu* 120 r. 16, *an-da-har* 239 i 21, *an-d]a-har* 239 i 20, *a-ta-ha-ar-ka-ma* 232 r. 3, *a[t]-ta-har* 233:16, *a-hu[r-ú-ni]* 26 r. 8, *a-hu-ru-ú-[ni* 66 r. 2, *im-hur* 229 r. vi 65, *[i]m-hur-ru* 128 r. 14, *i-ma-ha-ru* 234:9, *i-mah-har-šú* 120:11, *i-mah-ha-[ru* 36 r. 7, *i-ma-ah-h[ar* 205:3, *[in]-da-na-ha-[ru]* 241 e. 5, *lim-hur-ú-in-ni* 129:18, *[li]-ih-hur* 124:10, *li-hu-ru* 124 r. 4, *ma-ha-ra* 217:7, *ma-h]ir-u-ni* 152 r. 6, *ma-hi-ir* 232:1, *ma-hi-ru-u-ni* 243 r. 6, *mah-ru* 37 r. 6, 133:9, 229 r. vi 70, 237 r. 20, *[mah]-r[u]* 88:7, *m[u-hur]* 278 s. 1, *[mu-hur]-šú-ma* 74 r. 3, *ni-hu-ru* 162 r. 9, *ta]-mah-har-šú-nu-tú* 239 r. ii 25, *t]a-ha-ru-u-ni* 145:5,
mahāṣu "to strike, wound, fight; (Š) to make fight": *im-haṣ* 209 r. 5, *i]m-haṣ-ma* 204:4, *lim-ha-ṣ]u-ku-n[u]* 226:12, *lim-ha-ṣu-ku-u-nu* 229 r. vi 54, *us-sa-an-hi-ṣu* 120:10,
māhāzu "cult centre": *ma-ha-za-a-ni* 240:12,
mahīru "market price": *ma-hi-ri* 239 r. i 18, 19, *ma-hi-ru* 275:3,
mahru "front; before": *ma-har* 288 r. ii 17, *ma-har]* 230:8, *ma-hi-ru-u* 234 r. 9,
mahrû "previous, earlier": *mah-ri-i* 199 r. 8, 237 r. 18, *mah-ri-ti* 220:9, *mah-ru-ti* 243:6, *mah-ru-tu* 174 e. 5, *m]ah-ru-tu* 237 r. 19, *mah-ru-ú* 73:7,
mākālu "food, dish, meal": *ma-ka-la-ku-nu* 229 r. vi 73, *ma-ka-li* 229 r. vii 15,
mākassu "wooden dish, saucer": *ma-k[a-su* 288 ii 23,
maklulu (a kind of garment, perhaps "shawl"): *muk-lal.*[MEŠ] 288 r. i 11,
mala "once; (Bab.) everything that": *mal* 229 i 12, *ma-al-la* 239 i 6, *ma-la* 40:5, 80:7, 126 r. 13, 223:2, 229 r. vi 53, 717, 266:7, 280:12, *m]a-la* 164:8, r. 7,
malāku "to advise, counsel": *i]m-li-ku-u-ni* 145 r. 5, *li-mal-li-ku-nu* 229 r. vi 44, 712, *tam-tal-ku* 233:4,
maldu "born": *mal-du* 234:17,
māliku "advisor, counsellor": *ma-li-ki* 233:6,
malku "king": *mal-ki* 288 r. ii 21, *ma-al-ku* 233 r. 13,
malû "to be full; (D) to fill": *i]m-ma-li* 113:c5, *tu-un-da-al-[li]* 239 r. i 16, *un-de-el-li* 182 r. 10, *ú-me-il-li* 168:7,
māmītu "oath": *ma-mit* 229 r. v 40, 42, 43, 61, vi 5, 262:12, *ma-mit-su-un* 229 r. v 63, *ma-[mì]-tú* 229 i 79,
mamma "anyone": *mam-ma* 31 r. 7, 78 s. 1, 130:5, 168 r. 7, 10, 178:3, *mam-m[a]* 244 r. 3,
mammannu "relative": LÚ.*mam-ma-nu-šú* 275:8, *mam-ma-nu-šú* 283 r. 2,
mānahtu "toil": *[ma-na-ah-ti* 253 r. 3,
mandītu "information; surprise attack": *man-di-t[i]* 90 r. 4,
mannu "who?": *man-ni* 123 r. 8, 140:14, *man-nu* 21 r. 2, 72 e. 11, 82:3, 120 r. 17, 140 r. 16, 152:5, 232:1, 2, 235 r. 41, 238:3, 275:7, *[man-nu* 21 r. 8,
manû "mina": MA.NA 121 r. 4, 126:21, 165 r. 6, 275:3, e. 11, 276:4, MA.N]A 20 r. 3, MA].NA 77 r. 10, [MA.NA] 126:13, MA.NA.TA.ÀM 243 r. 3, M]A.NA.TA.ÀM 243 r. 4, 5,
manû B "to count, recite, deliver to": *i-man-nu-*

[*ú* 186 r. 4, *lim-nu-ku-nu* 229 r. vi 49, ŠID-*šú-nu* 247 r. 14, 248 r. 6, 250 r. 2,
manzaltu "post, office": *man-zal-ti-šú-nu* 263 r. 6,
manzassu "podium, stand": *man-za-si* 288 iii 21,
manzāzu "stand, station; personnel": KI.GUB-[*šú* 250 r. 11, NA 237 r. 12, 250:1, 252:1, 12, 253:4, [N]A 255:1,
maqātu "to fall, (Š) to overthrow, defeat": *an-qu-tu* 79 r. 4, *im-q*]*u-tu* 175:3, *in-da*]*q-tu-ni* 84 r. 2, *i*]*-ma-aq-qut* 199 r. 9, *li-in-qu-*[*tu* 186 r. 5, *li-šam-qit-ku-nu* 229 r. vii 8, *l*]*u-šam-qit* 226 r. 4, *mu-šam-qi-tu* 230:19, ŠUB.ŠUB-*u*[*t*] 253:1,
maqru "precious": *ma-aq-ru* 233:13,
mār "as much/many as, all that": *am—mar* 21:20, 146 e. 13, 226:9, 229 i 15, r. vii 18, *am—mar*] 229 r. vi 92, [*am—mar*] 124 r. 1, *mar* 19:6, 241:8,
marāru "to be bitter": *i-ma*]*r-ri-r*[*u*] 247:17, *mar-rat* 137:5, *mar-rat-u-ni* 229 r. viii 45,
marāṣu "to be ill, painful": *li-im-ri-iṣ-ku-nu* 229 r. vii 87,
mar'at šarri "princess": DUMU.MÍ MAN 233:17,
mar'atūtu "daughtership": [DUMU.MÍ-*ú-t*]*ú* 72 r. 9,
mar'u "son": A-*šú* 126:4, r. 5, DUMU 29:3, 64:6, 66:4, 75:5, 120 r. 26, 125:5, 6, 126:1, 5, 12, 149 r. 2, 153:3, 187:6, 189:7, e. 10, 212:3, r. 3, 229 i 2, 18, ii 3, iv 4, r. v 28, 45, 70, vi 79, 88, 703, 235 r. 15, 39, 237 r. 2, 247 r. 4, 280:8, 283:2, DUM[U 12:11, D]UMU 189:8, 210 r. 3, [DUMU 21 r. 7, 122 r. 5, 229 iv 10, DUMU-*i*[*a*] 22 r. 7, DUMU-*ka* 128 r. 5, DUMU.MEŠ 126:19, 184:3, 229 r. vi 81, viii 28, 287 iii 12, 13, DUMU.[MEŠ] 229 r. vii 4, DUMU.MEŠ-*ku-nu* 229 r. v 47, 60, vi 20, 26, 727, 30, 36, 43, 46, 55, 57, 61, 64, 68, 70, 74, 75, 78, 79, 83, 802, 13, 18, 33, 37, 46, 49, [DUMU.MEŠ]-*ku-nu* 229 r. v 52, [DUMU.MEŠ-*ni* 229 r. vi 92, DUMU.MEŠ-*šú* 74 r. 4, 146 e. 15, r. 2, 3, 227 ii 3, e. ii 11, 229 r. v 60, [DUMU.MEŠ-*šú* 228:5, [DUMU.MEŠ-*šú*] 147 r. 10, DUMU-*šá* 229 r. vii 41, DUMU-*šú* 38:9, 72 r. 5, 239 r. i 1, 267:5, 280 r. 1, DUM]U-*šú* 129:19,
mar'utu "daughter": DUMU.MÍ 154 r. 5, 15, 210 r. 1, 234 r. 18, DUMU.MÍ.MEŠ-*e-ku-nu* 229 r. vi 21, DUMU.MÍ.MEŠ-*ku-nu* 229 r. vii 31, 57, 61, 80, 83, viii 33, 37, 46, DUMU.MÍ.MEŠ-*ku-*(*nu*) 229 r. vii 43, 47, DUMU.M[Í.M]EŠ-*ku-nu* 229 r. vii 64, DUMU.[MÍ].MEŠ-*ku-nu* 229 r. vii 55, [DU]MU.MÍ.MEŠ-*ku-*(*nu*) 229 r. vii 28, DUMU.MÍ-*ti-šá* 229 r. vi 25, DUMU.MÍ-*šú* 72 r. 8,
mar'ūtu "sonship": DUMU-*ti* 249 r. 2,
mardû "successor": *mar-du-ú-ka* 239 r. i 31,
marrakunu: *mar-ra-ku-nu* 229 r. viii 47,
martakal (a medicinal plant): Ú.IN.N[U].U[Š 273 r. 7, [Ú.IN.NU.UŠ 262:3,
martu "gall (bladder), bile": *mar-tú* 229 r. viii 45, ZÉ 250:4, 5, 252:5, 6, 253:4, 11, Z[É 255:3,
martû "hardwood pole": GIŠ.MÁR.DA.ME 3 r. 1,
māru "son": DUMU-*ú-a* 235:47, DUM]U-*ú-a* 72 r. 7,
maruštu "trouble, hardship": *ma-ru-uš-tú* 229 r. vi 55, NÍG.GIG-*ku-nu* 229 r. vii 14,
mār banî "nobleman": LÚ].DUMU—DÙ.MEŠ 81:4,
mār damqi "nobleman; chariot fighter": LÚ.DUMU—SIG₅ 277 r. 5,
mār karšāni (an occupation): LÚ.DUMU—*kar-šá-a-ni* 243 r. 7,
mār mar'i "grandson": DUMU—DUMU.MEŠ-*ku-nu* 229 r. v 60, DUMU]—DUMU.MEŠ-*ni* 229 r. vi 92, DUMU—DUMU-*šú* 239 r. i 9,
mār šarri "crown prince": A—MAN 287:15, 287 ii 5, 6, 8, 16, DUMU—LUGAL 229 ii 2, iv 2, r. v 17, viii 67, 69, DUMU—[LUGAL 257:2, [DUMU]—LUGAL 56:2, DUMU—MAN 229 i 17, iii 5, r. v 6, 9, 26, 31, 35, 45, 57, 59, 66, 69, 80, vi 78, 87, 89, vii 4, viii 27, DUMU—MAN] 229 r. vi 93, DUMU—M]AN 228:4, DUMU—[MAN 229 i 63, r. vii 2, DUMU]—MAN 151:5, 229 iv 3, r. vi 90, DU[MU—MAN 227 ii 10, D]UMU—MAN 227 ii 2, [DUMU—MAN 229 iv 9,
mār šipri "messenger": LÚ].A—KIN 54:5, 214:3, LÚ.A—KIN 36 r. 6, 249 r. 3, LÚ.A—[KIN] 144:7, LÚ.A]—KIN 69 r. 8, LÚ.A—KIN-*i*[*a* 4:2, LÚ.A—KIN.MEŠ 294:8, LÚ.A—KIN.MEŠ-*k*[*a* 4:5, LÚ.A—*šip-ri* 246:9, LÚ.DUMU—*šip-ri* 3:2, LÚ.DUMU—*šip-*[*ri*] 151:2, LÚ.DUMU—*šip-ri-šú* 169 r. 3,
masāku "to be ugly, bad, rotten; (Š) to give a bad name": *šá-an-su-ku* 234:16, *ú-šam-sak* 298 r. 4,
masennu "treasurer": LÚ.IGI.DU]B 140:1, LÚ.[IGI.DUB 140:17, LÚ.IGI.UM 124:6,
masiru "purse": *i—ma-si-ri* 234:12,
maṣāru "to circle, enclose; (D) to limit, demarcate": *tu-ma-aṣ-ṣi-ru-ma* 73:7,
maṣhutu (a kind of scented flour): ZÍD.MAD.GÁ 247 r. 3,
maṣṣartu "watch, guard": EN.N[UN 136 r. 11, EN.N]UN 216:4, EN].NUN 37 r. 7, 198:7, EN.NUN.[MEŠ 67:2, EN.NUN-*šú* 229 r. v 11, 18, EN.NUN-*šú-nu* 287 iii 4, *ma-ṣar*]*-ti* 219 r. 6,
maṣṣaru "guard": *ma-ṣa-r*[*a* 73:8,
maṣṣuru "guard": LÚ.EN.NUN.MEŠ-*šú* 240:5,
mašāru "to drag": *li-in-da-šá-ru* 229 r. vi 64,
maš'ennu "shoe, sole" (reading uncert.): KUŠ.E.SIR 229 r. viii 55, KUŠ.E.SIR-*ku-nu* 229 r. viii 56, KUŠ.D[A].E.SÍR 288 r. i 9,
mašīri (a kind of chariot): *ma-ši-r*[*i*] 234:22,
maškanu "location, place(?)": *maš-ka-ni* 1 r. 7,
mašku "skin, hide": KUŠ 229 r. vi 28, 273 r. 10, K]UŠ 273 r. 5, KUŠ.MEŠ 124 r. 3, *maš*]*-ku* 7:8, *ma-áš-ki-šú-nu* 235:41,
mašqītu "potion, drink": *maš-qit-ku-nu* 229 r. vi 74,
maššê "twin": *maš-še-e* 230:13,
mašû "forgotten": *ma-š*[*u-ti*] 297:9, [*ma-šu-ti*] 297:5,
matāhu "to lift, pick up, use": *la-a*]*m-tu*[*h* 24:4,
matāqu "to be sweet": *li-im-ti-iq* 229 r. vii 61, *ma-ti-qu-u-ni* 229 r. vii 60,
matnu "tendon, penis": *mat-nat* 229 r. vi 62,
mātu "land, country": KUR 18:4, 29:10, 32 r. 7, 73:8, 74:6, 81:4, 126 r. 11, 133:2, 134:5, 185 e. 11, 216:3, 217:8, 229 r. vi 8, 44, 82, vii 31, viii 60, 235:47, 264:3, 265:1, 2, 5, 7, 267:4, KUR] 262:7, KU[R 79 r. 3, 286 iv 11, KU]R 265:7, [KUR 229 r. vi 17, KUR-*k*[*a*] 235:49, KUR-*ku-nu* 229 r. vi 10, 14, 16, 46, 725, 38, 59, 85, KUR-*ma* 264:1, 3, KUR.MEŠ 34:3, 140:4, KUR-*su* 252:4, 253:8, KUR-*šú* 235:12, 268:4, KUR.KUR 29:6, 126:2, r. 12, 14, 129:1, 135:1, 211:3, 228:2, i 29, 235:25, r. 12, 43, 239 ii 25, 33, r. i 10, 263:3, KUR.KUR] 229 i 26, KU]R.KUR 216:8, 239 i 12, K[UR.KUR] 135:3, *ma-ta-a-*[*ti* 64:3,

ma-ti-šú-nu 234 r. 5,
mâtu "to die": *a-ma-a-ta* 235:7, *a-m[a]-ta* 126 r. 16, *i-mat* 235 r. 5, *me-tu-ma* 30:4, *mi-ta-ku* 216:1, *ni-ma-at* 197:4, *ni-ma-ti* 182:9,
māt nakiri "enemy land": KUR—KÚR 195:2, KUR—*na-ki-r[i* 273 r. 12, KUR—*na-ki-ri-ka* 239 r. ii 15,
maṭû "to be defective, lacking": *ma-ṭi* 74:3, *ma-ṭú-ú-ma* 239 r. ii 18, *ú-ma-aṭ-ṭi* 177 r. 1,
mazû "to squeeze, press; to rape": *in-d]a-zu-ma* 74:6,
mazzā'u "squeezer, water-skin": KUŠ.*ma-za-œ* 124:8,
mazzassu "stand; presence": GUB.BA-*šú-nu* 280:2, *ma-za-su* 229 r. v 34, *ma-za-sú-šú-nu* 229 r. v 36,
mê "water": A.MEŠ 1 r. 13, 8:6, 21:18, 115 r. 1, 147 r. 11, 226:13, 229 r. v 74, vi 43, 44, 58, 60, vii 11, 13, 56, viii 4, 6, 23, 240:6, 7, 8, A.M[EŠ] 247 r. 3, [A.ME]Š 217:5, A.MEŠ-*ma* 161 r. 4, A.MEŠ-*šá* 229 r. viii 53, A.MEŠ-*ši-na* 229 r. vii 58, *me-e* 229 r. viii 54,
mê qāti "water for (washing) hands": A.MEŠ—ŠU.[2 273 r. 8,
meat "hundred": 1-*me* 286:2, 15, r. 7, 10, 286 iv 3, 1-*me*-20 120 r. 23, 2-*me* 31:70, 60 r. 1, 188:2, 236 r. 14, 291:3, 3-*me* 170:4, 219 r. 3, 287 ii1, 288 ii 30,
melammu "nimbus, splendour": *me-lam-mì* 233:14,
mēlû "stairway": *mi-lu-u* 288 iv 13,
memmēni "anybody, anything": *me-me-ni* 116 r. 6, 120:11, 12, 140 r. 12, 15, 227 ii 1, 6, 229 r. v 42, 720, *mi-mi-n[i* 10 r. 3,
meserru "band, belt, girdle": *me-se-ra* 299 i 4, 5,
mesû "to wash": *me-sa-a[t* 235:30,
meše'tu "measurement": *me-še-e'-tú-šu* 240:9,
mešrû "wealth": *meš-ru-ú* 239 r. i 15,
migru "favourite": *mi-gir* 237 r. 9,
mihhu (a type of beer): *mì]-ih-hu* 247 r. 3,
mihru "equal, counterpart": [GABA.RI 252:3, GA]BA.RI-*ka* 165:2, *mi-ha-ar-šú* 279:7, *mi-hir-šú* 239 r. i 6,
milku "advice, counsel": *mi-il-ki* 231:2, *mil-ku-ni* 17:7,
mimma "anything": *mim-ma* 200:4, 223 r. 3, 229 r. v 75, vi 72, 243:6, 288 r. ii 14, *mi]m-ma* 280:11, *m]im-ma* 204 s. 1, [*mim-ma* 247 r. 3, 5, 248:2,
mindēma "maybe": *mìn-de-e-[ma* 200:2, *mìn-de-[e-ma* 202:5, *mìn-d[e-e-ma* 185 e. 12,
minītu "count, number, length": ŠID.[MEŠ-*šú* 250:6,
mīlu "flood": A.KAL.MEŠ] 263 r. 4,
mīnu "what?": *am—mì-[ni* 217 r. 6, *am—mì-ni-i* 235:47, *mi-i-ni* 120:5, 139 s. 1, *mi-i-nu* 140:16, 154 r. 4, *mi-i-n[u* 140:15, 148 r. 7, *mi-i-[nu* 5 r. 3, 63:3, *mi-i-[nu]* 10:9, *mi]-i-nu* 21:5, *mi-nam-ma* 200:3, *mi-ni-i* 72 e. 10, 265:3, *mi-ni-i]* 128:12, *mi-ni-[i* 132:6, *mi-nu* 154:8, r. 14, [*mi-nu* 45:4, [*mi-nu*] 43 r. 1, [*mi-n*]*u* 43:2, [*mi*]-*nu* 111 r. 8, *mi-nu-ú* 73:8, *mi-nu-[ú* 132:11, *mì-i-[nu* 26 r. 6,
miqittu "downfall": [*mi-q*]*it-ti* 115 r. 3,
misru "boundary, border": *mi-iṣ-ri* 91:16, *mi-iṣ-ri-i-šú* 239 r. ii 14, *mi*]-*iṣ-ri-šú-nu* 72 e. 9, *mi-ṣir* 73:6, [*mi-ṣ*]*ir* 239 ii 33,
mīšaru "justice": [*mi-šá-ru* 268:4,
mītūtu "death": *mi-tu-tu* 93 r. 3, *mi-tu-su* 234 r. 16,
miṭṭu "mace": GIŠ.TUKUL.DINGIR 288 iv 3,
muātu "to die": *a-mu-at* 140:21, *mu-a-ti-šú* 229 iv 4, *mu-a-ti-šú-* 227 ii 4, *mu-a-tú* 139 s. 2, *mu-[u-ta*] 229 r. viii 54, ÚŠ 123:2, 264 r. 1,
muddû "to notify(?)": *ú-m*]*an-di* 174:7,
mūdû "knowledgeable": *mu-d*]*e-e* 267:4,
mugirru "chariot": GIGIR 287 ii 8, GIŠ.GIGIR 229 r. viii 7, 288 iv 1, 290 i 10, GIŠ].GIGIR.MEŠ 287 ii 10, GIŠ.GIGIR.MEŠ 1 r. 14, 140 r. 15, GIŠ.GIGIR.MEŠ-*ku-nu* 229 r. vii 66, GIŠ.GIGIR.MEŠ-*ku*-[*nu*] 229 r. viii 8,
muhhu "top, on": UGU 1:3, 5:2, 7, 8:4, 11:12, 15:5, 18:6, 26:4, 32:13, 18, 36:3, 38:1, 42:1, 44:6, 8, 47:3, 48:4, 7, 57:6, 66:1, r. 1, 74 r. 4, 91 r. 9, 93 r. 3, 99:4, 102:4, 105:3, 115 r. 5, 116 r. 3, 120:5, 7, 13, 14, r. 22, 124:6, 128:13, 136:5, 140 r. 4, 147 r. 2, 152:5, 154:5, r. 5, 10, 156:3, 159:4, 176 r. 1, 6, 189 r. 2, 213:3, r. 4, 7, 216 r. 7, 220:4, 6, 7, 223 r. 2, 227 ii 9, 229 i 17, ii 1, iii 5, r. v 37, 55, 56, 85, vi 25, 78, 702, 37, 50, 52, 847, 57, 66, 235:49, r. 14, 16, 17, 19, 22, 240:7, 14, 15, 247 r. 13, 249 r. 2, 250:6, 9, r. 10, 11, 253:6, 7, 261:8, 265:6, 273 r. 10, 274 e. 10, UGU] 91:2, 150:4, 151:1, 255:6, UG[U 44:10, 98:6, 130:7, 142:5, 144:1, 147:2, 199 r. 2, UG]U 8:4, 58:2, 62:3, 229 r. vi 87, 235 r. 21, U[GU 5:1, 128:12, 192:1, 195 r. 2, 229 i 48, 249 r. 4, U]GU 67:3, 120 e. 27, 239 r. i 3, 257 r. 1, [UGU 33:4, 246 r. 9, 247:7, 248 r. 7, [U]GU 247 r. 18, UGU-*hi* 21:19, 42:9, r. 2, 66 r. 4, 73:4, 8, 111 r. 5, 120:6, r. 10, 165 r. 8, 181 r. 10, 219 r. 1, 229 r. v 8, 231 r. 1, 235:38, 279:1, UGU-*h*[*i* 283 r. 3, UGU-[*hi* 163 s. 1, UG]U-*hi* 162 r. 12, [UGU-*hi*] 116 r. 1, UGU-*hi-ia* 5 r. 6, 120:10, r. 11, UGU-*hi-ia*] 111 r. 8, UGU-*hi-i*[*a* 163:5, UGU-*hi-iá* 278 s. 1, UGU-*hi-i*[*á* 147:6, UGU-*hi-ku-nu* 229 i 78, r. viii 48, UGU-*hi*-[*ku-nu* 229 i 67, UGU-*h*]*i-ni* 136:11, UGU]-*hi-ni* 153:7, U]GU-*hi-ni* 138:7, UGU-*hi*-[*šu*] 229 r. v 67, UGU-*hi-š* 240:1, UGU-*hi-šú* 92 e. 1, 120 r. 12, 136:6, 240:6, UGU]-*hi-šú* 229 i 19, UGU-*hi-šú-ni* 247:9, UGU-*hi-šú-nu* 120 s. 1, 127:2, 229 i 16, 243 r. 8, U]GU-*hi-šú-nu* 243:7, U]GU-*hi-šú*-[*nu* 228:7, UGU-*ia* 3:2, UGU-*iá* 204:4, UGU-*ka* 225:4, UGU-*ku-un* 229 r. vi 40, UGU-*šú*] 66:2, UG[U-*šú* 240:5, UGU-*š*[*ú-nu* 247 r. 11, UGU-*šú-un* 237:11, 15,
muk "thus": *mu-ku* 10:9, *mu-uk* 1 r. 2, 18:7, 120:4, 24, *mu-uk*] 66 r. 2,
mukīl appāti "chariot driver": DIB—PA 287 ii 5, DIB—PA.MEŠ 287 ii 2, LÚ.DIB—PA.MEŠ 229 i 5,
mukinnu "witness": *mu-kin-nu-tu* 129 r. 14, *mu-ki-nu* 279 r. 5, *mu-ki-nu-te-šú* 279 r. 4,
multābiltu "tongue(?)": *mul-ta-bíl-ta-ka* 230:17,
multēširu "orderly": *mul-t*[*e-ši-ru*] 239 r. i 28,
mundahṣu "warrior": [*mun-dah*]-*ṣu-ti* 38:7,
munnabbitu "refugee": LÚ.*mu-n*[*a-ab-bi-tu*] 38:2,
muntalku "circumspect, counselor": *mun-tal-ku*] 297:4,
mūnu "caterpillar": *mu-nu* 229 r. vii 84,
muraqqītu "female perfume maker": MÍ.*mu-raq-qí-tú* 286 r. 8,
murrānu "ash (tree)": *mur-ra-nu* 288 iv 5,

murru "myrrh": Ú.ŠEŠ 274:2,

murruru "to check, examine": *mur-[ru-ur* 196:5,

murṣu "disease": GIG 229 r. v 55, 83, vi 41, 72, 253:1,

muṣīptu "piece of cloth": *mu-ṣip-e-ti* 126 r. 7,

mušadbibu "agitator (of conspiracy)"": *mu-šad-bi-bu-ti* 229 r. vi 84,

mušamhiṣu "instigator of rebellion": *[mu-šam-hi]-ṣu-u-te* 229 r. vi 84,

mušēširtu "woman giving birth": *mu-šeš-è[r-tu* 199 r. 10,

mūšītu "night": *mu-ši-ti]* 234 r. 1,

muššuru "to let go, abandon": *tu-maš-ša[r* 235:48, *ú-maš-š[ar* 209 r. 7, *ú-[maš-šar]* 262:10, *ú-maš-šar-an-ni* 173:3, *ú-maš-šar-an-ni-ma* 126 r. 16, *ú-maš-šar-ú-ši-ma* 91:6, *ú-maš-ši-ru* 33 r. 1,

mūšu "night": *mu-ši* 231:6, MI 247 r. 2, 4, 288 ii 2,

mūtānu "pestilence": *mu-ta-nu* 229 r. vi 61, NAM.ÚŠ.MEŠ 229 r. vi 37, ÚŠ.MEŠ 229 r. vi 42, vii 60, viii 7, 9, 43,

mutīr ṭēmi "reporter": LÚ.*mu-tir—ṭè-me* 229 i 6,

mūtu "death": *mu-[ti]* 235:51, *mu-ú-tú* 239 r. i 11,

muza''izu "divider, allotter":*mu-za-'i-iz* 232:3,

na'ābu "to wither; (D) to make wither, knock down(?)": *ut-ta-'i-bu* 233:6,

na'ādu "to praise": *it-ta-['-du]* 29:7, *lu-na-'idi* 233:2, *lu-na-'i-id* 231:4, *[ú-na]-'a-du* 232:10,

nabalkutu "to rebel; (Š) to turn upside down": *lu-šá-bal-kit* 229 r. vii 39, viii 58, *lu-šá-bal-ki-tú* 229 r. vii 66,

nabāṭu "to shine": *it-ta-na-an-biṭ* 235:12,

nabnītu "creation": *nab-ni-ti* 229 r. vi 9,

nabû "to call; (D) to lament, wail, moan": *n]a-bu-ú* 230:31, *ú-nam-ba-a* 288 i 1,

nadānu "to give": *ad-din-šú-nu-ti* 288 iii 20, *at-ta-din* 79 r. 1, 192:4, *a-nam]-dak-ka* 91:13, *a-nam-din-ú-ka* 180 r. 7, *a-nam-di-na* 206:11, *a-nam]-di-na* 206:12, *in-na[m-di-nu* 31:6, *it-ta-din* 192:5, *[i]t-ta-din* 133:5, *i-nam-dan-ni-ma* 204:6, *i-nam-din* 164:5, 275 r. 1, *i-nam-d[in* 212 r. 4, *i-na[m-din]* 243:1, 6, *i-na]m-din* 172:10, *i-n[am-din* 34:9, *i-nam-dinu* 243 r. 5, *i-nam-di-nu* 243 r. 4, *i-nam-di-n[u* 175 r. 1, *i-nam-d[i-nu]* 243 r. 3, *i]-nam-di-nu* 243:5, *i-nam-di-nu-nik-[ka]* 206:10, *i-nam-di-nu-uš* 93 r. 2, *nad-na* 273 r. 6, *[na-d]a-nu* 217:7, *na-din* 229 r. vii 15, 275:5, 276:7, 280:11, *na-di-na-at* 229 r. vi 7, *na-ad-na-áš-šu-nu* 73:2, *[n]a-a[d-nu]-ni-ka* 233:18, *nit-t[a-din* 39:6, SUM-*in* 276:6, SUM-*ma* 251 r. 3, *ta-at-tan-n[a* 36:8, *ta-n]am-din* 31:11,

nadû "to throw, cast": *id-di* 71:8, *id-du-ú* 92 r. 9, 133:10, *i]t-ta-di* 83:2, *it-ta-du-uš* 239 i 22, *[i]t-ta-du-ú* 36:2, *lid-du-ú* 115:3, 7, *li-di-ku-nu* 229 r. viii 50, *lu[d-di* 134:6, *na-a-du* 229 r. viii 52, 237 r. 1, *na-de-e* 80:3, *[na-d]u-u* 80:5, ŠUB 252:12, ŠUB-*di* 252:13, 16, ŠUB-*di]* 262:3, 11, ŠUB-*ma* 253 r. 1, ŠUB.MEŠ 299:7, Š]UB-*ú* 258:4, *ta-na-da-a-ni* 229 r. v 74,

nādu "waterskin": *na-da-ku-nu* 229 r. viii 54,

nagarruru "to roll about, wallow": *it-tan-ga-ra-ár-ru* 237 r. 8,

nagbu "spring": IDIM 229 r. vii 11, 262:9, r. 2,

naggāru "carpenter": LÚ.NAGAR.MEŠ 140:10,

nāgiru "herald": L]Ú.NIGIR 165 r. 9, LÚ.NIGÍR 82 r. 1,

nagiu "district": *na-gi-i* 240:15, 246 r. 4, *na-gi-i]* 246 r. 4, *na-gi-ku-nu* 229 r. vii 39, *na-gi-u* 26 r. 7,

naglabu "shoulder blade": MAŠ.SILÀ.MEŠ-*ka* 230:27,

nahāsu "to recede, withdraw; (stat.) to be recessed": *i]h-hi-su* 83:7, *in-né-hi-i[s* 38:4, *lu-uh-hi-s[am-ma* 164:13, *ut-tah-[ha-su* 288 i 10,

nakāru "to be hostile; (D) to change": *tu-na-kar-a-ni* 229 r. v 73, *tu-nak-kar-a-šá-nu-u-ni* 229 r. v 32, *tu-nak-ka-ra-šú-u-ni]* 229 i 75, *ú-na-kar-u-ma* 229 r. v 65, *ú-na-kar-u-ni* 229 r. v 68, *ú-na-kar-u-šá-nu-ni* 229 r. v 36,

nakāsu "to cut": KUD-*su-ma* 237 r. 2, *na-kas* 229 r. vii 52, *(na-kas)* 229 r. vii 50, *ta-ki-is* 165:6, *ú-na-ki-is* 234 r. 4,

nakīru "enemy": *na-ki-ri* 235:28, *na-[ki-ri]* 81:4, *na-ki-ri-i-šu* 234:1,

nakkamtu "treasure, treasury": *na-kam-ti* 232:7,

nakru "enemy": KÚR 226 r. 4, 249:1, 251 r. 3, 253:3, 5, 255:7, 264 r. 1, [KÚR] 253:9, KÚR-*šú* 253:7, LÚ.KÚR 133:14, 247:8, 14, r. 10, LÚ.KÚR-*ku-nu* 229 r. vii 27, 65, 74, 78, 86, 87, viii 11, 25, 42, LÚ.KÚR-*ku-(nu)* 229 r. viii 9, LÚ.[KÚR-*ku*]-*nu* 229 r. vi 34, LÚ.KÚR.M[EŠ 133:10, LÚ.KÚ]R-*šú* 229 r. vi 83,

nalšu "dew": *na-al-šu* 229 r. vii 23,

namadu "measure": *[na-m]ì-di-šú* 41 e. 12, *na-mu-du* 42:5,

namāru "to be(come) bright; (Š) to let shine": *na-mar* 127:6, *na-ma-ri* 229 r. vi 68, ZALÁG-*ir* 262 r. 4,

namkūru "property": *nam-ku-ru* 233:11, 13,

nammušu "to set out": *nam-me-šá* 1:17, *nu-ta-mì-iš* 12:5,

namru "bright, shining": *na[m-ru-ti]* 230:20,

nāmurtu "audience gift": *na-mu-ra-ta* 126 r. 1, *na-mu-ra-ti* 126:11,

nannaru "brightness": *na-nar* 229 r. v 86,

napāhu "to blow, ignite, light up; to rise": *it-ta-ap-ha* 239 ii 26, *li-pu-hu-ku-nu* 229 r. vii 57, *na-bah* 265:8, *na-ba-hu* 234 r. 2, *na-pa-ah* 229 i 14, *ta-nap-pa-ha-a-ni* 229 r. vii 56,

napālu "to raze, demolish": *ú-na-pi-il* 234 r. 3,

naparšudu "to escape": *na-par-šu-di* 229 r. viii 50,

napharu "totality, sum": *nap-har* 229 r. v 85,

napištu "life": *na-piš-ta-šu* 232 r. 3, *n[a]-piš-ti-ku-nu* 229 r. vi 69, *na-piš-ti-šu-nu* 234:6, ZI-*su-nu* 217:8, see also *napšutu,*

nappāhtu "female smith": MÍ.SIMUG.MEŠ 286 r. 5,

nappāhu "smith": SIMUG 285 r. 6,

nappāh erê "coppersmith": LÚ.SIMUG—URUDU 140:8,

nappāh parzilli "ironsmith": LÚ.SIMUG—AN.BAR 140:8,

nappû "sieve(?)": *nap-pi-š[u* 40:5,

napšutu "life": *nap-šat-ka* 230:25, *nap-šat-ku-un* 229 r. vi 3, viii 51, *nap-šat-ku-nu* 229 r. vi 36, *nap-šá-te-ku-nu* 229 iv 11, ZI 246 r. 5, ZI.MEŠ 73 r. 2, 123:5, 229 r. vii 50, 53, 246 r. 1, ZI.MEŠ] 135:6, Z[I.MEŠ] 250 r. 1, ZI.ME[Š-*ku-nu*] 226:13, see also

napištu,
naptunu "meal": BUR 3:1,
napṭu "naphta": *nap-ṭi* 229 r. vii 76, *nap-ṭu* 229 r. vi 74,
naqbaru "burial place": *na-aq-bar-ku-n[u]* 229 r. vi 66,
naqû "to sacrifice; shed, pour, libate": BAL-*qí* 237:19, BAL-[*qí*] 261 e. 14, B[AL-*qí*] 262:13, BAL-*ú* 247 r. 5, *na-aq* 229 r. vi 31, *ni-qí* 234:20,
narāmtu "beloved": *na-ram-ta-šú* 229 r. v 80, *na-ra-am-tú* 230:23,
narāmu "beloved": *na-ram* 237 r. 15, 239 r. i 25, *na-ra-ma* 233 r. 13,
nargallutu "chief female singer": MÍ.NAR.GAL 286:18,
narkabtu "chariot": GIŠ.*nar-kab-tú* 239 i 17,
narmaku "bathtub" (rdg. and mng. uncert.): GIŠ.ŠÚ.NAGA 273 r. 7,
nāru "river": ÍD 9:8, 115:3, 7, 229 r. vi 75, Í[D 10 r. 5, Í]D 136 r. 13, ÍD.MEŠ-*ku-nu* 229 r. vii 58, ÍD-*šú-nu* 8:8, 15,
nâru "to kill, slay": *i-na-ru-ma* 237 r. 13,
nasāhu "to pull out, uproot; to extract, quote": *as-su-ha* 237 r. 18, *i-na-as-s[a-ah* 193:5, *lis-su-hu-ku-nu* 226:12, *li-sa-hu-u-ku-nu* 229 r. vi 57, ZI.MEŠ-*ha* 247 r. 6,
nasāqu "to choose": *na-as-qu-te* 120 r. 70, *tas-su-q[u* 73:7,
nasīku "sheikh": LÚ.*na-si-ka-t[i* 134:4, LÚ.*n[a-si-k]a-ti* 133:8, LÚ.*na-si-ka-tu* 133:4, LÚ.*na-si-ku* 133:9,
naspantu "devastation": *na-as-p]an-di* 136 r. 9, *na-as-pan-du* 235:31, *n]a-ás-pan-ta-ku-nu* 226 r. 3,
naṣāru "to watch, guard": *a-na]m-ṣar* 198:8, *a-na-ṣa-ru* 204:3, *it-ta-ṣa-ar* 239 r. i 34, *i-na-ṣu-ru* 229 r. v 11, *i-na-ṣu-[r]u* 229 r. v 18, *i-na-ṣu-ru-šu* 240:5, [*li-iṣ-ṣu*]*r* 37 r. 8, *taṣ-ṣu-ru-ma* 219 r. 6, *ta-na-ṣar-a-ni* 229 i 72, r. v 72,
naṣraptu "crucible; dyeing vat": NÍG.TAB 252:1, [NÍG.TAB] 247 r. 15,
naṣṣubu "drainpipe": *na-ṣa-*[*bat*.MEŠ] 288 iii 26,
našāku "to bite": *na-šik* 260 r. 2,
našāqu "to kiss": *ú-na-áš-šá-qu* 237 r. 11,
našpantu "devastation": *na-aš-pan-ta-ku-nu* 229 r. vi 71,
našpartu "message": *na-áš-par-ta* 30 r. 4, *na-áš-par-tu* 30:7,
našû "to lift, carry, take": *áš-šá-a* 165:10, r. 2, *iš-šá-[a* 34:7, *iš-šú-ú* 176 r. 8, *it-ta-ši* 176 r. 9, *i]t-ta-šu-u* 173:7, *it-ta-šu-u-n[i]* 162 r. 5, *it-ta-šu-ú* 197:3, *it-ti-ši* 279:6, *i-na-áš-šam-m[a]* 176 r. 11, *i-na-áš-ši* 140 r. 17, *i-na-á]š-ši* 22:3, *i-na-š[i* 146:3, *i-[ṣa]* 67:7, *i-ši* 1:10, *i-ti-ši* 281:10, *i-t[i-ši]* 281 r. 2, Í]L-*ma* 263:1, *liš-ši* 42:7, *lu-uš-ši-i-ma* 235 r. 24, *na-ṣu-u-ni* 148 r. 4, *na-šá-a-ni* 174 e. 6, *na-ši* 229 r. viii 59, *na-šú* 217:3, *na-[šú-ú* 269 r. 1, *t]a-áš-ši* 61:8, *ta-na-áš-ši-i-ma* 239 ii 32,
natāku "to drip, drop": *lit-tu-tuk* 229 r. vi 51,
nazāru "to curse; (Š) to make hateful": *tu-šá-an-za-ra-ni* 229 r. v 29,
nēbettu "girdle, sash": TÚG.IB.MEŠ 126:18,
nēbuhu "sash": TÚG.ÍB.LAL 299 i 7,
nekelmû "to look at angrily": *li-k]el-mu-šu-ma* 298 r. 5,
nēmal "because": *né-m[a-al* 66 r. 7,
nēmēqu "wisdom": *né-me-qí* 230:21,
nēmulu "profit, gain": *né-m[i-i]l* 240:1,
nērtu "murder": (*ni*)*-ir-ti* 128:9,
nērubu "entrance, pass": *né-ri-bi* 246 r. 3,
nēšu "lion": UR.MAH 229 r. vi 49, UR.MAH.ME[Š 236:14,
niālu "to lie, sleep": *e-tel* 233:1, *ta-tal-la* 229 r. vii 52, *uš-ni-il-šú* 288 r. ii 7,
niāru "papyrus": *ni*]*-a-ri* 248:2,
nidnakku "censer": NÍG.NA 242:1, 262:13,
nīd kussî "base of the throne": ŠUB]—AŠ.[TE 252:5,
nigûtu "music": *ni-gu-ti* 237 r. 4,
nikiltu "art, cunning": *ni-kil-ti* 229 r. v 76,
nikkassu "account(ing), assets, property": NÍG.ŠID.MEŠ-*ku-nu* 154:13, NÍG.ŠID.MEŠ-*ma* 140 r. 7,
niphu "sun disk, boss; rising, blaze; unreliable apodosis": IZI.GAR 255:5,
nipšu "breathing, snort; smell, odour": *ni-piš-ku-nu* 229 r. vii 91,
niqiu "offering, sacrifice": SISKUR.MEŠ 233 e. 19, r. 6, SI[SKUR.SISKUR 247:18, [SISKU]R.SISKUR.MEŠ 241:5, UDU.SISKUR.MEŠ 299 i 11,
nīru "yoke": *n]i-i-ri* 38:5, *ni-ri* 249:2, 250:7,
nisannu (Nisan, name of the first month): ITI.BARAG 239 i 16, 256:1, 262:1, ITI.BARAG] 245 r. 1, [ITI.B]ARAG 244 s. 1,
nissatu "worry": *ni-sa-tú* 229 r. v 84,
niṣirtu "secret": *ni-ṣir-ti* 288 r. ii 5,
niš "by": *ni-iš* 233 r. 12,
nīšī "people": UN.MEŠ 32:9, 120:7, 216:3, UN.[MEŠ] 1 r. 15, U]N.MEŠ 230:25, [UN.MEŠ 74:6, UN.MEŠ-*ia*] 134:2, UN.MEŠ-*šu* 234 r. 15, UN.MEŠ-*šú-nu* 62:3, 75:2,
nīš ili "oath": MU—DI]NGIR 129 r. 14,
nīš rēši "head lift": MU.SAG 237 r. 14,
niṭlu "sight": *ni-ṭil* 229 r. vi 63,
nizmatu "desire": *ni-iz-mat* 262 r. 3,
nuāhu "to calm, be quiet": *ta-nu-ha* 229 r. viii 37,
nuārtu "female singer": MÍ.NA[R.MEŠ] 285 e. 25,
nuāru "singer, musician": NAR.MEŠ 287 ii 11,
nubattu "evening": *nu-bat-ta*] 134:1,
nuhšu "abundance, affluence, prosperity": *nu-uh-ši*] 230:27,
nuk "thus": *nu-uk* 52:2, 145 r. 3, [*nu*]*-uk* 52:4,
nukurtu "hostility": LÚ.*nu-*[*kúr-ti* 241:4, *nu*]*-kúr-ti* 17 r. 6,
nūnu "fish": KU_6 262:11, 12, K]U_6 262:12, [KU_6 262:11,
nūru "light, lamp": *nu-ru* 214:4, 234 r. 15,
pagru "corpse, body": *pa-ag-ri* 124 r. 3, LÚ.ÚŠ 271:1, LÚ.ÚŠ.MEŠ-*ku-nu* 229 r. vi 65,
pahāru "to assemble": *pa-*[*hír*] 1:17, [*pu-u*]*h-hir-šú-nu-tú* 31:12, *pu-hu-ru-ti* 234:14, *ú-pah-hi*[*r-ú-ni* 217:2, *ú-pah-*[*hi-ru*] 90 r. 7, [*ú-pah-hi-ru*] 80:7, *up-tah-hi-ir*] 80:2,
pahhizu "boaster, braggard": *pah-hi-zi* 29:8,
pâhu "to caulk, block(?)": *ap-ti-ha* 232:13,
pāhutu "province; governor": LÚ.EN.NAM 25:6, 32:8, r. 2, 33:5, 14, 70:11, 90:4, 123 r. 4, 168 r. 9, 229 i 3, 280 r. 6, L]Ú.EN.NAM 76:2, 235 r. 22, 243 r. 8, L]Ú.EN.NA[M 85:3, [LÚ.EN.NAM] 139:3,

[LÚ.EN].NAM 39:8, LÚ.NAM 253 r. 7, LÚ.NAM.MEŠ 229 ii 4, NAM.MEŠ 287 ii 13, *pa-ha-ta* 126 r. 4,

pâhu "to caulk, block(?)": *ap-ti-ha* 232:13,

palāhu "to fear, respect, revere": *a-ba-làh* 8:13, *a-pa-làh* 130:7, *ip-t]a-làh* 211 r. 5, *lip-lu-hu* 229 r. v 60, *pal-h[u* 92 r. 10, *pal-hu-ma* 133:8, *pal-hu-ú-ma* 232:9, *pal-hu-uš* 229 r. v 10, 18, *pa]-làh* 129:6, *pa]-li-hu* 49 r. 1, *ú-pa-la-[x* 86:8,

palāzu "(D) to pierce, perforate, puncture": *pa-lu-za* 229 r. vii 83, *pa-lu-za-a-ni* 229 r. vii 81,

pallissu "female stone driller" MÍ.GAR.U.U.MEŠ 286 r. 5,

palû "reign, dynasty": *pa-le-e* 266:2,

pānāt "fore": *pa-na-at* 1:5,

pānīu "previous": *pa-ni-e* 59:2, *[p]a-ni-u* 6:7,

pānu "face, presence": *i–pa-[an* 101:4, IGI 11:14, 18:8, 44:3, 4, 5, 9, 11, 59:6, 67:6, 120 r. 24, s. 2, 127:7, 140 r. 15, 154:4, 229 i 20, 22, 46, r. v 2, 29, 31, 33, 35, 87, 726, 27, 90, viii 11, 235:51, 237 r. 5, 16, 240:1, 12, 13, 243 r. 6, 247:8, 18, r. 8, 9, 10, 248:3, r. 2, 3, 252:14, 257:1, 262:7, 13, 265:4, 267:7, 275 r. 2, 3, 4, 5, 6, 9, 276 r. 7, 8, 280 r. 2, 3, 4, 6, 7, 8, 9, 10, 11, 12, 13, 285 r. 7, 287 iv 11, IGI] 190:2, 237 r. 20, 279 r. 4, 280 r. 14, I[GI 276 r. 5, 6, [IGI 82 r. 2, 247:3, 266:1, 276 r. 4, 277 r. 5, 280 r. 5, IGI-*e-ku-nu* 229 r. viii 61, IGI-*ia* 139 s. 1, IGI-*ka* 154:12, IGI-*ki* 154 r. 13, IGI-*ku-nu* 229 r. v 72, vi 61, I[GI.MEŠ 263 r. 7, IGI.MEŠ-*šú* 233 r. 12, IGI.MEŠ-*šú-nu* 229 r. viii 21, IGI-*ni* 120:24, IGI-*š]a* 299 i 12, IGI-*šú* 229 r. v 2, 237:8, r. 8, 11, 279:5, *pa-an* 12:7, 36:9, 57:4, 64:5, 7, r. 4, 71:2, 133:8, 175 r. 4, 220:8, 235 r. 26, 38, 239 i 20, *pa-an]* 109:3, *pa]-an* 69:9, *p[a-an* 5 r. 2, *p]a-an* 10 r. 5, 33:20, 80:3, 132:3, 150:8, 167 r. 4, 180:2, 239 i 19, *pa-na* 88:6, *pa-ni* 1 r. 3, 35:6, 41:8, 117:9, 11, 126:17, 128:9, r. 1, 138:3, 4, 164 r. 4, 8, 176 r. 9, 208:6, 218:6, 229 r. vii 37, *pa-n[i* 31 r. 4, 130 r. 7, *pa-n]i* 182:5, *pa-[ni* 41:9, *p]a-ni* 179 r. 8, 183:11, *pa-ni-ia* 81:7, *pa-ni-ia]* 115 s. 1, *p]a-ni-ia* 8:11, *pa-ni-i-šú* 240:3, *pa-ni-ka* 61:5, 84:7, 235 r. 10, 239 r. ii 5, *pa-ni-ku-nu* 1:6, 229 r. v 38, *p]a-ni-ku-n[u* 222:2, *pa-ni-šu* 88:1, 234:4, *pa-ni-šú* 36 r. 8, 128:14, *pa-ni-[šú]* 128 r. 5, *p]a-ni-šú* 235 r. 9, *p a-ni-šú-nu* 280 r. 15, *pa-n[i-x* 263:2, *pa-[ni-x]* 146:2, *pa-nu-ka* 230:10, *pa-nu-šú* 133:13, *pa-nu-šú-un* 288 i 4,

paqādu "to appoint, entrust": *ap-t[i-qid* 66 r. 8, *ip-qid-ú-[ni]* 26:5, *ip]-qi-da-ni-ni* 50:2, *ip-qi-d[u-ni]* 7:11, *ip-qí-du* 216 r. 2, *ip-taq-du]* 250 r. 11, *ip-te-qid* 71:9, *lip]-qid* 121 r. 7, *lip-qid-su]* 250 r. 10, *li]p-qí-du* 168 r. 10, *lu-pa-aq-[qid-su-nu]* 58 r. 2, *paq-da-a-ni* 249 s. 1, *paq-da-at]* 230:7, *paq-du* 240:5, *pa-qi-da-at* 231:3, *pa-qi-di* 149 r. 4, *pa-qi-du* 229 r. vi 31, *pi-q[id]* 1 e. 21, *ta-pa-qid-da-a-ni* 229 r. v 74, *ú-paq-qid-ma* 126 r. 4,

paqāru "to challenge, contest": *pa-qa-ri]* 297:3, *pa-qa-a-ri* 228:4,

parādu "to frighten": *ip-tar-ri-du* 246 r. 1, 247 r. 6, *ú-pa-ra-du* 234:10,

parakku "dais, sanctuary": BARAG 231:1, BAR[AG.MEŠ 226:8, [BARAG.MEŠ-*šú-nu*] 263 r. 7, *pa-rak-ki* 232:11,

parāku "to bar, block, obstruct": *ip-rik* 72 e. 9,

parasrab "five sixths": 5:6 275:3,

parāsu "to separate, wean; to decide": *ip-ru-su* 280:5, KUD 232 r. 5, *lip-ru-us* 229 r. vi 10, 14, *ta-par-ra-sa-šú-u-ni* 229 r. v 3, *ta-ap-ta-na-ra-[as]* 163 r. 6,

parāṣu "to break, transgress": *i-par-ra-ṣu* 229 r. v 63,

parā'u "to sprout" *i-par-ru-'a* 229 r. vii 20, *i-par-[ru]-u-u-ni-ni* 229 r. vii 34,

parā'u B "to cut off, sever, slit": *li-p]a-ra-'u-ku-nu* 226:11,

parkiš "crosswise, athwart": *pár-kiš* 252:15,

parriṣu "criminal, traitor": LÚ.*par-ri-ṣu-te* 123 r. 5,

parṣu "function, ordinance; cult, rite, ritual": GARZA 239 i 23, r. ii 4, *par-ṣi-šú-nu* 230:6, *pa-ra-aṣ* 297:9, *pa-ra-a]ṣ* 297:5,

parzillu "iron": AN.BAR 20 r. 3, 229 r. vii 19, 38,

pasāsu "to erase": *i-pa-sa-su* 229 r. v 62,

paṣû "to be white": BABBAR.MEŠ 288 r. i 15,

pašāhu "to relent; (D) to calm, soothe": *ip-taš-hu* 33 r. 7, *pu-šú-hi* 288 iv 11,

pašālu "to creep, crawl": *piš-la* 229 r. viii 57,

pašāru "to solve, dissolve": *la-ap-šu-rak-ka* 120:19, *nap-šu-ri* 298 r. 5, *pa-ša-ri* 229 r. v 43, *pa-šá-a-ri* 229 r. vi 5, *pa-šá-ri* 229 r. v 40, *ta-pa-šar-a-ni* 229 r. v 42,

pašāšu "to anoint": *it-ta-nap-ša-áš* 262:3, ŠÉŠ-*šú* 247 r. 5, *ta-pa-šá-šá-ni* 229 r. v 39, [*ta-pa-šá-šá-šú-u-ni* 229 iv 6,

pašāṭu "to erase": *lip-šiṭ* 229 r. viii 60, [*pa-áš-ṭa* 250:1,

pašīratti "secretly": *pa-ši-r]a-at-ti* 131:6,

paššūru "table": BANŠUR 287 ii 6, GIŠ].BANŠUR.MEŠ 300 r. 3,

patāhu "to pierce, puncture, stab": *ú-pa-ta-hu-ka-[nu-ni]* 229 r. viii 42,

patru "sword": GÍR 56:4, 229 r. vi 38, 247 r. 13, 15, 250:2, 252:3, 5, 12, 253:6, 255:2, 3, GÍR.MEŠ 229 r. viii 31, GÍR.MEŠ-*me* 229 r. viii 32, GÍR-*šú* 229 r. vi 35, *pa-tar-šu* 234:6,

patû "to open": *i-pat-ti-a* 229 r. viii 62, see also *petû*,

paṭāru "to release; (Š) to cause to be released": DU$_8$ 249 r. 4, 252:15, 253:4, 258:5, 262:12, D[U$_8$ 247 r. 15, D]U$_8$ 300 r. 4, DU$_8$-*ár* 265:5, *i]-paṭ-ṭar* 267:9, *ip-pi-ṭir* 229 r. vi 61, *n]u-up-ṭir-ra* 77 r. 5, *pa-ṭu-ru* 19:13, 16, *š[up-ṭi-ra]* 262:9,

paṭīru "reed altar": GI.DU$_8$ 262 r. 5,

pāṭu "border": ZAG.M]U 251 r. 3,

pazzuru "to conceal": [*nu*]-*pa-za-ar-u-ni* 229 r. vi 90, *tu-pa-za-[ar* 115 s. 2, *up-ta-zi-i[r* 67 r. 4,

pēntu "charcoal, coal": *pe-e-na-a-ti* 229 r. vii 25,

pēthallu "cavalry": BAD.HAL 287 ii 14,

petû "to open": *ip-te-ma* 234 r. 18, 19, *ip-tu-ú* 128 r. 6, see also *patû*,

pilaqqu "spindle": *pi-laq-qi* 229 r. viii 10, GIŠ.*pi-laq-qa* 239 ii 32,

piqittu "check-up": SI.LAL 248 r. 6,

pir'u "offspring": *pi-ir-i-ka* 235:9, 239 i 2, 3, *pi-ir]-i-ka* 239 i 14,

pirittu "fright": ŠÀ.MUD 247 r. 2, 4, Š[À].MUD 247 r. 2,

pirku "injustice, obstruction(?)": *piš-k[i* 175 r. 2,

pirru "tax collection; (cavalry) unit": *pi-i-r[i* 7:8,

pirṣāti "deceit": *pir-ṣa-a-ti* 126:10,

pispisu "bug": *pi-is-pi-su* 229 r. vii 88,
piššatu "ointment" *pi-iš-šat-ku-nu* 229 r. vi 74,
pithu "wound": *pi-it-hi-ku-nu* 229 r. viii 44,
pitiltu "cord": *pi-til-[ti* 229 r. viii 2,
pitnu "string, chord": NA$_5$ 288 ii 20,
pitrudu "cautious, prudent, wary": *pi-it-ru-du* 234:16,
pitti "according to": *ap—pi-i[t-ti* 205:5, *[ap—pi-it-ti* 248:5, *pi-it-ti* 41 e. 11, 229 r. vii 59, *pi-ti* 43 r. 3, 46:2, 139 s. 1,
pû "mouth, utterance, command": KA 246:6, 247:5, 262:11, 288 iv 4, K]A 233 r. 15, KA-*ia* 247 r. 6, KA-[*ia* 246 r. 1, KA-*ka* 230:15, 18, KA-*šá* 229 r. vii 41, KA-*šú* 250 r. 12, KA-[*šú* 252:4, *pa-šú-nu* 41:5, *pi* 72 r. 6, 171 r. 1, *pi-i* 11:12, 57:6, 120:13, 14, 130 r. 6, 136 r. 5, 199:4, 209 r. 4, 213:2, 227 ii 6, 229 ii 3, 4, 239 ii 5, 241 r. 6, 264 r. 2, 280:4, 298 r. 4, *pi-ia* 85:7, *pi-i-ka* 119 e. 25, 128 r. 3, *pi-i-ku-nu* 229 r. vii 61, [*pi-i-ni* 229 r. vi 83, *pi-šú-nu* 80:1,
puāgu "to take by force": *ip-tu-ga* 279 r. 11, *ta-pu-ga-ni* 279 r. 13,
puhādu "(male) lamb": *pu-ha-di* 234:21,
puhattu "(female) spring lamb": MÍ.NIM-*tú* 229 r. vii 44,
puhru "assembly": *pu-hu-ur-ne* 234:10, UKKIN 229 r. v 37, 230:3,
pūhu "exchange, loan": *pu-u-[hi]* 66 r. 5,
puluhtu "fear": *pu-luh-tú* 229 r. v 13, 20, *pu-lu-uh-tu* 234:8,
puquttu "thorn plant, brier": *pu-qut-ti* 229 r. viii 56,
pursītu "(offering) bowl": *pur-si-t[e* 142:3,
purussû "decision": EŠ.BAR 79 r. 5, 264 r. 2, EŠ.BAR]] 261 r. 2, EŠ.BAR-*ka* 247:5,
pūtu "front, opposite": *pu-ut* 236 r. 9, 247 r. 2, [*pu-ut* 246:14, SAG.KI-*ka* 230:23,
puzru "shelter": *pu-uz-ri* 229 r. vi 59,
qa''û "to wait on; to await, wait for": *tu-qa-a* 244 r. 3,
qabassīu "middle, central": *qab-sa-te* 287 iii 9,
qābiānu "speaker": *qa-bi-a-nu-ti* 229 r. v 3,
qābiu "commanding": *qa-bi-u* 120:16,
qablu "middle (parts)": MURUB$_4$ 247 r. 14, 248 r. 5, 250:1, 251 r. 1, 252:10, 253:13, MU]RUB$_4$ 247 r. 16,
qablu B "battle": *qab-lu* 234:5, MURUB$_4$ 229 r. vi 32, viii 9 MURUB$_4$-*šú* 233:6,
qablû "middle": MURUB$_4$-*tum*] 258:2,
qabsi āli "city center": MURUB$_4$—URU 65:7,
qabû "to say, tell": *a-qa-bi* 140 r. 11, *a-qab-bu-ni* 120:3, *a-qa[b]-bu-ni* 120:6, *aq-bu-ni* 120 r. 23, *aq-bu-ú* 125:4, *aq-[bu-ú* 164:8, [*aq-ta*]-*bi* 85:8, *aq-ta-ba-áš-šú* 72 r. 6, *aq-ṭi-ba-áš-šú* 120:24, *aq-ṭi-bi* 120 r. 19, DUG$_4$-*ú* 237:18, DUG$_4$.GA-*u* 262 r. 2, *i-qa-ba* 235 r. 50, *i-qab-bi-iu-ú* 116:6, *iq-ba-a* 220:8, *iq-ba-a-ni* 154 r. 9, *iq-ba-ka-nu-u-ni* 229 r. v 4, *iq-bi*] 229 r. v 88, *iq*]-*bi* 90 r. 5, *i*]*q-bi* 277 r. 7, *iq-bu-ni* 150:6, *iq-bu-ni*] 140:17, *iq-[bu-u* 130:11, *iq-bu-u-ni* 58:3, 279 r. 9, *iq-b*]*u-u-ni* 42:2, *iq-[bu-u-ni]* 15:5, *iq-bu-ú* 168 r. 6, *iq-bu-[ú* 31:13, *i*]*q-bu-ú* 69:8, 130:8, *i*]*q-ta-ba-a* 164:11, *iq-tab-bu-ka-a-ma* 235:46, *iq-ta-bi* 128 r. 4, *iq-ta-b*]*i* 75 e. 8, *i[q-ta-bi]* 128:9, [*iq-ta-bi*] 31:8, *iq-ta-bu-[ú* 31:4, *iq-t[i-bi-a]* 19:12, *iq-ṭi-bi* 21:2, 17, r. 2, 7, 117:8, 147 r. 6, 240:13, *iq-ṭi-b[i]* 21:11, [*iq-ṭi-bi* 21:8, *iq-ṭi-bi-[a]* 21:3, [*i*]*q-ṭí-bi-a* 52:7, *i-qab*]-*ba-a* 71:7, [*i-qab*]-*ba-a* 183:10, *i*]-*qab-ba-áš-ši* 91:14, *i-q[ab-ba-ka-nu-ni]* 227 ii 5, *i-qab-bi* 126 r. 3, 223 r. 1, 280:10, *i-qab-b[i* 202:6, *i-qab-bi-ma* 265:3, *i-q[ab-bu-ni]* 146:4, *i-q[ab-bu-u-ni]* 63:4, *i-qab-bu-ú* 36:4, *i-qab-bu-[ú]* 37 r. 10, *i*]-*qab-bu-[ú* 189 r. 4, *i-qa-bu-ni* 17:6, *i-qa-bu-u-ni* 240:3, 6, *la-aq-ba-ka* 120 r. 3, *la-aq-bi*] 140:15, *liq-bi-ma* 164 r. 7, *liq-bu-ú* 129:8, *liq-bu-[ú* 200:5, [*liq-bu-ú* 136:5, *ni-qa*]-*bu-u-ni* 229 r. vi 91, *q[a-bi-i* 246:7, *qi-bi* 71:10, 122:2, 225:6, *qi-[bi]* 128 r. 3, *qi-bi-a* 120 r. 12, *qi-b[i-m]a* 239 r. i 12, *qí-ba-a* 239 r. i 21, *qí-bi-ma* 239 ii 3, *qí-bi-ma*] 125:1, *qí-b[i-ma]* 239 ii 16, [*qí-bi-ma* 239 i 9, *ta-qab-ba-a-ni* 229 r. v 2, 7, 29, 35, *ta-qab-[ba-a-ni]* 227 ii 7, *ta-qa-ba-a-ni* 229 r. v 33, *ta-qab-ba-a* 126:6,
qabūtu "cup": *qa*-ZAG 288 ii 27,
qaltu "bow": *qa-al-ti-šú* 234:14, see also *qassu,*
qalû "to burn": *li-qi-lu-ku-nu* 229 r. viii 34,
qâlu "to be silent": *qa-la* 123 r. 7,
qamû "to burn": *liq-mu* 229 r. vii 16, *liq-mu-[u]* 229 r. viii 5,
qannu "outside": *qa-ni* 9:9,
qan ṭuppi see *qarṭuppu,*
qanû "reed, cane": GI.MEŠ 229 r. viii 24,
qanû B "to acquire, buy": *li-qi-nu* 235 r. 38,
qaqānu (a worm): *qa-qa-a-nu* 229 r. vi 23,
qaqqadu "head": SAG.DU-*ka* 230:22,
qaqqaru "earth, ground": *qaq-qar* 132:9, 229 r. vi 51, *qaq-qar-ma* 73:5, *qaq-q[a-ri]* 226:7, *qaq-[q]a-[ri* 226:7, *qaq-q[a-ru* 130:4,
qarābu "to approach, arrive; (stat.) to be present; (D) to present, offer": *i-qar-ri-ba* 229 r. viii 39, *iq-ṭar-bu-u-ni* 1:16, *nu-qar-ra-[ab* 160:5, *qur-[bu* 140 r. 8, *ú-qa-rab* 110 r. 2,
qarābu B "battle, fight": *qa-ra-bu* 133:11, *q*]*a-ra-bu* 133:13,
qardu "heroic": *qar-d[a-ta* 239 ii 10,
qarnu "horn": SI 229 r. vi 44, 732, 288 iv 11,
qarrādu "hero": *qar-rad* 229 r. vi 35, *qar-r[ad* 235:20, *qar-r[ad]* 235:22, *qar-ra-du* 230:4, 9,
qarṭuppu "stylus": GI—*ṭup-pu* 270:1, GI—*ṭup-pi* 232:11, GI.DU[B].BA 129:3,
qarû "to invite": *qa-ru-t[i* 130:9,
qassu "bow": BA]N 211:2, GIŠ.BAN 235:11, GIŠ.BA[N 34:10, GIŠ.BAN-*ku-nu* 229 r. vi 33, GIŠ.BAN-*k*]*u-nu* 226 r. 3, GIŠ.BAN.MEŠ 219 r. 3, 235 r. 24, GIŠ.PAN 229 r. vii 66, GIŠ.PAN.MEŠ 288 iv 70, see also *qaltu,*
qatû "to end, finish": *liq-ti* 229 r. vi 69, TIL.MEŠ 265:4,
qātu "hand; responsibility (of)": *qa-ti*] 247 r. 5, *q[a-ti]* 115 e. 8, *qa-ti-ia* 232:13, *qa-[ti-ka]* 21:13, *q*]*a-ti-šú* 77 r. 3, *qa-tuk-k[a* 230:7, ŠU 3:2, 232:12, 252:15, Š[U 77 r. 8, 258:1, ŠU.2 77 r. 8, 83:7, 115 r. 5, 126 r. 15, 134:3, 146 e. 15, 170 e. 13, 186 r. 3, 229 r. vi 49, 774, 78, 86, 279:3, 290 i 8, 293 r. 1, [ŠU.2 93 r. 2, [Š]U.2 287 iii 10, ŠU.2-*i*-[*ka* 93 r. 1, ŠU.2-*ka* 229 r. v 30, ŠU.2-*ku-nu* 229 i 73, r. v 38, 728, 66, Š]U.2-*su-nu* 93 r. 1, ŠU.2-*š[u* 217 r. 5, ŠU.2-*šú* 77 r. 4, 6, 9, 120:20, 252 r. 5, 273 r. 6, ŠU.2-[*šú* 56:2, [ŠU.2-*šú* 229 i 11, ŠU.2-*šú-nu* 20 r. 3, 188:5, ŠU.2-*š*]*ú-nu* 173:3,
qebēru "to bury": [*iq-tib-ru*]-*šú-nu* 80:6, *qé-bé-r[i]* 288 iii 19,
qēmu "flour": ZÍD 188:2, 271:10, ZÍD.DA 176 r.

7,

qēpu "(royal) delegate": LÚ.*qe-[pa-a-ni]* 19:4,

qerbu "inside": *qer-bi* 234 r. 11, 13, *qé-reb* 237 r. 2, 13, *q]é-reb* 233 r. 2, 237 r. 16, *[qé]-reb* 288 r. ii 4, *qe-re-eb-ni* 234:10,

qerēbu "to approach": *[aq-te-ri]b-šú-nu-tú* 72 r. 2, *tu-qar-rib* 235 r. 10,

qiāpu "to entrust": *i-qi-pi* 128 r. 11, *ni-qip* 73:3,

qiāšu "to donate": BA-*eš* 232 r. 5, *[li-qí-šú]* 255 r. 10, *[ú]-qa-a-a-iš* 288 r. ii 24,

qibītu "command": *qí-bit* 297:6, *qí-bit]* 297:10, *qí-bit-ka* 230:16, *qí-bi-ti* 237:20, *qí-bi-t[i]* 237:21,

qilu "burning, burn-mark": *qi-lu* 232 r. 2,

qimmatu "hair, mane; topknot, top, crown": *qim-mat-ka* 230:10,

qinniš "backwards": *qí-in-niš* 229 r. viii 14, *qí-niš* 229 r. vii 58, 66,

qinnu "nest, family": *qí-ni-ia* 72 e. 11, LÚ.*qin-na-a-ti* 84 r. 8, *qin-ni-šú* 229 ii 3,

qīpu "delegate": LÚ.*q[í-i-pi* 170:5, LÚ.*qí-pa-a-ni* 40:2,

qīru "pitch": *qi-i-ri* 229 r. vii 76, *qi-i-ru* 229 r. vi 73,

qissu (qīštu) "gift": NÍG.BA.MEŠ-*te* 229 r. v 13, 20, *qi-šá-a-ti* 288 r. ii 21,

qītu "end": *qi-it* 234:6, *qí-it* 73 r. 2,

qû "litre": *qa* 64 r. 1, 218:1, 288 iii 11,

qulqulānu "cassia": Ú.*qul-qul-la-nu* 274:5,

qūlu "silence": *qu-lu* 11:6,

qundu (an object made of copper): *qu-un-di* 288 iv 9,

quppu "box, basket": *[qu-up-pa-ti* 42:3,

qurādu "hero": *qu-ra-de-e* 234:18,

qutru "smoke": *qu-tu-ru* 234 r. 5,

ra'āmu "to love": *i-ra-'a-mu-ú* 235:10, *i-ra-mu* 129:10, *i-ram-mu* 288 r. ii 16, *i-ram-mu-šú-ma* 237 r. 9, *i-r]a-mu-uš* 235:5, *i-ra-mu-ši-n[a-a-ta]* 239 ii 20, r. i 14, *i-r]a-mu-ši-na-a-ta* 239 i 9, *ra-i]m* 239 i 8, *tar-'a-ma-a]-ni* 229 iv 11, *ta-ra-man-ni* 176 r. 2, *ta-ra-a-[man-ni-ni]* 3:7,

rā'imānu "lover, supporter": *ra-a'-i-ma-ni-ka* 235 r. 42, LÚ.*ra-i-[ma-nu* 185:6,

rā'iu "shepherd": LÚ.SIPA.MEŠ 124:9, SIPA.MEŠ 287 iii 17,

rā'i iṣṣūri "gooseherd": LÚ.SIPA—MUŠEN.MEŠ 123:2, 8,

ra'û "to shepherd": *i-ra-'a* 279:5,

rabābu "(Š) to make languid, obedient, impotent": *t]u-šar-ba-ba* 235 r. 1,

rabannu "magnate": *rab-ban-na-ti-šú* 237 r. 7, 10,

rabāṣu "to lie (down), loll, lurk": *i-rab-bi-ṣu-u-ni* 229 r. vii 49,

rabbu "four": 4-*u* 283:2,

rābiṣu "lurker (demon); advocate": MAŠKÍM 229 r. vi 76,

rabiu "magnate": LÚ.GAL.MEŠ 241 r. 2, LÚ.GA]L.MEŠ 151:4, [LÚ.GAL.MEŠ 229 ii 4, [LÚ.GAL.MEŠ] 280:1, [LÚ.GAL].MEŠ 280 r. 15,

rabû "to be great, grow; (D) to rear, bring up; (Š) to magnify": GAL 65:6, 229 i 12, iii 5, iv 3, r. v 31, 57, 59, 66, 69, 249 r. 6, 286 iii 17, (GAL) 229 ii 2, [GAL 235:1, GAL-*e* 228:3, r. v 68, 297:8, GAL-*i* 246 r. 9, GAL.MEŠ 229 i 76, r. v 62, 65, vi 52, 707, 13, 15, 230:3, 233:4, 237:16, r. 15, 252 r. 11, 261 r. 2, GAL.MEŠ] 229 i 46, 230:18, GA]L.MEŠ 297:9, G]AL.M[EŠ 268:1, GAL-*ti* 239 i 25, 246:6, 247:3, 4, 5, 11, r. 9, 10, 18, 248 r. 7, GAL-*ti*] 246:6, r. 9, 248:3, GAL]-*ti* 247:7, GAL-*tu* 226 r. 10, GAL-*tú* 115 r. 3, 229 r. vi 41, 247:8, r. 8, GAL-*tu₄* 234 r. 12, GAL-*t[u₄]* 234 r. 10, GAL-*u* 229 i 17, 63, iv 2, r. v 6, 10, 17, 26, 35, 45, 80, vi 78, 87, 89, 90, 93, vii 2, 4, viii 27, 67, GAL-*u*] 229 iv 9, GAL-*ú* 246:1, 7, r. 2, 247:1, 5, r. 7, 18, 248:1, GAL]-*ú* 248 r. 7, *i-rab-b[i* 255 r. 1, *i-ra-bi-ú-[ni* 147 r. 4, *lu-rab-bi-šu* 221:3, *mu-ša[r-bu-u* 297:6, *nu-ra-ab-bi* 235 r. 25, *ra-bi-i* 280 r. 1, *ra-bu-ú* 239 r. i 4, *ru-ub-bi-iš* 235 r. 16, 18, 20, *r]u-ub-bi-iš* 235 r. 15, *šur-ba-a-ta* 231:2, *tu-rab-ba* 273 r. 4, *tu-ra-bu-šú-ni* 240:1, *ú-rab-bi-i* 288 iii 14, *[u]r-tab-biš* 280:6, *ú-šar-bi* 288 i 7, *ú-šar-bi-[ka* 230:3,

rab ālāni "village manager": LÚ.GAL—URU.MEŠ 229 i 6,

rab bārê "chief haruspex" GAL—LÚ.HAL 280 r. 7,

rab bēti "major-domo": GAL—É 126:5, LÚ.GAL—É 229 i 4,

rab bīrti "fort commander": LÚ.GA]L—URU.HAL.ṢU 282:7,

rab danībāti "chief victualler": LÚ.GAL—*da-ni-ba[t]* 8:2,

rab hanšā "commander-of-fifty": GAL—50 287 ii 18, GAL—50.[MEŠ 286 ii 10, LÚ.GAL—50 123:4,

rab kāri "chief of trade": LÚ.GAL—*ka-ri* 156:2,

rab kāṣiri "chief tailor": [LÚ.GAL—KA.KÉŠ 235 r. 19, LÚ.GAL—TÚG.KA.KÉŠ.MEŠ-*ni* 140:6,

rab kiṣri "cohort commander": GAL—*ki-ṣir* 287 ii 1, GAL—*k[i-ṣir* 287 iv 12, GAL—*ki*]-*ṣir*.MEŠ 287 ii 7, LÚ.GAL—*ki-ṣir* 40:4, 59:3, 284:5, LÚ.GAL—*ki-ṣir*.MEŠ 229 i 7,

rab mūgi "general (of cavalry)": LÚ.GAL]—*mu-gi* 295 r. 3, L]Ú.GAL—*mu-g[i]* 22 r. 4,

rab nuhatimmi "chief cook": GAL—MU 292:2, [LÚ].GAL—MU 284:2, LÚ.GAL—MU-*ú-ti* 284 r. 4,

rab piqitti "office holder": GAL—*pi-qit-ti* 126 r. 4,

rab šāqê "chief cupbearer": LÚ].GAL—KAŠ.[LUL 52:1, LÚ.GAL—KAŠ.LU[L] 278:2, LÚ.GAL—K]AŠ.LUL 53 r. 7,

rab ša-rēši "chief eunuch": GAL—SAG 287 ii 12,

rab ša-rēšūtu "office of chief eunuch": GAL—SAG-*ú-[ti* 250 r. 10,

rab ṭupšarri "chief scribe": LÚ.GAL—A.BA 279:4,

rab urāti "team commander": LÚ.GAL—ANŠE.*ú-rat* 284:3, L]Ú.GAL—*ú-rat* 284:9,

radû "to lead, rule; (D) to add to": *i-rad-di* 91:5, *ir-ti-di* 234 r. 1, *lu-ra-[ad-di]* 140:16, *ú-rad-du-[u-ni]* 161 r. 2,

ragāmu "to call (out), shout, raise claim": *ir-tu-gu-man-ni* 120:18, 21,

rahāṣu "to be confident, to trust; (Š) to encourage": *ra-ah-ṣa-ku* 211:5, *ú-ra-hi-ṣa-na-ši* 242 r. 3, *lu-šar-hi-ṣu* 229 r. viii 61,

rahāṣu B "to flood, inundate": *li-[ra-ah-ṣa]* 229 r. viii 9, *li-ir-hi-iṣ* 229 r. vi 16, *ra-[ah-sa-tu-u-ni]* 229 r. viii 7,

rakābu "to ride": *[li-ir]-ku-ba* 37 r. 9,

rakāsu "to bind, attach, gird; to decree (offerings)": HÉ.[KÉŠ-*a*]*s* 262:5, *i-ra-kas* 299 i 4, 5, KÉŠ-*as* 262 r. 5, KÉŠ-*is* 252:10, *li-ir-ku-us* 229 r. vi 39, *ta-[rak-kas-a-ni]* 229 r. v 39,

raksu "recruit, mercenary; bound, scheduled": LÚ.*rak-su* 76:6, LÚ.*rak-(su)* 293 r. 2, LÚ.*rak-su*.MEŠ 284:7,
ramāku "to wash": *ru-[u]n-ka* 229 r. vi 43, T[U$_5$] 262:2,
ramanu "self": *ra-man-ka* 163 r. 5, *ra-ma-ni-ku-nu* 229 r. v 12, 55, viii 9, *ra-[ma]-ni-k[u-n]u* 229 r. v 19, *r]am-ni-ia* 184:9, *ram-ni-iá* 176 r. 5, *ram-ni-i-ka* 235 r. 2, *ram-n[u* 191:5, *[ra-man-ga* 80:11, *ra-man-gu-nu* 88:5,
rammû "to leave, release": *ra-am-me-a* 148 r. 5, *r]a-am-mi* 12:10, *tu-ram-ma-a-ni* 229 r. viii 29, *tu-ra-ma-šú-u-ni* 229 r. v 5, *ur-ta-me-ú* 57:5, *u[r]-ta-mu-u-ni* 152 r. 7, *ú]-ra-ma-na-ši* 145:3, *ú-ra-me-šú-n[u]* 162 r. 12,
ramû "to settle, dwell, be seated": *ar-ma-a* 280 r. 5, *ra-ma-at* 234:12,
rapādu "to run (away), ramble, roam": *ru-up-da* 229 r. v 89,
rapāšu "to be wide, extensive": DAGAL 47:5, DAGAL-*[eš]* 253:8, *ra-pa-áš-ti* 239 r. i 27,
raqû "to hide": *i-ra-[q]u-ni* 22:6,
rašû "to get, obtain": *ir-ši* 229 r. vi 31, *ir-ta-ši* 71:6, TUKU-*[ši]* 252:3,
rebītu "square, plaza, main street": *re-bit* 229 r. vi 64, *re-bi-ti* 229 r. vi 11,
rēhtu "rest, remainder": *re-eh-te* 227 ii 3, *re-eh-te]* 228:4, *re-eh-ti* 226 e. ii 11, 229 r. vi 81, viii 28, *re-eh-t[i]* 162 r. 3, *re-eh-[ti* 26 r. 2, *re-e[h-ti* 14 r. 4, *[re]-eh-ti* 229 r. vii 4,
rēmu "mercy": ARHUŠ 229 r. vi 40, *re-e-mu* 235 r. 43, 240:1,
rēmuttu "grant, donation": *ri-mu-ú-tú* 235 r. 41,
rēṣu "helper": *re-ṣu-šu* 234:3,
rēṣūtu "help": *ri-ṣu-ti* 237 r. 21, *r]i-ṣu-ti* 237 r. 10,
rēšāti "first fruits": SAG.MEŠ 286 ii 13, 15,
reštu "top quality, first-class; summit, peak": *reš-ti* 226 r. 2,
rēštû "first-ranking, foremost, eldest": *reš-tu-ú* 229 r. vi 4,
rēšu "head, top, beginning": *re-eš* 1:9, *re-e-ši* 234:7, *re-e-šu* 140 r. 16, *re-eš-im-ma* 129:9, *re-ši* 130 r. 5, SAG 252:1, 7, 13, 14, 253:4, 267 r. 2,
riāmu "to grant, bestow, donate" *li-ri-man-ni* 235 r. 41,
riāqu "to be empty": *li-ri-iq* 229 r. viii 41, *ra-qu-u-ni* 229 r. viii 40, SUD 252:4,
riāšu "to rejoice": *i-riš-šú* 237 r. 4,
rihṣu "devastation": *ri-ih-ṣi* 229 r. vi 16,
riksu "setup; bond, agreement, obligation": *rik-sa-ni-ma* 33 r. 4, *rik-si* 229 r. viii 24,
rimṭu "venereal disease": *ri-im-ṭu* 229 r. vi 50,
rīmu "wild bull": AM 287 iv 1 ,
rittu "hand, wrist": *ri-ti* 260 r. 3,
ru'tu "spittle": ÚH-*su* 262:11,
rubê "increase, interest": *ru-bé]-e* 297:3,
rubû "ruler, prince": LÚ.NUN 164 r. 3, NUN 162 r. 4, 237 r. 1, 252:3, 4, 253:7, 8, r. 5, 262:9, r. 2, 265:4, 297:4, 298 r. 4, (NUN) 229 r. v 68, NUN-*e* 228:3,
rubûtu "rulership": *ru-ub-ta-ka* 230:8,
ruqqu "kettle, cauldron": SAL.LA 247 r. 15,
rūqu "distant, remote": *r[u-ú-qi]* 239 r. i 27,
rūṣu "help(?)": *ru-ṣa* 232 r. 1,
ruššû "red, reddish": *ru-uš-ši-i* 232:11, 12,
rūṭu "span": LAL 117:5, 247:18,
sabirru "ring, torc, bracelet": HAR 126:20, 232:12,
sadāru "to array; (Š) to accustom, maneuver": *la-as-di-ir* 120 r. 24, *[sad-ru-ti* 263 r. 5, *sa-ad-ra* 211:4, *ú-šá-as-dir* 130:3,
sāgu "sackcloth": *sa-ga-a-te* 124:7,
sagullu "herd": ÁB.GUD.HI.A.MEŠ 242 r. 2,
sahānu "(D) to sharpen": *sa-ha-an* 234:20, *ú-sa-ha-na* 234:6,
sahāpu "to overwhelm": *li-is-hu-up* 229 r. viii 49, *sah-hu-pu* 234 r. 16, *sah-pu-šú-nu* 233:14,
sahāru "to turn, go around, return; (D) to bring back": *lu-sa-hi-ra* 229 r. vii 58, NIGIN 252:16, 17, *ta-sa-har-u-ni* 229 r. vii 35, 70, *ú-sa-a]h-hi-ru-u-ni* 153:4,
sakāpu "to overthrow, defeat": *se-kep-šú-nu* 241 r. 3,
sakātu "to be silent": *su-uk-ku-tú* 83:3,
salāhu "to sprinkle": *sal-hu* 247 r. 14,
salāmu "to make peace; (D) to appease, reconcile": *is-si-lim* 239 i 11,
salīmu "peace, reconciliation": *[sa-li]-ma* 72 r. 1,
salmu "ally": *si-il-me-ka* 239 r. i 22,
samān "eight": 8 44:11, 129:21, 286:18, 290 i 8,
samānā "eighty": 80 34:5, 85 287 iii 16,
samuntu "one eighth": 8-*šú* 288 r. i 7,
sanāqu "to approach; (D) to question": *i-se-ni-qa-a-na-ši* 234:9, *is-si-ni-qi* 233:10, *lu-sa-an-[niq* 270:4, *ú-sa-niq-šú* 128 r. 7,
sangû "priest": L]Ú.SANGA 136 r. 4,
sapāku "to assail, seize, catch in": *i-sa-pak-u-ni* 229 r. vii 73, *i-sa-pa-ku-u-ni* 229 r. vii 77,
sapānu "to level, lay flat":
sarāhu "to range, rove(?)" *ta-sa-pa-na-a-ni* 229 r. v 77, *sa-ra-hu* 73 r. 1,
sarbu "slush": *sar-bu* 229 r. v 37,
sartu "fine": *sa-ri-it* 274 e. 11,
sasin qassi "bow-maker": LÚ.ZADIM—BAN 140:11,
sasin uṣṣi "arrow-maker": LÚ.ZADIM—GAG.TI 140:11,
sassu "base-board": *sa-se-šá* 229 r. viii 7,
sasû "to read": *i-si-si]* 147:11, *i-si-si-šú* 51:3,
seb'ā "seventy": 72 44:10,
seb'īšu "sevenfold": 7-*šú* 278 s. 1,
sēgallu "queen": MÍ.É.GAL 284:10,
segû "to go about, wander": *is-sag-gu-na* 40:3,
sehû "to revolt": *is-s]i-hu-ni* 90:3,
sekēpu see *sakāpu*,
SI4 (mng. uncert.): [SI$_4$-*m]a* 265:6,
siāmu "to be red": SA$_5$ 271:2, 288 ii 18, iv 5, [SA$_5$] 288 r. i 16, SA$_5$.MEŠ 263 r. 3,
siāqu "to be tight, narrow": *lu-si-qu-ni-ku-nu* 229 r. vii 19,
sihlu "thorn; piercing pain": *si-ih-lu* 229 r. vi 45,
sīhu "rebellion": *si-hu* 33:7, 229 r. vi 82, *si-hu]* 227 ii 3, *[si-hu* 228:7, *si-i-hi* 128:7,
sikkû "mongoose": ^{d}NIN.KILIM 229 r. vii 48,
sikkutu "yeast, leaven": *sik-kit* 229 r. vii 34, *sík-kit* 229 r. vii 32,
siliāti "lies, rubbish": *si-li-a-a-te* 240:6,
simānu "time, season": *si-ma-ni* 232:12,
simānu B (Sivan, name of the 3rd month): ITI.SIG$_4$ 263 r. 3, ITI.SI[G$_4$] 235 r. 3, I]TI.SIG$_4$ 50:4,

simmu "sore, wound": *si-mu* 229 r. vi 42,
simtu "propriety, ordinance": *si-mat* 288 r. ii 15,
siparru "bronze": *si-bar-ri* 140 r. 18, [*si-bar-ri* 140 r. 2, ZABAR 229 r. vii 21, viii 48,
sipru "letter-scroll, document": *sip-ri-šú* 36:7,
siqqurrutu "ziggurat": *si-qur-ri-te* 240:2,
siqru "word": *si-qi-ri-šú-nu* 234:16,
sīqu "lap": *si-qi-ku-nu* 229 r. v 39,
sirrimu "wild ass, onager": ANŠE.EDIN.ME[Š] 281:9, *sír-ri-me* 229 r. v 88,
sīru "plaster": *si-ri* 115:5,
sissiktu "hem": *ši-šik-ti-šú-nu* 126:17, TÚG.SÍG-*ka*] 262:5,
sissû "horse": ANŠ]E.KUR 288 iii 8, ANŠE.KUR.MEŠ 66 r. 5, 288 ii 28, ANŠE.KUR.MEŠ-*ma* 288 iii 17, ANŠE.KUR.RA 243 r. 1, 2, 262 r. 5, ANŠE.KUR.[R]A 243:7, A]NŠE.KU[R.RA 166:8, ANŠE.KUR.RA.MEŠ 122:8, 152 r. 5, 243:5, 247 r. 8, ANŠE.KUR.RA.M[EŠ 80:5, 180 r. 3, ANŠ[E.KUR.RA.MEŠ 170:4, ANŠ[E.KUR.RA.MEŠ] 238:5, A]NŠE.KUR.RA.M[EŠ 258:7, [ANŠE.KUR.RA.MEŠ] 249 r. 6,
sīsu "teat(?)": *si-si* 229 r. vi 62,
sittu "rest": [*si-i*]*t-ti* 39:3,
suāku "to pulverize": *ú-sa-ka* 176 e. 6,
su''u "dove": T]U.MUŠEN.[MEŠ 262:6, *su-'e-e* 229 r. viii 35,
sukkallu "vizier": LÚ.SUKKAL.MEŠ 129:11,
sullû "(D only) to appeal, pray": *ú-sa-li* 26 r. 3,
sunqu "want": *su-un-qu* 229 r. vi 60,
suppû "(D only) to pray": *ú-sap-pu-ma* 237:3,
sūqu "street": SILA 229 r. vi 11,
surrāti "lies, treason": *sur-ra-a-te* 229 r. vi 86,
sūsānu "horse trainer, chariot-man": LÚ.GIŠ.GIGIR 290 i 2, LÚ.*su-sa-ni* 290 i 6, LÚ.*su-sa-nu* 289 r. ii 2, LÚ.*s*[*u*] 290 i 4,
ṣabāru "to twitter": *lu-šá-aṣ-bir-ku-nu* 229 r. viii 10,
ṣabātu "to seize, capture; (D) to fasten": *a-ṣa-ba-at* 49 r. 2, *aṣ-ṣa-bat* 235:7, [*a-ṣa-bat-m*]*a* 72 r. 6, DI[B 247 r. 12, DI]B 247:10, DIB-*tu* 247:15, r. 12, DIB-*t*[*u* 247:10, *iṣ-ba-tu-nim-ma* 237 r. 16, *iṣ-ba-tú* 229 i 28, *iṣ-ṣa-ab-bat* 235:13, *iṣ-ṣa-bat* 233:8, *iṣ-ṣa-b*[*at* 160:4, *iṣ-ṣa-*[*bat*] 239 ii 21, *iṣ-ṣab-tu-ni* 120:9, *iṣ-ṣab-*[*tu-ni-šú*] 10:8, *i-ṣa-bat* 279:8, *i-ṣab-bat-ma* 136 r. 3, *i-ṣab-ba-tu-nim-ma* 245 r. 4, *i-ṣi-ba-ta* 229 r. v 82, *li-iṣ-bat* 183 r. 6, [*li-iṣ-bat* 37 r. 10, *na-ṣa-bi-ta* 229 r. vii 78, *ni-iṣ-bat-ma* 90:6, *ṣab-tú* 60:2, 4, *ṣa-bit-u-ni* 11:8, *ṣa-bi-ta-at* 231:1, *ṣi-bu-tu* 164 r. 11, *ṣ*]*i-bu-tú* 27:3, *ṣu-ub-bu-tu* 33 r. 3, *šá-aṣ-bu-ti* 229 r. vii 62, *ta-ṣa-bat-a-ni-ni* 227 ii 9, *ta-ṣab-ba-ta* 229 r. vii 28, *ta-ṣab-bat-su* 20 e. 21, *t*[*u-šá-aṣ*]*-bat-a-*[*ni* 229 i 77,
ṣabītu "gazelle": MAŠ.DÀ 229 r. v 89,
ṣabû "to wish": *ṣi-bi* 243:5, r. 3,
ṣābu "men, troops": ERIM 252:3, 253:5, ERIM.HI.A-*šú* 237 r. 12, ER[IM.HI.A-*šú*] 237 r. 1, ERIM.MEŠ 29:8, 71:7, 83:6, 120 r. 23, 125:3, 126 r. 12, 128 r. 9, 11, 129 r. 8, 15, 139:3, 164 r. 13, 181 r. 7, 187:2, 196:3, 227 ii 8, 247:2, 6, 7, ERIM.M[EŠ 189:5, ERI]M.MEŠ 37:6, 256:7, ER[IM.MEŠ] 247:12, ER]IM.MEŠ 84 r. 6, [E]RIM.MEŠ 76:1, ERIM.MEŠ-*šú* 37 r. 4, ERIM.MEŠ-*šú-nu* 229 i 13, 234 r. 5, ERIM.M[EŠ-*šú-nu*] 72:4, LÚ.ERIM.MEŠ 33:16, r. 2, 120 r. 70, 123 r. 2, 133:3, 229 i 11, 243 r. 2, 246 r. 2, 249 r. 6, 292:3, LÚ.ERIM.MEŠ] 246 r. 2, LÚ.ERIM.ME[Š 92 r. 3, 257 r. 1, LÚ.ERIM.ME[Š] 90 r. 9, LÚ.ERIM.M[EŠ 133:5, LÚ.ERIM.[MEŠ 254:8, LÚ.ERIM.[M]EŠ 243 r. 1, [LÚ.ERIM.MEŠ 247 r. 8, 258:7, LÚ.ER[IM.MEŠ-*šú* 133:9,
ṣahāru "to be small, young": *mu-ṣa-hi-ir* 229 r. vi 17, TUR 229 i 12, TUR] 250:6, TUR.MEŠ 229 i 76,
ṣalāu "to cast, throw, put down": *i-ṣ*]*a-li-ú-ni-ni* 299 i 10,
ṣalālu "to sleep": N]Á 288 ii 19, *ta-ṣa-la-la* 229 r. viii 38,
ṣalāmu "to be black; (D) to make black": *lu-ṣal-li-mu* 229 r. vii 76,
ṣalmāt qaqqadi "mankind": *ṣal-mat*—SAG.DU 235:39,
ṣalmu "statue, image, likeness": NU 271:3, 10, NU.M[EŠ 47:5, *ṣal*]*-ma* 77 r. 4, *ṣal-mu* 77 r. 9, 126:16, 233:13, *ṣa*]*l-mu* 77 r. 6, *ṣa-lam* 229 r. v 65, 66, 67, viii 3, 271:1, 288 iii 21, 297:9, *ṣa-la*[*m* 14:1, 3, *ṣ*]*a-lam* 297:8,
ṣâlu "to fight, quarrel, hassle": *lu-ṣa-lu* 226 r. 1, *ṣa-a-li* 229 r. v 12, 19,
ṣamādu "to harness, attach": *i-ṣi-mì-di* 234:22, *iṣ-ṣi-mid* 233:7, [*ṣa-mid* 250:4, [*ṣa-mid*] 252:6,
ṣamāru "to strive for": *ti-iṣ-m*[*u-ru-ma* 247:4,
ṣamû "(D) to make thirsty": *lu-ṣa-mu-ú* 226:13, see also *zamû*,
ṣappuhu "(D) to scatter, spill": *ṣa-pa-hu-u-ni* 229 r. viii 53,
ṣarāhu "to cry out, utter a cry": *ta-ṣar-ra-hu-ú-ma* 235:48,
ṣarāmu "to plan": [*l*]*i-iṣ-rim* 247:6,
ṣarbutu "poplar": GIŠ.*ṣar-*[*bi-ti* 61:6,
ṣarpu "silver": KUG.UD 3:4, 31:6, 56:4, 120 r. 15, 126:21, 165:7, 181 r. 3, 243 r. 3, 5, 251 r. 4, 271:9, 275:3, 5, e. 11, 276:4, 277:4, 283:1, 288 ii 19, 27, r. ii 13, KUG.UD] 31 r. 7, KUG.U[D] 288 iv 12, KUG.[UD 31:10, K[UG].UD 243 r. 4, K]UG.UD 216:6, [KUG.U]D 276:7, [KUG].UD 165 r. 5, KUG.UD.MEŠ 19:16, KUG.UD.MEŠ-*ni* 19:11,
ṣâtu "(scholastic) explanation": *ṣa-a-ti* 229 i 14, r. v 48, 58,
ṣehru "small, minor; child, apprentice": LÚ.TUR 120:20, 281:12, LÚ.TUR.ME[Š 212:2, *ṣe-eh-ru-t*]*e* 228:5, *ṣe-eh-r*[*u-te* 227 ii 3, *ṣ*[*e-eh-ru-te*] 226 e. ii 11,
ṣerru "snake": MUŠ 229 r. vii 48, MUŠ.MEŠ 236:16,
ṣēru "open country, plain, steppe": EDIN 229 r. v 89, 234:2, 249:6, 252:7, 13, 280:12, ED]IN 253:13, EDIN-*šú* 235 r. 48,
ṣētu "heat, light, drought": Ú.DA 229 r. vi 58, UD.D[A 226 r. 5,
ṣibtu "hold, grip, seizure; interest": *ṣib-ti* 19:7, *ṣi-ba-su* 239 r. ii 6,
ṣibûtu "wish, objective": ÁŠ 262:7, *ṣ*]*i-bu-ut-su* 216:7,
ṣillu "shadow": GIŠ.MI 226 r. 5, 229 r. vi 58, G]IŠ.MI 183:4, *ṣil* 120:23,
ṣimittu "team": LAL-*tum* 119:8,
ṣipirtu (a kind of textile, perhaps "scarf"): *ṣip-rat* 288 r. i 8,
ṣīru "emissary; exalted, noble": L]Ú.MAH 295 r. 2, LÚ.MAH.MEŠ 1:3, 14, 9:4, MAH 229 r. vi 1, MAH.MEŠ 252 r. 12, MAH.MEŠ] 255 r. 3, *ṣir-ta* 232:13,
ṣītu "exit, (pl.) distant times; loss": *ṣi-it* 228:5,

230:20, ZI.GA 252:15,

ṣit libbi "offspring, child": *ṣi-it—lib-bi* 229 r. vi 81, *ṣi-it*—ŠÀ-*bi* 229 r. vii 5, viii 28,

ṣīt šamši "east": ᵈUTU.È 262:10,

ṣubātu "cloth, garment": TÚG 246:14, 247 r. 2, 4, 262:4, 271:2, 4, TÚG.HI.A 299 i 6, TÚG-*s*[*u*] 115:2, TÚG.SìG 288 ii 33

ṣuddê "provisions": *ṣu-de-e* 271:6,

ṣuhāru "employee": LÚ.T[UR.MEŠ-*ia*] 281 r. 1,

ṣullû "to pray": *nu-ṣal-l*[*a* 171 r. 9, *nu-ṣal-l*[*a*] 135:7, *ú-ṣal-la* 218:5,

ṣumamītu "thirst": *ṣu-ma-mì-ti* 229 r. viii 53,

ṣummirāti "wish, objective": S]È.SÈ.KI-[*ka* 257 r. 6, ŠÀ.SÈ.SÈ.KI-*ka* 252 r. 16, ŠÀ.SÈ.SÈ.KI-*k*[*a*] 255 r. 6, ŠÀ.SÈ.KI-*šú* 253:5,

ṣummû "to thirst for, lack s.th.": *li-iz-za-ma-a* 229 r. vi 11, *li-iz-za-am-*[*m*]*a-a* 229 r. vi 15,

ṣummuru "wish, goal": *ṣu-um-mu-ru* 237 r. 10,

ṣūmu "thirst": *ṣu-um* 229 r. viii 54,

ṣupru "nail; nailmark": [UM]BIN.MEŠ-*ka* 230:31,

ša "that; what; of": *ša* 1:6, 8, 12, r. 6, 9, 14, 6:4, 5, 8, 7:4, 5, 7, 8, 8:7, 8:12, 9:4, 10, 11:3, 5, 12, 12:6, 9, 11, 14 r. 2, 15:5, 16:6, 18:4, 5, 6, r. 4, 5, 19:3, 8, 13, 18, 20:3, 20:5, 15, r. 2, 5, 8, 22:2, 25:1, 26:4, r. 7, 42:1, 5, 42:3, r. 1, 51 r. 1, 52:6, 58 r. 1, 59:4, 60:6, 60:7, 62:4, 5, 63:3, 66 r. 3, 5, 6, 67:4, 5, 100:4, 105:4, 5, 107 r. 1, 109 r. 1, 111 r. 8, 114 r. 4, 116:2, e. 7, r. 3, s. 1, 120:3, 5, 13, 14, 15, 17, r. 4, 18, 23, 26, s. 1, 123 r. 8, 124 r. 3, 126:1, 14, r. 3, 140:9, 13, 17, r. 7, 8, 13, 15, 18, 145:2, 147:11, r. 2, 4, 9, 148 r. 3, 6, 7, 150:5, 152 r. 10, 154:6, r. 5, 8, 156:3, 173:4, 227 ii 2, 4, 8, 10, 228:4, 228:2, 4, i 1, 13, 18, 19, 33, 48, 49, 50, 64, r. v 66, 67, vii 29, viii 68, 69, 70, 230:14, 231:4, 232:1, 233:3, 10, 234 r. 4, 6, 7, 240:1, 2, 3, 4, 5, 6, 7, 11, 12, 15, 246:13, 247:10, 256:3, 261 e. 14, r. 7, 279:3, 9, r. 6, 281:13, r. 4, 5, 282:6, 286:15, 286 ii 5, 14, iii 3, 288 i 3, ii 32, r. ii 16, 289 i 5, 8, 9, 292:2, 3, 297:3, 298 r. 4, 300 i 16, *ša*] 10:5, 26 r. 4, 139 e. 23, 229 r. vi 85, *š*[*a* 19:7, 228:1, *š*]*a* 6:8, 42:3, 105:2, 153:3, 226:8, 234:3, 240:10, 299 i 18, (*ša*) 8:4, 229 r. v 47, [*ša* 8:5, 18 r. 2, 42:2, 9, 46:1, 49:5, r. 2, 51:1, 60:2, 66:2, r. 1, 6, 102:5, 116:2, 121:6, 145 r. 2, 151:3, 228:5, 229 i 46, r. v 37, 263 r. 8, 298 r. 4, [*ša*] 1 e. 20, 124:9, [*š*]*a* 14 r. 3, 57:7, 58:3, 140:4, r. 5, 226:13, *šá* 10 r. 2, 16:2, 27:3, 29:3, 6, 9, 30:6, 7, r. 4, 5, 30:12, 13, 32:7, 8, 33:4, 11, 12, r. 17, 36:7, 37 r. 5, 6, 8, 15, 38:7, 9, 40:9, 52:3, 64:6, 73:7, e. 10, 11, 73:2, r. 3, 79 r. 5, 7, 80:3, 4, 9, 81:1, 2, 4, 5, 6, 81:3, 84 r. 7, 86:9, 91:2, 92 r. 2, 114 r. 8, 115:4, e. 8, r. 1, 125:3, 126:3, 4, 5, 7, 8, 13, 14, 15, 18, 20, 21, r. 1, 5, 127:2, s. 2, 128:3, 4, 7, r. 9, 11, 13, 129:4, 7, 13, 19, r. 9, 17, 130 r. 4, 8, 132:4, 5, 133:6, 11, 134 r. 6, 136:4, 158:1, 163 r. 2, 3, 164:9, r. 2, 4, 12, 14, 165:4, 7, 166:6, 7, 167 r. 1, 2, 168:4, 171:4, 9, 11, r. 6, 8, 172:5, 7, 175:4, r. 6, 176 r. 2, 5, 8, 178:4, 5, 182 r. 13, 183 r. 10, 184:7, 12, 185:8, 185 e. 10, r. 6, 187:3, 188:3, 6, 189:3, 7, r. 6, 192:1, 3, 197:7, 198:7, 206:15, 211:3, 212 r. 7, 213:1, 2, 5, 216:4, r. 7, 217:1, 5, 8, 220:3, 4, 6, 221:4, 229 i 33, 34, 35, 38, 47, 63, 66, ii 1, 2, iv 2, 3, 4, 9, r. v 1, 4, 6, 10, 17, 26, 28, 31, 34, 35, 37, 40, 43, 45, 46, 50, 53, 56, 57, 59, 61, 69, 71, 80, vi 22, 45, 50, 52, 62, 75, 79, 81, 88, 89, vii 1, 3, 4, 5, 13, 21, 26, 29, 30, 32, 33, 36, 37, 38, 40, 41, 43, 44, 46, 48, 50, 53, 54, 55, 56, 60, 62, 63, 67, 69, 72, 75, 77, 79, 80, 81, 82, viii 3, 4, 7, 9, 16, 18, 19, 20, 27, 29, 30, 35, 40, 45, 48, 52, 55, 67, 230:7, 9, 17, 22, 32, 232:6, 10, 234:8, 9, 10, 12, 13, 14, 15, 18, 19, 20, r. 14, 20, 235:4, 15, 19, 21, 22, 31, 39, 41, 49, 52, r. 3, 4, 5, 12, 14, 20, 22, 41, 49, 237:12, r. 1, 5, 9, 12, 14, 19, 20, 21, 22, 239 i 9, 14, 23, ii 6, 20, 26, r. i 1, 6, 9, 10, 13, 18, 19, 30, 31, 240:1, 241 r. 2, 3, 243:6, r. 6, 245 r. 1, 2, 3, 246:9, 10, 11, 12, 13, 14, r. 3, 4, 5, 8, 247:1, 2, 8, 9, 10, 17, 18, 19, r. 1, 2, 4, 10, 11, 12, 15, 248:1, 2, r. 3, 249:7, r. 7, 250 r. 8, s. 1, 252:4, r. 1, 2, 14, 253 r. 2, 3, 4, 254:5, r. 1, 255 r. 9, 260 r. 3, 6, 8, 10, 261:6, r. 5, 262:9, 263:2, 264 r. 2, 4, 265:1, 2, r. 10, 266:3, 5, r. 1, 271:1, 4, 10, r. 1, 273 r. 11, 274 r. 7, 275:7, 9, 279:2, 4, r. 11, 280:1, r. 2, 5, 6, 10, 15, 283:2, 284:10, 285 r. 7, 288 i 6, iii 12, 290 i 7, 298 r. 8, 300:11, *šá*) 229 i 36, *šá*] 32:3, 113:c 8, 115 r. 4, 134:4, 185:6, 229 r. vii 2, 84, 88, 247 r. 8, *š*[*á* 188 e. 10, 229 i 36, *š*]*á* 21 e. 11, 222:4, 226:4, 237 r. 15, 246:1, 247:10, [*šá* 129:10, 130:8, 135:7, 220:8, 229 iii 5, iv 1, r. vi 87, 91, 732, 235 r. 6, 237 r. 2, 7, 20, 247: 10, 258:8, 280:2, [*šá*] 229 r. vii 81, 247:3, [*š*]*á* 229 r. viii 32,

ša'ālu "to ask, consult": *a-sa-*[*'*]*a-al-šú* 10:9, *a-šal-ka* 245 r. 1, [*a-šal-ka* 247 r. 7, [*a-šal*]*-ka* 246 r. 2, *a-šal-lu-k*[*a* 247:1, *a-šal-lu*]*-ka* 248:1, *a-šal-l*[*u-ka* 246:1, *i-šá-a-*[*lu-šú*] 128:11, *a-šá-'a-al* 84 r. 13, *i-šá-'a-*[*al* 164 s. 2, *liš-al* 123 r. 4, 133:4, *liš-al-šú-nu* 120 r. 17, *liš-'a-al-šú* 33:6, *li-šá-al-la* 128 r. 12, *šá-'a-al* 84:9,

šabāru "to break": *liš-bir* 229 r. vi 33, *liš-bi-ru* 229 r. vii 65, *lu-ša-bir* 226 r. 3,

šabāṭu "to blast, hit, sweep": *liš-bi-ṭu-ma* 115:2,

šabû "to get sated, enjoy": *ši-ba-a* 239 ii 19,

šâbu "to sway": *šub-bat* 253:4,

šadādu "to drag, haul, extend": *il*]*-du-du* 189:4,

šadālu "to be broad; (D) to broaden, widen, increase": *lu-šá-di-lu* 229 r. vii 66, *lu-šá-di-lu-ku-nu* 229 r. viii 14,

šaddaqdiš "last year": [*i—šá-daq-di-iš* 117:10,

šaddû "mountain; east": KUR-*e* 105:2, 233:21, KUR-*i* 10:7, 234:2, 11, 15, KU[R]-*i* 32:5, K[UR-*i*] 10:4, *ša-du-e* 234:12,

šādidu (a stone): N]A$_4$.*šá-di-du* 288 iii 4,

šaggaštu "slaughter, massacre": *š*[*a*]*-ga-al-ta-šú-nu* 234:19, *šag-gaš-tú* 229 r. vi 36,

šahāhu "to disintegrate, waste away": *li-šá-hi-ha* 229 r. vi 47,

šaharšuppû "leprosy": SAHAR.ŠUB-*bu*] 229 r. v 86,

šahartu (a garment, perhaps "leggings"): *šá-har-rat* 288 r. i 6, 16,

šahātu "hiding place, inside corner": *šá-ha-ti* 229 r. vi 59,

šahāṭu "to strip, tear off; to become angry": *iš-hi-*[*ṭu* 31:16, *i-šá-hi-ṭu* 126 r. 14, *š*[*u-hu*]*-ṭu* 126 r. 7,

šahšahhu "slanderer, scandalmonger": *šah-šah-hi-ia* 232 r. 4,

šakānu "to place, set": *al-ta*]*-kan-na* 72 e. 10, *a-sa-kan* 145:7, *a-sa*[*k*]*-nak-ku-nu* 121:7, *as-sa-kan-na* 154 r. 11, *a-ša*[*k-kan* 73:6, GAR 237:1, 247 r. 13, 248 r. 3, 249 r. 4, 252:3, 9, 255:3, [GAR 250:3, GAR-*an* 273 r. 14, [GAR-*an* 262:13, GAR-*a-an* 250 r. 13, GAR-*át* 252:12, GAR-*in* 247 r. 16, 253:6, GAR-*ma* 252:14, 255:6, GAR.MEŠ 248 r. 4, GAR.MEŠ]

252:5, GAR.M[EŠ 255:5, GAR-*ni* 247 r. 8, GAR-*un* 248:3, 288 r. ii 20, GÁ-*ma* 232 r. 5, *i*]*l-ta-kan* 93 r. 5, [*il*]*-ta-kan* 178:3, *i-sa-kan-šú* 279:9, *is-sak-nu* 120 r. 8, [*is-sa*]*k-nu-šú* 11:13, *is-sa-ak-nu* 120 r. 8, *is-sa-kan* 147:5, 229 r. v 8, 15, 23, *is-sa-*[*kan* 153:7, *i-sa-at-ka-na* 234 r. 8, *iš-kun* 72 r. 1, 280:7, *iš-ku*[*n*] 206:9, *iš-ku-na-ni-ni* 8:5, *iš-ku-na-ni-ni*] 61:2, *iš-kun-an-na-ši*] 30 r. 5, *iš*]*-ku-na-*[*an-ni-ni*] 66:3, *iš-kun-ni-ni* 43:3, *iš-ku-nu* 237 r. 13, *iš-k*[*u-nu* 208:2, *iš-kun-u-ni* 229 r. vii 6, *iš-kun-u-*[*ni*] 229 i 19, [*iš-ku-nu-ni*] 229 i 28, *iš-ku-nu-uni*] 229 i 47, *iš-š*[*ak-nu* 261:6, *iš-šak-nu-ma* 260 r. 4, *it-taš-kan* 237 r. 14, *i-*[*sa-kan*] 146 e. 15, *i-ša*[*k-kan* 195:4, *i-ša*[*k-kan*] 132:6, *i-šak-ka-nu*] 247 r. 11, *i-šak-k*[*a-n*]*u* 247:9, *i-šá-kan* 229 r. vi 40, *liš-ka-nu-ku-nu* 229 r. vii 74, *liš-kun* 41:5, 208:7, 226 r. 3, 229 r. vi 51, 262:4, [*liš*]*-kun* 229 r. vi 37, *liš-k*]*u-na-an-ni* 69:18, *liš-kun-šu-ma* 69:13, *liš-ku-nu* 229 r. vii 14, *ni-iš-kun* 234:19, *ni-ša-kan-u-ni* 229 r. vi 83, *ni-šak-kan* 160 r. 3, *šak-na* 263:5, *šak-na-an-ni* 33:4, *šak-nu*] 247:3, r. 10, *šak-n*[*u*] 92 e. 1, *š*[*ak-nu*] 247:8, [*šak-nu*]*-ni* 229 r. vii 33, *ša-ak-nu* 229 r. viii 71, *šá-kan* 229 r. viii 44, *šá-kin* 83:5, 176 r. 10, 239 ii 12, *šá-kín* 230:27, 234 r. 15, *šá-kín-u-ni* 229 r. v 72, 742, *šá-ki-in* 140 r. 3, *šá-ki-nu-u-ni* 140 r. 19, *šuk-nam-ma* 248 r. 1, *ta-as-sak-na* 21:20, *ta-šak-kan* 235:36, *ta-šá-kan-a-ni* 229 r. v 55, *ta-šá-kan-a-*[*ni*] 229 i 78, *t*]*a-šak-kan-áš-šú* 91:18, [*ta-ša*]*k-ka-na-ma* 86:3, *taš-kun-nim-ma* 232 r. 1, *ul-ta-áš-kin-nu* 72 r. 9, *ú-šá-áš-kín* 234 r. 19,

šakkanakku "governor, viceroy": *šá-ga-na-ku* 233 r. 14,

šaklulu "to perfect; ungelded bull": [*mu-šak-lil* 297:5, *ú-šak-li-lu* 297:10,

šaknu "governor; prefect": GAR-[*nu-šú* 259:7, GAR-*nu*.MEŠ 287 ii 14, 16, LÚ.GAR 120:9, LÚ.GAR-*nu*.MEŠ 229 i 7, LÚ.GAR—KUR 229 r. viii 65, LÚ.GAR.KUR 279:2, 6, LÚ].*sa-gan* 81:6, LÚ.*šak-nu* 171 r. 13, LÚ.*ša*]*k-nu* 235 r. 14, L]Ú.*šak-nu* 178:5, L]Ú.*šak-nu*.MEŠ 70:6, LÚ.*šá-kin* 283 r. 1, LÚ.*šá-kin*.[*i*]*n-šú* 275:9,

šalālu "to loot": *áš-lu-la* 233:12, *i-šal-*[*la*]*l* 235 r. 4, *i-ša*]*l-lal-šú* 195 r. 3, *i-šal-lá-lu* 246 r. 6, 247:10, *i-šal-lá-lu*] 247 r. 12, *i*]*š-lu-lu* 235 r. 6, IR 247:10, r. 12,

šalāmu "to be sound, whole, safe; (D) to complete, repay": *il-te-lim* 33:19, *i-šal-li-*[*mu* 263 r. 4, SILIM-*im* 248 r. 6, 253:10, 12, SILIM-*im*] 258:2, SILIM-*tim* 246:6, SI[LIM-*ti*]*m* 255:5, SILIM-[*tim* 246 r. 8, SILIM.MEŠ 246 r. 7, [SILIM.M]EŠ 246 r. 8, *šal-ma-a-ti* 80:4, *šal-mu* 252 r. 13, [*šal*]*-mu* 247:5, *šal-mu-t*[*u* 36:5, *šá-lam* 239 r. i 8, *š*]*á-la-mu* 78 r. 1, *šá-lim* 252:11, 258:6, *ú-šal-li-mu* 33 r. 5,

šalānu "without": *š*]*á-la-nu-uš-šú* 239 r. ii 12,

šalāpu "to pull out, tear out": *li-šá-lip-ku-nu* 229 r. viii 25,

šalāqu "to cut, slit open": *šal-qa-at-u-ni* 229 r. vii 41, *šal-qa-tu-u-ni* 229 r. viii 52, *šal-qu-u-ni* 229 r. vii 45,

šalāšā "thirty": 30 126:21, 265:4, 6, 266:1, 267:7, 281:9, 288 ii 29, 33 287 r. 6,

šallussu "one third": 1:3 274 e. 11, 276:4,

šalmu "sound, whole, safe": *šal-m*[*e*] 234 r. 7,

šalšu "third": 3-*šú* 73:3,

šaluššeni "two years ago": *šá-lu-ši-ni* 117:10,

šamāru "to extol, praise": *il-ta-mar* 234:22,

šamaššammi "sesame": ŠE.GI[Š.Ì 263 r. 5,

šamê "heaven": AN 84:5, 89 r. 5, 171 r. 4, 192 r. 3, 226:2, 232:9, 273 r. 1, AN-*e* 162 r. 7, 229 i 25, 47, r. vi 52, 713, 230:18, 24, 231:4, 235:17, 239 ii 21, 22, 27, 262:8, AN-[*e* 229 r. v 86, AN-[*e*] 229 r. vii 21, AN]-*e* 239 i 10, 263 r. 6, A[N-*e* 257 r. 5, [AN]-*e* 229 r. vi 13, AN-*ú* 230:22,

šāmiu "hearer, listener": *šá-mi-u* 120:16,

šammu "drug, plant": *šam-me-šu* 234:21, *šam-mu* 229 iv 4, 261:9,

šamnu "oil": Ì.MEŠ 229 r. viii 16, 43, Ì.GIŠ 229 r. vii 13, 262:2, 3, 288 r. ii 6, Ì.GI[Š 298 r. 1,

šamšu "sun": ^{d}*šam-ši* 230:14, ^{d}*šam-šu* 230:10, ^{d}UTU-*ši* 229 i 14, 15,

šamû "to hear, heed; (Gtn) to listen": *a-šá-am-mu-ni* 120:5, *i-š*[*á-me*] 119 e. 25, *i-šam-me* 120:12, *i-šá-*[*mu-u-ni*] 139 e. 22, *liš-me* 283:4, *li-iš-me* 234 r. 9, *ni-iš-mu-u-ni* 238:4, *ni-šam*]*-mu-u-ni* 229 r. vi 89, [*še-ɑ*]*-i* 234:2, *ta-šá-m*[*a-a* 163:4, *ta-*[*šá*]*-qi-a-šú-ú-ni* 229 iv 5, *ta-šam-ma-a-ni* 229 r. v 1, *ta-ša*[*m-ma-a-ni*] 227 ii 6,

šamûtu "rain": *šam-u-te* 229 r. vi 13,

šandabakku (title of the governor of Nippur): LÚ.GÚ.EN.NA 263:4,

šaniš "alternatively; ditto": KI.MIN 227 i 2, 229 i 36, r. vii 17, 40, 60, 72, 812, 42, 55, 235:38, r. 21, [KI.MIN 235 r. 23, MIN 134 r. 1, 2, MIN] 229 i 30, 31, 32, 33, 34, 36, 38, [MIN] 229 i 35,

šaniu "deputy": LÚ.2-*e* 57:7, 229 i 4, LÚ.2-*u* 284:8, LÚ.2-*ú* 32:7, [L]Ú.2-*ú* 57:3,

šaniu B "second, other, different": MAN-*ma* 229 i 78, 79, MAN-*ma*] 229 i 77, *šá*]*-nam-ma* 130:5, [*šá-nim-ma*] 33:8, *šá-ni-t*[*i* 241 r. 11, *šá-ni-tu* 120 r. 18, *šá-ni-tu-um-ma* 120 r. 3, *šá-ni-iu-*[*u* 72 e. 9, 2-*u* 287 ii 6, 2-*u-te* 287 iii 5, 2-*ú* 284:4,

šanû "to be different, change; (D) to repeat; (Š) to change, alter": *li-il-tan-ni-šú* 126 r. 4, *lu-šá-an-*[*ni*] 234 r. 9, *šu-un-né-e*] 228:2, *tu-šá-an-na-a-ni* 229 i 62, *ul-te-en-ni* 178:7, *ú-šá-an-na-a* 260 r. 5, *ú-š*]*a-an-nu-ú-ši* 91:8,

šapal "under": KI.TA 229 r. vi 34, 765, K[I.TA 226 r. 4, *šap-la* 115 e. 8,

šapālu "to be low": *áš-šap-pil* 180:4,

šapartu "pledge": *šá-par-tu* 149 r. 3,

šapāru "to send": *al-ta-nap-pa-ra* 33:3, *al-tap-r*[*a* 86:7, *al-ta*[*p-ra* 86:4, *a*]*l-tap-ra* 172:5, 211 r. 3, *a*]*l-tap-r*[*a* 68 r. 6, *al-ta-áp-*[*ra* 83:4, *a-šap-p*[*ar*] 214 e. 3, *a-š*[*ap-par*] 161 r. 5, *a-ša*]*p-pa-rak-ku-nu-ši* 37 r. 11, *a-šap-par-*[*á*]*š-šú* 126:10, *a-šap-pa-ru* 126 r. 14, *áš-pur-an-ni* 140 r. 13, [*áš-pur-an-n*]*i* 145 r. 3, [*áš-pur*]*-an-ni* 105:5, [*áš-pu*]*r-an-ni* 18:7, *áš-pur-ka-a-ni* 154:6, *áš-pur-*[*k*]*e-e-ni* 154 r. 5, *áš-p*]*u-ram-ma* 78 r. 6, *á*]*š-pu-ru* 203:5, *a-sap-ra* 1:4, *a-sap-ra*] 1 r. 1, 44:2, [*a*]*-s*[*ap*]*-ra* 42 e. 6, *a-sa-par* 62:2, *a-sa-pa-ra* 152 r. 9, *a-šá-par-u-ni* 140 r. 20, *il-tapra* 126 r. 5, *il-tap-ra* 126 r. 6, *il-ta*[*p-ra* 138:8, *il-t*]*ap-ra* 82 r. 4, *i*]*l-tap-ra* 73:6, 221 r. 5, [*il-tap*]*-ra* 80:10, *i*]*l-tap-rak-k*[*a* 73 r. 3, [*il-tap*]*-ram-ma* 80:8, *il-tap-ra-an-na-šú* 182:6, *i*]*l-tap-ra-ni*[*š-šú* 137:6, *il-tap-ru* 247:7, *i*[*l-tap-ru* 175 r. 4, *il-t*]*ap-ru-ma* 247 r. 9, *il-*[[*tap-ru-ú-ni*]] 261 r. 4, *il-ta-n*]*ap-par-ru* 35:5, *i*]*l-ta-par* 40:8, *i*[*s-sa-par*] 67 r. 2, *iš-p*]*ur* 84 r. 9, *i*[*š-pur-an-na-ši*] 30 r. 4, *iš-pur-an-ni* 6:4, 12:6, 49:5, 62:4, 121:6, 217:6, 220:7, *iš-pur-an-*[*ni*] 9:5, *iš-pur-a*]*n-ni*

102:5, *iš-pur*]-*an-ni* 32:4, *iš-pu*[*r-an-ni*] 46:1, 151:3, *iš-*[*pur-an-ni*] 67:5, *iš-pu-ra* 82:3, *iš-pu-r*[*a* 172:6, *iš-pu-*[*ra* 68 r. 3, *iš*]-*pu-ra* 206:3, *i*]*š-pu-ra* 87:3, *i*]*š-pu-*[*ra* 172:11, [*i*]*š-pu-ra* 33:16, *iš-pu-ra-šú-ni* 51:2, *iš-pu-ru* 126:3, 128 r. 15, *i*[*š-pu-ru* 209 r. 3, [*iš-p*]*u-ru* 221 r. 11, *i-sa-ap-ar* 56:5, *i-sa-par* 240:13, *i-sa-pa-*[*ru-ni* 143:4, *i-šá-pa-ra-ni* 43 r. 2, *i*]-*šap-pa-ra* 17:3, *i-šap-pa-rak-kan-ni* 1:13, *i-š*]*ap-pa-ra-ni* 37 r. 12, *i-šap-pa-ru* 247 r. 9, *i-šap-pa-ru-nik-ka* 235:44, KIN 247 r. 18, KIN.NAM 262 r. 6, KI[N-*š*]*ú-ma* 247:4, *liš-pur* 106 r. 6, [*liš-pur* 120 r. 24, [*liš-pur*] 247:6, *liš-pur-an-ni* 129 r. 16, *liš-pur-na-a-*[*šú*] 139:3, [*liš-pu*]*r-ú-ni* 33:19, *liš-pu-ra* 124:7, [*lu-uš-pu-r*]*u* 129:17, *ni-šap-p*[*a-ra*] 189 e. 3, *šup-ra* 163 r. 8, 279 r. 5, *šup-ra*] 163:5, *šu*[*p-ra* 38:8, [*šu*]-*pur* 119 e. 25, *taš-pur-an-*[*ni*] 116 r. 3, *taš-pu-*[*ra* 5:5, *ta-*[*áš-pu-ra*] 144:2, *ta-š*]*ap-pa-ru* 86:4,

šaplāti "lower parts, netherworld": *šap-la-a*]*t* 226:7,

šapliš "below": *šap-liš* 229 r. vi 57,

šaplû "lower": KI.[TA-*tum* 254:11,

šapputu (a large wine jar, "jug"): ŠAB 212:1, *šap-pa-*[*a-te*] 288 iv 13,

šaptu "lip, edge": NUNDUN 164 r. 3, NUNDUN.2-*ka* 230:16, *šap-ti* 229 r. v 51,

šāqiu "cupbearer": LÚ.KAŠ.LUL 253 r. 8,

šaqû "to let drink": *ta-*[*šá*]-*qi-a-šú-ú-ni* 229 iv 5,

šaqû B "to be high": *šá-qa-ta* 230:9, 231:3, *šá-qu-ti* 234:11, *šá-q*[*u-ú* 230:30,

šarāhu "to be glorious; (D) to glorify": *lu-šá-ri-ih* 233:3, *šar-hu* 11:6, *ú-šar-ri-ha* 233:13,

šarāku "to bestow": *liš-ruk* 251:6, *liš-ru-ku-nik-ka* 127:8, *šá-ra-kim-ma* 232 r. 5, *šá-ri-k*[*at* 230:25,

šarāpu "to burn": *a*]*l-ta-ra-pi* 168:2, *iš-šar-rap-u-ni*] 229 r. viii 3,

šarāṭu "to tear; (D) to to tear into strips, shred": *ú-šar-ri-ṭi* 234 r. 3,

šarku "pus, suppuration": *šar-ku* 229 r. vi 42,

šarrāqu "thief": LÚ.*šar-ra-qa* 239 ii 30,

šarratu "queen, lady": *šar-rat* 235:6,

šarru "king": LUGAL 1:1, 6:3, 4, 6, 8:1, 3, 4, 9:1, 3, 10:3, 12:3, 4, 6, 9, 12:1, 3, 15:4, 17:5, 18:3, 4, 5, 6, 19:1, 2, 6, 21:2, 26:1, 3, r. 5, 27:1, 4, 28:3, 29:2, 7, 9, 29:5, r. 3, 4, 5, 31:2, 3, 4, 8, 13, 32:1, 4, r. 3, 33:4, 5, 12, 13, 18, 20, r. 6, 9, 37 r. 10, 38:6, 7, 40:8, 9, 41:2, 5, 43:4, 5, r. 1, 44:2, 45:5, 47:6, 48:1, 2, 48:5, r. 2, 53 r. 5, 58:3, 61:2, 63:3, 64:2, 64:4, 5, 66:2, 67:5, r. 2, 5, 69:9, 71 r. 2, 74 r. 3, 76 r. 4, 6, 82 r. 2, 85:5, 9, 86:3, 7, 92 r. 2, 94:1, 94:1, 3, 96:1, 3, 97:1, 3, 98:1, 2, 98:1, 3, 100:3, 102:1, 3, 5, 6, 103:3, 109:3, r. 1, 111 r. 6, 112 r. 2, 113:c 8, 114:1, 117:4, 7, 12, 119:1, 6, 120:1, 3, 4, 6, 8, 11, 14, r. 4, 13, 16, 17, 22, 23, 24, 25, 121:4, 6, 8, 124:1, 3, 5, 6, 126:2, 3, 16, r. 2, 11, 12, 14, 128:9, r. 12, 15, 129:1, 4, 7, 12, 16, 17, r. 13, 15, 17, 135:1, 3, 7, 146:3, 4, 149 r. 7, 150:5, 152 r. 9, 158:2, 162 r. 9, 11, 166:2, 6, 7, 167 r. 1, 2, 4, 168:8, r. 11, 13, 169 r. 4, 171:9, r. 6, 8, 175 r. 4, 176 r. 1, 177:3, r. 1, 178:7, 179 r. 6, 7, 182:3, 5, 183:4, r. 9, 184:7, 188:5, 195:5, 208:5, 6, 213:1, 5, 214 e. 3, 217:2, 3, 218:6, 7, 220:8, 221 r. 10, 223 r. 1, 3, 228:3, 228:1, i 77, 79, r. v 71, 87, vii 90, 231:5, 235:2, 5, 23, r. 23, 38, 43, 49, 51, 236:13, r. 11, 237 r. 1, 2, 5, 6, 7, 12, 18, 19, 20, 238:3, 239 ii 3, 15, 16, 25, 35, r. i 1, 10, 23, 30, 243:5, 6, 247:2, 5, r. 7, 248:4, 251:5, 252 r. 14, 253 r. 8, 255 r. 5, 258:1, 8, r. 2, 260 r. 8, 261 r. 3, 6, 262 r. 2, 263:3, 5, 6, 264:3, r. 1, 3, 265:1, 2, 3, 6, 266:5, 273 r. 4, 275 r. 8, 276 r. 12, 277 r. 6, 279:1, r. 5, 280:1, 4, 10, r. 10, 14, 15, 282:6, 288 ii 31, 295:2, 297:4, 299 i 4, 6, 7, 8, 9, 12, 13, 16, 300:8, LUGAL] 8:5, 12:1, 26:4, r. 7, 33:11, 77 r. 9, 105:4, 7, 109 r. 3, 114:4, 119:3, 121:1, r. 6, 128 r. 13, 133:8, 148 r. 6, 7, 202:5, 216:2, 217:5, 235:1, 2, 239 r. i 6, LUGA[L 30:7, 77 r. 5, 88:6, 103:1, 168 r. 9, 171:11, 217:8, 297:4, LUGA[L] 295:4, LUGA]L 68 r. 5, 93 r. 2, LUG[AL 133:2, 195 r. 1, 221 r. 11, 236 r. 13, LUG]AL 10:1, 15:5, 18:8, 22:5, 25 s. 1, 62:4, 67 r. 3, 121:3, 145 r. 2, 152 r. 10, 184:10, 206:9, 208:2, 216 r. 10, LU[GAL 30:6, 128 r. 14, 198:3, 7, 245 r. 3, 264:1, LU[GA]L 36:6, LU]GAL 15:2, 18:1, r. 2, 22 r. 9, 33 r. 8, 35:3, 118:5, 136 r. 10, 138:2, 151:3, 161:1, 195:2, 239 r. i 4, 262:9, LU]GA[L 213 r. 8, L[UGAL 52:6, 67:1, 100:4, 101:1, 114 r. 4, 147:11, 297:2, L[UGAL] 295:5, L]UGAL 177 r. 4, 182 r. 12, 299 i 5, L]UGA[L 41:3, [LUGAL 28:1, 33:1, 51:2, 58 r. 2, 64 r. 4, 66 r. 2, 68:13, 18, 94:4, 100:1, 114:3, 128 r. 10, 138:8, 149:1, 173:3, 179 r. 3, 189 e. 3, r. 1, 198:2, 239 ii 2, 249 r. 7, [LUGAL] 20:1, 27:3, 231:6, [LUG]AL 22 r. 2, 133:4, [LU]GAL 235:1, 255 r. 10, [L]UGAL 29:4, 33:3, 126 r. 15, LUGAL-*ka* 128:12, LUGAL-*ku-nu-*[*ma* 241 r. 7, [LUGAL-*ma* 125:2, LUGAL.MEŠ 74:2, 173:4, 235:10, 14, 40, 43, 51, r. 12, 44, 46, 239 i 4, 7, 8, ii 34, r. i 7, 20, 32, ii 8, 13, 19, 260 r. 6, LUGAL.MEŠ] 136:1, LUGAL.ME[Š 260 r. 7, LUGAL.ME[Š] 235:32, LUGAL.M[EŠ 236 r. 12, LUGAL.M[EŠ] 235:45, r. 2, LUGAL.[MEŠ 235 r. 40, LUGAL.[MEŠ] 235:26, r. 48, 239 ii 19, [LUGAL.MEŠ] 136:4, MAN 46:1, 4, 120:2, r. 12, 23, s. 1, 145:2, 226:3, 4, 227 ii 1, 10, 229 i 1, 2, 16, 18, 46, 64, iv 4, 10, r. v 24, 34, 45, 56, 64, 66, 70, 78, 83, vi 78, 82, vii 2, 5, 11, viii 26, 29, 233:1, 5, 6, 243 r. 6, 250 r. 9, 279 r. 8, s. 1, 2, 287 iii 10, 300 i 18, 300 r. 1, MAN] 226:8, [MAN 46:6, 228:6, 250 r. 8, 252 r. 5,

šarrūtu "kingship, kingdom": LUGAL-*te* 229 ii 1, LUGAL-*ti* 229 r. v 27, 288 r. ii 6, LUGAL-*t*[*i* 229 i 75, [LU]GAL-*tu* 119 e. 28, LUGAL-*u-t*[*u* 229 i 66, LUGAL-*u-tú* 229 i 16, LUGAL-*ú-tu* 126 r. 3, 129 r. 11, 239 i 5, LUGAL-*ú-tum* 230:7, LUGAL-*ú-tú* 180 r. 4, 239 i 14,

šāru "wind": *šá-a-ra* 234:13,

šarūru "radiance, ray": *ša-ru-ur* 230:14, *š*[*á*]-*ru-ru* 269 r. 1, *šá-ru-ru-šú* 264:1,

šasû "to shout, read": *al-si* 164:2, [*al*]-*ta-si* 33:2, *il-si* 239 ii 8, *i*]-*šá-as-si* 174:5, *li-il-s*[*u*] 70:10,

šāšu "him": *šá-a-*[*šú*] 128 r. 7,

šāšunu "them": *šá-šú-nu* 84:10,

šatammu "prelate": LÚ].ŠÀ.TAM 19:12, LÚ.ŠÀ.TAM 19:10,

šatāqu "to cut": DAR-*át* 252:17,

šattu "year": MU.AN.NA 176 e. 4, 235:35, MU.AN.N[A] 242 r. 1, MU.AN.[N]A 130:2, MU.[AN.NA] 239 r. i 17, MU].AN.NA 12:8, M[U.AN.NA] 256:3, MU.AN.NA.ME 133:15, MU.AN.NA.MEŠ 235:34, 239 r. i 33, M]U.AN.NA.MEŠ 239 r. ii 24,

šatû "to drink": *i-šat-t*[*u-ú* 217:5, *li-is-si-a* 1 r. 13, NAG 235 r. 43, 247 r. 5, N[AG] 262 r. 1, NAG-*e* 261:9, NAG-*ú* 247 r. 3,

šaṭāpu "to save, preserve": *šu-ṭi-ip* 232 r. 3,
šaṭāru "to write": *as-sa-ṭar* 120 r. 20, *a-sa-[ṭar]* 105:6, *[a]-sa-ṭar* 14 r. 4, *i]l-ta-ṭar* 194:2, *is-sa-ṭar* 229 r. v 15, 22, *iš-šá-ṭar-ni* 146 e. 14, *iš-ṭur-u-ni* 147 r. 10, *iš-ṭu-[ru]* 179 r. 3, *iš-ṭu-[ru-ni]* 107 r. 2, *liš-ṭ[ur* 150:4, *niš-ṭ[ur* 237 r. 22, SAR 77 r. 8, 247:10, r. 12, *šá-aṭ-ru* 14 r. 5, *šá]-aṭ-ru* 226:9, *šá-ṭí-ir* 233 r. 15, *šá-ṭir* 126:4, 264 r. 3, 276 r. 9, *šá-ṭir-u-ni* 229 r. v 70, *šaṭ-ru* 237 r. 18, 287 iii 19, *šaṭ-ru-ma* 247:3, 8, r. 8, *[šaṭ-ru-ma* 247 r. 10, *šaṭ-ṭa-ru-ú-ma* 248:2, *šu-ṭur* 120 r. 20, *š]u-ṭur-a-nim-ma* 38:8,
šaṭṭāru "copy, document, text": *šaṭ-ṭar-a-[ni* 270:5,
ša-arīti "shield-man, (regular) spearman" LÚ.*a-[ri-ti]* 229 i 10,
ša-KAR.SA (an object, rdg. unkn.): *šá*-KAR.SA 288 iv 10,
ša lā "without": *ša—la* 120:4, 8,
ša-lišāni "informer": LÚ.EME 10:5,
ša-muhhi-āli "city overseer": LÚ.*šá*—UGU—URU 120:13, 18, r. 11, s. 2, LÚ.*šá*—[UGU—URU] 1 e. 19,
ša-muhhi-[...] "overseer of [...]": LÚ.U[GU—*x* 81:2,
ša-pān-ēkalli "palace supervisor": LÚ.*šá*—IGI—É.G[AL] 141:1, LÚ.*šá*—IGI—KUR 284:4, L]Ú.*šá*—IGI—KUR-*ú-ti* 284 r. 2, *šá—pa-an*—É.GA[L] 280 r. 4,
ša-pān-sūqi "supervisor of the streets": *šá*—IGI—SILA 287 ii 17,
ša-pattûti "open chariotry": DU_8.MEŠ 287 ii 4, 8,
ša-qassi "bowman": LÚ.GIŠ.B[AN 137:7, LÚ.GIŠ.[BAN 89 r. 2, [LÚ].GIŠ.BAN.MEŠ 74 r. 1,
ša-qurbūti "royal bodyguard": LÚ.*qur-bu-te* 1:3, 120 r. 23, LÚ.*qur-bu-ti* 1:12, 5 r. 5, LÚ.*qur-[bu-ti* 5:7, LÚ.*qur-b[u-tu* 36 r. 3, *qur*-ZAG 284:5, 8, 287 ii 4,
ša-rēši "eunuch": LÚ.SAG 52:6, 65:4, 280 r. 10, LÚ.SA[G 282 e. 5, LÚ.SA[G] 177 r. 2, LÚ.S[AG 68 r. 1, 229 ii 5, L[Ú.SAG 228:2, LÚ.SAG-*ka* 235 r. 20, LÚ.SAG.MEŠ 81:5, 235 r. 14, LÚ.SA[G.MEŠ 81:6, LÚ.SAG.MEŠ-*šú* 235 r. 12,
ša-ṣilli "parasol": *ša*—GIŠ.MI 288 iv 2,
ša-šadādi "rickshaw": *šá—šá-da-di* 288 iv 12,
ša-šīmi "bought slave": LÚ.ŠÁM.M[EŠ] 243 r. 7,
ša-ziqni "bearded (courtier)": LÚ.*ša—zi]q-ni* 228:2, LÚ.*šá—ziq-ni* 279:3, LÚ.*šá—ziq-ni]* 229 ii 4,
šeʾu "corn": ŠE 105:3, 271:9, 279 r. 1, ŠE-*im* 263 r. 5,
šebû "to be satisfied; (D) to sate, satisfy": *šub-bi-ma* 237:5,
šēdu "genie": *še-e-du* 229 r. vi 76,
šēhu "frenzy(?); eminent": *ši-hu* 164 r. 11,
šelaltu "one-third": *še-lal-ti* 234 r. 1,
šemû "to hear, heed": *al-t]e-mu-ú* 129:16, *a-šem-mu-ú* 126 r. 13, *iš-me-e* 234:15, *iš-mu-ú* 29:7, 128:8, *[iš-mu]-ú* 80:2, *i-iš-mu-ú* 234:7, *i-šem-mu* 76:5, *i-še[m-mu-u* 298 r. 3, *i-šem-mu-ú* 211:7, *lu-uš-mu* 235 r. 46, *niš-me-e-ma* 33 r. 8, *ni-il]-te-mu-ú* 190:2, *nu-šá-áš-mu-ú* 197:5, [ŠE.GA-*ú* 246:8, *ul-t]e-eš-mi* 184:6,
šenu "shoe": K]UŠ.*še-n[i* 262:4,
šēpu "foot": GÌR.2 266:3, 287 ii 4, iii 3, 288 ii 21, GÌR.2-*ka* 235:13, GÌR.2.MEŠ 288 ii 32, GÌR.2.M[EŠ-*ka* 230:33, GÌR.2.MEŠ-*ku-nu* 229 r. vii 47, GÌR.2.MEŠ-*šú-nu* 229 r. viii 20, GÌR.2-*šú* 235:30, 237 r. 11, GÌR.2-*šú-nu* 229 r. vii 45,

šerʾtu (a divine garment): [TÚG.*še-er-ʾa-i-tu* 240:6,
šeššā "sixty": 61 285 e. 25,
šî "she, it": *ši-i* 104:4, 120:19, 122:5, 143:3, 235:25, *ši-i]* 240:9, [*ši-i* 240:1,
šiāmu "to decree, destine": *li-šim* 239 r. i 32, *li-ši-im* 229 r. vi 6, *li-ši-im-ku-nu* 229 r. v 79, *li-ši-mu* 229 r. vi 68, *mu-šim* 229 r. v 78,
šiāṭu "to be negligent, neglect": *i-š]i-ia-aṭ* 74 r. 2,
šiʾšiʾ "hush-hush": *ši-iʾ—ši-iʾ* '154:9,
šību "elder; witness": LÚ.IGI 21 r. 5,
šiddu "along(side); a unit of length, "stadium": *ši-da-at* 234:14, *šid-di* 31 r. 6,
šihlu "second-best; replacement": *ši-ih-li* 66 r. 8, *ši-ih-[li* 140 r. 4, *ši-ih-lu* 286:4, 9, 11, *ši-i]h-lu* 286:7,
šihṭu "attack, foray": *ši-ih-ṭu* 246 r. 5, 247:9, r. 11,
šikāru "beer": KAŠ 229 r. vii 32, 34, 262 r. 1, [KAŠ 262:3, KAŠ.S]AG 262:13,
šiknu "setting, nature": *šik-na-a-[ni]* 288 r. i 5, *šik-na-n[i]* 288 r. i 18, [[*ši-ik-ni* 261 r. 5, *ši-ik-nu* 261:7, *ši-kín* 230:15,
šīlu "hole": BÙR 252:12, 13, [BÙR 252:5,
šīmtu "fate, destiny": NAM.MEŠ 229 r. v 78, viii 59, *šim-ti* 229 r. v 25, *šim-ti-ku-nu* 229 r. vi 6, 68, *ši-mat* 229 r. v 79, *ši-mat-ku-nu* 229 r. vi 72, *ši-ma-a-ti* 126:6,
šīmu "price, purchase": ŠÁM 275:4, 276:5,
šina "1. they; 2. two": *ši-na* 11:10, 240:6,
šina B "two": 2-*ma* 248 r. 4, 253:6, 2-*m]a* 247 r. 13,
šīnāti "urine": KÀŠ 229 r. vi 74, 271:11, KÀŠ.MEŠ 115 r. 1,
šingutu (mng. unkn.): *ši-in-ga-ti* 229 r. v 42,
šinīšu "twice": 2-*šú* 73:3, 119 s. 1,
šinnu "tooth": ZÚ 288 ii 19, ZÚ.MEŠ-*ka* 230:19,
šipirtu "message": *ši-pir-ta-a* 33:8, *ši-pir-ti* 126:3, 4, 140 r. 12, *ši-pir-[ti* 171:3, *ši-pi[r-ti* 171:10,
šipru "art, ruse; message": *ši-pir* 229 r. v 76,
šiptu "incantation": ÉN 262 r. 6, *ši-pat-sa* 288 r. ii 12,
šiqlu "shekel": GÍN 165 r. 6, 181 r. 3, 271:8, r. 1, 274 e. 11,
širʾānu "muscle, sinew": *ši-ir-ʾa-an-šú-nu* 234:17,
šīru "flesh": UZU 127:5, 136:4, 229 r. v 84, vi 26, 28, 741, 80, 262 r. 1, 273 r. 13, UZU] 251:5, U]ZU 237 r. 14, UZU.ME 229 r. vi 45, UZU.MEŠ 229 r. vii 42, 63, 75, 79, 82, viii 16, 18, 246 r. 7, 261 r. 5, UZU.[MEŠ] 255 r. 8, UZU.MEŠ-*ku-nu* 229 r. vii 9, 63, 75, 79, 82, viii 17, UZU.M[EŠ]-*ku-nu* 229 r. vi 29,
šīti "she, it": *ši-ti* 49:1, *ši-ti]-ni* 45:4,
šitta "two": 2-*ta* 235:34,
šittūtu "remainder, rest": [*ši-i]t-tu-tu* 74 r. 6,
šizbu "milk": [*ši-iz-bu* 240:1,
šû "he": *šu-u* 120:3, 6, 20, r. 1, 4, 10, 21, s. 2, *šu-[u]* 242:2, [*š]u-u* 52:6, *šu-ú* 21 r. 2, 69:12, 71:3, 76 r. 1, 80:2, 84 r. 14, 128:13, r. 4, 204:8, 211:2, 212 r. 4, 235:47, 237 r. 10, 240:7, 9, 12, 14, 279:7, *šu-ú]* 21 r. 8, 116 r. 2, 240:6, 264 r. 2, *šu-[ú* 10:5, *šu]-ú* 173:6, [*šu-ú* 72 r. 3, [*šu-ú]* 140:19, *šú-ú* 17 r. 5, 72 r. 7, 136 r. 4, 172 r. 4, 188:6, *šú-[ú* 80:6, UR_5

2 37:12, r. 14,

šuātu "that": MU-*a-ti* 277 r. 4, MU-*tim* 276 r. 3, *šu-a-tu* 214:1, *šu-a-tú* 298 r. 4, *šu*]-*a-tú* 298 r. 4, *šú-a-tú* 288 r. ii 4, UR$_5$-*tú* 253 r. 2,

šuā'u "to float, fly": *li-šá-i* 234:13,

šubtu "seat, settlement; ambush": DAG.MEŠ-*š*[*ú* 255:2, *šub-tú* 239 ii 17, *šu-bat* 230:18, 252:12,

šuglû "deportee": *š*]*u-gu-lu-ú* 72 r. 3,

šuhattu "cloth, rag": TÚG.KUR.RA-*šú* 128:14,

šulmānu "present, bribe": *šul-m*[*a-ni* 89 r. 3, *šul-man-nu* 120 r. 15,

šulmu "health, well-being": DI-*mu* 6:3, 12:3, 13:3, 4, 19:2, 26:3, 28:4, 48:2, 95:3, 102:3, 113:c 6, 114:3, 6, 8, 119:3, 121:3, 124:3, 140:3, 155:3, 264 r. 1, DI-*m*[*u* 28:5, DI-[*mu* 103:3, DI-[[*mu* 261 r. 3, DI]-*mu* 131:3, D[I-*mu* 28:3, 141:4, D[I-*mu*] 18:4, D]I-*mu* 18:3, 27:4, 129:7, 145:8, [DI-*mu* 100:3, [DI-*mu*] 67:2, [DI]-*mu* 8:3, 113:c2, SILIM 248 r. 4, 252:5, *šul-mu* 29:2, *šul-m*[*u* 96:1, *šul*-[*mu* 97:3, *šu*[*l-mu* 94:3, 98:3, *šu*]*l-mu* 98:2, *š*]*ul-mu* 9:3, 10:3, *šu-lu*[*m* 239 ii 12, U]ZU.SILIM 196:5,

šuluhhu "purification ritual": *šu-luh-hi-šú-un*] 297:6,

šumēlu "left, south": GÙB 229 r. viii 30, 32, KAB 261 e. 14, 287 ii 1, [KA]B-*ka* 230:29, KAB-*šá* 91:3, KAB-*šú* 264:3, *šu*-[*me-li-ka*] 239 ii 7, 150 237 r. 12, 247 r. 13, 248 r. 3, 5, 250:4, r. 1, 252:6, 12, 13, 253:6, 255:3, 6, 258:2, 150] 252:1, 150-*šú* 237:12,

šumma "if": BE 248 r. 5, 6, 249:2, 4, 6, r. 2, 250:1, 2, 3, 4, 5, 6, 7, 8, 9, 10, 11, r. 1, 252:1, 5, 6, 7, 15, 16, 17, 253:4, 6, 254:1, 2, 4, 5, 6, 7, 8, 10, 11, 255:1, 2, 3, 6, 299:3, [BE 247 r. 13, 251 r. 1, 252:9, 10, 11, 12, 13, 258:2, [BE] 249 r. 5, BE-*m*[*a* 260 r. 2, *šum-ma* 115 r. 3, 229 i 62, 68, 80, iv 3, r. v 3, 5, 9, 16, 24, 31, 37, 41, 49, 54, 73, vi 77, 84, vii 1, viii 26, 243:5, [*šum-ma* 21:13, 229 iv 8, *šúm-ma* 18 r. 3, [*šúm-ma* 227 ii 1, 228:1, *šúm-mu* 60 r. 4, 67 r. 3, [*šúm-m*]*u* 46:4,

šumru "praise(?)": *šum-ru* 232:8,

šumu "name": MU 226 r. 6, 241 r. 10, 275 r. 7, 276 r. 11, MU-*ku-nu* 229 r. vi 8, vi í9, 36, viii 59, MU.MEŠ 6:5, 184:5, 231:7, 241 r. 9, MU.MEŠ-*ku-nu* 229 r. vi 67, 716, MU.NE 126:2, MU-*šú* 280:7, MU-*šú-nu* 226:9, 229 r. vii 18, MU-*šú*-(*nu*) 229 r. vi 54, *šum-ka* 239 i 4, *šu-mu* 128 r. 9, *šú-man-ni* 212 r. 5,

šunannu "a kind of tray": *šu-na-nu* 288 iv 11,

šunu "they": *šu-nu* 173:6, 240:3, 5, *š*[*u*]-*nu* 33:12, [*šu-nu* 240:14, [*šu-nu*]-*u-ni* 10:5, *šú-nu* 82:2, 122 r. 4, 136 r. 14, 221:8, 240:6, 10, *š*]*ú-nu* 181 r. 5,

šunūti "these, those, them": *šu-nù-ti* 247:6, 12, *šu-n*[*ù-ti*] 247:7,

šupālītu halluptu "reinforced lower garment": KI.TA—*hal*-[*pat*] 288 r. i 12, 14, KI.TA—*h*[*al-pat.*MEŠ] 288 iii 25, *šu-pa-li-ti* 220:5,

šupêlu "(Š only) to change, exchange": *uš-pe-el-lu* 247 r. 5,

šuptu "dwelling": *šu-pa-ta-ni* 234:12,

šuqdu "almond": *šuq-di* 288 iv 70,

šūr īni "eyebrow": SIG$_7$—IGI.2.MEŠ-*ka* 230:13,

šurbû "exalted": *šur-bu-tu* 252 r. 12,

šurkānu "gift": *šur-ka-a-na* 232 r. 1,

šurmēnu "cypress": GIŠ.ŠUR.MÌN 239 i 26,

šurruhu "glorified": *šur-ru-uh* 233:5,

šūši "sixty": I.ŠU 126:18,

šušuriš "straight away": *šu-šu-riš* 237:1,

šuttu "dream": MÁŠ.MI 120:19, [MÁŠ].MI 252 r. 1, MÁŠ.MI-*ia* 120:20, MÁŠ.MI-*šú* 262 r. 4, *šu-ut-ti* 220:10,

šūtu "he": *šu-tu-ma* 199 r. 4, *šu-tu-u* 240:14, *šu-tú* 121 r. 7, *š*]*u-u-tú* 240:7,

tabāku "to pour, shed": *i-t*[*a-bak*] 128 r. 8, *i-tab-ba*[*k* 187:9, *i-tab-ku* 182:5, *tab-kàt* 234:8, *tab-ku* 274 r. 4, *ta-ta-bak-a-ni* 229 iv 1,

tabālu "to carry away; (astron.) to disappear": *it-bal-ši-ma* 251 r. 1, *ta-bal* 262:12,

tabû "to rise, get up; (stat.) loose": *te-bi*] 255:6, ZI-*bi* 248 r. 5,

tadānu "to give": *ad-din* 208:5, *a-ta-na-áš-šu* 19:19, *at-ta-na-áš-šú* 120 r. 20, *at-ti-din* 143:1, *at-ti-d*[*i-in*] 162 r. 4, *di-in* 239 ii 26, 247:18, *di-i-ni* 280:3, [*d*]*i-i-ni* 280:5, *di-n*[*a* 168 r. 10, *di-ni* 151:5, *id-dak-ka* 239 r. ii 11, *id-da-áš-šú* 126:21, *id-da-na-ši* 145:6, *id-din* 275:5, *id-din-nu-ni-šú* 126:20, *id*]-*di-na* 200:2, *id-di-nu* 280:11, *id-di*-[*nu*] 280 r. 1, *i*]*d-di-nu* 200:4, *id-di-nu-ni* 120 r. 2, *id-du-nu-na-ši* 123 r. 6, *it-tan-n*[*a* 31 r. 5, *it-tan-nu* 185:4, *it-ta-an-na* 120:22, *it-ta-an-nu-ni* 19:17, *it-ta-an-nu-ni-šu* 120 r. 2, *it-ta-na* 235 r. 45, *i*]*t-ta-na-na-ši* 282:3, *it-ti-din* 120 r. 21, 123:6, 12, *i*]*t-ti-di-ni* 121 r. 5, *i-da-an* 120:12, *i-da-nu-ni* 124 r. 2, *i-di-na* 281:11, *i-di-ni* 196:4, *i-ta-na* 281:14, [*i-t*]*a-nu-ni-ši* 108 r. 2, *i-ti-d*[*in*] 281:16, *la-din-a*]*k-ka* 3:4, *lid-di-nam-ma* 164:9, *lid-di-nu* 1 r. 17, 120:2, 130 r. 3, *lid-di-nu-u* 239 i 3, *lid-di-nu-nu* 219 r. 5, *l*]*i-din* 22:7, *li-di-nu* 124 r. 5, *li-d*[*i-nu*] 255 r. 5, *nid-din* 33 r. 9, *n*[*i-id-din*] 31 r. 7, SU]M 285 r. 3, S UM-*nu* 275:1, 276:2, 277:2, *ta*]-*da-a-nu* 66 r. 7, *ta-da-na* 147 r. 8, *ta-du-nu* 88:3,

tāhāzu "battle": MÈ 226 r. 3, 229 r. vi 32, 237 r. 1, 15, *ta-ha-zi-šú* 233:9, *ta-ha-zu* 239 ii 10,

tahūmu "border, territory": *ta*]-*hu-mu-ma* 66 r. 9,

taiāru (mng. unknown, perhaps "leftover, revenue"): *ta-a-a-r*[*u*] 234 r. 14,

takālu "to trust; (D) to give confidence, faith": *tak-la*-[*x* 132:10, *tak-lu* 282:8, [*tu*]*k-ku-la-a-ta* 127:3,

takkussu "tube": *tak-ku-si* 229 r. vii 56,

takpirtu "purification": *t*[*ak-pir-tú* 115 r. 4,

taktīmu "cover, covering": *tak-ti-im-ku-nu* 229 r. vi 75,

talbuštu "clothing, costume": *tal-bu-uš-ti* 241 r. 1,

talittu "birth, natlaity": *ta-lit-tú* 229 r. vi 9,

tallultu "trappings": *tal-lul-tú* 288 iv 1,

tamhāru "battle": *tam-ha-ru* 237 r. 2, 13, 16,

tamirtu "meadow": *ta-me-ra-a-ti-ku-nu* 229 r. vi 14, *ta-me-ra-te*-[*ku*]-*nu* 229 r. vii 23,

tamītu "oath; oracle query": *ta-mit* 246 r. 1, 7, 247 r. 6, *ta-mì-ti* 229 r. v 49, *ta-mì-tú* 120 r. 8, 229 r. v 44, 50, vii 54, viii 17, [*t*]*a-mi-it-su-nu* 33:18,

tamkāru "merchant": LÚ.DAM.QAR 280 r. 14,

tamlû "terrace": *tam-le-e* 126:20,

tâmtu "sea": *tam-ti* 127:7,

tamû "to swear": *at*-[*t*]*a*-[*ma*] 117:8, *a*[*t-ta-ma*] 262:8, *it-ma-a* 235 r. 34, *it-mi-šum* 176 r. 6, *it-mu-n*[*in* 232:7, *ta-ɑ-ku-nu* 229 r. v 48, *ta-tam-ma-a-ni* 229 r. v 52, *ta-tam-ma-a-n*[*i*] 229 i 79, *ta-tam-ma-ni* 229 r. v 51, *ti-ma* 120 r. 9, [*ti-tam-ma*] 229 i 29, *ú-tam-ma-na-a-ši* 229 r. v 8, 15, 23,

tanattu "praise": *ta-na-da-te* 233:5, *ta-na-ta-*

k[*a* 230:2,

tanēhu "sighing, weariness, exhaustion": *ta-né-hi* 229 r. vi 69, *ta-né-hu* 229 r. vi 41, *ta-ni-hu* 229 r. v 83,

tangussu "small copper kettle": URUDU.ŠEN.TUR 271 r. 1,

tanittu "praise, eulogy": *ta-nit-ti-ka* 232:8,

tarāṣu "to stretch out": *i*]*t-ta-ra-aṣ* 31:14,

tarāṣu B "to be proper, in order, all right": *t*]*a-ra-ṣi* 242 r. 4, [*tar-ṣa-tú-u-ni* 229 ii 2, *ta-ri-*[*iṣ* 140:18,

tarbāṣu "courtyard, pen; halo": TÙR 287 iii 14,

tarbiu "trainee, apprentice": BULÙG.MEŠ 287 ii 15,

tārītu "nurse, nanny": *ta-ret-ku-un* 229 r. vi 12, *ta-ri-is-su* 229 ii 1,

tarsītu "proper preparation": *tar-si-it* 288 r. ii 14,

tarṣu "reach, time of": *tar-ṣi* 231:5,

târu "to return; to turn into": *i-tar-ma* 74 r. 5, *i-tur-r*]*u* 74 r. 7, *i*]*-tu-ru-nim-ma* 280:9, *l*]*i-tu-ra* 129:21, *lu-tir-am-m*[*a* 134:5, *ta-at-tur* 176 r. 4, [*ta-a*]*-ri* 280:10, *ta-a-ru-ú* 234 r. 20, *ut-tir* 165:8, 213:6, see also *tuāru,*

taṣlīltu "prayer, petition, plea": *ta-aṣ-lil-ti-šú* 288 r. ii 9,

tašlīšu "third man (in a chariot team)": LÚ.3-*šú* 284:6, LÚ.3-*šú*.MEŠ 122 r. 2, LÚ].3.U$_5$-*ia* 66 r. 4, LÚ.3.U$_5$.MEŠ 229 i 5, [L]Ú.3.U$_5$.M[EŠ] 140 r. 14, LÚ.3].U$_5$.MEŠ-*ni* 66 r. 1, 3-*šú*.MEŠ 287 ii 2, 18, iii 3,

tašrītu (Tishri, name of the 7th month): ITI.DU$_6$ 140 r. 8, 254 r. 4, [ITI].DU$_6$ 267 r. 10, ITI].DUL 12:5,

tēltu "saying, proverb": *ti-ìl-tu* 11:7,

têrtu "oracle, liver omen, liver": UR$_5$.ÚŠ 246 r. 9, 248 r. 7, UR$_5$.[ÚŠ-*ka*] 255:4,

tēšû "anarchy, confusion": *te-še-e* 265:5, *te-šu-ú* 234:9,

tibnu "straw": ŠE.IN.NU 271:10,

tību "attack": ZI-*bu* 247 r. 11, Z]I-*bu* 247:9, ZI-*ib* 249:1, 5,

tīku "raindrop, mist": *t*]*i-ki* 229 r. vi 51,

tillē "equipment, trappings": [G]IŠ.*til-li*.MEŠ 140:9, TÚG.*til-le-e-šú* 271:2,

tinūru "oven": [NINDU 229 r. vi 18,

tīrāni "coils, spirals": ŠÀ.NIGIN 248 r. 6, 248 e. 8, 250 r. 1, 252:11, [ŠÀ.NIGIN 247 r. 14, [Š]À.NIGIN 255:4,

tirku "throbbing": *ti-rik-ka* 239 ii 17,

tuāru "to turn, return; (D) to turn into, restore": G]UR 255:10, GUR.MEŠ 248 r. 6, 250 r. 2, *i-tu-ra*] 237 r. 4, [*mu-tir* 297:7, *tir* 232:10, *tur-ri* 229 r. v 43, *tur-ru* 275:6, *tu-tar-ra-a-ni* 229 r. v 41, *tu-tar-ra-a-ni-ni* 229 iv 2, *ú-tar* 243:4, *ú-tir-šú* 280:8, see also *târu,*

tubqu "corner, region": UB.MEŠ 226:8,

tuessu "maggot, worm": *tu-es-su* 229 r. vii 64, see also *tūltu,*

tukultu "trust, support": *tuk-lat-ka* 239 ii 5, *tuk-lat-su* 234:3,

tūltu "worm": *tul-t*[*u*] 229 r. vi 47, *tul-tú* 229 r. vii 62, see also *tuessu,*

tūrtu "backing out, turning": *tur-ti* 229 r. v 43, *tur-tu* 229 r. v 41,

ṭābiš "well": *ṭa-biš* 288 r. ii 7,

ṭābtu "goodness, favour; salt": MUN 136 r. 2, [M]UN 29:3, *ṭa-ab-ta-šu* 33:14, *ṭa-ab-ti* 237 r. 17, *ṭa-ab-tu*] 56:2,

ṭabû "to sink; (D) to immerse, sink": *i-ṭa-bu* 229 r. vi 23, *li-ṭa-bu-*[*u*] 229 r. viii 6

ṭâbu "to be(come) good, pleasant; (D) to make good, happy": *i-ṭib-bu-ni* 129 r. 8, *mu-ṭib-*[*bat* 230:23, *ṭa-bat-u-ni*] 229 ii 2,

ṭeānu "to grind, pulverize": *li-ṭ*[*e*]*-e-nu* 229 r. vi 21, *ṭe-a-ni* 229 r. vi 19,

ṭēhi "adjoining, adjacent to": *ṭé-eh* 230:20,

ṭehû "to approach": *i*]*ṭ-ṭah-ha-an-ni* 273 r. 2, TE-*ma* 265:4,

ṭēmu "order, report, mind": *ṭe-e*[*m* 172:4, *ṭè-e*[*m* 30 r. 5, *ṭ*]*è-em-ku-nu* 86:2, *ṭè-en-ga*] 163:4, *ṭè-en-šú-nu* 29:10, *ṭè-e-*[*ma-ni* 35:4, *ṭè-e-mi* 199 r. 3, *ṭè-*[*e-mi* 33:5, *ṭè-e-mu* 33:20, 69:17, *ṭè-e-*[*mu* 61:2, *ṭè-e-*[*mu*] 43:2, *ṭè*]*-e-mu* 69:13, *ṭ*[*è*]*-e-mu* 10:10, [*ṭè-e-mu* 66:3, *ṭ*]*è-e-mu-nu* 85:6, *ṭè-me* 22 r. 5, *ṭè-mu* 8:5, *ṭ*[*è-mu* 2:5, *ṭè-šú-nu* 234:16,

ṭerû "to strike, lash": *i*]*ṭ-ru-ú* 176 r. 7,

ṭiābu "to be good": DÙG 232 r. 5, 247:18, 286 iii 17, DÙG-*ab* 247:7, DÙG.GA 158:4, 229 r. v 84, vi 15, 46, 72, 86, 246:10, 247 r. 9, 251:3, 252 r. 7, 261:9, 288 iii 1, DÙG.G[A 261 r. 1, DÙ]G.GA 18:6, [DÙG.GA 241 r. 8, DÙG.GA-*ku-nu*] 241:6, DÙG.GA-*ti* 229 r. v 79, DÙG.GA-*tú* 229 i 74, r. v 1, 28, viii 15, *ṭa-a-ba* 8 r. 4, *ṭa*]*-a-ba* 113:c 10, *ṭa-ba* 239 i 4, *ṭa-bu-tu* 72 r. 5,

ṭubbāti "friendliness, goodwill": *ṭu-ub-ba-a-ti* 251 r. 2,

ṭūbu "goodness": *ṭu-*[*bi* 83:5, *ṭu-ub* 127:5, 251:4, 255 r. 8, *ṭu-u*]*b* 136:4, [*ṭu-ub* 136:4, 251:5,

ṭuhdu "abundance": *ṭuh-da* 239 r. i 15, *ṭuh-di* 263 r. 7,

ṭullummâ "treacherous, deceitful": [*ṭ*]*ùl-lum-ma-a* 269 r. 2, 0

ṭuppu "tablet": DUB 276 r. 3, 277 r. 4, 298 r. 4, IM 154:1, 163:1, 229 r. viii 4, 249:5, 271:1, 4, *ṭup-pi* 134:1, 179 r. 2, 229 r. v 61, 63, 64, vi 53, vii 17, viii 59, *ṭup-p*]*i* 163:3, *ṭup*]*-pi* 226:9, [*ṭup-pi* 32:3, [*ṭup-pi*] 131:1, [*ṭup-p*]*i* 267 r. 9, [*ṭup*]*-pi* 29:1,

ṭupšarru "scribe, secretary, omen-expert": LÚ.A.BA 267 r. 9, 275 r. 6, 276 r. 9, LÚ.A.BA.MEŠ 140:4, 229 i 5, LÚ.DUB.SAR 280 r. 3, 10, 12, 13, LÚ.DUB.S]AR 177:1, LÚ.UMBISAG 280 r. 5,

ṭupšarrutu "female scribe": MÍ.A.BA.MEŠ 286 r. 2,

ṭupšar ēkalli "palace scribe": LÚ.A.BA]—KUR 157:2, LÚ.DUB.SAR—É.[GAL] 176 r. 10, LÚ.DUB.SAR—[KUR] 176 r. 8,

u "and": *u* 6:8, 19:25, 70:2, 72:2, 84:5, 88:1, 93 r. 1, 114:4, r. 9, 115 r. 1, 119 e. 28, 127:1, 129:3, r. 14, 16, 135:3, 5, 136:3, 4, 162 r. 3, 164:10, r. 11, 165 r. 4, 168 r. 10, 171:4, 8, e. 12, r. 2, 5, 172 r. 5, 175 r. 5, 176 r. 1, 6, 7, 177 r. 4, 179 r. 10, 182 r. 11, 183:5, 209:2, 216:6, 217:7, r. 6, 221 r. 11, 229 i 12, 26, iv 7, r. v 64, 86, vi 7, 11, 18, 60, 79, 81, 88, vii 4, 13, 32, 34, 90, 230:11, 16, 232:3, 236:15, 237 r. 7, 11, 12, 239 r. i 12, 240:7, 247 r. 3, 14, 248 e. 8, r. 2, 4, 250 r. 2, 12, 252:1, 253:1, 4, 9, 255 r. 3, 8, 258:5, 260 r. 2, 262:6, 8, 9, e. 14, r. 2, 263:4, r. 5, 268:4, 271:11, 275:6, 280:4, 6, 8, 12, r. 16, 285 r. 7, 288 i 3, 299:3, *u*] 21:12, 229 r. v 87, 237 r. 9, 257 r. 4, [*u* 229 i 47, 230:13, 24, [*u*] 229 r. vi 58, *ú* 19:27, 22 r. 8, 70:8, 87:1, 180 r. 1, 222:3, 277 r. 3, *ù* 1 r. 9, 5 r. 4, 21:14, 26 r. 3, 4, 29:1, 5, 31:11, r. 2, 32:9, r. 7, 33:10, 11, 12, 15, r. 10, 34:9, 10,

11, 35:10, 39:2, 70:13, 71:4, 72 r. 2, 73:3, 5, 75:2, 77:4, 85:5, 88:5, 92 e. 2, r. 2, 4, 114 r. 13, 116 r. 3, 120 r. 23, 124:4, 126:19, r. 5, 127:6, 128:10, r. 8, 10, 129:21, 133:8, 9, 10, 12, 135:6, 136 r. 4, 138:2, 152:6, 153:2, 163:8, 164:3, r. 10, 165:11, 172:10, 173:6, 176 r. 3, 178:5, 179 r. 2, 186:5, 189:2, 190 r. 2, 199 r. 2, 205:2, 208:3, 212 r. 6, 218:4, 7, 221:3, 227 ii 3, 8, e. ii 11, 228:4, 229 r. vi 78, vii 3, viii 27, 28, 68, 233 r. 10, 235 r. 1, 21, 236:3, 4, 6, 7, r. 13, 237:1, 239 i 5, 10, 12, 26, r. i 8, 14, 15, 26, ii 21, 240: 12, 241 r. 6, 246 r. 4, 255:4, 258:7, 272 r. 4, 276 r. 9, 280:3, 8, 10, 282 s. 1, 288 r. ii 23, 294:7, 297:10, 30:9, *ù*] 239 r. i 24, [*ù* 129:7, 16, 297:9, [*ù*] 235 r. 7, 241:6, [[*ù*]] 297:6,

u lū "or": *ú—lu* 253 r. 5, *ú—l*]*u* 247:18, [*ú—lu* 246 r. 1, 247 r. 6,

udltu "(horizontal) tablet, report": *ú-ìl-ti* 276 r. 9,

ubālu "to bring": *bi-la* 120 r. 20, *it-tu-bil* 120 r. 21, *i-tu-bi*[*l* 149 r. 5, *lu-bi-la-šú* 119 s. 2, *lu-b*]*i-la-šú-nu* 120 r. 24, *lu-bi-lu-niš-šú-nu* 123 r. 3, *lu-še-bi-la* 141 r. 3, *lu-še-bi-l*[*a*] 177:3, *še-bil* 143:2, *še-bil-áš-*[*šú* 270:3, *še-bi-la* 3:3, [*še-bi-la*] 67:8, *tu-bal-a-ni*] 229 i 73, *ub-bal* 243:3, *u*]*b-bal-u-ni* 1 r. 10, *ub-ba-la* 119 s. 1, *ub-ba-la-áš-šú-nu* 1:7, *ub-ba-lu* 216:2, *ub-ba-lu-ni-ni* 1 r. 15, [*ub*]*-bu-lu* 57:2, *ú-bil* 229 r. v 30, *ú-se-bi-la* 105:7, *ú-*[*š*]*e-ba-lu-niš-šú* 119 s. 2, *ú-še-b*[*i-la* 208:3, *ú-šeb-bi-lam* 84 r. 16, *ú-še-bi-lu* 126 r. 2,

ubānu "finger": ŠU.SI 237:12, 265:8, [ŠU.SI 252:7, [Š]U.SI.MEŠ 230:30,

ubān hašê "finger of the lungs": U—MUR 248 r. 5, 250:10, 251 r. 1, U]—MUR 252:10,

ubārūtu "residency": *ú-ba-ru-ti-iá* 168 r. 5,

udduru "darkened": *ud-du-ru* 288 i 4,

udê "utensils": *ú-de-e* 147:12,

udē- "alone": *ú-*[*di-ia*] 140:20,

udû "to know": *lu-ú-du-ma* 255 r. 4, *ú-da* 6:7, 116 e. 13, 120:14, r. 13, [*ú-da* 15:3, [*ú-d*]*a* 22:5, *ú-di* 112 r. 2, [*ú-du-ni* 42:6, *ú-du-*[*ú*] 21:12,

uklu "overseer": LÚ.PA 280 r. 5,

ul "not": *ul* 10 r. 8, 31 r. 7, 32:3, 36 r. 5, 39:4, 40:6, 71:5, 72:5, 76:4, 86:5, 8, 138:7, 164:6, 178:8, 193:4, 202:1, 206:13, 209 r. 3, 213:4, r. 2, 214:2, 214 e. 5, 217:4, 220 r. 2, 234 r. 17, 235:17, r. 10, 239 ii 34, 241 r. 5, 243:1, 252 r. 7, 261 r. 1, 280:7, 8, *u*[*l* 30:8, 200:3, 209:6, *u*]*l* 168:7, 239 r. ii 17, [*ul* 280:9, [*ul*] 172:9, [*u*]*l* 29:10, 136 e. 8, 165:6,

ullû "that": *ul-la-ta* 232 r. 2, *ul-la-ti* 267:3, *ul-l*[*i*]*-t*[*i* 180 r. 8, *ul-lu-ti* 267:1, 2,

ulmû "axe": *ul-we-e* 233:6,

ultu "from": *ul-tu* 73:4, 79 r. 3, 220:6, 235:38, 241 r. 2, 297:8, *ul-t*[*u* 31:14, 163:3, *ul-t*[*u*] 235 r. 36, *ul*]*-tu* 184:5, *u*]*l-tu* 90 r. 3, [*ul-tu*] 129:9, [*u*]*l-tu* 138:4, *ul-tú* 229 r. vi 70,

ūmâ "now": *um-ma-a* 31:3, 125:2, *ú-ma-a* 22 r. 1, 120:8, 17, r. 6, 140 r. 10, 148 r. 2, [*ú-ma-a* 117:12, [*ú-ma-a*] 109:2, [*ú-ma*]*-a* 108 r. 3, 144:3,

umāmu "beast": *ú-ma*]*-me-ia* 106 r. 5, *ú-ma-mu* 229 r. vii 77,

umāšu "athlete": *ú-ma-še* 240:5,

umma "thus": *um-ma* 32 r. 2, 33:16, 37 r. 14, 71:3, 7, 72 r. 7, 73:6, 75:3, e. 8, 80:10, 84:8, 91:9, 126:6, 7, r. 3, 128:12, r. 2, 4, 130:8, 164:4, 8, 12, 167 r. 2, 172:9, 178:6, 187:6, 192 r. 2, 194:5, 235:42, r. 50, 239 ii 17, r. i 12, 31, 241 r. 7, 9, 260 r. 9, 280:5, *um-ma*) 235 r. 35, *um-ma*] 31:4, 239 ii 3, *um-m*[*a* 164 e. 13, *um-m*[*a*] 90 r. 5, 235:44, 46, *um-*[*ma* 85:1, 186:3, *u*[*m-ma* 30 r. 8, 36:4, *u*[*m-ma*] 31:9, 176 r. 9, *u*]*m-ma* 90:5, 183:3, 220:8, [*um-ma* 72 r. 7, 235:43, 280:11, [*um-ma*] 82 r. 1, [*um*]*-ma* 252 r. 2,

ummānu "army": ERIM-*ni* 237 r. 14, 15, [ERIM-*ni* 255:7, [*um-ma-ni* 264 r. 2,

ummânu "master, scholar; craftsman, expert": LÚ.*um-ma-a-ni* 229 i 10, LÚ].*um-ma-ni* 244:2, LÚ.*um-ma-ni* 60:5, 153:3, [LÚ.*u*]*m-ma-ni* 12:6, [L]Ú.*um-ma-ni* 140:7, LÚ.*um-ma-ni-i-ka* 239 ii 12, LÚ.*um-ma-ni-ka* 239 ii 9, *um-man* 287 iii 5, 10,

ummânūtu "scholarship": *u*]*m-ma-nu-ú-ti* 12:13,

ummatu "main body, collective mass; nation": *um-mat-k*[*u-nu* 226 r. 9,

ummi šarri "queen mother": AMA—LU[GAL 114 r. 10, 218:3,

ummu "mother; origin, source": AMA 34:9, 229 r. vi 25, AM[A 120 r. 1, AMA-*a* 176 r. 3, AMA-*šú* 229 r. v 28, vi 88, AMA-[*šú* 229 r. vii 3, AMA-[*šú*] 229 r. vi 79,

ūmu "day": UD 204:2, 247:18, 251:4, 252:4, 262 r. 6, U[D 260 r. 4, U]D 226 r. 8, UD-*me* 1:11, 116:2, 213:3, 229 r. v 46, 47, 58, 234 r. 1, 245 r. 1, 300:11, UD-[*me*] 135:6, [UD-*me* 229 r. vi 92, [UD]-*me* 229 i 14, UD-*me-ka* 21:20, UD-*me*.MEŠ-*ku-nu* 229 r. vi 66, UD-*mu* 1:8, 246:10, [UD-*mu* 7:7, UD-*mu-im-ma* 235:52, UD.ME 265:4, UD.MEŠ 120:2, 154:11, r. 12, 265:6, 275:7, UD.M[EŠ] 136:3, UD.M]EŠ 129:8, UD.MEŠ-*ka* 127:4, 239 i 9, ii 19, 20, r. i 13, [UD-*x*]-KAM 110 r. 1, UD-*x*-KÁM] 252 r. 8, UD-[*x*-KÁM 256:1, U[D]-*x*-[KÁM 116:3, UD.1.KÁM 245 r. 2, 262:1, 266:1, 271:4, UD].5.KÁM 231 r. 2, U]D.5.KÁM 206:13, UD.6.KÁM 275 r. 7, UD.7.KÁM 147:4, UD].9.KÁM 300:4, UD.10.[KA]M 253 r. 7, UD.10.K[ÁM] 290 i 3, UD.11.KÁM 254 r. 4, UD.12.KAM 245 r. 1, UD.12.KÁM 147:9, 244 s. 1, UD.17.KÁM 255 r. 2, UD.20.KÁM 235 r. 3, 267 r. 10, UD.24.K[ÁM 250 r. 5, UD.25.KÁM 120:17, [U]D.25.KÁM 293 r. 1, UD.26.KÁM 276 r. 10, [U]D.27.K[ÁM 63:2,

ūm bubbuli "new moon day": UD.NÁ.ÀM 229 r. vi 70, U]D.NÁ.ÀM 158:3,

ūmussu "daily": UD-*mu-us-su* 235:18, 252 r. 13, [UD-*mu-us-s*]*u* 135:5,

uniqu "young she-goat": MÍ.ÁŠ.QA[R 274 r. 13, MÍ.ÁŠ.QAR-*ma* 274 r. 5, MÍ.ÁŠ.QAR 274 r.8

unqu "signet ring, sealed order": *u*]*n-qa* 235 r. 23, *un-qi* 12:4, *un-qu* 147:11,

unūtu see *anūtu,*

upnu "fist": [*up-ni* 262:9, [*up-ni-ia*] 140:14,

uqnû "lapis lazuli": *uq-nu* 233:15,

ūqu "people, populace": *ú-qu-šú* 126:9,

urad-ēkalli "palace servant, courtier": L]Ú.ARAD—É.GA[L] 206:14,

urādu "to descend; (Š) to bring down": DUL.DU-*ma* 275:9, *nu-še-rid* 237 r. 20, [*šu-ri-di*] 262:12,

urāsu "brick mason, corvée worker": *ú-*[*ra-si* 44:1,

urbānu "papyrus": Ú.*ur-ba-an-ni* 247:3, 8, Ú.*ur-ba-an*]*-ni* 247 r. 10, Ú.*u*[*r-ba-an-ni* 247 r. 8,

urdu "servant, subject": ARAD 279:2, 4, ARAD-*ka* 8:2, 19:1, 26:2, 28:2, 31:1, 94:2, 97:2, 98:2, 103:2, 114:2, 120:1, 124:2, 141:3, 155:2, 247 r. 4,

ARAD-*ka*] 96:1, ARAD-*k*[*a* 20:2, 101:2, 149:2, ARAD-[*ka* 100:2, ARA[D-*ka* 98:1, [ARAD-*ka* 12:2, 13:2, 102:2, 119:2, 121:2, 136:2, 161:2, [ARAD-*ka*] 10:2, [ARAD-*k*]*a* 8:2, 95:2, 129:2, 140:2, [ARAD]-*ka* 18:2, [ARA]D-*ka* 6:2, 27:2, ARAD.M[EŠ 198:5, ARAD.MEŠ-*ka* 235:42, 242:2, [ARAD.MEŠ-*ka* 135:2, ARAD.MEŠ-*šú-n*[*u* 133:3, [ARAD-*šú*] 117:7, LÚ.ARAD 33:12, 152 r. 10, 277 r. 6, LÚ.ARAD.MEŠ 123 r. 8, LÚ.ARAD.ME[Š 33:11, 148 r. 6, [L]Ú.ARAD.M[EŠ 146:5, LÚ.ARAD.MEŠ]-*ni* 282:6,

urhu "month": IT[I 31:12, ITI.MEŠ 108 r. 1, 120:9,

urhu B "road": *ur-ha* 245 r. 4,

urki "after": EGIR 229 i 13, r. v 46, 53, 58,

urkīu "later, junior, future": EGIR.MEŠ 275:7, EGIR-*ú* 298 r. 4,

urputu "cloud": *ur-pi-ti* 232:11,

urqu "green": SIG₇.MEŠ 229 r. vi 44,

urû "team (of horses)": ANŠE.*ú-rat*.MEŠ 1 r. 16, *ú-rat* 241 e. 4, *ú-re-e* 290 r. ii 2,

ūru "roof": ÙR-*ri-šú* 129:20,

ussuku "to assign": *ú-ta-si-ku* 50 e. 4,

uṣṣuṣu "(D only) to investigate, look into": *u*]*ṣ-ṣi-iṣ* 84:9,

uṣû "to go out, emerge; (Š) to send out, banish": È 253 r. 4, *it-tu-ṣi-a* 120:21, *lu-ṣa-am-ma* 239 ii 14, *lu-ṣ*[*u-x* 239 ii 13, *nu-še-ṣi* 58 r. 3, *tu-ṣa* 154 r. 7, *uṣ-ṣa-a* 263:6, *ú-ṣa* 10:13, *ú-ṣa-a* 234 r. 17, *ú-ṣi* 221 r. 3, *ú-ṣ*[*u-ni*] 45:2, *ú-ṣu-*[*ú* 206:4, *ú*]*-ṣu-ú* 188:8, [*uṣ-ṣu-ú*] 217:4, *ú-še-ṣa-an-ni* 1 r. 10, *ú-še-ṣi* 229 r. viii 50, *ú*]*-še-ṣi* 181:2, *ú-še-ṣu-u-ni* 240:9,

uṣurtu "design, drawing, scheme": GIŠ.HUR 73 r. 1, GIŠ.HUR.MEŠ 246 r. 7,

ušābu "to sit, dwell; (Š) to enthrone, settle": [*áš-bu* 245 r. 4, *a-šib* 233:3, 267:4, *a-ši-bat* 234 r. 11, 13, *a-ši-bát* 229 r. vi 38, 40, *a-ši-bu-ut* 288 r. ii 23, *a-ši-bu*]*-ut* 226:7, *a-ši-b*[*u-ut* 226:7, *a-ši*]*-bu-ut* 226:8, *it-tu-šib* 229 r. v 27, *lu-še-ši-*[*bu*]*-ku-nu* 229 r. vii 65, *lu-še-eš-šib* 235 r. 12, *ú-še-si-*[*ib-u-ni*] 144:6, *uš-ab* 235 r. 43, *ú-šib* 237 r. 6,

ušandû "fowler" L[Ú.MUŠEN.DÙ 262:6,

ušpāru "weaver": LÚ.UŠ.BAR.MEŠ 140:12,

ušû "ebony": GIŠ.KAL 233:15,

ušuzzu "to stand": *it-ta-ši-iz-zu* 136:8, *šu-uz-ziz* 235 r. 13, *ul-te-zi-zi-šú* 128 r. 2,

utāru "to exceed; (D) to augment, increase, merit, gain": *ut-tar* 262 r. 4, *ut-ru* 44 r. 2,

utukku "ghost": *ú-tuk-ku* 229 r. vi 76,

uṭṭutu "barley": ŠE.BAR 188:3, 239 r. i 18,

uznu "ear, understanding": P]I.2 273 r. 14, PI.2.MEŠ 164:14, PI.2.MEŠ-*ka* 230:21, *uz-*[*ni*] 239 r. i 26, *uz-nu*] 33:3, *ú-za-an-šá* 234 r. 19, *ú-zu-un-šá* 234 r. 18,

uzuzzu "to stand, to be present": *at-ti-ti-zi* 117:11, *az-za-az* 120:17, GUB 265:4, 6, GUB.ME[Š 263 r. 6, GUB-*za-am-ma*] 246 r. 6, GUB-*zu* 262 r. 5, *i-ti-ti-su* 8:11, *iz-za-az-ma* 77 r. 3, *iz-zi-iz* 91:12, *iz-zi-zu* 126 r. 12, *i-za-zu* 211 s. 1, *i-za-zu-u-ni* 229 r. vii 26, *i-za-z*]*u-ú-ni* 240:5, *i-zi-iz* 91:11, *i-*[*zi-iz* 1 r. 4, *i-zi-zu-u-ni* 240:4, *li-iz-zi-zu* 1:11, *ta-az-za-az* 117:9, *ta-za-a-za* 229 r. vii 27, *ta-za-za-a-ni* 229 r. v 50, *ú-šú-uz-z*[*u*] 214 e. 4,

zabālu "to carry, haul, transport": *ta-za-bi*[*l*] 52:3,

zagindurû "greenish lapis lazuli": NA₄.ZA.GÌN.DURU₅ 262:5, [NA₄.ZA.GÌN.DURU₅ 262:2,

zakāru "to pronounce, call": *zak-ru* 229 r. vi 54, 718,

zakkāru "male": NITA 262:6, 272 r. 4, [NITA 262:10, NITA.MEŠ 19:18,

zakkû "exempt; frofessional (soldier)": LÚ.*zak-ku-e* 229 i 9,

zakû "to be clean, exempt (D); to exempt": *iz-ka-a* 280 r. 16, [*i*]*z-ka-a* 280:4, *ú-zak-ku-ni* 120 r. 13, *zak-ku* 8:9, *za-ku* 58:1,

zamāru "to sing": *a-za-mu-ru* 233:1, *la-za-mu-ru* 234 r. 7, *la-az-mur* 231:4,

zamru "fruit": G]IŠ.*za-ma-ru* 298 r. 6,

zamû "to thirst, yearn": *li-za-mu-u* 229 r. vi 58, see also *ṣamû,*

zanānu "to rain": *i-za-nun-a-ni* 229 r. vii 22, *li-*[*šá-az-nin*] 229 r. v 85, *li-iz-nu-na* 229 r. vii 25, *m*]*u-šá-az-*[*nin* 230:27, ŠUR 268:2, ŠUR-*an* 253 r. 4, *tu-šá-za*]*-na-a-ni* 229 iv 7,

zaqāru "to be high, elevated": *i-zaq-qa-ar* 234:18, *za-qu-ru* 6:6, *zuq-qúr* 252:1,

zaqīqu "phantom, ghost": *za-qi-ku* 117:2, *za-qí-qí* 235:52,

zarāpu "to purchase": *za-rip* 275:6,

zarāqu "to scatter, sprinkle, strew": *li-iz-ri-qu* 115 r. 2,

zar'u "seed, offspring": NUMUN 71 e. 12, 128:2, 129:7, 130 r. 2, 226 r. 6, 229 ii 3, r. vi 7, 729, 30, 32, 36, 84, 235:3, 4, NU]MUN 195:4, NUMUN-*ku-nu* 229 r. vii 30, 36, viii 60, NUMUN.MEŠ-*ku-nu* 229 r. vii 16,

zâru "to twist(?)": *zi-ri* 247 r. 16,

zâzu "to split, divide": BAR-*ma* 252:17,

zenû "to be angry": *ze-nu-ti* 263 r. 4,

zerretu "chain": *zer-re-tú* 288 ii 26,

zēru "seed, offspring": NUMUN-*a-ku-*[*n*]*u* 229 r. vi 8, NUMUN-[*ka*] 239 i 1, NUMUN.MEŠ-*ni* 229 r. vii 33, NUMUN-*šú* 117:5, NUMUN-*ú-ka* 235:8, *ze-ri-ka* 235:9,

zēru barmu "ladybug": NUMUN *bar-mu* 229 r. vii 84,

zēr halgatê "barbarians": NUMU]N—*ha-al-gat-e* 235:37,

ziāru "to hate": *i-zi-ir-ru-ni* 120:7,

zi'aru'u "ginger": *zi-i'-za-ru-'u* 229 r. viii 43,

zību "1. vulture; 2. sacrifice": *zi-i-bu* 229 r. vii 10,

zikāru "male": *zi-ka-ru* 234:17,

zikru "name; utterance, command": *zi-kir-ka* 232:10,

zīmu "appearance, countenance": *zi-im* 249:4, *zi-i-mi* 239 ii 24, *zi-i-mu* 235:19, 239 ii 23, *zi-mu-šú* 263 r. 3,

ziqqu "wineskin": KUŠ.SAL 287 iii 20, KUŠ.S[AL 287 iv 9,

zittu "share": HA.L[A 147:1,

zizibu "milk": GA 261 e. 14,

zumbu "fly": *zu-um-bi* 229 r. vii 86,

zummû see *ṣummû,*

zumru "body": SU 266:5, *zu-mur* 229 r. vi 46, *zu-u'-r*[*i*]*-ku-nu* 229 r. vi 42,

zunnu "rain": A.AN 229 r. vi 13, ŠÈG 229 r. vii 21, 23, 24,

zunzurahhu (a class of soldiers): LÚ.*zu-un* 290 i 7,

Index of Names

Personal Names

Abdâ (city overseer): ^{m}*ab-da-a* 120:18,
Abdabāni: ^{m}*ab-da-ba-a-ni* 276 r. 5,
Abī-[...]: ^{m}AD–[*x x*] 26:2, 27:2,
Adad-ēpuš: ^{md}IM–DÙ-*uš* 275 r. 5
Adad-kīn (*horse trainer*): ^{m}10–*ki-in* 290 i 4,
Adad-šumu-uṣur: ^{md}I[M–MU–PAB] 114:2,
Addî: ^{m}10-*i* 51:3,
Adrīa: ^{m}*ad-ri-i*[*a*] 139:2,
Adūnī-il (messenger):[^{m}*a-d*]*u-ni*–DINGIR 144:7,
Ahī-rāmu (deputy governor of Opis): ^{m}ŠEŠ–*r*[*a-mu* 32:6,
Ahu-milkī: [^{m}]*ah-ú–mil-ki* 284 r.3,
Ahū'a-lamur (of Halzi): ^{m}PAB-*u-a*–IGI 290 i 8,
Aha-iddina (son of Mar-biti-iṣṣur): ^{m}ŠEŠ–SUM-*na* 126:4,
Aha-iqīša: ^{m}ŠEŠ–BA-*š*[*á* 96:2,
Ahhēšâ: ^{m}ŠEŠ.M[EŠ-*šá-a* 187:7, 210 r. 4,
Aia-idā'a: ^{m}*a-a–i-da-a* 275:4, 6, 10,
Amat-Emūni: MÍ.*a-mat–e-mu-ni* 286:17,
Ambīa: ^{m}*am-bi-iá* 275 r. 2,
Amēl-Nabû: ^{m}LÚ–^{d}PA 276 r. 10,
Amēl-Nergal-kēn: ^{m}LÚ–ŠEŠ.GAL–GI.NA 77 r. 2,
Amēl-Šamaš: ^{m}LÚ–^{d}*šá-maš* 281:7, r. 5,
Ana-Nabû-taklāk (cf. Nabû-taklāk): ^{m}*a-na*–$^{d+}$AG–*tak-lak* 29:9,
Aplāia: ^{m}DUMU.UŠ-*a* 132:3, ^{m}DUMU.UŠ-*a-a* 67:4,
Aplu-uṣur (horse trainer): ^{m}DUMU.UŠ–PAB 290 ii 7,
Aqar-Aia (haruspex): ^{m}*a-qar-a* 280 r. 9, [^{m}*a-q*]*a*[*r*]*-a* 125:8,
Arad-Sutīti (majordomo of Nabû-ahhe-iddina): ^{m}ARAD–^{d}*su-ti-ti* 126:5,
Arda-Mullissi (murderer of Sennacherib): ^{m}ARAD–^{d}NIN.[LÍL-*ma*] 128 r. 1, ^{m}ARAD–^{d}NI[N.LÍL] 128 r.6, ^{m}ARAD–^{d}[NIN.LÍL] 128:13, r.4, ^{m}AR[AD–^{d}NIN.LÍL] 128 r.11,
Arie (ruler of Kumme): ^{m}[*a-r*]*i-e* 10:7,
Aššūr-ahu-iddina (Esarhaddon, king of Assyria): [^{m}AN].ŠÁR–ŠEŠ–SUM-*na* 247:3, ^{m}*aš-šur*–PAB–AŠ 229 i 1, 15, 18, v 34, 45, 56, 65, 229 r. vi 78, viii 26, 29, (^{m})*aš-šur*–PAB–AŠ 229 r. v 24, ^{m}*aš-šur*–[PAB]–AŠ 229 r. vi 81, vii 5, ^{d}*aš-šur*–PAB–AŠ 276 r. 11, ^{d}*aš-šur*(–PAB–AŠ) 275 r. 8,
Aššūr-bālti-nīšē: ^{m}*aš-šur*–TÉŠ–U[N.MEŠ-*ma* 1 r. 1,
Aššūr-bāni-apli (Assurbanipal, king of Assyria): ^{m}*aš-šur*–DÙ–A 229 i 17, iii 5, iv 1, 3, 8, r. v 6, 26, 31, 34, 44, 56, 59, 66, 69, vi 78, 87, 89, vii 2, viii 27, ^{m}*aš-šur*–DÙ–DUMU.UŠ 229 r. viii 66, [^{m}]^{d}*aš-šur*–DÙ–A 257:2, (^{m})*aš-šur*–[[*x*]]–DÙ–A 229 v 16, ^{m}AN.ŠÁR–*ba-an*–DUMU.UŠ 235:40, ^{m}AN.ŠÁR]–*ba-an*–DUMU.UŠ 235 r. 35, ^{m}AN.ŠÁR–DÙ–A 235 r. 51, 237 r. 3, 5, 6, r. 15, 238:3, ^{m}AN.ŠÁR–DÙ]–A237 r. 1, ^{m}AN.ŠÁR–DÙ–A-*ú* 252 r. 4, ^{m}AN.ŠÁR–DÙ–DUMU.UŠ 235:1, r. 23, 236 r. 16, 250 r. 8, 9, 237 r. 12, 16, ^{m}A]N.ŠÁR–DÙ–DUMU.UŠ 235:4, AN.ŠÁR–DÙ–DUMU.UŠ 280:1,
Aššūr-bēlu-taqqin (governor of Opis): ^{m}[AN.ŠÁ]R–EN–[LAL-*in*] 32:7, ^{m}AN.ŠÁR–EN–LAL-[*in* 32 r. 1, [^{m}]^{d}*aš-šur*–EN–LAL 33:14,
Aššūr-da''inanni (eponym): ^{m}*aš-šur*–KALAG-*i*[*n-an-ni*] 231 r. 2,
Aššūr-da''in-šarru (cupbearer): ^{m}*aš-šur*–KALAG]–LUGAL 253 r. 8, ^{m}*aš-šur*–KALAG-*in*–LUGAL 254 r. 5,
Aššūr-dūr-pānīa: ^{m}*aš-šur*–BÀD–IGI-*i*[*a*] 10:2,
Aššūr-dūru-uṣur (eponym): ^{m}AN.ŠÁR–BÀD–PAB 252 r. 8,
Aššūr-kallimanni (horse trainer): ^{m}*aš-šur–kal-lim-an-ni* 290 ii 8
Aššūr-mukīn-palēia (son of Esarhaddon): ^{m}AN.ŠÁR–[GIN–BALA.MEŠ-*a*] 114:7,
Aššūr-mušallim: ^{m}*aš-šur–mu-šal-l*[*im* 146:7,
Aššūr-nāṣir (servant of governor of Nuhab): ^{m}*aš-šur*–PAB 279:1,
Aššūr-nāṣir-apli (Assurnasirpal II, king of Assyria): ^{m}AŠ–PAB?–A 226:3, ^{m}AŠ–PAB–[A 226:4, ^{m}*aš-šur*–PAB–A 233:4, r. 13,
Aššūr-rēmanni: ^{m}*aš*]-*šur–rém-a-ni* 295 r. 4,
Aššūr-šar-šamê-erṣeti-muballissu (son of Esarhaddon): ^{m}AN.ŠÁR–LUGAL–AN–KI–T[I.BI] 113:3,
Aššūr-šarru-uṣur: ^{m}]*aš-šur*–LUGAL–PAB 24:3,
Aššūr-ukīn: ^{m}]*aš-šur–ú-ki-*[*i*]*n* 7:3,
Aššūr-zar'u-iddina: ^{m}]*aš-šur*–NUMUN–AŠ 285 r. 4,
Bābilāiu (eunuch, scribe of the king of Babylon): ^{m}TIN.TIR.KI-*a-a* 280 r. 10,
Bābilāiu (horse trainer): ^{m}KÁ.DINGIR-*a-a* 290 ii 9,
Balasî: ^{m}]*ba-la-si-i* 124:2,
Bēl-ahhē-rība (goldsmith): $^{md+}$EN–ŠEŠ.MEŠ–SU-*ba* 126.13,
Bēl-ahu-uṣur (recruit): ^{m}EN–PAB–PAB 293 r. 1,
Bēl-ašarēd: [^{m}]EN–MAŠ? 281:15,
Bēl-ēmuranni: ^{m}EN–IGI.LAL-*ni* 51 r. 1,
Bēl-ēpuš (scribe): ^{md}EN–DÙ-*uš* 275 r. 6,
Bēl-ēpuš (haruspex): $^{md+}$EN–DÙ-*uš* 247 r. 17,
Bēl-ēṭir (of Bīt-Ibâ): $^{md+}$EN–ŠUR 235 r. 15,
Bēl-Harrān-šadû'a: [^{md}EN?]–KASKAL–KUR-*u-a*

251:2,
Bēl-ibni: md+EN—*i*]*b-ni* 136:2, m]dEN—*ib-ni* 153:6,
Bēl-iddina: mEN—AŠ 281 r. 2, 4,
Bēl-iqīša (leader of the Gambulu tribe): md+EN—BA-*š*[*á*] 237 r. 2, mEN—NÍ]G.BA 121:2,
Bēl-qātū'a: m]dEN—Š[U.2-*u-a*] 15:9,
Bēl-taklāk: mEN—*tak-lak* 2:4,
Bēl-usātī: md+EN]—*ú-sa-ti* 210 r. 2,
Bēl-ušallim (haruspex): md+EN—SILIM-*im* 247 r. 17,
Bēl-u[...]: mEN—*ú-x x* 67:8,
Bēl-[...] (astrologer) md+EN—*x*[*x x x*] 266 r. 1,
Bēl-[...]: mEN—[*x x* 44:4, 5, 67:6,
Bēssu-Aia: m*bé-su—a-a* 279 r. 7,
Bibēa (son of Dugul-lakê): m*bi-bé-e-a* 126:19, m]*bi-bé-e-a* 275 r. 4,
Dabbî: m]*da-bi-i* 11:12, m*da*]*-bi-i* 11:7, m]*da-*[*bi-i* 10:5,
Dannāia (haruspex, reporter): m*dan-a* 250 r. 4, 253 r. 9
Dāri-[...]: m*da-r*[*i—x x* 149 r.2,
Didî: m*di-d*]*i-i* 152:2,
Dugul-lakê: m*du-gul—la-ke-e* 126:19,
Ezbu (servant of chief scribe): m*ez-bu* 279:4,
Gabbāru: m]*gab-bar* 162 r. 8,
Galbu: m*gal-bu* 80:8,
Gallulu: m*ga-lul* 123:9,
Gidgidānu (horse trainer): m*gíd-gíd-da-nu* 290 ii 13,
Gīru-Adad: m*gi-ru—*dIM 275:1, 2, 5,
Gula-ēṭir (sister of Rībāia): mdME—KAR-*ir* 154 r. 3, mdME.ME—KA[R]*-ṭirṣ* 154:1,
Hâ-ahu-uṣur: m*ha-a—a-hu*—ŠEŠ 294:4
Habūr-[...]: m*ha-bur—*[*x x* 134:10,
Hagatēte: m*ha-ga-te-te* 123:10,
Han-ṣarūru (third man): m*h*]*a?-an—ṣa-ru-ru* 285:4,
Huzālu (son of Šalamu): m*hu-za-la* 294:6,
Hur-waṣi (Egyptian): m*hur-u-a-ṣi* 225:6,
Ibâ see *Bīt-Ibâ,*
Iakīna: m*ia-ki-na* 34:8,
Illil-zēru-ibni: md+EN.LÍL—NU[MUN*—ib-ni* 214:3,
Ilu-iādi': mDINGIR*—ia-di-i'* 285:6,
Ina-pî-Bēl: m*ina—pi-i—*d+EN 134 r. 2,
Indabibi (king of Elam): m*i*]*n-da-bi-bi* 136:5,
Iqīša: mBA-*šá* 125:6,
Issār-šumu-ēreš (chief scribe): md15—MU—KAM-*eš* 262 r. 7,
Issār-šumu-ukīn (horse trainer): md15—MU—GIN 290 ii 11,
Išdī-Issār (horse trainer) mSUHUŠ—15 290 i 10,
Išdī-Libbāli: mSUHUŠ—URU.[ŠÀ—URU? 279:11,
Išdī-[...]: mSUHUŠ—[*x x x*] 44:11, mSU[HUŠ—*x x* 224:3,
Kabtīia: m*kab-ti-*[*ia* 210 r. 3,
Kandalānu: m*kan-dàl-a-nu* 300:10,
Kanūnāiu (governor of New Palace): mKI.NE.NE-*a-a* 280 r. 6,
Kibabiše: m*k*[*i-ba-bi-še*] 19:7,
Kiribtu-Aššūr: m*ki-rib-ti—*[*x* 125:7, m*k*]*i-rib-tú—aš-šur* 285:1, m]*ki-rib-tú—aš-šur* 285 r. 5,
Kudurru (son of Nabû-damqi-ilāni): mNÍG.GUB 294:5,
Kudurru (goldsmith): mNÍG.GUB 126: 14,
Kudurru (messenger): mNÍG.GUB 294:7,
Kuppuptu (father of Nabû-ahhe-iddina): m*ku-up-pu-up-ti* 126:1, 5,
Kur'e-rāmu: mdKUR*—ra-mu* 134 r. 6,
Kurigalzu: m*k*]*u-ri-gal-z*[*u* 180 r. 5,
Lā-qēpu (gooseherd): m*la—qe-pu* 123:7,
Lā-tubāšanni: m*la—tu-ba-áš-šá-n*[*i* 277:1,
Lā-tubāšanni-ilu (horse trainer): m*la—tú-ba-šá-ni*—DINGIR 290 ii 17
Lū-balaṭ (horse trainer): m*lu—ba-la-aṭ* 225:3, m*lu*—TI.LA 290 r. ii 1,
Lū-[...]: m*l*[*u?-x x x x*] 97:2,
Mahdê: m*mah-*[*de-e* 11:9,
Manīia: m*ma-ni-ia* 137:4,
Mannu-kī-Adad (horse trainer): m*man-nu—ki*—10 290 ii 5,
Mannu-kī-ahi: m*man-nu—ki*—PAB 276:6, m*man-nu—ki*—ŠEŠ 276:1,
Mannu-kī-ahī (horse trainer): m*man-nu—ki*—PAB.MEŠ 290 ii 14,
Mannu-kī-Aššūr (royal bodyguard): m*man-nu—ki—aš-šur* 1:12, m*man-nu—ki-i—aš-š*[*ur*] 1:2,
Mannu-kī-Issār-lē'i: m*m*]*an-nu—ki*—15—ZU 285:3,
Mannu-kī-Libbāli: m*man-nu*—GIM—URU.ŠÀ—URU 140:2,
Mannu-kī-[...]: m*man-nu—ki-i—*[*x* 213 r. 5,
Marduk (son of Dugul-lakê): m*mar-duk* 126:19, m*mar-du*[*k* 179 r. 4,
Marduk-apla-iddina (Merodach-Baladan, king of Babylon): mdAMAR.UTU—A—AŠ 21 r. 1, mdAMA]R.UTU—A—AŠ 17 r. 1, mdAMAR.UTU—DUMU.U]Š—SUM-*na* 21:3, mdAMAR.UTU—[A—AŠ?] 21:8,
Marduk-erība (foreman of an Aramean scribe): m]dAMAR.UTU—SU 280 r. 5,
Marduk-ēreš: mdŠÚ—KAM-*eš* 285:5,
Marduk-šarrāni: mdAMAR.UTU—MAN-*a-ni* 21 r. 1, 6, mdAMAR.UTU—LUGAL-*a*]*-ni* 21:7, m]dAMAR.UTU—LUGAL-*a-*[*ni*] 21:10,
Marduk-šarru-uṣur: mdAMAR.UTU—LUGAL—PAB 235 r. 13, 16,
Marduk-šumu-uṣur (chief haruspex, reporter): mdAMAR.UTU—MU—ŠEŠ 280 r. 7, [mdAM]AR.UTU—MU—PAB 245 s. 2, mdŠÚ—MU—PAB 253 r. 9,
Marduk-[...]: mdAMAR.UTU—[*x x* 170:3, mdAMAR.U[TU—*x x* 212:4,
Mār-Issār: mDUMU—[15?] 37:4, [mDUMU—15? 37 r. 7,
Mār-bīti-iṣṣur (father of Ahu-iddina): mdDU-MU—É—ŠEŠ-*ir* 126:4,
Meia (rdg. unclear): MÍ.ME-*ia* 154 r. 1,
Mētu-ādur (horse trainer): m*met-tú—a-dúr* 290 ii 6,
Milkī-rām (chief tailor): m*mil-ki-i—*ÁG-*am* 235 r. 18,
Mušēzib-ilu (horse trainer): m*mu-še-zib*—DINGIR 290 i 11,
Mutakkil-Aššūr: m*mu-tak*]*-kil—aš-šur* 296 r. 2,
Mutakkil-Marduk: m*mu-tak-kil—*dAMAR.UTU 267 r. 10,
Na'di-Aššūr (father of [...]-Ešarra): mI—*aš-šur* 285 r. 2,
Na'di-ilu: mI—DIN[GIR] 9:2,
Nabīia: m*na-bi-ia* 134:9,
Nabû'a (smith): mdPA-*u-a* 285 r. 6,
Nabû-ahhē-iddina (son of Kuppuptu): md+AG—

Šēp-[...]: ᵐGÌR.2—ᵈ[*x* 292:1,
Šērū'a-ēṭirat (daughter of Esarhaddon): MÍ.ᵈ[*še-ru-u-a*—KAR-*at*] 114 r. 11, MÍ.*še-ru-u-a*—KAR-*at* 300:9,
Šī-dannatī: MÍ.*ši-i*—*dan-na-ti* 276:5, M[Í.*ši-i*—*dan-na-ti*] 276:7,
Šiti-tabni: MÍ.*ši-ti*—*tab-ni* 286:16,
Šulāia: ᵐ*šu-la-a* 280:2, [ᵐ*šu-la-a*] 280 r. 16,
Šulmu-bēl-ašme: ᵐDI-*mu*]—EN—*áš-me* 8 r.3,
Šumāia: ᵐ*šu-m*[*a-a* 212 r. 3, [ᵐ*šu-m*]*a-a* 132:4,
Šumma-anni: ᵐ*šúm-ma*—*an-ni* 225:5,
Šumma-ilu: ᵐ*šum*]-*ma*—DINGIR 7 r. 10,
Šumma-ilā'ī: ᵐᵈ*šúm?-m*]*a*—DINGIR-*a-a* 295 r. 5
Šumu-kēn: ᵐMU—GIN 125:5,
Tabālītu: MÍ.*ta-ba-lit* 120 r. 26,
Tabnî: ᵐ*tab-ni-i*] 245 s. 2,
Tammarītu (king of Elam): [ᵐ*tam-mar*-ÍD 237 r. 5, ᵐ*tam-mar*-ÍD 237 r. 9, 11, 20, 22, ᵐ*tam-mar*-Í]D 237 r. 7,
Tattannu: ᵐ]*ta-at-tan-nu* 91:15,
Teumman (king of Elam): Te-*um-ma* 237 r. 2,
Tukultī-apal-Ešarra (king of Assyria): ᵐTU-KUL—A—É.ŠÁR.RA 231:5,
Tukultī-Inūrta (king of Assyria): GISKIM—ᵈ[MAŠ 226:3, G]ISKIM—ᵈ[MAŠ 226:4, ᵐTUKUL—MAŠ 233:5, ᵐ*tukul-ti*—[ᵈMAŠ? 120:27,
Ṭāb-ahī (horse trainer): ᵐDÙG.GA—PAB.MEŠ 290 ii 12,
Ṭāb-šār-Aššūr (treasurer) ᵐ[DÙ]G—IM—*aš-šur* 6:2,
Ṭudūti: ᵐ*ṭu*?]-*du-te* 66:4,
Ubār-Sebetti (royal merchant): ᵐ*ú-bar-ru*—ᵈ7.BI 280 r. 14,
Ubāru: ᵐ*ú-pa-ru* 275:2, r. 1, ᵐ*ú-bar-ru* 276:4, 277:3, ᵐ[*ú?-bar?*]-*ru* 277:5, ᵐ*ú*]-*bar-ru* 277 r. 2,
UD.NUN-[...]: ᵐUD.NUN-*x x*[*x* 134:9,
Ullubāiu: ᵐ*ul-lu-b*[*a-a-a* 31:1,
Umbakidinni: ᵐ*um*]-*ba*—*ki-din* 122 r. 5, ᵐ*um-b*]*a*—*ki-di-ni* 122:4,
Upāqa-Šamaš: ᵐ*ú*]-*pa-qa*—ᵈ*šá-maš* 13:2, ᵐ*ú-pa*]*q-qa*—ᵈ[UTU] 12:2,
Upāru see *Ubāru,*
Ummanigaš (king of Elam): ᵐ*um-man-i-gaš* 237 r. 5,
Urdu (scribe, omen-expert): ᵐ*ur-di* LÚ.A.BA 267 r. 9,
Urdu-Mullissi see *Arda-Mullissi,*
Ursâ (king of Urartu): ᵐ*ur-sa-a* 245 r. 3,
Zabāba-iškun (horse trainer): ᵐ*za-ba-ba*—GAR 290 ii 2
Zābāiu: ᵐ*za-ba-a-a* 275 r.3,
Zākir (sheikh): ᵐ*za-kir* 133:9,
Zākir (father of Nabû-le'i): ᵐ*za-kir* 280:5 [ᵐ*za-kir* 280 r.1,
Zanduru (horse trainer): ᵐ*za-an-du-ru* 290 ii 3,
Zērūtu: ᵐNUMUN-*ú-tu* 134 r. 1, ᵐNUMUN-*ú*-[*tu* 222:4,
Zīzî (reporter): ᵐ*zi-zi-i* 250 r. 4,
[...]-ahīia (son of Hâ-ahu-uṣur): [ᵐ*x*-Š]EŠ-*ia* 294:4,
[...]-ahhē-šullim (scribe): ᵐᵈ*x*—Š]EŠ.MEŠ—*šul-lim* 280 r. 3
[...]-Aššūr: ᵐ*x*]-*hi*—*aš-šur* 285:7,
[...]-bēlu-uṣur: ᵐ*x*]*x*—EN—PAB 285:8, ᵐᵈ*x*]—U—PAB 291:6,
[...]-dūrī: [*x x x*]—*du-ri* 25:1,
[...]-Ešarra (son of Na'di-Aššur): [*x x x*]—É.ŠÁR 285 r. 2,
[...]-ēṭir: [ᵐᵈ*x*—K]AR-*ir* 166:5,
[...]-iddina: [*x x*]—SUM-*na* 207:2,
[...]-ilu (son of Išdi-[...]): *x x*]*x*—DINGIR 224:3,
[...]kisu: ᵐ*x*]-*ki*?-*su*: 141:3,
[...]-Nergal: [ᵐ*x*]*x*—ᵈU.GUR 170:5,
[...]-siqrī: [*x x*]*x*—*siq-ri* 25:2,
[...]-šarru-uṣur: ᵐᵈ*x*]—MAN—PAB 11:4,
[...]-šumu-uṣur: ᵐ*x*]*x-zi*—MU—PAB 267:5,
[...]-ušēzib: ᵐᵈ*x*]—*ú-še-zi*[*b* 134 r. 4,

Place Names

Ahlamû "Aramean": LÚ.*ah-la-mu-ú* 241 r. 3,
Amqarrūna (Bibl. Ekron): *a-am-qár-ru-u-na* 229 r. vi 47,
Andārāiu "Andarian": MÍ.*an-dar-i-tú* 286 r. 2,
Arba'il (Gk. Arbela, mod. Erbil): *arba-il* 232 r. 10, URU.*arba-ìl* 229 r. vi 40, 287 iii 13,
Aramu "Aramean": LÚ.*a-ra-me* 241:7,
Arāši (region in Zagros): KUR.*a-ra-šú* 235 r. 19,
Armāiu "Aramean, Aramaic": KUR.*ár-ma-a-a* 140:5, *ár-ma-a-a*-[*te* 286:1, MÍ.*ár-ma-a-a-te* 286:19,
Arpad (now T. Rifa'at): *ár-pad-da-a-a-te* 286:10,
Arrapha (mod. Kerkuk): URU.*arrap-ha* 1 r. 7, 11,
Asdūdu (Bibl. Ashdod, mod. Esdud): MÍ.*as!-d*[*u-di*]-*tú* 286:12,
Aššūrāiu "Assyrian": *aš-šur-a-a-te* 286:3, *aš-šur*.KI-*a-a* 241 r. 8, KU[R].*aš-šur-a-a* 140:5, LÚ.*aš-š*]*ur*.KI.ME[Š 41:12, [L]Ú.*aš-šur*.KI-*a-a* 241:4,
Āl Aššūr (Assur, city on the Tigris, now Qalᶜat Širqaṭ): URU *aš-šur* 229 vi 64,
Aumeni (town near Lubda): URU.*a-ú-me-ni* 9:6,
Azai (district of Kunalia): KUR.*az-a-i* 229 r. vi 44,
Bābilāiu "Babylonian" DUMU—KÁ.DINGIR.RA.K[I] 21:1, LÚ.DUMU—K[Á.DINGIR.MEŠ] 19:8, LÚ.TIN.TI[R.KI.MEŠ 79:1, URU.TIN.TI[R.KI.MEŠ 128:5,
Bābili (Babylon): KÁ.DINGIR.RA.[KI 55 r. 1, TIN.TIR.KI 32:11, 138:2, 239 i 18, 280 r. 10 TIN.T]IR.KI 138:8, TIN.T]IR?.KI 193:6,
Bīt-Burnakka (city on the border of Elam): É—URU.*bu-ur-nak-ka* 235 r. 19,
Bīt-Hamban É—URU.*ha-am-ban*] 246 r. 3,
Bīt-Iakīni: DUMU—ᵐ*ia*-GIN 21:17, DUMU—ᵐ*ia*]-ki-ni 21:11,
Bīt-Ibâ (a Babylonian dynastic house near

Uruk): DUMU ᵐi-ba-a 235 r. 15, 39,
Bīt-Imbî (Elamite border city) URU.É–im-b[i-i] 122 r. 4,
Bīt-Zualza: É–zu-[al-za] 18 r. 4,
Dēru (city in Babylonia, now Tell Aqar): URU.de-ri 281:6, URU.de]-e-ri 122:3,
Diglat (Tigris): ÍD.di-ig-lat 9:9,
Dimašqa (Damascus):KUR.di-maš-q]a 231 r. 1,
Dū'ru (Bibl. Dor, city in Phoenicia):
Dūr-Kurigalzi: URU.ku-ri-gal-zi 120 r. 27,
Dūr-Šarrukēn (Khorsabad): URU.BÀD–MAN–GIN 232 r. 14, [UR]U.BÀD–LUGAL–GIN-a-a 54:2,
Dūr-Šarrukku (city in Babylonia, now Tell ed-Der): URU.BÀD–LUGAL-uk-ka 229 r. viii 65, URU.BÀD–LUGAL-uk-ki 21:18,
Eber nāri ("Trans-Euphrates," Upper Syria): KUR.e-bir–[ÍD] 7:5,
Elamtu (Elam): KUR.NIM.KI 300:12, r. 1, KUR.NIM.MA.KI 126:3, 216 r. 8, 219:4, 237:13, r. 5, 7, KUR.NI]M.MA.KI 235 r. 5, 237:2,KUR.NIM. M]A.KI 74:7,
Elamû (Elamite): LÚ.e-la-mi-i 237 r. 3,
Eridu (city S of Ur. now T. Abī Šahrāin) N]UN?.KI 193:2,
Etinu (district of Urarṭu) [KUR].e?-ti-na-a-a 10:11,
Gambūlu (Aram. tribe): [L]ÚṬ.gam-bu-li 25:4,
Gargamis (Carchemis): URU.gar-ga-mis 233:9,
Gimir (Bibl. Gomer, Cimmerians): L]Ú.gi-mir-a-a 238:4, [L]Ú.gi-mir-[ra-a-a 246 r. 3,
Halzi: URU.hal-zi 290 i 9,
Hamānu (Amanus): KUR-e ha-ma-na 233:19, ha-ma-n[a 233 r. 7,
Harrānu (Carrhae, mod. Harran): KASKAL.KI 252 r. 7, URU.KASKAL 232 r. 16,
Hattāiu (Hittite): hat-ta-a-a-te 286:13, MÍ.hat-ta-a-a-te 286:20,
Hatti: KUR.hat-ti 233:10,
Haza[t? (Gaza?): KUR.ha-za-[x 180 r. 4,
Hīdalu (Elamite royal city): URU.hi-da]-lu 235 r. 16,
Hilimmu (town on the border of Elam): URU.hi-li-im 235 r. 21,
Hindiru (Aram. tribe) LÚ.hi-in-di-[ru] 25:3,
Ilu-[...]: URU.DINGIR–[x 26:4,
Indarāiu (tribe in Elam): in-da-ra-a-a 235 r. 22, 52, LÚ.in-d]a-ra-a-a 235:41,
Irgistiani (Urarṭian city): URU.i]r-gi-is-ti-a-ni U10:6,
Iškuza (Scythia): LÚ.iš-ku-za-a-a 246 r. 2
Itu'u (Aram. tribe): L]ÚṬ.i-tu-'a-[a-a] 12 r. 14,
Kaldāiu "Chaldean/Babylonian": [LÚ?.ka]l-da-a-a 120:26,
Kaldu (Chaldea, Chaldean): L]Ú.kal-di 191:3, LÚ.k]al-di?191:1,
Kalhu (Calah, mod. Nimrud): URU.kal-ha 232 r. 13, URU.kal-hi 233:7, URU.kal-h[i 191:4,
Kaššû (Kassite): MÍ].káš-šá-a-a-te 286:6, MÍ.kaš-šá-[a-a-te] 286:24,
Kibrâ: LÚ?.k]i-ib-ra-a 216 r. 3,
Kiltāta (Elamite city): URU.ki-il-ta-a-ta 235 r. 17,
Kissik (city E of Eridu, Tell Lahm): LÚ.ki-i]s-s[ik-a-a] 135:2,
Kummuhi (class. Commagene): KUR.ku-mu-ha-a-a 233:14,
Kunalia (T. Tayinat): KUR.ku-na-li-a 229 i 3,
Kurbail (city in Assyria): kur-ba-(ìl) 232 r. 17, URU.kur-ba-ìl 229 r. vi 45,
Kūsu (Cush, Nubia): ku-sa-a-a-t[e 286:2,
URU-kutallu: URU.ku-tú-li 281:3,
Kutû (Cutha): GÚ.DU₈.A 232 r. 21,
Labnāna (Lebanon):
Libbi āli ("Inner City," an appellative of Assur): ŠÀ–URU-a-a 287 iii 12, URU.ŠÀ–URU 120:13, 17, 229 i 35, URU.Š[À–URU] 120:27, 162 r. 2, URU].ŠÀ–URU 51:1, URU.ŠÀ–URU-a-a 120 r. 7, 14, URU.ŠÀ–URU-iá 279 r. 7,
Lubda (city S of Arrapha, mod. Tauq?): URU.lu-ub?-d[a?] 9:7,
Mandiru: URU].man-di-r[a-a-a 23:1,
Manna (Mannea, Bibl. Minni, kingdom S of lake Urmia) KUR.man-na-a-[a 6:8,
Marratu (Persian Gulf): mar-rat 137:5,
Māt Akkadî (Babylonia): KUR–URI.KI 229 i 26, 231:24, 235 r. 5, 6, 263:2, KUR–UR]I.KI 263 r. 5, KUR]–URI.KI.ME 263 r. 4,
Māt Amurrî (Westland): KUR].MAR.TU.KI 33:4, KUR–MAR.TU.[KI 266:8,
Māt Aššūr (Assyria): KUR–AN.ŠÁR 235:2, 246:5, 247:2, KUR–aš] 249 r. 7, KUR–aš-šur 229 i 1, 2, 16, 18, 25, 275 r. 8, KUR–aš]-šur 252 r.5 KUR–aš-šur-ma] 225:3, 4, KUR–aš-šur.KI 21 r. 2, 231:5, 241:8, 280:1, 4, 10, KUR–aš-šu[r.KI 258:8, KUR–aš-[šur.KI 184:11, KUR–aš?-[šur.KI 68:5, KUR]–aš-šur.KI 248:4, KUR]–aš-šur.[K]I 21 r. 8, KUR–aš]-šur.KI 193:9, KUR–ᵈaš-šur.KI 275 r. 12, KUR–ᵈaš-š[ur.KI] 21:15,
Māt Šumeri (Sumer): KUR–šu-me-ri 229 i 26,
Māt tāmti (Sealand): KUR–tam-ti[m 34:5,
Māzamua (province of Assyria, mod. Sulaimaniya): KUR–za-[mu-a 14:2, 4,
Nāṣir: URU.na-ṣir 162 r. 6,
Nīnua (Nineveh): URU.ni-ná-a 280 r. 2, URU.ni-[nu-a 114 r. 14, URU.n]i-nu-a 11:8, NINA 232 r. 9, NINA.KI 229 r. vi 38, 287 iii 12, NIN]A.KI 237 r. 8, URU.NINA 11:11, 232 r. 12, 237 r. 4,
Nippur (Babylonian city, mod. Nuffar): EN.LÍL.KI 232 r. 23,
Nuhab: nu-uh-ba-iá 279 r.10, URU.nu-hu-ba-a-a 279:2
Padānu: URU.pad-an 30 r. 7,,
Pattina: pa-te-na-a-a 233:14, [pa-t]e-na-a-a 233:17,
Pillat (town on the Elamite border): URU.pi-il-la-at 235 r. 21,
Puqūdu (Aram. tribe, Bibl. Pekod): LÚ.pu-q[u-du 201:2,
Ru'ua (Aram. tribe): [LÚṬ].ru-'u-a-a 25:3,
Qarnīna (Bibl. Qarnaim) KUR.SI 228 r. vi 44,
Qidru (Bibl. Qedar): [KUR.qe-d]a-ra-a-a 53:7,
Si'immê (Ass. provincial capital in the upper Habur area): URU?].si-im-me-e 16:5,
Sinnu (city in Mesopotamia, location uncert.):
Sippar (city in Babylonia, mod. Abu Habba): LÚ.DUMU–si-na-a-a 31:5, [LÚ.DU]MU–si-na-a-a 31:10,
Ša-amēlē (city in Bit-Amukani): URU.šá–a-[me-le-e] 203:4,
Šama'ūna (city in Arāši): URU.šá-ma-[ú-nu 130:12,

Šamaš-nāṣir (city in the Diyala valley): URU.^{d}UTU—P[AB-*ir* 246 r. 5,
Tamūnu (Elamite city): URU.*t*]*a-mu-ú-nu* 235 r. 17,
Šušan (Susa): URU.*šu-šá-an* 235 r. 3, 14,
Tarbiṣu (city in Assyria, Sherif Khan): *tar-bi-ṣi* 232 r. 18,
Te[...]: URU.*te-x*[*x x* 32:2,
Til-Libanāna *til-li-ba-na-na* 70:12,
Til-qanê: URU.*til—qa-né-e* 123:11,
Ṣurru (Tyre, now Ṣur): MÍ.*ṣur-ra-a-a-te* 286:5, MÍ.*ṣur-ra-*[*a-a-te*] 286:21,
Upî (Opis): U[RU.*ú*]-*pi-ṭiṣ* 32:8,
Urarṭu (Bibl. Ararat, Armenia): KUR.*ur-ár-#u* 245 r.3, KUR.URI 288 ii 31, KUR.URI-*a-a* 1:4, KUR.URI-*a-*[*a*] 9:4, KUR.U[RI-*a-a*] 10:10,
Uruk (city in Babylonia, Bibl. Erech, now Warka): LÚ.UNUG.[KI-*a-a* 31:15, UNUG.K[I 133:6,
Urzuhina: URU.*ur-zu-hi-na* 1:7, 15, URU.*ur-zu-h*[*i-na*] 1:20, URU.*ur-zu-*(*hi*)-*na* 1:18,
Zikkû (town in Assyria): URU].*zi-ik-ku-ú* 252 r. 3,

God, Star, and Temple Names

Adad (weather god): ^{d}IM 229 i 23, r. vi 13, 230:22, 234:3, 22, 255 r. 3, 258 r.4, 297:6, 10,
Adad-Šala (divine couple worshiped in Kurba'il): ^{d}IM ^{d}*ša-la* 229 r. vi 45,
Allātu (a name of Ereškigal): ^{d}*al-la-tum*] 299: 1,
Anat-Baiti-il (tutelary goddess of Bethel): (^{d})*a-na-an-ti—*^{d}*ba-a-a-ti*—DINGIR 229 r. vi 48,
Antu (consort of Anu): *an-tum* 230:16,
Anu (god of heaven): ^{d}*a-num* 229 i 22, 30, v 81, 230:16, 236:90,
Anunītu (a war goddess; part of Pisces): ^{d}*a-nu-*[*ni-tum* 239 ii 9,
Anunnakkī (netherworld gods): ^{d}*a-nun-na-ki* 231:2, 288 r. ii 22,
Anzû (lion-headed eagle, a mythological creature| a star):
Aramiš (Syrian god): ^{d}*a-ra-miš* 229 r. vi 44,
Asakku (a demon): ^{d}*a-sak-ku* 240: 12,
Aššūr (father of gods, national god of Assyria): ^{d}*a-aš-šur* 234:3, ^{d}*aš-šur* 229 r. v 78, 240:12, ^{d}]*aš-šur* 229 i 22, *aš-šur* 120:2, 229 i 29, r. v 72, 232 r. 6, 234 r. 7, ^{d}*a-šur*$_{4}$ 229 i 1, AN.ŠÁR 297:8, 235:8, 236:11, 240:13, A]N.ŠÁR 238:7, AN].ŠÁR 297:2,
Baiti-il (Bibl. Bethel): ^{d}*ba-a-a-ti—*DINGIR 229 r. vi 48,
Bēl ("Lord," an appellative of Marduk): ^{d}EN 117:2, 172:7, 219 r. viii 19, 240:12, $^{d+}$EN 124:4, 127:1, 235 r. 50, EN 232 r. 7,
Bēlet balāṭi ("Lady of Life"): ^{d}*be-lit—*TIN 159:3, ^{d}NIN—TIN 214:5
Bēlet ilī ("Lady of Gods", creation goddess): ^{d}*be-let—*DINGIR.MEŠ 229 i 24, r. vi 9, ^{d}*be-let—ì-lí* 230:12,
Bēl ṣarbi ("lord of the Euphrates poplar," city god of Šapazzu): ^{d}LUGAL—GIŠ.[ASÁL] 32:4, ^{d}LUGAL—[GIŠ.ASÁL 32 r. 5,
Bēl-šarru: ^{d}EN—MAN 299 i 2,
bēt Marduk (temple of Marduk): É—^{d}AMAR.UTU 115:8,
Dagān (Canaanite god syncretized with Aššur) ^{d}*da-gan* 230:32,
Damkina (consort of Ea): ^{d}*dam-ki-na* 230:21,
Dilbat (Venus): MUL.*dil-bat* 229 i 20,
Ēa (god of wisdom): ^{d}[É.A] 229 i 22, 30, r. vii 11, 230:21, ^{d}É.A? 268:2,
Ereškigal (queen of netherworld): *áš-ri-gi-in-gal* 234 r. 12,
Esaggil (main shrine of Marduk): É.*sag-gíl* 229 r. vi 2, É.SAG.ÍL 2 240:5, É.SAG.Í[L 132:4,
Ešarra (main shrine of Aššur): É.ŠÁR.RA 233:3, r. 8, 11, 297:5, 9, É.ŠÁ]R.RA 297:7,
Ezida (temple of Nabû): É.ZI.DA 280:6,
Girru (fire-god): ^{d}GIŠ.BAR 229 r. vii 15, 16,
Gula (goddess of healing): ^{d}*gu-la* 229 r. vi 41, 230:12,
Illil (Enlil, king of gods): ^{d}BAD 229 i 22, 30, 233:3, ^{d}EN.LÍL 229 r. viii 58, $^{d+}$EN.LÍL 230:11,
Iltēru: ^{d}*i*]*l-te-e-ru* 235 r. 7,
Inurta (son of Enlil, celestial crown prince): ^{d}MAŠ 232 r. 11, 234:4, [^{d}M]AŠ 299 i 8, ^{d}NIN.URTA 230:4,
Issār (Ištar, goddess of love): ^{d}*iš-tar—arba-ìl*.KI 252 r. 2, ^{d}IŠ.TAR 229 r. vi 32, IŠ.TAR URU.[*x* 207:3, ^{d}U.DAR 226 r.2, ^{d}15 229 r. vi 40, 234 r. 11, 13, 237 r. 1, 9,
Issār kakkibī (Ištar of stars): ^{d}IŠ.TAR—MUL.MEŠ 230:15, ^{d}U.DAR—MU]L.MEŠ 299 i 11,
Issār ša Arba'il (Ištar of Arbela) ^{d}15 arba-*ìl* 232 r. 10, ^{d}15 ša arba-[*ìl* 229 i 33,
Issār ša Nīnua (Ištar of Nineveh): ^{d}15 šá URU.[NINA].KI 229 i 33, ^{d}]15 šá URU.*ni-nu-a* 240:1, ^{d}15 NINA 232 r. 9,
Ištarān (chief god of Der): AN.GAL 19:9,
Kaimānu (Saturn, "The Steady One"): MUL.UDU.IDIM.SAG.[UŠ] 229 i 20,
Karhuha (Hittite god): ^{d}*kar-hu-ha* 229 r. vi 50,
Kippatu ("disc," a symbol of Ištar): [^{d}*kip-p*]*a-tum* 299 i 9,
Kubāba (Hittite god): ^{d}*ku-*KÁ 229 r. vi 50,
Lahmu ("The Hairy One," a primordial god, porter of the abyss): ^{d}*làh-mu* 240:114,
Manungal (a netherworld god): [^{d}*ma-nu-g*]*al* 299 i 13,
mārat Ani (a name of Lamaštu): DUMU.MÍ ^{d}*a-nim* 240:8,
Marduk (chief god of Babylon) ^{d}AMAR.UTU 91 r. 4, 129:3, 136:12, 172 r. 2, 218:2, 229 r. vi 4, 230:24, 235:3, 8, 15, 21, 23, 236:7, 241 r. 6, ^{d}AMA[R.UTU 114 r. 8, 235:52, 236:4, ^{d}MES 229 i 33,
Mullissu (queen of heaven, consort of Aššur): ^{d}NIN.LÍL 154:4, 229 r. v 80, vi 38, ^{d}NIN.L[ÍL 229 i 32, ^{d}[NIN.LÍL] 230:11,

Nabû (Nebo, son of Marduk, keeper of celestial records): ^{d}AG 124:4, 229 r. viii 59, $^{d+}$AG 127:1, 241 r. 6, $^{d+}$A[G] 70:2, $^{d+}$A[G? 209 r. 4, [^{d}]$^{+}$AG 33:6, ^{d}PA 21:12, 114 r. 9, 129 r. 3, 181 r.5, 229 i 13, 230:26, 232 r. 8, 12, 13, 14,

Nanāia (goddess of erotic love): ^{d}*na-na-a* 235 r. 7,

Nergal (lord of the netherworld): ^{d}U.GUR 229 r. vi 35, 235:22, 240:13, ^{d}U.GU[R] 79 r. 5, ^{d}U.[GUR 229 i 31,

Nikkal (consort of Sin): ^{d}NIN.GAL 135:5 ^{d}NIN. G]AL 135:3,

Ninpanigarra (an appellative of Ninkarrak): ^{d}NIN.PAB.NIGÌN.GAR.R[A 230:29,

Nisaba (goddess of writing): ^{d}[NISABA] 230:10,

Nūru ("Light", consort of Šamaš): ^{d}GIŠ.NU$_{11}$.[GAL] 287 iii 15,

Nušku (son of Sîn): [^{d}P]A.TÚG 299 i 7,

Pabilsag (Sagittarius): ^{d}PA.BÍL.SAG 230:17,

Pālil (Mesopotamian war god): ^{d}IGI.DU 229 r. vii 9,

Qingu (husband of Tiamat): ^{d}*qi-in-gu* 240: 12,

Sagmegar (Jupiter): ^{d}SAG.ME.[GAR 229 r. vi 1 MUL.SAG.ME.GAR 118:3, 263 r. 3, MUL.SAG].ME. GAR 219 i 20,

Sebetti (Pleiades): ^{d}7.BI 230:19,

Sîn (moon god): ^{d}30 135:5, 229 i 23, 39, r. v 87, 232 r. 15, 16, 234 r. 18, 30 266:1, 267:7,

Siusa: ^{d}*si-ú-sa* 299 i 3,

Ṣalbatānu (Mars): MUL.*ṣal-bat-a-nu* 229 i 21,

Šala (consort of Adad): ^{d}*ša-la* 229 r. vi 45, 230:23,

Šamaš (sun, god of justice): ^{d}*šá-maš* 234:22, r. 2, ^{d}*šam-ši* 230:14, ^{d}*šam-šu* 230:10, ^{d}UTU 174:3, 179 r. 10, 193:7, 229 i 23, 235:8, 255 r. 3, 262:7, 13, 264 r. 2, 288 r. ii 17, 297:10 ^{d}]UTU 129:3, 297:6, ^{d}UT[U 120:2, 262:7, 20 264:1, 3,

Šarrat Amqarruna (city god of Ekron): ^{d}*šar-rat—a-am-qár-ru-u-na* 229 r. vi 47,

Šarru (Regulus) ^{d}LUGAL 230:27, MUL.LUGAL 265:4, 6,

Šērū'a (morning star, daughter of Aššur): ^{d}*še-ru-u-a* 229 i 24, ^{d}*še*]*-ru-u-a* 229 i 32, [^{d}*še-ru-i*]*a* 299 i 6, ^{d}UZU-*ú-a* 231:6,

Šiḫṭu (Mercury): MUL.UDU.IDIM.GUD.UD 229 i 21,

Šimālia: ^{d}*ši-ma-a-l*[*i-a*] 235:31,

Šukūdu ("arrow", Sirius): MUL.[GAG.SI.SÁ] 229 i 21,

Uraš (city god of Dilbat, equated with Ninurta): ^{d}IB 229 i 31,

Urgal (Constellation of Leo): UR.GAL 239 ii 24,

Uta'ulu (a name of Jupiter): ^{d}UTU.U$_{18}$.LU 230:28,

Zabāba (city god of Kiš): ^{d}*z*[*a-ba$_{4}$-ba$_{4}$* 230:3,

Zappu (Pleiades): MUL.[MUL 265 r. 1,

Zarpānītu (consort of Marduk): ^{d}NUMUN—DÙ-*tú* 229 r. vi 7, ^{d}*zar-pa-ni-ti* 235:6, ^{d}*zar-pa-ni-tum* 230:25, ^{d}*zar-pa-*[*ni-tum* 236:6,

List of Text Headings

1. Urarṭian Emissaries Meet Captives
2. Fragment Mentioning Bel-taklak
3. Silver Requested
4. Messengers
5. ———
6. Names of the City Lords on Reliefs
7. Fragment Related to the West
8. Chief Victualler Waters Terebinth Trees
9. Urarṭian Emissaries on Their Way
10. A Captured Informer
11. Ninevite Dealings
12. Urged by the King's Sealed Order
13. ———
14. Images in Mazamua
15. Fragment Mentioning Snow and Defeat
16. Fragment Mentioning Si'immê
17. Fragment Mentioning Merodach-baladan
18. Fragment Referring to Kibabiše and Bit-Zualza
19. Cultic and Economic Dealings in Der
20. ———
21. Marduk-šarrani Conspires with Merodach-Baladan
22. Fragment Mentioning Scouts and Rab mugi
23. Fragment Mentioning Mandireans
24. Fragment Mentioning Aššur-šarru-uṣur
25. Visiting Aramean Tribes
26. Petition Concerning Towns and Orchards
27. ———
28. ———
29. Joining the Royal Entourage
30. ———
31. We Have not Sold Sinneans for Silver!
32. Seating Bel-ṣarbi
33. Loyal Servant's Report
34. Fragment Mentioning Westland, Sealand and Yakin
35. ———
36. ———
37. Fragment Concerning Military Matters
38. Problem with Fleeing Fugitives and Refugees
39. ———
40. ———
41. ———
42. Mounting [...] of Gods with Sinews
43. Doing the King's Work
44. Corvée Workers for the King
45. ———
46. ———
47. Details on Statues
48. ———
49. Punishing the King's Foes
50. ———
51. Official Sent to Assur
52. Transporting in Secrecy
53. Dealings with the Qedarites
54. Fragment Mentioning the People of Dur-Šarruken
55. Tablet from Babylon
56. A Silver Dagger
57. Fragment Referring to the Deputy (Governor?)
58. Work for Officials
59. ———
60. Taking Care of Mares
61. ———
62. ———
63. ———
64. They Are not Speaking the Truth
65. ———
66. Accusations about Horses
67. Writing-Board of Aplaya
68. ———
69. ———
70. The Governor in Til-Banana
71. I Did not Sin
72. Adopting a Deportee's Children
73. A Border Dispute
74. Raping and Resettling People
75. ———
76. ———
77. Inventory of Royal Statues and Treasures
78. ———
79. Deserting from a Foreign Land
80. Burying Massacred Corpses
81. Noblemen of the Enemy Country
82. ———
83. ———
84. ———
85. ———
86. ———
87. ———
88. ———
89. ———
90. Men Revolting
91. ———
92. ———
93. Problem with the Harvest
94. ———
95. ———
96. Fragment of a Letter by Ahu-iqiša
97. ———
98. ———
99. ———
100. ———
101. ———

102. ———
103. ———
104. ———
105. ———
106. ———
107. What NN Wrote
108. ———
109. ———
110. ———
111. ———
112. ———
113. Medical Report
114. Another Medical Report
115. Purification of a House
116. Do Not Conceal from Me What You See!
117. Phantom of Bel
118. Fragment Mentioning Jupiter
119. Fragment of a Letter by Nabû-šumu-iddina
120. Plotting in the Upper Echelons of Assur
121. Fragment of a Letter by Bel-iqiša(?)
122. Fragment Mentioning Umban-kidinni and Bit-Imbî
123. Denouncing Crimes
124. ilku-duty of the Shepherds
125. A Royal Order Concerning Men
126. Conspiracy against Esarhaddon
127. Blessings
128. Your Son Is Going to Murder You
129. Petitioning the King Again
130. ———
131. Fragment from Nergal-naṣir to Nabû-ušallim
132. ———
133. Sheikhs Are Afraid
134. Returning People to the Sheikhs
135. ———
136. Fragment of a Letter by Bel-ibni
137. ———
138. King of Babylon, Natan and Nabû-bel-šumati
139. Men Requested
140. All Is Lost
141. Fragment of a Letter to the Palace Supervisor
142. ———
143. Send it to the Palace!
144. ———
145. ———
146. ———
147. Royal Decision on the Division of Inheritance
148. We Are the King's Servants
149. Fragment of a Letter Concerning a Person as a Pledge
150. Fragment Referring to the City Gate
151. ———
152. ———
153. Fragment Mentioning a Bel-ibni
154. Two Private Letters on One Tablet
155. ———
156. Fragment Mentioning the Chief of Trade
157. Fragment of a Letter to the Palace Scribe
158. Day of the Disappearance of the Moon
159. Fragment Mentioning Belet-balaṭi
160. Setting to Work
161. ———
162. Appealing to the King
163. Harvesters Requested
164. ———
165. ———
166. ———
167. NN Should not Kill Me
168. ———
169. ———
170. ———
171. ———
172. ———
173. Do not Forsake Me in Their Hands
174. ———
175. ———
176. Fragment Concerning the Palace Scribe
177. Bowls to the King
178. ———
179. ———
180. ———
181. ———
182. ———
183. ———
184. ———
185. ———
186. ———
187. ———
188. ———
189. ———
190. ———
191. Chaldeans in Calah
192. Fragment of a Letter about Blood Money
193. ———
194. ———
195. ———
196. ———
197. Performing Extispicy
198. Keeping the King's Watch
199. ———
200. ———
201. Fragment Mentioning the Puqudu
202. ———
203. ———
204. Hit on the Head
205. ———
206. ———
207. Fragment Mentioning the Ritual of Ištar of [...]
208. ———
209. ———
210. ———
211. ———
212. ———
213. Fragment about a Possible Quarrel
214. Fragment Mentioning Belet-balaṭi
215. ———
216. ———
217. ———
218. ———
219. Fragment Mentioning Babylon, Elam, and Bows
220. A Message from Bel
221. ———
222. ———
223. ———
224. ———
225. Fragment of a Private Letter about a Legal Case
226. Treaty of Assurnasirpal II

Index of Texts

By Publication Number

By Museum Number

List of Joins

List of Illustrations

COPIES AND COLLATIONS

K 5333B + K 9813 (= no. 21)

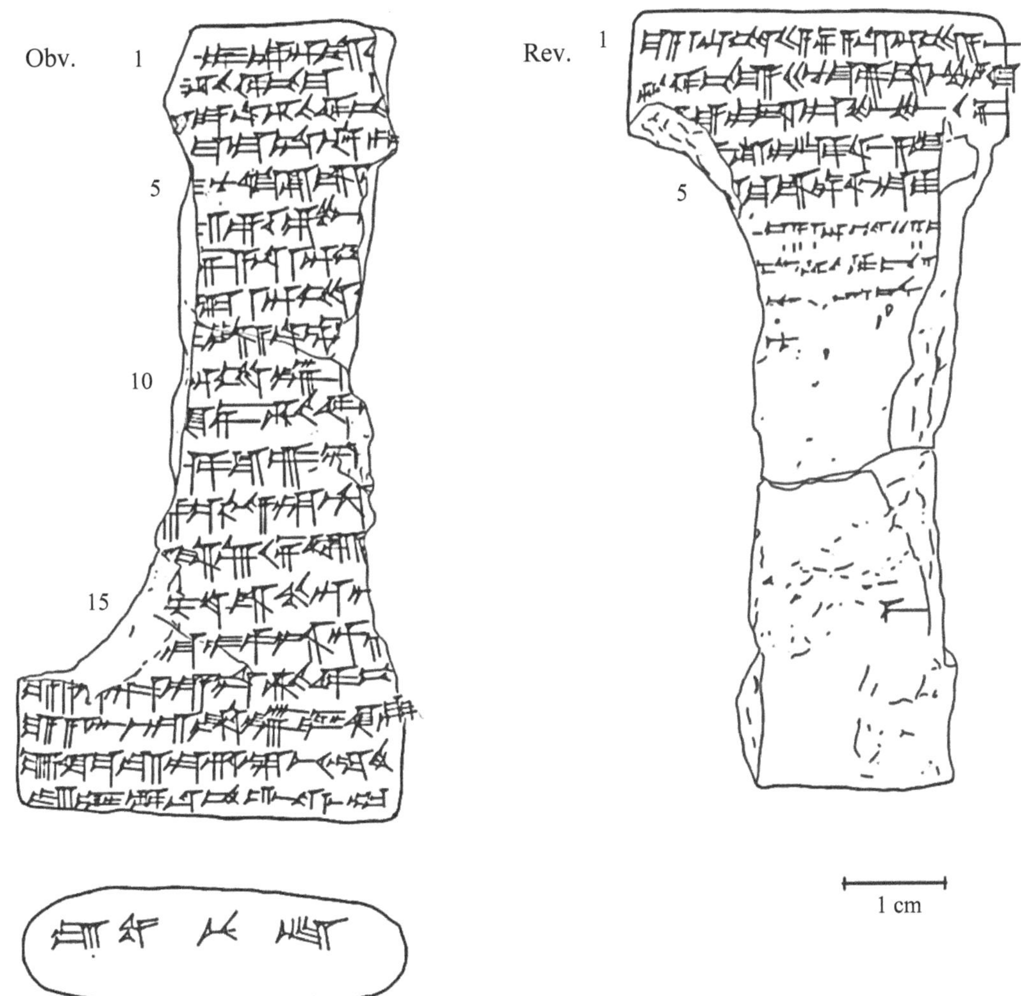

K 115 (= no. 262)

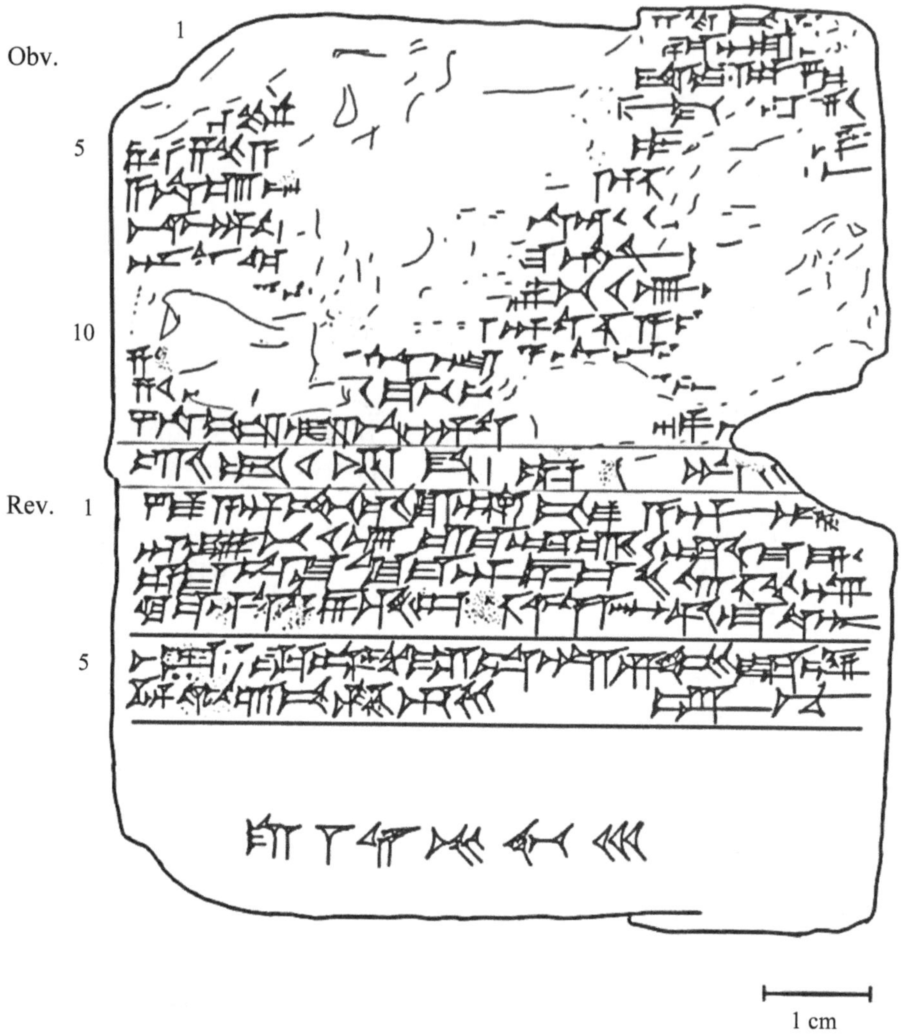

Obv.

Rev.

1 cm

K 11974 (= no. 270)

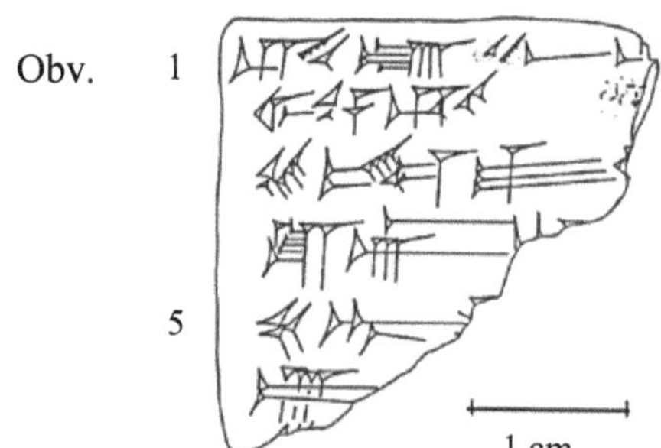

K 6609 + K 9899 (= no. 243)

Obv.

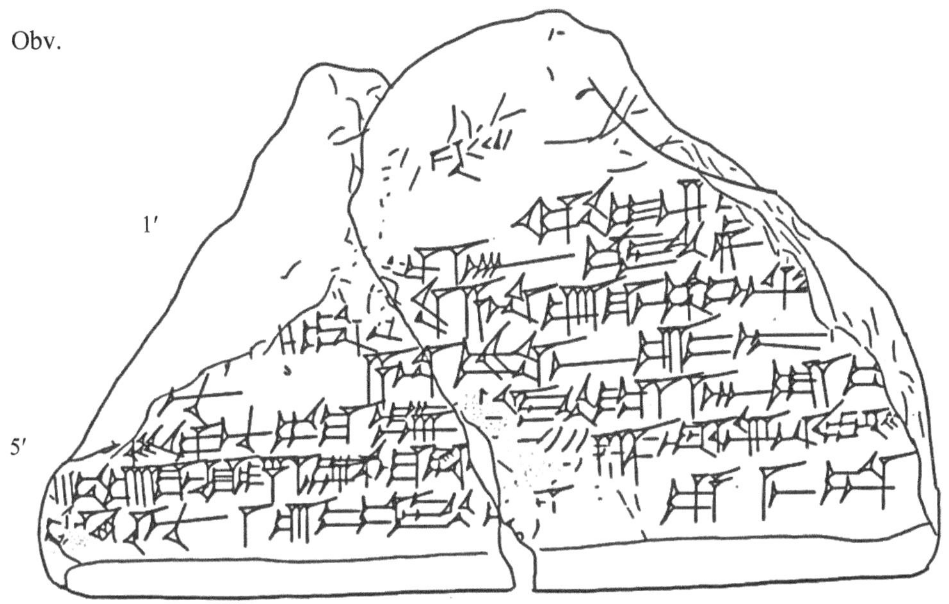

Rev.

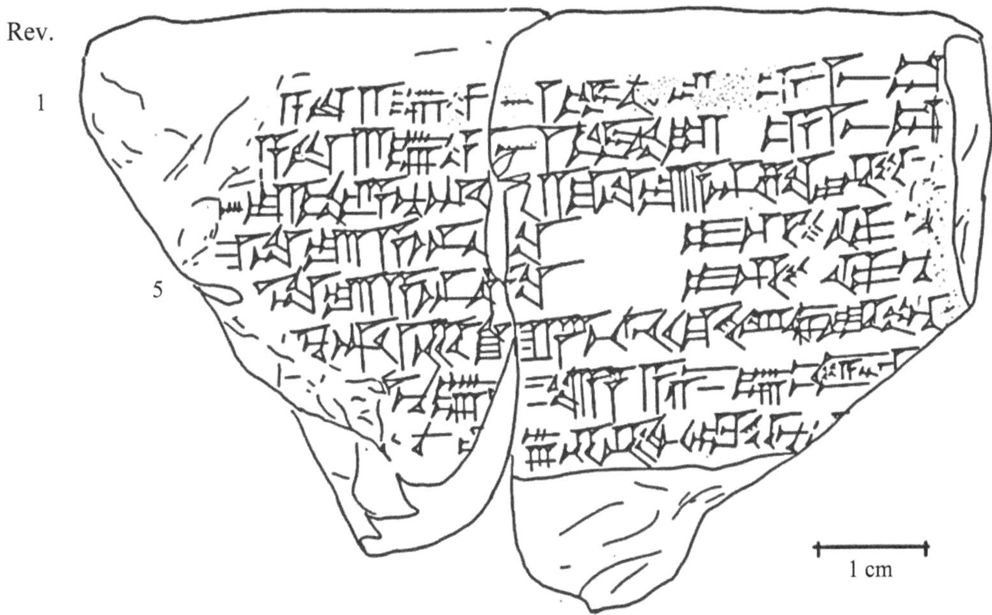

1: 10	*ha-an-ni-i i-*
r.7	*ina* -*ka*-⸢*ni*⸣
r.12	NINDA.M[EŠ *l*]*e-e-*
r.13	A.MEŠ -*is-si-a a-* ⸢É *a*⸣-[*na*]-
r.15	*a-na* .[MEŠ]
r.16	*a-na* ANŠE.*ú-* .MEŠ
6: 5	LÚ*.EN– .MEŠ *ša* URU.MEŠ
26: 1	*a-na* LUGAL *be-* -[*ia*]
30 r.1	[*x x x*]
r.2	[*x x x*] [*x*
r.3	[*x x*]- *a-na* LUGAL *b*[*e-*
r.4	*šá* LUGAL -[*pur-an-na-ši*]
r.5	*ki-i šá* LUGAL
32: 5	*ki-i* -⸢*i*⸣
r.1	*a-ki* ^{m}AN.ŠÁR–EN– -[*in*
34: 6	[*x x*].MEŠ-*ši-na* [*x x x*]
10	[*x x*] NIN GIŠ.BA[N? *x x*]
59: 6	*ina* IGI ^{m} [*x*
66: 2	[*be-lí*]
67 r.5	LUGAL *hi-ṭu le-* -[*ni*]
117: 2	[*x x x*]
5	*a-na* *x*[*x x x*]
6	[*x x x*]
12	*ú-* -*a* LUGAL
e.13	[*x x x*]
133: 2	*ina* KUR
5	LÚ.ERIM.
6	-*i*
10	[*x x*] ⸢*id*⸣-*du-ú*
134: 6	-*ia lu*[*d-di* 0]
136: 3	UD.
r.7	*a-na* [*x* (*x x*)]
r.8	*ú-* -[*ṣip*
r.13	*x*] *x*[*x* (*x*)]
162: 8	*x* $^{m?}$] -*bar*
165: 2	[*x* GA]BA. -*ka* [*x x x*]
235 r.9	N]A4.AN.ZA.
239 r. i 26	*a-na* -[*ni*]
r. ii 24	M]U. .MEŠ
241 r.3	*šá* [*x*
245 r.1	-*šal-ka* ^{d}UT[U
247 r.3	*mì*]-⸢*ih*⸣- .MAD.GÁ
r.14	*u* -*hu*
250 r.4	^{m}*zi-zi-i* EN. –UMUŠ
255 r.4	*lu-* -*du-ma*
r.5	*a-na* *be-lí-iá*
r.7	*lu*-⸢*šak*⸣-*ši-du-* -[*ka*]
279: 3	*ša* ŠU.2 ^{m}*qu-u-a* LÚ*.*šá*– -*ni*
7	*šu-ú da-a-ni mi-ha-ar-*
r.5	LUGAL -*ra*
s.2	.[*x* (*x*)]
281: 12	1 LÚ.TUR *ku-*
286: 1	*ár-ma-a*-⸢*a*⸣-[*te x x x*]
2	*ku-sa-a-a-t*[*e x x x*]
3	7 *aš-šur-* -*a-te*
5	[*x*]3 MÍ. -*ra-a-a-te*
6	[*x* MÍ]. -*šá-a-a-te* :.
12	1 MÍ. -*d*[*u*?-*di*]-*tú* [*x x x*]
15	*ša* AD-*šú*
16	MÍ.*ši-ti*– -*ni* GÉME.MEŠ :.
18	8 MÍ. .GAL
20	MÍ.*hat-ta-a*-⸢*a*⸣-
r.3	MÍ.*an-dar-i-tú*
r.6	1 MÍ. .I PAB 33
r.8	1! MÍ.*mu-* –*qí-tú* 0!
r.10	PAB 1-*me-* [*x x x*]